Margaret
Avromeer
2017

SALES MANAGEMENT

SALES MANAGEMENT
Building Customer Relationships and Partnerships

JOSEPH F. HAIR
Kennesaw State University

ROLPH E. ANDERSON
Drexel University

RAJIV MEHTA
New Jersey Institute of Technology

BARRY J. BABIN
Louisiana Tech University

Houghton Mifflin Company
Boston   New York

To my son, Joe III, and my grandson, Joe IV.

—Joe Hair

To my talented and supportive wife, Sallie, and our wonderful children, Rachel and Stuart.
—Rolph Anderson

To the memory of a wonderful father, R.K., for his unconditional love; and to my mother, Kamlesh, for her love and sacrifice.

—Rajiv Mehta

To my family.

—Barry Babin

Executive Publisher: George Hoffman
Executive Sponsoring Editor: Lisé Johnson
Sponsoring Editor: Michael Schenk
Marketing Manager: Nicole Mollica
Senior Development Editor: Joanne Dauksewicz
Associate Project Editor: Deborah Thomashow
Cover Design Director: Tony Saizon
Senior Photo Editor: Jennifer Meyer Dare
Senior Composition Buyer: Chuck Dutton
New Title Project Manager: James Lonergan
Marketing Assistant: Lauren Foye

Cover image: ColorBlind Images/Getty Images

Printed in the U.S.A.

Library of Congress Control Number: 2007941450

ISBN-10: 0-618-72101-0
ISBN-13: 978-0-618-72101-6

2 3 4 5 6 7 8 9—CRK—12 11 10 09 08

Brief Contents

Preface xv

About the Authors xxiii

PART ONE   Twenty-First Century Sales Force Management   1

CHAPTER **1**   Introduction to Sales Management and Its Evolving Roles 2

CHAPTER **2**   Managing Ethics in a Sales Environment 28

CHAPTER **3**   Customer Relationship Management and Building Partnerships 56

CHAPTER **4**   The Selling Process 88

PART TWO   Organizing and Developing the Sales Force   117

CHAPTER **5**   Sales Forecasting and Budgeting 118

CHAPTER **6**   Sales Force Planning and Organizing 148

CHAPTER **7**   Time and Territory Management 180

CHAPTER **8**   Recruiting and Selecting the Sales Force 210

PART THREE   Managing and Directing Sales Force Efforts   247

CHAPTER **9**   Training the Sales Force 248

CHAPTER **10**   Sales Force Leadership 282

CHAPTER **11**   Sales Force Motivation 322

CHAPTER **12**   Sales Force Compensation 356

PART FOUR   Controlling and Evaluating Sales Force Performance   387

CHAPTER **13**   Sales Volume, Costs, and Profitability Analysis 388

CHAPTER **14**   Sales Force Performance Evaluation 422

Notes N1

Glossary G1

Subject Index I1

Name Index I13

Contents

Preface xv
About the Authors xxiii

PART ONE Twenty-First Century Sales Force Management 1

CHAPTER 1

Introduction to Sales Management and Its Evolving Roles 2

Inside Sales Management: Joel Hollenbeck, VP, Eastern Division Manager, Houghton Mifflin Company 2
What Is Sales Management? 3
Types, Titles, and Hierarchical Levels of Sales Managers 4
Responsibilities and Duties of Sales Managers 4
  Twenty-First Century Sales Force Management 5
  Organizing and Developing the Sales Force 6
  Managing and Directing Sales Force Efforts 8
  Controlling and Evaluating Sales Force Performance 9
Expanding Roles of Sales Managers 10
  Managing Customer Relationships 10
  Serving as Customer Consultants 10
  Managing the Hybrid Sales Force 11
What Qualities Are Needed to Be a Sales Manager? 11
Integrating Sales Management and Marketing Management 11
  The Field Sales Force and Headquarters Marketing Support Team 12
  Integrated Marketing Communication 14
Monitoring and Adapting to the Macroenvironment 15
  Megatrends Affecting Sales Management 16
How Well Are Sales Managers Performing? 18
  Illogical Selection of Sales Managers 18
  Inadequate Sales Management Training 19
  Lack of a Long-Run Customer Relationship Orientation 20
  Insufficient Blending of Sales, Marketing, and Financial Knowledge 20
Developing Sales Managers for the New Millennium 20
Chapter Summary 22

Review and Application Questions 23
It's Up to You 23
  Internet Exercise 23
  Role-Playing Exercise 23
  In-Basket Exercise 24
  Ethical Dilemma 24
  ■ **CASE 1.1** Simpson Machine Tool Company: Sales Management Seminar 25
  ■ **CASE 1.2** Centroid Computer Corporation: The New Sales Manager 26

CHAPTER 2

Managing Ethics in a Sales Environment 28

Inside Sales Management: Robert Perry, Vice President of Sales, PokerTek Inc. 28
What Is Business Ethics? 29
  Business Ethics, Sales, and Sales Management 30
Salespeople Are Boundary Spanners 30
  Customer Vulnerability 31
Applying Professional Sales Codes of Ethics 32
  Types of Codes of Ethics 33
  Do Codes of Ethics Affect Behavior? 33
Ethical Philosophies and Moral Judgments 34
  Idealism 35
  Relativism 35
  Teleology 35
  Moral Judgments 36
  Are Salespeople More Unethical than Anyone Else? 36
  Potentially Unethical Behaviors 36
  Dealing with Unethical Behavior 38
Creating an Ethical Work Climate 38
  Policies and Rules 39
  Trust and Responsibility 39
  Peer Behavior 39
  Bottom-Line Sales Emphasis 39

Managing the Ethical Climate 40
Legal Considerations in the Sales Environment 41
  Federal Regulation 41
  Price Discrimination 41
  International Regulation of Sales 46
  Personal Selling 47
  State and Local Regulation 47
Practicing Good Ethics Among the Sales Force 47
  Understanding Ethics 48
  Measuring the Ethical Climate 48
  Leading by Example 49
  Sales Manager Ethics Checklist 49
Chapter Summary 50
Review and Application Questions 51
It's Up to You 52
  Internet Exercise 52
  Role-Playing Exercise 52
  In-Basket Exercise 53
  Ethical Dilemma 53
  ■ CASE 2.1 Billings Pharmaceuticals: Customer Vulnerability and Moral Equity 53
  ■ CASE 2.2 J&R Company: Unethical Sales Practices 54

CHAPTER 3

Customer Relationship Management and Building Partnerships   56

Inside Sales Management: Julie Wroblewski of eFunds 56
What Is CRM? 57
Relationship Orientations and CRM 58
  Mass Marketing 59
  Differentiated Marketing 59
  Niche Marketing 59
  One-to-One Marketing 60
  Using Information to Meet Customer Needs: The Basis of CRM 60
  Production Versus Marketing Orientation 61
CRM and Repeat Business 62
  Transactional View 62
  Relational Selling 63
  Strategic Partnerships 64
  Mechanisms That Govern Exchanges 66
CRM, Customer Loyalty, and Lifetime Value 67
  Customer Loyalty 68
  Computing the Value of a Customer 68

Risks of Relational Selling 69
CRM and Selling 70
  CRM and Sales 70
  The Salesperson and Managing Customers 70
  Product Portfolios 72
  Customer Portfolios 72
  CRM and Production 72
  CRM and Technology 73
  Web Technologies and CRM 73
  Integrated Web Solutions 74
Technology and CRM Programs 74
  Sales Force Automation 74
  CRM Hardware 76
  CRM Software 77
CRM Successes and Failures 78
Chapter Summary 80
Review and Application Questions 81
It's Up to You 82
  Internet Exercise 82
  Role-Playing Exercise 82
  In-Basket Exercise 83
  Ethical Dilemma 83
  ■ CASE 3.1 Cosair Gas Distributors: Problems with a CRM System Installation 83
  ■ CASE 3.2 TC's Bookings: Getting the Most Out of a CRM System 84

CHAPTER 4

The Selling Process   88

Inside Sales Management: Anne Hubbell at Kodak 88
Updating the Roles of Salespeople 89
  Customer Relationship Management 90
  Opportunities in Personal Selling 91
  Careers for Different Types of Individuals 91
  Everyone Sells Something 91
What Salespeople Do: Stages of the Personal Selling Process 92
  Continuous Cycle or Wheel of PSP 92
  Prospecting and Qualifying 93
  Planning the Sales Call: Preapproach 93
  Approaching the Prospect 96
  Making the Sales Presentation and Demonstration 98
  Negotiating Sales Resistance or Buyer Objections 100
  Confirming and Closing the Sale 103

Following Up and Servicing the Account 106

Applying CRM to the Personal Selling Process 108

Empowering Salespeople for CRM 108

CRM Training and Rewards 110

Chapter Summary 111

Review and Application Questions 112

It's Up to You 112

Internet Exercise 112

Role-Playing Exercise 113

In-Basket Exercise 113

Ethical Dilemma 113

■ **CASE 4.1** Solex-Digital: Effective Negotiation Strategies 114

■ **CASE 4.2** Dasseaux Pharmaceuticals: Relationship versus Transactional Selling 114

PART TWO   Organizing and Developing the Sales Force   117

CHAPTER **5**

Sales Forecasting and Budgeting   118

Inside Sales Management: Ewell Hopkins, Principal Partner, Morgan Holland & Company 118

Sales Forecasting and Its Relationship to Operational Planning 119

Sales and Operational Planning: S&OP 121

Estimating Consumer Demand 123

Estimating Industrial Demand 123

Forecasting Approaches and Techniques 124

Nonquantitative Forecasting Techniques 126

Quantitative Forecasting Techniques 129

Evaluating Forecasting Approaches 136

Sales Budget Planning 137

The Planning Function 137

The Coordinating Function 137

The Controlling Function 138

Preparing the Annual Sales Budget 138

Step 1: Review and Analyze the Situation 139

Step 2: Communicate Sales Goals and Objectives 140

Step 3: Identify Specific Market Opportunities and Problems 140

Step 4: Develop a Preliminary Allocation of Resources 140

Step 5: Prepare a Budget Presentation 140

Step 6: Implement the Budget and Provide Periodic Feedback 140

Chapter Summary 141

Review and Application Questions 142

It's Up to You 143

Internet Exercise 143

Role-Playing Exercise 143

In-Basket Exercise 144

Ethical Dilemma 144

■ **CASE 5.1** AKAMAI Corporation: Developing Sales Forecasts 144

■ **CASE 5.2** Global Container Corporation: Creative Sales Forecasting 146

CHAPTER **6**

Sales Force Planning and Organizing   148

Inside Sales Management: Nikki Verna of Beiersdorf 148

Purpose and Levels of Organization Planning 149

Why Should Sales Managers Plan? 149

Levels of Organizational Planning 150

Sales Management Planning Process 151

Analyze the Situation 152

Set Goals and Objectives 153

Determine Market Potential and Forecast Sales 154

Develop Strategies 155

Allocate Resources and Develop Budgets 157

Implement the Plan 157

Evaluate and Control 159

Causes of Unsuccessful Planning 160

Dialectic Planning 160

Contingency Planning 161

Organizing the Sales Force 161

Types of Organizations 161

Types of Sales Department Organizations 163

Team Selling 166

Guidelines for Developing Sales Organizations 167

Size of the Sales Force 167

Developing a High-Quality Sales Organization 171

Chapter Summary 172

Review and Application Questions 173

It's Up to You 173

Internet Exercise 173

Role-Playing Exercise 173

In-Basket Exercise 174

Ethical Dilemma 174

■ **CASE 6.1** PlayMart Toyz: Building a Sales Organization 174

■ **CASE 6.2** Wild Willie "Juiced" Drinks: Planning for Sales Growth 177

CHAPTER **7**

Time and Territory Management   180

Inside Sales Management: Jean Berdis of DHL 180

Improving Sales Productivity 181

Establishing Sales Territories 182

Reasons for Sales Territories 182

Reasons for Not Having Sales Territories 184

CRM and Sales Territories 184

Setting Up Sales Territories 184

Selecting a Geographic Control Unit 185

Conducting an Account Analysis 188

Developing a Salesperson Workload Analysis 188

Combining Geographic Control Units into Sales Territories 190

Assigning Salespeople to Territories 190

Revising Sales Territories 191

Signs Indicating the Need for Territorial Revisions 191

Impact of Territory Revision on Salespeople 192

Self-Management 193

How Salespeople Spend Their Time 193

New Sales Manager Roles 196

Customer Reviews of Performance 197

Time Management and Routing 197

Managing Salesperson Time 198

Routing 201

Time Management for Sales Managers 202

Chapter Summary 203

Review and Application Questions 204

It's Up to You 204

Internet Exercise 204

Role-Playing Exercise 204

In-Basket Exercise 205

Ethical Dilemma 205

■ **CASE 7.1** Manufacturers Insurance Group: Developing Territories 205

■ **CASE 7.2** SalesTech, Inc.: Coping with Growth 206

CHAPTER **8**

Recruiting and Selecting the Sales Force   210

Inside Sales Management: Tere Blanca de Ulloa of Codina Realty Services 210

Importance of Recruiting and Selection 211

What Is Recruitment? 212

The Recruitment Process 212

Job Analysis 213

Preparing a Job Description 213

Developing a Set of Job Qualifications 214

Attracting a Pool of Applicants 217

Sources of Salespeople 218

Persons within the Company 218

Competitors 218

Non-Competing Companies 219

Educational Institutions 219

Advertisements 220

Online Recruiting 220

Employment Agencies and Professional Recruiters 221

Factors to Consider in Evaluating Sources 222

The Sales Force Selection Process 222

Initial Screening 223

Checking References 225

In-Depth Interviewing 227

Employment Testing 231

Follow-Up Interviewing 234

Making the Selection 234

Sales Force Socialization 235

Initial Socialization 238

Extended Socialization 239

Chapter Summary 240

Review and Application Questions 241

It's Up to You 241

Internet Exercise 241

Role-Playing Exercise 241

In-Basket Exercise 242

Ethical Dilemma 243

■ **CASE 8.1** Vector Marketing Corporation: Recruiting and Selecting College Students 243

■ **CASE 8.2** R^3 Technology: Improving Recruitment and Selection 244

PART THREE Managing and Directing Sales Force Efforts 247

CHAPTER 9
Training the Sales Force 248

Inside Sales Management: Robert Brodo, Executive Vice President, Advantexe Learning Solutions 248
Importance of Sales Training 249
Benefits of Sales Force Training 250
Keys to Sales Training Success 250
Developing and Implementing Sales Training 251
Sales Training Development Process 252
Conduct a Training Needs Assessment 253
Determine Training Objectives 254
Determine Training Program Content 255
Making Training Delivery Decisions 258
Determine Responsibility for Training 259
Select Group or Individual Training 260
Choosing Instructional Methods 260
Traditional Training Methods 261
Emerging Training Methods 263
Location of Training 266
Timing of Training Programs 266
Preparing, Motivating, and Coaching Trainees 266
Preparing Trainees for Training 267
Motivating Trainees during Training 267
Conducting Post-Training Reinforcement 268
Evaluating Training Programs 269
Continuous Training Programs 272
Refresher Training 272
Retraining 273
Managerial Training 274
Sales Training Challenges for Global Companies 274
Chapter Summary 276
Review and Application Questions 277
It's Up to You 277
Internet Exercise 277
Role-Playing Exercise 277
In-Basket Exercise 278
Ethical Dilemma 278
■ **CASE 9.1** Hops Distributors, Inc.: Getting the Blend Right! 278
■ **CASE 9.2** Midwest Auto Parts, Inc.: The Value of Sales Training 279

CHAPTER 10
Sales Force Leadership 282

Inside Sales Management: Jim Travis, Vice President of Sales, Green Mountain Coffee Roasters 282
Foundations of Leadership 284
Supervision, Management, and Leadership 284
Leadership and Power 285
Position Power Sources 286
Personal Power Sources 286
Sales Management Implications 286
Applying Classical Leadership Theories to Twenty-First Century Sales Management 287
Trait Theory 287
Behavioral Styles Theory 288
Contingency Theories of Leadership 290
Applying Contemporary Leadership Theories to Twenty-First Century Sales Management 299
Transformational (or Charismatic and Visionary) Leadership 299
Pygmalion Leadership 302
Leadership and Empowerment: Distributive Power Sharing through Participative Management 303
Other Emerging Issues in Twenty-First Century Sales Force Leadership 306
Mentoring 306
Women as Sales Managers 308
Communication 309
Listening 310
Understanding Nonverbal Communication 312
Breaking Down Communication Barriers 312
Chapter Summary 314
Review and Application Questions 316
It's Up to You 316
Internet Exercise 316
Role-Playing Exercise 316
In-Basket Exercise 317
■ **CASE 10.1** School Suppliers, Inc.: Leading a Diverse Sales Force 317
■ **CASE 10.2** Öhlins Chemicals: Leadership and Communication Problems 319

CHAPTER **11**

Sales Force Motivation   **322**

Inside Sales Management: Lance Perkins of GE Medical Systems 322

Foundations of Motivation 323

Applying Contemporary Motivation Theories to Sales Management 324

Contents Theories of Motivation 324

Process Theories of Motivation 326

Reinforcement Theory of Motivation 330

Using Rewards and Incentive Programs for Sales Force Motivation 330

Extrinsic Rewards 331

Intrinsic Rewards 332

Sales Force Motivation Strategies and Tools 335

Sales Contests 335

Sales Meetings 340

Additional Perspectives in Twenty-First Century Sales Force Motivation 343

Organizational and Job Commitment 343

Organizational Climate 344

Learning Orientation versus Performance Orientation 344

Salesperson's Career Cycle 345

Empowerment and Participative Management 347

Chapter Summary 347

Review and Application Questions 348

It's Up to You 349

    Internet Exercise 349

    Role-Playing Exercise 349

    In-Basket Exercise 349

    Ethical Dilemma 350

■ **CASE 11.1** Schindler Pharmaceuticals: Motivating the Sales Force 350

■ **CASE 11.2** Sales Actions Software, Inc.: Motivating Salespeople in Different Career Stages 352

CHAPTER **12**

Sales Force Compensation   **356**

Inside Sales Management: J. B. Shireman, Executive Vice President of Sales and Marketing, New Belgium Brewery 356

Sales Force Compensation Plans 358

Variable Pay Compensation Systems 360

Developing the Compensation Plan 360

Preparing Job Descriptions 361

Establishing Specific Objectives 361

Determining General Levels of Compensation 363

Developing the Compensation Mix 364

Pretesting the Plan 367

Administering the Plan 367

Evaluating the Plan 368

Advantages and Disadvantages of Different Compensation Methods 368

Straight Salary 368

Straight Commission 370

Combination Compensation Plans 373

Trends in Sales Compensation 374

Compensation for Productivity and Retention 374

Inclusion of Customer Satisfaction in the Compensation Plan 374

International Sales Compensation 375

Commission for Sales Managers 375

Expense Accounts and Fringe Benefits 376

Acknowledging the Importance of Selling Expenses 376

Designing the Expense Plan 376

Controlling Expenses through Reimbursement 377

Curbing Abuses of Expense Reimbursement Plans 379

Adjusting to Rising Selling Costs 379

Chapter Summary 379

Review and Application Questions 380

It's Up to You 380

    Internet Exercise 380

    Role-Playing Exercise 381

    In-Basket Exercise 381

    Ethical Dilemma 382

■ **CASE 12.1** Syntel, Inc.: The Role of Compensation in Salesperson Turnover 382

■ **CASE 12.2** Sun-Sweet Citrus Supply, Inc.: Compensation and Sales Expenses 384

PART FOUR   Controlling and Evaluating Sales Force Performance   387

CHAPTER 13

Sales Volume, Costs, and Profitability Analysis   388

Inside Sales Management: Mike Andrews, Vice President of Sales and Marketing, J. A. Riggs 388

Framework for Sales Force Organization Audit 390

Sales Volume, Costs, and Profitability Analysis 391

Sales Volume Analysis 392

Profitability Analysis 399

Underlying Problems 412

Return on Assets Managed (ROAM) 412

Increasing Sales Force Productivity and Profits 414

Chapter Summary 414

Review and Application Questions 415

It's Up to You 415

Internet Exercise 415

Role-Playing Exercise 416

In-Basket Exercise 416

Ethical Dilemma 416

■ **CASE 13.1** Fabrizia Pasta Company: The Value of Financial Reports 417

■ **CASE 13.2** J.B.'s Restaurant Supply: How CRM Data Is Used to Justify Change 419

CHAPTER 14

Sales Force Performance Evaluation   422

Inside Sales Management: Tom Cunningham, Senior Sales Manager, Boeing Rotorcraft Systems 422

Sales Force Performance Appraisal 423

Purpose of Salesperson Performance Appraisals 423

Challenges in Salesperson Performance Appraisals 424

Timing of Salesperson Performance Appraisals 424

A Contemporary Approach to Sales Force Performance Evaluation 425

Establish Sales Goals and Objectives 426

Develop the Sales Plan 426

Set Sales Force Performance Standards 426

Allocate Resources and Sales Force Efforts 432

Measure Sales Force Performance Against Standards 441

Providing Feedback and Improving Sales Force Performance 448

Providing Feedback on Salesperson Performance 448

Improving Sales Force Performance 450

Emerging Perspectives in Twenty-First Century Sales Force Performance Appraisals 452

360-Degree Performance Appraisals 452

Performance Appraisals of Team Selling 453

Performance Review Ranking System 454

Chapter Summary 454

Review and Application Questions 456

It's Up to You 457

Internet Exercise 457

Role-Playing Exercise 457

In-Basket Exercise 457

Ethical Dilemma 458

■ **CASE 14.1** FUTSUCO Electronics: Rewarding Performance 458

■ **CASE 14.2** Midwest Risk Management: Performance Evaluation Systems 461

Notes N1

Glossary G1

Subject Index I1

Name Index I13

Preface

I t is an exciting and challenging time to be—or anticipate being—a sales manager! Sales managers and salespeople are facing more opportunities and challenges than at any time in the past. No jobs will be more important than sales or sales management in the effort to increase our global competitiveness. It's safe to say that the successes of sales managers and salespeople will affect not only their careers, but also the economic health of the United States.

Sales managers play pivotal, multifaceted roles in planning, organizing, managing, directing, and controlling the sales departments of their organizations. They are virtually the only managers in the firm directly responsible for generating revenues and profits. Indeed, the sales manager's responsibility for managing the sales force and its interface with customers is possibly the most crucial of all functions in terms of determining the firm's success.

Successful sales professionals will have to adapt to several emerging developments. Probably the most obvious developments impacting sales management today and in the near future are technological innovations, particularly information technology. Technological trends directly impacting sales managers and salespeople include Internet-related developments impacting training, communication, and customer interactions; sales force automation; mobile virtual sales offices; and electronic sales channels. Other emerging developments include growing buyer expertise; rising customer expectations, particularly service quality standards; intense global competition, especially from China and India; and the influx of minorities into sales careers. Appropriate responses to these trends will be based on a significant broadening of the concept of sales management.

Sales managers will not find a comfort zone in their past knowledge, experience, or success. Instead, to keep pace with the extraordinary changes ahead, they will need to establish a continuous learning environment for themselves and their salespeople. There will be closer interaction of marketing and sales activities. Sales managers will require a greater knowledge of strategic marketing functions, and the marketing team must increasingly include selling and sales management perspectives in their planning efforts. The most successful sales managers will develop and apply marketing concepts, strategic planning processes, financial analysis techniques, motivation and leadership skills, effective communication methods, interpersonal capabilities, and the latest information technology applications. We are confident that *Sales Management: Building Customer Relationships and Partnerships* will help current and future sales managers to perform their duties much more effectively and efficiently.

Sales Management: Building Customer Relationships and Partnerships integrates selling and sales management while illustrating how the entire marketing organization must function as a team, working with customers and other stakeholders to develop solutions to problems and to pursue opportunities. The emphasis is on relationship selling, which seeks to establish long-run partnerships with customers based on professionalism, trust, quality, service, and mutual respect. More attention is given to Business-to-Business (B2B) selling than to Business-to-Consumer (B2C) selling because most graduating students will be selling products and services to businesses. Discussions and examples of the diverse sales concepts, issues, and activities strive to provide an appropriate balance among the theoretical, analytical, and pragmatic approaches by blending the most progressive applications from the sales practitioner's environment with the latest research findings from academia.

To provide both instructors and students with an exciting, up-to-date text and a comprehensive set of supplements, we conducted interviews with professors, students, salespeople, and sales managers. Although *Sales Management: Building Customer Relationships and Partnerships* is designed primarily for use at upper-level colleges and universities, some progressive junior colleges may wish to adopt it for students planning to enter sales careers. All chapters of the text have been pre-tested by undergraduate- and masters-level students at several universities, and the suggested improvements were included where appropriate.

Organization of the Book

The overall goal of this book is to help sales managers and salespeople prepare for the challenging and exciting years ahead, so that the transition from personal selling to sales management to marketing management is a natural progression, not a traumatic step. To this end, *Sales Management: Building Customer Relationships and Partnerships* is divided into four major parts, with a total of fourteen chapters.

Part One provides and overview and integration of personal selling and sales management. Chapter 1 covers the eclectic, expanding role of professional sales managers who are quickly becoming respected members of the marketing management team and increasingly are assuming a long-run, strategic perspective for their organizations. Chapter 2 focuses on the ethical and legal issues increasingly faced by salespeople and sales managers. It provides an overview of the concepts of business ethics and the conflicts confronted in responding to the ever-changing environment, including dealing with the company, coworkers, customers, and other stakeholders. Finally, the legislation affecting selling and sales management in local, state, federal, and international selling situations is examined. Chapter 3 begins by discussing the different ways companies deal with customers in an effort to build customer relationships that lead to repeat business. Next, we relate customer loyalty to customer lifetime value, with particular emphasis on applying CRM and other technology to improve the selling process. Chapter 4 provides a comprehensive, in-depth analysis of the personal selling process and presents a variety of techniques and real-world examples of ways to improve selling performance.

Part Two covers planning, organizing and developing the sales force. Chapter 5 focuses on sales forecasting and budgeting. Sales forecasting is viewed as the starting point for all sales and marketing planning, production scheduling, cash-flow projections, financial planning, capital investment, procurement, inventory management, human resource planning, and budgeting. After analyzing the major concepts and methods of estimating demand, we illustrate the application of the most widely used forecasting techniques. Finally, the purpose, benefits, and preparation of an annual sales budget are discussed. Chapter 6 explains strategic sales planning and organizing. Planning is represented as a basic function of the sales manager because it creates the essential framework for all other sales decision making. The value of a sales management information system for strategic and tactical planning is illustrated, and the proactive planning process is explained step by step. The various approaches for organizing the sales force are summarized and illustrated, as well as techniques for determining the optimal sales force size. Chapter 7 presents alternative approaches for assigning and managing sales territories to achieve sales objectives effectively and efficiently. It also outlines the procedures for setting up and revising sales territories, and for routing and maximizing productive sales time. Chapter 8 explains the sales force recruitment and selection process. The sources of good sales candidates, the legal rights of sales applicants, the differences between job analysis and a job description, and the basic qualifications necessary for sales positions are all covered. These are followed by a description of the procedures and tools used to select the best applicants and an explanation of what sales managers look for in application forms and interviews. Legal considerations in interviewing and testing are summarized, as is the important step of socialization of new recruits.

Part Three covers managing and directing sales force efforts. Chapter 9 presents the many aspects of training and retraining sales reps. The major topics include who is responsible for training, training program content, approaches for training, evaluation of training, and the benefits of continuous training and retraining, as well as executive training. Chapter 10 is concerned with the important topic of leading the sales force. First, the essential differences between leadership and management are considered, and the sources of leader power are identified. Major classical and contemporary leadership theories including the increasingly popular concept of empowerment that can be used to influence the sales force towards the attainment of sales and organizational goals are discussed. The chapter concludes with a discussion of how communication—both verbal and non-verbal—can be used by sales managers for interacting with salespeople. Chapter 11 focuses on motivating the sales force. It describes the various theories of motivation and considers non-financial as well as financial rewards that can be used to effectively increase the effort of salespeople for attaining sales goals. Perhaps most important, it demonstrates why blanket approaches to motivation are ineffective and recommends unique ways to individualize motivation using incentives based on the career stage of salespeople. Chapter 12 examines the major types of compensation plans and how they need to be modified with changing market conditions. We also consider what can be done to slow the rise in sales costs and analyze alternative ways to achieve the optimum balance of personal sales calls and other means of managing customer relationships. The chapter ends with a discussion of different approaches to reimbursing sales expenses incurred by sales reps.

Part Four discusses controlling and evaluating sales force performance. Chapter 13 demonstrates the relationship between sales volume, costs, and profitability. Sources of sales information and the collection of sales data are described. Then the value of cooperation between marketing and accounting is shown, as well as procedures for conducting sales, cost, and profitability analyses. Methods of allocating costs as well as return on assets are examined in terms of their influence on measuring productivity. Chapter 14 summarizes techniques for setting performance standards for salespeople and how to objectively measure actual performance, including the topic of sales quotas. Various performance appraisal techniques are discussed as well as the value of performing sales force audits.

Objectives and Features

We wrote this text because of our belief that the market needed a comprehensive, up-to-date text on sales management. As a result, our goal has been to

- Emphasize the role of sales managers in the tough, highly competitive selling environment companies face today and will face in the future.
- Analyze key behavioral, technological, and managerial forces and long-run trends in the sales environment.
- Underscore the increasing importance of ethical considerations for sales managers and salespeople.
- Stress the important analytical, communication, relationship, and leadership skills today's sales managers need.
- Illustrate the latest information technology developments and innovations impacting the sales manager's job, particularly in the areas of recruitment, selection, training, sales force planning, and forecasting.
- Emphasize the importance of developing long-run, win-win customer relationships and partnerships.
- Summarize the latest statistics and trends in sales force management.
- Communicate the necessity for sales managers to learn marketing and financial skills and perspectives in order to contribute to marketing strategy development.

To accomplish these objectives, we have incorporated a number of innovative features to assist instructors in achieving *Assurance of Learning Objectives,* including:

- Real world examples summarized in *Sales Management in Action* boxes.
- Ethics in sales management scenarios.
- In-basket exercises to illustrate and develop sales management skills.
- Role-play exercises to facilitate understanding sales management challenges.
- Chapter cases by leading sales management scholars to reinforce the chapter material.
- Pedagogical supplements to help students learn and professors teach, including a comprehensive Instructor's Resource Manual, Test Bank, and PowerPoint Slides that are unmatched by other texts on sales management.

An Effective Supplements Package

We are pleased to provide a comprehensive set of supplements to help both instructors and students.

- *HM MarketingSPACE*TM *Student Website.* The student site includes complete and chapter-by-chapter glossaries, flashcards and crossword puzzles for reviewing key terms, and ACE self-tests.
- *HM MarketingSPACE*TM *Instructor Website.* The instructor site provides downloadable versions of the complete Instructor's Resource Manual (in PDF format) as well as by chapter (in MS Word) that can be edited or used as is. It also pro-

vides a set of Basic PowerPoint slides and Premium PowerPoint slides for each chapter. In addition, the site includes Classroom Response Systems content, sample syllabi, and the complete Video Guide.

- HM MarketingSPACE™ content for Blackboard® and WebCT® courses allows delivery of text-specific content online using your institution's local course management system.

- *Instructor's Resource Manual.* This resource includes for each chapter the list of learning objectives, a detailed lecture outline, and suggested answers to all text questions and end-of-chapter activities.

- *Test Bank.* The Test Bank includes a wealth of both recall and application-oriented multiple-choice, true-false, and essay questions.

- *HM Testing CD.* The electronic version of the printed *Test Bank,* HM Testing, powered by Diploma™ allows instructors to easily generate and edit tests. The program includes an online testing feature instructors can use to administer tests via their local area network or over the Web. It also has a gradebook feature that lets users set up classes, record and track grades from tests or assignments, analyze grades, and produce class and individual statistics.

- *PowerPoint Slides.* PowerPoint slides on the instructor website provide an effective presentation tool for lectures. The PowerPoint program provides an outline of each chapter with key figures and tables from the main text plus short relevant videos embedded within the PowerPoint slides. A Premium PowerPoint program includes all of these slides as well as additional slides containing unique supplementary content.

- *DVD Program.* To illustrate important concepts from the text, real-world video examples from leading organizations are provided. The video segments run from 10 to 20 minutes to allow time for classroom discussion. The Video Guide provides suggested uses, teaching objectives, an overview, and issues for discussion for each video segment.

Acknowledgements

Extensive efforts are required from many talented people to write a college level textbook. The authors gratefully acknowledge the contributions made by those who helped in finalizing *Sales Management: Building Customer Relationships and Partnerships.* First, for their support and encouragement, we would like to thank our deans and chairs at our respective universities—Dean Tim Mescon, Kennesaw State University, Dean George Tsetsekos and Marketing Department Head Trina Larsen Andras at Drexel University, Dean David Hawk and Associate Dean Barbara Tedesco at New Jersey Institute of Technology, and Dean James Lumpkin at Louisiana Tech University. Second, several colleagues have contributed very personally to our development as teachers, researchers, and writers, including the following professorial colleagues: Nabil Tamimi, Mark Somers, Bruce Kirchhoff, Julia Callaway, Jennifer Barr, Alan Dubinsky, Paul Christ, Jim Strong, Myroslaw Kyj, Srini Swaminathan, Burt Brodo, Stan Kligman, Joe Rocereto, Mary Shoemaker, Khalid Dubas, Frederick Hong-kit Yim, and Barry Dickinson. Third, we are especially appreciative to our marketing colleagues who contributed case material or read early versions of the book and offered candid and constructive suggestions. Among these people our special thanks go to

Sarah Baker Andrus, *Vector Marketing Corporation*
Charles Besio, *Southern Methodist University*
Jim Boles, *Georgia State University*
Aberdeen Leila Borders, *University of New Orleans*
Ron Bush, *University of West Florida*
José Casal, *New Jersey Institute of Technology*
Paul Christ, *West Chester University*
Mary Collins, *Strayer University*
Bobby Davis, *Florida A&M University*
Bob Erffmeyer, *University of Wisconsin, Eau Claire*
Karen Flaherty, *Oklahoma State University*
Lucas Forbes, *Western Kentucky University*
Susan Geringer, *California State University, Fresno*
Dan Goebel, *Illinois State University*
Rajesh Gulati, *St. Cloud State University*
Christopher D. Hopkins, *Clemson University*
Mark Johlke, *Bradley University*
Andrew Klein, *DeVry University*
Balaji Krishnan, *University of Memphis*
Mark Leach, *Loyola Marymount University*
Terry Loe, *Kennesaw State University*
James Mullen, *Villanova University*
Paul Myer, *University of Maine*
Frank Notturno, *Madonna University*
Joseph Ouellette, *Bryant University*
Michael Pearson, *Loyola University New Orleans*
Ossi Pessama, *Luleå University of Technology, Sweden*
Kathrynn Pounders, *Louisiana State University*
Woodrow D. Richardson, *Ball State University*
K. Randall Russ, *Belhaven College*
Dheeraj Sharma, *Ball State University*
C. David Shepherd, *Georgia Southern University*
G. David Shows, *Louisiana Tech*
J. Gary Smith, *Middle Tennessee State University*
Michelle D. Steward, *Wake Forest University*
Jim Strong, *California State University–Dominguez Hills*
Brian Tietje, *California Polytechnic State University*
Mike Weber, *Mercer University*
Vicki West, *Texas State University*
John Whelpley, *Vector Marketing Corporation*
Scott Widmier, *Kennesaw State University*
Mike Williams, *Illinois State University*
Mike Wittmann, *University of Southern Mississippi*
Andy Wood, *West Virginia University*

Most important to the initiation and completion of *Sales Management: Building Customer Relationships and Partnerships* were the members of the Houghton Mifflin and Lachina Publishing Services team who diligently and creatively guided us throughout the various stages of development. These included Lisé Johnson, Mike Schenk, Joanne Dauksewicz, and Nicole Mollica, as well as Deborah Thomashow and Annie Beck who coordinated the production efforts. A special thanks also goes to Elisa Adams, who helped us with manuscript development and with many of the opening profiles. Finally, we want to acknowledge our students—past, present and future—who make our teaching and writing enjoyable and meaningful.

Joseph F. Hair, Jr.
Rolph E. Anderson
Rajiv Mehta
Barry J. Babin

About the Authors

Joseph F. Hair, Ph.D.

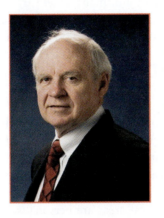

Joseph Hair is Professor of Marketing at Kennesaw State University. He previously held the Copeland Endowed Chair of Entrepreneurship and was Director, Entrepreneurship Institute, Louisiana State University. He was a United States Steel Foundation Fellow at the University of Florida, Gainesville, where he earned his Ph.D. in Marketing in 1971. He has published over 30 books, including *Marketing,* South-Western Publishing Company, 9th edition 2008; (South African, Portuguese, Malaysian, Australian, and Spanish-language editions also available); *Marketing Essentials,* South-Western Publishing Company, 5th edition 2007; *Multivariate Data Analysis,* Prentice-Hall, 6th edition, 2006 (this text cited over 6,500 times according to Google Scholar, January, 2007); *Essentials of Business Research Methods,* Wiley, 2003; *Research Methods for Business,* Wiley, UK, 2007; *Marketing Research,* McGraw-Hill/Irwin, 3rd edition 2006; *Essentials of Marketing Research,* McGraw-Hill/Irwin, 2007; *Sales Management,* Houghton-Mifflin, 2008; *Sales Management,* Random House, 1983; and *Effective Selling,* South-Western Publishing Company, 8th edition, 1991. He also has published numerous articles in professional journals such as the *Journal of Marketing Research, Journal of Academy of Marketing Science, Journal of Business/Chicago, European Business Review, Management Decision, Journal of Advertising Research, Journal of Business Research, Journal of Marketing Theory and Practice, World Journal of Tourism and Small Business Management, European Business Review, Journal of Personal Selling and Sales Management, Industrial Marketing Management, Management Decision, Journal of Experimental Education, Business Horizons, Journal of Retailing, Marketing Education Review, Journal of Marketing Education, Managerial Planning, Medical and Marketing Media, Drugs in Health Care, Multivariate Behavioral Research, Journal of Medical and Pharmaceutical Marketing,* and others.

Dr. Hair is a Distinguished Fellow of the Academy of Marketing Sciences, the Society for Marketing Advances, and Southwestern Marketing Association. He also has served as President of the Academy of Marketing Sciences, the Society for Marketing Advances, the Southern Marketing Association, the Association for Healthcare Research, the Southwestern Marketing Association, and the American Institute for Decision Sciences, Southeast Section, and has been Program Chairperson and Proceedings Editor for several scholarly associations.

Dr. Hair was recognized as the Innovative Marketer of the Year in 2007 by the Marketing Management Association. In 2004 he was awarded the Academy of Marketing Science Outstanding Marketing Teaching Excellence Award. The Louisiana State University Entrepreneurship Institute under his leadership was recognized nationally by

Entrepreneurship Magazine in 2003 as one of the top 12 programs in the United States, and also was ranked #3 in the U.S. in 2004 and 2005 by *Forbes Magazine/ Princeton Review.* Dr. Hair has been retained as a consultant for numerous companies in a wide variety of industries, as well as by the U.S. Department of Agriculture and the U.S. Department of Interior. He also has provided expert testimony, most often in the areas of marketing, entrepreneurship, and economic analysis, and has planned/ presented executive development and management training programs. Finally, he is often invited to give lectures on research techniques, data analysis, and marketing issues for organizations in Europe, Australia, and other locations outside the U.S.

Rolph Anderson, Ph.D.

Rolph Anderson is the Royal H. Gibson Sr. Chair Professor and former Head of the Department of Marketing at Drexel University. He earned his Ph.D. from the University of Florida and his MBA and BA degrees from Michigan State University, where he was a member of the varsity basketball team. His primary research and publication areas are personal selling and sales management, customer relationship management, and customer loyalty. He is author or co-author of 22 textbooks, including *Multivariate Data Analysis,* 6th ed., the most referenced textbook in academic marketing.

Dr. Anderson's research has been widely published in the major journals in his field, including articles in the *Journal of Marketing Research, Journal of Marketing, Journal of Retailing, Journal of the Academy of Marketing Science, Journal of Experimental Education, European Journal of Marketing, Psychology & Marketing, Journal of Global Marketing, Journal of Marketing Education, Journal of Business-to-Business Marketing, Business Horizons, Journal of Managerial Issues, Industrial Marketing Management, Journal of Business & Industrial Marketing, Journal of Personal Selling & Sales Management,* and others. His classic *Journal of Marketing Research* article titled "Consumer Dissatisfaction: The Effect of Disconfirmed Expectations on Perceived Product Performance" was one of the pioneering articles in the study of customer satisfaction. In 1988, he won the national Mu Kappa Tau award for the best article published in the *Journal of Personal Selling & Sales Management.* Dr. Anderson has been selected twice by Drexel's LeBow College of Business students to receive the Faculty Appreciation Award, and he serves as a distinguished fellow of the Center for Teaching Excellence. In 1995, he was recipient of the national "Excellence in Reviewing Award for the *Journal of Personal Selling & Sales Management.* In 1998, he received the American Marketing Association Sales Special Interest Group inaugural "Excellence in Sales Scholarship" award. He received Drexel's LeBow College of Business "Research Achievement" award in 2000–2001, and its "Academic Leadership in Textbook Publishing" award in 2003.

Dr. Anderson has served several professional organizations as an officer, including President, Southeast Institute for Decision Sciences (IDS); Secretary and Board of Directors, Academy of Marketing Science; Vice-President for Programming and Board of Directors, American Marketing Association (Philadelphia Chapter); National Council, Institute for Decision Sciences; Board of Directors, Northeast IDS;

and Co-Chairperson, 61st International American Marketing Association Conference. He serves on the Editorial Boards of six academic journals, and on the Faculty Advisory Board of the Fisher Institute for Professional Selling.

Prior to entering academia, Dr. Anderson worked in sales and managerial positions for three Fortune 500 companies. Active as a business and government consultant, he is also a retired U.S. Navy Supply Corps Captain. With wife, Sallie, they are parents of two current college students, Rachel and Stuart. Professor Anderson's biographical sketch appears in *Who's Who in American Education, Who's Who in Finance and Industry,* and *Who's Who in America.*

Rajiv Mehta, Ph.D.

Rajiv Mehta is an Associate Professor of Marketing at New Jersey Institute of Technology. Previously, he served on the faculty of Loyola University New Orleans. He earned his Ph.D. in Marketing from Drexel University in 1994. He is co-author of *Personal Selling: Building Customer Relationships and Partnerships,* 2nd Edition, with Rolph Anderson and Alan Dubinsky.

Dr. Mehta's research has been widely published in major academic journals and presented at national and international academic conferences. His research, which focuses on the areas of selling and sales management, marketing channels, and global marketing, has appeared in *Journal of Business Research, Industrial Marketing Management, Journal of Personal Selling and Sales Management, Business Horizons, European Journal of Marketing, International Marketing Review, Journal of Business to Business Marketing, Journal of Business and Industrial Marketing, Journal of Marketing Channels, Journal of Global Marketing, International Journal of Physical Distribution and Logistics Management, Journal of Managerial Issues, Journal of Services Marketing, Management Bibliographies and Reviews, Journal of Shopping Center Research,* and others.

In 2001, his co-authored the article "Leadership and Cooperation in Marketing Channels: A Comparative Empirical Analysis of the United States, Finland, and Poland," which received the award for excellence as the outstanding paper in *International Marketing Review.* He also received the Stanley Hollander Best Retail Research Paper Award for another co-authored article entitled "Leadership Styles, Culture, and Cooperation in Global Marketing Channels" that was published in the *Journal of Shopping Center Research.*

At New Jersey Institute of Technology, his contributions to teaching were recognized by the alumni when he has awarded the university-wide Robert W. Van Houten award for Teaching Excellence in 2005. He also received the University Award for Excellence in the Category of Teaching in Upper Division Undergraduate Instruction in 2004. While at Loyola University, New Orleans, its College of Business Administration chose him three straight years to receive the Excellence in Research award.

Prior to entering academia, Dr. Mehta worked in sales and marketing for a major international manufacturer of steel wire ropes and cables.

Barry J. Babin, Ph.D

Barry Babin is the Max P. Watson, Jr. Professor and Head of the Department of Marketing and Analysis at Louisiana Tech University. He earned his Ph.D. and B.S. degrees from Louisiana State University and his MBA from the University of Central Florida. He previously served as the Chair of the Management and Marketing Department at the University of Southern Mississippi.

Dr. Babin's research has been published in over 70 scholarly and professional publications, including articles in the *Journal of Marketing, Journal of Retailing, Journal of Consumer Research, Journal of the Academy of Marketing Science, Journal of Business Research, Journal of Retailing and Consumer Services, Research in Marketing, Journal of International Consumer Marketing, Journal of Services Marketing, Journal of Marketing Theory and Practice,* and the *Journal of Consumer Behaviour.* He is co-author of *Exploring Marketing Research,* 9th Edition, and *Essentials of Marketing Research,* 3rd Edition, with the late Bill Zikmund; *The Essentials of Business Research* with J. Hair, A. Money, and P. Samouel; and the frequently cited *Multivariate Data Analysis,* 6th Edition with J. Hair, R. Anderson, R. Tatham, and W. Black.

Dr. Babin has served as President, Vice-President, and Program Chair for The Academy of Marketing Science and President and Program Chair of The Society for Marketing Advances; he has also been serving as the Associate Editor of Marketing for the *Journal of Business Research* since 1999. He was three times awarded the USM Louis K. Brandt Award for Outstanding Faculty Research as well as the Omerre DeSerres Award for Outstanding Research in Retailing in addition to many other honors.

Before entering academia, Dr. Babin was a weapon systems and specifications auditor for a Defense Contract Audit Agency in Orlando, Florida, and Operations Manager at Kean's in Baton Rouge, Louisiana. He was also a sales representative for Ruello and Associates and performed retail management and buying for Armel, Inc.

SALES MANAGEMENT

Twenty-First Century Sales Force Management

CHAPTER **1**
Introduction to Sales Management and Its Evolving Roles

CHAPTER **2**
Managing Ethics in a Sales Environment

CHAPTER **3**
Customer Relationship Management and Building Partnerships

CHAPTER **4**
The Selling Process

Introduction to Sales Management and Its Evolving Roles

LEARNING OBJECTIVES

When you finish this chapter, you should be able to:

1   Summarize the basic responsibilities and evolving roles of sales management.

2   Demonstrate how sales managers can better integrate their roles with marketing management.

3   Identify and prepare for megatrends that will affect your future in sales management.

4   Evaluate the selection criteria for sales management and compare them to your present and potential qualifications.

5   Analyze how the sales manager's job is expanding and what it will mean for your career.

INSIDE SALES MANAGEMENT

Joel Hollenbeck, VP, Eastern Division Manager, Houghton Mifflin Company

Joel Hollenbeck enjoys wearing a lot of different hats. The vice president and Eastern Division Manager of Houghton Mifflin Company, a Boston-based publisher, he manages fifty-two sales reps and six district managers as they call on customers across the East Coast. Therapist, coach, sales analyst, motivator, and trainer are some of the roles Hollenbeck plays.

The best part of the job for him? "Motivating and challenging people, all with different strengths and weaknesses, and getting them across the finish line at the end of the year," he says. That's the rewarding moment when all the hard work and strategy discussions come to fruition in sales that meet quota.

With a master's degree in government, Hollenbeck didn't initially think of himself as a sales manager. But he found himself intrigued by the challenges of the hiring and recruiting process, and by what he calls the "ultimate test"—the opportunity to take a brand-new hire and shape him or her into a successful sales rep. "It's like watching someone graduate," he says of that proud managerial accomplishment.

The spirit of teamwork in selling was another powerful draw of a career in sales, as was the opportunity to develop both teamwork and leadership skills while managing a group of eight or nine people toward a common goal. His satisfaction in organizing their efforts, budgeting the group's resources, setting goals, selecting new hires, and evaluating each rep's performance were experiences that motivated Hollenbeck to aspire to a higher level of responsibility as a sales manager. They also prepared him to tackle it successfully.

In the end, though, says Hollenbeck, "the job is all about communication. Communication is 75 percent of what I do." Communicating consistently with reps and customers—coaching, problem solving, guiding, motivating, persuading—are still among the most important of his everyday tasks. Another big responsibility is listening—to complaints, concerns, questions, suggestions, problems, reports, and feedback of every kind. Sometimes there's even good news to take in and pass along to the rest of the team.

Looking back on his education, Hollenbeck has no regrets about his liberal arts background, which prepared him well for work in the publishing industry. "I'd probably have benefited from a few more business courses," he admits, but he also credits learning on the job with giving him the skills in analysis and forecasting that he now relies on every day. "Analysis, forecasting, those skills can be taught," he says. "Those are the means by which you get better information for your people, so they can do their job."

While a lot can be learned, the traits Hollenbeck feels a good sales manager should bring to the job are competitive drive, good communications skills, willingness to be a team player, and the empathy and insight that make a good coach. How does he feel about his career as a sales manager? Right now, he says, "I can't imagine myself doing anything else."

What Is Sales Management?

What an exciting time it is to be—or anticipate being—a sales manager! Sales management today is one of the most challenging, versatile, and rewarding of all possible careers. Few jobs are more crucial to the ultimate success of a business than sales management, because it shapes and determines nearly all the firm's interactions with customers.[1] Sales managers are respected marketing professionals who oversee the sales force—the direct income producers who determine the financial health of their organizations. Working together, salespeople and sales managers generate direct revenue for their organizations while carrying out their company's marketing strategies in their day-to-day interactions with customers.

In its "Dictionary of Marketing Terms" (www.marketingpower.com), the American Marketing Association (AMA) defines sales management as "the planning, direction, and control of the personal selling activities of a business unit, including recruiting, selecting, training, equipping, assigning, routing, supervising, paying and motivating as these tasks apply to the personal sales force." This definition, however, fails to capture the fast-paced, expanding roles of sales management in satisfying customers and achieving company objectives. In today's highly competitive markets, sales managers are trying all kinds of new ideas, sales channels, and technologies to develop mutually profitable long-run relationships with customers. At the same time, technological innovations, dynamic buyer behavior, and managerial creativity are dramatically changing the way sales managers understand, prepare for, and accomplish their jobs.[2] The opportunities and challenges ahead for sales managers appear to be awesome!

Types, Titles, and Hierarchical Levels of Sales Managers

Sales Management
The function of planning, directing, and controlling the personal selling activities of a business unit, including recruiting, selecting, training, equipping, assigning, routing, supervising, paying, and motivating as these tasks apply to the sales force.

Depending on the nature of the organization and its managerial philosophy, **sales management** types and titles can vary widely. In some organizations, the sales manager may be little more than a supervisor of the sales force, a kind of "supersalesperson" who shows the salespeople how best to do their jobs.[3] In other organizations, the sales manager is the marketing manager in all but name. Most sales management positions fit somewhere between these two extremes.

In a national study, sales managers were asked, "If you couldn't use the term 'sales manager', what might you use to describe the job you do?" They gave themselves various titles, including account manager, problem solver, channel manager, business manager, team leader, group psychologist, resource coordinator, sales department administrator, change manager, director of income, contact manager, staff development specialist, trainer/coach, and customer relationship manager.[4] Clearly sales managers see themselves as wearing a lot of hats and doing everything from traditional leadership and coaching of the sales force to taking on new roles in sales channel management and customer relationship management.

Many not-for-profit organizations also employ salespeople—no matter what their job title—to generate income and/or achieve organizational goals, so they also need people to do sales manager types of activities. For instance, recruiters for all-voluntary military services, fundraisers for political parties, institutional development officers, and college admissions representatives are all engaged in various forms of "selling." Not surprisingly, then, selling and sales management concepts and techniques apply to non-commercial as well as to commercial organizations.

There are various titles and hierarchical levels of sales managers across diverse organizations. Typical position titles and responsibilities of sales managers in business organizations are shown in Table 1.1.

Responsibilities and Duties of Sales Managers

Macroenvironment
Largely uncontrollable factors—such as technology, competition, economy, laws, culture, and ethics—that are continuously changing and to which sales managers must adapt in overseeing the sales force.

Stakeholders
Company employees, suppliers, financial community, media, stockholders, special interest groups, governments, and the general public—all of whom have a stake, interest, and frequently an opinion about sales force activities.

While sales managers' roles are constantly evolving in response to changing market conditions, they still center on traditional sales management responsibilities and duties. Essentially, sales managers are paid to plan, lead, and control the personal selling activities of their organizations. They carry out these responsibilities and duties within the larger framework of organizational objectives, marketing strategies, and target markets. At the same time, they must continuously monitor and adjust to various changing **macroenvironment** factors (technological, competitive, economic, legal, cultural, and ethical) and the company's **stakeholders** (employees, suppliers, financial community, media, stockholders, special interest groups, governments, and the general public). In sum, sales managers today have an eclectic and increasingly challenging job that requires flexibility, adaptability, and ongoing learning. Let's take a closer look at the responsibilities and duties of contemporary sales managers. To facilitate our discussions, Figure 1.1 presents an overall conceptual framework for sales management decision making and indicates the chapter in the text where each component is discussed.

TABLE 1.1 Sales Management Hierarchies: Titles and Responsibilities

Vice President of Sales	This is the highest-level sales executive who, depending on the company organization, reports to the vice president of marketing or the company president. The vice president of sales is usually involved in longer-run, top-level planning for the company and is directly responsible for sales strategy. In companies with no vice president of marketing, the vice president of sales is responsible for all marketing activities.
National Sales Manager	This position provides the link between the highest-level company decisions on overall strategy and the line sales managers responsible for carrying out sales plans in their respective regions. Participating in both strategic and tactical planning, the national sales manager provides overall direction to the sales force and renders top-level decisions on sales operations to regional sales managers.
Regional, Division, or Zone Sales Manager	As the titles indicate, these managers are responsible for line sales activities for successively smaller subdivisions of company sales operations. Starting with the smallest subdivision, zone sales managers report to division sales managers, who in turn report to regional sales managers.
District, Branch, or Field Sales Manager	These are the first-level line sales managers responsible for handling day-to-day activities of salespeople. Usually (but not always), the titles "district," "branch," and "field" indicate successively smaller territorial responsibilities.
Sales Supervisor	This more experienced salesperson is charged with providing general guidance and advice to a few salespeople in a given branch or field territory.
National Account Manager (NAM), Key Account Manager (KAM), Senior Account Executive	These are top-performing, usually more senior salespeople who are responsible for handling one or only a few major customers, such as large national retail chains (Sears, K-Mart, J.C. Penney, or Wal-Mart).
Marketing Representative, Sales Representative, Account Manager, Sales Engineer, Salesperson	These are only a few of the titles for front-line salespeople, as used by various companies that sell consumer or industrial products and services.
Assistant Sales Manager, Sales Analyst, Sales Training Manager	These titles are representative of the many staff positions needed to support the line functions of sales. Staff people function at every level in the sales organization, from corporate headquarters to the smallest branch office. Many have impressive titles, such as corporate vice president of sales or assistant national sales manager, yet have no line sales management authority. Usually, staff members in these positions assist in performing various related functions at different levels in the sales organization (sales planning, sales promotion, sales recruiting, sales training, and sales analysis). Sales staff people often receive opportunities to switch to line management positions.

■ Twenty-First Century Sales Force Management

Chapters 1–4 will help you understand the overall roles of sales managers (chapter 1) and salespeople (chapter 4) while professionally and ethically (chapter 2) building customer relationships and partnerships (chapter 3). Specific sales management responsibilities and duties are discussed in chapters 5–14, but a short overview is offered at this point to help you anticipate and appreciate what lies ahead.

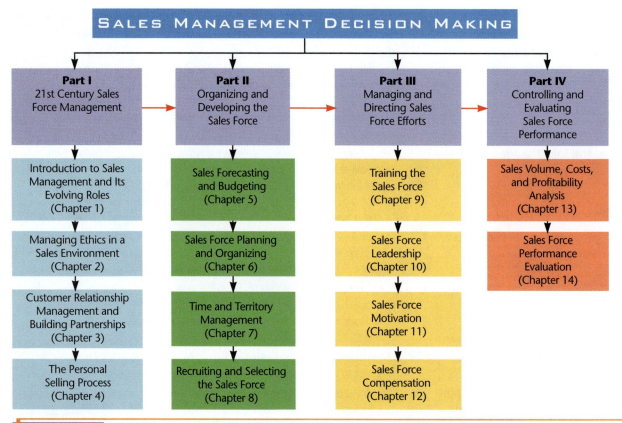

FIGURE 1.1 Responsibilities and Duties of Sales Managers: A Conceptual Framework

■ Organizing and Developing the Sales Force

Sales forecasting and budgeting (chapter 5) are the cornerstones supporting virtually all sales management decisions and activities. Sales managers must estimate *market potential* for their industry and *sales potential* for their company before developing a final *sales forecast* on which to base operational planning and budgeting for their sales force. Savvy sales managers employ both quantitative and qualitative approaches and study the similarities and differences between the two sets of results before deciding on the final sales forecast. Funds are needed to implement any sales plan, so preparing a realistic sales budget is essential. A *sales budget* is simply a financial plan of expenditures needed to accomplish the organization's sales goals and objectives. The purpose of the sales budget is to ensure that organizational resources are allocated in the most efficient and effective way over the period of the plan. Accurate sales forecasting and budgeting are critical to the success of any organization.

Sales force planning and organizing (chapter 6) are essential functions of sales managers because they provide guidelines and direction for most other sales decisions and activities. As planners, sales managers must set sales goals and objectives, establish sales policies and procedures, devise sales force strategies and tactics, and implement controls to ensure that sales goals and objectives are achieved. Planning requires sales managers to anticipate the possible outcomes and future implications of current decisions, so in many ways, planning is an attempt to manage the future. As organizers, sales managers must determine the optimal number of salespeople to hire and the best way to structure the sales force (geographically, by product, by customer type, or by some combination of these factors). Determining the appropriate number of salespeople and how to organize them affects several sales management decision areas, including job descriptions, compensation methods, sales forecasts, budgets, territory assignments, supervision, motivation, and evaluation of sales force performance. In some companies, the sales manager must also decide whether to substitute independent *manufacturers' agents* (who receive commissions only) for some or even all members of the direct sales force. Adjustments may be needed in sales force size as well as structure in response to changes in marketing strategy or fluctuations of uncontrollable variables in the marketing environment. In all cases, the overriding purpose in selecting a particular sales organizational structure and size should be to optimize the achievement of sales objectives and goals.

Time and territory management strategies (chapter 7) help sales managers determine which accounts their salespeople should call on, when, and how often. To effectively allocate sales force efforts, the sales manager must first design sales territories. A *sales territory* is a market segment or group of present and potential customers who usually share some common characteristics relevant to purchasing behavior. Territories should be compared on the basis of sales potential, which in turn decides individual *sales quotas* (the motivational targets assigned to the sales force as a whole and to salespeople individually). After sales territories have been determined, management may design a formal *routing* pattern for salespeople to follow in calling on customers. Some sales managers prefer to have the salespeople assume responsibility for efficient scheduling and routing themselves, but in either case a predetermined plan should be carried out. Few salespeople make optimal use of their most precious resource: time. Thus, one of the most important jobs of sales managers is to train and retrain their salespeople in techniques for improving the management of their time and territory.

© Stock Connection Blue / Alamy

● **Because the sales manager's job is so eclectic, it is critical that he or she be trained in an array of activities such as sales forecasting, budgeting, leadership, motivation, compensation, and performance evaluation—essential skills for successful sales management.**

Recruiting and selecting the sales force (chapter 8) includes identifying sources of potential sales recruits, methods of reaching them, and strategies for attracting them to apply for a sales job. Once applicants have been recruited, the sales manager must devise a system for measuring applicants against predetermined job requirements. This involves analysis of the numerous tools and techniques available for processing applicants. Finally, the decision to select or reject each applicant must be made. New salespeople need to be assimilated or blended smoothly into the sales organization. Included in the assimilation process are an explanation of job responsibilities and managerial expectations, introduction to coworkers, and help for the new salesperson as he or she adjusts socially and psychologically to the organization—and sometimes to the community as well.

■ Managing and Directing Sales Force Efforts

Traditionally, *training the sales force (chapter 9)* has focused mainly on selling techniques. But customers today are more knowledgeable than ever, competition is more intense, and customers are demanding more service, so progressive companies have intensified their sales force training and are using the latest telecommunications advances to enhance learning and provide "real-world" sales practice. Sales managers are also trying to broaden the perspectives of their salespeople by blending sales, marketing, and finance concepts into sales training. This broader-based training not only helps salespeople to see how their jobs fit into the overall organization but also prepares them for future responsibilities when they may be promoted to sales or marketing managers, or perhaps eventually to top management. Anytime a salesperson is promoted to sales manager or receives significantly broader or different responsibilities, it is a good idea to consider additional training. In designing a training program, the sales manager must answer several questions: Who should receive the training? Who should do the training? Where, when, and how should the training be accomplished? What should be taught? Sales training programs should seek to help salespeople continually grow in knowledge, selling skills, and customer understanding while reinforcing good attitudes about themselves and their jobs, companies, and customers.

Sales force leadership (chapter 10) may be thought of as the emotional process of exercising psychological, social, and inspirational influence on individual salespeople and the sales force collectively toward the achievement of organizational objectives, goals, and values. In today's intensely competitive markets, organizations have become flatter and leaner, thereby requiring greater leadership skills at all organizational levels. Supervision, management, and leadership are all related but quite different concepts. Supervision entails performing tasks that deal with monitoring the daily work activities of subordinates. Management is primarily a *learned* process whereby subordinates are guided by formally prescribed duties toward achieving organizational goals. In contrast, leadership is more of an *emotional* process that seeks to inspire salespeople to greater achievements by providing a positive vision for the future. Several different theories, concepts, and approaches to effective sales force leadership will be explored. It is up to the individual sales manager to choose those most appropriate in any given situation.

Sales force motivation (chapter 11) deals with the set of dynamic interpersonal processes that stimulate the initiation, direction, intensity, and persistence of work-related behaviors of salespeople toward attaining organizational goals and objectives.

Several theories of motivation offer intuitively appealing, but slightly different, explanations for why salespeople exert high levels of effort under varying circumstances to reach personal and organizational goals. We analyze three types of theories (content, process, and reinforcement oriented) as particularly relevant to sales managers. Depending on the situation and the composition of the sales force, sales managers will need to exercise their individual judgments in deciding which motivation approach applies best.

Sales force compensation (chapter 12) is widely recognized as the most important and least ambiguous way to motivate salesperson performance. It can be viewed as all monetary payments and benefits used to remunerate salespeople. The sales force compensation plan is the "steering wheel" that enables management to directly influence salesperson performance and should reflect the company's goals. While there are a variety of ways to compensate salespeople, most companies use three main methods: (1) *Straight salary*—a fixed amount of money at fixed intervals, such as weekly or monthly; (2) *Straight commission*—an amount that varies with results, usually sales or profits, and (3) *Combination*—a mix of salary and commission. Besides salary and commissions, *financial compensation* also should include reimbursement of sales expenses and transportation. *Non-financial incentives* may include use of a company car, office space, secretarial help, and special company benefits such as life insurance, a retirement plan, and health care. Sales force compensation plans should be reviewed frequently and revised, when appropriate, to ensure they continue to be effective.

■ Controlling and Evaluating Sales Force Performance

Sales volume, costs, and profitability analysis (chapter 13) is essential to ensure the organization's bottom-line goal of improving profitability. Sales managers need to analyze sales volume, costs, and profit relationships by product lines, territories, customers, and salespersons as well as across sales and marketing functions. These analyses seek to identify unprofitable sales units so that sales managers can take timely corrective action to allocate sales force efforts better and improve profitability.

Sales force performance evaluation (chapter 14) is perhaps the single most important activity for sales managers and their salespeople. Sales force performance must be measured and evaluated to determine commissions and bonuses for salespeople and to make promotion decisions. The overall purpose of performance evaluation, however, is to improve organizational profitability by improving sales force productivity. For effective managerial control and evaluation, standards of performance must be established, actual performance compared to the predetermined standards, and appropriate corrective action taken to improve performance.

Not to be overlooked in evaluating sales force performance is how well ethical guidelines and standards of social responsibility are being met. A salesperson's reputation for ethical behavior and integrity is one of the most valuable assets he or she can bring to negotiations with prospects and customers. Nothing will destroy the credibility and performance of salespeople faster than the perception that they do not operate in an ethical or socially responsible manner. Most companies understand the importance of ethical behavior and provide written ethical codes and training for all their employees.[5]

Expanding Roles of Sales Managers

Marketing
An organizational function and a set of processes for creating, communicating, and delivering value to customers and for managing customer relationships in ways that benefit the organization and its stakeholders.

For nearly two decades, the official AMA definition of **marketing** was "the process of planning and executing the conception, pricing, promotion, and distribution of ideas, goods and services to create exchanges that satisfy individual and organizational objectives." In 2004, the board of directors of the American Marketing Association approved a new definition:[6] "Marketing is an organizational function and a set of processes for creating, communicating, and delivering value to customers and for managing customer relationships in ways that benefit the organization and its stakeholders."

■ Managing Customer Relationships

What's the difference? The old definition viewed marketing largely from the seller perspective by emphasizing management of the marketing mix and creating exchanges. But the new definition shifts the perspective to the customer by focusing on delivering value and managing customer relationships. As Northwestern University marketing professor Philip Kotler puts it, "Current marketing is moving from a transaction-orientation to a customer-relationship-building orientation"[7] **Customer relationship management** (CRM) is based on the idea that developing closer relationships with customers is the best way to earn purchasing loyalty, and that loyal customers are more profitable than non-loyal customers.[8] CRM can be defined as "a cross-functional process for achieving a continuing dialogue with customers, across all their contact and access points, with personalized treatment of the most valued customers, to increase customer retention and the effectiveness of marketing initiatives."[9]

Customer Relationship Management (CRM)
A company-wide effort to satisfy customers across all "touch" points and provide personalized treatment of the most valued customers in order to increase customer retention and profitability.

Although we discuss CRM in chapter 3, you might want to visit the websites of companies such as Salesforce.com (www.salesforce.com) and Oracle (www.oracle.com) to gain a greater appreciation of how firms can gain a competitive edge by adopting innovative, cutting-edge approaches to manage sales information and serve their customers better.

● **Salesforce.com (www.salesforce.com) is an example of a company website that advocates attaining a competitive edge by adopting innovative, cutting-edge approaches to manage sales information and better serve customers.**

■ Serving as Customer Consultants

In line with their company's CRM orientation, contemporary sales managers are training salespeople to think longer term by striving to build ongoing relationships and mutually profitable partnerships with customers. Salespeople are being asked to go beyond merely selling, toward serving and a role more like that of customer consultant and business partner. What's more, as companies stress the value of customer relationship management, sales managers and their sales forces are taking on greater roles in carrying out CRM strategies in the selling situation.[10] That means today's sales managers are responsible for helping their salespeople devise and carry out strategies for building these profitable long-term relationships with customers. At the same time, they also need to skillfully develop their in-house relationships by "selling" sales force goals and customer requirements within their own companies to ensure the timely service and technical support their salespeople need. Fortunately, many contemporary senior executives recognize that the whole organization needs to have a customer orientation in order to retain customers and enhance profitability.[11]

■ Managing the Hybrid Sales Force

For the foreseeable future, sales managers will be under tremendous pressure to adjust to rapidly changing market forces. For one thing, instead of merely directing the *field* sales force, many sales managers now oversee salespeople across multiple online and offline marketing channels. They work with telesalespeople, telemarketers, e-commerce salespeople, direct mailers, international salespeople, missionary salespeople, technical salespeople, manufacturers' agents, and multicultural and international salespeople. To illustrate, SPX Cooling Technologies (www.spxcooling.com), a manufacturer of industrial water-cooling towers headquartered in Overland, Kansas, employs a full-time direct sales force of 40 people in 9 North American locations. But the company also employs about 70 manufacturers' agents in what it calls "a hybrid sales force approach." As more emphasis is placed on long-term customer relationships, SPX recognizes how important it is to minimize turnover of the salespeople calling on its customers, so that buyer-seller relationships are not disrupted. Unlike its direct sales force, with annual turnover above 20 percent, SPX's manufacturers' agents work solely on commissions and tend to stay in one sales territory and develop it for life.[12] In this era of closer customer relationships and multiple sales channels, such hybrid sales forces will be more common, and sales managers will need to develop the diverse skills to lead them.

What Qualities Are Needed to Be a Sales Manager?

Exactly what qualities, skills, and attitudes are required to be a successful contemporary sales manager? The nearby *Sales Management in Action* box describes the eclectic abilities needed to be a sales manager today.

Integrating Sales Management and Marketing Management

Sales management is a specialized set of responsibilities and activities within the larger field of marketing management. In a broad sense, sales managers are really *marketing* managers with the specific task of managing the sales force.[13] Should the link between sales and marketing be closer? Well, in international surveys across a wide range of business-to-business industries, senior executives identified sales and marketing integration as one of the organizational changes that would do the most to improve sales force performance.[14] Many experts believe the sales manager heads the most important of all marketing activities—the critical revenue-generating and customer relationship functions—that ultimately determine the success or failure of the overall marketing plan.[15] But without thoroughly understanding the company's goals and marketing strategy, few sales managers can successfully integrate marketing and sales. Let's look at how headquarters marketing and the field sales force support each other.

SALES MANAGEMENT IN ACTION

What It Takes to Be a Sales Manager

First and foremost, sales managers have to be effective leaders and motivators of people. In addition, they must be good decision makers, creative problem solvers, and outstanding communicators. As part of the overall marketing team, they must work closely with other functional areas, helping to coordinate and focus the efforts of product development, manufacturing, market research, and promotion. For example, sales managers help develop national marketing objectives and strategy with the advertising department, and then offer insightful advice on how to tailor these plans to match regional differences, the competitive environment, and consumer preferences. Sales managers use findings from market research to better demonstrate the benefits of their products to their customers while helping generate strong brand support. Based on feedback from customers and monitoring of competitive offerings, sales managers make recommendations for new or improved products (better functional design, safety enhancements, or user-friendly packaging). Sales managers must spend many hours in their offices poring over financial data to analyze costs and profits by products, customers, territories, and salespeople to decide how best to allocate budgets and human resources to enhance productivity and profitability.

To be successful in sales management, you have to enjoy challenges and solving problems because you'll be encountering them almost every day. Moreover, you have to be resilient enough not to become discouraged when a customer doesn't buy, resourceful enough to find solutions for customer problems, motivated enough to set lofty goals for yourself, and then driven enough to surpass them. Most important, you have to love working with people within and outside your company because that's the heart of this critical boundary-spanning job. Because sales managers' responsibilities require working closely with customers and with people in nearly all departments of the company while trying to control costs and improve profits, a career in sales management provides the kind of broad experience and skills important to assuming senior management responsibilities.

SOURCE: www.brodart.com; www.complinet.com; http://jobs .monstergulf.com; www.servepath.com; www.sandmanhotels.com; www.blackboard.com; www.destingyp.com; www.shoreypr.com

■ The Field Sales Force and Headquarters Marketing Support Team

An organization's marketing team usually consists of two basic groups: (1) the field sales force and (2) the headquarters marketing support team. While the field sales force is working with customers out in their sales territories, the headquarters marketing team is providing critical support and service functions. This headquarters support includes contributions from the following areas:

- **Advertising.** Coordinates product or service advertising, usually through an outside agency
- **Sales promotion.** Develops brochures, catalogs, direct-mail pieces, and special promotions
- **Sales aids.** Prepares videos, podcasts, product samples or prototypes, flip charts, PowerPoint presentations, and other audio-visual materials for sales presentations
- **Trade shows.** Coordinates arrangements for participation in exhibits and trade shows
- **Product publicity.** Prepares and distributes news releases to various media about products and services

- **Marketing research.** Collects and interprets data about markets, products, customers, sales, competitors, and other factors
- **Marketing and sales planning.** Assists in the preparation of marketing and sales objectives, strategies, and tactics
- **Forecasting.** Prepares sales forecasts and predicts market trends
- **Product planning and development.** Helps in planning, developing, and testing new and improved products
- **Market development.** Provides support for deeper penetration of current markets and entering new markets
- **Public relations.** Explains the actions of the sales force to the company's various stakeholders, including employees, the media, special interest groups, suppliers, government agencies, legislators, the financial community, company stockholders, and the general public
- **Internet communications.** Assists with online customer service, website development, and customer databases

Specific responsibilities can vary widely across marketing support teams, and some companies may outsource tasks to external specialists such as advertising agencies, marketing research houses, consulting organizations, and public relations firms. Sales managers need to keep in close touch with these headquarters marketing support people, and with the outside specialists. Having friendly, cooperative relationships with these teams can make it easier to obtain extra support and services to measurably improve sales force performance. Promoting or continuing cold or contentious relationships here can only do a disservice to the sales force.

● **Salespeople and sales managers work together to generate revenue for their organizations—which often involves customer relationship management (CRM) activities such as promoting their products at trade shows and conventions.**

▪ Integrated Marketing Communication

Integrated Marketing Communication (IMC)
The coordination of promotional elements (advertising, personal selling, sales promotion, public relations, direct marketing, and publicity) with other marketing mix elements (product, pricing, and distribution).

Another important reason for maintaining cooperation between the field sales force and headquarters marketing support is to improve communication with customers. The coordination of promotional elements (advertising, personal selling, sales promotion, direct marketing, and public relations) and other marketing efforts is called **integrated marketing communication** (IMC). Many companies today are recognizing that they need to integrate the wide range of promotional tools and other marketing efforts in order to communicate effectively and efficiently while presenting a consistent brand image and message to customers. Thus, they're planning and coordinating the total set of marketing communication programs simultaneously, instead of planning each one separately.[16] Since personal selling is the most important and highest-cost component of the promotional mix for business-to-business selling, progressive sales managers should work closely with other promotional mix areas in integrating the firm's message for its target customers. When implemented properly, IMC can improve sales force effectiveness and increase company profitability, as illustrated in the nearby *Sales Management in Action* box.

SALES MANAGEMENT IN ACTION

Impact of IMC on the Sales Force and Profits

Red Star Yeast Co. (www.redstaryeast.com) specializes in developing flavor enhancers for large food manufacturers. Historically, Red Star's marketing communication program consisted of spending several hundred thousand dollars yearly for traditional advertising in trade magazines and business periodicals. After Red Star assessed the effectiveness of its trade advertising, however, its managers were surprised to learn that only 10 percent of those who responded to the ads were considered "A" leads or top prospects for the firm's products. A startling 70 percent were "C" leads—people or companies that weren't worthwhile cultivating profit-wise. The inefficiency of Red Star's trade advertising caused its executives to completely revise its marketing communications program. One major limitation, however, was that its marketing budget could not be increased, so Red Star decided to adopt an *integrated marketing communications* (IMC) program.

In the past, the company had no formal sales presentations but instead relied on ad hoc one-to-one selling with food technologists. This led to a great deal of confusion and inconsistencies about how to use Red Star products in day-to-day customer applications. Therefore, Red Star decided to allocate some of its advertising budget to developing educational materials such as brochures and newsletters that more fully addressed customer issues and concerns. These materials were sent to clients and key customers before they met with the salespeople. In addition, the company developed a sales presentation for its salespeople targeted at clients and prospective research and development (R&D) departments.

Red Star also drastically reduced spending on ineffective television and radio advertising, diverting dollars instead into direct mail advertising, trade shows, and customer relationships to build a strong customer database. For customer education and sales promotion, Red Star developed an interactive computer software tutorial on flavor enhancers and specific Red Star products. About 3,000 of these software programs were sent to customers and prospects in advance of sales calls. Its IMC program led Red Star to new promotional channels, fresh messages, and a yearly double-digit increase in revenue and profits. Importantly, Red Star achieved all this without increasing its marketing communications budget.

SOURCE: Knight Ridder Tribune Business News (November 5, 2005), p. 1; Chemical Market Reporter (June 12, 2000), p. 31; *The Business Journal-Milwaukee* (August 18, 2000), p. 6; *Business Wire* (April 27, 1998), p. 1.

Monitoring and Adapting to the Macroenvironment

Sales managers work within the larger framework of their organization's objectives, marketing strategies, and target markets. And they must respond to the concerns of their company's stakeholders—including employees, suppliers, financial community, media, stockholders, special interest groups, government, and the general public. Every corporation has many stakeholders who share a vested interest in corporate activities, and an increasing number of companies are becoming proactive in dealing with these indirect partners. Large companies, for example, usually have public affairs departments that try to influence legislation and promote the company to stockholders, the financial community, and the media. Beyond these publics or stakeholders is the larger macroenvironment, which often brings dramatic, unexpected changes in technology, economic conditions, resource availability, competitors, laws, culture, and ethical standards.[17] Sales managers must continuously monitor and adjust to these changing domestic and global variables because they can sharply affect sales.

Successful sales managers need to be alert for new market opportunities as well as threats to existing markets. As the organization's "eyes and ears" in the marketplace, the sales force has a special responsibility to identify opportunities and threats and report them back to headquarters. The sales manager thus operates a kind of early warning system that, if successful, is invaluable to achieving the organization's short-run and long-run objectives. Organizations usually earn their highest profits by capitalizing on opportunities, not just solving problems. Cisco Systems exploited a marketing opportunity to build customer relationships and sales while reducing selling costs, as explained in the nearby *Sales Management in Action* box.

SALES MANAGEMENT IN ACTION

Cisco Systems: Building Customer Relationships via the Internet

Cisco Systems (www.cisco.com) sells the networking products that make the Internet and most corporate intranets work, so naturally it uses the Web to grow its customer relationships. While most other companies are still using the Web primarily as an information channel, Cisco's website is a tool for its salespeople to build customer relationships while making sales. It allows customers to track the status of their orders and get up-to-date pricing and availability information as well as technical advice, freeing up the salespeople to do what they do best—sell. Cisco's site receives hundreds of thousands of hits a month, translating into millions of dollars in sales and over 50 percent of its total revenue. Exploiting this channel opportunity has greatly reduced selling and customer service costs for Cisco. Instead of spending a lot of time answering customer questions about orders and technical problems, Cisco's salespeople focus on maintaining existing customer relationships and finding new prospects.

SOURCE: Rahul Bhaskar and Yi Zhang, "CRM Systems Used for Targeting Market: A Case at Cisco Systems." IEEE International Conference on e-Business Engineering (October 2005), 183–186; www.quovera.com/case/cs_ciscoCCA.html; http://www.cisco.com/web/partners/pr11/pr66/crm_express/ partners_ pgm_concept_home.html

■ Megatrends Affecting Sales Management

What lies ahead for sales managers? Today and for the foreseeable future, several inexorable forces or megatrends will continue to dramatically impact personal selling and sales management. Sales-related megatrends fall into three major categories—*behavioral, technological,* and *managerial,* as shown in Table 1.2.[18]

Behavioral Forces. Among the most important megatrends affecting the sales manager's job are changing behavioral forces, which are leading to more expert and demanding buyers, rising customer expectations, globalization of markets, empowerment of customers, and micro-segmentation of domestic markets. As customers become increasingly empowered and their purchasing expectations rise, they are becoming more sophisticated in their purchasing decisions and intolerant of poor product quality or service. Both domestic and global competitors remain ever alert to capture customers from companies that are not fully satisfying them, so there is no room for seller complacency in today's intensely competitive markets.

Technological Forces. U.S. companies and consumers spend over $400 billion annually on computer hardware, software, and technology services.[19] Thus, sales managers and their salespeople have their work cut out for them in trying to keep up with the

TABLE 1.2 Megatrends Affecting Sales Management

BEHAVIORAL FORCES

- More Expert and Demanding Buyers
- Rising Customer Expectations
- Globalization of Markets
- Empowerment of Customers
- Micro-Segmentation of Domestic Markets

TECHNOLOGICAL FORCES

- Sales Force Automation
  - Portable computers (notebook, hand-held, and pocket PCs)
  - Electronic data interchange
  - Videoconferencing (via desktop, laptop, or hand-held computers)
  - Multi-function cell phones and satellite pagers
  - Voice mail, e-mail, and instant messaging
- Mobile Virtual Sales Offices
- Electronic Commerce
  - Internet
    - Blogs
    - Podcasting
    - Screen sharing
    - WebEx
  - Extranets
  - Intranets

MANAGERIAL FORCES

- Selling Cost Reduction Efforts
- Shift to Direct Marketing Alternatives
  - Direct mail (catalogs, brochures, and sales letters)
  - Telemarketing
  - Teleselling
  - Personalized e-mail
  - Kiosks
  - Facsimile
- Shortage of Business-to-Business Salespeople
- Developments in Information Management
  - Database marketing
  - Data warehousing
  - Data mining
  - Push technology
  - Professional Certification of Salespeople

Sales Force Automation (SFA)

The use of high-tech sales tools by salespeople to work more effectively and efficiently.

technology their prospects and customers are using. **Sales force automation** (SFA) is the use of high-tech tools that help salespeople work effectively and efficiently. Sales managers who make skillful and efficient use of swiftly developing SFA technology to increase the productivity of their salespeople in selling to and serving customers are most likely to be successful in the years ahead.[20] To gain a critical understanding of how SFA technologies can augment revenues and increase bottom-line performance, examine the website of Dendrite (www.dendrite.com), a global sales technology solutions provider to clients in the health-care industry.

As seen in Table 1.2, sales managers and salespeople already use a host of SFA innovations. Over 60 percent of the managerial respondents in one study indicated that their companies were generating more revenue by using sales technologies.[21] When innovations come along that promise to cut costs and increase efficiency, many companies will adopt them promptly, so sales managers must also adopt them rapidly to keep pace with customers. Instant messaging, for example, is being used by sales teams in different cities around the world to query coworkers and customers anywhere for an instant response without picking up the phone or logging into e-mail. No company can afford to lag behind in adopting technological advances that can increase its effectiveness and efficiency in profitably satisfying customers.

Reprinted by permission of Dendrite.

● **Dendrite (www.dendrite.com), a global sales technology solutions provider to clients in the health-care industry, helps companies implement sales force automation technologies to increase sales revenues and improve bottom-line performance.**

© Edward Bock / Corbis

● **By deploying SFA technology to salespeople and using the latest information management tools, sales managers can increase productivity while reducing sales and marketing costs to improve profitability.**

Managerial Forces. How are sales organizations responding to these relentless behavioral and technological megatrends? As revealed in Table 1.2, they're trying various strategies such as reducing selling costs, shifting from field selling to direct-marketing alternatives, hiring and developing specialized sales personnel to cope with the shortage of business-to-business (B2B) salespeople, requiring salespeople to obtain professional certification to enhance their credibility with customers, and using the latest developments in information management. Sales manager creativity in promptly responding to evolving behavioral and technological megatrends can give the sales force a significant competitive advantage.

Information Management Tools. Fortunately, sales managers have valuable new data collection and analysis tools that are helping them respond to the domestic and global megatrends affecting the operation of their sales organizations. Among the most widely used of these information management tools are database marketing, data warehousing, data mining, and push technology—all discussed in chapter 3.

How Well Are Sales Managers Performing?

Sales managers have a challenging job, and they're bound to be criticized by some organization members no matter how well they handle their duties. A study reported in *Sales & Marketing Management* identified a number of complaints that salespeople have about their own sales managers. Some of the most common were that sales managers did not take their salespeople's concerns seriously, demanded too much paperwork, and failed to follow up on problems.[22]

Some major reasons why sales managers can fail to perform at higher levels are (1) illogical selection of sales managers, (2) inadequate sales management training programs, (3) lack of a long-run customer relationship orientation in handling sales operations, and (4) insufficient blending of sales, marketing, and financial knowledge.[23]

■ Illogical Selection of Sales Managers

Through no fault of their own, newly selected sales managers are probably marketing's best example of the Peter Principle: "In a hierarchy, every employee tends to rise to his level of incompetence."[24] Despite articles by marketing scholars and practitioners who stress that a super salesperson does not necessarily make a good sales manager, the reward for a sales rep who does an outstanding selling job for a couple of years or so is still usually promotion to sales management—a position for which he or she may be ill prepared. Ironically, the very skills that enable a person to be an excellent salesperson may inhibit him or her from being a good sales manager. As Figure 1.2 indicates, as individuals climb up the managerial staircase, the skills needed to excel change. But at all levels, interpersonal skills are critical to serving effectively as the vital link between the sales force and higher management.

Some sales organizations suffer because the sales manager remains too involved in doing instead of managing. Time devoted to determining how to accomplish work through other people is "managing." Time spent on performing activities that subordinates could do is "doing." New sales managers often unconsciously become involved in doing because they feel comfortable in continuing to apply the same skills that earned them promotion to sales management. Even in small businesses where the size of the sales force restricts the amount of time they can devote to managing, sales

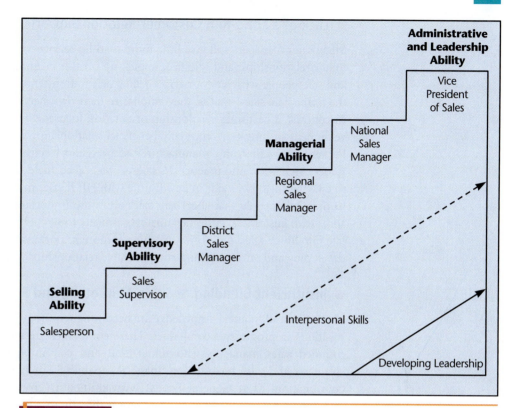

FIGURE 1.2 Sales Management Hierarchy: Skill and Ability Requirements

managers still should recognize that managerial tasks come first. For example, when sales managers make sales calls on their own, they are not managing. But when they make calls with the salespeople to analyze the latter's presentations, they are performing management duties. Subordinates usually recognize when a manager is doing rather than managing, and few sales managers enhance their own stature with the sales force by preempting salespeople's jobs.

■ Inadequate Sales Management Training

Compounding the problem of poor selection criteria for promotion to sales management is the inadequacy of sales management training programs. While many companies spend thousands of dollars to train new salespeople, many of these same companies fail to train sales managers adequately. In studies of sales managers from a cross section of sixteen industries, fewer than half indicated that their companies provided any sales management training at all.[25] Even when they do, it often emphasizes company policies and procedures. Seldom is adequate and sound training provided in what constitutes effective management practice or what the holistic role of the successful sales manager should be. As the linchpin between the selling and buying organizations, sales managers are too essential to organizational success to be excluded from managerial training. In fact, over the long run, managerial training for sales managers is even more critical to the organization because such a high percentage of company CEOs come from sales backgrounds. One study of 1,000 companies by the executive search firm Heidrick and Struggles found that over 30 percent of CEOs came from selling and marketing backgrounds.[26]

▪ Lack of a Long-Run Customer Relationship Orientation

Many sales managers still give little more than lip service to developing long-run customer relationships, and salespeople pick up on this attitude quickly. Sales managers and salespeople who have a narrow *selling* orientation tend to focus on products and the immediate sale—that is, they emphasize their own needs, not those of customers. In contrast, a customer relationship orientation focuses on the buyer's needs and development of long-term mutually beneficial relationships and partnerships. Hewlett-Packard (www.hp.com), manufacturer of precision electronic devices, puts the customer orientation into practice. Its salespeople, called "field engineers," are encouraged to take the customer's side in any dispute with HP. If sales managers convey even subtly to their salespeople that short-run sales are more important than long-run relationships with customers, customer turnover is likely to be high; and this will soon translate into lower sales and profits. Nothing is more important to sales force success than developing and nurturing long-run profitable relationships with customers.

▪ Insufficient Blending of Sales, Marketing, and Financial Knowledge

Marketing and financial knowledge are becoming requirements for sales management positions in progressive companies. These companies are looking for versatile, well-rounded sales managers who understand and can implement overall marketing strategies and who have strong financial capability. For better sales and marketing coordination, Kraft General Foods (www.kraft.com) gives division sales managers dual reporting responsibilities. They report directly to a national sales manager, and they also have a direct relationship with the head of the marketing division. The idea is to keep division managers more closely informed about how their particular product lines are being marketed and what their relative profitability is. Yet, in some companies today, sales managers still are kept in the dark when it comes to sharing marketing and financial information. For example, control reports sent to sales managers often contain only overall sales performance, sales expense, and budget data—not profit figures, which are too often solely for the eyes of top management. To do their jobs well, sales managers need profit information by customer, product, territory, and other market segments. Otherwise, they will tend to focus on generating the largest sales volume, which may be more unprofitable for the company than smaller, more specialized sales.

Both the field sales and headquarters marketing groups need to appreciate that they are key players on the same team, and that they must cooperate to achieve organization objectives. If either job is viewed as an activity isolated and remote from the other, poor communication and even rivalry can separate the marketing staff and sales force and reduce overall company performance. Cross-disciplinary training is one approach to achieving organizational synergism. Some companies periodically bring sales managers into headquarters for training in finance and operations as well as marketing. Broad managerial training in several functional areas can greatly increase the value of sales managers to their companies and help prepare them for promotion to higher management levels.

Developing Sales Managers for the New Millennium

To succeed in the years ahead, sales managers will need to learn fresh roles and reinvent some old ones, such as (1) developing closer relationships with customers, both domestically and internationally, and more in-depth understanding of their different businesses and organizational cultures; (2) treating salespeople as newly empowered equals and partnering with them in achieving sales, profitability, and customer satisfaction/loyalty goals; (3) applying flexible motivational skills in working with a multi-cultural, hybrid sales force of telemarketers, telesellers, missionary salespeople, direct marketers, manufacturers' agents, field salespeople, international salespeople, and others; (4) keeping up-to-date on the latest technologies affecting buyer-seller relationships, (5) learning marketing and financial skills in order to identify potential business opportunities and recommend competitive strategies; (6) working closely with other internal departments as a member of the total corporate team dedicated to satisfying customers profitably; (7) continually seeking ways to exceed customer expectations and bring *added value* profitably to the ongoing buyer-seller relationships, and (8) creating a flexible, learning, and adapting environment for all members of the sales team.[27] Table 1.3 contrasts today's sales managers with yesterday's sales managers.

A primary goal of this sales management text is to help current and future sales managers successfully adapt to the inexorable technological, behavioral, and managerial forces that will affect sales forces in the years ahead. Upcoming chapters provide realistic guidance and learning experiences to help current and future salespeople move into professional sales management careers in an era of rapid technological advances and multiple sales channels to better serve diverse customers—globally as well as domestically.

TABLE 1.3 Yesterday's versus Today's Sales Manager

Yesterday's Sales Managers Focused On:	Today's Sales Managers Focus On:
■ Conducting sales transactions	■ Developing profitable customer relationships
■ Following short-run objectives—current products, markets, customers, and strategies	■ Monitoring and adjusting to long-run trends, opportunities, and challenges to serve new markets and customers as well as current ones
■ Achieving sales volume and quotas	■ Analyzing profitability by customers, products, territories, and salespeople
■ Serving as the information conduit between senior management and the sales force; little use of technology other than the telephone	■ Using management information systems (MIS) and the latest telecommunications technology to effectively and efficiently manage the sales force and carry out CRM activities
■ Working in sales territories with salespeople and handling their own set of large accounts	■ Devising plans and strategies to achieve organization goals through effective leadership of the sales force
■ Managing field sales activities *only*, since marketing was considered company headquarters' responsibility	■ Developing marketing and financial skills to identify, assess, and recommend market opportunities and strategies to senior management
■ Accepting detached or even adversarial relationships with internal departments, which were perceived as not sufficiently responsive to sales force needs	■ Working closely with internal departments as a member of the total corporate team dedicated to fully satisfying customers profitably
■ Looking for ways to increase sales volume	■ Looking for ways to bring *added value* profitably to ongoing buyer-seller relationships
■ Driving and motivating the field sales force to achieve their assigned quotas	■ Creating a flexible, learning, and adapting environment for all members of the hybrid sales team across multiple sales channels

CHAPTER SUMMARY

1. Summarize the basic responsibilities and evolving roles of sales management. Sales managers are instrumental in building relationships with an organization's customers. More specifically, sales managers plan, lead, and control the personal selling activities of the organization. Their basic duties are to prepare sales plans and budgets; set sales goals and objectives; estimate demand and forecast sales; determine the size and structure of the sales force; recruit, select, and train salespeople; determine sales territories, sales quotas, and performance standards; compensate, motivate, and lead the sales force; conduct sales volume, cost, and profit analyses; and evaluate sales force performance, including ethical and social conduct.

Sales managers' responsibilities and titles vary widely depending on the nature of the organization. Most organizations assign traditional duties—such as forecasting, planning, budgeting, and profit responsibilities—to the sales manager. But in some organizations, the sales manager is the marketing manager in every way except position title. The sales management position hierarchy usually starts at the branch level and moves up through district, zone, division, regional, and national sales manager to vice president of sales in some organizations—with increasing managerial, administrative, and leadership responsibilities at each higher sales management level.

2. Demonstrate how sales managers can better integrate their roles with marketing management. Sales managers are essentially marketing managers with the specific task of managing the sales force in its interactions with prospects and customers. Cooperation between the field sales force and headquarters is vital, given the trend of integrated marketing communications and customer relationship management. Many companies today are taking a broader perspective when planning marketing communication programs and coordinating the total set of communication functions rather than planning each one separately. Thus, the integration of sales and marketing is more important than ever.

3. Identify and prepare for megatrends that will affect your future in sales management. Accelerating megatrends in the marketing environment are making the sales manager's job more complex than ever. These inexorable megatrends include *behavioral, technological,* and *managerial* forces that are leading to higher customer expectations and buying expertise, globalization of markets and microsegmentation of markets, advances in telecommunications technology, cultural diversity in the sales force and among customers, emphasis on controlling selling costs, and the shortage of qualified business-to-business salespeople. It is critical for sales managers to stay flexible, adaptable, and in a continuous learning mode as they oversee hybrid sales forces in rapidly changing markets.

4. Evaluate the selection criteria for sales management and compare them to your present and potential qualifications. Sales managers in many organizations may not be performing as well as they could, for four major reasons: (1) illogical selection of sales managers, (2) inadequate sales management training programs, (3) lack of a long-run customer relationship orientation in handling sales operations, and (4) insufficient blending of sales, marketing, and financial knowledge. Unless these four problems in sales manager selection, training, orientation, and integration with marketing are resolved, newly selected sales managers may not be equipped to handle their expanding responsibilities.

5. Analyze how the sales manager's job is expanding and what it will mean for your career. With the empowerment of salespeople through the Internet and sales force automation, sales management jobs are shifting more toward customer relationship management while directing a hybrid sales force across multiple sales channels in selling to diverse customers. Sales managers will need more intense training not only in traditional managerial duties but also in blending marketing, finance, and sales perspectives to increase profitability of sales force operations. Only those sales managers who are flexible, adaptable, and continually learning will thrive in the years ahead.

REVIEW AND APPLICATION QUESTIONS

1. Why and how do you think the sales manager's job will change as we move further into the twenty-first century? [LO 5]

2. What domestic and global forces or megatrends are affecting sales managers now and in the foreseeable future? [LO 3]

3. You work for a large machine tool manufacturer and have been recently promoted from the sales force to the position of sales manager in another region. How would you go about ensuring a good working relationship with your salespeople and the headquarters marketing staff? [LO 4]

4. What criteria would you propose for progressive companies to use in selecting salespeople for promotion to sales manager? [LO 4]

5. What kind of training would you provide to new sales managers? What about additional training for more experienced sales managers? [LO 1, 2, 5]

6. If you were the vice president of sales or the national sales manager for a large corporation, what criteria would you use to evaluate the performance of subordinate sales managers? [LO 1, 2, 4]

7. Write a job description for the position of sales manager. What responsibilities and duties do you consider most important? Why? [LO 1]

8. Describe how sales managers can use the latest telecommunications technology and developments in information management to more effectively and efficiently lead and direct the sales force. [LO 3, 5]

9. How might sales managers use the latest technological developments in information management to better satisfy and improve relationships with prospects and customers? [LO 3, 5]

10. Assume you are the national sales manager for a medium-size company. How will you improve the selection and preparation process for new sales managers? Outline a training process, including topics to cover, to provide new sales managers with the knowledge and skills to succeed. [LO 1, 2, 3, 4, 5]

IT'S UP TO YOU

 ## Internet Exercise

Use an Internet search engine (e.g., Google or Yahoo) to find three companies that are marketing sales management training courses. For each course, answer these questions: What is the length and cost of the training course? Where is it held—online or offline? What are the credentials of the people doing the training? What does the training cover that sounds most interesting? Is the focus of the sales training B2B or business-to-consumer (B2C)? Does the training cover customer relationship management? What does the training promise that's new? Based on the online information, which of the training courses would you choose to attend? Explain why.

 ## Role-Playing Exercise

Explaining CRM to New Salespeople

Situation:

You're a relatively new district sales manager for a large consumer products company on the East Coast. The firm sells mainly through wholesalers, but also direct to giant chain retailers like Wal-Mart and Target. Today, as a guest lecturer, you'll talk for an hour to eight newly hired field salespeople who are taking your company's basic sales training program. You've been asked to talk about the company's customer relationship management (CRM) initiative as it relates to the way field salespeople do their jobs. You want to talk with the salespeople in a down-to-earth, pragmatic way, so that they will grasp what CRM is, why it's so important to the company, and what they can do in their interactions with prospects and customers to further the company-wide CRM initiative.

Role-Play Participants and Assignments

Guest lecturer District sales manager invited to talk about the company's CRM program and the role of salespeople in implementing it in their interactions with prospects and customers.

Salespeople Eight people in their twenties with different backgrounds who are just starting their sales careers, so they are likely to have many questions about CRM and their roles.

In-Basket Exercise

You are a district sales manager for a large consumer products company that sells its products largely through wholesalers and directly to a few giant retailers. Your company also has an extranet where business customers can order online. Today, your company's national sales manager sent you an e-mail saying that the CEO is upset because of poor customer retention rates. Last year, the company lost over 20 percent of its regular customers through attrition of various kinds. At the same time, promotional costs to attract replacement customers are increasing dramatically, causing profit margins to suffer. The CEO has found this loss of customers and declining profits unacceptable, and he has demanded that all the company's sales managers start focusing more on customer retention. In addition, he is launching customer relationship training programs for all company managers. Large bonuses will be awarded to those sales managers and their salespeople who can reduce customer attrition most. You have called a sales meeting for all your salespeople to discuss this new initiative by the CEO.

What will you tell your sales force? Outline the points that you plan to make to them.

Ethical Dilemma

You're the sales manager for a large chemical company, with reason to suspect that one of your top salespeople isn't always playing by the rules. You know that occasionally Jared has taken friends out to lunch and charged it to the company. At other times, you've caught him conducting personal business on company time with company resources (long-distance telephone calls and charging car mileage to the company for personal business and pleasure). At the end of last year, you discovered that Jared had persuaded one of his best customers to order extra product quantities so he could make his sales quota for the year. In mid-January, that customer returned the excess products for a full refund.

You've overlooked these things in the past because of the large sales volume Jared usually generates in his sales territory. One evening, though, on your way out of the office, you overhear a conversation between Jared and another of your salespeople. Jared comments: "I personally think it's okay to withhold negative information about a product in order to make a big sale, as long as no one can get injured by using the product. Things are getting really tough in our industry—if you're going to survive, you've got to do whatever it takes to get a sale!"

QUESTION

1. As Jared's sales manager, what will you do? Should you reprimand him, retrain him, or fire him? Why?

CASE 1.1

Simpson Machine Tool Company: Sales Management Seminar

It was a beautiful autumn day in downtown Philadelphia as the three recently appointed sales managers were enjoying a hearty breakfast in the hotel restaurant. While sipping their second cup of coffee, Jerry Kline, Grace Gallo, and Paul Swenson were discussing the events of the first day in the three-day sales management seminar Simpson Machine Tool Company now requires all its new sales managers to attend.

Jerry Kline: I wonder why we spent so much time talking about sales force performance this morning. They're making it sound like sales force success is a big mystery. All that talk about developing long-term prospects and customer relationships and internal company support is a lot of ivory tower stuff that'll just distract our salespeople and their sales managers. All week I'm running around like a deer on opening day of hunting season just pushing my salespeople to make their sales quotas. I've got a couple of guys in the office making sales calls by phone on our smaller prospects and customers, and I don't have time to monitor them since I'm out of the office so much. Working with my people in the field and helping them make sales presentations and handle customer complaints keeps me from even finding time to do all the paperwork headquarters keeps demanding. And those automated intranet sales reports that we're supposed to prepare each week are no easier to do online than by hand like we've been doing for years. I guess this seminar is supposed to make us more sensitive to our salespeople, prospects, and customers, but I sure don't have much time to worry about subtle things like role perceptions and developing long-term customer relationships. In my opinion, there's only one thing that really matters, and it's spelled M-O-N-E-Y. You make the carrot big enough and any donkey will get the job done. And the same goes for customers—you offer products at lower prices than competitors do, and you'll get a sale whether you've got a warm and fuzzy relationship with the customer or not.

Grace Gallo: Yeah, I know what you mean, Jerry. Seems like the sales training manager is trying to impress the big boss by bringing in these glib consulting whizzes, who probably never carried "the sales bag," to tell us in fancy terms what we should be doing and

thinking about besides our pressure-cooker jobs. I'd like to see them try running a sales force. It's a lot easier talking about managing salespeople than actually doing it. Today, the schedule says we're going to discuss "inexorable megatrends in the macromarketing environment"—whatever that string of gobbledygook means. My people know that I'm the only megatrend they have to worry about. If I'm happy, they're happy. They know what they have to do if they want their commissions and bonuses. If they make their quotas, I leave them alone. If they don't, then I come down hard on them. Most of my salespeople would laugh in my face if I told them they had to concentrate more on developing long-term relationships with prospects and customers. I'm not even sure how we would measure it! In five years, half or more of my salespeople will have moved on, so they're focused on the short term. With salespeople, you're always going to have 20 to 30 percent turnover a year because a lot of people just can't cut the mustard in sales.

Paul Swenson: I have to admit that I'm learning some things I'm going to try when I get back to the office next week. Top management doesn't allow us to match some of the discounts our competitors are offering, so I know we have to learn to sell on some basis other than price. By focusing on developing closer customer relationships and better service, maybe we can overcome our price disadvantage. I know a lot of salespeople don't think long run because they're opportunists, but maybe I can find a way to reward them for doing a better job in cultivating customer relationships and keeping customers from leaving us for a competitor's latest discount offer. But, like you said, it would be difficult to come up with a good way to measure whether they have done a better job or not. I know that I'm probably going to be at Simpson for the foreseeable future since my kids are just now entering grade school and I don't want to disrupt their lives. So, I've got to figure out a way to keep my profitable loyal customers. Simpson's marketing director told me that the company loses almost 20 percent of its customers each year, and that it costs about ten times as much to win new customers as to keep our current ones. She said: "If we could cut back just a little on customer defections each year, our company's profits would soar and we'd probably all get big bonuses."

Maybe these trainers can tell us how to get early warnings about coming market trends and how to do this customer relationship management stuff that's supposed to help us keep profitable loyal customers. Anyway, I'm willing to listen because I sure don't have all the answers . . . especially since I'm so new to sales management. That increase in gasoline prices last year caught me off-guard and ran my selling expenses way over budget. If I'd known in advance about the sharp rise in gas prices, I would have had more of my salespeople making telephone calls or sending e-mails to my small customers instead of driving out to their offices.

Grace Gallo: Hey, it's almost 8:00! We'd better get over to the seminar room, so we don't make a bad impression by coming in late.

QUESTIONS

1. Based on the brief conversation between Jerry Kline, Grace Gallo, and Paul Swenson, what kind of sales manager do you think each of them is? What do you think is the level of performance of the sales force each person heads? How do you think each of them will benefit from the sales management training seminar?

2. If you were a top executive for a company, how would you go about selecting your new sales managers? What specific criteria would you use? How would you determine whether your candidates had the qualities desired?

3. Do you think that outstanding salespeople newly appointed to the position of sales manager need any special training? If so, what should the training cover? Why?

4. Do you think that sales managers can have much impact on the performance of individual salespeople? Specifically, what might new sales managers do to increase the performance of their sales force?

Case prepared by Terry Loe, Kennesaw State University.

CASE 1.2

Centroid Computer Corporation: The New Sales Manager

Centroid Computer Corporation is a Dallas-based manufacturer of personal computers, monitors, interactive terminals, disk drives, and printers. In the past five years, Centroid has expanded into the development of a variety of software packages for small businesses. The firm's growth in the past three years can only be described as explosive—Centroid sales have grown from less than $32 million to over $98 million. Centroid distributes its products through office supply wholesalers and large retailers. It also has a sales force of fifty-two salespeople who call directly on small businesses up and down the East Coast. Most major metropolitan cities have at least one Centroid salesperson assigned, and a few have two. There are four regional sales managers and one national sales manager.

Six months ago Alan Champion was promoted to regional sales manager for the southeastern region. Alan grew up in Athens, Georgia, and graduated from the University of Georgia. He spent two years with IBM as a salesperson and then joined Centroid three years ago. He was based in Atlanta and has consistently been among the top five salespersons in the company, winning sales awards every year. Alan's region includes Georgia, Florida, Alabama, Mississippi, Tennessee, North Carolina, and South Carolina. As regional sales manager, Alan must supervise fourteen salespeople in the seven states. He is also permitted to do some personal selling himself, but his primary responsibility is managing the sales force. Since being promoted to sales manager, Alan has spent a great deal of time in the field working with his salespeople. His years of selling computers have given him many innovative ideas, and he wants to pass along his insights so that all his salespeople can perform better. Alan typically spends two or three days per month with each salesperson, showing them how to best approach customers and negotiate sales.

Since Alan was such a "super salesperson," his national sales manager saw little need to train him after his promotion to sales manager. Besides, the company is so busy handling the rapid sales growth that little thought has been given to training needs for sales managers. The firm has been promoting outstanding salespeople like Alan to sales manager mainly because it knows people like him can teach the sales force "how to sell." In the past few months, the national sales manager has received a couple of complaints from salespeople in the southeastern region about Alan's spending so much time with them. In fact, they said that several times, Alan actually made the sales presentations to their customers for them. Some salespeople say that he is confusing their customers and belittling their efforts.

One of the salespeople complained that she now has a credibility problem with several clients. She stated, "When we made sales calls together, he would allow me to take the lead and handle the call as I normally would. And that was fine, but the perception of the prospects was that Alan was there to observe and evaluate me. Three of my most promising clients asked why Alan was not satisfied with my performance." Other salespeople offered similar comments and even reported that if Alan disapproved of their presentation, he would take over right in the middle in such a manner that "it was clear he was there to teach me a lesson." One salesperson said that Alan's manner was so negative that one of her customers asked: "Was your boss here to help you sell us equipment or to put you in your place?"

QUESTIONS

1. Do you believe Alan is doing a good job in his new sales management position? Why or why not?

2. Describe the functions Alan should be performing as sales manager. What should the approximate allocation of his time be in performing these functions?

3. Do you believe that Alan's behavior will have a long-term negative effect on those salespeople who have had a problem with his way of field supervision and training? If so, what could Alan do to moderate the situation? How could technology be used here?

4. As the national sales manager, how would you handle this problem with Alan?

5. Do the issues in this case raise any ethical concerns the national sales manager should consider? If yes, how would you suggest handling those concerns?

Case prepared by Andy Wood, West Virginia University.

Managing Ethics in a Sales Environment

LEARNING OBJECTIVES

When you finish this chapter, you should be able to:

1   Define ethics and defend its importance to sales and sales management.

2   Show how salespeople are boundary spanners.

3   Apply a code of ethics to sales and sales management situations.

4   Apply the criteria for making moral judgments.

5   Create and manage an ethical climate.

6   Observe legal regulations that affect the sales environment.

7   Model good ethical behavior among the sales force.

INSIDE SALES MANAGEMENT

Robert Perry, Vice President of Sales, PokerTek Inc.

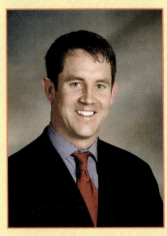

Poker is hot. The game's popularity has been growing dramatically, and casinos all over the country are adding it to their gaming offerings to meet popular demand fueled by the success of the *World Series of Poker* and World Poker Tour, the game's prominence in recent hit movies, and even the spread of online play. PokerTek Inc.—a software development and engineering company based in Charlotte, North Carolina—supplies automated poker tables to casinos eager to cash in on the trend. The tables make play more profitable by eliminating the need for a dealer; there's no shuffling of cards, and thus the game can't be compromised. It also moves faster so it can accommodate more players.

As PokerTek's vice president of sales, Robert Perry is responsible for overseeing sales planning, budgeting, goal setting, evaluation, and compensation of the company's sales force. Recruiting and hiring are also part of his job, and he oversees the extensive background checks the company runs on all potential sales hires. That's a major change from a generation ago, when gaming and its related industries were unregulated and rife with questionable practices of all kinds.

Today, as the gaming industry restructures itself under more accountable corporate ownership and stringent FTC oversight, suppliers like PokerTek Inc.—and often all their sales employees—must apply for licenses in every jurisdiction where the company wants to sell. License applications aren't trivial paperwork—they can run to sixty-five pages long and must include corporate and personal tax and bank records going back several years. And licenses must be renewed every year.

Thus the higher ethical standards applied to the gaming industry now apply to supplier firms as well. Perry explains, for instance, that the background checks he runs will uncover anyone who's ever been convicted of a crime related to gaming. "That person will simply not be hired," he says.

Once hired, new PokerTek employees learn in the employee orientation process that unethical behavior—such as unfair selling practices, bribes, and kickbacks—won't be tolerated, and that the company could lose its licenses if any of its employees failed to meet its tough ethical standards. The news would spread throughout the industry, too, and the result could be financial disaster for the firm.

Normal business entertainment of customers is acceptable, of course, and a certain amount is expected. But "to have unethical people on the team is just not worth it, no matter what level of sales they could bring," Perry says. "If a rep started even talking about doing something wrong like taking a bribe, I think the rest of the team would report it—the company norm to stick to the right way of doing business is just that strong.

"It's ironic, in a way," he says. "An industry that used to be rather unscrupulous is now being run according to the very highest standards."

What Is Business Ethics?

A hallmark of the world's greatest golfers is that they never cheat. Jack Nicklaus, Arnold Palmer—and today, Tiger Woods—play golf strictly by the rules and with the greatest respect for their competitors. Why have they never cheated? Certainly, part of the story is in their strong upbringing, which instilled core values of honesty and integrity. However, another part of the story is their success.

Let's look at Tiger. Tiger Woods earned the number one ranking in golf when he was just twenty-one years old and has now kept that rating for all but a few weeks for over a decade. Tiger is odds-on better than nearly all his competitors. Maybe when you're that good, you don't need to cheat. Playing the game fairly comes easy when you are so much better than your competitors.

The same is probably true in the world of sales. When you are a successful sales manager for a very successful company, what motivation is there to cheat? But, what happens when you are a struggling sales manager for a struggling company? Perhaps an honest person still would not be tempted to blatantly cheat a customer—in particular, a customer who is at some disadvantage relative to the salesperson. However, sometimes the shades of gray present more temptation. Maybe the sales manager would be tempted to condone or practice behaviors that could somehow be justified as "not really so bad." These might include

- Misleading customers by leaving out important facts
- Using guilt tactics such as telling older people they should have life insurance policies for many relatives
- Making a product seem more complex than it really is
- Using excessive jargon and fine print to make the terms of sale unclear

If you're uncertain about getting your next paycheck, might you view some of these acts as acceptable?[1] Should there be different standards for different sales managers?

Perhaps more than any other legitimate occupation, sales has long been linked with "sleazy" activities. You might have had personal experiences that confirmed this impression. Do salespeople deserve this dubious place in society? The answer to this question is not the point of this chapter, because the past cannot be undone. We can and should, however, learn from the past. This chapter defines key variables that together explain how business ethics and sales management are interrelated. In explaining this link, we offer advice that enables the sales manager to avoid a selling environment that encourages unethical selling.

■ Business Ethics, Sales, and Sales Management

Business Ethics
The study of how businesspeople behave when facing a situation with moral consequences.

Ethics describes the moral content of behavior. **Business ethics is the study of how businesspeople behave when facing a situation with moral consequences.** It's easier to think of selling situations *with* moral consequences than to think of situations without them. For instance, whenever salespeople represent a product benefit, they are implicitly saying the customer can rely on or trust that these benefits will indeed result from purchasing and consuming the product. Thus, any situation involving trust also inherently involves business ethics.

Sales Management Ethics
The specific component of business ethics that deals with ethically managing the sales function.

Sales management ethics is the specific component of business ethics that deals with ethically managing the sales function. When a customer and a salesperson communicate in an ethical selling situation, both parties treat each other honestly. Neither person tries to take unfair advantage of the other. The sales manager has the special duty of overseeing this process.

Although many recent business scandals such as Enron, Daewoo, and Arthur Andersen did not involve salespeople directly, the principles of ethical action in the marketplace do go beyond the selling environment. All these situations revealed motivations that can lead other people, too, to participate in questionable behaviors. Specific behavior by employees of a company eventually contributed to the harm of others. Were the people involved morally corrupt, or did the system simply encourage morally corrupt behavior?

Salespeople Are Boundary Spanners

Boundary Spanner
Someone who performs his or her job in the "boundary" between a company and a customer.

A **boundary spanner** is someone who performs his or her job in the "boundary" between a company and a customer. Salespeople represent the company to the customer and the customer to the company. For example, consider a situation in which a salesperson for an aviation parts supplier is trying to win a contract from Boeing. The salesperson represents her company to Boeing. But she also represents Boeing to her own company. Whenever Boeing asks for information about how the company can satisfy a particular need for parts, the salesperson can face an ethical dilemma. Often the dilemma means weighing telling the truth versus winning business. With either option, however, the salesperson is exposed to the wrath of either her customer or her sales manager should a conflict occur. In this sense, boundary spanners perform their job in a proverbial no-man's land, as illustrated in Figure 2.1.

Sales managers have a special role in maintaining an ethical work and sales environment. It's their duty to make sure morally corrupt individuals are not employed by

Big Customer   **Salesperson**   **Big Company**

FIGURE 2.1 Salespeople Work in the Boundary Between the Company and the Customer

the firm and to put a check on any system providing an incentive for immoral behavior. Sales managers are also responsible for the way the firm's sales force treats its customers. Thus, sales management and business ethics are very much interrelated—they manage the firm's behavior in the boundary.

■ Customer Vulnerability

Customer Vulnerability
State in which customers are at a disadvantage relative to the company.

Consider a salesperson working for a financial services firm. Customers in such situations are often **vulnerable**, meaning they are at a disadvantage relative to the company. Most often, the disadvantage comes in these forms:

- Ignorance—a lack of some vital knowledge, often product knowledge, needed to participate in a fair exchange
- Naiveté—a lack of experience or the ability to conduct a transaction or negotiate terms of a fair deal
- Powerlessness—a lack of either competition within a marketplace or sufficient assets with which to be persuasive

Table 2.1 illustrates these sources of disadvantage.

TABLE 2.1 Sources of Potentially Unfair Advantages and Disadvantages in the Sales Arena

SOURCE OF CUSTOMER VULNERABILITY	SALESPERSON ADVANTAGE	CUSTOMER DISADVANTAGE
Ignorance	Salesperson has superior technological knowledge.	Customer is technologically challenged and cannot understand salesperson.
Naiveté	Salesperson allows room for negotiation in setting prices.	Customer doesn't understand the negotiation process.
Powerlessness	Salesperson works for an exclusive supplier to the customer who is under contractual obligation to purchase from the supplier.	Customer represents a small retail company with few assets and little access to other markets.

Recently several financial services firms have come under scrutiny based on the vulnerability of their customers. One lost its license to sell securities because it followed unscrupulous sales practices in the sale of annuities to older customers.[2] This customer segment prefers conservative investment strategies, but salespeople for the firm succeeded in selling risky annuities by misrepresenting the returns. Thus, the customers were victims of both ignorance and naiveté, and many lost much of their life's savings on these investments.

Did the company have a duty to prevent salespeople from taking advantage of this situation? Or did the salespeople themselves, even if the company condoned selling to vulnerable customers without adequately informing them of the products they were buying, have a duty to intervene on the customer's behalf? As we shall see later, answers to such questions often are not as clear as they may seem.

Applying Professional Sales Codes of Ethics

Codes of Ethics
Written expression of a firm's values, listing specific behaviors that are consistent or inconsistent with those values.

Codes of ethics express the values of a firm by specifying, in writing, specific behaviors that are consistent or inconsistent with those values. Whether codes of ethics are effective is often debated, their mere existence alone does not guarantee a more ethical environment. Codes must not only be adopted, they must embody values truly epitomized by top management. How can a sales manager expect a salesperson to conform to a code of behavior the manager openly behaves inconsistently with?

Textbook discussions of ethics can make the topic sound quite simple. However, amid the turmoil and emotion of the real-life workplace, making the "right" decision can often be extremely complex. For instance, most people would agree that honesty is an important ethical principle. Consider, however, an otherwise honest salesperson faced with a looming end-of-the-month quota and needing to close one big deal to avoid a severe reprimand for falling short of the number. A customer might ask a question about some benefit such as compatibility of the products being sold. The salesperson, rather than being completely honest about issues related to compatibility, may skirt the issue or become blatantly dishonest to avoid missing the quota. Realize that the salesperson may be facing other ethical dilemmas. Perhaps there are issues concerning providing for his family or meeting personal financial obligations. Factors such as these make ethics much more gray than black and white. However, ethical codes spelling out specific actions that will not be tolerated under any circumstance can prove helpful in shaping a virtuous outcome.

Some ethics codes are simple and straightforward, relying mostly on the individual's good judgment and character. For example, insurance company Cigna (www.cigna.com) tells employees only that they "will abide by the highest legal and ethical standards without exceptions." Other codes, such as the General Dynamics (www.generaldynamics.com) code for worldwide business conduct, are complex and lengthy. Some companies have used creative approaches to providing their employees with ethical guidelines. Texas Instruments (www.ti.com) has an ethics officer who answers employee questions in a weekly electronic news column.[3] An ethics hotline at Verizon Corporation (http://www22.verizon.com/), then NYNEX, received over 2,700 calls in one year.[4]

■ Types of Codes of Ethics

There are four basic types of ethical codes:

1. Company codes that define ethical boundaries for employees.
2. Professional codes that define ethical boundaries for occupational groups such as advertisers, marketing researchers, sales representatives, doctors, lawyers, accountants, and so on.
3. Business association codes that define ethical boundaries for people engaged in the same line of business. Examples are codes established by the Direct Selling Association of America and by the American Association of Advertising Agencies.
4. Advisory group codes suggested by government agencies or other special interest groups.

Codes often list employee behaviors that the firm does not condone or accept. Each industry is confronted with somewhat unique ethical situations. The following behaviors are generally prohibited in sales-related codes of ethics:

- Bribes, gifts, kickbacks
- Conflicts of interest
- Illegal political payments
- Violation of laws in general
- Use of insider information
- Violations of secrecy agreements
- Falsification of sales accounts
- Moonlighting
- Violation of antitrust laws
- Fraud and deception
- Illegal payments abroad
- Justifying the means by the intended end

■ Do Codes of Ethics Affect Behavior?

What happens when sales managers work for companies with an effective code of ethics? The nearby *Sales Management in Action* box describing pharmaceutical sales training illustrates how far some sales managers will go to get their sales force to learn the code of ethics. Clearly, such a code does alter the way sales managers view questionable behaviors among the sales force.

Consider two sales managers, one who works for a firm with an effective code of ethics and one who works for a firm that does not have a code of ethics. Each manager discovers that a salesperson has intentionally misled a customer about delivery dates when trying to win a sale. The manager in the firm with a code of ethics will consider the same offense unethical and discipline the employee more severely.[5] In the firm where no code exists, the outcome depends entirely on the sales manager's ethical standards. And since a code of ethics typically does not cover minor issues, it may not influence outcomes in such situations. For example, a salesperson may not be able to rely on a code of ethics in deciding whether taking an extra thirty minutes at lunch represents ethical misconduct.

Many companies practice discriminatory acts. For instance, airlines treat their high-mileage flyers differently from other customers. "Platinum" flyers get access to first-class lounges in airports and are upgraded to first class on many flights. In addition, when flights have to be rearranged, the best customers are likely to be inconvenienced the least. Is this treatment ethical? The code of ethics should address how far salespeople can go to satisfy the company's best customers.

SALES MANAGEMENT IN ACTION

Good and Bad Drug Sellers

As professional sales jobs go, pharmaceutical selling is considered a glamorous job. Pharmaceutical sales managers have a special duty to ethically manage the sales force, given the obvious implications of selling customers a less than appropriate product. Pharmaceutical salespeople often offer to buy lunch for a physician or other prospective customer. Is this an ethical act? A lunch probably creates no feeling of obligation on the part of the physician to choose one drug over another more effective drug. But what happens when the gifts become quite large? What if a vacation to Rio is offered instead of lunch?

Abbot Laboratories is taking a novel approach to instilling proper ethical beliefs and behaviors among its salespeople. Sales and marketing employees are asked to play a videogame involving a virtual sales-person—Joe Salesguy. During the game, Joe is confronted with multiple ethical dilemmas including the opportunity to provide tickets to a big game to a physician from a major medical group. Is this action appropriate? When the Abbot employee chooses incorrectly, Joe, the animated salesguy, is lit up with about a thousand volts of electrical shock. This is an innovative way to teach ethical standards to the video game generation. Some may question the tactic just as debate rages over videogame violence in general. However, the technique speeds up compliance among sales and marketing people.

SOURCES: Gregg Cebrzynski, "Targeting Pharmaceutical Reps Gives Sales a Shot in the Arm, Chains Report," *Nation's Restaurant News,* July 25, 2005, p. 12; and T. Kary, "Straighten Up and Fry Right," *Psychology Today,* January–February 2005, p. 35.

© 2007 Indexstock.com

Ethical Philosophies and Moral Judgments

How can a situation like the one just described involving financial services sales come to be? Were the salespeople acting on their own, or was management so concerned with sales they created a system that rewarded unscrupulous behavior? Part of the answer lies in understanding the everyday moral stress people face when they must decide between actions that may be beneficial to themselves, or even to their families, and actions that are virtuous.[6]

Moral philosophy deals with the systematic ways that individuals recognize and resolve decisions having moral content. Many books have been written on this topic alone. Our interest here is to describe how different sales managers, salespeople, channel partners, or even customers may behave quite differently when faced with the same ethical problem. Let's look at the concepts of idealism, relativism, and teleology as the basis for different moral philosophies.[7]

■ Idealism

Moral Philosophy
A systematic tool for recognizing and resolving decisions about what is right and wrong.

In moral philosophy, **ideals** are a set of principles by which individuals determine morality. The golden rule is considered a widely held moral principle—or moral absolute.[8] A *moral absolute* represents a rule that should always be applied with no exceptions or excuses. But a sales manager may also develop other rules. For instance, some may believe that all customers should receive complete and full information. Others may believe "the customer is always right" or "salespeople should always be truthful." Or someone who is highly idealistic would have a difficult time consciously doing something inconsistent with the terms of a sales contract. Strict idealism is associated with universal standards, meaning they should be applied in all relevant situations regardless of context.

Ideals
A set of principles by which individuals decide morality.

Certainly, there are many, many other principles. Just imagine how such a set of principles might vary with national culture. We wouldn't expect sales managers in South Korea to hold the same set of principles as sales managers in New Zealand.

We can certainly debate the merits of each possible principle, but idealism as a moral philosophy deals more with how people use these principles than with whether any individual principle itself is universally valid. Idealism is thus a mechanism by which principles become tools for decision making. It's sometimes called a **deontological** process, signifying that it is rule based.

Deontological
Another term sometimes used to represent decision processes that are rule based or idealistic.

■ Relativism

"It's all relative." You've probably used this expression thousands of times without giving it much thought. It's another way of saying, "It depends." **Relativism**, as a moral philosophy, is a process by which individuals reach moral decisions based more on the actions they perceive to be acceptable *given a particular situation*. Those who are highly committed to relativism usually reject moral absolutes or imperatives.[9] In this sense, relativism and idealism are competing moral orientations.

Relativism
A moral philosophy by which individuals reach moral decisions based more on the actions they perceive to be acceptable *given a particular situation*.

Relativism is sometimes called **situational ethics**, meaning that a behavior acceptable in one situation can be unacceptable in another. Relativism rejects "absolutes" or moral imperatives. Acceptability could be based on the cultural context, for instance. A bribe may be unacceptable in Kansas but acceptable in Guatemala. Or it can be based on the social situation. An individual may perceive few social sanctions with illegally downloading a movie from an unauthorized site. But the same person likely would not consider going to a store and shoplifting a DVD containing the same movie.

Situational Ethics
A behavior acceptable in one situation can be unacceptable in another.

■ Teleology

Teleology
A philosophy that defines morality based on the *consequences* of the behavior.

Teleology is a philosophy that defines morality based on the *consequences* of the behavior. It allows some indiscretion based on the argument that the "good" that results is more important than the harm caused. In other words, the end justifies the means. Sales managers sometimes use teleological norms in making decisions.[10]

■ Moral Judgments

Ethical Dilemma
A situation with alternate courses of action, each having different moral implications.

Moral Judgment
A person's evaluation of the situation from an ethical perspective.

Moral Equity
The inherent fairness or justice in a situation.

Acceptability
How culturally or socially acceptable we perceive an action to be.

Contractualism
The extent to which an act is consistent with stated or implied contracts and/or laws.

Regardless of your moral philosophy, situations with moral content require you to make a judgment. An **ethical dilemma** is a situation with alternate courses of action, each having different moral implications. Choices about hiring, firing, and performance evaluations often have moral content, as do many other business decisions. A **moral judgment** is a person's evaluation of the situation from an ethical perspective. We usually base moral judgments on three criteria:[11]

1. **Moral equity** is the inherent fairness or justice in a situation.
2. **Acceptability** describes how culturally or socially acceptable we perceive an action to be.
3. **Contractualism** is the extent to which an act is consistent with stated or implied contracts and/or laws.

The first criterion—moral equity—spans moral philosophies and comes closest to representing an act's inherent rightness or wrongness. Relativists, on the other hand, are more likely to perform a behavior they view as acceptable. Idealists will have a difficult time with behavior they see as inconsistent with a contract or law. These three dimensions have been used to study salespeople and sales managers across a wide range of business situations ranging from puffery to bribes.[12]

■ Are Salespeople More Unethical than Anyone Else?

Do salespeople and sales managers deserve the popular perception that they have low moral standards and will do anything to make a sale? Are dishonest people attracted to sales jobs, or do they become dishonest because of the work they do? Or are those involved with sales just like people in other occupations? How do moral philosophies relate to the ethical decisions of sales managers?

Several researchers have examined these issues. Here are some of their findings:

- Sales managers and salespeople are *not* more likely to engage in unethical practices than are people with other marketing and management jobs.[13]
- Age is positively related to ethical behavior among sales managers—older sales managers tend to make more ethical decisions.[14]
- Relatively high levels of relativism are associated with less ethical decision making among sales managers.[15]
- Relatively high levels of idealism are associated with a lower likelihood of hiring a controversial job candidate.[16]

Research does not support the popular belief that sales professionals are more unethical than others. Further, findings show that personal characteristics associated with unethical behavior are found across the population in general. In other words, morality lies not in the occupation so much as in the individual, and misconduct can occur in all jobs and professions.

■ Potentially Unethical Behaviors

What kinds of selling-related behaviors might be perceived as unethical? Consider the twenty actions listed in Table 2.2. Undergraduate students rated offering a bribe and using expense accounts to pay for personal spending as more serious lapses than mis-

TABLE 2.2 Potentially Unethical Selling-Related Behaviors

	BEHAVIOR	PERCEIVED SERIOUSNESS
1	Offering better prices and terms for customers who buy exclusively from one person	Not serious
2	Using customers to get information about competitors' activities	Not serious
3	Using shadow prices—attracting customers with lower-priced products, then trying to shift them to more expensive products at the sale	Not serious
4	Pretending to have a personal or even a romantic interest in a potential customer in an effort to close a sale	Not serious
5	Misrepresenting the motivation for a contact with a customer when the real intent is solely trying to make a sale (pretending to be conducting research, checking on a previous item sold)	Not serious
6	Offering a bribe in return for signing a purchase agreement	Serious
7	Exaggerating performance of a product offered to customers	Serious
8	Disparaging a competitor's products	Serious
9	Disparaging a competitor's sales and service people	Serious
10	Misleading someone about potential product shortages in an effort to stimulate current sales	Serious
11	Using expense account to pay for personal expenses	Serious
12	Creating, repeating, or embellishing unsubstantiated rumors reflecting negatively on coworkers or competitors	Serious
13	Overstating list prices to give a customer a "refund"	Serious
14	Misrepresenting how frequently a service should be performed or the quantity of a product that should be used	Serious
15	Intentionally misreporting one's work activities to the sales supervisor	Serious
16	Withholding key facts about a product from consumers in an effort to keep them uninformed	Serious
17	A sales manager condoning payment of bribes in order to increase sales	Very serious
18	Padding an expense account	Very serious
19	Calling in sick when well only to take a day off	Very serious
20	Misleading someone about product safety by withholding truthful information	Very serious

SOURCE: Some items taken from John R. Sparks and Mark Johlke, "Factors Influencing Student Perceptions of Unethical Behavior by Personal Salespeople: An Experimental Investigation," *Journal of Business Ethics* 15 (1996): 871–87.

representing intent, price discriminating, and faking a personal relationship. Interestingly, some of the behaviors they rated most severely were those that take advantage of the firm more than the customer, such as padding an expense account or falsely calling in sick.

Perhaps developing an exhaustive list of unethical behaviors is impossible. But salespeople and managers should see any behavior that unfairly takes advantage of another party in an exchange as a serious breech of ethical conduct. For free exchange to work efficiently, all parties involved need to treat each other with respect and honesty. If either party violates the standards of moral conduct, someone is harmed. Therefore, salespeople, sales managers, government officials, and even customers must operate with integrity. Then the free exchange system is efficient and is the best governance system that exists.

SALES MANAGEMENT IN ACTION

Used, Pre-Owned, Certified, Second Hand?

Over the past two decades, the "used-car" business has been transformed. Car resellers have coined phrases like "pre-owned" and "certified program cars" to avoid any stigma that might be associated with the idea of a "used car."

Sales managers at both Ford and Daimler-Chrysler have come under scrutiny for developing and implementing a program that sells used automobiles as "Certified Used Cars." Certified used-car salespeople were instructed to tout the cars' greater reliability and lower prices compared to similar offerings by competitors. Unfortunately for both Ford and Daimler-Chrysler, research failed to support their claims, and both companies were charged with offenses including unfair pricing and false advertising. The moral of the story . . . call a duck a duck and a lemon a lemon!

SOURCES: Kim-Mai Cutler, "Certified Used Car Superiority Questioned," *Wall Street Journal*, July 12, 2005, pp. D1–D3; "Isn't Pre-Owned Just Another Word for Used?" *Money*, September 2005, p. 141.

■ Dealing with Unethical Behavior

Sales managers should not encourage or tolerate sales behaviors inconsistent with professional sales standards or with the moral standards of the firm. But what happens when sales managers must choose between ethics and sales success? While someone outside the situation might easily condemn a sales manager for looking the other way while a salesperson pays a kickback to gain business, who knows how we might behave when faced with the prospect of taking action that may damage job performance?

Research shows that sales managers tend to discipline poor performers more severely than they do more effective salespeople.[17] In other words, when two salespeople have violated the same ethical code, the one with the better sales performance is more likely to escape with little to no reprimand or punishment than is the one with the lower sales record. Sales managers also appear to adjust their disciplinary tactics based on salesperson demographics. For example, given the same violation, a sales manager, particularly a male, will tend to discipline a male salesperson more severely than a female salesperson.[18]

An effective sales manager will strive to discipline all salespeople with the same standards. Although unethical selling tactics may benefit firms in the short run, they almost always end up being detrimental in the long run. Not only do good ethical principles dictate avoiding discrimination in disciplinary actions, but fair treatment will help the sales manager avoid litigation by disgruntled employees.

Creating an Ethical Work Climate

What determines a sales manager's or even a salesperson's tolerance for unethical actions among employees? Why does one firm seem to promote selling behaviors that are consistent with high moral standards while another seems to promote pushy techniques that take advantage of sources of vulnerability among consumers? The answer lies in a salesperson's ethical work climate.

Organizational Climate
Employees' perceptions of and attitudes about the organizational culture.

The **organizational climate** is the way employees perceive the organizational culture. When a culture is very strong, employees will tend to share the same perceptions. When a culture is not as strong or identifiable, perceptions may vary considerably from one employee to another. The organizational work climate ultimately affects an employee's well-being.

Ethical Work Climate
The way employees view their work environment on moral dimensions.

The **ethical work climate** is a specific aspect of the organizational climate. Specifically, it's the way employees view their work environment on moral dimensions. Ethical climate is a multidimensional concept, with four unique aspects.[19]

■ Policies and Rules

Policies and Rules
Principles that govern selling and marketing conduct within the firm, sometimes summarized in a code of ethics.

When sales managers and salespeople internalize the **policies and rules** that govern selling and marketing conduct within the firm, they are more likely to behave ethically.[20] Sometimes, the policies and rules are summarized in a code of ethics. Employee perceptions of the type and severity of sanctions that follow violations of the code of ethics also go along this dimension.

■ Trust and Responsibility

Trust and Responsibility
Dimension that defines how far people are trusted to behave in a responsible way and are held personally responsible for their actions.

The **trust and responsibility** dimension defines how far people are trusted to behave in a responsible way and are held personally responsible for their actions. Consider a sales manager supervising a dozen outside salespeople. Trust is increased when salespeople are allowed to set their own schedules and are not constantly being monitored. However, this freedom should be accompanied by a sense of responsibility. Salespeople who take advantage of freedom by participating in behaviors such as those in Table 2.2 should be held responsible for their actions. Under conditions like these, the ethical climate dimension of trust and responsibility will be high.

Experiencing trust and responsibility also means carrying out the job responsibly. When employees frequently avoid work or find ways to pass it on to others, they are behaving unethically. Value creation, the reason the company exists, is a primary responsibility of employees. In fact, one of the surest ways of avoiding unethical actions among sales managers and salespeople is to make sure their actions are directed toward maximizing the value provided by the firm's products.

Peer Behavior
A dimension of ethical climate that is the extent to which employees view coworkers as having high moral standards.

■ Peer Behavior

Peer behavior, as a dimension of ethical climate, is the extent to which employees view coworkers as having high moral standards. Employees who observe other employees doing things that bother them from a moral point of view will perceive the workplace as having a more negative ethical climate, and the peer behavior dimension of ethical climate will be reduced.

Sales Emphasis
A dimension of ethical climate that is the extent to which employees feel pressured to prioritize increased sales, profits, margins, or other financial returns over all other concerns.

■ Bottom-Line Sales Emphasis

Sales emphasis is the extent to which employees feel pressured to prioritize increased sales, profits, margins, or other financial returns over all other concerns. A strong sales emphasis or *bottom-line orientation*, coupled with a control system based on sales quotas, leads to a more negative ethical work climate.[21] When sales goals are overly aggressive or even unrealistic, closing the sale becomes more important than creating

© Tony Freeman / PhotoEdit

● See http://www.realtor.org/mempolweb.nsf/pages/printable2006Code for the full version of the professional real estate agent's code of ethics. Would you expect that it is widely accepted?

value for customers by providing a product that best matches their needs. Over time, sales managers and salespeople will behave consistently with the compensation system, since it defines which goals are rewarded. Thus, the compensation system does much to determine the ethical climate in a sales environment.[22]

Managing the Ethical Climate

Each dimension just described can be a tool to help create a positive, healthy, ethical work climate. Sales managers should make sure employees are aware of rules and policies and, based on employees' actions, reward and reprimand them with no favoritism or bias. Employees should also be aware of the extent to which they foster a bottom-line orientation.

Besides increasing performance and creating a more contented, more motivated sales force, a positive ethical climate generates less stress among salespeople.[23] Sales managers and salespeople who internalize policies and rules experience less ambiguity because they are more likely to know how to respond to a given ethical dilemma. When sales managers and salespeople trust each other, they experience less conflict on the job. As a result, sales managers should face fewer problems with turnover.[24]

Promoting an ethical climate is the responsibility of management at all levels of the organization. If top management is unconcerned about ethics in developing strategies, then sales managers are likely to be unconcerned with the way their sales force behaves. Similarly, salespeople are not likely to be concerned with the way they treat customers.[25] In the end, managing the ethical climate should be a top priority for firms.

General Electric (www.ge.com) actively manages its ethical climate. In 2002, the company appointed the first Vice President for Corporate Citizenship.[26] This means GE monitors its own sales force as well as its suppliers' sales forces to make sure they act consistently with GE values and comply with health, safety, and environmental standards. GE is recognized by Dow Jones as a leader in responsible management and is a member of the Dow Jones Sustainability Index (www.sustainability-index.com), a list of 300 firms worldwide that are noted for responsible management practices.

Legal Considerations in the Sales Environment

Domestic and international selling and sales management activities are regulated by local, state, and federal laws and regulations, as well as legislation within each foreign country. Some laws are designed to prevent unfair competition, while others protect consumers and society from harmful business practices. This section summarizes the most important federal laws and regulations affecting sales and sales management.

■ Federal Regulation

We can divide U.S. legislation regulating business into two major categories:

1. Laws protecting companies from each other
2. Laws and policies protecting consumers and society from unfair business practices

The first category tries to ensure that a competitive marketplace exists. Among many federal laws regulating business competition, the Robinson-Patman Act, the Sherman Antitrust Act, and the Clayton Act are the most important. These acts deal with issues including price discrimination, collusion, price fixing, exclusive dealing, restraint of trade, reciprocity, tie-in sales, unordered goods, orders and terms of sale, business descriptions, product descriptions, secret rebates, customer coercion, disparaging competitors' products and services, and business defamation.

Table 2.3 shows major federal legislation that affects selling and sales management activities directly and indirectly. More recent laws have limited the extent to which sales managers can mine customer information using new technologies. For example, COPPA (Children's Online Privacy Protection Act) and the Telephone Record Protection Act are aimed at adjusting regulation to account for advances in Internet and mobile phone technologies.

■ Price Discrimination

Price Discrimination
Discriminating among different customers on price or terms of sale when the discrimination has a harmful effect on competition.

The Clayton Act prohibits a seller from discriminating on price or terms of sale among different customers when the discrimination has a harmful effect on competition. This practice is known as **price discrimination**. Clayton makes it unlawful for a buyer to knowingly induce or receive a discriminatory price. Sellers are required to treat similar buyers equally with respect to price and terms of sale.

Section 3 of the Robinson-Patman Act goes even further by criminalizing behaviors that facilitate discrimination among competing purchasers. Robinson-Patman limits a seller's ability to sell at different prices in different markets, or charge different buyers different prices for the same quality and quantity of goods. However, the act

TABLE 2.3   Key Legislation Affecting Selling and Sales Management

LAWS INTENDED TO REGULATE BUSINESS COMPETITION

Sherman Antitrust Act (1890)—prohibits (a) "monopolies or attempts to monopolize" and (b) "contracts, combinations, or conspiracies in restraint of trade" in interstate and foreign commerce.

Federal Trade Commission Act (1914)—established the FTC as a body of specialists with broad powers to investigate and to issue cease-and-desist orders to enforce Section 5, which declares that "unfair methods of competition in commerce are unlawful."

Clayton Act (1914)—supplements the Sherman Act by prohibiting certain specific practices (certain types of price discrimination, tying clauses, and exclusive dealing, inter-corporate stockholdings, and interlocking directorates) "where the effect . . . may be to substantially lessen competition or tend to create a monopoly in any line of commerce." Provides that violating corporate officials can be held individually responsible.

Robinson-Patman Act (1936)—amends the Clayton Act by strengthening the prohibition of price discrimination (subject to certain defenses). Gives the FTC the right to establish limits on quantity discounts, to forbid brokerage allowances except to independent brokers, and to prohibit promotional allowances, services, or facilities except where made available to all "on proportionately equal terms."

Wheeler-Lea Act (1938)—Amends the FTC act; prohibits unfair and deceptive acts and practices regardless of whether competition is injured.

Lanham Trademark Act (1946)—regulates brands and trademarks.

Consumer Goods Pricing Act (1975)—repeals federal "fair-trade laws" and state laws allowing manufacturers to set retail prices.

FTC Improvement Act (1980)—enables the Senate and House of Representatives to exercise joint veto power over FTC trade regulations; limits FTC power to regulate unfairness issues.

LAWS DEREGULATING SPECIFIC INDUSTRIES

■ Natural Gas Policy Act (1978)	■ Staggers Rail Act (1980)
■ Airline Deregulation Act (1978)	■ Depository Institutions Act (1981)
■ Motor Carrier Act (1980)	■ Telecommunications Act (1996)

LAWS INTENDED TO PROTECT CONSUMERS

Pure Food and Drug Act (1906)—regulates labeling of food and drugs and prohibits manufacture or marketing of adulterated food or drugs. Amended in 1938 by Food, Drug, and Cosmetics Act.

Meat Inspection Act (1906)—regulates meatpacking houses and provides for federal inspection of meats.

Textile Labeling Laws—require the manufacturer to indicate what their product is made of:
- ■ Wood Products Labeling Act (1939)
- ■ Fur Products Labeling Act (1951)
- ■ Flammable Fabrics Act (1953)
- ■ Textile Fiber Products Identification Act

Automobile Information Disclosure Act (1958)—prohibits car dealers from inflating the factory price of new cars.

Kefauver-Harris Drug Amendments (1962)—requires that (a) drugs be labeled with their generic names, (b) new drugs be pretested, and (c) new drugs get approval of Food and Drug Administration before being marketed.

TABLE 2.3 (continued)

LAWS INTENDED TO PROTECT CONSUMERS

Fair Packaging and Labeling Act (1966)—provides for regulation of the packaging and labeling of consumer goods. Requires manufacturers to state what the package contains, who made it, and how much it contains. Permits industries' voluntary adoption of uniform packaging standards.

National Traffic and Motor Vehicle Safety Act (1966)—provides for safety standards for tires and automobiles.

Fair Packaging and Labeling Act (1966)—the "truth in packaging" law that regulates packaging and labeling to disclose name and address of manufacturer or distributor, and information about the quality of contents.

Child Protection Act (1966)—bans sale of hazardous toys and other unsafe articles. Amended in 1969 to include articles that pose electrical, mechanical, or thermal hazards.

Federal Cigarette Labeling and Advertising Acts (1967, 1971)—requires manufacturers to label cigarettes with written health warnings (1967); prohibits tobacco advertising on radio or television (1971).

Consumer Credit Protection Act (1968)—"Truth in lending" law that requires lenders to state the true costs of a credit transaction, outlaws the use of actual or threatened violence in collecting loans, and restricts the amount of garnishments.

Fair Credit Reporting Act (1970)—ensures that a consumer's credit report will contain only accurate, relevant, and recent information and will be confidential unless requested for an appropriate reason by a proper party.

National Environmental Policy Act (1970)—established the Environmental Protection Agency (EPA) to deal with various types of pollution and organizations that create pollution.

Consumer Product Safety Act (1972)—established the Consumer Product Safety Commission and authorizes it to set safety standards for consumer products as well as exact penalties for failure to uphold the standards.

Consumer Goods Pricing Act (1975)—prohibits the use of price maintenance agreements among manufacturers and resellers in interstate commerce.

Magnuson-Moss Warranty/FTC Improvement Act (1975)—authorizes the FTC to determine rules concerning consumer warranties and provides for consumer access to means of redress, such as the "class action" suit. Also expands FTC regulatory powers over unfair or deceptive acts or practices.

Equal Credit Opportunity Act (1975, 1977)—prohibits discrimination in a credit transaction because of sex and marital status (1975), and because of race, national origin, religion, age, or receipt of public assistance (1977).

Fair Debt Collection Practice Act (1978)—makes it illegal to harass or abuse any person and make false statements or use unfair methods when collecting a debt.

Nutrition Label and Education Act (1990)—requires food manufacturers and processors to provide detailed information on the labeling of most foods.

Children's Television Act (1990)—limits the advertising shown during children's television programs to no more than 10.5 minutes per hour on weekends and not more than 12 minutes per hour on weekdays.

Americans with Disabilities Act (1991)—protects the rights of people with disabilities by making it illegal to discriminate against them in public accommodations, transportation, and telecommunications.

Brady Law (1993)—Imposes a five-day waiting period and a background check before a purchaser can receive a gun.

does not make price discrimination necessarily illegal. Price differences or different terms of sale are allowed under two conditions:

1. The price differential is given in good faith to meet a price offered by a competitor
2. The price differential is based upon cost savings reflecting a difference in the cost of manufacture, sale, or delivery resulting from the differing methods or quantities in which products are sold or delivered

Price reductions based on volume ordered, closeout sales, lower shipping costs, good-faith meeting of competition, and lower commissions paid by the seller to its employee salespeople are generally allowable. All these defenses can justify a difference in price or terms of sale. For legal protection, however, sellers should be sure their accounting procedures reflect cost differences that permit the firm to reduce prices or terms of sale to certain customers. Price discrimination laws are particularly applicable to business-to-business sales (B2B), although business-to-consumer (B2C) marketers also could be found culpable in a price discrimination suit.

The terms described in the following sections look at different behaviors associated with discrimination in the marketplace.

Collusion. When competitors conspire to set prices, agree to divide territories on a noncompetitive basis, or join together to act to the detriment of another competitor, they are practicing illegal collusion.

Price Fixing. Competitors who conspire to set or maintain uniform prices and profit margins are fixing prices. Even informally exchanging price information with competitors or discussing pricing policies at trade association meetings has been found illegal by the courts.

Exclusive Dealing. Agreements in which a manufacturer or wholesaler grants one dealer exclusive rights to sell a product in a certain trading area or insists that the dealer not carry competing lines are illegal under the Clayton Act.

Restraint of Trade. Under the Sherman and Clayton acts, competitors colluding to divide a market into noncompetitive territories or to restrict competition in a market are in restraint of trade. Nor can dealers be required to refrain from selling competitors' products as a condition of receiving the right to sell the manufacturer's product. However, a unilateral refusal to deal with a price-cutter is not illegal so long as the manufacturer does not raise or maintain prices in doing so.

Reciprocity. Selecting only suppliers who will also purchase from the buyer—"You buy from me and I'll buy from you"—can be considered illegal. The FTC took nearly a year to investigate the competitive practices of American Standard Company, a manufacturer of plumbing, heating, and air conditioning products. American had a director of sales coordination whose job was to coordinate its reciprocal trade agreements. Beyond this, American kept its funds in banks whose borrowers were involved in building projects utilizing American Standard products. Since these practices are prohibited by Section 5 of the Federal Trade Commission Act, American Standard (www.americanstandard.com) agreed to stop such activities and even eliminated the position of sales coordinator. Most buyers and salespeople believe reciprocity should be illegal.

Tie-in Sales. Purchasers cannot be forced to buy an unwanted item or items in return for being allowed to purchase a product in heavy demand.

Unordered Goods. Section 5 of the FTC Act (see Table 2.3) prohibits companies from shipping unordered goods or shipping larger amounts than ordered, hoping the buyer will pay for them.

Orders and Terms of Sale. The FTC Act makes it illegal to sell substitute goods different from those ordered, intentionally misrepresent delivery dates, fail to actually fill an order, and not fill an order in a reasonable time. Terms of sale or conditions of sales offers cannot be misrepresented. Key terms of sale include warranties and guarantees, the ability of the buyer to cancel a contract or obtain a refund, and important facts in a credit or financing transaction.

Business Descriptions. Salespeople must never misrepresent the company's financial strength, length of time in business, reputation, or facts concerning its plant, equipment, or facilities.

Product Descriptions. Salespeople must not misrepresent the method by which a product is produced. For example, it is illegal to state that a product is "custom-made" or "tailor-made" when it is ready-made. Furthermore, no statements can be legally made about "proven" claims unless scientific or empirical evidence has been obtained to establish their truth.

Customer Coercion. Coercing a customer into a sale can be illegal when sales practice places undue pressure, intimidation, or fear on the buyer. This behavior includes practices such as badgering a customer with repeated sales calls.

Business Defamation. Hundreds of company and manufacturing agents have been sued for making slanderous statements about a company that result in financial damages, lost customers, unemployment, or lost sales. For example, a competitor to Starbucks can't say that Starbucks' coffee tastes like swill without some means of supporting the statement. Customers can bring private lawsuits, and the FTC is empowered to impose a cease-and-desist order or injunction on companies that engage in unfair or deceptive practices through their salespeople. Business defamation includes these offenses:

1. *Business slander*—when an unfair and untrue oral statement is made about a competitor, the statement becomes actionable when it is communicated to a third party and can be interpreted as damaging the competitor's reputation or the personal reputation of an individual in that business.
2. *Business libel*—when an unfair and untrue statement about a competitor is made in writing (usually a letter, sales literature, advertisement, or company brochure), the statement becomes actionable when it is communicated to a third party and can be interpreted as damaging the competitors' reputation or the personal reputation of an individual in that business.
3. *Product disparagement*—false or deceptive comparisons or distorted claims are made concerning a competitor's product, services, or property.
4. *Unfair competition*—injury to a competitor can result from the false advertising of one's own product, misrepresentation of the qualities or characteristics of the product, or related unfair or deceptive trade practices.

False statements made by a salesperson during or after the sales presentation can be especially troublesome. The law treats certain kinds of statements as defamatory per se. A company or defamed individual does not have to prove actual damages to successfully win a verdict. All that needs be proved is that the statement is untrue. Here are the types of statements considered personally defamatory:

- Untrue statements insinuating that a competitor engages in illegal or unfair business practices
- Untrue statements insinuating that a competitor fails to live up to contractual obligations and responsibilities
- Untrue statements regarding a competitor's financial condition
- Untrue statements insinuating that a principal in the competitor's business is either incompetent, of poor moral character, unreliable, or dishonest

A company's, salesperson's, or sales manager's reputation for integrity and high ethical standards in dealing with all people at all times is an invaluable attribute for long-run business success. Nearly all customers prefer to do business with a company whose representatives they can trust to be ethical and honest in all their negotiations.

■ International Regulation of Sales

International sellers must cope with three different sets of laws restricting their operations. First, U.S. laws sometimes forbid U.S. companies to trade with foreign countries. For example, the U.S. government imposed an embargo on trade with Vietnam in 1975 that wasn't lifted until 1994,[27] and a trade embargo has been in force with Cuba since the early 1960s. Most recently, trade embargoes have been placed against Serbia and Montenegro, two survivor states of the former Yugoslavia, and against North Korea.

Second, the multinational firm also must obey the laws of any country in which it operates, even though these may differ sharply from U.S. laws. Many times, foreign laws are less stringent, allowing sale of products banned in the United States or openly permitting bribery. Considering what U.S. law considers bribes, for instance, Germany holds such payments legal and tax deductible as long as they are made outside Germany. According to a survey by the Hong Kong–based Political and Economic Risk Consultancy, China, Vietnam, and Indonesia have the most relaxed standards regarding bribery, while Switzerland, Australia, Singapore, the United States, and Britain have the most stringent.[28] Notice how this difference affects the ethics of a sales situation. While bribery may be more acceptable and consistent with the law in Indonesia, the moral equity may be unchanged. Consider the material on ethical philosophies from the beginning of the chapter. Does greater acceptability and consistency with the law necessarily make a bribe fair or just?

On the other hand, foreign laws are sometimes *more* restrictive. For example, France restricts door-to-door selling and television advertising more than the United States does. Thus in France, a sales firm that wishes to supplement its sales efforts with television promotion will probably be unable to do so.

Finally, the multinational firm is subject to international laws that are enforced across national boundaries. Both the United Nations and the European Union are standardizing commercial codes, such as environmental and product safety standards, that are binding on all companies whose nations consent.

■ Personal Selling

International salespeople will find a wide variety of business practices as they travel across countries and cultures. But sales managers should also be aware that different ethical standards may exist from culture to culture. The interrelationships between cultural elements and ethical climate vary as well. A positive ethical climate, for instance, is associated with greater commitment among U.S. salespeople. However, an increased ethical climate negatively influences commitment among Mexican salespeople.[29]

Why is this difference important for sales managers? Sales managers have a duty to protect the salespeople under their direction, as well as the reputation of the firm. Although certain practices may be acceptable, legal, and even expected in other cultures, the sales manager should be leery of condoning actions that are unethical at home. Once a company establishes ethical standards, those standards should transcend culture. While sales managers will train and educate salespeople to adapt to other cultures, adaptation should fall short of requiring salespersons to act inconsistently with company values or condoning it when they do.

■ State and Local Regulation

Uniform Commercial Code
A basic set of guidelines adopted by most states that set forth the rules of contracts and the law pertaining to sales.

Green River Ordinances
Local ordinances requiring nonresidents to obtain a license from city authorities to sell goods or services direct to consumers in that vicinity.

Cooling-Off Rules
FTC regulation requiring door-to-door salespeople to give written notice to customers placing orders of $25 or more that they can cancel their purchase within three days.

Among the most important state and local laws and ordinances designed to regulate selling activities are the Uniform Commercial Code and the Green River Ordinances. The **Uniform Commercial Code** is a basic set of guidelines adopted by most states that set forth the rules of contracts and the law pertaining to sales. The code regulates the performance of goods, sellers' warranties, and the maximum allowable rates of interest and carrying charges. Court actions under this code usually concern buyers' claims that salespeople misrepresented the goods or made promises that were not kept. In defending itself, the selling organization must be able to provide the court with substantiating sales documentation, including contracts, letters of agreement, and the like.

Green River Ordinances, originally passed in Green River, Wyoming in 1933, are local ordinances requiring nonresidents to obtain a license from city authorities to sell goods or services direct to consumers in that vicinity. Adopted by most metropolitan areas, the laws tend to discourage many companies from trying to distribute their products and services door-to-door on a national basis.

Cooling-Off Rules are closely connected to the Green River Ordinances and require door-to-door salespeople to give written notice to customers placing orders of $25 or more that they can cancel their purchase within three days. This FTC ruling came after years of complaints about high-pressure tactics in selling magazines, jewelry, encyclopedias, cosmetics, and other merchandise house-to-house.

Practicing Good Ethics Among the Sales Force

Few topics discussed in this book are more complex than ethics. We might be tempted to follow simple rules like "always obey the law." But sometimes legal actions may be unethical, and illegal actions can be ethical. For instance, a pharmaceutical rep may be tempted to leave disproportionately large amounts of samples with physicians who administer care to populations containing high proportions of illegal immigrants.

Many may consider this ethical since these people could not obtain the medicine otherwise. However, the practice could be illegal. Also, consider how inadequate simple rules could become when the sales manager is responsible for salespeople operating in different countries—each with a different set of laws and a different culture. Some countries have strict rules concerning the types of behaviors that women should exhibit, for instance. Something as simple as a dress code may violate cultural norms in some cultures.

Ethical Stress
Ambiguity about not knowing what to do in a given situation; conflict between multiple courses of action, each with different moral implications for the people involved.

With this in mind, a sales manager often experiences **ethical stress** in the form of ambiguity or conflict. Ambiguity occurs when the sales manager simply does not know what to do in a given situation. Conflict arises when the sales manager is torn between multiple courses of action, each with different moral implications for the people involved. Next we present advice for maintaining a positive ethical climate. Ultimately, this is the best way to deal with ethical stress.

■ Understanding Ethics

Marketing is often criticized for failing to train employees adequately before "turning them loose" on customers. Sales managers have many things to teach professional salespeople before they can carry out their individual jobs. Indeed, ethics training may not seem to be a very high priority. But if the firm has strong ethical values, then ethics training is essential. Even if the company's salespeople already believe they know the difference between right and wrong, training can increase their sensitivity to ethical issues and make them more aware of potential ethical implications. Awareness is an essential part of morally virtuous behavior.

Ethical Maturity
State achieved when individuals place the moral treatment of others ahead of short-term personal gain.

Salespeople reach **ethical maturity** when they place the moral treatment of others ahead of short-term personal gain. Interestingly, as we saw earlier, age is one of the strongest causal factors of ethical actions. Older managers generally behave more ethically than younger sales managers.[30] This doesn't mean older employees are always more honest, dependable, and fair than younger employees. Each person carries with him or her a set of values that shape personal ethical standards. However, individuals tend to become more ethical with the wisdom of experience.

■ Measuring the Ethical Climate

A reduction in the ethical climate could signal problems. Fortunately, managers can monitor the ethical climate, for instance with surveys. Figure 2.2 shows some items that capture the dimensions of ethical climate. By measuring multiple dimensions, the sales manager may be able to diagnose particular areas needing attention. For example, if the score on policies and rules drops, the sales manager may consider

Reprinted by permission of Consumer Federation of America.

● **In addition to government and industry regulations, consumer groups, like The Consumer Federation of America, look out for consumer interests.**

Example Item	Strongly Disagree	Disagree	Neutral	Agree	Strongly Agree
Trust/Responsibility Employees are held accountable for their actions.	☐	☐	☐	☐	☐
Peer Behavior Employees here sometimes perform unethical acts.	☐	☐	☐	☐	☐
Policies and Rules Employees are reminded of company policies regarding fair treatment.	☐	☐	☐	☐	☐
Sales Emphasis Employees here are strongly encouraged to "up-sell" customers.	☐	☐	☐	☐	☐

FIGURE 2.2 Sample Items for Measuring the Ethical Climate as Perceived by Employees

holding training sessions that clearly outline the firm's ethics policies and the implications of violating these policies. Likewise, if salespeople begin to sense a climate increasingly typified by a bottom-line sales orientation, sales managers may wish to reconsider the motivational tactics they use to shape job performance.

■ Leading by Example

A positive, healthy, and moral ethical work climate begins at the top. Likewise, salespeople should realize that the people they supervise look to them in forming expectations of their own moral behavior. If the sales manager does not treat salespeople honestly, fairly, and equitably, salespeople are likely to have a low regard for fair, equitable, and honest treatment of customers, suppliers, channel partners, or even coworkers. Similarly, sales managers must thoroughly know and practice the company code of ethics (assuming one exists) if they expect salespeople to follow it.

■ Sales Manager Ethics Checklist

What is a sales manager to do, given the complexity of ethical behavior? How can you be sure you recognize situations and actions that may violate ethical standards?

Table 2.4 provides a sample ethical checklist tailored specifically to the sales manager's job. Try to avoid situations leading to yes answers to the questions given there.

TABLE 2.4 Sales Manager's Ethical Checklist

Briefly describe the decision you face:

_____

_____

Use the following questions to analyze the situation:

1. Will the action I take diminish the value of the product we are selling?
   ☐ YES
   ☐ NO

2. Will the action I take result in inequitable or disrespectful treatment of a salesperson?
   ☐ YES
   ☐ NO

3. Will this action place a greater emphasis on sales or profits than on the ethical treatment of the customer?
   ☐ YES
   ☐ NO

4. Will the action take unfair advantage of vulnerabilities among customers, suppliers, employees, or shareholders?
   ☐ YES
   ☐ NO

5. Will my action, either intentionally or unintentionally, motivate a salesperson to treat someone unethically?
   ☐ YES
   ☐ NO

6. Would I be comfortable telling my children about the way I acted in this situation?
   ☐ YES
   ☐ NO

CHAPTER SUMMARY

1. **Define ethics and defend its importance to sales and sales management.** Business ethics determines how companies resolve dilemmas with moral consequences. Sales managers cannot escape dealing with these types of ethical dilemmas and should make sure customers' vulnerabilities in the exchange are not exploited.

2. **Show how salespeople are boundary spanners.** Salespeople are considered boundary spanners because they work in the "boundary" between customers and the organization. As such, they perform actions that link the customer to the firm. In this position, the salesperson often faces an ethical dilemma involving the fair treatment of customers, the organization, or both.

3. **Apply a code of ethics to sales and sales management situations.** Codes of ethics express the values of a firm by specifying in writing specific behaviors that are consistent or inconsistent with those values. Their effectiveness is a debated topic, since the mere existence of a code does not guarantee a more ethical environment. Codes must not only be adopted, but top management must truly epitomize the values embodied by the codes. A sales

manager cannot expect a salesperson to conform to a code of behavior the manager openly behaves inconsistently with. There are four basic types of ethical codes: (1) company codes that define ethical boundaries for employees; (2) professional codes that define ethical boundaries for occupational groups such as advertisers, marketing researchers, sales representatives, doctors, lawyers, accountants, and so on; (3) business association codes that define ethical boundaries for people engaged in the same line of business; and (4) advisory group codes suggested by government agencies or other special interest groups. Each industry is confronted with unique ethical issues and must adapt its code to meet the situation.

4. **Apply the criteria for making moral judgments.** Every person has a particular ethical philosophy. Idealism is a philosophy by which we judge actions against some applicable, universal standard or guiding principle. Relativism is a philosophy by which we judge the acceptability of actions in the context of some situation. Teleology is the philosophy that the end justifies the means. Three dimensions of moral judgments are (1) moral equity, or the fairness or justness of some behavior; (2) acceptability, or how socially or culturally acceptable an employee views certain types of behavior; and (3) contractualism, or whether an act violates written or implied policies, contracts, or laws.

5. **Create and manage an ethical climate.** Ethical climate concerns the way employees view their work environment on moral dimensions. Four dimensions of ethical climate are policies and rules, trust and responsibility, peer behavior, and a bottom-line sales orientation. In particular, a strong bottom-line orientation—heavy emphasis on making the numbers—is responsible for motivating unethical actions. The sales manager can work toward a more positive ethical climate by emphasizing four workplace outcomes: (1) employees should know and understand ethics, (2) management should measure the ethical climate and use the measure to diagnose potential problems, (3) managers should lead by example, and (4) managers should use an ethics checklist to avoid making poor decisions when faced with ethical dilemmas.

6. **Observe legal regulations that affect the sales environment.** Observation of legal regulations begins with knowledge. The chapter covers many legal regulations that affect the sales environment. Key regulatory acts include the Sherman Antitrust Act and the Child Protection Act. These regulations are largely intended to make sure that a competitive marketplace is maintained or to protect populations perceived as vulnerable. Sales managers must be aware of key legal regulations that are relevant in their respective industries.

7. **Model good ethical behavior among the sales force.** Sales managers have many things to teach professional salespeople before they can carry out their individual jobs. Ethics training may not seem to be a high priority, but if the firm has strong ethical values, then ethics training is essential. Even if the salesperson already believes he or she knows the difference between right and wrong, training increases ethical sensitivity and makes the salesperson more aware of potential ethical implications. A positive, healthy, and ethical work climate begins at the top. If the sales manager does not treat salespeople honestly and fairly, salespeople are likely to have low regard for equitable and honest treatment of customers, suppliers, channel partners, or even coworkers. Similarly, sales managers must thoroughly know and practice the company code of ethics (assuming one exists) if they expect salespeople to follow it.

REVIEW AND APPLICATION QUESTIONS

1. Define business ethics. [LO 1]
2. Why are salespeople considered boundary spanners? [LO 2]
3. Describe why business ethics is such an important topic in sales management. [LO 1]
4. Define vulnerability in a business context. Provide an example for each of these scenarios:
   a. Salesperson is vulnerable to a customer based on a knowledge deficit.
   b. A customer is vulnerable to a salesperson based on naiveté.

    c. A sales manager is vulnerable to a salesperson based on a power discrepancy.

    d. A customer is vulnerable to a salesperson based on a power discrepancy. [LO 1, LO 3]

5. A sales manager sends a salesperson to a Latin American country, noted for corruption in business, to work on closing a deal to supply parts to a heavy equipment manufacturer. The salesperson will be able to close the deal only if his company provides a bribe (a new Cadillac) to a buyer from the manufacturer. How would you resolve this decision? Based on your decision, would you say your moral philosophy leans more toward idealism or relativism? How would a person with the other moral philosophy resolve the situation? [LO 4]

6. List and define each dimension of moral judgment. [LO 4]

7. List at least ten salesperson behaviors that would generally be considered unethical. [LO 5]

8. What is the Clayton Act? [LO 6]

9. When is price discrimination considered legal? [LO 6]

10. Define *ethical climate*. List two local companies that you are somewhat familiar with. What do you think the ethical climate is like in these companies? [LO 5]

11. If your university was a workplace, what would the ethical climate be regarding each of its four dimensions? [LO 5]

12. What is ethical stress? How can ethical stress be resolved in the workplace? [LO 7]

13. Do you believe that the common negative perception of salesperson ethics is fact or fiction?

14. Question for Thought: Consider the material in the chapter describing the sales manager and the salesperson's role as a boundary spanner. Do you believe the boundary-spanning nature of selling is responsible for the bad reputation of salespeople? [LO 2]

IT'S UP TO YOU

Internet Exercise

Use a search engine such as ask.com or google.com to find some company or industry codes of ethics. Do these codes of ethics appear more consistent with idealism or relativism? Do you think the codes are effective?

Role-Playing Exercise

Situation

A sales manager receives a call from a customer. The customer is concerned because the company salesperson has not made a call to her business in over ten weeks. As a result, she is out of stock on some critical items, causing her own production to become inefficient. When the sales manager confronts the rep about this action, he does not deny the story. Instead, he insists he was acting consistently with company policy that places a high value on maximizing shareholder wealth. His quotas are tied to this goal, and he believes that providing sales and service support to small customers undermines his effort to obtain sales from better customers. Assume you were the sales manager; how would you react to the salesperson? What tools or knowledge might assist you in resolving the dilemma?

In-Basket Exercise

You are a district sales manager for an electronics firm that markets to industrial users, and you have recently been receiving complaints from customers about late deliveries. It appears that, occasionally, several of your salespeople promised customers certain delivery dates without checking with the product and shipping departments. As a result, the products reached the customers a day or two after the promised delivery date. When you confronted your salespeople with this issue, they claimed, "Everyone in the industry does it," and said, "The competition is getting so intense that we have to do it to compete." Moreover, your salespeople told you that an "on-time delivery" is more of an exception than the rule for the industry.

Questions

1. Should anything be done in this situation? Why or why not?

2. Would establishing a code of ethics on the issue of "over-promising" help in this situation? Why or why not?

3. How would you develop a code of ethics for your company in this situation, and how would you enforce it?

Ethical Dilemma

Consider a sales manager working for a small manufacturing firm. A salesperson in the field phones with a problem. Yesterday he committed to a deal to provide products to a retail chain operating in three states with two dozen stores. Today, he can close a deal with a nationwide retailer with over 100 stores, but he wonders whether his firm can supply enough product to fulfill both customers' demands. The sales manager knows the answer to this question. There is no way the company can fulfill the deal signed yesterday and meet the demands of the larger retailer. So the sales manager is considering whether to have the salesperson mislead the smaller retailer while diverting deliveries to the larger retailer. What should the sales manager do?

CASE 2.1

Billings Pharmaceuticals: Customer Vulnerability and Moral Equity

It was the biggest quarterly sales bonus check she had received in the year since joining Billings Pharmaceuticals, but it sat unopened on the breakfast table. Rather than being excited, Beth Simmons had mixed emotions. Beth, like many of her peers in college, longed to work in pharmaceutical sales. The industry and Billings Pharmaceuticals seemed to fit with her career goals and core values. She had always wanted to work for a company that helped people—and did so in a highly ethical manner. During the recruitment process, she was particularly impressed by the code of ethics at Billings that stressed integrity, excellence, and respect for people. Beth is now having second thoughts about the company, and some events in the recent past are troubling her.

Beth joined Billings after receiving an undergraduate degree in psychology and an MBA from a major state university. Because of her background in psychology, the company trained Beth specifically to represent its portfolio of products to physicians practicing in the area of mental health. She called on psychiatrists in private practice, in mental health units at private and public hospitals, and at state and federal prisons, as well as primary-care physicians. In the eyes of these doctors, Beth Simmons was Billings Pharmaceuticals, because they trusted her to give them timely and accurate information about new and existing products.

The leading product in the company's portfolio of psychiatric drugs is Depolara. This product was designed to treat schizophrenia and bipolar disorder. In the five years since its approval by the Food and Drug Administration (FDA), Depolara had become Billing's best-selling product, accounting for 25 percent of company revenues or $4 billion annually. Beth was proud to discuss the features and benefits of Depolara after learning in her training program that the drug works much better than competitive offerings do for certain patients. But she remembered that in one of her first appointments after training, a psychiatrist asked if she had any information on Depolara being associated with obesity and increased blood sugar—both risk factors for diabetes. The doctor indicated that about a third of his patients gained 20 pounds while taking the drug for a year and that some gained as much as 100 pounds. He also said that he was very concerned because patients had become diabetic while on Depolara. Beth wrote down his concerns in her notes, but didn't think much about it until she began to notice a pattern. During her first several months of making sales calls, more and more doctors began asking her about this problem.

Beth had reviewed all of her documentation on Depolara and could find no references to these side effects. So she decided to ask her sales manager, Bob Pearce, what he knew about the issue. Bob had just returned from a sales managers' meeting and told Beth that concerns about Depolara and diabetes did come up, but that the company's president had said, "There is no scientific evidence establishing that Depolara causes diabetes." "Besides," Bob said, "It's FDA approved, so why worry about it?"

Beth reiterated that most of her psychiatrists were talking about these side effects, and many were beginning to change patients to a major competitor's products. In response, Bob suggested that she downplay concerns about obesity and diabetes with these doctors. He also encouraged her to make more calls on primary-care doctors and prison-based physicians because Billing's market research showed that they were less aware of Depolara's side effects. He even gave her sales brochures to use that promoted Depolara as a "safe, gentle psychotropic suitable for people with mild men-

tal illness." "After all," Bob said, "Billings Pharmaceuticals is counting on us to make our numbers." However, Beth knew that "making the numbers" was increasingly difficult to do; doctors were becoming more aware of the side effects, and the issue was becoming more public.

Although at first she had been excited about working for Billings, Beth was now beginning to question the company's leadership. She knew that the doctors' concerns were real, and she wondered how seriously senior management believed in the principles of integrity, excellence, and respect for people. She glanced down one more time at the newspaper headline, "Billings Pays $1.2 B to Settle Depolara Lawsuits," and then she left for work.

QUESTIONS

1. Briefly describe the moral dilemma that Beth Simmons is facing.

2. Does the code of ethics at Billings Pharmaceuticals seem to be influencing sales management decisions in a meaningful way? Why or why not?

3. In her boundary-spanning role, what is Beth's responsibility for customer vulnerability of the physicians and their patients?

4. Describe the ethical climate in the sales organization at Billings.

5. Complete the Sales Manager's Ethical Checklist in Table 2.4. If Bob Pearce had followed this checklist, how would it have changed the direction he gave Beth?

6. Beth is debating her commitment to a career with Billings Pharmaceuticals. If she stays and nothing changes at Billings, how will this affect her career in pharmaceutical sales over the long run in the market she presently serves?

Case prepared by K. Randall Russ, Belhaven College.

 ## CASE 2.2

J&R Company: Unethical Sales Practices

Tom Peterson is an industrial sales representative for J&R Company, a large company in the pipe, valve, and fitting industry. J&R Company serves customers with facilities in which gases or liquids are moved from one place to another in the manufacturing process. Tom

returned to his office from visiting a large potential customer in the paper and pulp industry. During his drive, Tom decided to call his weekly golf partner Sam McNeil, a reporter for the trade publication for Tom's industry. Tom planned to ask Sam to run a story about his company's new product and the two largest companies that Tom believed would soon sign a contract with J&R to purchase the product. J&R Company had developed a new valve system that they believed would reduce spills and leaks in customers' manufacturing facilities. However, the product was slow to take off in the market. While J&R's system was shown to reduce leaks by 0.4 percent (0.5 percent with the additional purchase of an extended service contract), Tom believed those reports significantly underestimated the value of the system.

Valve leak detection systems had become extremely popular in manufacturing facilities in recent years. Tom sensed that the product was slow-moving on the market because companies felt that the leak detection systems were more cost-effective than purchasing a completely new valve system and stopping production while the new system was installed.

Earlier in the day, Tom had visited one of his company's largest prospective customers—Biddle Inc., a major pulp and paper company. Tom told Biddle Inc. that one of its closest competitors would soon begin using J&R's new valve system. While Biddle Inc.'s competitor had not yet signed a contract or committed to J&R, Tom felt that they soon would come around and agree to purchase the system as well as the extended service contract. Tom offered Biddle Inc. a low price on the initial system. He knew the initial system would be obsolete in the next year as the company refined the system and significantly decreased its spill/leakage rate. But Tom felt that if Biddle Inc. agreed to buy the initial system, they would see how well the product performed and naturally upgrade to the refined system once it was placed on the market. Tom explained to Biddle Inc. that the new system substantially reduced the risk of leaks and spills, which slow down production and are costly. Tom built his sales presentation around the costs of leaks or spills across all industries in which liquids and gas are somehow processed. He mentioned several times in his sales presentation that as compared to purchasing the new valve system only, purchasing the extended service contract would offer Biddle Inc. a 20 percent reduction in the spill rate.

Tom hoped that if Sam, his golfing partner, would help him with media coverage for J&R's new valve system, the product might start to pick up some momentum on the market. He planned to use coverage of the story as an additional lever to close the deals with Biddle Inc. and its competitor. While neither potential customer had committed, and both frankly told Tom they had serious reservations about the new product, Tom thought a product review published in a respected trade publication would offer the product the credibility it needed to jump-start sales. In any case, Sam owed Tom a favor.

If the valve system did not do well in the market during the next quarter, J&R had made clear that the company would be forced to downsize its sales force. The company had an extended line of products and services, and while senior management hoped the new valve system would become a flagship product for the company, they would not sacrifice the reputation of their other products in attempts to force a lackluster product to market. Tom has worked for J&R for ten years. Nevertheless, he felt his job was vulnerable. He had shifted his sales emphasis entirely to the new valve system, giving up territory and smaller customers who purchased other products and services from the company. In Tom's city, industrial sales positions were limited. With two children—one in high school, the other in middle school—and a wife with a secure position at a large law firm in the area, Tom did not welcome the prospects of job change. He had to find a way to make the new valve system a marketplace success.

QUESTIONS

1. Briefly describe the issues that, in your opinion, are raised in the case.

2. For each issue you listed in question 1, if any, rate how important you believe that issue is on the following scale:

Very Important   Unimportant

   7 6 5 4 3 2 1

3. How could a company code of ethics aid Tom in his decisions? What are some examples of what the company code of ethics might contain to assist sales representatives in situations similar to Tom's?

4. What questions might Tom have asked himself during this situation to determine whether his actions were ethical?

5. Recommend a course of action that Tom might have taken, and support your recommendations.

Case prepared by Michelle D. Steward, Wake Forest University.

Customer Relationship Management and Building Partnerships

INSIDE SALES MANAGEMENT

Julie Wroblewski of eFunds

Julie Wroblewski obtains most of her sales leads from a technology that barely existed ten years ago—and some of the services she sells are even newer. Wroblewski is an account executive for eFunds, which provides electronic payment software and processing solutions as well as the data and analysis tools to help companies make decisions about financial risk (fraud, for example). Customers include banks, financial services firms, retailers, electronic funds networks, government agencies, and e-commerce firms.

Technology is a vital part of the personal selling environment for eFunds. "I get most of my leads through our website," Wroblewski says. Prospects visit the site (www.efunds.com) and then call or e-mail the company for more information. A group at eFunds headquarters screens these requests and sends them on to reps for personal contact.

Because they've browsed the website, prospects usually have a general idea of what eFunds can do for them. Still, Wroblewski carefully investigates each prospect's unique needs and situation. To save time and money, she schedules as many as ten conference calls per week so that various eFunds technical specialists can discuss solutions to prospects' problems. For a typical conference call, she says, "I learn about the prospect's needs and expectations ahead of time, gather a pool of eFunds experts, and we work through the agenda with the prospect's businesspeople." A growing number of prospects do business globally, which means people in other countries sometimes participate in these conference calls.

To spot sales opportunities, Wroblewski reads the *Wall Street Journal, Fast Company,* and several technology magazines. "But what is really new for sales folks in today's environment are Internet sources like *Wall Street Journal Online* and online newsletters," she observes. "I can have news about particular firms forwarded to my e-mail inbox. This keeps me up-to-date about prospects and companies where I'm trying to make an appointment."

Technology also affects what Wroblewski sells. One of eFunds' newest offerings is a service that allows online shoppers to pay with electronic checks that look much like ordinary bank checks. Consumers without credit cards like the convenience, and merchants pay lower fees than they would for processing credit card payments.

Not long ago, Wroblewski began talking with an education company that wanted to start accepting Internet checks. After an initial phone call to discuss the prospect's situation, "We set up a time for eFunds experts to meet face-to-face with their management," she says, "and we presented our proposal using a PowerPoint electronic presentation." She followed up with periodic conference calls to address technical issues, supplemented by e-mails to provide additional details. After nine months, she closed the deal—and now eFunds powers the electronic checks on this customer's website.

SOURCE: Anderson, Rolph E., Alan J. Dubinsky, and Rajiv Mehta, *Personal Selling: Building Customer Relationships and Partnerships*, 2/e, pp. 34–35. Copyright © 2007 by Houghton Mifflin Company. Reprinted with permission.

What Is CRM?

Business is famous for inventing catch phrases. Do you remember these?

- "Think outside the box!"
- "Work smarter, not harder!"
- "Downsize"
- "Pushback"
- "Total Quality Control"—also known as Total Quality Management (TQM)

The newest is CRM—for customer relationship management.[1] CRM's roots have been around for many years. As long ago as 1969, *Reader's Digest* kept files on over 10,000,000 customers segmented into three groups based on the likelihood of their responding to promotional appeals. The system answered the question: "If a customer is sent a new book to review, how likely will they be to respond by purchasing the book and buying others?" One group was highly likely to respond, another group responded only with more prodding, and a third group was highly unlikely to respond. While primitive by today's standards, this example captures the basic notion of CRM.[2]

CRM is more than a catch phrase. For sales managers, CRM means a wide array of solutions for handling sales and customer information. Thus, finding a universally accepted definition of CRM is difficult.[3] Here, we focus on CRM from a sales and sales management perspective. In this sense, **CRM** is a systematic integration of information technology and human resources designed to provide maximum value to customers and to obtain maximum value from customers. In other words, a CRM system

CRM
A systematic integration of information, technology, and human resources, all oriented toward (1) providing maximum value to customers and (2) maximizing the value obtained from customers.

helps salespeople match customers with the products that are best for them, and in doing so leverages company resources into higher sales. Indeed, companies adopting CRM programs often experience higher business performance.[4]

As the name implies, CRM deals with managing relationships. Thus, just as people have different relationships with other people, businesses also have different relationships with customers. So before explaining CRM systems, let's consider the nature of relationships between selling approaches and customers.

Relationship Orientations and CRM

Businesses approach customers in many ways. But we can summarize almost all these relationships into a few types, shown in Figure 3.1.

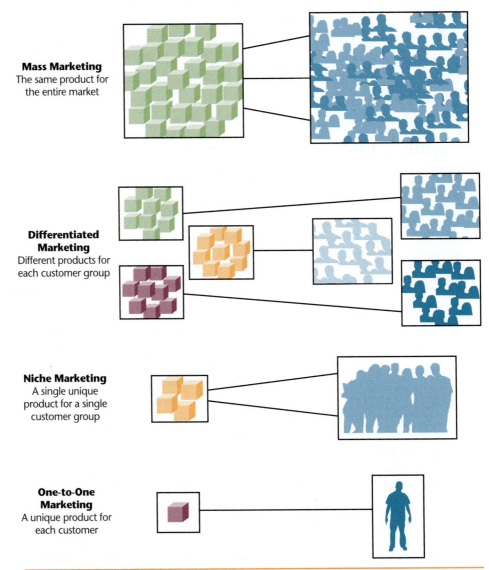

Mass Marketing
The same product for the entire market

Differentiated Marketing
Different products for each customer group

Niche Marketing
A single unique product for a single customer group

One-to-One Marketing
A unique product for each customer

FIGURE 3.1 Relationships Between Businesses and Customers

■ Mass Marketing

Mass Marketing
A way of dealing with customers by offering the same product to the entire market.

When we think of marketing, we often think of mass marketing. **Mass marketing** is a way of dealing with customers by offering the same product to the entire market. All customers get the same treatment. The company may make small variations in the products sold, but the main concern is efficiency in production and distribution. Mass marketing evokes the images of large factories with high-volume assembly lines. You may have heard the expression, attributed to Henry Ford, that "the customer can have any color car he wants as long as it's black!"

Mass marketing focuses on efficiently distributing products to large numbers of consumers. As a result, the orientation is maximizing market share and minimizing costs by distributing them over sales to large numbers of customers. Sales managers serve a large number of customers with a limited sales force. Marketing expenses are generally minimal, and the sales effort becomes routine. Many firms selling basic commodities still operate as mass marketers today.

Differentiated Marketing
Dealing with different groups of customers by offering a unique product for each group.

■ Differentiated Marketing

Differentiated marketing is selling to different groups of customers by offering a unique product for each group. Many consumer-goods firms use differentiated marketing. For example, Coca-Cola has products for traditional cola lovers, cola lovers with concerns about calories, energy drinks, products without caffeine, and even products for water lovers! Coke also sells different products for institutional customers and individual consumers.

Niche Marketing
Offering a specialized product to an individual customer segment with specialized needs.

Differentiated marketing requires a more customized sales effort and greater attention to customer research than does mass marketing. Sales managers must decide, for example, whether to assign salespeople based on customer similarities or product similarities, or whether the same salespeople calling on fast-food restaurants should also call on hypermarts. CRM influences these decisions, as we will see later.

© Patterson Graham/Corbis

● Brands like Cesar and Miss Lilly's have marketing strategies that cater to a niche market: female dog owners who wish to pamper their pets like the consumer shown here!

■ Niche Marketing

Niche marketing offers a specialized product or a small range of products to an individual customer segment with specialized needs. For instance, some insurance companies focus on providing insurance for specific circumstances. AFLAC (www.aflac.com) sells supplementary disability insurance for people who are unable to work. Salespeople for niche marketers must be very knowledgeable about the needs of the niche market the company serves.

■ One-to-One Marketing

One-to-One Marketing
Involves matching individual products with individual customers.

One-to-one marketing, as the name implies, matches individual products with individual customers. This way of dealing with customers takes differentiated or niche marketing to the extreme. The result is a product personalized for each customer in some way.[5] Many textbook publishers customize textbooks for individual courses at different universities. Perhaps some of your textbooks contain material and/or pictures depicting things specific to your school. If so, chances are the publisher has agreed to produce a special version of the book for use only at your university. This is an example of one-to-one marketing.

Successful one-to-one marketing requires detailed knowledge of customers. A custom home builder, for example, relies on the customer to provide all the details desired in the home. A mobile home manufacturer, obviously not a one-to-one marketer, provides customers very little opportunity to choose features. Custom home builders add features based on feedback customers provide directly. But manufacturers of many other types of products rely on technology to gather detailed customer information and feed it directly into the design of a customized product.

© Bonnie Kamin / PhotoEdit

● **Wal-Mart remains a mass marketing icon. However, companies that tie the scanner data to individual customers can target segments for individualized promotions.**

■ Using Information to Meet Customer Needs: The Basis of CRM

Many companies that formerly practiced mass marketing now are moving quickly toward differentiated marketing—and sometimes even one-to-one marketing. Through the middle of the twentieth century, U.S. television was dominated by three national networks, each offering a single programming option for the entire viewing audience. Networks have now diversified and offer many programming options for different customer segments. Most of the major networks own news channels (CNBC, Fox News) and sports channels (ESPN, ESPN2, ESPN-Classic). Sky Network (www.sky .uk) operates many different cable options.

Even supermarket giants such as Tesco (www.tesco.uk.com) and Sainsbury's (www .sainsbury.uk.com) are adopting some one-to-one marketing practices. Tesco, for example, sends its entire market traditional flyers with weekly specials. But Tesco also sends flyers with over 5 million variations, each tailored for a specific customer based on his or her buying patterns.

How can a company try to match up 5 million different promotional products with 5 million individual customers? With technology! Companies like Unica (www.unica.com) offer software that tracks individual customer activities and ties those activities to targeted communications. The information is gathered through scanner data or Internet cookies. Industrial customers, in particular, are realizing that giving a firm access to their cookies can be a win-win situation. In this way, information that salespeople once had to collect in the field can be gathered easily and inexpensively using technology.[6]

■ Production Versus Marketing Orientation

Production Orientation
Companies focus on processes allowing large-scale, efficient, and economic production.

Market Orientation
Companies focus on making what could be sold, not selling what is made. A market-oriented firm focuses all activities on providing value for customers.

The production and marketing orientations are complementary ways to look at business. The industrial revolution enabled businesses to manufacture in high volumes efficiently and at lower costs. This is the essence of a **production orientation**. Companies with this outlook focus on processes allowing large-scale, efficient, and economic production. They need little customer research because they don't have to change their products to fit the demands of any particular market.[7]

Table 3.1 illustrates the similarities between mass marketing and a production orientation. Sales managers in mass-marketing firms concentrate on moving large quantities of products through traditional distribution channels that allow for economical shipping, such as trucking and railroad freight. Sales practices rely heavily on price promotions such as trade allowances and discounts, since the products often are seen as somewhat interchangeable.

The production orientation dominated industry in the United States and other developed economies through the mid-twentieth century. Indeed, a production orientation helped the Allies win World War II as factories turned out large quantities of B-17s, Sherman tanks, and Liberty ships at an unprecedented pace. Production capacity more than satisfied the demand for basic goods. But eventually businesses had to do more than just sell whatever they could make.

The answer emerged from a new way of doing business called **market orientation**. With this approach companies focus more on making what they can sell.[8] Market-oriented firms seek success in a competitive marketplace by focusing on providing value for customers. This means knowledge of consumers must be shared through all areas of the firm. Sales managers play an important role not only in carrying outbound communications to customers but also in steering inbound communications that flow from customers back through various organizational levels within a company. When a firm becomes market-oriented, these communications can end up altering the design and production of products as well as promotion and distribution strategies.

TABLE 3.1 Production Orientation to Market Orientation in the Twentieth Century				
1900–1940	1941–1945	1946–1959	1960–1990	1991–beyond
Industrial capacity increases—the production orientation is born.	Industrial capacity reaches its highest productivity in war time.	The economy is strong, but firms can make more than can be sold.	Better marketing research techniques allow more input from consumers prior to making key marketing decisions—the marketing orientation is born.	Firms become more customer-centric as many firms move from transactional exchange to relational exchange—the marketing orientation leads to CRM.

Customer-Centric
The customer becomes the heart of the business process.

Customer Value
The net positive worth resulting from participation in exchange.

Sales-Oriented Salesperson
Motivated to maximize sales from each contact even if a product does not best match customer needs and desires.

Market-oriented firms are **customer-centric**—customers are the heart of the business process. These firms focus on **customer value**, which is the net positive worth resulting from participation in exchange. Differentiated marketers and one-to-one marketers follow the market orientation, since their products must closely match consumer desires or a competitor will move in to better meet the demand. General Electric is often credited with developing the concept of a marketing orientation in the early 1960s. GE emphasized the critical role played by customer research prior to launching new products. This was a revolutionary concept in the mid-twentieth century.

Salespeople can be more or less customer-oriented. **Sales-oriented** salespeople are motivated to maximize sales from each contact even if a product does not best match customer needs and desires. But **customer-oriented** salespeople are motivated primarily to match customers with products that best meet their needs. Research generally supports the idea that positive outcomes come from both firm market orientation and salesperson consumer orientation.[9] The positive outcomes include better relationships through customer service and improved performance.[10]

CRM and Repeat Business

Customer-Oriented Salesperson
Motivated primarily by matching up customers with products that best address their needs.

Touchpoint
Refers to points in time when the customer and the company come together, either personally or virtually.

Sales Exchange
The act of trading economic resources (usually money) for a specific set of benefits offered by a company.

CRM is based on the premise that companies interact with customers more than one time and in more than one way. Businesses that assume they'll contact each customer one time are less motivated to provide excellent service than those that assume they'll be in touch with customers many times over an extended period. The extra motivation is based on the likelihood of repeat business.

A **touchpoint** is a situation in which the customer and the company come together, either personally or virtually. For example, a touchpoint occurs when a salesperson calls on a customer at his or her place of business; when a customer phones the business for sales assistance or service; when a customer visits the company's website, and even when the customer hears a radio advertisement for the company. With CRM, touchpoints become critical parts of the service delivery process.

Perhaps the most critical touchpoint is at the point of exchange. A **sales exchange** is the act of trading economic resources (usually money) for a specific set of benefits offered by a company. Marketing facilitates exchange, and salespeople play the key functional role in conducting exchanges for the organization.

■ Transactional View

Transactional Selling
Exists when a sales firm acts consistently with the view that each and every interaction with a customer is a unique and independent event.

One view of exchange is that each and every interaction with a customer is a unique and independent event. Companies that consistently follow this view are practicing **transactional selling**. Here, the salesperson is concerned most with winning business from a particular exchange touchpoint.

Transactional selling is at the low end of the relationship involvement continuum (see Table 3.2).[11] The exchange environment is characterized by short-term customer needs. Sales reps make periodic sales calls, with high-volume customers receiving more frequent visits than low-volume customers. Buyers and sellers remain independent, and each transaction is conducted as a new event. Thus, the *relationship* lasts only as long as necessary to complete the sales transaction. No long-term commitment or loyalty is involved, and little value is assigned to understanding long-run buyer needs and expectations.

TABLE 3.2 **Contrasting Types of Exchange Relationships**			
NATURE OF EXCHANGE RELATIONSHIP			
	Transactional →	Relational →	Partnership
Exchange environment	Competitive	Cooperative	Collaborative
Timing of contact	Periodic sales calls	Frequent contact—near daily	Intensive contact—dedicated sales associate(s)
Service level	Good	Very good	Intensive
Trust	Moderate	High	Complete
Interdependence	Low	High	Extreme—vertical integration possible
Sales pattern	Independent	Renewing contract	Ongoing contract
Governance	Market forces	Contract	Relational

Transactional selling can be more adversarial than cooperative. Price becomes a key consideration—neither the salesperson nor the customer is looking for much beyond the immediate transaction, and issues like service after the sale are relatively less important.[12] Thus, the most common way to increase value is to lower price.

Although buyers and sellers participate in transactional exchanges many times over a period of years, they negotiate prices and other terms each time an exchange takes place. Interpersonal trust may develop over time, but the transactional exchange does not require high trust levels. If customers have a bad experience, they simply exclude the company from the consideration set next time. Selling firms with this orientation generally have to touch large numbers of customers to generate business. In this sense, risk is reduced because the selling firm is less dependent on any one customer or a small number of customers.

■ Relational Selling

Relational Exchange
Recognition, by both buyer and seller, that each transaction is merely one in a series of purchase agreements between a buyer and a seller.

Attracting new customers costs significantly more than reselling to current customers. In **relational exchange**, both buyer and seller recognize that each transaction is just one in a series of purchase agreements. Thus, relational selling is more customer-centric than transactional exchanges are.[13] The exchange environment is characterized by a spirit of cooperation between buyer and seller. Firms seek to develop profitable, ongoing relationships with customers by delivering high value and creating a sense of loyalty. In fact, loyal customers frequently become a company's best unpaid salespeople by referring other prospects and spreading positive word-of-mouth messages.[14]

Customer Retention
Refers to the percentage of customers who will repeatedly purchase products from the selling firm.

Sales managers must be committed to providing exceptional service. This relatively high level of customer service is influential in customer retention. **Customer retention** is the percentage of customers who repeatedly purchase products from the selling firm. Any relationship, whether social or business, requires regular attention and nurturing. Poorly served or neglected customers are likely to start looking for alternate suppliers. Thus, relational exchange relationships are characterized by frequent, even daily contacts between the sales force and the customer, or by electronic systems that enable the seller to monitor various aspects of the buyer's business, such as inventory levels and reorder points.

Relational exchange has a longer-term focus than does transactional exchange. As a result, salespeople can develop ties that generate repeated transactions. These relationships require higher levels of trust, since the switching costs are increased due to greater dependence. Consider a computer manufacturer that purchases processor chips via transactional exchange relationships. Over time, the company will use many different suppliers.

Relational exchanges should result in win-win sales solutions. Sales managers emphasize the importance of understanding customer needs and requirements. This corporate knowledge must be communicated to salespeople in the field. CRM provides a more high-tech approach to staying in touch with customers. The next *Sales Management in Action* box provides some insight into this process for a new pharmaceutical rep.

Strategic Partnership
Occurs when the goals, strategies, and resources of buyers and sellers become so interconnected and intertwined that they develop an integrated, symbiotic relationship although still retaining their independent identities.

■ Strategic Partnerships

In relational exchanges, the buying and selling firms are so closely intertwined they sometimes become partners. This type of exchange environment is a **strategic partnership**. Strategic partnerships arise when the goals, strategies, and resources of buyers and sellers are so interconnected they develop an integrated, symbiotic relationship while retaining their independent identities.[15]

Strategic partnerships and other inter-firm collaborative arrangements are commonplace in today's global economy. As companies increasingly specialize, they

SALES MANAGEMENT IN ACTION

Merck Goes High Tech

Jane Smart is about to begin a sales training class for new hires at Merck. She has been a sales manager for twenty years and is reflecting on how things have changed. She recalls her first sales calls to physicians' offices. Each new sales call was a nerve-racking experience. She had no information from previous reps about the types of products each doctor was likely to respond positively to, no knowledge of who the key people in the office were or how to actually get access to the physician, no clue about the physician's demeanor and whether she would be greeted warmly or rudely or be thrown out of the office because of something another rep had done. She quickly learned that taking notes following a sales call was essential to making the next call more effective.

Merck's training class will add a couple dozen people to the more than 90,000 pharmaceutical reps selling drugs across the United States. In contrast to Jane Smart's early experiences, each rep will receive sophisticated training, including a detailed history of

each existing account. This history will be instantly available from computers that store information about physicians, regulations, clinical drug trials, and potential competing products. The system is the result of a partnership between Microsoft and Accenture to produce a product especially for Merck sales reps. Following each sales call, reps enter notes about what happened. The information is integrated into the system, enabling each rep to use time more effectively, managing customers with a combination of technology and personal attention. Although the selling process is more complicated than when she began, Jane realizes new Merck reps will be more productive and get more out of the limited time each of them has with a customer. How things have changed!

SOURCES: Adapted from David Myron, "Pharmaceutical Firms Find a Spoonful of CRM Helps the Sales Pitch Go Down," *CRM Magazine,* May 2004, pp. 14–17; *Medical Marketing & Media,* Update, 39, no. 7 (2004): 9.

are moving away from rigid, control-based structures and adopting more flexible, relationship-based partnering arrangements that capitalize on the relative strengths of each partner. In fact, many companies have re-engineered their business processes to create coalitions and partnerships with their customers' companies, thus developing tightly interwoven and interdependent value chains.

Strategic partnerships are at the opposite end of the exchange continuum from transactional exchanges. They are based more on inter-organizational *collaboration* than on arm's-length aggressive bargaining and are not viewed as competitive. In fact, decision making often is collaborative, and firms share managerial resources and expertise when solving key strategic and tactical issues. Companies that skillfully establish strategic partnering agreements can shore up weaknesses and capitalize on strengths together, thereby making both partners stronger.[16]

Strategic partnerships result in continuous, recurring exchanges. This requires intensive levels of communication, relationship openness, information sharing, joint problem solving, strategic integration, and mutual learning.[17] Strategic partnerships also exhibit high levels of collaboration among partners, equality, shared vision, benefits and goals, and high levels of trust.

Mutual Loyalty
Occurs when both buyer and seller are committed to each other and avoid behaviors that may damage the relationship.

Mutual loyalty occurs when both buyer and seller are committed to each other and avoid behaviors that may damage the relationship. Sun Microsystems (www.sun.com) is an example of a firm that has developed strategic partnerships. Sun has strong brand identity and is known as a key technology provider that manufactures server hardware, workstations, and storage devices. Sun salespeople partner with software vendors and system integrators to provide complete technology solutions for their customers. Because Sun almost never takes a "prime contractor" role, it does not compete but rather cooperates with its partners.[18]

© Julio Etchart / Peter Arnold

● **Joint stores typify the strategic partnership between these units of KFC and Pizza Hut.**

Companies that rely on strategic partnerships may actually reduce the need for salespeople.[19] Sales managers in strong strategic partnerships can end up functioning more as employees of the buyer's firm than as a traditional salesperson. In this way, reps acquire detailed knowledge needed to maintain healthy relationships with customers. Much information—including sales histories, forecasts, and even market research results—is shared between firms, often in real time.

Strategic partnerships often result in vertical integration. **Vertical integration** is a pattern of controlling and perhaps acquiring assets and resources at different levels of the marketing channel enabling the manufacturer to tightly control production and distribution processes, creating value for the customer. The increased control means customer needs are more precisely met.

Bridgestone Tire Company (www.bridgestone-firestone.com) creates strategic partnerships with customers. Bridgestone even manages inventories for customers, eliminating their need to place orders. Thus, sales reps don't need to call on dealers for routine order taking. Bridgestone also controls many aspects of the distribution channel including its own fleet of trucks and a customized delivery system that makes twenty-four-hour delivery possible. Bridgestone also owns manufacturing assets, including rubber farms. All these steps help Bridgestone provide value for customers.

■ Mechanisms That Govern Exchanges

All types of exchanges are accompanied by some type of **governance**, the mechanism that helps ensure the exchange is fair to all parties involved. As shown earlier in Table 3.2, transactional exchanges are controlled by market forces, relational exchanges are governed by contracts, and strategic partnerships are governed by a mechanism known as relational governance. Market forces are the simplest because they require no artificial mechanism. When problems occur in exchange, the parties simply look for another place to do business. Contracts complicate exchange by specifying the legal obligations of buyers and sellers. Fair exchange proceeds so long as each party fulfills these obligations. If not, legal action is possible.

Relational governance includes arrangements for sharing information and tasks between the buying and selling firms, but it does not include specific obligations for each party. There is a written commitment between buyer and seller, but the agreement allows greater flexibility than a contractual governance structure does.[20]

In all relationships, one firm eventually takes advantage of the other. When this occurs, the firm has behaved in an **opportunistic manner**. Figure 3.2 shows survey scale items measuring whether a customer believes a supplier has behaved opportunistically. Generally, written agreements and greater trust result in less opportunism. But when a selling situation is characterized by high ambiguity, relational-based governance creates a high degree of opportunistic behavior.[21] For example, cross-cultural exchanges include considerable amounts of ambiguity due to cultural uncertainties and unfamiliarity with legal systems, regulations, and infrastructures.[22] In these situations many opportunities exist for one firm to take advantage of another.

For instance, consider a company that supplies combustion engine parts including regulators, release valves, and water pumps to original equipment manufacturers (OEM). The company's largest customer is John Deere (www.johndeere.com), which competes with Caterpillar (www.cat.com). Suppose a sales rep develops a relationship with Caterpillar representatives and has the opportunity to sell them water pumps.

Vertical Integration
A pattern of controlling and perhaps acquiring assets and resources at different levels of the marketing channel.

Governance
The mechanism that helps ensure the exchange is fair to all parties involved.

Relational-Based Governance
Involves arrangements for sharing information and tasks between the buying and selling firms, but falls short of spelling out specific obligations for each party.

Opportunistic Behavior
One fact of all relationships is that sometimes, one firm may take advantage of another firm.

	Strongly Disagree	Disagree	Neutral	Agree	Strongly Agree
The distributor has not kept some promises that were made when we began the relationship.	1	2	3	4	5
The distributor has ignored some aspects of the contract that were designed to increase our ability to reach and service customers.	1	2	3	4	5
The distributor has interpreted terms of the contract in [its] favor at our expense.	1	2	3	4	5
The distributor has coerced us unfairly in order to gain concessions.	1	2	3	4	5
The distributor has violated contractual terms.	1	2	3	4	5

FIGURE 3.2 Measuring Opportunism in a Relational Exchange Environment

SOURCE: Cavusgil et al. (2004).

But if the company does so, it will be unable to meet the needs of John Deere. How should the sales manager react to this situation?

The type of exchange relationship the company has with John Deere should govern this decision. Market exchanges would leave the company free to move its business to Caterpillar with no fear of legal problems. One consequence is that John Deere will have reservations about future business with the company.

If the relationship between the company and John Deere is relational, a legal obligation exists to live up to the contract terms. If the contract specifies that 1,000 water pumps must be delivered each month, then the company must deliver this quantity or face legal problems. This type of arrangement should discourage opportunistic behavior, at least for the length of the contract.

If the relationship between the company and John Deere is based on an ongoing contract, the relational governance for opportunism is altered somewhat. When the company acts opportunistically, it risks losing the John Deere contract. Under a strategic partnership, however, mutual benefit is tied to performance. In other words, when one company performs well, the other is rewarded. Thus, the company is less likely to behave opportunistically if doing so lowers the partner's performance.

CRM, Customer Loyalty, and Lifetime Value

CRM makes sense only when a firm expects to do business with a customer repeatedly over an extended period of time. Thus, companies succeed by offering superior value to customers over repeated sales exchanges. In return customers become more valuable to the firm.

■ Customer Loyalty

Loyal customers are like money in the bank because their purchases provide revenue into the future. Customer loyalty is a function of two components—customer share and customer commitment.

Customer Share
Represents the proportion of resources a customer spends with one among a set of competing suppliers.

The behavioral component of customer loyalty is **customer share**,[23] the proportion of resources a customer spends with one among a set of competing suppliers. For example, if Walgreens (www.walgreens.com) purchases generic heart medicine from a supplier of generic drugs such as Cypress Pharmaceuticals (www.cypressrx.com), customer share is the amount Walgreen purchases from Cypress compared to the amount it purchases from Cypress's competitors. If Walgreens purchases half (in terms of revenue and units) from Cypress and half from other generic suppliers, customer share is 50 percent. As Cypress becomes more and more an exclusive supplier to Walgreens, customer share increases. High customer share is an important component of true loyalty. It's a tangible component of loyalty because it's based on actual behavior.

Customer Commitment
Represents the bonding, or affective attachment, between a customer and a sales firm.

The second component of customer loyalty is intangible and based on emotion. **Customer commitment** is the bond between a customer and a sales firm that builds up over time as a customer continues to have rewarding sales exchanges with a supplier. Trust develops, as do comfort and favorable emotions.

Part of the commitment is toward the firm and part toward the sales rep or other company representatives. Thus, one consideration for a sales manager in reassigning reps is the amount of commitment customers may feel toward the current reps. High commitment builds switching costs, since the customer feels less comfortable with and has a more difficult time understanding a new rep or supplier. Customer commitment, although less tangible than customer share, is very real.

■ Computing the Value of a Customer

CRM implies that firms should manage different customers differently. Valuable customers deserve special treatment. "Platinum" flyers, whom an airline identifies by recording information in a database each time they fly, get access to special waiting areas with complimentary food and drink, preferred seating where they receive more complimentary food and drink, and a higher degree of service. While infrequent flyers may not see things the same way, the special treatment is worthwhile because platinum flyers provide a disproportionate amount of revenue based on their frequent flying behavior.

Customer Lifetime Value
The monetary amount representing the worth of a customer to a firm over the foreseeable life of a relationship.

Thus, with CRM the company should determine how much each customer is truly worth. **Customer lifetime value** is a monetary amount representing the worth of a customer to a firm over the foreseeable life of a relationship. Let's look at some different approaches for determining customer lifetime value (CLV).

Consider a firm that takes a transactional view of customers. It assumes each exchange is a unique and independent event. Therefore, the life of a relationship is one sale. In this case, we can think of the value of each customer as

$$CLV_1 = (R_1 - C_1)$$

The CLV for customer 1 is the amount of revenue generated by this particular sale (R) less the costs associated with selling to and serving this customer (C).

Relational exchange and strategic partnerships are based on the idea that repeated transactions with customers will result from sales efforts. Thus, we adjust the basic equation to reflect this notion:

$$CLV_i = \sum_{t=1}^{p} (R_t - C_t)$$

where

CLV = the lifetime value of customer i

t = the time period

p = the total number of time periods of the relationship

R = the revenue gained from the customer in a time period t

C = the cost of the sales and service effort directed at the customer in a time period t

Knowing the value of a customer is critical within CRM. For example, a firm can determine how much should be spent to acquire a new customer. If the costs of acquiring a customer are high relative to the estimated CLV, those resources might be better spent elsewhere.[24] In this way, CLV estimates the potential return on investment in a customer. Similarly, we can see that loyalty pays off in the form of higher CLV. In fact, if we sum the CLV values for all current and future customers for a given firm, we have an estimate of total customer equity.[25]

With CRM we can use CLV to identify customers with more desirable characteristics. These customers may have higher CLV values, or they may be less price sensitive than other customers, making each exchange more profitable. In fact, a company may be tempted to implement a pricing strategy in which these customers are actually charged higher prices than other customers. Even Coca-Cola has considered such a move by creating vending machines that automatically adjust prices based on the temperature. Customers purchasing in hot weather would be asked to pay more than customers approaching the vending machine in cool weather. Research on this topic, based on CLV concepts, demonstrates that customers are actually more valuable when prices are increased in several small increments rather than all at once.[26]

■ Risks of Relational Selling

Relational selling and strategic partnerships clearly have advantages. As mentioned earlier, most businesses find selling to existing customers less expensive than selling to new customers. It's also easier to predict the future because long-term commitments ensure future business for the company.

These advantages do not come without a price.[27] Relational selling can increase dependence on partners. Consider the case of an auto parts supplier forming a strategic partnership with Ford. The partnership requires the company to divert over 75 percent of its production capacity to satisfying the demand from Ford. The fortunes of this firm now become heavily dependent on Ford. If Ford does well, so will the supplier. In contrast, if the auto parts supplier avoids the partnership and instead sells auto parts to various wholesalers throughout North and South America, its fortunes are not likely to be hurt if one of its many customers falls on hard times. Therefore, relational selling increases risk when either the buying or selling firm is small relative to the other firm.

Firms may also alter their way of doing business to better satisfy a relational or strategic partner.[28] For example, a relational partner may demand some type of automated self-service communication system that allows them to process orders without the intervention of the selling firm's employees. This system can be costly and may require changing other company procedures. As a result, the company could lose flexibility and be less able to capitalize on future business opportunities with new customers. Firms cannot customize systems for each and every customer. Sales managers need to be careful not to commit to a change for the sake of one customer that will affect the way business is done with other good customers.

Another danger arises when companies that form relationships and strategic partnerships with a few large customers grow complacent with current customer(s) and become less creative. They may not see opportunities to extend their business to new customers or into new business areas. In contrast, sales managers taking a transactional view are constantly looking for new business opportunities.

CRM and Selling

Although CRM stands for customer relationship *management*, the "M" may just as easily represent *marketing*. A CRM system greatly facilitates exchange between a customer and the selling firm, and therefore it is a marketing system. CRM's roots are in marketing and the technologies designed to better communicate with customers.

Nintendo (www.nintendo.com) has adopted a CRM approach to managing key market segments. College students are a key customer group. Nintendo not only maintains a database of information about customers, much of it acquired through product registration information, but also creates websites where customers can obtain product knowledge that enhances the value of the gaming experience. These websites can record customer activities to provide even more information about gamers. With this information Nintendo can offer complementary products and services. For instance, Nintendo reps are targeting college campuses to organize virtual dog shows—extremely popular among customers of *Nintendogs,* an electronic dog design game. Students enter their dogs in a show, and other students vote to identify the "best in show." All the while, Nintendo reps gather information from customers that will lead to even more opportunities to extend this concept into more value opportunities among this customer segment.[29]

■ CRM and Sales

The salesperson's role changes across different business orientations. With a production orientation, the salesperson may be primarily an order taker. The products are essentially homogeneous across all customers, as are ancillary services that accompany product purchase. With a customer orientation, the salesperson becomes much more involved with each customer. CRM requires the salesperson to have greater knowledge of customers and generally provides greater flexibility in making decisions that enhance customer satisfaction. In addition, many mundane tasks are performed automatically through electronic tracking and/or communication devices. This frees up the sales team for more important tasks. Thus, with CRM the salesperson becomes a value manager, managing the benefit customers obtain from exchanges.

■ The Salesperson and Managing Customers

Marketing strategy is one way firms go about creating value. The salesperson plays a key role in this process. Although *value* is often used in everyday language as a syn-

Value
An individual's selective perception of the worth of some activity, object, or idea.

onym for *low* price, this view is far too narrow. **Value** is an individual's selective perception of the worth of some activity, object, or idea. The consumer creates this perception by weighing all costs, both monetary and non-monetary. The great thing about providing customers with value is that it is the single best way to provide value for the firm.

With CRM the salesperson does more than just create sales.[30] The salesperson has four important goals, all of which help create value for the customer:

1. Gather important data about the customer and the market.
2. Identify the types of data needed to give the customer better service.
3. Provide input into how the CRM system should utilize data to create value for the customer.
4. Manage the relationship between the firm and the customers to whom the salesperson is assigned.

A CRM approach means the salesperson is responsible for balancing high-tech processes against high-touch approaches that personalize service offerings. Salespeople must spend more time with profitable, individual customers. The nearby *Sales Management In Action* box discusses how this can be a successful strategy.

SALES MANAGEMENT IN ACTION

High Tech–High Touch at HP

While technology can allow customers to perform some traditional selling tasks through self-service, only a human being can create the positive emotions that lead to strong, long-lasting commitment. Indeed, when a salesperson takes effective advantage of technology, his or her performance improves.

© Susan Van Etten / PhotoEdit

Recently Hewlett Packard (HP—www.hp.com) underwent a successful turnaround under the management of Mark Hurd. Hurd was startled by statistics showing that HP salespeople spent only slightly more than 30 percent of their time with customers. The rest was spent dealing with internal HP matters or in transit. True relational selling became difficult as salespeople failed to spend enough time with individual customers, even the very best customers, to develop a deep understanding of their businesses. Hurd reorganized HP and actually slashed the size of the sales force. But he freed reps from red tape and changed the reward system in a way that enabled salespeople to focus on their best customers. As a result, HP reps became as intimately involved in their best customers' businesses as were employees of those businesses themselves. The bottom line: by increasing customer contact so that salespeople spend about half their time with customers, HP increased profits as a reward for the value the salespeople created.

SOURCES: Michael Ahearn, Narasimhan Srinivasan, and Luke Weinstein, "Effect of Technology on Sales Performance: Progressing from Technology Acceptance to Technology Usage and Consequence," *Journal of Personal Selling & Sales Management* 24 (Fall 2004): 297–310; Pui-Wing Tam, "Hurd's Big Challenge at HP: Overhauling Corporate Sales," *Wall Street Journal*, April 3, 2006, p. A1.

Product Portfolio
The set of products that a customer is responsible for selling.

■ Product Portfolios

A **product portfolio** is the set of products a salesperson is responsible for selling. For instance, Novartis (www.novartis.com) has a portfolio of over 800 drug products.[31] Like most drug companies, the portfolio includes both branded and generic products. A salesperson might be responsible for selling the entire portfolio or just some subset. For a pharmaceutical firm, some sales managers might oversee only branded medications, while others oversee salespeople responsible only for generic products. The key is a salesperson's responsibility to sell a portfolio of products to customers within some geographic region. By narrowing down the range of products a salesperson is responsible for, the sales manager has organized the selling effort based on product knowledge. Therefore, the customers in these territories can be better served.

■ Customer Portfolios

Customer Portfolios
Sets of customers who have something in common.

With CRM, sales managers are more interested in having their salespeople know customers than products. Thus, salesperson responsibilities are more likely to be arranged by customer portfolios. **Customer portfolios** are sets of customers that have something in common. Instead of assigning salespeople based upon product characteristics, as might be the case in a generic-branded product assignment, the manager assigns salespeople based on customer characteristics. Pharmaceutical salespeople may be assigned to customer groups defined by areas of medical specialties such as pediatrics or cardiology. Or they might be assigned to private physician groups, institutional medical facilities, or even HMOs. Thus, if a salesperson calls only on physician groups, he or she develops an in-depth knowledge of the factors contributing to success in that particular business environment.

IBM has a sales force numbering over 12,000 employees that it recently reorganized based upon specific industries rather than product characteristics or territories.[32] IBM product development has evolved into developing industry-specific products as a result. It has financial industry solutions, medical industry solutions, education industry solutions, and so on. The more intimate knowledge enables salespeople to generate more value for customers.

Cross-selling and up-selling also become easier using customer portfolios rather than product portfolios.[33] A customer's past behavior is the single best indicator of future purchasing behavior. When salespeople are assigned to small numbers of similar customers, they become very familiar with past behavior. In addition, if the firm adopts CRM systems, it can integrate information about previous purchasing behavior into its decision support systems. Customer portfolio assignments enable salespeople to empathize with the customers' problems and quickly suggest solutions. This approach not only increases sales but, more importantly, the customer realizes greater value, strengthening the relationship even further.

Analytical CRM
Focuses on aggregating customer information electronically, allowing for better identification of target markets and opportunities for cross-selling.

■ CRM and Production

CRM systems can be either analytical or operational.[34] **Analytical CRM** focuses on aggregating customer information electronically, enabling the company to better identify target markets and opportunities for cross-selling. In contrast, **operational CRM** is more focused on using information to improve internal efficiencies. Information about a transaction with a customer is automatically fed into a decision support

Operational CRM
Focuses on using information to improve internal efficiencies.

system that schedules logistical and production operations. One advantage of automating certain sales and service operations using an electronic interface is that information the customer enters is also automatically used to adjust schedules. These adjustments are made with no incremental cost to the firm.

Consider companies like Bridgestone or Michelin. Their primary product is tires. Increasingly, new car models are made with unique specifications for tires—meaning a dramatic increase in the numbers of specific tires that must be produced. Without CRM, a production manager might have to carefully devise a production schedule calling for certain models of tires to be produced on certain days of the month. With CRM the production manager doesn't worry about this decision. Information from customer orders is automatically fed into the decision support system, and production schedules are determined just in time. In other words, the number and types of tires produced are based on real-time sales information. CRM integration is one of the keys to CRM success.[35]

■ CRM and Technology

Companies adopting CRM cannot avoid high-technology solutions. CRM on any large scale is impossible without electronic storage and processing of large quantities of data that all functional areas of the firm can share. Considering the salesperson is the direct agent interacting with customers, the sales manager as a supervisor is responsible for managing many inputs into this system. Indeed, when CRM fails, some aspect of technology or its use is almost always responsible. Thus, the sales manager must be familiar with basic CRM technology components.

■ Web Technologies and CRM

Although CRM's roots are older than the widespread adoption of the Internet, Web-based technologies have contributed a great deal to the design and effectiveness of CRM systems. A primary role played by the Internet in CRM implementation is to allow the sharing of information between buying and selling firms. This takes place in several ways.

E-mail is useful in managing customer contact information and becomes critical in customer service efforts. Many leads are generated from e-mails. E-mail also helps with **push technology**, which uses data stored about a particular customer or customer group to send information and promotional material at a time when the data suggests the customer will be interested in a purchase. The customer does not initiate the sales contact. Rather, an automated system invites the customer into a sales transaction.

A decade or so ago, e-mail was a relatively safe, reliable communication vehicle. Today, with the siege of SPAM e-mails, firms must use systems to curtail the volume of junk messages. Unfortunately, network SPAM filters often identify e-mail from legitimate businesses as SPAM, based on issues that are difficult to control. For example, as a company sends e-mails to more undeliverable addresses, its chances of getting put on a SPAM list increase. In fact, the more e-mail a company sends in general, the greater the e-mail's chance of being identified as SPAM. As a result, e-mail communication has become increasingly unreliable, and firms are looking for solutions to these technology problems.

Push Technology
Involves using data stored about a particular customer or customer group; helps send the particular customer information and promotional material when the data suggests the customer will be interested in a purchase.

One solution is for salespeople to closely monitor the customer list and identify each customer as a valid address. This means firms must make sure their customer lists are constantly updated and verified by salespeople—which can be difficult. Another partial solution is to send e-mails that are going out to groups of customers in small batches. WebEx, Inc. (www.webex.com) recently used this method to increase its e-mail deliverability rate to 96 percent.[36] **Deliverability** describes the proportion of e-mail sent that is successfully delivered to the intended recipient. But even with a 96 percent success rate, 4 percent of communications are not delivered as expected. Certainly, every undelivered communication could lead to lost business or lower customer satisfaction.

Deliverability
Refers to the proportion of e-mail sent that is successfully delivered to the intended recipient.

■ Integrated Web Solutions

When firms take a relational approach or become strategic partners, they may avoid e-mail for key communications. Instead, they use the Internet to develop an integrated Web-based database. How does this work? Well, if you've taken an online course, you probably submitted completed assignments by depositing them into an Internet drop box. Your instructor receives your assignment without using e-mail. An integrated information system works in much the same way. Information is deposited onto the Internet in ways that give the strategic partner secure access. Some of the information becomes integrated into the strategic partner's decision support system, particularly when dealing with issues like inventory systems. This type of communication is more reliable than e-mail.

The challenge for the CRM system is to take information from the various touchpoints and integrate it into relevant databases that act as a single information system. Figure 3.3 illustrates the process of integrating information from these touchpoints,[37] including customers phoning a call center, salespeople recording information from a sales call using a PDA or pager, customers sending an e-mail to a service center or leaving a response at the company's website, and an inventory system recording stock rates. All this information is stored on the Internet, where a Web service helps integrate the information and transforms the content so sales managers, salespeople, and other employees can access what they need on any type of electronic device.

Technology and CRM Programs

■ Sales Force Automation

CRM invites numerous information technology (IT) applications. But sales managers are concerned with **sales force automation** (SFA). SFA is an integrated system of computer software and hardware that performs routine sales functions formerly performed by independent and often manual systems. An integrated SFA system ties together some or all of these functions:[38]

Sales Force Automation (SFA)
An integrated system of computer software and hardware used to perform certain routine sales functions that formerly were performed with independent and often manual systems.

1. Expense reports
2. Presentation software
3. Sales call scheduling (contact management)
4. Territory management
5. Proposal generation
6. Order entry

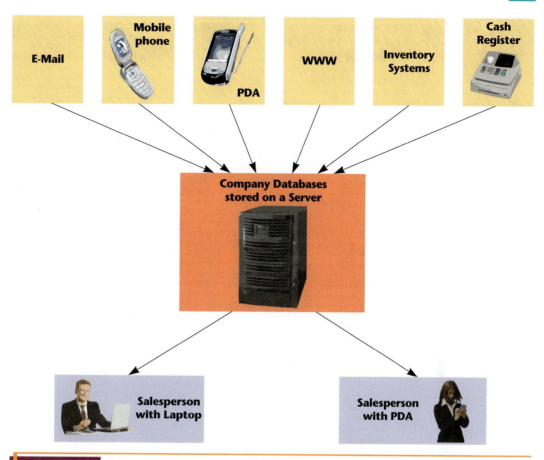

FIGURE 3.3 Customer Data Integrated and Disseminated Using Web Devices and Services

7. Data entry
8. Team selling materials
9. Sales tracking

All information recorded by the SFA system is integrated into other CRM systems. Thus, salespeople *must* use the SFA tools, or the company will be operating with inaccurate information. In fact, getting salespeople to actually adopt SFA procedures is among the most difficult steps in implementing CRM—presenting a challenge for sales managers to overcome. Salespeople mistakenly believe SFA means salespeople will no longer be needed. This isn't the case at all.

An effective SFA program is really a way of making salespeople more productive. Although salespeople may feel taking the time to enter information into an SFA system would be better spent actually selling to customers, in reality the system enables them to be more certain that each sales call will actually produce sales. By carrying company data with them on a PC device, salespeople have the information they need in the right place—wherever they are! Research on sales forces using SFA is mixed. Although job performance does seem to improve with SFA, salespeople also report more rather than less stress on the job as they go through growing pains in learning and using new technologies.[39] Sales managers can facilitate adoption of SFA systems

SALES MANAGEMENT IN ACTION

SFA at Harris Interactive

Harris Interactive is known for providing public opinion about all manner of subjects and now produces over $200 million in revenue annually. Until 2000, Harris did not have a sales force as such. Rather, it relied on marketing researchers to do the selling. Eventually, Harris realized that sales professionals could better handle the job of selling its products and services.

SFA is a big part of sales at Harris—though its salespeople, like those at many other organizations, originally resisted adoption of the technologies. Harris spared no expense in putting together a system that would add value for customers and therefore add value for the salespeople. Its managers suggest the following guidelines for making sure SFA is effective:

- Make SFA procedures mandatory for all salespeople.
- Focus on how much value is produced for the salespeople, not on how much SFA improves the company's bottom line.
- Build SFA into the corporate culture, getting buy-in from all levels of the organization.
- Make the transaction easy, and make allowances for drops in performance in the short term.

SOURCES: Mark Cotteleer, Edward Inderrieden, and Felissa Lee, "Selling the Sales Force on Automation," *Harvard Business Review,* 2006, 84 (October), pp. 18–22; *PR Newswire,* "Harris Interactive Expresses Continued Confidence in Full Year 2007 Results; Noteworthy Points," November 3, 2006, www.prnewswire.com (accessed November 3, 2006).

by working with salespeople to be receptive to change and by providing training as needed on the value of effective SFA.

Salespeople already use a host of SFA innovations, including portable notebook or hand-held computers, electronic data interchange, videoconferencing, multi-function mobile phones, satellite pagers, voice mail, and electronic mail to increase their productivity. SFA tools provide many benefits for resourceful and creative sales managers and salespeople. Over 60 percent of the managerial respondents in one study indicated their companies were generating more revenue by using sales technologies.[40]

A complete list of the benefits of SFA would be difficult to compile. However, here are some:[41]

- Ease of spotting opportunities based on the information available through the SFA system
- Increased ability to monitor, coach, and mentor salespeople
- Greater ability to assess, analyze, and react to results of sales calls

Marketing Automation Systems
Taking SFA even further, these systems monitor and integrate all aspects of a firm's marketing program.

Marketing automation systems take SFA even further. The goal of **marketing automation systems** is to integrate all aspects of marketing. Thus, the SFA must be integrated into a system that also monitors other aspects of promotion, pricing, logistics, and production.

■ CRM Hardware

PDAs, laptops, and servers are all important CRM products. But CRM is more, and its benefits are the technological breakthroughs. CRM has given the sales manager a new terminology to match these new products.

Database Marketing
A computerized process for analyzing customer databases in a way that allows more effective selling by tailoring product and promotional offerings to a specific customer's sales patterns.

Database marketing is a computerized process for analyzing customer databases in a way that allows more effective selling by tailoring product and promotional offerings to a specific customer's sales patterns. Database marketing is the starting point for a CRM system. The sheer size of a single database can be amazing. Ford Motor Company (www.ford.com) has 50 million names in its customer database. Citicorp (www.citicorp.com) has 30 million, Kimberly Clark (www.kimberly-clark.com) 10 million, and Kraft General Foods (www.kraft.com) 2.5 million customer records. General Motors (www.gm.com) has 12 million GM credit card holders in a database yielding detailed data on customer buying habits. For each name in the database, the companies have an average of twenty separate pieces of information. Detailed customer information can be translated into effective strategies for field salespeople.

Data Warehouse
An electronic storage center containing data records from diverse information systems that are shared across all functional departments.

A **data warehouse** is an electronic storage center containing data records from diverse information systems that are shared across all functional departments. American Airlines (www.aa.com) gathers customer information from all its customer touchpoints. Data collected includes demographics, takeoff points and destinations, prices paid, and hotel accommodations. When customers call, e-mail, or connect to the American Airlines website, they are immediately recognized and classified as to their relative profitability to AA. Then, based on their past purchase preferences, they are offered a customized package that might include recommendations for hotels, car rentals, and vacation packages in addition to flight options.

Data Mining
Exploratory statistical analysis of the data in the data warehouse; aimed at revealing relationships that allow customers to be targeted more accurately.

Data mining is exploratory statistical analysis of data in the data warehouse. The objective is to identify relationships that enable customers to be targeted more accurately. Multivariate statistical tools such as cluster analysis, discriminant analysis, multiple regression, and automatic interaction detection[42] analysis help with data mining. For instance, data mining techniques discovered a relationship between diaper sales and beer purchases. This finding was explained by the fact that fathers often buy beer when sent to the store to buy baby diapers. So, displaying beer near the diaper aisle can increase sales of both products.

Harrah's Entertainment, Inc. has individual profiles of millions of customers. The models include ages, gender, zip codes, amount of time spent gambling, and how much the person has won or lost. Analyses of these data enable Harrah's to target individuals with special offers, like getaway weekends and gourmet restaurant meals, to attract them back to the casinos to gamble more. Sophisticated modeling of customers has enabled Harrah's to average 22 percent growth for the past five years, while its stock price has tripled.[43] Resourceful sales managers make use of these systematically designed and implemented database technologies to help salespeople develop long-term, personalized, and profitable relationships with each of their customers.

■ CRM Software

The real heart of CRM technology is the software. Software makes information stored in a CRM system useful by allowing sales managers to act with greater intelligence than they could otherwise. When CRM software converts information into data that can be used in solving a sales manager's problem, we have **CRM Intelligence**. Here we review a few software applications to illustrate types of products available.

CRM Intelligence
Results when CRM software converts information into data that can be used in solving a sales manager's problem.

The CRM industry is a multi-billion-dollar entity with numerous vendors. Perhaps the best known are Siebel Systems (www.oracle.com/siebel/index.html), Salesforce.com (www.salesforce.com), and SAP (www.sap.com). Table 3.3 provides a list of application software vendors.[44]

TABLE 3.3	CRM Software Application Vendors and Characteristics		
APPLICATION TYPE	**COMPANY**	**RELATIVE STRENGTH**	**LEADING INDUSTRIES**
Data quality and integration	Firstlogic (www.firstlogic.com)	High customer satisfaction	Financial services, retailing
Marketing automation	Aprimo (www.aprimo.com)	Functionality	Pharmaceuticals, media/entertainment
SFA	Salesforce.com (www.salesforce.com)	Reputation	Financial services, communications
Large enterprises	Siebel Systems (www.siebel.com)	Functionality	Professional services, public sector
Small businesses	Maximizer Software (www.maximizer.com)	Customer satisfaction	Real estate, manufacturing

What should sales managers look for in a CRM software system? Certainly, no one size fits all CRM applications. Here are a few things sales managers should consider before recommending a particular CRM application:[45]

1. *Flexible sales effectiveness processes*—Sales managers should develop sales processes that salespeople in different areas and selling different portfolios can apply.
2. *Easy coaching*—Make step-by-step advice available for salespeople in the field.
3. *Easy data access*—All salespeople should enter data accurately and in a timely fashion so they can work with accurate data in the field. That is, data entry should be made easy.
4. *Advanced analytics*—The system should analyze current sales performance along with past performance data. The result should provide diagnostic information so a salesperson can spot and correct potential problems.

Click-Stream Analysis
Involves drawing conclusions based on the path a customer takes while navigating information on the company website.

Click-stream analysis draws conclusions based on the path a customer takes while navigating the company website. In other words, to identify and classify sales prospects, the software uses information about which pages a customer clicked through and how long he or she spent on each one. A customer who reads product specifications in some detail is a hotter sales prospect than one who doesn't even click through to this information. The software may automatically send out e-mail responses to leads who provide an e-mail address but who do not appear very engaged with the company or its products based on the click-through analysis. Customers showing a more promising pattern of "clicks" may be placed on a list with the recommendation that a company representative phone them. The software provides a report identifying the most promising prospects for a face-to-face sales call.

CRM Successes and Failures

Despite CRM's popularity, its adoption is no guarantee of success. Some estimates suggest that over half of the firms that try CRM are unhappy with the results.[46] CRM is not for all firms. For example, it won't benefit firms using a transactional approach because they treat all exchanges as independent. Thus, tracking information about customers isn't consistent with their approach.

CRM is also not for firms whose customers won't realize added value from the benefits provided by the CRM process. For instance, some business-to-business (B2B) firms now sell significant portions of their inventories through reverse auctions.[47] Through this process, buyers have sellers compete for a sale based exclusively on price. When price competition dominates a market, CRM may not be advantageous.

Factors Contributing to Success or Failure. CRM offers the promise of complete information integration, which is undeniably a good thing. As in many aspects of business, when CRM fails, it does so not because the idea is bad, but because implementing it creates many difficult hurdles. Table 3.4 lists some factors contributing to success or failure of CRM implementation.[48]

CRM is successful only when the people who work for the business truly believe the benefits will be worth the added expense and effort. This begins with the CEO or top management. If top management is often heard disparaging the CRM system, how can they expect other employees to support CRM applications?

Sales managers and sales staff often resist CRM applications. They believe that tasks like entering electronic notes into a PDA aren't worth the trouble, or that the system will eliminate the need for them. If information about customers is now available through the company's information system, the salesperson may also feel less job security. Sales managers can overcome this problem by convincing employees they will benefit from CRM. For example, a CRM system should allow salespeople to spend more time with more profitable customers. As a result, each salesperson should sell more and collect higher bonuses and/or commissions. The fact that all areas of the firm must buy into CRM means that CRM should always be a cross-functional effort.

TABLE 3.4 Success or Failure in CRM Implementation

	FACTOR	EFFECTIVE	INEFFECTIVE
1	Top management gives its support.	Top managers believe in CRM and are truly customer oriented.	Top managers have doubts about the technology, or lack customer orientation.
2	Sales managers and sales force buy in to CRM.	Sales managers and salespeople share top management's enthusiasm and religiously follow CRM procedures.	Sales managers or salespeople fail to see how the added complexities of CRM will enhance their job performance—or they see CRM as a threat.
3	CRM system does not fit the firm's situation.	CRM system matches the focus and size of the organization.	CRM either too elaborate or too simple for firm's needs.
4	Confidence in CRM vendor	Everyone has faith in the added value that the system provides.	People doubt the system will really enhance value for anybody.
5	Training	Training is adequate and ongoing.	Training is looked at as expensive and of relatively little value.
6	A well-defined sales process	Sales process is widely known and practiced.	No identifiable sales process exists.
7	Expectations	Sales managers have realistic expectations for what a CRM system can do for them.	Sales managers believe CRM is the answer to all prayers.

Firms should select a CRM vendor carefully. Different software products have features making them more or less suitable to different types of organizations. Systems that are difficult to use lead to disgruntled employees who dread having to deal with CRM. As a result, they become less cooperative in following its procedures. Only careful research can ensure that the CRM solution fits the particular company. When the company has checked out alternate vendors to validate its choice, employees are more likely to have confidence in the system.

Training also is critical. The CRM vendor should provide ongoing training on how to apply CRM and why it is important. But, the firm should also make its own training available to employees who feel they cannot adequately perform the CRM tasks.

Neither CRM nor the SFA components replace sales management or selling processes. These high-tech components merely enhance the activities of sales managers and salespeople. The sales process also extends beyond salespeople. Hitachi (www.hitachi.com) data systems recently increased sales effectiveness by implementing a new sales process[49] through training sessions for salespeople, service techs, sales managers, and top management. The process not only improved sales and customer satisfaction, but it also helped increase compliance with CRM maintenance procedures. The sales process helps make sure companies are truly both *high tech* and *high touch.*

Finally, CRM implementation may fail because top management has "pie in the sky" expectations. CRM is not a panacea. Expectations for sales increases should be realistic. Also, given that CRM is oriented to the long term, management should not expect benefits to occur too soon. Management may feel the CRM system is ineffective because sales increased only 20 percent in five years when the goal was an unrealistic 40 percent. If the goal had been 15 percent, management might feel quite different. Thus, CRM vendors should help establish realistic expectations for what CRM can do.

CHAPTER SUMMARY

1. **Master the different ways sales companies deal with customers.** CRM is a systematic integration of information, technology, and human resources all oriented toward (a) providing maximum value to customers and (b) maximizing the value obtained from customers. A *production*-oriented sales manager focuses a sales force on selling products. A *customer*-oriented sales manager, more typical of a marketing-oriented firm, focuses a sales force on providing value by filling a customer's needs. The greater use of information and knowledge of customers that comes with a CRM program is vital to understanding how best to provide a customer with value.

A firm that practices *transactional* selling treats each and every interaction with a customer as a unique and independent event. In a transactional view, loyalty is not necessary. In a *relational* view, each exchange between a salesperson and a customer is but one in a series. The customer is seen as a customer for life, not a customer for today. In a third option, the company views each customer as a *strategic partner.* Strategic partners are generally considered loyal to one another.

2. **Build customer relationships that lead to repeat business.** CRM is based on the premise that companies interact with customers more than one time and in more than one way. Businesses that assume each customer will be contacted one time are less motivated to provide excellent service than are those that assume they will contact customers many

times over an extended period. The extra motivation is based on the likelihood of repeat business.

A CRM system should be both high tech and high touch. The salesperson should use information technology, including CRM-related hardware and software, to serve the customer better—not as a replacement for true service to the customer. Good customers deserve personal attention. While technology can help personalize products, regular contact with the customer is necessary to help build the bond that represents true commitment. The combination of high tech and high touch helps create value for the customer. Sales managers must realize that CRM technology and systems are not a replacement for a true sales process.

3. **Relate customer loyalty to customer lifetime value.** True customer loyalty exists when the customer exhibits both high customer share and high customer commitment to the relationship. Customer commitment represents the bonding, or affective attachment, between a customer and a sales firm. Loyalty contributes to customer lifetime value by guaranteeing a larger stream of sales over the lifetime of a relationship. Commitment, for example, means that the customer will stick with the selling firm even if others are offering similar products for a lower price. Committed customers also work like salespeople in spreading positive word of mouth about the firm.

CRM makes sense only when a firm expects to do business with a customer repeatedly over an extended period of time. Thus, companies succeed by offering superior value to customers over repeated sales exchanges. In return customers become more valuable to the firm. Loyal customers are like money in the bank because they will continue to purchase in the future. Customer loyalty is a function of two components—customer share and customer commitment. The behavioral component of customer loyalty is *customer share,* the proportion of resources a customer spends with one among a set of competing suppliers. In a CRM framework, a firm can determine how much it should spend to acquire a new customer. If the costs of acquiring the customer are high relative to the estimated customer lifetime value (CLV), those resources might be better spent elsewhere.

4. **Apply CRM to the selling process.** An effective CRM system uses physical devices like PDAs, notebook computers, servers, and other types of communication and storage devices. Many companies also specialize in software allowing all the information gathered in these communications to be harvested and stored in a data warehouse. The integration of this information, making it available to employees throughout the firm, is a key function of CRM technology. Companies must match the right CRM system to the particular characteristics of the firm. Software products in particular specialize in firms of certain sizes and in certain industries. The risk of CRM failure from choosing the wrong product is real. So time and effort invested in getting the CRM technology right is well spent.

5. **Use technology successfully in CRM programs.** Table 3.4 summarized factors contributing to the success or failure of CRM implementation. These factors suggest that CRM is not merely a technology issue. If the technology is right, but the human element is lacking, CRM will fail. Thus, implementing CRM requires getting buy-in from all members of the organization—from the top through entry-level sales personnel.

REVIEW AND APPLICATION QUESTIONS

1. Define CRM. What are the two key goals of CRM? [LO 1]

2. How would a sales manager's approach in motivating a sales force differ based on the way the company approaches customers? [LO 1]

3. Define a relational view to exchange relationships and a transactional view to exchange relationships. [LO 1]

4. Use the Internet to find a list of the ten most successful companies in two different industries. Do you think the firms are generally more production or market oriented? Do you think they tend to emphasize a transactional or relational approach to customers? Discuss in terms of the role of CRM in a company with either a production or market orientation. [LO 1]

5. What does it mean for a company to be customer-centric? [LO 2]

6. Would a company that views its customers as strategic partners tend to have a larger or smaller sales force than that of a similar-sized company with a more transactional view of customers? Explain. [LO 2]

7. What is meant by the term *opportunistic behavior* in the context of an exchange relationship? [LO 3]

8. What are some risks associated with relational selling (including strategic partnerships)? [LO 3]

9. From a sales manager's perspective, what is the difference between a customer portfolio and a product portfolio approach? [LO 4]

10. What are four things a sales manager should look for when choosing a CRM vendor? [LO 4]

11. List and briefly explain factors associated with an unsuccessful CRM implementation. [LO 5]

12. Use the list of CRM success/failure factors to describe how a pharmaceutical firm might implement a CRM system. [LO 5]

IT'S UP TO YOU

Internet Exercise

Go to the website at www.1000ventures.com/business_guide/mbs_mini_spartnerships.html and review the articles, case studies, and slide shows on developing strategic partnerships. How does the material enhance your understanding of this cutting-edge business philosophy?

Role-Playing Exercise

Capital Wireless

Situation

Capital Wireless invested thousands of dollars last year in a new SFA system. It has all the latest technology, and the sales rep for the SFA vendor promised account closing ratios would double and customer satisfaction increase substantially. The system has been in place and operational for about eight months, but there are lots of problems. The sales force had three 1-hour training sessions, and the sales manager has suggested more. Unfortunately, most of the sales force does not see the value of the system. After entering the basic customer profile data, the salespeople pretty much ignore the system, saying they know their customers and do not need a computerized system. The vendor and the company CEO are taking a hard line, saying the manager should just fire all the salespeople who will not use the system. On the other hand, the sales manager says firing these

salespeople is unrealistic and will create serious problems. But other than pushing for additional training, the sales manager as yet has offered no further ideas.

Role-Play Participants and Assignments

Alvin Burns, CEO Alvin argues to just get rid of the salespeople who will not use the SFA system. The firm paid a lot for it, and the need for it is clear. After all, it is the salespeople's job to do what the company says, and not complying with company guidelines is grounds for dismissal.

Sheri Ahuja, Sales Manager Sheri wants to find another way to solve the problem. She poses and offers justification for several alternatives short of firing salespeople, or at least a large number of salespeople. She is concerned the CEO will say other alternatives (besides firing salespeople) will take too long, so she needs to be prepared to defend her plans.

In-Basket Exercise

Zenon is an oil-field service company that specializes in well cementing and acid and hydraulic fracturing treatments. The oil industry typically goes through boom and bust cycles, often attributed to the price of a barrel of oil. During boom times the demand far outstrips the supply of services for the entire industry. In fact, the sales manager has urged salespeople to avoid making commitments to some customers and be more selective in seeking future business. One possible solution is to implement a CRM system to make the sales force more efficient in serving current customers and to more effectively target future customers.

QUESTIONS

1. Prepare an e-mail to your boss encouraging the adoption of a CRM program for Zenon.

2. In your e-mail, be sure to outline how CRM has the potential to improve customer service and increase repeat business.

Ethical Dilemma

Drexel Pharmaceuticals manufactures and sells several generic drugs designed to treat high blood pressure, arthritis, and similar diseases. The company has a positive relationship with many of its patients. They can learn about its medications and other current issues from its website and newsletter, which provide the latest developments on new medical research and treatments as well as general health and fitness materials. Drexel was recently acquired by an investment banking group that also owns another company that sells hydrotherapy spas and hot tubs. The sales manager from the spa company has asked to use the e-mail and regular mail lists to promote that firm's products.

What should Drexel Pharmaceuticals do?

CASE 3.1

Cosair Gas Distributors: Problems with a CRM System Installation

The gasoline industry in the United States is confronting many challenges. Not a single new gas refinery has been built in this country in over thirty years. Several well-known companies own refineries. But in addition, quite a few independent oil companies have developed alliances to process and distribute petrochemicals, mostly from plants located in the Southeast. Gasoline is distributed through a vast convoy of trucks that fan out across the country. Deliveries to retail gas stations can occur as infrequently as once a month for a small gas station to once or even twice a week for large stations in high-traffic areas.

Cosair Gas Distributors is an independent oil distributor located in Houma, Louisiana. With a fleet of 50 trucks running 24 hours a day, the firm purchases gas from distributors and transports it to a network of 360 stations spread across five states. Business has been good for Riley Sayer, founder of the company. "We've weathered it all," said Riley at the last company Christmas party. "We survived the boom and bust of the '80s, the consolidation in the '90s, and then 9-11. Heck, we survived Katrina and the crazy prices. We proved that we have a place."

Riley attended the recent Louisiana Gas and Oil Exposition in Lafayette, Louisiana, and saw a demonstration of the latest CRM system. The demo wowed him to the point of purchasing it on the spot, handing the installation over to his sales manager, T-John, and telling him to have it running in three months.

It's four months down the road, and the CRM system is installed. But there are some in the company who feel that it may have been money poorly spent. The company's other managers were surprised when T-John told them the new system would affect not only sales, but distribution, inventory, order entry, and purchasing. These departments weren't sure why they had to be included when the software is designed for salespeople to track their customer base. On top of that, the number one salesperson hasn't even used it! He keeps up with his customers using the old tried-and-true Excel spreadsheets he has on his computer in his office. Some managers are asking Riley, "How good can it be if your own number one salesperson doesn't use it?"

The distribution side of the business is having a difficult time as well. The software was "generic" in nature, with updates and customization written in the contract. The old printouts gave the drivers their invoices by route, so they could plan their stops. However, the new printouts don't sort properly—forcing drivers to review their list before leaving to make sure they don't miss a stop. The slowdown is delaying deliveries and has already resulted in the loss of one customer after a truck arrived a day late.

Cosair Distributors needs to make a decision, and quickly. The cost of purchasing and trying to implement the system has been enormous, from installation to upgrading computers to training the staff. If the decision is to continue with the CRM system, Cosair knows changes will need to be made. Moreover, if the firm does continue with the project, its managers are unsure where to start in trying to get it on the right track.

QUESTIONS

1. Where do you think the first mistake was made in the decision to purchase the new CRM system?

2. What would you do if Cosair hired you to get the project completed? Prepare a list of steps indicating the sequence to be completed and why.

3. You have a meeting tomorrow with the company that installed the CRM software. What issues would you cover with its salespeople that need to be resolved to get the project back on schedule?

Case prepared by G. David Shows, Spring Hill College, Mobile, AL.

 ## CASE 3.2

TC's Bookings: Getting the Most Out of a CRM System

Tony Charles owns TC's Bookings, an independent booking agency servicing four states—Wisconsin, Illinois, Indiana, and Michigan. These four states include large metro areas like Chicago, Detroit, Milwaukee, and Indianapolis, as well as several university towns. Tony operates TC's Bookings part-time, as a way of pursuing two of his passions—music and marketing—and to supplement his income as a marketing professor. The business also allows him to apply many of the marketing principles and skills he has studied, practiced, and taught for many years, particularly in managing his salespeople. Tony can be successful in this business part-time because much of his efforts involve managing four salespeople—one for each state in which he operates.

Tony also represents his clients to music venues. His clients are nine bands (ranging from three to five members) and three acoustic duos. All of the musicians focus on classic rock, but some of the bands play the blues, country, or folk music as well. Two of the duos specialize in traditional Irish folk music, as well as classic rock. Most of the songs the bands play are commercial hits ranging from the 1960s to the 1990s. These include hits from such stars as Led Zeppelin, The Rolling Stones, The Beatles, Aerosmith, and Bad Company, to name a few. Four of the bands create and perform their own original songs.

TC's Bookings is a full-service agency, booking not only shows or "gigs" for the bands but also creating their promotional packages or "kits" as well. The kits usually include a biography of the band and its members, a group photo as well as individual photos, a song list, and a demo. The demo usually has 4 to 5 songs the band has recorded live or in a studio. Some bands, though, might want an entire CD marketed as a demo—or perhaps an entire set (usually 10 to 12 songs) that was recorded live at one of its shows.

Booking agents serve as a liaison between the client (the bands) and the music venues (customers). Some agents represent only the bands; some represent only the venues. The difference relates to how the agent gets paid. If working for the bands, the booking agent is basically a sales representative responsible for getting maximum pay for the bands and gets paid a percentage, usually 10–15 percent of the price of the gig. If working for the venue, the booking agent plays the role of a purchasing agent responsible for negotiating the lowest price. In this situation, the agent may be paid a percentage or a flat fee per show or may be on a retainer to the venue. TC's Bookings, aside from the twelve musical groups, also represents two venues. In dealings between his clients and these two venues, Tony tries to reach a fair compromise for both parties by substituting some of the pay for the bands with more shows at these venues. This keeps both the bands and the venues satisfied. The venues are Tony's customers, and he markets his bands to them. Venues include bars, restaurants, nightclubs, casinos, and, in the summertime, local festivals. Basically, anyone who hires live music can be a customer for TC's Bookings.

Tony maintains an extensive database on the venues that offer live music in the four states he serves. He'd like to say "all of the venues," but in fact live music is a dynamic industry. Venues such as bars, nightclubs, and restaurants go out of business all the time, while new ones start up seemingly out of thin air. If a venue hits a slump, it might decide to go to a less expensive form of entertainment such as a DJ or karaoke. Both of these cost about half the price of a live band and, depending on the venue, can be a viable alternative. In fact, most venues the company deals with will offer a karaoke night to satisfy those wannabe rock stars; a DJ night for the younger crowd that wants to dance to the thump-thump beat of electronic or techno dance music, and live music nights for those customers who really enjoy watching and listening to musicians perform. If the venue's business slows down, the first thing to go is live entertainment—the club will likely substitute DJs or karaoke for the band, thereby cutting its cost of entertainment in half.

The database consists of the following information on each customer:

- Venue name
- Address
- Contact (the decision maker; usually the owner, but sometimes a manager or another booking agent)

- Best time to contact
- Phone number and e-mail address
- Which days the venue has live music
- Size of the bands the venue is looking for
- Genre(s) of music the venue hires
- Venue's budget
- How far in advance the venue books musicians (some book 1 month, some 3 months, some 6 months in advance)
- When the venue does bookings (some book continuously, others book 3 months in the course of 2–3 days)
- Whether the venue books one-nighters or weekends
- Whether the venue has its own public address (PA) system or the band must supply one (The former situation is rare but is very appealing to a band. Setting up and tearing down a PA could take 30–45 minutes before and after a show.)
- Whether the venue has a strong regular crowd or is expecting the band to promote and bring lots of customers
- Any other peculiarities about the stage or the venue, like the size of the stage, size of the venue, whether the band needs to play "quieter" or with volume controlled

Tony also maintains a database on his bands. This database is like a small CRM system. It includes the band's name, members, phone numbers, e-mail addresses, genre(s) of music, song list, which geographical areas the band wants to play, a schedule of the band's gigs, dates that the band has blocked off as not available, acceptable minimum price the band is willing to play for, and photos, logos, and songs used in the band's demo. TC's Bookings has done very well using its CRM system to build and maintain relationships with its customers. But there are still many venues whose doors are closed to the agency. And while Tony realizes the agency cannot serve every venue, he knows the industry is dynamic and customers today may be out of business tomorrow. Therefore, the agency must always be seeking to establish new relationships as well as trying to enhance the relationships that already exist. As a small business with only four salespeople, TC's Bookings does not have the budget for and realistically does not need a larger, more expensive CRM system with many features. Tony does, however, need a better way of accessing and using his databases to communicate with his salespeople and support their sales efforts, as well as to attract more bands and serve additional venues.

QUESTIONS

1. What methods of maintaining and enhancing customer relationships do you think the company is missing?

2. How might you use these methods?

Case prepared by Frank Notturno, Madonna University.

The Selling Process

LEARNING OBJECTIVES

When you finish this chapter, you should be able to:

1 Evaluate the benefits and opportunities available in a sales career.

2 Compare and contrast today's sales professional with yesterday's.

3 Describe the seven stages of the personal selling process (PSP).

4 Use various searching methods to find new prospects.

5 Apply several sales presentation strategies.

6 Overcome prospect objections and resistance through negotiation.

7 Demonstrate closing techniques from each of five closing categories.

8 Explain how to empower salespeople for customer relationship management (CRM) roles.

INSIDE SALES MANAGEMENT

Anne Hubbell at Kodak

Anne Hubbell never expected to be in sales; "I went to art school!" she says. Now an account executive in Kodak's entertainment imaging group, Anne sells motion picture negative film stock to independent filmmakers from Maine to Virginia. Hubbell loves movies, and after college she ran a nonprofit media center, organizing film festivals that showcased independent films. Later, she produced for television and made a documentary that went into theatrical release. Then she joined Kodak and began calling on filmmakers who are not part of the big movie studios—a customer base she understands well because of her background.

Hubbell spends much of her time building and maintaining relationships with prospects and customers. "One of the nice things about my job is that I go to a lot of film festivals and industry events," she says. Not only does she increase awareness of Kodak's diverse line of imaging products, but she is always available to consult with filmmakers about their needs as they prepare for production. She usually reads the scripts to understand what each movie is about and what each customer wants to achieve.

In fact, she says, "I do more educating than selling. If a prospect calls to say, 'I have $100,000 to make a feature film,' I'll explain what can be done within that budget." Product knowledge is critical, Hubbell observes: "I need to know exactly how our film stock is going to perform under specific conditions." For example, filmmakers who shoot outdoors at night must use a different stock from those who shoot indoors, where the lighting can be controlled. "I have to be able to advise customers, especially low-budget filmmakers, on what will work best for their situation—not simply for the best look for their film, but also how to work within their budget," she notes.

Because Hubbell travels extensively throughout her territory, often visiting movie sets where Kodak stock is being used, she depends on her cell phone and personal digital assistant to stay in touch and on schedule. She uses database software to organize the complete contact information for every sales lead and every customer, adding links to previous projects that these filmmakers have worked on so she can refresh her memory before a meeting or phone call. To track sales opportunities, she follows the progress of dozens of upcoming productions and makes detailed notes about communications with customers and prospects. Whenever she finds out that a production is about to begin (and Kodak is making the sale), Hubbell updates the database "so there is a record of the entire sales process."

SOURCE: Anderson, Rolph E., Alan J. Dubinsky, and Rajiv Mehta, *Personal Selling: Building Customer Relationships and Partnerships,* 2/e, pp. 1–2. Copyright © 2007 Houghton Mifflin Company. Reprinted with permission.

Unless you're a tremendous athlete with a chance to turn professional, or a super-talented entertainer who may become the next American Idol, you're probably going to start your career after college making an average salary, receiving annual raises approximately matching inflation, and working hard for many years or decades trying to climb the corporate ladder. Of course, other college graduates in your company will be doing the same thing, and only a few will be able to climb very high up the ladder. You may be the one to make it, and we hope you are! But how would you like to learn about another career opportunity that will give you a great chance to make a six-figure income in your twenties, plus many other exceptional benefits, while having the gratifying job of helping people solve their problems?

If you start in personal selling after college, you'll likely be able to receive these opportunities and benefits at an early age. What's more, after only a few years as a successful salesperson, at most companies you're eligible for promotion into multiple career paths, including sales management, marketing management, and high-level professional selling, that is, national or key account executive positions with only one or two major customers such as Procter & Gamble (www.pg.com) or DuPont (www.dupont.com). Nearly all sales managers began their sales careers in personal selling, so we're going to take a close look at professional selling in this chapter to help you understand the exciting things ahead for you in your first sales job.[1]

Updating the Roles of Salespeople

Be honest now, what are your impressions of salespeople? Do you picture the flamboyant caricatures of salespeople in television shows, or Willy Loman in the play, *Death of a Salesman?* Do you visualize salespeople going door-to-door to sell encyclopedias, cosmetics, or life insurance? If so, you have a real awakening ahead as you learn about contemporary business-to-business (B2B) salespeople.

Stereotypical "door-to-door" salespeople have essentially been replaced by various forms of direct marketing including e-mails, e-commerce websites, teleselling, catalogs, and sales letters. College graduates who enter sales today are most likely to be calling on professional buyers working for manufacturers, producers, retailers, wholesalers, distributors, government agencies, and various not-for-profit institutions. With access to various online and offline sources to gather information and compare offerings before buying, customers have become empowered. They expect greater value at lower prices while demanding better service.

At the same time, salespeople themselves are empowered by technology, and they are increasingly independent of their sales managers. No matter where they are, salespeople have instant access to all the information they and their customers need via computer laptops or multi-function cell phones. They can serve prospects and customers much like trusted consultants or business partners. Present-day salespeople are also developing a new level of professionalism and sensitivity to customer concerns, as they face diverse and sophisticated buyers whose expectations continually rise.

■ Customer Relationship Management

We've seen in earlier chapters that salespeople are essential in providing added value for customers while creatively managing the buyer-seller interface. Salespeople generally have the greatest influence in reducing customer defection, and their efforts largely determine the effectiveness of customer relationship management (CRM) strategies aimed at creating customer loyalty.[2] Thus, in their boundary-spanner roles, salespeople must continuously keep in touch with customer expectations, organizational goals, and changes in the macromarketing environment. Top-performing salespeople are not focused on merely mastering the standard seven stages of the personal selling process discussed in this section. They also are heavily involved in CRM for their companies.[3] To appreciate the differences between yesterday's and today's salespeople, see Table 4.1.

TABLE 4.1   Contrasting Yesterday's and Today's Salespeople

YESTERDAY'S SALESPERSON	TODAY'S SALESPERSON
Was Product oriented	Is Customer oriented
Focused on *selling* to customers	Focuses on *serving* customers
Did little sales call planning	Develops sales call strategies to achieve specific objectives
Made sales pitches without listening much to customers	Listens to and communicates meaningfully with customers
Stressed product features and price in sales presentations	Stresses customer benefits and service in sales presentations
Often used manipulative selling techniques	Tries to help customers solve their problems
Sought to make immediate sales and achieve quotas	Seeks to develop long-term, mutually beneficial relationships with customers
Disappeared after the sale was made until the next sales call	Follows up with customers to provide service and ensure satisfaction leading to customer loyalty
Worked largely alone and had little interest in understanding customers' problems	Works as a member of a team of specialists to serve customers

SOURCE: Adapted from Anderson et al. (2007), 10.

■ Opportunities in Personal Selling

The demand for business-to-business salespeople is expected to grow sharply over the next several years.[4] Even relatively new salespeople (those with less than three years experience) earn about $50,000 annually and the average income across all levels of salespeople currently exceeds $100,000.[5] Skilled technology salespeople, who are in short supply, may receive six-figure signing bonuses, and some top performers can earn over $1 million a year.[6]

Unlike most jobs, which offer annual raises reflecting the change in the cost of living or a superior's subjective performance evaluation, the sales profession offers salaries, commissions, bonuses, sales contest prizes, and relatively objective performance evaluations. In addition, salespeople may receive many "perks," including expense accounts, club memberships, company credit cards, automobiles, cell phones, and laptop computers. Beyond tangible rewards, high-performing salespeople also enjoy a high degree of recognition within their companies. At some companies, top-performing salespeople are invited to special meetings with the CEO to discuss organizational issues. Other benefits of a sales career include consistently high demand, job freedom and independence, the adventure of interacting with new prospects and buying situations, personal satisfaction in doing a job that contributes directly to the welfare of one's company and the economy, and excellent promotion opportunities.

Because they interact with and know customers best, successful salespeople are among the employees most likely to be promoted to senior management positions. Many CEOs of Fortune 500 corporations began their careers as sales representatives, for example, Anne Mulcahy of Xerox (www.xerox.com) and Mark Hurd of Hewlett-Packard (www.hp.com).[7] As direct revenue generators, salespeople are vital to the well-being of their companies. Unless its products and services are profitably sold, a company cannot stay in business long, and its employees will lose their jobs. Thus, in many ways, the success of every business depends on the success of its salespeople.

■ Careers for Different Types of Individuals

No particular cultural background, ethnic group, gender, age, physical appearance, or personality ensures success in selling to diverse customer types. Studies have found that sales effectiveness is most related to the degree of similarity between the customer and salesperson[8]—such as in age, gender, personality, and thought patterns.[9] As a result, many sales managers try to match their salespeople with similar customer types.[10] It follows then that women and minorities may be especially effective salespeople when calling on female and minority customers, particularly if they are alike in other characteristics relevant to the buying situation.

■ Everyone Sells Something

Robert Louis Stevenson, the well-known novelist, once said: "Everybody lives by selling something." Tens of millions of salespeople are working in all types of profit-oriented and not-for-profit organizations selling products, services, and ideas. But what Stevenson recognized is that all of us, whether we earn our living in sales or not, must engage in persuasive two-way communication to convince (sell) others in various situations at different times about various things. For example, when you graduate from college or a university, even if you're not applying for a sales job, you'll still need to "sell" potential employers on hiring *you*, rather than someone else with similar credentials who may apply for the job. In other situations, you may need to "sell" someone on voting for your favorite political candidate, attending your alma mater, allowing you to take an exam early, giving you a day off work, donating to your charitable organization, or loaning you money. Learning the principles of selling will improve anyone's chances for success in all these situations and in virtually every career. Jay Leno, long-time host of "The Tonight Show," planned from early childhood to become a salesperson, and he attributes much of his success as a standup comedian and in-demand corporate speaker to his knowledge of selling techniques.[11]

The good news for most of us is that, although some people may have more natural ability than others, selling is not an art or innate talent but a discipline that almost anyone can learn. There's a specific selling process to learn, and all you need is a disciplined, organized approach to carry it out. If you have that, you'll outperform others who don't understand the process nearly every time.[12]

What Salespeople Do: Stages of the Personal Selling Process

Although there are diverse types of customers, products, services, and sales situations, there are only seven basic interacting, overlapping stages that form the personal selling process (PSP). Here they are, in order:

1. Prospecting and qualifying
2. Planning the sales call (preapproach)
3. Approaching the prospect
4. Making the sales presentation and demonstration
5. Negotiating sales resistance or buyer objections
6. Confirming and closing the sale
7. Following up and servicing the account[13]

■ Continuous Cycle or Wheel of PSP

Wheel of Personal Selling
Depiction of the seven stages of the personal selling process (PSP) as a continuous cycle of stages carried out by professionals in the field of sales.

The seven stages of the PSP are best depicted as a continuous cycle or wheel of overlapping stages, as shown in Figure 4.1. Once the **wheel of personal selling** is set in motion, it continues to rotate from one stage to the next. Thus it's easy to see that stage seven isn't really the end of the cycle but rather a new beginning, because the salesperson's follow-up and service activities can generate repeat sales or purchases of new products and services as customer needs grow. The wheel is not a rigid mechanism that can't be stopped, changed, or reversed if necessary. Sometimes, the salesperson may need to skip over, redesign, or return to a previous stage in the PSP when an initial approach or turn of the wheel fails to work. Sensitivity and flexibility in responding to feedback from customers about their needs and wants is critical for the salesperson to make the most effective and efficient use of the PSP process. As seen in Figure 4.1, at the wheel's center axle are prospects and customers. Without them, the wheel would have nothing to revolve around. Let's discuss each of the seven stages in the PSP.

FIGURE 4.1 The Personal Selling Process

SOURCE: Anderson et al. (2007), 136.

■ Prospecting and Qualifying

Customers are continually leaving for various reasons—death, bankruptcy, relocation, or switching to other suppliers. From 10 to 30 percent of a company's current customers leave each year.[14] To increase or even maintain sales volume, salespeople must continually search for potential new customers, called *prospects*. **Prospecting** requires salespeople to first obtain *leads*. A **lead** is basically the name and address or telephone number of a person or organization potentially needing the company's products or services. Before considering a lead to be a valid prospect, the salesperson must qualify it in terms of *need or want, authority to buy, money to buy,* and *eligibility to buy* (e.g., salespeople who call on wholesalers cannot bypass them to sell directly to retailers without disrupting channel relationships). One way to remember these four qualifiers is the acronym *NAME,* which consists of the first initial of each prospecting stage. When companies or individuals pass all four of these screens, they become prospects for a sales call. Many salespeople consider prospects their "pot of gold nuggets" that they can draw from when sales slow down, and most spend more time on prospecting than on any other selling activity. Various random-lead and selective-lead searching methods for finding new business or organization prospects are presented in Table 4.2.

■ Planning the Sales Call: Preapproach

In the **preapproach** or planning stage, salespeople carry out seven basic steps as outlined in Table 4.3. An effective way to prepare the prospect for the first sales contact is called *seeding.* With this technique, the salesperson mails pertinent news articles to the potential buyer over several weeks, thereby establishing a kind of "pen pal" relationship before calling to ask for an appointment. Prospects do not want their time wasted, so salespeople must learn to "sell" the sales call. A step beyond seeding is a technique called *prenotification,* in which the salesperson makes a telephone call or

Prospecting
First step in the PSP, wherein salespeople find leads and qualify them on four criteria: need, authority, money, and eligibility to buy.

Lead
The name and address or telephone number of a person or organization potentially needing the company's products or services

Preapproach
The approach-planning stage of the PSP.

TABLE 4.2 Looking for Business and Organization Leads

RANDOM-LEAD SEARCHING METHODS

Door-to-door canvassing of organizations	Advertising (print or broadcast media)
Territory blitz of organizations	Websites
Cold calls on organizations	Electronic mail

SELECTIVE-LEAD SEARCHING METHODS

Direct Sources	Indirect Sources
Networking through friends, neighbors, colleagues, and acquaintances	Postal or electronic sales letters
Personal observation	Trade shows, fairs, and exhibitions
Spotters, or "bird dogs"	Professional seminars and conferences
Current satisfied customers and former customers	Contests
Endless chain (obtaining referrals from prospects and customers)	Free gift offers
Centers of influence (joining social or business groups to meet potential prospects)	Unsolicited inquiries
Surveys	Telemarketing
Internet (World Wide Web)	
Sales associates and professional sales organizations	
Company records, directories, mailing lists, newsletters	

SOURCE: Anderson et al. (2007), 105.

sends a letter, e-mail, or fax to request permission to send sales materials and pique the prospect's interest in scheduling the face-to-face sales call.

Before developing a sales call strategy, it's especially important to gather detailed information about the prospect and the buying situation. As Table 4.4 shows, selective information sources may include trade associations, chambers of commerce, credit bureaus, mailing list companies, government and public libraries, investment firms,

TABLE 4.3 Seven Steps in Preapproach Planning

1. Prepare the prospect for the initial sales call (for example, by using the seeding technique).
2. "Sell" the sales call appointment to the prospect through prenotification.
3. Gather and analyze information about the prospect.
4. Conduct a Problems and Needs Assessment for the prospect.
5. Identify the product *Features, Advantages,* and *Benefits* likely to be of most interest to the prospect, with major focus on the benefits.
6. Select the best sales presentation and demonstration strategy for the prospect.
7. Plan and rehearse your approach to the prospect.

SOURCE: Adapted from Anderson et al. (2007), 139.

© Jeff Greenberg / PhotoEdit

● **The more information salespeople have regarding a prospect, the better prepared they will be to handle any situation during a sales call.**

and numerous Internet search engines like Google and Yahoo. For instance, visit www.thomasnet.com, the website of the *Thomas Register of American Manufacturers,* where you'll find a wealth of information for planning your sales call (Figure 4.2). One of the most direct ways to obtain information is a low-profile preliminary call at the prospect's business site. There, salespeople can talk to receptionists or other employees, gather company brochures and materials, and simply observe the way the business operates. Such efforts must be diplomatic and gracious, though, to avoid the impression of spying or snooping. Ask the prospect's permission to visit and gather basic information about product or service needs, so you can offer appropriate problem solutions in a later sales call.

SALES MANAGEMENT IN ACTION

Sales-Savvy Telemarketers Generate Best Leads

Sales managers at DuPont, the chemical giant, have a unique approach to prospecting and supporting the field sales force. Former field salespeople are hired as telemarketing reps to identify "hot prospects" for the field sales force, answer customers' technical questions, help resolve distribution problems, and even sell some products. Having knowl-edgeable former salespeople make the initial telephone contact with potential customers has sharply increased the conversion rate of leads to prospects to customers. More than 50 percent of the leads passed on to the field sales force by these sales-savvy telemarketers become DuPont customers.

TABLE 4.4 Selective Electronic Sources of Information

NAME	TYPE OF INFORMATION	WEBSITE
Thomas Register of American Manufacturers	Listing of manufacturers based on product classifications	www.thomasnet.com
Yellow Pages	Listing of more than 10 million businesses	www.yellowpages.com
Fortune Magazine	Fortune 500 firms	www.fortune.com
Forbes Magazine	Forbes 500 firms	www.forbes.com
Inc. Magazine	*Inc.* magazine fastest-growing small firms	www.inc.com
U.S. Census Bureau	Information on industrial activity	www.census.gov/cir/www/
Dun & Bradstreet	Information on small and large firms	www.dnb.com/us/
Moody's Industrial Manuals	Data on over 10,000 corporations	www.moodys.com/cust/default.asp
Hoover's Online	Information on small and large businesses	www.hoovers.com
ABI-Inform	Data on industries, companies, products, and current business topics from 550 publications	www.proquest.com
COMPUSTAT (Standard & Poor's)	Detailed balance sheet and income statement information for more than 5,000 firms	www.compustat.com
Industry Data Sources	Trade association reports, government publications, and industry studies by brokerage firms on 65 major industries	www.virtualpet.com/industry/data/data.htm
Economic Information Systems	Data on about 400,000 organizations	http://fisher.lib.virginia.edu

SOURCE: Anderson et al. (2007), 148.

■ Approaching the Prospect

Approach
The first face-to-face contact with the prospect.

Salespeople make their critical, often long-lasting, impressions in the **approach** stage. As you see in Table 4.5, several methods for approaching the prospect can succeed, ranging from a referral by a mutual acquaintance to beginning an immediate product demonstration. For example, while walking or driving to a prospect's office, a salesperson may call the prospect and say something like this: "Hi John, I'm calling you on our new Celestrial 3000 cell phone. How's the sound coming through? I think you'll like the phone's exciting new features, and it's very compact. You can see for yourself in just a few minutes when I'll be knocking on your door for our appointment."

Whatever the approach, successful salespeople must tailor it to each prospect. Successful salespeople often set a *primary objective* (targeted outcome), a *minimal objective* (lowest acceptable outcome), and an *optimal objective* (best possible outcome) before approaching the prospect. It's a good idea to use **SMART** steps to set objectives:[15]

SMART Objectives
A method of setting sales call objectives that are **s**pecific, **m**easurable, **a**chievable, **r**elational, and **t**emporal.

- *Specific*—Establish a specific, major objective for the sales call.
- *Measurable*—Ensure that your major objective is measurable or quantifiable—for example, a certain number of units or dollar sales volume.
- *Achievable*—Make sure the goals you set are realistic and achievable.

FIGURE 4.2 Salespeople can find a wealth of information for planning sales calls from various sources, such as trade associations, chambers of commerce, or the website of the *Thomas Register of American Manufacturers.*

■ *Relational*—Always try to further a positive long-term relationship with the prospect whether you achieve your major objective on this sales call or not.

■ *Temporal*—If you can, establish with the prospect a specific time frame for achieving the major objective. For instance, arrange for trial use of the product or service for a designated time period, with the prospect's purchase decision to follow.

Ultimately, most sales calls should achieve one or more of three overall objectives:

1. *Generate sales*—Sell particular products or services to target customers on designated sales calls.
2. *Develop the market*—Lay the groundwork for generating new business by educating customers, gaining visibility, and developing relationships with prospective buyers.
3. *Protect the market*—Learn competitors' strategies and tactics and protect relationships with current customers to keep them satisfied and loyal.

TABLE 4.5 Strategies for Approaching Prospects	
NON-PRODUCT-RELATED APPROACHES	
Mutual Acquaintance or Reference	Mention the names of satisfied customers whom the prospect respects.
Self-Introduction	Smoothly and professionally greet the prospect.
Free Gift or Sample	Offer a free gift, sample, or luncheon invitation.
Dramatic Act	Do something dramatic or memorable in a positive way to capture the prospect's attention.
PIQUING-INTEREST APPROACHES	
Customer Benefit	Offer the potential customer a benefit immediately.
Curiosity	Offer the prospect a benefit that appeals to the prospect's curiosity.
CONSUMER-DIRECTED APPROACHES	
Compliment or Praise	Subtly but sincerely compliment the prospect.
Survey	Ask permission to obtain information about whether the prospect might need your product.
Question	Involve the prospect in two-way communication early on by asking a question.
PRODUCT-RELATED APPROACHES	
Product or Ingredient	Show the prospect the product or a model of the product.
Product Demonstration	Begin demonstrating the product upon first meeting the prospect.

SOURCE: Anderson et al. (2007), 157.

■ Making the Sales Presentation and Demonstration

Persuasive communication is at the heart of the selling process, and the sales presentation/demonstration is the critical center stage or "showtime" for salespeople. After asking the customer qualifying questions to uncover specific needs, the salesperson presents the products and services that will best satisfy those needs; highlights their features, advantages, and benefits; and stimulates desire for the offerings with a skillful demonstration. Prospects are primarily interested in the benefits being offered them. Product features and advantages are important only if they can be tied directly to a specific benefit the prospect is seeking. For instance, pointing out a flat-screen monitor feature when demonstrating a new desktop computer does not mean much to a prospect unless the salesperson explains the related benefits of taking up less desk space, reducing eye strain, and increasing employee productivity.

Success in this stage requires development of carefully tailored and practiced strategies, including a convincing product demonstration. It's been said that a picture is worth a thousand words, and a demonstration is worth a thousand pictures. One successful sales representative always carried a hammer and a plate of his company's unbreakable glass with him to demonstrate its strength. One day, instead of hitting the glass with the hammer himself, he let the prospect do it. From then on, his sales soared as he continued letting customers swing the hammer. Salespeople should always try to get their prospects involved in demonstrating the product or "trying it out," so they can gain confidence in using it. A dog-and-pony show, no matter how elaborate, seldom succeeds because prospects usually see its focus as selling the product instead of solving their problems.

Salespeople who use skillful questioning and reactive listening while prospects describe their needs can often adjust their sales presentation and demonstration on the fly to provide the best customer solutions. Various sales presentation strategies are presented in Table 4.6, but most professional B2B salespeople find the consultative problem-solving strategy to be most effective, along with tactics that anticipate likely interactions between buyer and seller. Like an actor or athlete, the salesperson needs to diligently practice the sales presentation with a sales associate or friend. Some salespeople enroll in sales presentation training programs offered by companies like Empowerment Group (www.empowermentgroup.com/presentation_training.html) as a way to further develop their proficiency (Figure 4.3).

FIGURE 4.3 Salespeople can enroll in sales presentation training programs, offered by companies like Empowerment Group, to learn about various sales presentation strategies.

Adaptive versus Canned Sales Presentations. Traditional salespeople tend to make relatively standard sales presentations that don't vary much from one prospect to another. Top-performing salespeople try instead to adapt each presentation to the particular prospect and selling situation.[16] Salespeople who modify their presentations according to specific prospect or customer needs and behaviors are more effective than those who do not.[17] This point may seem obvious, but only salespeople who

TABLE 4.6 Sales Presentation Strategies

STRATEGY	APPROACH	ADVANTAGE OR DISADVANTAGE
Stimulus-Response	Salesperson asks a series of positive leading questions.	Customer develops habit of answering "yes," which may lead to a positive response to the closing question. Can appear manipulative to sophisticated prospects.
Formula	Salesperson leads the prospect through the mental states of buying (AIDA: attention, interest, desire, and action).	Prospect is led toward purchase action one step at a time, as the prospect participates in the interview. May come across as too mechanical and rehearsed to win prospect's trust and confidence.
Need Satisfaction	Salesperson tries to find the prospect's dominant but often latent buying needs; skillful listening, questioning, and use of certain image-producing words will help the salesperson uncover the critical need or needs to be satisfied if the sale is to be won.	Salesperson listens and responds to the prospect while "leading" the prospect to buy; the salesperson learns dominant buyer needs and motivations. Salesperson must not overlook latent needs of prospect that are not articulated.
Consultative Problem Solving	Salesperson carefully listens and asks probing questions to more fully understand the prospect's problems and specific needs and then recommends the best alternative solutions.	Through the parties working together to understand and solve problems, the salesperson forges a trustful, consultative relationship with the prospect. Salesperson and buyer negotiations focus on a "win-win" outcome and a long-run relationship.
Depth Selling	Salesperson employs a skillful mix of several sales presentation methods.	A customized mix of the best features of all of the strategies that draws on most of their advantages. Depth selling requires exceptional salesperson skill and experience.
Team Selling	Salesperson, in concert with other company personnel, sells the product/service benefits and avoids intra-group conflicts by promoting harmony, identifying and catering to the needs of each interest group.	Team selling involves counterparts from both the buyer and seller organizations interacting and cooperating to find solutions to problems. Salesperson serves as coordinator of the buyer-seller team interactions.

SOURCE: Anderson et al. (2007), 197.

Adaptive Selling
Modifying each sales presentation and demonstration to accommodate each individual prospect.

Canned (or Programmed) Selling
Any highly structured or patterned selling approach.

are inclined to adjust their sales presentation to the customer are likely to do so during the sales call.[18] Successful salespeople regularly practice adapting their sales presentation to different customer types and sales situations, and they stay alert to prospects' verbal and nonverbal feedback during the presentation. For example, if the purchasing manager for Hertz (www.hertz.com) shows more interest in safety than in gas mileage, then an observant salesperson for General Motors (www.gm.com) can quickly adapt the sales presentation by emphasizing the safety benefits of GM cars. Although **adaptive selling** is generally best, **canned** (or programmed) **selling** can be appropriate for some types of prospects, selling situations, and salespeople. In fact, the most effective sales presentations often blend the canned and adaptive approaches.[19] Many professional salespeople use programmed multimedia to present general information efficiently and effectively and to enliven their sales presentations.

During the multimedia presentation, salespeople are able to closely observe the prospect's reaction and accordingly better adapt later stages of the sales presentation. To gauge how adaptive you are as a salesperson, take the test in Table 4.7.

■ Negotiating Sales Resistance or Buyer Objections

Even after an effective sales presentation and demonstration, most prospects and customers are not ready to sign a purchase agreement. Instead, they're likely to ask more questions and resist making the purchase. However, you shouldn't be discouraged by prospect resistance or **objections.** Experienced salespeople know the sale doesn't really begin until the prospect says no. Usually, objections are simply a request for more information so that the prospect can justify a purchase decision. Before you make a sales call, it's always a good idea to anticipate prospect objections and prepare appropriate responses to win the sale.

Sales resistance can consist of either valid or invalid objections, and salespeople need to recognize each type in negotiating with prospects or customers. Table 4.8 summarizes various forms of common **valid** and **invalid objections** that you're likely to encounter in your selling efforts. It's generally futile for salespeople to try to negotiate invalid or hidden objections.

Objection
Anything that the prospect or customer says or does that impedes the sales negotiations.

Valid Objections
Sincere concerns that the prospect needs to have addressed before he or she will be willing to buy.

Invalid Objections
Irrelevant, untruthful delaying actions or hidden reasons for not buying.

TABLE 4.7 How Adaptive Are You?

Assume you're a salesperson, and respond to each of the following statements to determine how adaptive you would be in dealing with a prospect or a customer using the following scale:

5–Strongly Agree   4–Agree   3–Neither Agree nor Disagree   2–Disagree   1–Strongly Disagree

1. Each customer requires a unique approach.
2. When I feel that my sales approach is not working, I just change to another approach.
3. I like to experiment with different sales approaches.
4. I am very flexible in the selling approach I use.
5. I feel that most buyers can be dealt with in different ways.
6. I change my approach from one customer to another.
7. I can easily use a wide variety of selling approaches.
8. I use varied sales approaches.
9. It is easy for me to modify my sales presentation if the situation calls for it.
10. Basically, I use a different approach with most customers.
11. I am very sensitive to the needs of my customers.
12. I find it easy to adapt my presentation style to most buyers.
13. I vary my sales style from situation to situation.
14. I try to understand how one customer differs from another.
15. I feel confident that I can effectively change my planned presentation when necessary.
16. I treat each of my buyers differently.

Add your scores for the sixteen questions. A score of 64 or higher indicates that your adaptability is strong; a score of 48 or lower indicates that your adaptability is weak and needs work.

SOURCE: Adapted from Rosann L. Spiro and Barton A. Weitz, "Adaptive Selling: Conceptualization, Measurement, and Nomological Validity," *Journal of Marketing Research,* 27 (February 1990): 60–61. Reprinted with permission of the American Marketing Association.

TABLE 4.8 Types of Valid and Invalid Objections

VALID OBJECTIONS

Product Objections	■ Product characteristics and benefits are perceived as less than ideal by the prospect.
	■ The proposed product is not superior to the product currently being used.
	■ Product characteristics and benefits are not competitive.
Price Objections	■ Price is too high for the perceived value offered.
	■ Price isn't competitive.
	■ Price exceeds the prospect's budget limitations.
	■ Discounts are inadequate.
	■ Payment terms are out of line.
Promotion Objections	■ Cooperative advertising is insufficient.
	■ Free display merchandise is not offered.
	■ No "push money" is provided for reseller salespeople.
	■ No advertising support is offered.
Distribution Objections	■ Delivery lead time is too long.
	■ Minimum order size requirements are unacceptable.
	■ Delivery arrangements are inadequate.
	■ Questions regarding who pays transportation costs.
	■ The salesperson's company is unwilling to provide consignment sales.
	■ Inadequate damage and return goods policy.
	■ Prospect's fear of being overstocked.
Capital Objections	■ Required investment outlays are too high.
	■ Customer credit rating is too low to obtain favorable interest rate for capital fund loans.
	■ The prospect company's capital budget has not yet been approved.
	■ Customer has cash flow problems, so is currently unable to buy capital goods.
Source Objections	■ Source company's reputation is poor.
	■ Buyer prefers a local supplier.
	■ Buyer wants to do business with a national company.
	■ Lingering concerns over past problems in doing business with the seller.
	■ Buyer prefers to stick to the status quo in supplier relationships.
	■ Vendor has a reputation for manufacturing low-quality products.
	■ Vendor is known to be unethical.
Needs Objections	■ Buyer has no need for the seller's product or service.
	■ Buyer is satisfied with the products currently being purchased.

INVALID OBJECTIONS

Latent Objections	■ Buyer usually purchases from an old friend.
	■ Prospect does not have the authority to make the purchase but is embarrassed to let salesperson know this.
	■ Prospect resents the salesperson making an unannounced visit.
	■ Prospect simply doesn't like the salesperson or his or her company and doesn't want to start a business relationship.

(continued)

TABLE 4.8 (continued)	
INVALID OBJECTIONS	

Stalling Objections	■ To put off the salesperson for the time being or get him to leave and not return, the prospect says something like:
	  • "Thanks for coming in, we'll get back to you if we decide to consider purchasing your products."
	  • "Purchasing decisions are made by a buying committee, so I'll let you know if the committee decides to consider your company as a supplier."

Time Objections	■ Prospect says he has to prepare for a meeting. ■ Prospect claims he needs time to assess the purchase specifications and requirements. ■ Prospect says he is just too busy to meet with the salesperson.
Unethical Objections	■ Prospect does not do business with people from a particular ethnic group or religion. ■ Prospect makes sexual overtures to the salesperson. ■ Prospect solicits bribes or kickbacks.

SOURCE: Anderson et al. (2007), 218–19.

There are too many specific techniques for negotiating buyer objections to discuss in this overview (see Table 4.9), but a couple deserve special mention. One especially useful technique is called *Feel, Felt, Found.* To illustrate, if a prospect says: "This new fax machine is too complicated for me to operate," the salesperson can respond: "I know just how you *feel,* I *felt* the same way when I first saw it, but I've *found* that you need to concern yourself with only three buttons to do over 90 percent of the operations."

© Jeff Greenberg / PhotoEdit

● **Salespeople can use various negotiating techniques to achieve "win-win" agreements.**

TABLE 4.9 Specific Techniques for Negotiating Buyer Objections	
PUT-OFF STRATEGIES	**PROVIDE PROOF STRATEGIES**
■ I'm Coming to That ■ Pass-Off	■ Case History ■ Demonstration ■ Propose Trial Use
DENIAL STRATEGIES	**SWITCH FOCUS STRATEGIES**
■ Indirect Denial ■ Direct Denial	■ Alternative Product ■ Feel, Felt, Found ■ Comparison or Contrast ■ Answer with a Question
OFFSET STRATEGIES	
■ Boomerang ■ Compensation or Counterbalance	■ Agree and Neutralize ■ Humor

SOURCE: Anderson et al. (2007), 231.

Reprinted by permission of High Probability® Selling.

FIGURE 4.4 Firms like High Probability Selling offer seminars that can help improve salesperson closing abilities.

Another surprisingly useful technique is called *boomerang,* or turning an objection into a reason for buying. For example, assume an automobile dealership is considering buying new garage doors for its large repair facility, and the manager says: "Your garage door is slower and noisier going up and down than all your competitors' doors." In response, the salesperson might say: "Yes, our 'safety first' brand door is the slowest and noisiest for a good reason. Our safety engineers learned that most accidents with heavy garage doors are the result of their coming down too fast and too quietly, so all our doors were redesigned to come down more slowly and to make a loud noise in doing so. No one has been injured by our 'safety first' doors since we began selling them six months ago."

To learn more about closing sales and to improve their sales closing performance ratio, sales managers can enroll their salespeople in skill improvement workshops offered by companies such as High Probability Selling (www.highprobsell.com/html/closing_ sales.html), shown in Figure 4.4.

■ Confirming and Closing the Sale

Close
The stage in the PSP where the salesperson tries to obtain the prospect's agreement to purchase the product.

For most salespeople, a successful **close** is the exciting high point in the personal selling process. Like scoring the winning goal in a game, it's the exhilarating reward for which the salesperson has worked so hard. Skillful salespeople learn a variety of closing techniques, as set forth in Table 4.10, to help prospects make decisions in the buying process.

TABLE 4.10 Types of Closes

CLOSING TECHNIQUE	EXPLANATION
Clarification Closes	
Assumptive Close	Assume that the purchase decision has already been made so that the prospect feels compelled to buy.
Choice Close	Offer the prospect alternative products from which to choose.
Success Story Close	Tell a story about a customer with a similar problem who solved it by buying the product. Alternatively, provide satisfied customers' written or verbal testimonies supporting the product. Especially effective are endorsements from people well known and respected by the prospect.
Contingent Close	Elicit the prospect's agreement to buy if the salesperson can demonstrate the benefits promised.
Counterbalance Close	Offset an undeniable objection by balancing it with an important buying benefit.
Boomerang Close	Turn an objection around so that it becomes a reason for buying.
Future Order Close	If a prospect does not have a current need, but may have one in the future, the salesperson can ask for a commitment from the prospect to purchase at a future time.
If/When Close	Asking the prospect to provide a clarification as to *when* an order will be placed, as opposed to *if* an order will be placed.
Probability Close	Although seemingly comparable to the if/when close described above, the probability closing technique asks the prospect to assign a quantified likelihood of signing a sales contract in the near future.
Suggestion Close	Gets the prospect to accept the advice offered without giving it a great deal of thought. A salesperson could suggest that many customers who have purchased the product have reported high levels of satisfaction, thereby suggesting that the prospect should purchase it.
Psychological Closes	
Stimulus-Response Close	Use a sequence of leading questions to make it easier for the prospect to say yes when finally asked for the order.
Minor Points Close	Secure favorable decisions on several minor points, leading to eventual purchase of the product.
Standing Room Only (SRO) Close	Suggest that the opportunity to buy is brief because demand is high and the product is in short supply.
Impending Event Close	Warn the prospect about some upcoming event that makes it more advantageous to buy now.
Advantage Close	This variation of the impending event close emphasizes the specific advantages of making a timely decision, while still stressing a sense of immediacy.
Puppy Dog Close	Let the prospect use the product for a while and, as with a puppy, an emotional attachment may develop, leading to a purchase.
Compliment Close	Praise prospects for raising interesting and intelligent questions to flatter their egos and lead them to sign the sales order.
Reserve Advantage Close	In this slight variation of the advantage close described above, salespeople identify a number of merits for purchasing a product, but save a few to use if the prospect exhibits resistance yet again.
Dependency Close	Used to break the "choke-hold" that a competing firm has over a prospect's business by suggesting that the prospect needs an alternative supplier to reduce the risk of being dependent on one supplier.

CLOSING TECHNIQUE	EXPLANATION

TABLE 4.10 (continued)

Straightforward Closes

Closing Technique	Explanation
Ask-for-the-Order Close	Ask for the order directly or indirectly.
Order Form Close	While asking the prospect a series of questions, start filling out basic information on the contract or order form.
Summary Close	Summarize the advantages and disadvantages of buying the product before asking for the order.
Repeated-Yes Close	This variation of the summary close requires a salesperson to pose several leading questions to which the prospect has little choice but to respond in an affirmative manner.
Benefits Close	Also a variation of the summary close, it requires the salesperson to identify and present a synopsis of the various salient benefits that the sales solution offers.
Action Close	The salesperson simply hands the prospect a pen along with the contract, and frequently the prospect, almost by reflex, will sign.
Negotiation Close	Both the buyer and the salesperson negotiate a compromise, thus ensuring a "win-win" agreement.
Technology Close	The salesperson more impactfully and effectively summarizes key value-added benefits for the prospect by using technologies such as PowerPoint, Excel, or other multimedia tools.

Concession Closes

Closing Technique	Explanation
Special Deal Close	Offer a special incentive to encourage the prospect to buy now.
No-Risk Close	Agree to take the product back and refund the customer's money if the product doesn't prove satisfactory.
Management Close	When salespeople do not have the authority to make the prospect's requested commitments or concessions, they can elicit the assistance of a senior sales manager who has the authority to make the necessary decisions to close the sale.
Takeaway Close	Used as an emotional fear appeal to cause anxiety that the prospect may lose out on a special deal or incentive. A salesperson could suggest that the special offer to provide an ancillary product or service free of charge is available only for another week, thereby evoking an immediate purchase.

Lost-Sale Closes

Closing Technique	Explanation
Turnover Close	Turn the prospect over to another salesperson with a fresh approach or a better chance to make the sale.
Pretend-to-Leave Close	Start to walk away, and then "remember" another benefit or special offer after the prospect has relaxed his or her defenses.
Ask-for-Help Close	When the sale seems lost, apologize for not being able to satisfy the prospect and ask what it would have taken to secure the sale. Then offer that.

SOURCE: Anderson et al. (2007), 258–60.

One of the most *straightforward* closing approaches, when the salesperson and the prospect seem to be in agreement, is simply to ask, "Shall we write up the order?" But the close need not be that blatant. Often, the salesperson can accomplish the same result with a more subtle *assumptive close* question, such as "When do you need the product delivered?" Another concern for many new salespeople is determining *when* to try to close the sale. There's no single best time. The close can happen at any time during the sales process—in the first few minutes of the first sales call, or in the last few seconds of the sixth. An old axiom for salespeople is to recite your ABCs (that is,

● **Salespeople should be looking for verbal and nonverbal signals from customers that indicate it's time to close a sale.**

Trial Close
Any well-placed attempt to close the sale; can be used early and often throughout the PSP.

"always be closing"), which advocates making **trial closes** throughout your interaction with the prospect. Trial closes are simply attempts to test the prospect's *readiness to buy*. Examples include statements like "Do you think this product will meet your needs?" or "So, what do you think?"

A *puppy dog close* can be especially effective. With it, the salesperson simply lets the prospect use the product for a while—and hopes that, as with a puppy, an emotional attachment may develop and lead to a purchase. Even when the sale seems lost, salespeople still can use the *ask-for-help close*. Simply apologize for not being able to satisfy the prospect, and ask what it would have taken to secure the sale. When the prospect answers, offer that.

Nonverbal trial closes can also be effective. Even a small physical act such as moving the order form and pen in front of prospects may generate a reflex action to pick up the pen and sign the order. Most salespeople also learn to read and closely observe prospect body language to spot an opportune time to try a close. Some verbal and nonverbal signals indicating it's time for a trial close are presented in Table 4.11.

■ Following Up and Servicing the Account

After making the sale, top salespeople don't disappear. Instead, they maintain close contact with the customer to handle any complaints (see Table 4.12 for basic rules about handling customer complaints) and to provide customer service such as installation, repair, or credit approvals. It's far easier—and less costly—to keep present customers satisfied than to search out and acquire new customers. Fully satisfied customers are the ones most likely to become loyal repeat buyers who cut costs for companies in various ways.[20] They are generally easier to work with and satisfy because your relationship has reached a high level of understanding about what the customer expects. Moreover, loyal customers will buy additional products and refer

TABLE 4.11 Trial Closing Signals

VERBAL SIGNALS

When the prospect asks

- about product price, delivery, installation, or service.
- about any special discounts, deals, or special incentives to buy.
- a hypothetical question about buying: "If I do decide to buy . . ."
- who else has bought the product.
- what other customers think about the product.
- whether a special feature is included or available.
- whether the product can accomplish a particular task.
- the salesperson's opinion about one product version versus another.
- what method of payment is acceptable.

When the prospect says

- something positive about the product.
- that he or she has always wanted some special product feature.

When the salesperson

- successfully answers one of the prospect's objections.
- asks whether the prospect has any more questions and the prospect says no or is silent.

NONVERBAL SIGNALS

When the prospect

- begins closely studying and handling the product.
- tests or tries out the product.
- seems pleased by the product's performance or by some product feature.
- looks more relaxed.
- becomes more friendly.
- increases eye contact with the salesperson.
- looks over the order form or picks up the pen the salesperson has handed him or her.
- nods his or her head in agreement or leans toward the salesperson.
- begins to listen more intently to the salesperson.
- lends the salesperson a pen.
- picks up, fondles, smells, tastes, or closely studies the product.
- unconsciously reaches for his or her checkbook or wallet.

When the salesperson

- finishes the sales presentation.
- completes a successful product demonstration.
- hands the order form and a pen to the prospect.

SOURCE: Anderson et al. (2007), 254.

you to other excellent prospects, so you can reduce expenditures on promotion to attract new prospects. Over their lifetimes, they can be worth up to ten times as much to a business as the average customer.[21] Companies as diverse as Pizza Hut (www.pizzahut.com), Home Depot (www.homedepot.com), and General Motors

> ## TABLE 4.12   Basic Rules for Handling Customer Complaints
>
> - Anticipate customer complaints and try to resolve them before the customer expresses them.
> - Listen closely and patiently to customers' complaints without interrupting.
> - Never belittle a customer's complaint. Few customers actually complain, and those who do are a valuable source of feedback and information that can help improve the quality of your product and service.
> - Encourage customers to talk and fully express their feelings so that they can vent their emotions.
> - Don't argue with customers or take their complaints personally. You gain nothing by making a customer angry, and there is no surer way to do so than to argue over the customer's version of the complaint.
> - Record the facts as the customer sees them. If you take the complaint over the telephone, let him or her know that you are carefully recording the facts without passing judgment.
> - Reassure customers that you hear and understand their complaints accurately by verbally repeating the information as you record it. This repetition reassures customers about your accuracy and interest. Asking non-threatening and nonjudgmental questions to clarify their various points can also help them to know that they are communicating successfully.
> - Empathize with customers and try to see the situation from their point of view.
> - Don't make excuses for service problems or criticize your firm's service personnel.
> - Ask customers how they would like to have their complaint resolved instead of volunteering what you're going to do. Customers may have quite different expectations about how to solve their problem, and you may offer the wrong solution or much more than they expect. By asking customers what they want, you'll meet their expectations and not overdo it in making amends.
> - Resolve problems promptly and fairly, even if that means the sale will become unprofitable.
> - Thank customers for voicing the complaint. Welcome them as people who care enough to try to help you improve your products and services.
> - Follow up to ensure that a customer's complaint has been resolved to his or her satisfaction.
> - Keep records on all customer complaints and their outcomes so that, through analysis, you can spot patterns of problems.

SOURCE: Anderson et al. (2007), 307.

Follow-Up
Customer service provided not just after the sale is closed, but throughout the PSP.

(www.gm.com) are working not only to satisfy customers but also to keep their loyalty. Pizza Hut estimates that the lifetime value of its loyal customers is over $8,000; Home Depot figures $23,000; the Cadillac (www.cadillac.com) division of General Motors reports $332,000; and Lexus (www.lexus.com) calculates over $600,000.[22] Frequent and comprehensive **follow-up** is a primary means of retaining long-run, satisfied, loyal, and profitable customers—and of keeping the *personal selling process wheel* revolving.

Applying CRM to the Personal Selling Process

■ Empowering Salespeople for CRM

As their companies' front-line representatives, salespeople are the ultimate customer relationship builders. In recent years, their roles have shifted from merely selling goods and services to building and maintaining long-term, mutually profitable relationships with valued customers. Yet, despite their expanding responsibilities for CRM, most salespeople have not been sufficiently trained or empowered by their companies to perform effectively and efficiently in this challenging new role. Even sales managers may not have a CRM attitude toward serving customers. To see how customer oriented you are, assume that you are a salesperson or sales manager and honestly answer the questions in Table 4.13.

TABLE 4.13 How Customer Oriented Are You?

Determine how customer oriented you are by responding to the following statements, using this scale:

5–Strongly Agree   4–Agree   3–Neither Agree nor Disagree   2–Disagree   1–Strongly Disagree

1. I want to help my customers achieve their goals.
2. I want to serve my customers so well that they will come back to buy more from me.
3. It's more important to satisfy a customer than to make a big sales commission on a product that won't satisfy the customer.
4. I use a canned sales pitch for most sales.
5. I try to influence customers by providing information rather than by applying pressure.
6. I try to sell the product best suited to my customer's problem even if my commission is lower on that product.
7. I listen to customers more than I talk to them so I can understand their needs.
8. I try to answer a customer's questions about products as honestly as I can.
9. I try to help customers solve their problems even if I occasionally have to recommend a competitor's product.
10. I am willing to politely disagree with a customer in order to help him or her make a better decision.
11. I try to give customers accurate expectations about what the product will do for them.
12. I try to resolve customers' complaints promptly so that they want to remain my customers.
13. I want customers to be fully satisfied so they will become repeat buyers from me.
14. I try to sell customers all I can convince them to buy, even if it's more than they really need.
15. I keep alert to spot weaknesses in a customer's personality so I can use them to apply buying pressure at the right time.
16. If I'm not sure whether a product is right for a customer, I still pressure him or her to buy because it's not my job to figure out whether or not the product's right for the customer.
17. I usually try to persuade customers to buy the product on which I make the most commission.
18. I sometimes paint too rosy a picture of my products to make them sound as good as possible to customers.
19. If a customer doesn't ask about a particular product weakness, I don't think it's my job to mention it.
20. It's sometimes necessary to stretch the truth a little in describing a product to a customer.
21. Even when I know they're wrong, I generally pretend to agree with customers in order to please them.
22. I sometimes imply to a customer that something is beyond my control when it's not.
23. When customers come back to complain about a product I sold them, I often try to avoid them.
24. In negotiating with customers, my main focus is on winning the sale.
25. I never let customers assume something that's incorrect because over the long run, my integrity and honesty are among my best sales tools.

The higher your score for items 1 through 3, 5 through 13, and 25, the more customer oriented you are. Total scores of 52 or higher on these items indicate a strong customer orientation; a score lower than 39 indicates a weak customer orientation. The lower your score for items 4 and items 14 through 24, the more customer oriented you are. Total scores of 24 or lower indicate a strong customer orientation; a score of over 36 indicates a weak customer orientation.

SOURCE: Adapted from Robert Saxe and Barton A. Weitz, "The SOCO Scale: A Measure of the Customer Orientation of Salespeople," *Journal of Marketing Research*, 19 (August 1982): 343–51. Reprinted with permission of the American Marketing Association.

Kotler and Armstrong define CRM as "the overall process of building and maintaining profitable customer relationships by delivering superior customer value and satisfaction."[23] CRM has been called an inevitable—literally relentless—movement because it represents the way customers want to be served, and offers a more effective and efficient way of conducting business.[24] Many companies are developing complex CRM strategies that integrate sales force automation (SFA), data warehousing, data mining, push technology, and other tools to more fully understand and serve their most valuable customers. For example, KeyCorp (www.keycorp.net) achieved a return of over 350 percent by collecting customer profiles, interests, activities, and goals on its website and then designing strategies to cross-sell products via direct mail, teleselling, and the Internet.[25] It is critical for sales managers to empower salespeople by enabling them to promptly address customer needs and negotiate mutually satisfying agreements with them. In practice, empowerment should seek to strengthen the flexibility, self-confidence, authority, and effectiveness of salespeople as they try to fully satisfy customers and achieve CRM objectives. One important way to empower salespeople is to give them more financial flexibility to commit company resources in serving customers—approving reimbursements for unsatisfactory products, negotiating price discounts, providing purchase incentives, and resolving customer complaints. By being able to make on-the-spot decisions, salespeople can enhance their image and competence with customers and thereby feel more psychologically empowered and motivated for CRM.[26]

In sum, managers can foster a CRM orientation among salespeople by increasing their perceptions of empowerment, releasing managerial power and control of resources to salespeople, providing continual empowerment and CRM training, keeping recognition and reward systems current with organizational goals, and eliminating barriers in the organizational structure and work environment that affect empowerment of both salespeople and customers.[27]

■ CRM Training and Rewards

To develop the skills of empowerment and customer relationship building needed for effective CRM, salespeople need appropriate training programs. They must be trained and rewarded for proactively taking initiatives that build customer relationships. Customer expectations are continually rising and tend to be infinitely elastic.[28] Therefore, CRM training for salespeople must be ongoing to keep up with the increasingly higher-level buying experience and relationship expectations of customers. Salespeople need to be empowered to make on-the-spot decisions that respond to customer requests. Delaying responses because managerial approval is required visibly undercuts the salesperson's power before customers and can hurt his or her CRM dedication and performance.

Traditional sales quota systems for motivating, evaluating, and rewarding the sales force need updating to include tangible goals and rewards for cultivating and retaining key customers through empowered CRM activities. To achieve this, salespeople ought to be empowered with profit figures by different market segments—information that some management teams still are reluctant to share. Finally, in designing reward systems, perceived managerial fairness or evenhandedness is essential for maintaining highly motivated, satisfied, and committed CRM salespeople.

CHAPTER SUMMARY

1. **Evaluate the benefits and opportunities available in a sales career.** Among the many benefits available to salespeople are high earnings potential from salaries, commissions, and bonuses; various "perks;" and interaction with senior management. Other benefits of a sales career include consistently high demand, job freedom and independence, the adventure of interacting with new prospects and buying situations, and personal satisfaction in doing a job that contributes directly to the welfare of one's company and the economy. In addition, after performing successfully for a few years, salespeople usually have opportunities to be promoted into sales management or marketing management or to become a national account manager for one or two major customers.

2. **Compare and contrast today's sales professional with yesterday's.** Yesterday's salespeople were largely product oriented, focused on selling, did little sales call planning, made sales pitches without listening much to customers, stressed product features and price, often used manipulative techniques, worked largely alone, showed little interest in understanding customers' problems, and usually disappeared after the sale was made until the next sales call. By contrast, today's professional salespeople are customer oriented, focus on serving customers, develop sales call strategies with specific objectives for each sales call, listen to and communicate meaningfully with customers, stress customer benefits and service, try to help customers solve their problems, follow up with customers to ensure full satisfaction leading to customer loyalty, and work as a member of a team of specialists to serve customers.

3. **Describe the seven stages in the personal selling process (PSP).** The PSP is depicted as a revolving wheel of seven overlapping, interacting stages. *Stage 1,* prospecting and qualifying, involves finding organizational leads and qualifying them based on four criteria. *Stage 2* is planning the sales call, or the preapproach. Here, the salesperson obtains detailed information from diverse print and electronic sources about the prospect and the buying situation, and then develops a strategy for a favorable recep-

tion. *Stage 3,* approaching the prospect, can include various strategies ranging from a referral from a mutual acquaintance to a customer benefit approach. *Stage 4* is making the sales presentation and demonstration. Of the various sales presentation options, business-to-business (B2B) salespeople most often use *consultative problem solving. Stage 5* is negotiating sales resistance or objections. There are many ways to handle objections; the savvy salesperson will anticipate objections and prepare techniques to overcome them. *Stage 6,* confirming and closing the sale, is the culmination of all the salesperson has worked so hard to achieve. There are many types of closes, ranging from directly asking for the order to the puppy dog close, where the prospect is allowed to try out the product before making a purchase decision. *Stage 7* is following up and serving the account after the purchase. This stage is critical in ensuring customer satisfaction and retention.

4. **Use various searching methods to find new prospects.** *Random-lead searching methods* for prospects include door-to-door canvassing, a territory blitz, cold calls, general e-mails, advertising through print and broadcast media, and websites. *Selective-lead searching methods* include *direct sources* (i.e., pre-targeted organizations or people) and *indirect sources* where organizations or people must identify themselves by responding.

5. **Apply several sales presentation strategies.** The most important sales presentation strategy for B2B salespeople is *consultative problem solving,* where the salesperson carefully listens and asks probing questions to more fully understand the prospect's problems and specific needs and then recommends the best alternative solutions. By working together with prospects to understand and solve problems, the salesperson forges a trustful, consultative relationship focused on a win-win outcome and a long-run customer relationship.

6. **Overcome prospect objections and resistance through negotiation.** Negotiating prospect objections or resistance is an essential skill for today's salesperson. Objections should not be feared since they are usually pleas for more information in order

to justify a purchase. Although there are many types of prospect objections, negotiation strategies can be categorized under five headings: (a) put off, (b) denial, (c) offset, (d) provide proof, and (e) switch focus.

7. Demonstrate closing techniques from each of five closing categories. The many closing techniques can be divided into five basic categories: (a) clarification, (b) psychological, (c) straightforward, (d) concession, and (e) lost sale.

8. Explain how to empower salespeople for customer relationship management (CRM) roles. Empowerment of salespeople can strengthen their flexibility, self-confidence, authority, and effectiveness in striving to fully satisfy customers and achieve CRM objectives. An important way to empower salespeople is to give them more financial flexibility to commit company resources in serving customers—for example, approving reimbursements for unsatisfactory products, negotiating price discounts, providing purchase incentives, and resolving customer complaints.

REVIEW AND APPLICATION QUESTIONS

1. Why do you think so many successful CEOs of top companies have come up through sales? [LO 1]

2. What qualities do you think are needed by top-performing salespeople of today and tomorrow? [LO 2]

3. Describe the seven stages in the professional personal selling process (PSP). Why are they depicted as a revolving wheel? [LO 3, 4, 5, 6, 7]

4. Salespeople spend more time on prospecting than on any other of the seven PSP stages. Why do you think this is so? [LO 4]

5. Describe the different sales presentation strategies, including the advantages and disadvantages associated with each one. [LO 5]

6. How should salespeople view buyer objections and resistance? [LO 6]

7. Identify the five basic techniques for handling buyer objections, and give examples of each one. [LO 6]

8. What is a trial close? Give some examples of trial closes. When should they be used? [LO 5, 7]

9. Name and explain as many closing strategies as you can. [LO 7]

10. Why should salespeople be empowered in their dealings with prospects and customers? [LO 8]

IT'S UP TO YOU

 ### Internet Exercise

You have been appointed to work as a U.S. sales representative for Airbus Industrie, which has just developed the Airbus 380—a state-of-the-art, double-decker aircraft that carries from 550 to 900 passengers. Using the websites provided in Table 4.4, conduct a Web-based search for detailed information about the airline industry. More specifically, to help you plan the sales call and make your approach successful, find the following information:

- Addresses and locations of the headquarters of major players in the airline industry (passenger airlines and cargo carriers)

- Sales, market share, profits, and size of each major competitor

- Regions of the United States, and of the world, where each airline operates

- Type of aircraft the airline currently uses

- Names, addresses, e-mail addresses, and telephone numbers of purchasing managers for all of the airlines and cargo carriers

Role-Playing Exercise

Handling Customer Complaints

Situation

Alex Webster, a sales representative for Tectron Scientific Software (TSS) Corporation, recently sold an expensive new software program to a new account, the Biology Department of the University of Western Pennsylvania. A week after the software was installed, Alex called the department chairperson, Dr. Kim Feng, to see how the program was working out.

Role-Play Participants and Assignments

Dr. Kim Feng Graduate students have complained that the TSS software is not working right, and they suspect there are some errors in the software program. Dr. Feng can't tolerate any bugs in the software, which is being used for high-precision work under a National Science Foundation research grant. Due to time pressures to complete this research, Dr. Feng wants Alex to pick up this software and refund the purchase price, so the department can buy a competitor's product.

Alex Webster What should he say to Dr. Feng? How could he have prevented the problem in the first place?

In-Basket Exercise

You have recently been promoted to district sales manager. You now have responsibility for the performance of thirty salespeople who call on industrial distributors in Pennsylvania, New Jersey, and Delaware that sell mainly to independently owned hardware stores and franchises. Perhaps because you recently earned an MBA in Marketing, your national sales manager has asked you to develop a program to empower the company's field salespeople in carrying out the CEO's mandate for a total sales force customer relationship management (CRM) program to retain profitable business customers. Prepare a bulleted outline or executive summary of your proposed sales force empowerment program to submit to the national sales manager.

Ethical Dilemma

Clive Farley sells multi-function machines that print, copy, scan, and fax. On Friday night, he's preparing his sales presentation and demonstration before making the third sales call on a medium-size manufacturer who has asked for a product demonstration this coming Monday morning. Clive knows that his company's machine is very slow compared to competitors in making copies on both sides of the paper. Although many companies are trying to save copying costs by using both sides of the paper, Clive doubts that his prospect will ask for a demonstration of this feature, nor is it likely to come up in their discussions. So, Clive is thinking that he should avoid mentioning or doing any demonstration of two-sided copying because his machine is about 10–15 percent less expensive than the competitors and is equally good on all other features. He fears that a direct comparison of his machine with competitors on two-sided copying will probably cost him the sale. What would you advise Clive to do?

CASE 4.1

Solex-Digital: Effective Negotiation Strategies

Marilyn Boldt, a sales rep for Solex-Digital—a large semiconductor manufacturer—is negotiating with the chief buyer for National Computer Company (NCC). The buyer, Howard Logan, a thirty-year employee of NCC now nearing retirement, is such an aggressive, greedy bargainer that most salespeople hate to negotiate with him. He views each sales negotiation as a contest to be won, so he won't agree to sign a contract unless he feels that he's gotten the best of the supplier. Salespeople who do agree to the usual "seller lose–buyer win" agreement with Mr. Logan usually try to salvage a little profit on the contract by cutting some corners, usually on product quality or service. But this strategy often leads to dissatisfaction by NCC, so Mr. Logan usually moves on to another supplier for the next contract. The NCC account could be very valuable since its annual purchases of semiconductors exceed $4 million and are steadily increasing by about 5 percent a year. Mr. Logan, however, makes sales to NCC very dicey by insisting on squeezing out most of the profit margin and then switching suppliers if performance is less than fully satisfactory. Mr. Logan's assistant, Dale Mobley, seems to be much more reasonable, but he doesn't say much in negotiations since Logan always dominates. Most of the sales reps who call on NCC seem to be looking forward to the day when Mr. Logan retires because they often subtly ask receptionists about his retirement plans.

Mr. Logan has just demanded that Marilyn give him a whopping 20 percent discount on all NCC purchases—or, as he bluntly states, "I won't be buying anything from Solex-Digital." If the 20 percent discount is provided, Mr. Logan promises to give Solex-Digital all of NCC's semiconductor business this year. Marilyn knows that her company can't make any profit if she agrees to a 20 percent discount, and she's quite sure that no other semiconductor supplier will offer such a large discount. While Mr. Logan continues talking, Marilyn wonders how to respond to his demand.

QUESTIONS

1. Is it worthwhile for Marilyn to negotiate with Mr. Logan when his demands are so unreasonable—and unprofitable, if she agrees to the 20 percent discount? Explain.

2. Should Marilyn do like most salespeople who "win" orders from Mr. Logan—simply cut back on product quality and/or service and be relatively unresponsive to complaints, so that her company can make a little profit? If she follows this strategy, Marilyn realizes that she probably won't get any orders from Mr. Logan next year, and it may hurt her company's reputation—not only with NCC, but with other companies through negative word of mouth.

3. Marilyn wants to keep NCC as a customer because it could become a valued account when Mr. Logan retires. So, she's thinking about calling her sales manager to ask if she can offer the 20 percent discount and accept a loss on the contract in order to keep the customer relationship going with NCC. As her sales manager, what advice would you give Marilyn?

4. What role, if any, does customer relationship management play when dealing with difficult buyers like Mr. Logan?

Case prepared by Dheeraj Sharma and Woodrow D. Richardson, Ball State University.

CASE 4.2

Dasseaux Pharmaceuticals: Relationship versus Transactional Selling

Dasseaux Pharmaceuticals is a French-owned firm that entered the U.S. market about five years ago. Using two separate sales groups, the company markets over-the-counter ophthalmic products east of the Mississippi River. One sales group concentrates its efforts on independently owned retail drugstores; the other, much smaller group focuses on selling to chain drug stores such as Walgreen's, Rite Aid, CVS, and Sav-On. The primary promotional thrust of Dasseaux Pharmaceuticals is on trade advertising to create brand awareness with pharmacists at independent drugstores and chains, as well as with purchasing agents for large drugstore chains. Dasseaux also provides point-of-purchase display materials and offers coop advertising programs. The retail price of the company's products is competitive with similar products available in the market. But the retail margin for drugstores is a little higher than on other brands typically sold in the stores. Package design and color are contemporary, and product quality meets or exceeds competitive offerings.

Along with providing an extensive array of in-store promotional materials, Dasseaux Pharmaceuticals relies on the pharmacists to recommend its products. The success of this strategy depends a lot on how effective salespeople are in communicating to the pharmacists that margins, and therefore profits, are higher with Dasseaux products.

QUESTIONS

1. Is a relationship selling approach or transactional selling approach best in this situation? Would the same approach work for independent and chain drugstores, or should a different selling approach be used? Justify your recommendation.

2. How would the method of prospecting differ between the independent drugstores and the chain drugstores?

Case prepared by Balaji Krishnan, University of Memphis.

PART TWO

Organizing and Developing the Sales Force

CHAPTER 5
Sales Forecasting and Budgeting

CHAPTER 6
Sales Force Planning and Organizing

CHAPTER 7
Time and Territory Management

CHAPTER 8
Recruiting and Selecting the Sales Force

Sales Forecasting and Budgeting

LEARNING OBJECTIVES

When you finish this chapter, you should be able to:

1 Relate sales forecasting to operational planning.

2 Use the most popular quantitative and qualitative sales forecasting tools.

3 Evaluate the various sales forecasting techniques.

4 Identify the purpose and benefits of sales budgets.

5 Prepare an annual sales budget.

INSIDE SALES MANAGEMENT

Ewell Hopkins, Principal Partner, Morgan Holland & Company

Ewell Hopkins is as a principal partner of Morgan Holland & Company, a boutique consulting company that specializes in the financial services and information technology industries. His thirty-member firm is all about services, and to Hopkins, "while selling a product is an event, selling a service is creating a relationship." After committing the same amount of effort and investment that's needed for a product

sale, he says, in services the handshake that closes the deal is only just the beginning, not the end, of the story.

That means that the process of qualifying, closing, and satisfying customers is an ongoing one, with many projects under way at all times, all in different stages, and with reps working leads and prospects far in advance. How does Hopkins forecast sales in order to meet clients' future needs, keep projects flowing in, and ensure he has the right in-house and freelance staff available in the right numbers when they're needed?

At his weekly forecast meeting, Hopkins reviews all the company's current sales prospects. His report lists four stages of the sales process and includes detailed comments about each potential client, such as who the rep is using for technical help, who the primary customer contact is, who the influencers are, and when the selling process started. Stage 1 projects are the top of the "sales funnel"—these are potential clients who have expressed an interest in talking with Morgan Holland about a problem the company might be able to solve for them. Stage 2 prospects have an identified need and a time frame in which they must solve it—and Hopkins knows enough about the project at this stage to predict who he'll need on the team to get the job done.

In Stage 3, prospects have identified Morgan Holland as their preferred supplier. From this point, says Hopkins, no sales prospect should ever fall out of the ever-increasingly narrowing sales funnel. In the last stage, Stage 4, the deal has been struck, and paperwork awaits completion. Now Hopkins knows exactly who he needs to do the work. Where does he get them? Some team members are on staff, and some are independent contractors who come in on an as-needed basis.

The company is constantly tracking outside workers it can call upon as needed. In a service business like consulting, "nothing kills profitability faster than a deep bench," says Hopkins. "Keeping the company lean might mean giving up some opportunities, but it won't kill you like overstaffing will." So one of the company executives carefully tracks the status of current-current engagement teams, as well as freelancers' availability for current and future projects, during its weekly staffing meeting. The key to accurate sales forecasting, says Hopkins, is successfully putting the project forecast and the staffing plan together. That's what gives him a picture of the ongoing sales effort, and reveals where the all-important momentum of the business is directed.

Forecasting is important to practically all marketing organizations. Without a short-term forecast, sales managers would not have a logical basis for assigning workloads or deciding where to concentrate the sales effort. Without a long-term forecast, sales managers would not know how many salespeople the firm will need or how many should be promoted to a sales management position. The mere fact that a forecast has to be done admits that uncertainty exists in the process. In other words, forecasting is important, but the art and science of forecasting is imperfect, and every forecast can be only so accurate.

In many industries, managers still determine sales forecasts by comparing this year's sales with last year's sales at the same time period. But consider how much information is not taken into account with this approach. For companies like Toyota, Eli Lilly Pharmaceuticals, and IBM, a simple prediction will be useful only when conditions like economic trends and consumer tastes remain unchanged. How likely is this? In the pharmaceutical industry, predicting demand for a new drug depends on variables like how many people are likely to contract a certain disease, the life expectancy of someone with the disease, and even the likelihood of getting Food and Drug Administration (FDA) approval. Thus, forecasting is not only important, but it can be complex too. This chapter introduces the topic of sales forecasting.

Sales Forecasting and Its Relationship to Operational Planning

The Weather Channel may not provide the most exciting programming on television. But more U.S. viewers tune in to the Weather Channel at some time during the week than they do to practically all other topical cable networks.[1] Why? Well, people need to plan and organize their day, and the Weather Channel's local weather forecasts tell them what type of clothing to wear and whether taking an umbrella is a good idea. A quick trip to the Weather Channel website (http://www.weather.com) can also be helpful when deciding what activities to choose for an upcoming weekend. Weather forecasts make planning and organizing family activities much easier.

Sales forecasts work in much the same way. Many operational and strategic decisions are made much riskier without some type of forecast. A **sales forecast** is a prediction of the future market potential for a specific product. Simply put, it sets the sales expectations for a given time period. And just like the weather forecast, a bad sales forecast may expose you to some stormy times ahead.

Companies sometimes go forward with strategic planning while paying little or no attention to forecasting. This is a bit like getting in the car without directions. The odds are better you'll end up in a pleasant place if you start out with some idea of how far away and in what direction a pleasant place might be. A forecast provides the "how far" by estimating the amount of sales possible in a given situation. It also gives the direction by indicating what types of products customers are likely to want.

Sales managers are much more likely to arrive at a pleasant outcome if they begin with valid data about the marketplace. Sales forecasts provide an assessment of both market potential and sales potential. **Market potential** is a quantitative estimate, in either physical or monetary units, of the total sales for a product within a market. **Sales potential** is the portion of market potential that one among a set of competing firms can reasonably expect to obtain.

Sales managers use market and sales information in making critical operational decisions, like setting logical sales goals for different sales territories and individual salespeople. Sales goals of this type are sometimes known as sales **quotas**. Sales managers should use this term with some caution, however, because salespeople often interpret *quota* to mean, "Do this or else."

Forecasting is important for giant multinational corporations as well as small entrepreneurial firms. The forecast of sales potential becomes a starting point for sales and marketing planning, production scheduling, cash flow projections, financial planning, capital investment, procurement, inventory management, human resource planning, and budgeting. For example, before developing a production schedule, a company must know how much is expected to be sold. This production schedule, in turn, determines how much material it will order and how much labor will be scheduled for the period. Sales managers must know their operating budget before they can determine how many new salespeople to hire.

Accurate sales forecasts are also important for avoiding unfavorable inventory situations. The purchasing department schedules purchases of supplies and raw materials according to sales forecasts. A large inventory of unsold goods piles up when the forecast is too high. Plant shutdowns, employee layoffs, and deteriorating raw materials can soon follow. On the other hand, a sales forecast that *underestimates* demand causes stockouts. Sales are lost as a result, and customers may be lost permanently as they are forced to seek products elsewhere. Table 5.1 summarizes the impact of erroneous sales forecasts on planning in various functional areas.

Here is an example of using a sales forecast to calculate how many salespeople are needed for an upcoming year. We'll use the sales potential approach. Suppose a company expected $500,000 in annual sales. Over time the sales managers have learned that a typical salesperson can sell $50,000 per year and that 10 percent of the sales force will quit during the year. Here's how you would plan the number of salespeople needed:

Sales Forecast
A prediction of the future market potential for a specific product.

Market Potential
A quantitative estimate, in either physical or monetary units, of the total sales for a product within a market.

Sales Potential
The portion of market potential that one among a set of competing firms can reasonably expect to obtain.

Quotas
Sales goals for different sales territories and individual salespeople.

TABLE 5.1 Impact of Erroneous Sales Forecasts

FUNCTIONAL AREA	FORECAST	
	Too High	**Too Low**
Production	Excess output, unsold products	Inadequate output to meet customer demand
Inventory	Overstock	Understock
Finance	Idle cash	Cash shortage
Promotion	Wasted expenditures	Insufficient expenditures to cover the market
Distribution	Costly, insufficient to sell excess products	Inadequate to reach market
Pricing	Reductions to sell excess products	Price increases to allocate scarce products
Sales Force	Too many salespeople, high selling costs	Too few salespeople, market not covered
Customer Relations	Money wasted on unneeded activities, resulting in lower profits	Unsatisfactory due to out-of-stock products
Profits	Lower unit profits since expenses are high	Lower total profits because market not covered

$$NSP = \left(\frac{Sales\ Potential}{Sales\ per\ SP}\right) \times (1 + TO) = \left(\frac{\$500,000}{\frac{\$50,000}{SP}}\right) \times (1 + .1) = 10 \times 1.1 = 11$$

where

NSP = Number of Salespeople
Sales per SP = Sales per Salesperson
TO = Turnover

■ Sales and Operational Planning: S&OP

Sales and Operational Planning Process (S&OP)
An organized process that uses sales inputs to forecast business for upcoming periods of varying length.

More and more firms are realizing how important sales are to operational planning. Many have adopted a formal **sales and operational planning process**, or **S&OP**, an organized process that uses sales inputs to forecast business for upcoming periods of varying length. The S&OP then adjusts planning parameters (purchasing, labor schedules, capital requirements) based on the forecast.

Figure 5.1 illustrates how the S&OP works.[2] The sales team starts with data from various sales records, such as orders or shipment data, that help them develop the initial sales forecast. Managers from various functional areas—including marketing, sales, production, and finance—review the preliminary forecast and suggest any necessary adjustments. For example, a marketing manager may possess knowledge from a market research report that suggests some change from the previous period. The team then builds a sales plan around the resulting forecast. The plan includes operational parameters and potential trigger points for various contingencies. A **contingency** in this sense refers to events that are conceivable, but less likely than those based directly on the forecast. For example, a resort hotel may build in a plan to shift sales efforts away from vacationers and more toward business meetings if vacation bookings are not materializing as expected. This event may even be tied to a long-range seasonal weather forecast. In the end, operational actions and adjustments are driven by this plan.

Contingency
Events that are conceivable, but less likely than those based directly on the forecast.

Analyze sales records   Develop a preliminary forecast   Have managers review forecast and adjust   Build a sales plan around the forecast   Make adjustments to operating plans

FIGURE 5.1 Sales and Operational Planning Process

Manufacturing, marketing, procurement, customer service, and sales all improve with an effective S&OP.[3] Successful S&OP programs improve customer fill rates, customer retention, and gross margin. Here are five characteristics of successful S&OP programs:[4]

1. *People*—All managerial levels must support the S&OP process and the plans that result. Each department in the firm must also cooperate and respect the process.
2. *Process*—Regular meetings are an important part of developing a successful operational plan. The process also includes metrics to monitor progress and provide benchmarks.
3. *Technology*—Market intelligence and other key information is integrated into a decision support system that automates some decisions and provides reports

© Bill Bachmann / Photo Researchers, Inc.

● **Sales teams rely on accurate customer and project data to prepare their sales plans.**

that assist in planning. Companies must maintain sufficient technological sophistication to ensure an efficient S&OP process.

4. *Strategy*—Effective strategy goes beyond finance and should align supply and inventories with demand. The strategy should also make continuous improvement possible and integrate customer data to highlight exactly where the company can create value.

5. *Performance*—Firms don't know how well they're doing unless they measure outcomes. Managers should derive metrics from the firm's goals, monitor progress to assess the plan's effectiveness, and include feedback in subsequent S&OP processes.

S&OP can extend beyond the walls of the firm, since the task of integrating data systems and planning processes often needs to include suppliers and downstream customers too. Delta Air Lines (www.delta.com) invested over $1 billion in a "nervous system" that tied together multiple databases to help it forecast sales for given routes, labor demand, fuel purchases, and baggage-moving demands.[5]

■ Estimating Consumer Demand

Buying Power Index (BPI)
A weighted combination of population, income, and retail sales, expressed as a percentage of the national potential, to identify a given market's ability to buy.

Sales managers estimate consumer market potentials from basic economic data. *Sales & Marketing Management* (S&MM) magazine's **Buying Power Index (BPI)** uses a weighted combination of population, income, and retail sales, expressed as a percentage of the national potential, to identify a given market's ability to buy. Sales managers need not make any calculations themselves, because *S&MM* magazine's (www.salesandmarketing.com) annual "Survey of Buying Power" reports the BPIs by metropolitan area, county, and city. National sales managers can compare a BPI figure with their company's actual sales in that market (as a percentage of total company sales) to determine whether present sales results are adequate.

■ Estimating Industrial Demand

Standard Industrial Classification (SIC)
A uniform numbering system for categorizing nearly all industries according to their particular product or operation.

Two approaches show how firms estimate industrial demand. One relies on the government's **Standard Industrial Classification (SIC)**—a uniform numbering system for categorizing nearly all industries according to their particular product or operation. The second approach conducts surveys of buyer intentions, carried out by the sales force, the in-house marketing research staff, or an outside research agency.

Standardized Classification Systems. The most widely used approach to estimating industrial demand was traditionally based on information provided in *The Standard Industrial Classification Manual,* published by the U.S. Office of Management and Budget (OMB) every five years. The manual provides codes classifying all industries into several divisions, identifying industry and product subgroups with increasing specificity by up to seven digits. If sales managers could classify current and potential customers with a standardized classification system, they could more easily locate prospective new customers, determine market potentials, and improve the accuracy of their sales forecasts.[6]

NAICS (North American Industrial Classification System)
A system for categorizing firms, formally adopted beginning with the 2002 Economic Census and the publication of the *2002 U.S. NAICS Manual.*

More recently, the **North American Industrial Classification System (NAICS)** has replaced the original SIC. Canada, Mexico, and the United States worked together to create this system for categorizing firms, which was formally adopted beginning with the 2002 Economic Census and the publication of the *2002 U.S. NAICS Manual.* NAICS

TABLE 5.2 Sample NAICS Codes

INDUSTRY DESCRIPTION	NAICS CODE
Transportation	481
Scheduled Air Service	48111
Scheduled Freight Air Service	481112
Scheduled Passenger Air Service	481111
Wholesalers	424
Pharmaceutical Wholesalers	424210
Wine Wholesalers	424820
Technical or Scientific Services	541
Management Consulting Services	5416
Sales Management Consulting Services	541613

codes can be accessed online through the U.S. Census Bureau (www.census.gov)[7] and greatly facilitate statistical comparisons across industries. Table 5.2 illustrates how the NAICS uses a numerical system for identifying industries in an increasingly specific manner.

North American Product Classification System (NAPCS)
A system for categorizing consumer products and service industries.

The **North American Product Classification System (NAPCS)** is currently being developed with a focus on consumer products and service industries.[8] Once complete, the NAPCS is expected to work in much the same way as the NAICS.

Once you find the NAICS designation for a targeted industry, you can identify firms in that industry using sources like *Sales & Marketing Management's* annual survey of industrial purchasing power and various government publications, including the *U.S. Census of Manufacturers*, the *U.S. Survey of Manufacturers*, the *U.S. Industrial Outlook*, and *County Business Patterns.*

Purchase Intentions
The likelihood customers will actually purchase a given product.

Buyer Intentions. The second approach is more focused and surveys potential industrial customers, such as those identified via a NAICS classification, to measure their **purchase intentions**—the likelihood they will actually purchase a given product. A company can send questionnaires to prospective customers from selected NAICS codes to measure purchase intentions over a given forecast period. Response rates (whether responses come by "snail mail," e-mail, or other electronic transmission format) are usually sufficiently high to estimate market potential accurately. We discuss surveys of buyer intentions in more detail in the next section.

Forecasting Approaches and Techniques

Managers can develop forecasts with either the breakdown approach or the build-up approach. The **breakdown approach** starts with a forecast of general economic conditions, typically projected gross national product (GNP) in constant dollars, along

Breakdown Approach
A way of developing forecasts based on general economic conditions, typically projected gross national product (GNP) in constant dollars along with projections of consumer and wholesale price indexes, interest rates, unemployment levels, and federal government expenditures.

with projections of consumer and wholesale price indexes, interest rates, unemployment levels, and federal government expenditures. An industry forecast, company forecast, and product forecasts follow in succession. Here are the "top-down" steps in developing a sales forecast using the breakdown approach:

1. Forecast general economic conditions.
2. Estimate the industry's total market potential for a product category.
3. Determine the share of this market the company currently holds and is likely to retain in view of competitive efforts.
4. Forecast sales of the product.
5. Use the sales forecast for operational planning and budgeting.

A model of the breakdown approach is shown in Figure 5.2.

Build-Up Approach
A way of developing forecasts based on *primary research,* new data collected for the specific purpose at hand.

The **build-up approach** is based on *primary research,* which is new data collected for the specific purpose at hand—in this case, a specific forecast for a specific company. The research either surveys individual salespeople about what they expect to sell in a future time period, or surveys customers about their purchase intentions. Managers then sum the individual estimates to provide a sales forecast.

Industrial buyers are generally cooperative, and a survey response rate of 50 percent or higher can be achieved. Consumers are usually less cooperative and a response rate of even 33 percent would be good. When a representative random sample is

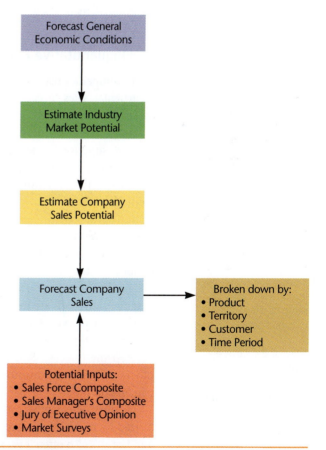

Factors to consider:
• Economic influences
• Demographic changes
• Social changes
• Competitive developments
• Legal developments
• Political developments
• Internal company factors

Forecast General Economic Conditions

Estimate Industry Market Potential

Estimate Company Sales Potential

Forecast Company Sales

Broken down by:
• Product
• Territory
• Customer
• Time Period

Potential Inputs:
• Sales Force Composite
• Sales Manager's Composite
• Jury of Executive Opinion
• Market Surveys

FIGURE 5.2 Sales Forecasting Model

Nonquantitative

✧ **Judgment methods**
- Jury of executive opinion
- Sales force composite

✧ **Counting methods**
- Survey of customers' buying intentions
- Test marketing

Quantitative

✧ **Time-series methods**
- Moving averages
- Exponential smoothing
- Trend analysis using ARIMA

✧ **Causal or association methods**
- Correlation-regression
- Econometric models
- Input-output models

FIGURE 5.3 Classification of Sales Forecasting Approaches

impossible or impractical, firms rely on nonprobability sampling techniques. The response rate with these is usually sufficiently high to develop a good estimate of the potential market. When using nonprobability samples, however, firms need to closely examine profiles of respondents to assess their representativeness.

Since there is no consensus on which approach is better, some companies prefer to use both the breakdown and the buildup-up approach to increase their confidence in the sales forecast. In general, the breakdown approach is less expensive because aggregate, publicly distributed forecasts from secondary sources provide the basis for decision making. Secondary sources such as university repositories, policy agencies, and the federal government make many forecasts available to the public, often free of charge and sometimes through the Internet. The breakdown approach is particularly useful and reliable when forecasting for periods of six months or longer. The build-up approach becomes more attractive as the time frame gets shorter. Primary data collection can be tailored specifically for the company, and for the particular time frame of interest.

We classify the more common sales forecasting techniques as either quantitative or nonquantitative, as shown in Figure 5.3. The nonquantitative methods rely primarily on judgment or opinion, whereas the quantitative methods use statistical techniques with varying degrees of complexity.

■ Nonquantitative Forecasting Techniques

Nonquantitative Forecasting Techniques
Subjective forecasts based on knowledgeable people's opinions instead of being analytically derived.

Many companies use several methods to compare sales projections before settling on a particular sales forecast. **Nonquantitative forecasting techniques** are often called *subjective forecasts,* because they're based on knowledgeable people's opinions instead of being analytically derived. Results range from very good to poor, but in some cases they are superior to expensive, sophisticated, quantitative techniques. Nonquantitative forecasts are popular and can be a practical alternative to quantitative approaches. Two major types of nonquantitative forecasts are judgment methods and counting methods.

Naïve Forecast
The simplest judgment method, which assumes, naively, that the next period's sales will be the same as they were in the previous period.

Judgment Methods. The simplest judgment method is the **naïve forecast**. It assumes, naively, that the next period's sales will be the same as they were in the previous period, and that an extrapolation of the last period's sales will give an acceptable estimate of the next period's sales. This method provides some initial insights, but other judgment methods are more accurate.

Jury of Executive Opinion
Sales forecast method based on key managers' best estimates of sales in a given planning horizon.

The **jury of executive opinion** method asks key managers within the company for their best estimate of sales in a given planning horizon and combines the results to develop the forecast. Some managers may support their opinions with facts, while others may rely on intuition alone. The consensus is generally better than any single person's opinion.

The jury of executive opinion can be done quickly and easily. In industries characterized by rapid changes, it may be the best forecasting approach because it's flexible and fast. It's also often less expensive than other methods.

But the executive opinion method has several disadvantages. Since it's based on opinions and not facts, it can be unscientific and little better than a guess. Second, the technique diverts top managers from other tasks that may be more important, and often they are not in touch with developments in local markets anyway. For example, could we expect the CIO or CFO to know about future sales in a particular market? Despite these disadvantages, smaller companies most often use the jury of executive opinion method.

The **sales force composite** method is similar, but it asks the *sales force* for their best estimates of sales in the planning horizon. Managers evaluate and adjust each salesperson's estimate before combining them to form an overall forecast. Here are the advantages of this approach:

Sales Force Composite
Sales forecast method based on sales force estimates of sales in the planning horizon.

- Assigns forecasting responsibility to those held responsible for making the sales
- Uses specialized knowledge of salespeople in the field
- Helps salespeople accept sales quotas assigned to them because they participate in developing forecasts
- Yields results that are often more reliable and accurate because a larger number of knowledgeable individuals contribute to them
- Allows estimates to be prepared by products, customers, and territories so a final, detailed forecast is readily available

Here are the disadvantages of the sales force composite method:

- Relies on input from salespeople who are not trained in forecasting, so forecasts are often too optimistic or too pessimistic
- Allows salespeople to deliberately underestimate their forecast so they can reach their quotas more easily
- Yields forecasts based on present rather than future conditions, because salespeople often lack the perspective for future planning
- Requires a considerable amount of sales force time that otherwise could be spent in the field attracting new customers
- Relies on salespeople who may not be interested in forecasting and so put little effort into their sales predictions

Counting Methods. Forecasting approaches that tabulate responses to questions on surveys or count the numbers of buyers or purchases are called **counting methods.** Two types of counting methods are surveys of customer buying intentions and test marketing.

Counting Methods
Forecasting approaches that tabulate responses to questions on surveys or count the numbers of buyers or purchases.

Surveys of Buying Intentions
Surveys that ask customers about their intentions to buy various products over a specified period.

Surveys of buying intentions sample customers and ask about their intentions to buy various products over a specified period. Managers then combine the responses into one forecast, generally by products, customers, and territories. This method of forecasting is particularly useful for companies selling industrial products, because their customers are easily identified and few in number, able to estimate their purchasing requirements well in advance of ordering, and highly likely to follow through on buying intentions. Here are some advantages of using surveys of buying intentions:

- The actual product users determine the forecasts.
- Forecasts are relatively fast and inexpensive when only a small number of customers are surveyed.
- Research gives the sales forecaster a good prediction of customers' buying intentions and some of the subjective reasoning behind their answers.

■ Research gives the forecaster a viable forecasting basis when others may be inadequate or impossible to use, such as when there is no historical data.

Here are some disadvantages:

■ Surveys can be expensive and time-consuming in markets with a large number of customers who are not easily located.

■ Buyer intentions can be inaccurate, since what people say they're going to buy and what they actually buy can differ.

■ Forecasts depend on the judgment and cooperation of the product users, some of whom may be uncooperative or uninformed.

■ Buying intentions, especially for industrial products, often are subject to multiple effects because the demand for industrial products is derived from the demand for consumer products.

Test Marketing
A popular counting forecasting method for consumer packaged goods products.

Estimating sales for a new product is the most difficult type of forecast since no historical sales data is available. It is particularly difficult when the product is very different from the company's current product mix. A popular forecasting method for consumer packaged goods products is a counting method called **test marketing**. This is similar to a full dress rehearsal in a limited market area, to obtain consumer reactions before expanding to the regional and national markets. By carefully selecting a few representative market areas, marketing managers can observe the impact on sales of various combinations of the marketing mix and use measures of market share in these small markets to forecast the total market. For example, if Nokia (www.nokia.com) achieves a 10 percent market share in the test markets for a new mobile phone, it will assume it can achieve approximately this share in the expanded market. In fact, Nokia recently joined with Coca-Cola to test a new mobile marketing solution that

© David Young-Wolff / PhotoEdit

● **It takes the combined knowledge of managers and the sales force to develop accurate sales forecasts.**

brings services to customers' smart phones via Bluetooth.[9] The objective was to assess mobile phone users' interest in downloadable wallpapers, mobile coupons, video clips, and other mobile content.

Some managers argue that test marketing takes too long (often a year or more), costs too much, and reveals too much to competitors, who often monitor the test markets and may even attempt to disrupt the test or distort results. To minimize this likelihood, some companies use laboratory testing of products instead of field tests. Laboratory methods ask a panel of customers to evaluate different marketing mix combinations and choose a particular product. Laboratory tests provide more privacy, lower costs, and quicker answers than traditional test marketing does, particularly when the tests can be carried out over the Internet.

■ Quantitative Forecasting Techniques

User-friendly statistical software enables sales managers to develop forecasts that only trained statisticians used to do, and to "crunch the numbers" with numerous quantitative sales forecasting techniques. Two broad categories of methods are time-series analyses and causal or association methods.

Time-Series Technique
Use of historical data to predict future sales.

Time-Series Methods. **Time-series techniques** use historical data to predict future sales. We'll discuss three types: moving averages, exponential smoothing, and ARIMA.

When using time-series methods, forecasters look for four factors:

1. *Trends*—Upward or downward movements in a time series as a result of basic developments in population, technology, or capital formation.
2. *Periodic movements*—Consistent patterns of sales changes in a given period, such as a year, generally called *seasonal variations*. Snow skis and boats are examples of products that have seasonal patterns.
3. *Cyclical movements*—Wave-like movements of sales that are longer in duration than a year and often irregular in occurrence, such as business recessions. The housing market is characterized by cyclical fluctuations.
4. *Erratic movements*—One-time specific events—such as wars, strikes, snowstorms, hurricanes, fires, and floods—that are not predictable.

All these factors can affect sales forecasts. Time-series methods attempt to separate their impact from random variations and identify true trends in data.

Moving Average
Forecasts developed mathematically based on sales in recent time periods.

Moving Averages. Forecasts developed using a **moving average** predict future sales as a mathematical function of sales in recent time periods. The statistical approach is based on an average of several months' sales, where the high and low values are made less extreme. As the forecasters add each new period's sales data to the average, they remove from the total the data from the oldest period. They compute a new average for each period, and the new average is the moving average. Consider a sales manager trying to project sales for the year 2009. Data is available showing the total sales obtained in each year from 1995 through 2008. One method of forecasting is to predict that sales in 2009 will be the same as sales in 2008. Alternatively, the sales manager could base the forecast on one of the other years' results or take an average of all the data. The moving average provides a compromise between these approaches by assuming the information from the most recent years' sales performance is more likely to reflect the current situation than data from many years ago.

| | | | THREE-YEAR | FIVE-YEAR |
YEAR	ACTUAL SALES	SIMPLE AVERAGE	MOVING AVERAGE	MOVING AVERAGE
1995	1500			
1996	750			
1997	1250			
1998	800			
1999	1750			
2000	900			
2001	1400	**1158**	**1150**	**1090**
2002	750			
2003	900			
2004	1000			
2005	500			
2006	650			
2007	1150			
2008	850			
2009	1200	**1023**	**883**	**830**

TABLE 5.3   Time-Series Forecasts Using Several Average Methods

Table 5.3 illustrates predictions made using the moving average and several other methods. The data is from years 1995 through 2009. The forecasted sales are for years 2001 and 2009. The "Simple Average" column simply takes the mean of the previous years' sales. So, the prediction for 2001 is based on data from 1995 to 2000. The prediction for 2009 is based on data from 1995 to 2008. The three-year moving averages use the average of only the most recent three years. So, the 2009 forecast is based only on sales data from 2008, 2007, and 2006. Similarly, the five-year moving average is based on an average from 2004 through 2008.

Notice that in this particular example, the forecasts are not equally accurate. Sales for this company seem particularly volatile. When this is the case, an average containing more data, rather than less, is likely to be more accurate. Thus, the overall average proves most accurate in this case. However, for firms experiencing growth or a decline in sales, the moving averages will generally be more accurate. For instance, three-month moving averages are generally used to predict semiconductor sales in a given month.[10]

Exponential Smoothing.   Like the moving average, exponential smoothing is useful in spotting trends. **Exponential smoothing** is in fact a type of moving average that represents the weighted sum of all past numbers in a time series, with the heaviest weight placed on the most recent data. Exponential smoothing modifies the moving-average method by systematically stressing recent sales results while de-emphasizing old sales data. Exponential smoothing overcomes a significant disadvantage of the moving average. That is, the moving average is *not* more responsive to the most recent sales trends. The forecasting equation then would contain a larger number to weight the

Exponential Smoothing
A type of moving average that represents the weighted sum of all past numbers in a time series, placing the heaviest weight on the most recent data.

more recent data points. Thus for example, if we use a three-year weighted average, we can compute the forecast (FC) for 2009 as follows:

$$FC = \frac{1}{6}(Sales_{2006}) + \frac{1}{3}(Sales_{2007}) + \frac{1}{2}(Sales_{2008})$$

Notice that the most recent year (2008) is weighted with the largest of the three numbers (1/2). The most distant data year, 2006, has the smallest weight (1/6).

Using data from Table 5.3, this yields a prediction of 916 units for 2009, which we compute as follows:

$$FC = \frac{1}{6}(Sales_{2006}) + \frac{1}{3}(Sales_{2007}) + \frac{1}{2}(Sales_{2008}) = \frac{1}{6}(650) + \frac{1}{3}(1150) + \frac{1}{2}(850)$$
$$= 916 \text{ units}$$

Sophisticated algorithms exist to help determine the weighting scheme that is most accurate in a given situation.[11] Exponential smoothing is particularly appropriate in industries experiencing high growth and can also reflect seasonality in short period forecasts. Exponential smoothing, like moving averages, is being used by more sales managers because many easy-to-use point-and-click options are available in standard software packages. With these, sales managers need not even enter a formula—they simply select the years to be included, and the software does the rest.

Other Trend Analyses. Managers can use many other statistical approaches to prepare forecasts using trends over time. Simple regression predicts sales for a period using time as an independent variable. An **ARIMA** (autoregressive integrated moving average) model is a sophisticated forecasting approach based on the moving average concept. The model incorporates information about trends by spotting patterns in the fluctuations in data. The exact process for conducting an ARIMA forecast is beyond the scope of this text. However, ARIMA models have been useful in predicting many types of sales, including the demand for tourism to China.[12]

Causal/Association Methods. Instead of predicting directly on the basis of judgment or historical data, **causal/association methods** attempt to identify the factors affecting sales and to determine the nature of the relationship between them. Causal or associative methods include correlation-regression analysis, econometric models, and input-output models.

Correlation analysis is a statistical approach analyzing the way variables are related to one another or *move together* in some way. A **correlation coefficient** is a measure of how much two variables are related to one another. Correlations do not imply cause and effect. **Regression analysis**, which you may be familiar with, is a statistical approach to predicting a dependent variable such as sales, using one or more independent variables such as advertising expenditures. It can examine, for example, whether a change in sales is associated with a change in advertising expenditures. Managers often use scatter diagrams with correlation and regression analyses. A **scatter diagram** plots one variable against another to see whether there is a relationship. The variable used to make the prediction is the independent or X variable, displayed along the horizontal axis of the graph. The variable being predicted is the dependent or Y variable on the vertical axis. Figure 5.4 shows a typical scatter diagram. Notice how the plotted points tend to line up. This alignment indicates the two variables are related.

ARIMA (Autoregressive Integrated Moving Average)
A sophisticated forecasting approach based on the moving average concept.

Causal/Association Methods
Methods that attempt to identify the factors affecting sales and determine the nature of the relationship between them.

Correlation Analysis
A statistical approach analyzing the way variables are related to one another or *move together* in some way.

Correlation Coefficient
A measure of how much two variables are related to one another.

Regression Analysis
A statistical approach to predicting a dependent variable such as sales, using one or more independent variables such as advertising expenditures.

Scatter Diagram
Graph that plots one variable against another to see whether there is a relationship.

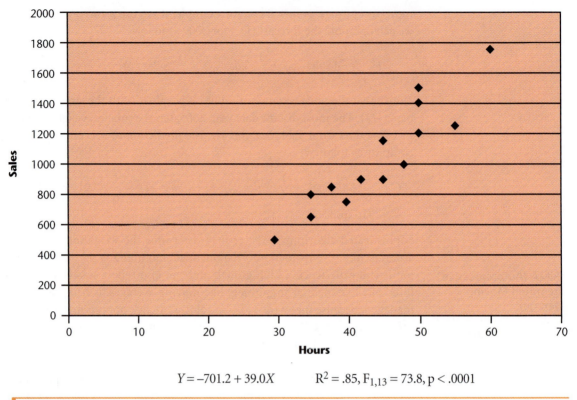

$$Y = -701.2 + 39.0X \qquad R^2 = .85, F_{1,13} = 73.8, p < .0001$$

FIGURE 5.4 A Scatter Plot of Sales Against Labor Expenditures

Simple Regression. The relationship between two variables is shown by fitting a straight line to plotted points. We can use visual inspection to draw the line with a ruler, but this may not be the most reliable approach, since different people may put the line in different places. Simple regression finds the best-fitting line mathematically using the least squares estimation formula for a straight line, $Y = a + bX$, where a is the *intercept* (intersecting with the vertical axis) and b is the *slope* or trend of the line. The least squares method estimates coefficients (a, b) by mathematically minimizing the squared differences between actual plotted sales and the values predicted by the regression line.

Trend Analysis
A quantitative forecast whereby the dependent variable is sales, and the independent variable is time.

A **trend analysis** can provide a quantitative forecast. In a trend analysis forecasting sales, the dependent variable is sales, and the independent variable is time. If such a model produced an estimated regression equation of $Y = 33.5 + 10.5X$, we could predict sales for any year by inserting the desired time period for X. We derive Year 5 sales, for example, by multiplying 5 by the trend (slope) of 10.5 and adding the constant term (intercept) of 33.5. The result is a forecast of 86.

Multiple Regression. Regression can also use something other than time to produce a forecast. In Table 5.3, sales are forecasted with labor hours. If a salesperson works 50 hours, the regression model predicts $1,249 in sales. The model explains a significant portion of sales, as evidenced by the small significance value ($p < .0001$), meaning that labor hours explains a significant portion of variance in sales. Another way of looking at this is that, by knowing labor hours, we can predict sales with some accuracy.

Simple regression describes the relationship between a single independent variable and a single dependent variable. In our example, *time* is the independent variable and *sales* is the dependent variable. More realistically, sales are probably associated with several independent variables (advertising expenditures, number of sales calls, prices, or interest rates). **Multiple regression** is a tool for forecasting a dependent variable like sales using several independent variables simultaneously. Software programs like Excel (www.microsoft.com) and SPSS (www.spss.com) simplify forecasting by performing the mathematical calculations needed to estimate a multiple regression model. The results show the strength of relationships between the independent variables and the dependent variables. We can make forecasts using multiple regression for any given values of the independent variables.

EMCO sells mobile telecommunications equipment and has fifteen years of data in its data warehouse. The single dependent variable is sales, and three independent variables are advertising, price, and number of salespeople. The output from the SPSS multiple regression appears in Figure 5.5. Like simple regression, SPSS produces coefficient estimates that represent the relationship between each independent variable and the dependent variable, annual sales. Using the constant term (*Y* intercept) of

Multiple Regression
A tool for forecasting a dependent variable like sales using several independent variables simultaneously.

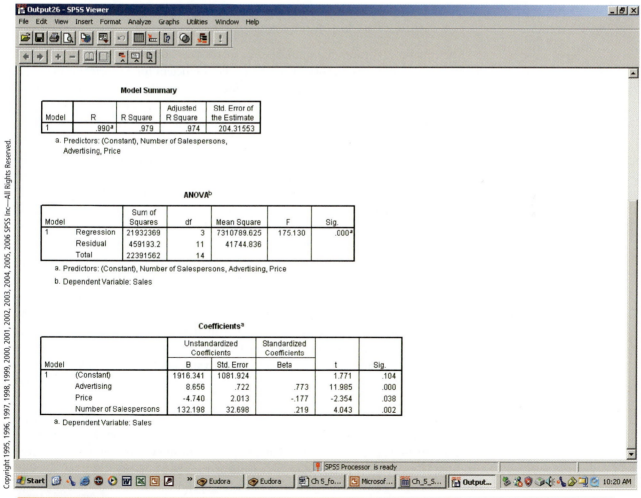

Model Summary

Model	R	R Square	Adjusted R Square	Std. Error of the Estimate
1	.990[a]	.979	.974	204.31553

a. Predictors: (Constant), Number of Salespersons, Advertising, Price

ANOVA[b]

Model		Sum of Squares	df	Mean Square	F	Sig.
1	Regression	21932369	3	7310789.625	175.130	.000[a]
	Residual	459193.2	11	41744.836		
	Total	22391562	14			

a. Predictors: (Constant), Number of Salespersons, Advertising, Price

b. Dependent Variable: Sales

Coefficients[a]

Model		Unstandardized Coefficients B	Std. Error	Standardized Coefficients Beta	t	Sig.
1	(Constant)	1916.341	1081.924		1.771	.104
	Advertising	8.656	.722	.773	11.985	.000
	Price	-4.740	2.013	-.177	-2.354	.038
	Number of Salespersons	132.198	32.698	.219	4.043	.002

a. Dependent Variable: Sales

FIGURE 5.5 Example Multiple Regression Results

1916.341 and the unstandardized coefficients (weightings) for the three variables = 8.656, −4.740 and 132.198, we derive this forecasting equation:

$$Y = 1916.341 + 8.656\,X_1 + -4.740\,X_2 + 132.198\,X_3$$

where

Y = annual sales
X_1 = advertising expenditures
X_2 = price
X_3 = number of salespersons

We can generate a forecast for any values of the independent variables. Suppose the independent variables take on the following values:

- X_1 − 10 ($100,000 in advertising)

- X_2 = $100

- X_3 = 5 salespeople

Then, substituting these values into the regression equation yields the following result:

$$Y = 1916.3 + 8.656\,(10) - 4.740\,(100) + 132.20\,(5)$$
$$Y = 1916.3 + 86.56 - 474.0 + 661 = 2189.9$$

The equation indicates that annual sales increase as advertising expenditures and number of salespersons increase. The sign of the coefficient for X_2 (price) is negative, which indicates that as we lower price, sales increase. A *multiple R* of 0.990 is a correlation coefficient reflecting the degree of association between the dependent variable and the three independent variables. The *multiple R-square,* also called the coefficient of determination, indicates the percentage (97.9 percent) of total variation in Y (sales) explained by the three independent variables (X_1, advertising; X_2, price; and X_3, number of salespersons).

The *standard error of the estimate* is a measure of the accuracy of the prediction. That is, it's the range of error around the sales forecast. The standard error 204.316 means there is a 68 percent chance (one standard deviation) that actual dollar sales will be within ±$204,316 of any forecast made with our derived equation. A model F statistic also demonstrates that a significant (significance level is less than .000) portion of the variance in sales is explained by the independent variables.

We can analyze forecasting quality by computing standard errors for the coefficients for our three independent variables. These error coefficients show the expected dispersion (or scatter) around the coefficient estimates. *F-values* indicate that all three independent variables are highly significant in forecasting sales. Thus, advertising expenditures and number of salespersons are key variables in understanding and predicting sales from period to period. Similarly, price is important too; and as we expected, lower prices are associated with higher sales.

When using multiple regression for forecasting purposes, the model R^2 is an important diagnostic tool for estimating the accuracy of prediction. R^2 values range from 0 to 1. A value of one means that 100 percent of the variance in the dependent variable is explained by the set of independent variables—in this case, the forecast would be exact. Conversely, if the R^2 is 0, the independent variables do not enable us to predict with any accuracy. In other words, we may as well use a wild guess. In practice, R^2 values below .2 suggest poor forecasting ability. Values between .2 and .5 indicate modest predictive power, values above .5 to .75 indicate good predictive power, and values above .75 indicate excellent predictive power. Thus, the equation in our example shows very high predictive power.

Econometric Models
Models developed to trace economic conditions in the United States by industry, with the objective of capturing, in the form of equations, complex interrelationships among the factors affecting either the total economy or the industry's or company's sales.

Econometric Models. **Econometric models** are based on a series of regression equations. The number of equations can range from 1 to 1,000 or more. These models have been developed to trace economic conditions in the United States by industry, and their objective is to capture, in the form of equations, complex interrelationships among the factors affecting either the total economy or the industry's or company's sales. For example, consumer spending is related to disposable income and interest rates, while fixed capital spending is explained by the past value of capital, interest rates, and economic activity. Another purpose of such models is to predict the future. Large corporations like General Motors, General Electric, and IBM develop their own econometric models. Econometric models can be very expensive to develop. Therefore, the simpler regression approaches offer a less expensive alternative for firms with fewer resources.

Input-Output Models
Complex systems showing the amount of input required from each industry for a specified output of another industry.

Input-Output Models. **Input-output models** are complex systems showing the amount of input required from each industry for a specified output of another industry. This type of model is expensive and tedious to develop, but it generally provides good intermediate and long-range forecasts for industries such as metals, energy utilities, and automobiles. Due to the difficulty of building large input-output models, this type of forecasting typically is outsourced to specialized experts.

SALES MANAGEMENT IN ACTION

How Many Drugs Can We Sell?

New product development is very important in the pharmaceutical industry. Not only does new product development ensure the health of the firm, but the quality of life and even the survival of many consumers depend on continued advancement in pharmaceutical products. For a host of reasons, however, accurate sales forecasts for any given drug, in particular a new drug, are complicated by many uncertainties. Not the least of these is that an entirely separate forecasting process is likely needed to predict the timing of release of the new drug. Even once the product has been refined, FDA approval can take years. In addition, new therapeutic treatments may make the drug obsolete. Competition from generic drug companies also affects sales, making up a dynamic but growing market that has grown about 20 percent a year in recent years.

Managers in the pharmaceutical industry are constantly trying to improve their sales forecasts. Multiple regression enables them to consider infor-mation about the lifestyles of market segments, aspects of the approval process, and even information about competing companies, among other things. In addition, Internet technology allows firms to harvest, from the "information market," information that they might not otherwise have found. Eli Lilly is using such processes to forecast which developmental products are most likely to win FDA approval. Information may also include insights into potential consumer reactions. In either event, pharmaceutical forecasts that take into account more information than simple trends are likely to lead to greater accuracy.

SOURCE: Derived from information in Steven Ostrover, "Employing Information Markets to Achieve Truly Collaborative Sales Forecasting," *Journal of Business Forecasting* (spring 2005): 9–12; IMS Health, "5.4% Dollar Growth in 2005 U.S. Prescription Sales," *Medical Benefits*, February 22, 2006, p. 9, and Anti-Aging Products—Market Research, Market Share, Market Size, Sales, Demand Forecast, Market Leaders, Company Profiles, Industry Trends, June 2005, p. 323, http://www.freedoniagroup.com/Anti-aging-Products.html.

Evaluating Forecasting Approaches

Quantitative sales forecasting techniques use a variety of sophisticated mathematics and statistics. Some of the techniques are expensive, time-consuming, and require considerable forecaster expertise. In fact, using a complex forecasting technique is no promise of predictive accuracy. Some companies with limited historical data or in rapidly changing markets use less-sophisticated techniques.

Nonquantitative techniques have been criticized for their lack of consistency. But with the more widespread availability of user-friendly software and historical data, their use is increasing. In selecting a forecasting method, sales managers should consider several criteria:

■ *Comprehensibility*—Sales managers must understand the basic methods of developing forecasts. This understanding provides confidence in the estimates of different approaches. It's harder to be confident when using highly complicated quantitative techniques. If only statisticians can understand the way the estimates are derived, sales executives and other decision makers will not trust the results as much as they would a process they at least partially understand.

■ *Accuracy*—A forecasting method must provide results that are sufficiently accurate for the purpose desired. Most forecasts contain inaccuracies but still furnish valuable information for managerial decision making. A projection within 10 percent accuracy is considered acceptable by many sales forecasters. In fact, S&OP programs generally are based on an outcome forecasted under pessimistic conditions and one under optimistic conditions. Thus a forecast is actually a range of values instead of one number.[13]

■ *Timeliness*—The forecasting method must generate forecasts in time for managers to use them. Complex quantitative techniques or surveys can require weeks to deliver a forecast. Thus, sales managers who need answers quickly may resort to faster but potentially less accurate estimates.

■ *Quality and quantity of information*—Any forecasting method is limited by the amount and quality of information available to the organization. In forecasting as in other areas, "garbage" input leads to "garbage" output (GIGO).

■ *Qualified personnel*—Experts can give opinions on qualitative techniques like the jury of executives' opinions or the Delphi method. The Delphi method polls a small panel of experts concerning future events. Unlike the jury of executive opinion, these experts are generally from outside the firm and often from closely related industries. Once the company has collected the experts' opinions, an analyst summarizes the results in a report. Thus, companies like Blackberry, Motorola, and Samsung might use the Delphi technique to estimate the effect of the Apple iPhone (introduced from the iTunes platform in 2007) on the demand for their own products. The specialists in this case might be top executives at media, entertainment, and telecommunications companies. But other trained specialists may be needed for some advanced quantitative forecasting approaches. Sales managers hiring people to consult on the sales forecast must be sure that consultants are fully qualified for the job.

■ *Flexibility*—Managers continually monitor actual sales for any deviations from forecast that may indicate the need for revised sales forecasting tools. Their sales forecasting methods should be flexible enough to adapt to changing conditions.

■ *Costs/Benefits*—The benefits from forecasting must more than offset the costs of generating the sales forecast. And if the cost of an incorrect forecast is high, then sales managers should spare little expense in deriving an accurate forecast.

Once again, forecasters should use more than one method so they can compare the results of several techniques. Finally, it's good to examine several "what-if" scenarios that incorporate all the bad assumptions as well as all the good ones.

When the sales manager has an acceptable sales forecast, the next area of concern is to obtain sufficient funds (i.e., a budget) to execute the sales strategy. Our next discussion topic, therefore, is sales budget planning.

Sales Budget Planning

Sales Budget
A financial sales plan outlining how to allocate resources and selling efforts to achieve the sales forecast.

Sales managers must decide either what level of sales they can obtain with a given budget, or what level of expenditures they will need to reach forecasted sales. A **sales budget** is a financial sales plan outlining how to allocate resources and selling efforts to achieve the sales forecast. Sales forecasts and sales budgets are interdependent planning tools that require close coordination with other marketing activities. If a sales budget is inadequate, the sales forecast will be accurate only by pure chance. As the importance of a forecast increases, so must the sales budget.

Sales budgets are used in planning, coordinating, and controlling selling activities. Sales managers should appreciate the significance and value of sales budgets in the overall planning and administration of a sales territory.

■ The Planning Function

Budgeting
An operational planning process expressed in financial terms.

Sales managers must translate department goals and objectives into actionable tasks. Each task is associated with an estimated cost. **Budgeting**, therefore, is an operational planning process expressed in financial terms. The budget provides a guide for action toward achieving the organization's objectives.

Budgets exist for different planning horizons. A long-range budget may require a forecast for five years or more. Typically, a one-year operational budget includes a forecast for the upcoming twelve months. Short-range budgets may cover periods of six months or less. A quarterly budget is commonly required. Thus, firms should have both long-range and short-range budgets.

For a smooth transition from one period to another, some sales budgets overlap— that is, a twelve-month budget might include a three-month overlap period at the beginning and end of the year so the actual budget plan covers eighteen months. Other sales organizations operate on a continuous budget by projecting a month or a quarter ahead as each month or quarter ends. This procedure forces sales managers to continuously revise and update the budget in response to external and internal opportunities and problems.

■ The Coordinating Function

Sales budgets must be closely integrated with budgets for other marketing functions. Personal selling is only one element in the promotional mix, and promotion is only one element in the marketing mix. We can't develop distribution plans, for example, until we know the amount of products that must be distributed. This number

TABLE 5.4 Budget Variances				
	VARIANCES			
	Budget	Actual	Favorable	Unfavorable
Sales Expenses	$715,000	$733,000	$18,000	
■ Direct Selling	384,000	375,900	8,000	
■ Sales Promotion	107,250	117,328		$10,078
■ Advertising	87,000	93,281		6,281
■ Administrative	44,500	43,617	883	
Total Expenses	$622,750	$630,126		7,376
Profits (before taxes)	$ 92,250	$102,874	$10,624	

depends on the sales forecast, which is part of the budget. The sales budget should reflect a well-thought-out allocation of resources and efforts designed to meet goals and objectives.

■ The Controlling Function

Budget Variances
Differences between actual results and sales budget expectations.

The control function of a sales budget is to evaluate actual results against sales budget expectations. Differences between them are **budget variances**. Favorable variances reflect a positive budget outcome, such as lower actual costs than were anticipated to produce a forecasted amount of sales. In this case, the sales manager might reduce future budgets in an effort to maintain accuracy. Unfavorable variances result from actual costs that are higher than anticipated costs and require corrective action. If the firm cannot avoid the higher costs in future periods, a budget adjustment is needed.

An illustration of budget variances is shown in Table 5.4. You can see that unfavorable variances are easy to identify. Sales managers are responsible for determining why actual promotional and advertising expenses exceeded budgeted amounts. This doesn't mean managers should always avoid unfavorable expense variances. For example, actual sales may also be higher in the same period that expenses are higher than expected. Notice in the table that sales are $18,000 more than budgeted or forecast. Thus, as long as expenses are proportionately higher or less, the higher expenses are likely justified. Using the budget variances approach enables a sales manager to more quickly spot potential problems or to better plan for unexpected developments like higher-than-expected sales.

Preparing the Annual Sales Budget

Preparing the annual sales budget is often considered one of the most tedious and unrewarding jobs the sales manager does. Yet managers should view the sales budget instead as an opportunity for profit planning, and for obtaining the resources needed to achieve projected sales. Budgets benefit the sales department in the following ways:

- Ensure a systematic approach to allocation resources.
- Develop the sales manager's knowledge of profitable resource utilization.

- Create awareness of the necessity of coordinating selling efforts with other divisions of the company.
- Establish standards for measuring the performance of the sales organization.
- Obtain input from all areas of the company in the profit-planning process.

Most sales organizations have specified procedures and timetables for developing the sales budget. The following sections describe a typical set of steps.

■ Step 1: Review and Analyze the Situation

Beginning with the last budget period's variances, *where, when,* and *how much* were the deviations from planned performance, and *who* was responsible? Review of past budget performance helps the sales manager avoid variances in the coming period. Changes in the current budget period, such as introduction of new products, marketing mix adjustments, or developments in the uncontrollable marketing environment, must be anticipated and worked into the sales budget. Here are some common line items in sales budgets:

- *Salaries*—for salespeople, administrative support, sales supervisors, and managers
- *Direct selling expenses*—travel, lodging, food, and entertainment
- *Commissions and bonuses*
- *Benefit package*—social security, medical insurance, retirement contributions, and stock options
- *Office expenses*—mailing, telephone, office supplies, miscellaneous
- *Promotional materials*—selling aids, premiums, contest awards, product samples, catalogs, price lists, and so on
- *Advertising*

SALES MANAGEMENT IN ACTION

Big Predictions

Not all forecasts are directed specifically toward some company's sales. *Sales & Marketing Management* magazine each year makes predictions about the sales and marketing industry. Here's a sample of what *Sales & Marketing Management* has predicted in recent years:

- National and regional TV advertisers will shift emphasis away from traditional broadcast television to cable television and Internet advertising. This trend depends in part on the capability of the sales force for these promotional channels.

- Durable goods will increasingly be sold directly out of the back of trailers. This will result because of shortages in warehouse space and the lessened likelihood of damage.

- New product development will increasingly be a team effort between traditional new product developers (engineers) and salespeople—since they are most in contact with customers.

How accurate are these "forecasts?"

SOURCES: http://www.ibm.com (accessed November 2006); "S&MM Predictions," *Sales & Marketing Management,* May 2006, p. 158; Mike Thacker, "Why They Are Wrong, Why Does That Matter?" *Logistics and Transportation Focus,* November 2001, pp. 24–29.

▪ Step 2: Communicate Sales Goals and Objectives

All management levels must be fully informed about sales goals and objectives, including their relative priorities, to ensure everyone is developing their budgets using the same assumptions and general guidelines. Encourage participation of all supervisors and managers in the budget process so that, having been a part of its development, they will accept responsibility for the budget and enthusiastically implement it.

▪ Step 3: Identify Specific Market Opportunities and Problems

Sales managers and salespeople should use budget resources to pursue specific market opportunities. Budgets also should be allocated to dealing with problems in a timely manner.

▪ Step 4: Develop a Preliminary Allocation of Resources

Initially, assign resources to particular activities, customers, products, and territories. Later, you can make revisions in the initial sales budget. But make all budgets as realistic as possible at each development stage to maximize their favorable impact on the organization. When you accomplish budget goals through a cooperative team effort, you create a feeling of organizational confidence. Instead of emphasizing punishment for failure to stay within budgets, sales managers should stress rewards and public commendations for staying within budgets, thereby encouraging positive attitudes toward budget goals and pride in their achievement.

▪ Step 5: Prepare a Budget Presentation

All organizational divisions clamor for an increased allocation of funds. Unless sales managers can justify each line item in their budgets on the basis of its profit contribution, the item will be ripe for higher management to cut. Succinct, well-reasoned written and oral budget presentations are worth the preparation they require. They're even more effective when supported by alternate budget scenarios that are easy to develop with spreadsheet software.

▪ Step 6: Implement the Budget and Provide Periodic Feedback

Although salespeople can be trained to be more budget conscious and provide early warning of budget overruns, the sales manager must ensure that sales revenue and cost ratios remain within reasonable budget limits. Sales managers might consider a monthly or quarterly sales budget and control chart (illustrated in Table 5.5) to monitor budget variances and make timely corrective actions. They can post this on the company website or automatically distribute it via the company intranet.

Budget preparation is easier and more systematic today because many software packages are available to facilitate the process. For example, the IBM sales and support environment solution integrates existing customer and research information across the firm, so it's available in real time for budgeting as well as for other selling objectives.[14] SAP (www.sap.com) also offers an integrated sales budgeting option in its enterprise software platform. These two alternatives are more complex, but you can find many options that are available off the shelf by using a search engine and entering the keywords "sales budget software."

TABLE 5.5 Monthly Sales Budget

	JANUARY			FEBRUARY		
Line Items	Budget	Actual	Variance	Budget	Actual	Variance
Sales Expenses						
■ Salaries						
■ Commissions						
■ Bonuses						
■ Social Security						
■ Medical Insurance						
■ Retirement						
Travel						
■ Food						
■ Lodging						
■ Entertainment						
Office Expenses						
■ Mail						
■ Telephone						
■ Miscellaneous						
Promotion						
■ Samples						
■ Premiums						
■ Technology						
Advertising						

CHAPTER SUMMARY

1. **Relate sales forecasting to operational planning.** Planning is the most basic function that sales managers do because it creates the essential framework for all other decision making. Organizing, sales forecasting, and budgeting are all integral parts of the planning process. A sales forecast is the cornerstone of all operational planning, and the sales budget represents the conversion of the sales forecast into meaningful financial terms. If a sales budget is inadequate, the sales forecast probably will not be met, and the overall sales plan may not be accomplished. An effective, flexible organizational structure is necessary to achieving sales force goals and objectives, and to efficiently using the allocated budget.

If a sales forecast is too high, it can lead to excessive production, unsold products, excess inventory, idle cash, wasteful promotion expenditures, price reductions, too many salespeople, and lower unit profits. Conversely, if a sales forecast is too low, it may cause inadequate output to meet customer demand, understock, cash shortages, insufficient promotional expenditures to cover the market, price increases, too few salespeople, out-of-stocks, dissatisfied customers, and lower total profits.

2. **Use the most popular quantitative and qualitative sales forecasting tools.** Qualitative forecasting tools still play an important role for many sales managers. But by using computers and user-friendly statistical software, sales managers can apply numerous quantitative sales forecasting methods. Thus, sales managers can serve the managerial role of data analyst in using sophisticated forecasting tools, without having to become adept in statistical procedures.

3. **Evaluate the various sales forecasting techniques.** When considering the use of a particular sales forecasting method, sales managers should compare the method to alternative methods with respect to comprehensibility, accuracy, timeliness, availability of information, qualified personnel required, flexibility, and cost-benefit trade-offs. Several approaches often are used so the results can be compared and a more accurate forecast prepared.

4. **Identify the purpose and benefits of sales budgets.** A sales budget puts the sales forecast into dollar terms by serving as the financial sales plan outlining how resources and selling efforts should be allocated to achieve the sales forecast. Sales budgets can provide several benefits, such as (1) improve morale, (2) provide direction and focus for organizational efforts, (3) improve cooperation and coordination, (4) develop individual and collective standards for measuring performance, and (5) increase sales organization flexibility.

5. **Prepare an annual sales budget.** The steps in systematic budget planning are (1) review and analyze the situation, (2) communicate sales goals and objectives, (3) identify specific market opportunities and problems, (4) develop a preliminary allocation of resources, (5) prepare a budget presentation, and (6) implement the budget and provide periodic feedback.

REVIEW AND APPLICATION QUESTIONS

1. What assumptions might a sales manager make (sometimes subconsciously) about the marketplace in preparing the annual plan? How would you ensure that these assumptions are valid? [LO 1, LO 5]

2. Do you think the role of the sales manager in sales planning, organizing, forecasting, and budgeting will become less or more important with the ever growing power of computers and software sophistication? Explain. [LO 1, LO 2]

3. What are the characteristics of a successful S&OP program? [LO 1]

4. Using the sales potential approach, how many salespeople will be needed if the company sales forecast is $22 million, annual sales volume productivity for the average salesperson is $400,000, and the anticipated annual rate of sales force turnover is 25 percent? [LO 2, LO 1]

5. Which of the forecasting techniques do you feel are most appropriate for small business operations? Which for a large corporation? Which for nonprofit organizations, such as museums or public libraries? [LO3]

6. Assume that you are an entrepreneur who owns a small machine tool company with fourteen employees. Describe the kind of problems you will encounter if your sales forecast for the coming year turns out to be 25 percent too high. Describe the scenario if your sales forecast turns out to be 25 percent too low. [LO 1]

7. Go to the library and ask the business reference librarian for the North American Industrial System Classification Manual. Then sequentially follow an NAICS code all the way through to seven digits. Write down the increasingly detailed descriptions that accompany each additional NAICS classification. Step by step, explain how you can use this information to identify potential customers. [LO 5]

8. Go to the Cisco Systems website at http://www.cisco.com/global/EMEA/ciscoitatwork/pdf/Cisco_IT_Case_Study_ESales.pdf#search='sales%20forecasting%2C%20Cisco'. Review how the company uses sales forecasting to improve productivity. What problems might Cisco Systems have with its approach? [LO 1, LO 3, LO 4]

9. Consider the following data:

YEAR	SALES
2000	900
2001	1400
2002	1750
2003	1900
2004	1700
2005	1500
2006	2000
2007	1950
2008	2250
2009	2300

Suppose you wished to forecast sales for 2010. At first glance, which time-series forecasting method would you suggest as appropriate for this data? Compute the forecast using a simple average, a three-year weighted average, a five-year weighted average, and a five-year exponentially smoothed weighted average. Suppose actual sales for 2010 were 2500. Which forecasting technique is most accurate in this case? [LO 2, LO 5]

10. Consider a consumer goods company introducing a new product. The sales manager argues for a conservative forecast, meaning that care should be taken not to overestimate sales for the first six months of the product's life. What is the danger in making too conservative an estimate? Assuming an equally inaccurate forecast, is it better to underestimate or overestimate demand? [LO 1]

11. What are the key purposes and benefits of sales budgets? [LO 4]

IT'S UP TO YOU

Internet Exercise

Use a search engine such as Ask.com to search for sales forecasting software on the Internet. Locate at least three different software packages, each from a different company. Read the overviews of each product. If possible, also find the price. Would you recommend any of these for a small, start-up business that supplies industrial products to CAT-scan manufacturers?

Role-Playing Exercise

Sales Forecasting

Situation

Toni King is a sales manager for a restaurant supply firm and receives an annual sales forecast from the home office each year. Top management expects Toni to use this forecast to establish sales quotas for each salesperson in the territory. The forecast is a simple, five-year moving average. Management takes the forecasted sales amount and then adds 5 percent to "stretch" the goals and motivate the sales force. Each year, as sales manager, Toni is pressured to eliminate salespeople who do not meet their goals. Personally, Toni is considering establishing her own goals based on a five-year exponential smoothing forecast—with no stretch. Toni is unsure how top management would perceive this move. However, she feels such a forecast would be both more accurate and more equitable to the sales force.

Role-Play Participants and Assignments

Toni King Assume you are Toni. Do you believe a moving average or an exponential smoothing forecast would be more accurate in a restaurant-related business? Do you consider stretch goals ethical? Playing the role of Toni, consider your options and decide what to do—will you go along with the company policy, or establish your own goals and risk conflict with your superiors?

In-Basket Exercise

You are a sales manager for a consumer goods company that has just launched a new product. Although all the staff members are extremely excited about its potential, after only a few months on the market the product is generating disappointing responses from buyers. One of your salespeople recently heard a major wholesaler, serving over five hundred supermarkets, say: "We've had this product three months, and it's not moving, so we're going to yank it from the stores!"

QUESTIONS

1. What possible factors may be contributing to this situation?

2. What steps can you take to ensure a more accurate forecast for a new product?

Ethical Dilemma

Forecasting is one task that presents ethical dilemmas for sales managers. Consider a sales manager faced with endorsing a forecast for a new high-tech radio frequency identification (RFID) tracking device being developed by the company. We'll call the sales manager Abby. Abby has asked an outside firm to present a sales forecast for the new product. The forecast is rosy, suggesting enough demand to warrant the hiring of about ten new salespeople. Abby is very excited about the prospects for this new product and plans a meeting with top management to present the plan for hiring additional salespeople. The meeting goes well, and Abby is given authority to expand the sales force immediately. Three salespeople are hired within the week, with plans for more.

A few weeks after the presentation, Abby reads an article about the business cycle. Many forecasters believe managers must take the business cycle into account when making predictions about high-ticket items because inevitable peaks in the health of the economy are followed every few years by a period of decline. The article predicts an upcoming decline. Abby also reads in a trade magazine that a competing firm with even more resources is developing a similar RFID device. After going back and reading the commissioned forecast report, Abby realizes the outside firm has not taken either of these pieces of information into consideration. If either is true, the forecast almost certainly overstates sales for the RFID tracking device.

Abby now faces the dilemma of either informing management that the forecast may be wrong, and the product will not live up to sales expectations, or trying to take corrective action that could include layoffs. Either of these courses could deal a blow to Abby's career, and many questions enter her mind: "Maybe the business cycle doesn't exist? Maybe the other company won't be able to get the product to market quickly? Or maybe other companies are secretly working on the product as well?"

What is Abby's best course of action from this point?[15]

CASE 5.1

AKAMAI Corporation: Developing Sales Forecasts

AKAMAI Corporation is a diversified producer of performance chemicals for the petroleum industry. Performance chemicals are designed to meet rigid specifications to enhance the performance of a variety of end-use products. AKAMAI also produces plastics and aluminum products. The company is organized into three groups—Chemicals, Plastics, and Aluminum.

To maintain growth, AKAMAI manages its various groups with the goal of maintaining a healthy mix of businesses in different life-cycle stages. New products must be in the pipeline, either in development or ready for commercial introduction to replace declining ones. Equally important is managing growing and mature products to extend their life cycle and maximize cash flow to support new product development requiring substantial investment. The Chemicals Group has experienced dramatic growth and changing market conditions in the last three years, and AKAMAI has recently replaced the vice president of that group. Because of the importance of this group to overall corporate growth and profits, sales forecasts must be accurate.

The Chemicals Group is managed by Gabriel Perez and is organized into three operating divisions—industrial intermediates made up of polymers and detergents, specialty chemicals, and bromine. The three divisions are managed by separate general managers who have product managers reporting to them. For the Industrial Intermediates Division, total polymer intermediates sales reached 62 billion pounds in 2002, and 2003 sales are expected to exceed 75 billion pounds. This will be almost a 40 percent increase over a two-year period. The market for detergent intermediates, on the other hand, is mature and stable. The market has become increasingly competitive, with an annual growth of only about 3 percent. But AKAMAI is a leading competitor and has recently been gaining in market share.

The Specialty Chemicals Division has a diverse product mix. The performance polymers market is the primary revenue-producing unit and is highly dependent on market conditions for crude oil. Agricultural chemicals are a growth market too, but they also are dependent on the crude oil market. The pharmaceuticals market is growing, and the company has a strong market position as the only domestic producer of the active ingredient for one of the best-selling over-the-counter analgesics.

Performance of the Bromine Division is expected to be very good. The AKAMAI sales force has been successful in securing some major new accounts. The success has been achieved based on the company's favor-

able reputation as a quality producer of industrial chemicals and from an aggressive sales effort.

In the past, sales forecasts were prepared by the general manager of each division based on a percentage increase determined by the VP of the Chemicals Group. In approaching this task for the first time, new Group VP Perez believes improvements are necessary in the sales forecasting method. Because market conditions for each division are diverse, Perez believes different methods of forecasting should be considered for each of the three divisions.

Group VP Perez began his market analyses with a review of sales data for each division. The Industrial Intermediates Division represents about 54 percent of sales, Specialty Chemicals about 39 percent, and Bromine the remaining 7 percent. Perez also examined sales data by year for each division to track market trends. Table 1 summarizes sales of the Industrial Intermediates Division by quarter for a ten-year period from 1998 to 2007.

Relevant sales data for the Specialty Chemicals Division was available only for a six-year period because the division is relatively new and experiences somewhat unstable market conditions. Quarterly sales data are provided in Table 2 for 2002 through 2007.

The Bromine Division is entering its third year in operation, so little sales history is available. Perez has therefore asked for input from the sales force as well as industry data from trade publications. Following is a summary of the sales and market conditions prepared for each division.

Industrial Intermediates Division

- Recent increase in sales and market share for polymers
- Large number of competitors
- Many customers

TABLE 1 Industrial Intermediates Division: Sales Summary

QUARTER	1998	1999	2000	2001	2002	2003	2004	2005	2006	2007
1	54.2	55.2	56.0	59.9	63.4	65.2	68.3	68.2	71.4	79.8
2	53.2	56.1	59.0	61.6	63.8	67.4	71.2	73.1	88.7	100.2
3	54.2	56.1	58.1	59.0	62.5	64.1	67.5	74.1	87.4	95.8
4	53.5	55.2	57.1	59.6	59.9	63.4	66.8	73.2	73.7	84.4
Total	215.1	220.6	230.2	240.1	249.6	260.1	273.8	288.6	321.2	360.2

TABLE 2 Specialty Chemicals Division: Sales Summary						
QUARTER	2002	2003	2004	2005	2006	2007
1	11.0	15.0	22.7	29.6	34.9	43.3
2	14.0	15.1	23.8	31.3	41.7	52.7
3	11.5	16.3	20.7	31.5	40.3	50.7
4	13.5	14.2	21.9	32.2	36.6	45.2
Total	50.0	60.6	89.1	124.6	153.5	191.9

- Strong, stable, mature market for detergent intermediaries
- No foreseeable significant market changes for detergents
- Extensive historical sales data
- Represents 54 percent of sales

Specialty Chemicals Division

- Growth market
- Uncertain market conditions
- Highly dependent on crude oil market
- Represents 39 percent of sales

Bromine Division

- New market
- No historical sales data
- Only a few key customers
- Small sales force

- Need for accurate forecast by product line
- Limited number of products
- Few competitors

QUESTIONS

1. What recommendations would you give Mr. Perez to develop more precise sales forecasts?
2. What forecasting methods would you use for each division, and why?
3. Prepare a sales forecast for the Specialty Chemicals Division and justify your results.
4. What additional information would enable you to develop a more precise forecast for the Industrial Intermediates Division? Which method would you use?

Case prepared by Christopher D. Hopkins, Clemson University.

 ## CASE 5.2

Global Container Corporation: Creative Sales Forecasting

Global Container (GC) is a large manufacturer of plastic containers for a variety of liquids, from beverages to industrial fluids. Its products are marketed worldwide through a well-established channel of distribution. Recently Maiko Sakane, Director of New Product Development for GC, returned from a vacation in the Bahamas with what she thought was a great new product idea. After a week of lying on the beach and watching the sights, Maiko discovered something interesting about snorkelers. Most of them bring their snorkeling equipment to the beach in a rather haphazard way. Either they attempt to carry their masks, fins, gauges, and so on loosely—often dropping several of the items into the sand—or they put everything into a mesh bag. The divers' gear is a bit disorganized in the mesh bag, but the carrier appears to work well. The only problem is finding a place to put the bag once the gear is removed.

Maiko believes there is unfulfilled need in the marketplace for a product that will help snorkelers carry their gear onto the beach. Therefore, she created the "Snork-All," a lightweight plastic device that easily carries a diver's fins, mask, knife, various gauges, an underwater camera, and related equipment. The Snork-All could easily snap on to any belt or bathing suit the diver is wearing. Being an expert in plastics, Maiko believes this product represents an opportunity for GC to diversify its product line and expand into new markets.

Once back in the States, Maiko presented her new product idea to a somewhat disenchanted CEO and senior management team. Several of the management team liked the idea, and so did the sales manager and other salespeople. But management was uncertain about what action to take since the company's previous experience was in an entirely different industry. Management's major concerns were the potential sales of the proposed new product. With no knowledge of total market potential, and ultimately without a sales forecast for Snork-All, GC management resisted backing the idea. While Maiko is a brilliant idea person, her expertise in marketing planning and forecasting is limited.

QUESTIONS

1. How would you estimate the total market potential for Snork-All? What kind of historical data might help with this project?

2. How would you estimate GC's sales potential for Snork-All? Who from GC should be involved in developing the sales estimate?

3. What type of forecasting methods might work best in developing a sales forecast for Snork-All?

4. What would you recommend that Maiko do now? What other information could be used to help develop a better sales forecast for Snork-All?

Case prepared by Susan Geringer, California State University, Fresno.

Sales Force Planning and Organizing

LEARNING OBJECTIVES

When you finish this chapter, you should be able to:

1 Understand the purpose and levels of organizational planning.

2 Apply the sales planning process, including strategic and tactical sales planning.

3 Avoid unsuccessful sales planning.

4 Describe different ways to organize the sales force, including calculating its optimal size.

INSIDE SALES MANAGEMENT

Nikki Verna of Beiersdorf

To be successful, Nikki Verna must understand not only the products she sells and the needs of her customers but also what her customers' customers might want. As a national account manager for Beiersdorf AG, Verna sells two main product lines to large retailers: Curad bandages and Futuro elastic braces and supports. She builds strong relationships with her customers by helping them determine which specific Curad and Futuro products each store should carry and providing support for the retailers as they present and sell these products to consumers.

Market knowledge is critical: "If we don't know what the consumer is looking for," Verna explains, "we're not going to get our products into the store." In addition to examining broad market trends and analyzing consumers' historical buying patterns, she receives analytical reports from researchers who visit hundreds of stores to count every bandage and support product on the shelves. This kind of information reveals, for example, that bandage sales typically increase during March, April, and May as people begin spending more time outside and stock their medicine cabinets for summer cuts and scrapes.

Understanding market dynamics enables Verna to balance two key customer concerns. Retailers do not want to have large quantities of Curad or Futuro products sitting unsold on store shelves, nor do they want to run out of a product and have consumers walk away empty-handed. For this reason, a member of Verna's team monitors each account's sales—item by item, day by day. At one retailer, for example, the goal is to have Beiersdorf products in stock 98.5 percent of the time. "If we see that a certain item is about to dip below that level," she says, "we check the inventory in each individual store and immediately restock those that are running low."

Understanding her company, products, and markets helped Verna sell Curad to a recalcitrant buyer. "We had a fantastic relationship with him on Futuro elastics," she remembers, "but he was carrying two other bandage brands and wasn't interested in carrying a third. We made at least ten sales presentations about profit opportunities, unique products, and other reasons to carry the Curad line. Yet we simply couldn't get anywhere."

Verna ultimately convinced the buyer to try a no-risk test of three Curad products as a way to demonstrate consumer interest. "We promised to take the products back if they didn't sell," she says, "but the test went very well. This retailer ended up expanding the order and now carries twelve of our items." Just as important, the buyer has even more respect for Beiersdorf as a company because "we stood behind our products, we used the facts to tell our story, and it worked."

SOURCE: Anderson, Rolph E., Alan J. Dubinsky, and Rajiv Mehta, *Personal Selling: Building Customer Relationships and Partnerships*, 2/e, p. 354. Copyright © 2007 by Houghton Mifflin Company. Reprinted with permission.

Purpose and Levels of Organization Planning

Planning creates the essential framework for all other decision making. Without well-thought-out plans, getting anything accomplished efficiently and effectively is difficult, especially in larger companies. Effective sales managers are usually good planners.

■ Why Should Sales Managers Plan?

Planning requires sales managers to anticipate the possible outcomes and future implications of current decisions; thus planning is an attempt to manage the future. In fact, a succinct definition of planning is "making decisions today to create a desired tomorrow."

Some sales managers argue the marketplace changes too fast for planning to be of much value. These managers are fooling themselves, because without a plan to provide direction, decision making tends to be merely reactive, especially in rapidly changing markets. For example, sales managers who recruit and select a sales force without planning are likely to find themselves continually under-hiring, over-hiring, and firing employees. Similarly, sales managers who organize, train, motivate, or evaluate salespeople without a plan are likely to be frequently reorganizing, retraining, and suffering poor morale and high sales force turnover.

Sales managers make decisions in an environment where change is continuous—whether in competitive, technological, political, economic, or social arenas. Planning minimizes environmental shocks such as energy price increases, raw materials or component parts shortages, or major changes in tax laws. If sales managers don't anticipate marketplace changes, they'll be caught up in a whiplash decision-making process where they are batted back and forth by a rapidly changing marketing environment. Instead, they must ensure that salespeople collaborate with customers to create solutions neither would have been able to put together by themselves.[1]

Planning has several potential benefits for the sales manager. First, morale improves when the entire sales organization actively participates in the planning process. Second, planning provides direction and focus for organizational efforts. Third, it improves cooperation and coordination of sales force efforts. Fourth, planning helps develop individual and collective standards by which sales force performance can be measured and deviations can be identified in time to take corrective action. Fifth, planning increases the sales organization's flexibility in dealing with unexpected developments.

■ Levels of Organizational Planning

Every manager should plan, and more effective planners tend to be more effective managers. At the top, CEOs, boards of directors, presidents, and vice presidents spend more time planning than do middle managers. Similarly, middle managers spend more time planning than do supervisory level people. Top management focuses on strategic planning for the company, while middle managers—such as regional and district sales managers—spend most of their planning time on shorter-run tactical plans. Table 6.1 illustrates types of planning at different levels in the organization.

As planners and administrators, sales managers must (1) define goals and objectives, (2) set policies, (3) establish procedures, (4) devise strategies, (5) direct tactics, and (6) develop and enforce controls. Let's turn our discussion to these essential planning and administrative roles.

Goals and Objectives. Effective sales department planning requires communication of clear-cut goals and objectives to all organizational members involved in planning. **Goals** are general, long-range destinations, while **objectives** are specific results desired within a designated time frame—usually the period covered by the annual sales plan. One sales goal for IBM (www.ibm.com) is to be recognized as the most service-oriented sales force in its industry. In fact, sales executives at IBM think the company's

Goals
General, long-range destinations.

Objectives
Specific results desired within a designated time frame—usually the period covered by the annual sales plan.

TABLE 6.1 Planning at Different Levels of Management		
TYPE	PARTICIPANTS	FOCUS
Strategic planning	CEO, boards, president, senior VPs	Company mission, vision, goals, primary strategies, overall budgeting
Tactical planning	General sales manager, director of marketing	Departmental, yearly, and quarterly plans, policies, procedures, budgets
Monthly and weekly planning	Regional sales managers	Branch plans and budgets
Daily planning	Sales supervisors and sales reps	Unit plans and budget

best advertisement declares simply: "IBM means service." Objectives for most companies are expressed in terms of annual sales volume targets or quotas, market share, return on assets managed (ROAM), earnings per share of common stock, inventory turnover, back orders, accounts receivable, or employee turnover.[2] Without clearly communicated goals and objectives, sales efforts may not be synergistic with those of other departments and can even be conflicting.

Policies
Predetermined approaches for handling routine matters or reoccurring situations.

Procedures
Detailed descriptions of specific steps for carrying out actions.

Strategy
An overall program of action for using resources to achieve a goal or objective.

Tactics
Day-to-day actions that make up the strategic plan.

Policies and Procedures. Predetermined approaches for handling routine matters or reoccurring situations are called **policies**. For example, there should be a policy regarding product trade-ins, any warranties, and credit terms when customers purchase new products. Policies enable sales managers to avoid answering the same questions over and over, so they can focus on more important decision making such as strategic sales planning.

Detailed descriptions of specific steps for carrying out actions are called **procedures**. For example, when offering a refund on a defective product, salespeople should follow a clear-cut series of steps to ensure the transaction is handled correctly.

Strategies and Tactics. A **strategy** is an overall program of action for using resources to achieve value-creating goals or objectives. **Tactics** are day-to-day actions that make up or implement the strategic plan. One example of a sales strategy is Honeywell's (www.honeywell.com) decision to concentrate its field sales force in smaller cities to compete against other manufacturers whose resources are located in larger cities. In this way, they could compete better in a head to head competition with these firms. Special sales presentation formats designed to approach different customer categories and communicate more effectively are examples of sales tactics.

Controls. For effective control, sales managers must develop performance standards so they can compare actual performance to predetermined standards. If there are gaps between actual and planned results, the sales manager has two options: (1) increase sales efforts to accomplish the plan, or (2) revise the sales plan to conform to a new "reality" in the marketplace. The appropriate course of action depends on the reasons for the gap. In analyzing the situation, the sales manager needs to consider the following: Were planning assumptions used in preparing the sales forecast and performance objectives realistic? Have there been major strategic or tactical changes by competitors? Have customer tastes or preferences changed? Are product quality, price, and service satisfactory? Are advertising and other support activities effective? Are salespeople properly trained and motivated? Is the sales force optimally organized? Only after sorting through the myriad possibilities can the sales manager decide which approach to use to realign planned and actual sales performance.

Sales Management Planning Process

Sales management planning is never completed and requires several sequential steps. The process never comes to an end because the process is really continuous. As soon as the first plan is prepared, something has changed in the marketing environment—perhaps a competitor's actions—that calls for an adjustment in the original plan. Planning enables a sales manager to be proactive rather than reactive.

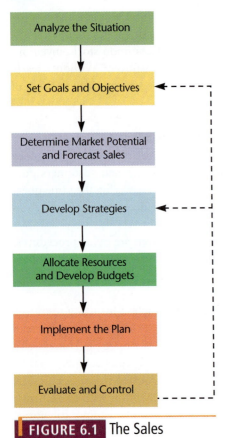

FIGURE 6.1 The Sales Management Planning Process

When beginning the planning process, sales managers should consider six basic questions:

1. *Diagnosis*—Where are we now?
2. *Prognosis*—Where are we headed if no changes are made?
3. *Objectives*—Where should we be headed?
4. *Strategy*—What is the best way to get there?
5. *Tactics*—What actions need to be taken by whom, and when?
6. *Control*—What measures must be monitored so we know how we're doing?

Let's examine the flowchart in Figure 6.1 as we discuss each of the stages in the sales management planning process.

■ Analyze the Situation

The planning process begins with an analysis of where the organization is today and where it is headed if no changes are made. Managers learn this by reviewing the organization's past performance, judging its progress versus the competition, and reviewing its success in accomplishing objectives and goals. Here are some key variables to study in the situation analysis:

- *Market characteristics*—number and types of potential buyers, their demographic and behavioral profiles, their attitudes and buying patterns, and their servicing needs.
- *Competition*—number and types of competitors; their strengths and weaknesses; their products, prices, and brands; and their market shares, characteristics, and sales trends for each competitive brand.
- *Sales, cost, and profit data for current and recent years*—by product, market, territory, and time period.
- *Benefits offered as perceived by potential customers*—products, brand names, prices, packages, and service.
- *Promotional mix*—personal selling, advertising, sales promotion, and publicity programs, particularly emerging website strategies.
- *Distribution systems*—channels of distribution, channel partners, storage and transportation facilities, and intensity of distribution.

Sales managers and others engaged in the planning process at any level need to monitor internal and external events that directly or indirectly affect the organization. It's particularly important to match the organization's strengths and weaknesses against the opportunities and threats facing it. By building on strengths and shoring up weaknesses, the organization puts itself in a good position to counter market challenges and exploit opportunities. Understanding comparative strengths and weaknesses is essential for survival and growth, but management must be aware of emerging marketplace trends. General Electric (www.ge.com) relies on its website's sales portal to assemble information for use in sales planning. The portal accesses multiple databases simultaneously to obtain everything from sales tracking and customer data to parts pricing, production schedules, and external data from news and trade industry RSS feeds. To do so, it dynamically assembles personalized "portlets," such as a

● **This GE Sales Portal improves sales planning.**

customized view of industry news, customer profiles, and sales performance year-to-date, and presents them in a unified way. The result is less time spent preparing for sales calls and more time spent face-to-face making sales and building partnerships.[3]

■ Set Goals and Objectives

Organizations usually have multiple goals and objectives. In many cases, especially in smaller companies, goals are often vague or inadequately defined, for example, "We want to become one of the best in the industry." Without a clear understanding of what "one of the best" means, the goal is not very meaningful.

All units and employees in an organization should understand overall goals and objectives as well as individual goals and objectives. One way to improve development of goals and objectives is by using interactive sales force automation (SFA) applications. Companies like Acumen Software Services Inc. (www.acumen-software.com/) sell Interactive Sales Manager (ISM) packages as an add-on to many SFA applications. They make a salesperson's goals and expectations easier to confirm, and then managers can prepare plans that serve sales territories and accounts to best meet goals and expectations. The ISM tool tracks performance against plans, current activity, and future commitments, and it even identifies mentoring opportunities.[4] The *Sales Management in Action Box* illustrates this point further.

Goals and objectives must be spelled out explicitly and in order of priority. They also must be consistent, particularly between different company divisions and

SALES MANAGEMENT IN ACTION

Using SFA to Monitor and Plan

Technology is changing nearly all aspects of sales management. Planning and monitoring used to be handled by referring to information on index cards filed in boxes. Today, sales force automation (SFA) programs have made these processes much easier and more effective for many sales managers. While salespeople once had to do the best they could in interpreting ways to implement company strategies, today the SFA can help plan salesperson activities in a way that makes their behavior more consistent with company desires. During the sales call, the SFA also provides more of the key information the salesperson needs to accomplish key goals. In Australia, for example, a pharmaceutical salesperson might make only one sales call ("detail") per year to many rural physicians. The frequency of sales calls and the

information that should be conveyed during the visit are all provided by the SFA.

Additionally, the SFA allows the sales manager to track progress toward key goals in real time. When a salesperson is lagging on some goal, or emphasizing nonproductive accounts too much, the sales manager doesn't have to wait for a paper report to take corrective action. Instead, the real-time data in the SFA provides the guidance needed to nip many problems in the bud.

SOURCES: "The Automator," *Pharmaceutical Executive* 27 (February 2007), pp. 36–40; "What Does the Sales Force Do?" *Builder's Merchant Journal*, October 2006, p. 35, and Sales Force Automation, http://www.businesscreatorpro.com/articles/sales_force_automation_sfa.php, accessed August 2007.

TABLE 6.2 Sample Goals and Obectives for a National Sales Manager

GOALS	OBJECTIVES
■ Implement a sales management training program for new sales managers within two years.	■ Increase sales by 15 percent next year.
■ Expand our market coverage over the next five years to include all U.S. primary metropolitan statistical areas.	■ Reduce customer complaints by 10 percent next year.
■ Reduce sales force turnover to below the industry average over the next five years.	■ Increase the number of new customer accounts by 20 percent in the next six months.

departments. Sample goals and objectives for a national sales manager for a large office supply manufacturer might include those in Table 6.2.

We discuss individual salesperson goals and objectives in chapter 14 on sales force performance evaluation.

■ Determine Market Potential and Forecast Sales

Market Potential
The maximum possible sales for an entire industry.

Sales Potential
The maximum possible sales for a company.

Market Capacity
Refers to the units the market will absorb if the product or service is free.

After managers and salespeople have agreed on goals and objectives, the next step in the planning process is to assess **market potential**—the maximum possible sales for an entire industry—and **sales potential**—the maximum possible sales for a company. We usually estimate both market and sales potentials for a specified period of time based on favorable assumptions about the marketing environment and marketing expenditures. Some sales managers, however, prefer to develop separate (1) optimistic, (2) expected, and (3) pessimistic assumptions for market and sales potential using different possible scenarios.

Market capacity refers to the units the market will absorb if the product or service is free. Since market potential assumes a competitive pricing structure, the market potential number will always be less than market capacity. Potentials developed for an organization are generally grouped for planning purposes, for example in geographic or customer terms such as sales territories. Thus, sales managers know where sales potential is highest and can better allocate the sales force and set sales quotas. Estimates of customer potential also help in scheduling sales calls and implementing promotional support.

Market potential determination starts with the study of present customers and their characteristics—for example, place of purchase, method of payment, product size, and usage rate. Sales managers can then estimate usage rates if the current product is modified for existing customers or repositioned for potential new customers. Finally, they estimate market potential for new products. Analysis of market potential leads to the development of more realistic sales forecasts for the next quarter or year.

Sales forecasts predict future sales for a specified period as part of a marketing plan based on a set of assumptions about the marketing environment. Since an accurate sales forecast is vital to an organization, most firms are constantly seeking more reliable sales forecasting methods. Sales forecasting can be quite complex, utilizing sophisticated mathematical models. Some firms have established separate departments specializing in sales forecasting, but many firms rely on off-the-shelf packages available with customer relationship management (CRM) systems. For small- and medium-sized firms, IBM (www.ibm.com) and its channel partners provide free sales planning solutions on topics such as defining market opportunities, targeting the most attractive market segments, identifying appropriate sales coverage, and assigning sales responsibilities during each step of the sales cycle, from demand generation to post-sale support.[5]

Strategy Planning
The process of setting overall objectives, allocating resources, and developing broad courses of action.

Market Penetration
A strategy focusing on increasing sales of current products in current markets by more intensive marketing efforts.

Market Development
A strategy for opening up new markets for current products.

Product Development
The creation of new or improved products for current markets by adding new sizes, models with new features, alternative quality versions, or creative new alternatives to satisfy the same basic needs.

■ Develop Strategies

After organizational objectives have been determined and sales forecasts developed, the next step is to determine the best way to achieve the targets. **Strategy planning** is the process of setting overall objectives, allocating resources, and developing broad courses of action. Strategic decisions give the organization a plan of action to serve customers better by creating value, taking advantage of competitors' weaknesses, and capitalizing on the firm's strengths.

Growth Strategies. Figure 6.2 depicts four types of growth strategies. **Market penetration** focuses on increasing sales of current products in current markets by more intensive marketing efforts. As an example, AFLAC recently refocused its marketing effort by allocating more resources to sales. The hope was to get salespeople to spend more time in the organizations where AFLAC's core product, supplemental disability insurance, is sold. In this way, AFLAC might capitalize on the name recognition created through advertising, by educating employees on the actual product that AFLAC sells.

Market development seeks to open up new markets for current products. To illustrate, the A. T. Cross (www.cross.com) continues to enjoy good earnings growth because it has concentrated on developing an upscale market among corporations (beyond the traditional retail consumer market) for its high-quality pens as special gifts for customers and awards for employees.

Product development creates new or improved products for current markets by adding new sizes, models with new features, alternative quality versions, or creative new alternatives to satisfy the same basic needs. For example, farmers are increasingly using biogenetics and hydroponics for applications formerly involving chemical fertilizers and pesticides. Biogenetics is the breeding of strains of plants that are resistant to pests and diseases, thus eliminating the need for pesticides or herbicides. Hydroponics is the science of growing plants indoors in a controlled environment that requires no herbicides, pesticides, or fertilizers. New products from biogenetics and hydroponics offer exciting growth opportunities.

Above the sales management level, two other growth strategies are to diversify by purchasing new businesses or product lines, and to obtain ownership or control over different levels of distribution channels. For example, the Firestone Division of

Reprinted by permission of A. T. Cross Company

● **A. T. Cross pursues an upscale market as part of the marketing strategy**

	Current Products	New Products
Current Markets	Market Penetration	Product Development
New Markets	Market Development	Diversification

FIGURE 6.2 Growth Strategies for Sales Management

Market Share/Market Growth Matrix
A matrix displaying alternative methods of growing sales.

Strategic Business Units (SBUs)
Logical divisions of major businesses within multiple product companies.

Business Portfolio Matrix
A method of segmenting the company's activities into groups of well-defined businesses for which distinct strategies are developed.

Bridgestone (www.bridgestone.com) integrated forward through ownership of its retail outlets in the United States, while Holiday Inns, a division of InterContinental Hotels Group (www.ichotelsgroup.com), integrated backward into manufacturing by acquiring carpet mills and furniture plants.

Business Portfolio Approach. Two major growth concepts are the *strategic business unit* and the **market share/market growth matrix**. **Strategic business units (SBUs)** are logical divisions of major businesses within multiple product companies. SBUs are evaluated on the basis of their profit and growth potential just as if they were standalone companies. SBUs have several characteristics: (1) distinct mission, (2) separate management, (3) unique customer segments, (4) their own competitors, and (5) planning that is largely independent of other units in the company. Many of the largest U.S. manufacturing corporations use the SBU concept. For example, Campbell Soup Co. set up eight SBUs: Soups, Beverages, Pet Foods, Frozen Foods, Fresh Produce, Main Meals, Grocery, and Food Service.

In evaluating a company's SBUs, the most popular approach is the **business portfolio matrix**. This method segments the company's activities into groups of well-defined businesses for which distinct strategies are developed. The most widely used is Boston Consulting Group's (BCG) growth-share matrix, which plots market share on the horizontal axis and market growth potential on the vertical axis. It evaluates a company's businesses based on market share and market growth and then puts them in one of four quadrants labeled *cash cows, stars, dogs,* or *problem children* (also referred to as question marks), as shown in Figure 6.3.

Strategies based on the four quadrants suggest the following:

- *Stars* produce large amounts of cash because of high market share but consume large amounts of cash because of high growth. If stars maintain or extend market share, they become cash cows.

- *Cash cows* are leaders in mature markets and produce much more cash than they consume. Companies "milk" business units so they can invest cash in other products or services. For example, the cash might be used to turn problem children into stars.

- *Problem children* are growing rapidly and consume large amounts of cash. Also known as "question marks," they have the potential to increase market share and become stars. But if they do not increase market share, they may become dogs.

Relative Market Share (Cash Generation)

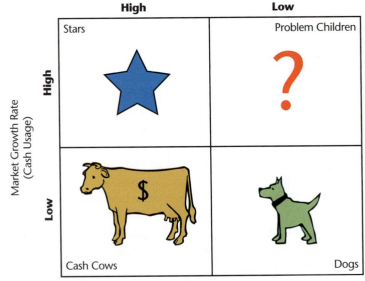

FIGURE 6.3 The BCG Growth-Share Matrix

■ *Dogs* have low market share and low growth rates. They do not consume much cash but also do not produce any. These business units are likely to be sold.

Stakeholders. Marketing planning and strategy must consider an organization's relationship with all stakeholder publics, not just customers. Government—whether federal, state, or local—can change a company's structure, pass laws, issue regulations, and become either a customer or a competitor of the organization. Government actions have ranged from the Product Safety Commission demanding numerous product recalls to the Food and Drug Administration banning sale of certain products as possible cancer-causing agents to the Department of Agriculture subsidizing tobacco growers while at the same time the Department of Health and Human Services campaigns against cigarette smoking. Special interest groups battle either for or against handgun control, nuclear power plants, and tax reform, while the general public protests wasteful government spending. Company employees demand higher wages and better working conditions. Stockholders vote against extravagant executive salaries and benefits or commercial dealings with governments that violate human rights. The financial community provides either easy or tight credit terms. Suppliers make decisions on allocation of scarce commodities. Investigative reporters for the independent print and broadcast media expose legal, moral, and ethical violations by business—whether they are misleading advertising claims, faulty product designs, or insider stock trading. Each of these stakeholders influences sales force operations for better or worse. Thus managers must consider each stakeholder in planning overall marketing strategy and tactics.

After the overall strategy has been decided, the planning process incorporates more detailed activities—tactics. Tactics focus on implementation of the strategic plan and are really the functional sub-plans that underlie and accomplish the strategy plan. Tactical action plans identify what needs to be done, who is responsible, what resources are needed, and what benefits are expected. The *Sales Management in Action* box on teamwork illustrates one approach. Figure 6.4 shows a sample action plan.

■ Allocate Resources and Develop Budgets

Given detailed sub-plans and tactics, managers must allocate resources—money, people, materials, equipment, and time—to carry out the plans. Budgets are the formal expression of managerial support. The sales budget is the expected expenditures required to achieve projected sales revenues. It must support the sales forecast. If budgeted resources are inadequate, the entire plan—including the sales forecast—must be scaled down. As we pointed out in Chapter 5, budgets coordinate and control company resources during the period covered by the sales forecast.

■ Implement the Plan

Goals, objectives, strategies, and tactics need to be communicated throughout the organization. Upper-level management wants to be sure departmental plans are consistent with overall corporate objectives. Sales managers often use management by objectives (MBO) to involve subordinates in planning and budgeting, since subordinates are more apt to accept and carry out plans if they're involved in their preparation. A PERT (program evaluation and review technique) network is commonly used for planning and scheduling. PERT diagrams specify a project's **critical path**—the

Critical Path
The sequence of tasks to be completed, the time to complete each activity, and the responsible individuals.

SALES MANAGEMENT IN ACTION

Developing Successful Cross-Functional Teams

Comprehensive sales plans may need cooperation from many camps if they are to be implemented successfully. Some companies have turned to cross-functional teams (CFTs) and charged them with implementing an action plan aimed at accomplishing major sales and marketing objectives. The cross-functional team involves marketing, innovation, engineering, research, and financial personnel. A CFT can better ensure that all issues involved in a sales contract are covered with sufficient expertise. But CFTs are not always effective. Here are some hints to make a CFT work:

1. Spread the work around to avoid bottlenecks. Each member of the CFT should be charged with approximately the same amount of responsibility. If someone on the CFT does not have responsibility, then perhaps they don't belong on the team.

2. Provide quantitative success goals. Each member of the team should have a benchmark allowing progress to be noted.

3. Celebrate success. When goals are met, the entire CFT should be recognized for achievement. This is time to celebrate!

Cross-functional teams can be a good solution in a CRM environment. However, like most tools, they don't apply to every action plan.

SOURCES: D. Antonucci and K. Kono, "High Energy: Sustain the Momentum of Your Cross-Functional Team," *Marketing Management* (April 2006), pp. 14–16. Reprinted with permission of the American Marketing Association; Matthew Schwartz, Fundamentals of Sales Management for the Newly Appointed Sales Manager, New York: AMACOM Division of American Management Association, 2006, p. 192; and Impact Report, "Cross-Functional team focus on marketing is key to success," http://csdd.tufts.edu/_documents/www/Doc_309_20_892.pdf, accessed August 2007.

Tactical Action Plan

Velop Manufacturing Co.
Eastern Region

Goal: To call on 200 new accounts during the first quarter of fiscal year 2009.

Strategy/Tactics:
- Develop list of potential new accounts.
- Contract with telemarketing firm to pre-screen list to determine likely prospects.
- Assign pre-screened prospects to sales force by territory.
- Hold a training workshop to make sure all salespeople know what background material to develop on prospects and where to obtain it.
- Develop timetables and quotas for each salesperson.

Responsibility: Sales Manager, Eastern Region

Start Date: October 1, 2008

Completion Date: December 31, 2008

Resources Needed: $28,000 to develop list and contract with telemarketing firm.

Benefits:
- Ensures new accounts are called upon.
- Facilitates achieving projected 5 percent increase in sales for FY 2009.

FIGURE 6.4 Sample Action Plan

sequence of tasks to be completed, the time to complete each activity, and the responsible individuals. Managers can often create this scheduling tool through a Web-based portal for increased control and dissemination of information.

Regardless of the approach, it is essential to closely monitor project progress. Some companies assign full-time project coordinators to follow up with those responsible for completing each task. Since the planning process is based on many assumptions about the external environment, changes or modifications may be necessary at various points in the implementation stage. Sales managers who anticipate the unexpected can adjust plans and implementation quickly.

■ Evaluate and Control

A sound planning process requires a built-in monitoring device for management evaluation and control. The device should include regular measurements to check progress toward specific objectives and signal deviations in time to take corrective actions and get back on track. Whenever possible, managers should quantify measurements.

Performance Standards and Measures. In Table 6.3, we show three types of performance standards and relate them to eight performance measures. One measure of performance is comparisons to *industry averages.* Of course, when the total industry is performing poorly, it is small consolation to be doing as well as the average company. Another type of standard is *past performance,* which can indicate trends either favorable or unfavorable. Probably the most important standards are *managerial expectations,* because they are based on the organization's objectives, forecasts, and budgetary support. Even if sales exceed past performance and industry norms, management may still view failing to meet expectations negatively.

These performance measures are unlikely to all be used in any specific situation. But managers do need multiple measures to adequately monitor and control progress toward achieving goals and objectives.

TABLE 6.3 Performance Standards and Performance Measures for Sales Managers

	PERFORMANCE STANDARD		
Performance Measures	Industry Averages	Past Performance	Managerial Expectations
Sales volume	Trade publications Annual reports	Sales records	Sales forecast
New accounts	Trade publications	Sales records	MBO contract
Selling costs	Trade publications	Sales records	Budgeted costs
Sales force turnover	Trade publications	Personnel records	MBO contract
Market share	Trade publications	Marketing department	Forecast
Profit margins	Trade publications Annual reports	Accounting department	Pro forma statement
Customer service	Trade publications Customer surveys	Complaint records Products returned Number of service calls	MBO contract
Website visits	Trade publications Customer surveys	Data warehouse	Marketing plans

Each of these standards reflects the organization's internal measures. But two *external* measures may be even more critical to the organization's long-run survival: *customer satisfaction* and *societal satisfaction.* Indicators of customer satisfaction or dissatisfaction include purchase frequencies and quantities, repurchase rates, brand or store loyalty, customer perceptions of product quality and service, number of customer complaints, and overall organizational reputation. Satisfaction of society is more difficult to measure or even set standards for, since societal expectations for all levels of performance seem to rise continually. Nevertheless, an organization can track areas most likely to affect societal perceptions, such as product safety and quality standards, equal employment and promotion opportunities, nondiscriminatory treatment of customers and suppliers, promotional truthfulness and disclosure, energy conservation, and environmental policies. Remaining alert and responsive to government initiatives and public interest groups helps organizations satisfy societal expectations.

By establishing standards, organizations can regularly compare the gap between actual performance and benchmarks to ensure timely corrective action. Unless performance is continuously monitored, planning is likely a waste of resources.

Causes of Unsuccessful Planning

Some plans are poorly prepared, filed away, and not looked at again until next year's plan is due. This kind of planning doesn't represent much real planning and is a big waste of time and resources. Merely "going through the planning motions" is probably not much better than having no plan at all.

Many organizations devote substantial time and effort to the planning process. They also use computer simulations and quantitative analyses to improve the process. Despite the serious commitment and sophisticated effort, however, unsuccessful plans are too often the outcome. Poor results are not limited to small or new companies. Global corporations have had drastic planning failures, too—as witnessed by the failure of both Texas Instruments and AT&T in personal computers. Probably the most universal cause of unsuccessful planning is making one or more erroneous assumptions in each stage of the planning process. To illustrate, before the oil shortage of the 1970s, Texaco decided to stop exploring for oil and concentrate on refining and distributing oil products. Management's erroneous assumption was that there would be a cheap, plentiful supply of oil for the foreseeable future. In planning, management *must* make assumptions about the future, so it's important that they be systematically considered. Let's look at two tools.

■ Dialectic Planning

Dialectic Planning
An approach to planning that calls for making a new set of assumptions—sometimes directly opposite—and reevaluating all previous planning decisions.

One approach to examining the validity of assumptions in a forecast is called **dialectic planning.** This approach calls for making a new set of assumptions—sometimes directly opposite—and reevaluating all previous planning decisions. Plans are rigorously challenged at every step, and a second plan with different assumptions is prepared. Forcing management to come up with a different second plan enables them to view the planning process from two contrasting views and reduces the chance of mistakes. With two alternative plans, however, management uncertainty may increase, sometimes resulting in delayed decision making or a compromise that produces undesirable results.

■ Contingency Planning

Contingency Planning
A backup plan to the one adopted; a contingency plan is executed only if events occur beyond the control of the major plan.

Another tool used to reduce the risk of future problems is **contingency planning**. A contingency plan is a backup plan to the one adopted, and it will be executed only if events occur beyond the control of the major plan. For example, electrical systems in many hospitals have "redundancy" or "backup" systems in case the primary system fails. Contingency planning is expensive and time-consuming, but its value has been proven many times. When preparing plans, management must therefore anticipate and prepare for an emergency or unlikely turn of events.

Organizing the Sales Force

A proper organizational structure is necessary to effectively implement the sales manager's plan. *Organizational structure* determines how well activities are coordinated in serving customers profitably, and how quickly the organization can adapt to changes in the marketing environment. The purpose of the sales organization is to facilitate the accomplishment of marketing and sales objectives by (1) shortening the time a sales manager needs to evaluate and respond to changing market needs, (2) arranging activities efficiently, and (3) establishing and maintaining open channels of communication with customers, salespeople, support staff, and concerned stakeholders. No sales organization can remain stagnant and expect long-run success. The success of companies such as Coca-Cola, Microsoft, Dell, and General Electric can be partially attributed to their continuously adapting their organizational structures to market conditions.

■ Types of Organizations

Depending on its objectives, an organization can be structured in many ways. But most organizations are one of three types: line, line and staff, or functional. A variation of these three is the matrix organization. Management can modify these structures as needed to decentralize or to organize by product, customer, function, territory, or a combination. In addition, all organizations have an informal network.

Line Organization. A line organization is the simplest design and the one most often used by smaller firms (Figure 6.5). It typically consists of only a few managers who

FIGURE 6.5 Line Organization for Marketing and Sales

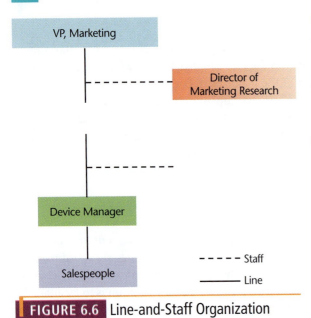

FIGURE 6.6   Line-and-Staff Organization

have authority over specific functional areas of the business, such as production, finance, or sales. When a firm is small and managers interact frequently, line organizations are efficient and flexible. But as firms grow, line organizations are much less effective because decision making is slower and managers have too many responsibilities.

Line-and-Staff Organization. A line-and-staff organization creates more functional areas and adds staff assistants to complete specialized support activities, such as marketing research or sales forecasting (Figure 6.6). A vice president of marketing or a sales manager heads the department. Staff people provide specialized skills for the sales manager and enable them to spend more time working with salespeople. Line managers have direct authority over the operations of the organization, while staff managers only make recommendations or assist line managers.

Functional Organization. In functional organizations, staff specialists have line authority, as shown in Figure 6.7. The sales manager directs salespeople through district managers, but the director of sales training also has authority over the sales force for training, as does the manager of technical services. In functional structures, managers are highly qualified specialists whose job is to make sure their function is accomplished. This type of organization creates many conflicts for salespeople, who must react to several bosses.

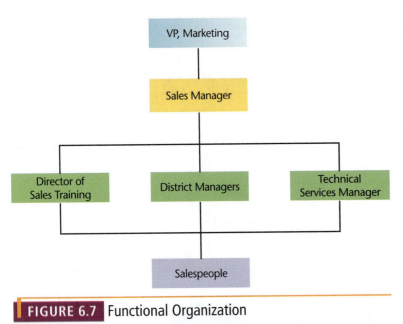

FIGURE 6.7   Functional Organization

Matrix Organizations. Matrix organizations are typical in industries confronted with rapid technological changes and the need to quickly develop new products or services. Traditional organizations are designed around functions, while matrix organizations revolve around projects. The firm's efforts focus on a specific project, and the functional areas are integrated into the project structure. Figure 6.8 shows a matrix organization that focuses on specific products and projects. While the functional aspects are still present, they are secondary. Project managers head a team of individuals from different functional areas and have responsibility for coordinating these functions toward project completion. Individual team members still have a functional superior such as the sales manager, but they also report to their project managers. Matrix organizations are much easier to implement today, thanks to enterprise software applications like Matrix Manager (www.matrixmanager.com). These applications facilitate management overview of all activities, streamline processes, and empower employees.[6]

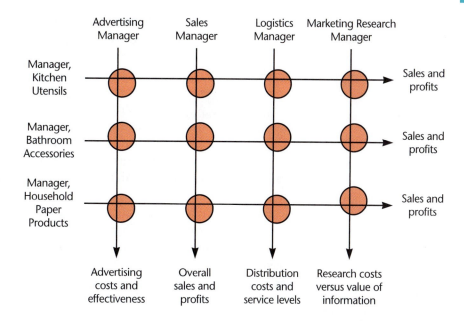

EVALUATION CRITERIA

FIGURE 6.8 Matrix Organization Focusing on Products or Projects

Matrix organizations encourage teamwork to maximize individual contributions. They view team leaders as coordinators of efforts rather than as bosses. Matrix organizations are most effective when projects or products are unique, team members are professionals in terms of expertise and skills, the project is of short duration, and speed and creativity are as important as cost.[7] Companies as diverse as Shell Oil (www.shell.com), Kraft Foods (www.kraft.com), IBM (www.ibm.com), Alcoa Aluminum (www.alcoa.com), and Westinghouse (www.westinghouse.com) have made effective use of matrix organizations. Matrix organizations provide flexibility, encourage interdepartmental cooperation, and develop employee skills as well as motivating and challenging them.[8]

Informal Organization. Despite the existence of formal organizational structures, the informal organizational structure is the network by which things often get done. Healthy organizations are dynamic and self-adjusting. They find the most efficient methods to accomplish objectives, without regard to how the objectives are supposed to be achieved. Employees adapt to the way the organization actually works rather than to the way the organization structure indicates it should. Real power and authority in an organization may belong to a strong staff manager or junior line manager who works with weaker or less competent senior managers. The way an organization really functions is eventually reflected in the organization structure, but the actual chains of authority can take a long time—perhaps years—to develop.

■ Types of Sales Department Organizations

Sales organization efforts center on products, markets, and functions. These elements are blended together differently by various industries and companies in the same industry. Sales departments have traditionally been organized into five basic types: geographic, product, function, market, or some combination of the four. Let's look briefly at each one.

FIGURE 6.9 Geographic Sales Organization

Geographic Organizations. Geographic sales organizations are the most common (Figure 6.9). But they often are used in combination with product-, function-, or market-oriented structures. Some examples of geographic organizations are banks with suburban branches, magazine publishers with regional editions, hotel chains with regional divisions, or companies with international and domestic sales divisions. A sales manager has authority over a specific geographic area, and several salespeople assigned a separate part of the territory report to him or her.

Geographic organization has advantages and disadvantages. Advantages come from a decentralized line authority structure, ensuring flexibility in adapting to needs, problems, buying patterns, service requirements, and competitive conditions in the regional markets. Disadvantages include the overhead costs of management as more levels of geographic executives are created, and problems in coordinating total company sales efforts when several sales divisions operate with considerable autonomy. Lack of functional specialists can also be a problem, since territorial managers are expected to operate as "jacks of all trades" and handle advertising, sales analysis, billing, credit, and collection in addition to managing the sales force.

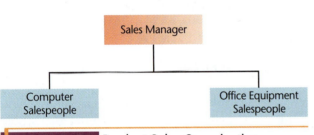

FIGURE 6.10 Product Sales Organization

Product-Oriented Organizations. Product-structured sales organizations (Figure 6.10) are useful when product lines are complex or distinct and require increased individualized attention. Under this setup, products compete among themselves for profit, market share, and company resources. Procter & Gamble (www.pg.com), one of the world's most successful consumer products companies, uses a product-oriented structure. Competition among P&G products, which are sometimes sold to overlapping market segments, is encouraged.

Disadvantages of product structures are the additional expense—increased specialization usually requires additional management—and the possible irritation of customers who lose time because more than one salesperson from the same company calls on them for different products. Also, using multiple salespeople to call on a single customer tends to confuse the image of the seller.

FIGURE 6.11 Functional Sales Organization

Function-Oriented Organizations. Function-oriented sales organizations are structured by major functions, such as development of new accounts or maintenance of current customers (Figure 6.11). This structure offers specialization and efficiency in performing selling activities, and it is best for companies selling only a few or very similar products to relatively few customer types. Generally, this structure is used by medium to large companies that can afford for salespeople to focus on a small number of activities.[9]

A common problem among growing companies is motivating salespeople to call on potential new accounts, since that requires a different set of sales skills than does selling to existing customers. Assigning these two functions to separate sales groups would be an appropriate use of the functional organization. Unlike a pure line-and-staff organization, function-oriented structures give specialists line authority over salespeople.

The cost effectiveness of a function-oriented organization is questionable. Small companies seldom find it practical to have such a high degree of specialization. In large organizations, however, it's difficult to coordinate functions throughout the sales department due to size of the sales force. Furthermore, when several functional specialists have line authority over salespeople, as shown in Figure 6.7, conflicts are likely among the function managers, as well as confusion and frustration in the sales force.

Customer/Market-Oriented Organizations. Customer/market-oriented sales organizations (Figure 6.12) are appropriate for companies whose products are purchased in multiple combinations by several customer types with unique needs. Aircraft manufacturers such as Boeing (www.boeing.com) and Lockheed-Martin (www.lockheedmartin.com) have different marketing efforts for government, military, and commercial markets. Similarly, electric utilities separate their markets into residential and commercial accounts.

FIGURE 6.12 Customer/Market Sales Organization

As we discussed in chapter 3, CRM is more effective when salespeople are organized by market or type of customer. Customers are frequently classified by industry, channel of distribution, or importance of the account (national or local). A market-oriented sales structure can often more successfully reach different industries with unique needs. But the other two classifications—distribution channels and account size—are less obvious. Organization by distribution channel is appropriate when a company sells through several competing channels that use different pricing strategies such as drugstores, supermarkets, and discount stores. Under these conditions, it may be advantageous to create separate sales units for each channel to reduce customer complaints and divided salesperson loyalties. The organizational structure for IBM is customer/market-oriented because salespeople specialize in serving a customer type in one industry. The objective of this approach is for salespeople to better understand, through specialization, how customers/markets purchase and use their products and services. Salespeople are then more effective in building long-term relationships with customers.[10]

Key Accounts
High-volume, important customers that require added attention from the sales organization.

Many companies use a variation of customer/market-oriented structures called *key account selling*. **Key accounts** are high-volume, important customers that require added attention from the sales organization. This type of organization is based on the 80-20 rule that says a large percentage of a firm's sales (80 percent) come from a relatively small number of accounts (20 percent). Organization by national or key accounts is appropriate when a company's customers centralize buying at national or regional offices. Companies such as Gillette (www.gillette.com) prefer a customer-focused sales structure to give special attention to large accounts. Key account organization also avoids duplication of sales efforts because only one salesperson calls on a particular customer. With the trend in business toward concentrated industries, large customers, centralized purchasing, and fewer new markets to enter with existing products, ensuring the satisfaction of the largest and most important customers is becoming a critical concern. Thus, many sales organizations are moving toward organizing by customers/markets because it enables them to create competitive advantages and achieve superior financial performance.[11]

Market-oriented structures overcome some limitations of product structures, but still have disadvantages. Market-oriented structures result in expensive overlapping of territorial sales coverage when customers are geographically dispersed. Higher overhead from added layers of management and increased compensation for salespeople who represent a full line of products also adds cost. Overall, however, market-oriented sales organizations match the problem-solving approach of today's consultative sales reps.

FIGURE 6.13 Combination Sales Organization—Organized by Geography, Products, and Customers

Combination. Combinations of basic types of sales organizations are common. Figure 6.13 depicts a sales force organized by territories, products, *and* markets. Many companies use a combination structure for the sales organization as they grow in size and complexity. Kraft Foods (www.kraft.com) and DuPont (http://www2.dupont.com/DuPont_Home/en_US/index.html) are successfully using a combination sales structure. Similarly, Coca-Cola (www.coca-cola.com) uses a product-by-market structure. For many years, Coca-Cola was produced as a single product made according to a secret formula and sold at one retail price. However, with the demand for sugar-free soft drinks, large bottles, and new flavors, Coca-Cola began marketing a range of sizes, prices, and new products to specific market segments.

■ Team Selling

Today decisions occur at many levels in medium- and larger-sized businesses. A single salesperson seldom knows enough about all products and services to close the sale at all the various levels. At the same time, customer expectations are escalating, and many companies are looking for ways to reorganize traditional sales functions and processes.[12] To increase the likelihood of closing sales and to deliver superior value consistently in today's highly competitive conditions, companies increasingly are relying on team selling. **Team selling** relies on several individuals in an organization to sell products and services to all relevant decision makers. The goal of team selling is to develop long-term, mutually beneficial relationships between people, products, and companies.[13]

Team selling is often used by firms that have a key account or customer/market-oriented sales organization. Reasons for adopting a team selling approach are that information needs of customers are large, several people are involved in the decision to buy, the potential sale is large for the selling or buying company or both, and the complexity of the products or services is high and therefore beyond a single individual's capabilities.[14] Selling teams frequently include individuals from diverse functional areas such as operations, finance, R&D, marketing, and sometimes even the CEO. In fact, an increasing number of companies have offices located in or near the

Team Selling
The grouping of several individuals in an organization to sell products and services to all relevant decision makers.

customer's facilities. One of the best examples of this concept is the large number of companies that have set up offices in Bentonville, Arkansas, to sell to Wal-Mart (www.walmartstores.com). Procter & Gamble, for instance, has a team of two hundred people who work solely on the Wal-Mart account.[15]

■ Guidelines for Developing Sales Organizations

Well-designed sales organizations encourage effectiveness, efficiency, intra-organizational cooperation, customer loyalty, and profitability. New sales reps should all be given a copy of the organization's manual, which includes the organizational chart and describes the duties of each job and reporting relationships. There is no perfect sales organization, but here are suggestions for developing a sound sales organization:

- ■ *A market-oriented approach*—Recognize the customer as the organization's reason for being, and make the organization customer-centric.

- ■ *An approach designed around sales activities*—Do not ignore the people who will perform the work. Design sales organizations to accomplish major sales activities, such as sales planning, sales development, and customer service. In practice, it may be necessary to adapt an organization to take advantage of human strengths or to work around weaknesses.

- ■ *Defined areas of authority and responsibility*—Clearly communicate individual responsibility, and allocate sufficient authority to accomplish work assigned. For example, if branch sales managers are given sales quotas, they should be able to select their sales members and allocate their efforts.

- ■ *A reasonable span of control*—Besides handling administrative responsibilities, sales managers must be able to control the sales force adequately through frequent contact. While there is no magic number of people a manager can control, keep the number at ten or fewer, depending on the abilities of the sales manager and salesperson as well as on the challenges encountered.

- ■ *Flexibility*—An organization needs to be flexible enough to survive stress, such as sales declines or the loss of key personnel. Enhance flexibility by ensuring a trained replacement is ready to move into any position and by using staff specialists to give the manager more time for other tasks.

- ■ *Coordination and balance*—Sales managers should not allow any unit or individual to have excessive influence on operations. Ensure coordination and balance in all relationships involving sales and marketing as well as other functional areas of the business.

Not every possible sales organizational form can be listed here. The *Sales Management in Action* box provides in an interesting idea to add creativity to the sales organization.

■ Size of the Sales Force

An important consideration in managing the sales force is its size. Some companies may have too many salespeople and need to reduce the size of their sales force; others may have too few salespeople and need to increase. The number of salespeople in a company directly influences the nature of sales planning, as does the type of salespeople. Companies must consider not only the optimal number of salespeople but also

SALES MANAGEMENT IN ACTION

Going Outside

Big firms are often not the most creative. While corporate culture can be a good thing, a strong culture also can create a climate where all employees think and act the same way. Some innovative companies involved in sales and marketing actually go outside—literally—in search of innovative ideas. One CEO has recruited people who come from all walks of life and have expertise in drastically different areas from the task at hand. For example, an "idea generator" might be pulled from working behind the bar to sit in on a planning team for the day. A bartender is sure to generate thoughts that VPs would never come up with alone. A mechanic and a mom are recruited to assist in developing new automotive sales approaches. The key to making this method effective is that these people are from outside the organization and are not restricted by the corporate culture existing on the inside. The CEO or sales manager who adopts this approach can avoid a major sales bias of the past—emphasizing conformity over creativity.

SOURCES: J. Rooney, "Tapping the Brilliance of Ad-Hoc Experts," *Advertising Age,* September 4, 2006, p. 18.; D. Mayer and H. Greenberg, "What Makes a Good Salesman," *Harvard Business Review,* July–August 2006, pp. 164–71, and John Agno blog, "Looking outside for executives," http://coachingtip.blogs.com/coaching_tip/2006/02/looking_outside.html, accessed August 2007.

the number of inside sales reps versus outside sales reps. Other issues affecting sales force size include productivity of salespeople, turnover, and company strategies such as increasing market share or cutting costs. Sales managers generally welcome increases in the sales force. They usually oppose decreases, even when necessary, because they fear giving competitors an advantage.[16]

Several methods are available to determine optimum sales force size, including equalized workload, incremental productivity, and sales potential. Each approach has strengths and weaknesses, as we'll see next.

Equalized Workload. In the equalized workload method, each salesperson is assigned a set of customer accounts that demand about the same total sales time and effort. This approach assumes that the total workload in covering the market consists of three factors: customer size, sales volume potential, and travel time. The workload calculation consists of six steps:

1. *Classify present and prospective customers according to sales potential.* For example, there are 500 total customers (present and potential) classified by sales volume potential:

   Class A (large)   = 100 accounts
   Class B (medium) = 180 accounts
   Class C (small)   = 220 accounts

2. *Estimate the length of time per sales call and desired call frequency for each customer class.* Assume both present and potential customers require the same time per sales call and the same sales call frequency.

   Class A: 30 minutes/call × 150 calls/year = 75 hours/year
   Class B: 20 minutes/call × 210 calls/year = 70 hours/year
   Class C: 15 minutes/call × 160 calls/year = 40 hours/year

3. *Compute the total work necessary to cover the market.*

Class A: 100 accounts × 175 hours/year =   7,500 hours/year
Class B: 180 accounts × 170 hours/year = 12,600 hours/year
Class C: 220 accounts × 140 hours/year =   8,800 hours/year
Total = 28,900 hours/year

4. *Calculate the total work time available per salesperson.* Assume the sales manager specifies that salespeople work 40 hours per week, 45 weeks per year (allowing 7 weeks for vacations, holidays, illness, and the like). So each salesperson has the following hours available each year.

40 hours/week × 45 weeks = 1,800 hours/year

5. *Divide the total work time available per salesperson by sales task.* Assume management requires salespeople to apportion their time as follows:

Selling tasks: 55% =   990 hours
Non-selling tasks: 20% =   360 hours
Traveling: 25% =   450 hours
Total   100% = 1,800 hours

6. *Determine the total number of salespeople required.* Divide the total market workload by the total selling time available per salesperson.

$$\text{Salespeople needed} = \frac{28,900 \text{ hours}}{990 \text{ hours}} = 29.2$$

Assuming the company now has 20 salespeople, it should hire 9 new people to equalize the workload.

Despite its apparent simplicity, the workload method requires up-to-date and accurate input data. Estimating the number of potential customers and the ideal frequency of calls can be especially difficult. Furthermore, the approach does not consider the cost-profit ratio associated with a sales call and the cost of increasing the sales force size. Nevertheless, it provides valuable input to decision making when combined with managerial judgment.

Incremental Productivity. The incremental productivity method is based on economic marginal analysis theory. It assumes the sales force should be increased until profits added by the last salesperson hired equal the costs of employing that salesperson. Managers must compare the costs of training a new salesperson, his or her salary, and selling expenses with the marginal revenue generated by that salesperson. In short, marginal revenue equals marginal cost in the ideally sized sales force.

To illustrate this method, consider a company whose total sales volume varies directly with the number of salespeople in the field. Costs of goods sold remain constant at 70 percent of sales. All company salespeople receive a straight salary of $25,000 yearly plus commissions of 5 percent of total sales volume. Each salesperson also receives $1,000 per month for travel expenses. Currently, there are thirty-two members of the sales force, and the sales manager wants to determine whether to add more. To make this decision, the manager must first estimate the increases in sales volume, costs of goods sold, and gross margin from the addition of each salesperson.

Salesperson #	Sales Volume −	Cost of Goods =	Gross Margin
33	$300,000	$210,000	$90,000
34	225,000	157,500	67,500
35	150,000	105,000	45,000
36	75,000	52,500	22,500

Next, the sales manager calculates the net profit contribution with the addition of each salesperson:

Salesperson #	Gross Margin −	Salaries +	Commissions +	Total Expenses	Net Profit Contribution
33	$90,000 −	$25,000 +	$15,000 +	$12,000	= $ 38,000
34	67,500 −	25,000 +	11,250 +	12,000	= 19,250
35	45,000 −	25,000 +	7,500 +	12,000	= 500
36	22,500 −	25,000 +	3,750 +	12,000	= −18,250

The incremental analysis shows it would pay to add three more salespeople but not four. While the third salesperson (#35) would add $500 of marginal revenue, the net profit contribution of the fourth (#36) would be a negative $18,250.

Limitations of this approach include lack of cost data in most organizations, the assumption of no increase in efficiency as new salespeople become more experienced, and not including the effect of territorial assignment on the marginal revenue produced by new salespeople. Nevertheless, the incremental productivity concept can help sales managers think pragmatically about sales force size, even if the relationship between marginal cost and revenue is imprecise.

Sales Potential. The sales potential approach to determining sales force size starts with the sales manager's assumption of what the average sales representative will achieve in annual sales volume. Divide the total sales forecast for the year by this figure to obtain the number of salespeople needed. In equation form, the relationship is

$$N = \frac{S}{P} \times (1 + T)$$

where

N = number of salespeople needed
S = annual sales forecast for the company
P = estimated sales productivity of the average salesperson
T = estimated percentage of annual sales force turnover

For example, if the company sales forecast is $10 million, annual sales volume productivity for the average salesperson is $500,000, and the anticipated annual rate of sales force turnover is 20 percent, the calculation is

$$N = \frac{\$10,000,000}{\$500,000} \times 1.20 = 24$$

Twenty-four salespeople are needed.

In using the sales potential approach, the sales manager must consider several limitations. First, lead time will be needed for training and field experience before new salespeople reach average productivity. Second, since all salespeople are not equally productive, the manager must account for the relative quality of each salesperson hired. Third, the sales manager must estimate resignations, retirements, and promotions in estimating sales force turnover. Finally, any adjustments in the sales forecast will require changes in the size of the sales force.

Instead of relying on just one method to determine sales force size, sales managers will probably employ all three approaches to see how closely they coincide before making the final decision.

Manufacturer's Representatives. One relatively low-risk way to increase the sales force is to use manufacturers' representatives. Entrepreneurial, independent salespeople who sell products for several noncompeting companies, manufacturers' reps usually become specialists in certain markets before starting their own sales operations. Many companies use manufacturers' reps to do specialized selling or to increase call frequencies on certain customers.[17] In the frozen foods market, Quaker Oats (www.quakeroats.com), a division of PepsiCo, Inc., believes manufacturers' reps enable the company to increase call frequencies on supermarkets so in-store stocks are replenished at least weekly. Along with providing specialized selling experience and expertise, a fixed cost-to-sales ratio, and rapid penetration of new markets, reps may also bring problems. They sometimes are reluctant to handle customer service problems, to go to training, or to allow control over their sales activities. Moreover, they tend to emphasize major product lines where minimal selling is necessary. Finally, their time with customers is divided because they also sell other manufacturer's products.

Small companies often start out using agents to sell their products instead of spending their limited resources on maintaining their own sales force. Manufacturers' reps offer a way to minimize selling costs so more funds can be allocated to new product development, sales forecasting, and pricing. Thus manufacturers' reps can be a substantial benefit to companies they represent.

■ Developing a High-Quality Sales Organization

The overall quality of the sales organization is contingent on effective organization in general. The sales manager should consider the following practical guidelines in developing and managing the sales organization.

- *Be sure authority equals responsibility.* Salespeople find it difficult to perform effectively without the authority to make necessary decisions.
- *Put salespeople where they fit best.* Consider geography and personality types, and compare aptitude for inside and outside positions or national and local accounts.
- *Be willing to delegate.* The sales manager's task is to accomplish objectives through the efforts of the sales force.
- *Be more than just an efficiency expert.* Don't ignore qualitative considerations while focusing on quantitative issues. The human element must be considered.
- *Hold sales force personnel accountable for what they do.* This is the basic means of maintaining control.
- *Be flexible.* An organizational structure effective today may not be the best for tomorrow. The sales force organization must be open to new ideas.
- *Know what needs to be done.* Organization of the sales force should be directed toward accomplishing sales goals.

■ *Organize the sales force to avoid unequal workloads.* Inequitable distribution of work for salespeople creates a potential source of dissatisfaction and reduces productivity.

These guidelines should result in a highly productive sales force. A well-thought-out and carefully developed sales organization can be invaluable to salespeople, customers, and the company. But the really critical part of any sales organization is the quality of its people.[18]

CHAPTER SUMMARY

1. Understand the purpose and levels of organizational planning. Planning creates the essential framework for all other decision making. It requires sales managers to anticipate the possible outcomes and future implications of current decisions; thus planning is an attempt to manage the future.

Every manager should plan, and more effective planners tend to be more effective managers. Top management focuses on strategic planning for the company, while middle managers—such as regional and district sales managers—spend most of their planning time on shorter-run tactical plans. As planners and administrators, sales managers must (1) define goals and objectives, (2) set policies, (3) establish procedures, (4) devise strategies, (5) direct tactics, and (6) develop and enforce controls.

2. Apply the sales planning process, including strategic and tactical sales planning. Sales planning is the primary function of sales managers because the sales plan provides basic guidelines and direction for all other sales decisions and activities. In their role as planners and administrators, sales managers must set goals and objectives, establish sales policies and procedures, devise strategies and tactics, and implement controls to ensure that goals and objectives are achieved. Before the planning process begins, sales managers should think through the six-stage process of diagnosis, prognosis, objectives, strategy, tactics, and control. The actual steps involved in the sales planning process are (1) analyze the situation, (2) set goals and objectives, (3) determine market potential, (4) forecast sales, (5) select strategies, (6) develop detailed activities, (7) allocate necessary resources (budgeting), (8) implement the plan, and (9) control the plan.

Strategic sales planning is the process of setting the sales organization's overall objectives, allocating total resources, and outlining broad courses of action. Strategic decisions give the organization a total plan of action to serve customers better, to take advantage of competitors' weaknesses, and to capitalize on the firm's strengths. Tactical sales plans are the functional sub-plans that underlie and accomplish the overall strategic plan. Tactical action plans identify what needs to be done, who is responsible, what resources are needed, and what benefits are expected. It's been said that generals do strategic sales planning while soldiers do tactical sales planning.

3. Avoid unsuccessful sales planning. Probably the major cause of unsuccessful sales planning is the number of unchallenged and often erroneous assumptions made in each stage of the planning process. Dialectic and contingency planning can help overcome the inherent problems of underlying assumptions in sales planning. Another reason for planning failures is the often perfunctory approach to the planning process whereby the plan is simply filed away after being prepared, without having much impact on actual operations.

4. Describe different ways to organize the sales force, including calculating its optimal size. Most sales forces can be organized in four ways: (1) by geography, (2) by function, (3) by market or customer type, or (4) by a combination of two or more of these ways. Many sales organizations also are supplemented by manufacturers' agents or reps. Optimal sales force size is estimated using one of three approaches: (1) equalized workload method, (2) incremental productivity, or (3) sales potential. Probably the easiest approach to apply is the sales potential approach, which requires only an annual sales forecast, estimated sales productivity of the average salesperson, and an estimate of anticipated annual sales force turnover. The best decision is based on comparing the results of all three approaches and then selecting the optimum size.

REVIEW AND APPLICATION QUESTIONS

1. What assumptions might a sales manager make (sometimes subconsciously) about the marketplace in preparing the annual plan? How would you ensure that these assumptions are valid? [LO 1]

2. Do you think the role of the sales manager in sales planning, organizing, forecasting, and budgeting will become less or more important with the ever growing power of computers and software sophistication? Explain. [LO 1]

3. What are the potential benefits of sales management planning? [LO 2]

4. What are the essential planning and administrative roles of the sales manager? [LO 2]

5. What is the difference between a sales strategy and a sales tactic? Give recent examples of each using a source like the *Wall Street Journal.* [LO 2]

6. What are three types of performance standards relevant for sales managers? When is each type particularly appropriate? [LO 2]

7. What are the biggest sources of unsuccessful sales planning? [LO 3]

8. When is it appropriate to organize departments by distribution channel? [LO 4]

9. If a sales firm has 200 "A" customers and 200 "B" customers, and each sales call to an A consumer takes 1 hour and each sales call to a B consumer takes 2 hours, the firm expects 75 sales calls per year to A customers and 100 sales calls per year to B customers. The salespeople spend 20 percent of their time on non-selling tasks and 25 percent of their time traveling from sales call to sales call. How large should the sales force be? [LO 5]

IT'S UP TO YOU

Internet Exercise

Think of thee companies that you consider "sales organizations." List them and describe the business that each is in. Use Internet resources to find the mission statement for each organization. Try to determine as best you can what form of organizational structure exists in this company. What type of organizational structure would you recommend for each company? Have they selected the best type of organizational structure for their given industry?

Role-Playing Exercise

Denman Business Forms

Situation

For many years Denman has been a leader in manufacturing and selling business forms and related products directly to industrial users. The past ten years could be characterized as a "change" decade for this industry. The current situation facing Denman can be summarized as follows:

- Demand for business forms has declined in recent years due to increased affordability and usage of desktop publishing.

- Denman's market share has been steadily shrinking for the past five years.

- Future growth in sales and profits is not expected to come from business form sales.

- The sales force has little autonomy or authority,

and training historically has been in areas such as order taking and inventory control.

■ Denman has three major product lines—business forms, office supplies, and office equipment—and sales reps sell only one product line so they can specialize, even though each customer gets sales calls from three separate Denman sales reps.

Role-Play Participants and Assignments

Rick Andrews, CEO and owner, is in his mid-fifties and argues that the entire problem is at the sales level.

He thinks the sales reps must be out of touch with what's happening with their customers, and they need to work harder.

Patrick Schul, recently hired sales manager with ten years' experience at Cisco, says they have a loyal sales force and need to be careful what actions they take. While the situation they are facing is difficult, he believes more information is needed to make the right decision.

In-Basket Exercise

You are a sales manager for a consumer goods company that has just launched a new product. Although all the staff members are extremely excited about its potential, after only a few months on the market the product is generating disappointing responses from buyers. One of your salespeople recently heard a major wholesaler, serving over five hundred supermarkets, say: "We've had this product three months, and it's not moving, so we're going to yank it from the stores!"

Consider these questions: How do you respond to this situation? What do you tell your salespeople? What tools are available to help you in the rather gloomy scenario? Prepare a list of things you will discuss in a meeting with your salespeople to deal with this issue.

Ethical Dilemma

Bruce is a branch sales manager in a traditional line organization. He decides to assign the sales force based on products rather than geographic territories. He believes this will increase the perceived expertise of the sales force. However, his supervisor approaches him upon hearing of the plan. "The problem is that you ended up assigning some salespeople predominantly cash cows, others are getting problem children, while still others are assigned only stars." Bruce replies that he has thought of this and assigned only the most experienced

salespeople to stars and the least experienced people to problem children. Some of the salespeople have begun to complain to Bruce after only a few months of the plan.

QUESTIONS

1. Does this situation present any moral dilemmas for Bruce or his supervisor? Explain.

2. Can any moral issue be resolved without scrapping Bruce's organizational plan completely?

CASE 6.1

PlayMart Toyz: Building a Sales Organization

It was December of 2007, and Pam Siira found herself contemplative and somewhat detached. On the outside, she was able to join her new husband and friends in the celebrations of the holiday season. But inside, her mind was working nonstop—organizing, planning, and strat-

egizing. She had accepted a challenging yet exciting new role that was to begin the first week of January, and she was responsible for achieving a major objective.

In November, Siira had accepted an offer to be senior vice president of sales for PlayMart Toyz. She had a previous working relationship with PlayMart, having sold the company's famous water guns and dart guns for ten years, but she had never been an employee. As an independent manufacturers' representative, Siira represented several toy manufacturers, along with PlayMart. Now, she was working solely for PlayMart as an executive reporting to the owner—and she was responsible for doubling sales to $100 million over the next five years.

The change in employment status required Siira to organize her thoughts and efforts a bit differently. She was no longer "independent" in the sense of working for herself. She was now responsible to a company that had invested its future in her, and her new role focused on managing the other North America PlayMart sales reps. This would involve hiring and firing when necessary, training them properly, troubleshooting any issues along the way, motivating them to give maximum effort to reach objectives, and evaluating their efforts. This was going to be a change from what she was used to, but she felt ready for the challenge! While getting used to the new role and status, she considered how to organize the fifty independent sales representatives that represented the PlayMart Toy Company in North America to achieve the 100 percent sales volume increase.

PlayMart's sales representatives are all independent manufacturers' representatives who work on a commission basis. Each representative receives a 3 percent commission of total dollar sales volume. Sales representatives are currently divided according to geographic territories based on potential sales volume. In more population-dense areas like the Northeast there might be two or more PlayMart reps in a particular state, while in the Plains region one rep might handle several states. The goal is to enable each sales rep to earn a worthwhile commission in the area that he or she covers.

Another issue that comes into play in determining territory allocation is the location of the headquarters for its "key" accounts. PlayMart Toyz has five major "key" accounts: Wal-Mart, Wal-Mart Canada, K-Mart, Toys 'Я' Us, and KB Toys. Consequently, PlayMart has established regional offices in Bentonville, Arkansas, where Wal-Mart headquarters is located; and in Chicago, where K-Mart is located. Other smaller key accounts include Meijer, Kohl's, Target, J.C. Penney, Sam's Club, Costco, and Shopko. The rest of the customer base includes regional drug outlets, regional chains, and toy distributors. The company is seeking to break into the pool and spa and sporting goods chains in the future.

The PlayMart Toyz product line started with large water guns that kids could use to "blast" streams of water at each other during the hot summer months. Sales of this product are highly seasonal and skewed toward warmer climates. Over the years, the company has added products that would provide balanced sales throughout the year and would reach different age groups. For example, dart guns, young girl's makeup kits, and play horse action figures are items that are sold year-round. Mobiles, soft crib toys, and musical toys are targeted to infants and toddlers and are also sold year-round. And sporting goods such as pogo sticks and foam balls are targeted to children in their formative years and are slightly skewed toward the summer months. Products are all manufactured in China according to PlayMart Toyz specifications and are shipped to the United States and Canada.

PlayMart is well established in major retail chains, so much of the sales rep's job is really one of inventory management. Each sales rep monitors inventory at the chain level and therefore is responsible for seeing that:

- The chain's yearly forecast is accurate.
- Actual sales are on par with historical data.
- Current inventory levels are sufficient to handle demand.
- The proper amount of new shipments are in transit.
- The proper amount of product is on order.

The bottom line for the chain is that it needs to have product available on each store's shelf when customers come looking. Being out of stock on a particular item means the store has failed to properly satisfy customers and runs the risk of sending that customer to a competing chain. The PlayMart rep's job is to work in partnership with each chain to make sure this does not happen. What makes this task difficult is the seasonality of certain items.

The toy industry has two seasons: summer and the winter holidays. Planning and strategizing for summer occurs in June and July, when decisions are made about what will be on the shelves for spring and summer of the following year. Orders must be placed, product manufactured and shipped, and product received and sorted at the distribution centers for each of the stores.

In the final step, product is shipped to the stores and placed on the shelves. The entire process is repeated in December and January for the next year's holiday season. That merchandise is shipped in June. Basically, PlayMart needs to plan one year in advance. During the two seasons, the sales representative needs to be working with the chain to make sure enough product is planned for shipment and that it will be delivered on time. Failure to do this accurately can result in several problems including:

- product arriving too late
- having too much product left unsold at the end of the season
- having to order additional inventory from China at the last minute

The first situation results in missing the period of highest demand. If a retailer doesn't have what the customers want when they want it, customers will look elsewhere. The second situation forces the retailer to discount heavily to unload product. This eats into profits. The last situation can be a major problem due to increased risk. Should the product not arrive in a timely fashion, it too could mean drastic markdowns potentially meaning that product is sold at a price below its cost. Any of these situations can disrupt the harmony of the relationship.

Siira knows most salespeople are motivated by money, and they might be interested in encouraging a customer to over-order to increase sales volume and the amount of the commission check. Some, she knows, might be motivated to keep the customer happy and will stay silent when the chain under-orders, even though they know it will leave the company out of stock early in the selling season. Consequently, Siira has been wondering how she can get her salespeople to work together with the chains to plan properly for the good of both parties in the relationship.

The remainder of the sales rep's job is to find and cultivate new business. Since new chains don't just crop up overnight, it becomes more of an issue of finding new markets. One new market to explore is pool and spa chains that sell water guns and other water-related toys. While some of the objective to increase sales might be achieved through better planning with the current chains and by expanding some of those chains, Siira realizes the bulk of the increase will have to come from developing new markets. That means she has to develop a strategy for determining which new markets to develop, how to approach those markets, and how to sell product in those markets. Once the strategy is developed, she has to develop an incentive plan to motivate the PlayMart reps to implement the strategy.

So as Pam Siira was celebrating the holidays and relocating her office in December 2007, all of these issues regarding her new job rolled around in her head:

- Is the territory alignment the best means of organization for her sales force? If not, what alignment should she install?
- How can she get her sales reps to plan properly with their customers so that PlayMart Toyz can maintain a harmonious relationship with all its customers?
- What new markets would be best to pursue? Which ones will allow the company to grow the fastest?
- What new strategies can she employ over the next five years to achieve the 100 percent increase in sales that the company has set forth as her objective?
- How can she properly motivate the reps to achieve the objective?

As these issues roll around in her head, Siira is sure of one thing—she does not want to make any personnel changes for at least six months, so initially she has to focus on organization, planning, and strategy.

QUESTIONS

1. What is the best sales and territory organization for PlayMart Toyz?

2. How could PERT and/or the critical path method help the sales manager be more effective in this situation?

3. Should Siira focus only on the United States and Canada to achieve PlayMart sales increase objectives, or should she pursue the toy market in other countries as well? Justify your choice.

Case prepared by Frank Notturno, Madonna University.

CASE 6.2

Wild Willie "Juiced" Drinks: Planning for Sales Growth

Soft drinks, dominated by Coca-Cola and Pepsi, are a huge industry in the United States. As a category of beverages they sell more than coffee, tea, and fruit juices combined. But the soft-drink product category is mature, and alternative beverages have emerged in recent years. The first alternative beverage was sports drinks, followed later by bottled water and then flavored waters. The most recent entry into the beverage category is energy drinks.

Energy drinks are beverages featuring a combination of ingredients such as B vitamins, caffeine, and exotic herbal extracts like guarana, ginseng, maltodextrin, creatine, and ginkgo biloba. Some contain high levels of sugar. Most brands also offer an artificially sweetened version. They are designed to provide consumers the benefit of a quick burst of energy. Brands offering energy drinks target young people, students, and people "on the go." The most popular brands of energy drinks are Red Bull, Monster Assault, No Fear Gold, Rhinos Energy Gummies, Wired X3000, Bawls Energy Drink, Killer Buzz, Mad Croc, Red Rhinos, and Rockstar Energy Cola.

Most energy drinks differ from sports drinks in several important ways. Sports drinks are designed to replenish electrolytes, sugars, water, and other nutrients. Gatorade and Powerade are the leading brands in the sports drink category. Some beverage brands have now introduced new products that combine energy and sports drink ingredients, having both electrolytes and herbal extracts.

Wild Willie Juiced Drinks is one of the latest entries into this rapidly growing niche beverage category. Wild Willie is currently sold only in New England. It was developed by two friends and recent graduates of Boston College—one a chemistry major and the other a business major. They had hired two other friends to work as telemarketers, and another to make personal sales calls on two channels of distribution—convenience stores and independent grocers. Sales were growing steadily, but the two entrepreneurs have noticed a seasonal influence in sales volume with a double-digit decline in the winter months. This seasonality is due to some consumers switching to hot beverages during the winter months. Therefore, they believe major markets in the Southern and Western states may provide more consistent year-round sales volume and growth for their brand. They would like to expand into these larger markets but are not sure how to do so.

Another major problem is brand awareness and distribution. Because the organization is small, none of the larger chains like Wal-Mart and Target, or supermarkets like Publix and Kroger, will talk with them. In addition, major convenience store chains like Exxon-Mobil's "On-the-Run" have been difficult to penetrate. The owners know that syndicated category sales data shows that convenience stores account for over 60 percent of sales volume. Unfortunately, most potential discount, grocery, and convenience store chain customers say the brand is unknown and is not supported by much marketing, including brand-building advertising and store-level sales promotions.

Some popular brands use a distribution method called "direct store door" delivery or DSD, in which company representatives or independent distributors check shelf inventory levels for their brand, restock and rotate product for freshness, manage displays and point-of-purchase materials, and set up in-store sales promotions and sampling. Retail chains generally welcome DSD service as "value added," because it helps them reduce in-store labor costs. However, for efficiency and cost reasons, Wal-Mart prefers that food and beverage products be distributed through its own distribution centers.

While DSD is an effective method of distribution, it requires a major up-front investment since a sales organization must be created, local warehousing must be established, and a fleet of trucks must be purchased. Wild Willie's owners find this situation frustrating because in blind taste tests, most consumers prefer their product over those of leading competitors. The owners believe they can become market-share leaders in this emerging category if they can figure out the brand awareness and distribution puzzle.

QUESTIONS

1. What should the two entrepreneurs do first to decide how to expand their business?

2. If a sales plan is developed, what should it include?

3. One business associate told the owners to get a loan to expand their business and start "direct store door" delivery. If they can find the capital to expand, which states and customer segment(s) should they distribute in first, how many salespeople and truck drivers should they hire, and how should they be organized?

4. Are there other alternatives to expand geographically and build the brand with DSD service without incurring the large up-front investment? If so, how would this alternative still allow the owners to meet their sales plan?

Case prepared by K. Randall Russ, Belhaven College.

Time and Territory Management

INSIDE SALES MANAGEMENT

Jean Berdis of DHL

"Prospecting," says Jean Berdis, "is a huge part of my day-to-day job." Berdis is an account representative for DHL, the leading global express delivery and logistics company. She attracts new customers and keeps current customers satisfied by improving DHL's small-parcel shipping programs, covering everything from letters to packages weighing as much as 150 pounds.

Berdis averages twenty new business calls a week and spends about 40 percent of her time looking for leads as well as following up on promising prospects. She identifies potential customers in a variety of ways, such as looking at Internet sites, following up on lead campaigns generated through DHL's customer relationship management system, and using DHL's database tools. In addition, she uses telemarketing, area-specific canvassing, and cold calling—visiting businesses without an appointment.

Leads from DHL drivers are particularly valuable, because the drivers often develop relationships with employees of the companies where they make deliveries. Berdis tracks the results "to determine which methods have proved most successful in obtaining appointments with prospects and which have resulted in new business. Over time, this has allowed me to understand where my energy should be spent," she notes.

To qualify a prospect, Berdis visits the company's website, studies its brochures, and reads its annual report. "We're looking for two things," she explains. "We want to identify a company's need for transportation and shipping. We also want to understand its organizational structure. Is this a multi-location account or a single site? Who are the key players within that organization, and what are their concerns?" Berdis's research helps her identify not only the people in the company who use shipping services but also the person who actually has the authority to make buying decisions about shipping.

Not long ago, one of DHL's drivers returned from a delivery with a lead. He had learned that a beauty products distributor was unhappy with its current shipping company. Next, Berdis says, "I visited the distributor's website to learn more about its business, customer base, and distribution network." Armed with this background information, she phoned the company's president and asked a number of qualifying questions.

As a result of that phone call, "I was able to schedule a meeting with the president and his key managers," Berdis remembers. "It also helped me plan my sales call." During her visit with the shipping manager and other executives, she developed a more detailed understanding of the company's requirements and expectations. Then she presented a couple of specific alternatives for solving the current problem—and closed the sale. "If you can position yourself as a consultant, someone who wants to understand the customer's business and help address the challenges that keep its managers awake at night, you will be viewed as a real partner."

SOURCE: Anderson, Rolph E., Alan J. Dubinsky, and Rajiv Mehta, *Personal Selling: Building Customer Relationships and Partnerships,* 2/e, pp. 99–100. Copyright © 2007 by Houghton Mifflin Company. Reprinted with permission.

Improving Sales Productivity

George likes to unwind and reward himself during the middle of the week by taking a leisurely two-hour lunch on Wednesdays. He feels this helps motivate him to work for the rest of the week. On Fridays, after working hard all week making sales calls and providing customer service, George usually takes the afternoon off to play golf. Although he has convinced himself that these habits actually help his productivity by keeping him motivated, it's more likely they are "time traps" that can seriously diminish George's performance as well as the efforts of the whole sales force team.

Time and territory management strategies help sales managers determine which accounts are called on, when, and how often. Rising fuel prices have had a domino effect, increasing the prices of many other products and services—and sales costs have consistently increased. The average sales call costs almost $300, a figure that can be as much as $1,500 for some high-tech firms. Managers are therefore searching for less expensive ways to sell products and services. For instance, they increasingly use electronic channels such as telemarketing, Internet, intranets, and extranets to perform many steps in the selling process. As a result, many traditional sales forces have become hybrids, relying on these electronic channels to support field salespeople.[1] Simultaneously, managers are equipping their salespeople with laptop computers, mobile phones, PDAs, MP3 players, and similar technology enabling them to access websites, blogs, wikis, podcasts, webinars, and other support mechanisms. Along with these technological innovations, there is renewed emphasis on better training for salespeople to help them use technology to improve time and territory management.

© ThinkStock LLOC / Index Stock

● **Salespeople rely on technology to improve their time management.**

Technology enables salespeople to become increasingly independent from sales managers. But time and territory management will continue to be among the sales manager's most important roles.[2]

Establishing Sales Territories

Sales Territory
A specific geographic area that contains present and potential customers and is assigned to a particular salesperson.

One of the most important tasks in time and territory management is effective assignment of salespeople to territories. A **sales territory** is usually a specific geographic area that contains present and potential customers and is assigned to a particular salesperson. Because the total market of most companies is usually too large to manage efficiently, territories help the sales manager in directing, evaluating, and controlling the sales force. Assigning sales territories also helps the sales manager achieve a match between sales efforts and sales opportunities

Most companies establish territories on a geographic basis. Customers and prospects are grouped so the salesperson serving the accounts can call on them as conveniently and economically as possible. But geographic considerations are only the initial focus. Companies determine their markets based on the number of customers and their purchasing power, not on square miles.

■ Reasons for Sales Territories

Sales territories facilitate planning and controlling selling activities. But sales managers have other reasons for developing them.

Enhance Market Coverage. Sales calls should be planned as efficiently as possible to ensure proper coverage of current and potential customers. Coverage is more thorough when each salesperson is assigned to a well-designed sales territory rather than when all salespeople are allowed to sell anywhere. A sales territory should not be so large that the salesperson spends a great deal of time traveling, or has time to call on only a few of the best customers. On the other hand, a sales territory should not be so small that the salesperson is calling on customers too often. Sales territories should be big enough to represent a reasonable workload but small enough to ensure that the salesperson can visit all potential customers as often as needed.

Minimize Selling Costs. Inflation affects the price of food, lodging, and transportation—and selling costs. Sales managers must design cost-effective territories by eliminating or minimizing overnight travel and by finding alternate methods of reaching customers. Alternatives to face-to-face interaction with customers include teleconferencing, Internet/website, e-mail, fax, and inside sales reps. These options enable salespeople to work from office or home, thereby curtailing travel, hotel, and dining expenses.

Strengthen Customer Relations. Efficient territories enable salespeople to spend more time with present and potential customers and less time on the road. The more salespeople learn about their customers by spending time with them, the better they understand customers' problems and the more comfortable their relationship becomes—until it evolves into a partnership. Sales territories facilitate regularly scheduled sales calls on customers. Regular contact with prospects or infrequent buyers via alternative methods can turn infrequent buyers into more frequent buyers, and prospects into customers.

Build a More Effective Sales Force. Well-designed sales territories motivate salespeople, improve morale, increase interest, and build a more effective sales force. When salespeople are assigned a territory and given responsibility for it, they become the manager of the territory. Clearly defined responsibility is a powerful motivator for many people, and when territories are distributed equitably among the salespeople, with specific accounts assigned to each, fewer conflicts arise about which accounts belong to whom.

Better Evaluate Sales. Assigning salespeople to specific geographic areas improves performance evaluation because salespeople can be evaluated on their performance compared with the territory's potential. Historical databases enable sales managers to access past information and compare it with current performance in each territory. By examining sales performance territory by territory, sales managers can spot changing market conditions and make needed adjustments in sales tactics. Giving salespeople a specific geographic area facilitates efficient routing, helps establish a strong customer base by building rapport with each customer, and helps determine the best call frequency for each customer.

Coordinate Selling with Other Marketing Functions. Well-designed sales territories enable management to better perform other marketing functions. Sales and cost analysis is easier on a territory basis than for the entire market. Market research on a territory basis is also more effective for setting sales quotas and expense budgets. If salespeople are able to help customers launch advertising campaigns, distribute point-of-purchase displays, sell channel partners on cooperative advertising, or perform other work related to sales promotions, the results often are better when work is managed on a territory-by-territory basis rather than for the market as a whole. Finally, if the company uses inside sales reps to support the field sales force, territory assignments enable them to pinpoint whose territory the customer or potential customer is in, rather than just randomly assigning a salesperson to the account. In this way salespeople can respond to customers more quickly.

■ Reasons for Not Having Sales Territories

Despite the advantages, geographic sales territories are not needed in all situations. For example, small companies with only a few people selling in a local market do not need territories. Assigning sales territories in this case would only slow decision making by sales managers. Territory assignments generally become necessary only as the sales force increases in size.

Individuals may not be assigned sales territories when sales coverage is far below the sales potential of the market—that is, when there is more than enough business for every salesperson. This is often the case for small companies, those selling products that everyone needs (such as insurance), and those introducing a new product. Not assigning sales territories in such situations, however, could mean a potential segment of the market is neglected, thereby inviting competition into the market. If this is the case, the firm should hire additional salespeople as soon as possible.

Other reasons have been used to justify not establishing territories. For example, sales territories may not be needed when sales are made primarily on the basis of social contacts or personal friendships, or if territories eventually will have to be revised, thereby resulting in disagreement among the salespeople.

■ CRM and Sales Territories

As we discussed in chapter 3, companies that have adopted a customer relationship management (CRM) perspective see benefits in assigning territories based on customer characteristics rather than geography. Thus, a tire manufacturer may assign one sales manager to deal with all U.S. OEM customers, while another may be assigned responsibility for a single retailer like Sears. The principle here is that the enhanced knowledge that comes when a salesperson deals only with very similar customers more than compensates for any additional costs arising from an inefficient geographic assignment. Thus, in this situation, geography is not the primary factor in assigning responsibilities for customers.

Trust between customers and sales reps is critical with CRM. Thus, the frequency of contact needed between a customer and a salesperson is another important factor in making assignments. Wyeth (www.wyeth.com) found that maintaining this high level of trust with traditional territory management practices was very difficult. The solution the firm adopted was to use part-time reps to call on customers located in rural areas or not designated as "best" customers.[3] "Best" customers were given full-time reps.

Setting Up Sales Territories

Whether a company is setting up geographic sales territories for the first time or revising ones that already exist, the same procedure applies: (1) select a geographic

SALES MANAGEMENT IN ACTION

Cisco's Web Portal Improves Sales Productivity

Salespeople are much more successful if they have complete and up-to-date customer information. Cisco Systems has about 12,000 salespeople and over 300 local offices worldwide, as well as numerous employees at the regional and corporate headquarters. To increase sales productivity, Cisco wanted a new sales management tool to help salespeople work more efficiently and spend more time with customers. One problem was that reps were spending a lot of time identifying high-volume customers. Another was that the reps' daily status reports did not have relevant, real-time customer information to help them develop close customer relationships. The solution was the E-Sales Web portal initiative, which created Internet-based information-sharing tools.

E-Sales included a portal with a collection of sales information and forecasting applications, in a single location and a single format, to help salespeople work more effectively and efficiently. Personalized alerts, reports based on user type, sales projections based on realistic customer opportunities, and other specialized features were designed to meet the needs of the sales, finance, marketing, production planning, and executive divisions. One feature for salespeople was the *My Bookings Reports* that deliver near real-time information (every 15 minutes) about customer orders. The *My News* application provides daily information about customers, market issues, competitor activity, and the latest Cisco sales-related information. *Personalized Customer Alerts* notify account managers of time-sensitive customer information that requires a salesperson's immediate attention, such as order status, warranty expiration dates, end-of-sale announcements, and so forth. The *Sales Territory* application uses account and geographic data to track sales activities by salesperson and territory. Both qualitative and quantitative assessments of E-Sales portal results demonstrate its value in improving salesperson productivity and improving sales forecasting.

SOURCES: http://www.cisco.com; E-Sales portal; and http://www.cisco .com/web/about/ciscoitatwork/case_studies/business_applications_dl2 .html (accessed November 2006).

control unit, (2) conduct an account analysis, (3) develop a salesperson workload analysis, (4) combine geographic control units into territories, and (5) assign salespeople to territories.

■ Selecting a Geographic Control Unit

The starting point in developing territories is selecting a geographic control unit. Units most often used are states, counties, Zip Code areas, cities, metropolitan statistical areas, trading areas, major accounts, or a combination of these. Control units should be as small as possible, for two reasons. First, smaller units help management pinpoint the geographic location of sales potential. Second, small geographic areas make adjusting territories much easier. One salesperson's territory can be increased and another's reduced, and adjustments are easier if the control unit is smaller—for example, a county rather than a state.

Political units (state, county, or city) are often used as geographic control units because census data and other market information for them are available. Political units and market factors like buying habits and patterns of trade flow also serve as geographic control units. For example, sales territories can be based on a trading area that lies within county lines. This location makes data for a particular trading area easy to collect.

States. Firms sometimes use state boundaries to develop territories, especially in the early stages of territory development. A state may be an adequate control unit for companies with a small sales force covering the market selectively rather then intensively. States as territory boundaries also work well for companies seeking nationwide distribution for the first time. In fact, in these situations salespeople may be assigned to territories that consist of more than one state. This arrangement typically is temporary until the market develops, at which time the firm switches to smaller control units.

State sales territories are simple, convenient, and inexpensive. But few companies use them. Customers from one state often cross boundaries into another state to do their purchasing. For example, hundreds of thousands of shoppers a year cross from New York into northern New Jersey to make their purchases because shopping malls are centrally located and easy to get to, there is less traffic, and New Jersey has a lower sales tax. In the other direction, the tourist appeal of New York City and its diversity of goods and services attract millions of shoppers from around the country.

Another reason for not using states as territories is that some states are just too large. Most companies would need more than one person to handle California or Texas. If one person did cover California, another salesperson would have to cover a dozen or more Rocky Mountain States to have a territory equal to California in sales potential. Finally, a state may simply be too large and diverse in market potential for management to control or evaluate salesperson performance.

Counties and Zip Codes. Counties are much smaller units than states, and they are better for dividing territories. There are over 3,100 counties in the United States but only 50 states. Territories with approximately equal sales potential are easier to develop in smaller control units.

Counties as control units offer several other advantages. Counties typically are the smallest units for which government data are available. Many government, commercial, and private sources report market data (like population, retail sales, income, employment, and manufacturing information) by county. Also, counties are usually small enough so that management can better identify problems. Finally, the small size of counties makes shifting salespeople from one territory to another easier because fewer customers are affected.

Counties have some of the same drawbacks as states. Not all counties are similar in size, sales potential, or ease of market coverage. Some may be too large for practical use as control units. For example, Cook County (Chicago) may require several salespeople to cover the market adequately. In such cases, a company may divide a county into several territories, so the control unit is smaller than a county.

D&B—Dun's Market Identifiers (DMI)
A directory file produced by D&B, Inc. that contains basic company data, executive names and titles, corporate linkages, DUNS Numbers, organization status, and other marketing information on over 17 million U.S. business establishment locations, including public, private, and government organizations.

Territories based on Zip Codes are flexible and typically reflect the economic and demographic characteristics of individual areas, whereas political subdivisions, such as states and counties, do not. **D&B—Dun's Market Identifiers (DMI)** is a directory file produced by D&B, Inc. that contains basic company data, executive names and titles, corporate linkages, DUNS Numbers, organization status, and other marketing information on over 17 million U.S. business establishment locations, including public, private, and government organizations. Dun & Bradstreet also produces other databases available on DIALOG, including D&B Duns Financial Records Plus. Non-U.S. businesses can be found in several D&B files accessed via the *DIALOG Database Catalogue*. In designing territories, sales managers can use this directory to pinpoint companies by geographic area.

Metropolitan Statistical Areas (MSAs)
Areas that serve as territories; they can include a major city as well as the surrounding suburban and satellite cities.

Consolidated Metropolitan Statistical Area (CMSA)
An MSA that has a population of 1 million or more.

Trading Area
A geographic region consisting of a city and the surrounding areas that serves as the dominant retail or wholesale center for the region.

Cities and Metropolitan Areas. Instead of establishing sales territories using city boundaries, some firms use **metropolitan statistical areas (MSAs)**. MSAs are boundaries that include the major city as well as the surrounding suburban and satellite cities. Each MSA must have at least:

- One city with 50,000 inhabitants or more, or
- A census-defined urbanized area of at least 50,000 inhabitants and a total MSA population of at least 100,000 (75,000 in New England)

An MSA that has a population of 1 million or more is considered a **consolidated metropolitan statistical area (CMSA)**. The large concentration of population, retail, industry, and income in MSAs and CMSAs is a justification firms use to choose them as control units for territories.

Trading Areas. Another control unit for establishing sales territories is the trading area. A **trading area** is a geographic region consisting of a city and the surrounding areas that serves as the dominant retail or wholesale center for the region. Trading areas are a logical control unit, since they are based on the natural flow of goods and services rather than on political or economic boundaries. Firms that sell through channel partners often use trading areas as a control unit.

Customers in one trading area typically do not go outside its boundaries to buy merchandise, nor will a customer from outside enter the trading area to purchase products. This is not always the case, however, because sometimes trading areas overlap, and buyers in the overlapping areas make purchases in one or both areas.

A trading area as a geographic control unit has several advantages. Since trading areas are based on economic considerations, they are representative of customer buying habits and patterns of trade. Trading areas also facilitate planning and control. For

● A trading area is a geographic region that consists of a city and the surrounding areas that serves as the dominant retail or wholesale center for the region.

example, the same salesperson usually calls on all wholesalers in a trading area. Thus, the likelihood that salespeople will steal each other's accounts is minimized.

Several disadvantages are associated with using trading areas as control units. Two of the main problems are defining trading areas and obtaining statistical information to use in forecasting the sales potential in each area. The difficulty of defining trading areas has been reduced by companies such as Rand-McNally (www.randmcnally.com/), which publishes a map of the United States delineating several hundred trading areas. *Sales & Marketing Management* magazine also publishes maps relating to trading areas—one provides consumer market information by county, while another shows industrial market data by county. Companies can reduce limitations in available statistical data by adapting the dimensions of the trading areas to the counties included. While county market information may not fit the trading area exactly, it often is the best and most readily available data.

■ Conducting an Account Analysis

After a company selects a geographic control unit, the next step is to audit each geographic unit. The purpose of the audit is to identify customers and prospects and determine the sales potential of each account.

Accounts must first be identified by name. Many sources containing this information are available. For example, the *Yellow Pages* is one of the best sources for identifying customers quickly. One service, the *Instant Yellow Pages Service* (www .instantyellowpages.net/), contains a database of over 6 million U.S. businesses. This service can, for example, tell sales reps how many doctors are in any city in the United States—complete with names, mailing addresses, and phone numbers. Other sources include company records of past sales; trade directories; professional association membership lists; directories of corporations; publishers of mailing lists; trade books and periodicals; chambers of commerce; federal, state, and local governments; and personal observation by the salesperson. Most of this information is available electronically so it can quickly be stored for analysis in the firm's database.

After the firm has identified potential accounts, the next step is to estimate the total sales potential for all accounts in each geographic control unit, using one of the methods discussed in chapter 5. Then the company determines how much of this total it can expect to get. Estimated sales potential for a company in a particular territory is often a judgment call based on the company's existing sales in that territory, the level of competition, any differential advantages enjoyed by the company or its competitors, and the relationship with current accounts.

Sales managers forecast sales potential in a territory using data mining and other statistical techniques. Firms can store and organize the information they gather about potential and existing accounts in a variety of ways: name, Zip Code, account size, purchase frequency, or primary business. Once it is stored, they can retrieve the information in seconds in whatever form or basis of analysis they need, such as estimated sales potential based on predetermined criteria. Sales managers classify accounts based on annual buying potential in order to determine appropriate sales call patterns.

Salesperson Workload Analysis
An estimate of the time and effort required to cover each geographic control unit.

■ Developing a Salesperson Workload Analysis

The third step in setting up sales territories is to develop a **salesperson workload analysis**, an estimate of the time and effort required to cover each geographic control unit. The estimate is based on an analysis of the number of accounts to be called on, the frequency of the calls, the length of each call, the travel time needed, and the non-selling time required. The outcome of a workload analysis is a sales call pattern for each geographic control unit.

Several factors affect the number of accounts reps can call on in each geographic control unit. One is the length of time required to call on each account. This factor in turn is influenced by the number of people to be seen during each call, the amount of account servicing needed, and the length of waiting time. The sales manager can find information about these factors by checking company records or talking with salespeople. Non-selling time also must be included in a workload analysis. Non-selling activities include preparing for sales calls as well as processing orders and servicing accounts after the sale.

Another factor affecting the number of accounts a rep can call on is travel time between accounts. Travel time will vary considerably from one region to another depending on transportation, highway congestion, weather conditions, and the density of present and potential accounts. The objective of workload analysis is to minimize travel time and thereby increase the number of accounts reps can visit and/or the frequency of sales calls.

The frequency of sales calls is influenced by a number of factors. Accounts generally are divided into several groups according to sales potential and assigned to a category—often A, B, or C. For example, accounts with potential annual sales of over $1 million would be called on most frequently and placed into group A; accounts with potential sales of $250,000 to $1 million would be put into group B and called on less frequently; and finally group C accounts, with potential annual sales under $250,000, would receive the lowest number of sales calls. Other factors influencing call frequency are the nature of the product, the level of competition, and estimates of a seller's ability to win the business. For example, supermarkets purchasing canned food products require frequent calls because of the high inventory turnover rate, whereas a private high school purchasing textbooks requires only two or three calls a year. Of course, if there is strong competition within the market, more frequent sales calls may be needed.

An alternative to the analytical rigor of mathematical models is the portfolio analysis approach presented in Figure 7.1. This method classifies accounts into one of four types based on competition and opportunity, and each account type merits different sales call frequencies.[4] Segment 1 (top left) represents what most companies call key accounts. Segment 2 (top right) is considered a potential customer or prospect. Segment 3 (lower left) is a stable account, and Segment 4 (lower right) represents a weak account. Although the portfolio analysis approach is logical and easy to use, it is limited by having only four account categories.

Strength of Position

	Strong	Weak
High	Attractiveness: Accounts are very attractive, offer high opportunity, and sales organization has strong position. Call Strategy: Frequent sales calls	Attractiveness: Accounts are potentially attractive based on high opportunity, but sales organization has weak position. Call Strategy: Frequent sales calls to strengthen position.
Low	Attractiveness: Accounts are somewhat attractive since sales organization has strong position, but future opportunity is limited. Call Strategy: Moderate frequency to maintain current position	Attractiveness: Accounts are very unattractive since they offer low opportunity and sales organization has weak position. Call Strategy: Minimal sales calls and migrate personal sales calls to telephone or Internet.

Account Opportunity

FIGURE 7.1 Account Analysis

■ Combining Geographic Control Units into Sales Territories

Up to this point the sales manager has been working with the geographic control unit initially selected for setting up sales territories. Whether the unit is a state, county, MSA, or some other geographic area, the sales manager is now ready to consider grouping adjacent control units into territories of roughly equal sales potential. Numerous territory mapping software packages are available to align territories quickly and equitably. One of these packages is described in the *Sales Management in Action* box.

Sometimes territories have equal sales potential, but each territory has its own level of coverage difficulty, such as poor highways. With almost any realignment, sales managers will have to make compromises, because some territories may have a higher sales potential than others. Territories with unequal sales potential are not necessarily bad. Salespeople vary in ability and experience as well as initiative, and some can be assigned heavier workloads than others. Sales managers should assign the best salespeople to territories with high sales potential, and newer or less-effective salespeople to the second- and third-ranking territories. Some further adjustment in sales quotas and commission levels may be necessary, depending on the relative sales potential of a specific area and the types of selling or non-selling tasks required.

■ Assigning Salespeople to Territories

Once the sales manager has devised an optimal territory alignment, it's time to assign salespeople to territories. Salespeople vary in physical condition as well as ability, initiative, and effectiveness. A reasonable and desirable workload for one may overload another and frustrate another. In addition, interactions of an individual salesperson with customers and prospects may be affected by factors such as customer character-

SALES MANAGEMENT IN ACTION

Sales Territory Alignment and Optimization

Since sales calls often cost as much as $1,000 each, the sales force is one of the most expensive human resource investments for many companies. As a result, companies have turned to sales force automation (SFA), customer relationship management (CRM), enhanced sales training, and account management programs to increase sales force productivity. While all these approaches can produce benefits, sales territory alignment often increases productivity and sales at a relatively lower cost.

Sales territories are most often based on geographic considerations. When they are out of balance, some areas with high potential can be underserved while other areas are saturated. Similarly, too much effort may be devoted to low-potential cus-

tomers. Sales and service people need to spend more time seeing and listening to customers, and less time driving.

Empower Geographics sells mapping software that can improve sales force performance by optimizing the shape and content of territories. This approach minimizes travel time, balances sales opportunities, and maximizes returns. Empower Geographics, along with many others, leverages available information and company criteria with its sophisticated software to develop optimal sales territory solutions. Other tools such as automatic e-mail notification can enhance productivity.

SOURCE: http://www.empower.com/territory_management.htm (accessed May 2007); Pharmaceutical Executive (2004), vol. 24 (11), 132.

istics, market traditions, and social influences. Thus, a salesperson may be outstanding in one territory and weak in another, even though sales potential and workload for the two territories are similar.

In assigning sales personnel to territories, managers should rank them according to relative ability. When assessing a salesperson's relative ability, look at factors such as product and industry knowledge, energy level, persuasiveness, and verbal ability. All good salespeople rate high on these factors, though some are better than others. What ultimately determines the salesperson's assignment to a territory, however, is his or her potential sales effectiveness within that territory. To judge a salesperson's effectiveness within a territory, the sales manager must look at the salesperson's physical, social, and cultural characteristics and compare them to those of prospects and customers in the territory. For instance, a salesperson raised on a farm in Iowa is likely to be more effective with rural clients than with urban customers because he or she shares the same values as the rural clients. The goal in matching salespeople to territories in this manner is to maximize the territory's sales potential by making the salesperson comfortable with the territory and the customers comfortable with the salesperson.

Revising Sales Territories

Firms consider revising established territories for two major reasons. When a firm is just starting in business, territories are not designed very precisely. Often, the firm is unaware of problems in covering a territory, and sometimes the territory's sales potential and workload are over- or underestimated. But as the company grows and gains in experience, the sales manager recognizes where territory revision is needed. In other situations, territories may become outdated because of changing market conditions or other factors beyond management control.

Before making revisions, the sales manager should determine whether the problems with the original alignment are due to poor territory design, market changes, or problems in other areas. For example, if the cause is the compensation plan or training program, then it would be a mistake to revise sales territories. Generally, however, appropriate redesign of sales territories will have a positive impact on the bottom line.

■ Signs Indicating the Need for Territorial Revisions

As a company grows, it usually needs a larger sales force to cover the market adequately. If the company does not hire additional salespeople, the sales force is likely to only skim the cream in the territory instead of covering it intensely. If sales managers have not estimated territorial sales potential accurately, sales performance may be misleading. Also, morale problems will emerge if there are wide variations in territory potential.

Territories may also need revision when sales potential has been overestimated or changes have occurred. Sometimes, a territory may be too small for even a good salesperson to earn an adequate income. Overlapping territories are another reason for revision. This problem usually occurs when territories are split, and it can cause a tremendous amount of friction in the sales force. Salespeople are reluctant to have their territories divided because that generally means they must hand over accounts they have built up and nurtured. The thought that another salesperson is reaping the benefits of their hard work can lead to bitterness. The organization should correct this problem in a way that will benefit the existing rep and the new rep. No one should be unfairly penalized in a territorial revision. Overlap should be minimized or eliminated for other reasons, too. For example, overlapping territories usually mean higher traveling costs and wasted selling time, which increases overall selling expenses and reduces profitability.

Territory revisions may be necessary when one salesperson jumps into another salesperson's territory in search of business. This is an unethical practice, and it will cause severe problems within the sales force unless dealt with quickly. Territory jumping is usually a sign that salespeople are not developing their territory satisfactorily. If salespeople are doing a good job covering their own market but contiguous markets have more potential, reps may be unable to resist the temptation to enter adjacent markets. But this behavior can also indicate that sales potential in one territory is greater than in another. If territories have been designed properly, there should be no need for jumping. Before making territory realignments, however, the sales manager should evaluate whether using closer supervision or refusing to pay commissions on orders outside a rep's territory is a better solution to the problem.

Territory jumping may also be a sign of poor management. Some salespeople are interested only in quick and easy sales. Instead of developing their own territories, they will jump into another area unless management stops them. Unless quickly halted, territory jumping often leads to higher costs, selling inefficiencies, bitterness, and low morale in the sales force.

■ Impact of Territory Revision on Salespeople

Salespeople dislike change because of the uncertainty that accompanies it. Management must decide whether it is preferable to avoid territory revisions for fear of damaging morale, or to revise the territories to correct problems. When territories are reduced, salespeople often face a reduction in potential income and the loss of key accounts developed over years. The result is likely to be low morale. Therefore, before making revisions, firms may want to consult their salespeople for suggestions that might avoid or reduce other problems.

Compensation adjustments sometimes can avoid morale problems. Salespeople whose territory is being reduced need to be shown that a smaller territory can be covered more intensely, thereby offering a higher sales volume for the same travel time. Most firms talk with sales reps before making a change but make no salary adjustments until the territory develops. The problem here is that developing the territory may take some time, and the salesperson's income may suffer in the meantime. During this transition period, additional compensation or increased commissions may be needed to maintain morale and loyalty.

One approach to compensating salespeople during the transition period is to guarantee the previous level of income. For example, a sales rep covering the entire state of Texas may be earning an excellent commission, even though she is only skimming the territory. The sales rep will probably resist the idea of having the territory split in two in order to get better coverage. Thus, the company may guarantee the salesperson's level of commission until she has had reasonable time to penetrate the smaller territory and achieve a satisfactory commission level. While this approach may maintain morale and loyalty, it also can reduce the salesperson's aggressiveness in gaining new accounts. Another solution is to compromise. For example, if the transition period is three years, the company guarantees a portion of the salesperson's income but the guaranteed portion declines in the last two years. As the salary guarantee declines, the salesperson's incentive to develop the territory to its full potential increases.

Self-Management

Few jobs allow, or require, more self-management than personal selling does. This observation is particularly true as technology enables salespeople to cover their territories from mobile virtual offices.[5] Instead of fighting what may seem like a loss of control over the sales force, sales managers must recognize that more self-management gives them additional time to spend on other managerial tasks.

● Technology allows salespeople and sales managers to enhance productivity with a virtual office.

David Young-Wolf/PhotoEdit

Sales managers must make sure salespeople understand that self-management is more difficult than getting direct feedback and motivation. But salespeople increasingly must decide what, how, and when to do their sales tasks. Most field salespeople set their daily agenda, sales call objectives, and even performance standards. Empowering salespeople enables them to serve prospects and customers faster and better. A tool like CRM On Demand, by Siebel (www.crmondemand.com), can improve sales productivity by helping salespeople manage their activities more efficiently. They can quickly and easily create to-do lists, schedule activities and appointments, and track priorities and due dates. By streamlining these and other administrative tasks, salespeople have more time to focus on what they are paid to do—sell![6]

■ How Salespeople Spend Their Time

Effective and efficient use of time is critical to successful performance for both sales managers and salespeople. Many sales managers spend too much time in the field because they feel most comfortable using the same skills that earned them promotion to sales manager. When managers make sales calls on their own, they are "doing" (as opposed to managing) because this is work salespeople could and likely should perform. Time devoted instead to determining how to accomplish work through other people is managing. Sales managers who make sales calls with their salespeople to observe, analyze, and coach them in improving their presentations are performing managerial duties. The difference between a skillful sales manager and a mere "doer" can make a substantial impact on the success of sales force efforts.

Salespeople who work for firms like Cisco, General Electric, and IBM spend a large proportion of their time gathering information about potential customers, planning sales call activities, working with other departments, and servicing existing customers. Indeed, it is difficult to identify all the activities salespeople perform, but the list in Table 7.1 summarizes the main types:[7]

Table 7.2 shows the breakdown by category of the ways in which salespeople spend their time.[8] You may have thought salespeople spend most of their time selling, but in fact two-thirds of it is spent traveling, waiting, or doing administrative tasks.

Whether salespeople spend a quarter or a third of their time in face-to-face selling can have a tremendous impact on their sales effectiveness and efficiency.[9] For example, assume the typical salesperson works 40 hours per week and takes a two-week annual vacation. That leaves just 500 hours a year ($40 \times 50 \times 0.25 = 500$) for face-to-face selling for salespeople who devote 25 percent of their time to selling. Salespeople whose efficiency allows them to devote 33 percent of their time to face-to-face selling spend 660 hours a year ($40 \times 50 \times 0.333 = 660$), or 160 hours more. Given these assumptions, how much is an hour of the salesperson's time worth at different earning levels? For someone earning $50,000 a year, each hour of selling time costs $100 if only 25 percent of working time is spent in face-to-face selling, but that cost

TABLE 7.1   Activities of Salespeople

SALES	COMMUNICATION	RELATIONSHIP	TEAM	CRM/DATABASE
Setting appointments	E-mail	Website	Conferencing	Collect data
Preparing sales appeals	Internet	Work with channel partners	Mentoring	Enter data
Obtain customer background	Voice mail	Help customers	Selling	Update files
Use technology for presentations	Mobile phone	Call on CEOs	Coordinate sales support	
Share technology with customers	Fax	Build rapport with buying center		
Adaptive and consultative selling	Pager	Build trust		
Call planning	Websites	Network		
Respond to referrals	Conferencing	Work with others within their company		
Identify key accounts	Provide technical information			
Listen	Practice presentation skills			
Ask questions	Maintain/develop virtual office			
Assess nonverbal communications				
Traveling				

| TABLE 7.2   How Salespeople Spend Their Time ||
ACTIVITY	PERCENTAGE
Prospecting	14%
With customers	15
Administrative tasks	34
Service calls	5
Waiting/Traveling	32
Total	100%

SOURCE: Dave Kahle, "Strategic Planning for Salespeople," http://www.davekahle .com/article/strategic.htm (accessed October 2006).

drops to $76 an hour if selling time is increased to 33 percent, as depicted in Table 7.3. Thus, finding ways to increase face-to-face selling time yields a substantial payoff in efficiency.

Salespeople can increase interactions with prospects and customers by using combinations of selling aids such as Web conferencing, e-mailing, telephone contacts, and faxing. If a sales rep can increase interactions by 20 percent, it seems reasonable that sales volume might also increase by 20 percent. Thus, an increasingly important role for sales managers is coaching salespeople on how to be successful self-managers. Some of the most important concepts to teach salespeople in helping them manage their activities are (1) finding an optimal combination of effectiveness and efficiency, (2) calculating the return on time invested (ROTI), and (3) setting priorities for objectives and activities. Let's briefly discuss each of these topics.

Effectiveness
Describes results-oriented behavior that focuses on achieving sales goals.

Achieving Effectiveness and Efficiency. A basic concept sales managers need to convey to salespeople is that successful territory management depends on an optimal combination of effectiveness and efficiency. **Effectiveness** is results oriented and focuses

| TABLE 7.3   Dollar Cost of an Hour of a Salesperson's Selling Time |||
EARNINGS	SALESPEOPLE WHO SPEND 25% OF THEIR TIME IN FACE-TO-FACE SELLING (500 HRS./YR.)	SALESPEOPLE WHO SPEND 33% OF THEIR TIME IN FACE-TO-FACE SELLING (660 HRS./YR.)
$20,000	$40	$30
30,000	60	45
40,000	80	61
50,000	100	76
60,000	120	91
70,000	140	106
80,000	160	121
90,000	180	136
100,000	200	152

Efficiency
Describes cost-oriented behavior that focuses on making the best possible use of the salesperson's time and efforts.

ROTI, or Return on Time Invested
A financial concept that helps salespeople spend their time more profitably with prospects and customers.

Parkinson's Law
A theory that work tends to expand to fill the time allotted for its completion.

Concentration Principle
Belief that most of a salesperson's sales, costs, and profits come from a relatively small proportion of customers and products.

on achieving sales goals, while **efficiency** is cost oriented and focuses on making the best possible use of the salesperson's time and efforts. Together, the two equal selling success:[10]

$$E_1 \text{ (Effectiveness)} + E_2 \text{ (Efficiency)} = S_1 \text{ (Selling Success)}$$

Measuring Return on Time Invested. **ROTI**, or **return on time invested**, is a financial concept that helps salespeople spend their time more profitably with prospects and customers. Return can be measured in various ways, such as dollar sales to a customer, profits on a certain product category, or new customers won. ROTI is the designated return divided by the hours spent achieving it. For example, if a salesperson spends 60 hours in preparing a sales call, making a sales presentation, and providing service to a customer who orders $90,000 worth of products, that salesperson's ROTI is $90,000 divided by 60 or $1,500. Another salesperson who invests 30 hours of time to make a sale of $25,000 has an ROTI of $833.

To determine their ROTI for different activities, customers, and products, salespeople need to keep accurate hourly records. Although this may sound like tedious record keeping, it takes only a few minutes a day to record this information. Moreover, PDAs and similar devices can store the information as well as the software to provide real-time updates for sales call planning.

Setting Priorities. Setting priorities is essential. Salespeople who don't set priorities often work on relatively minor tasks first because they are the easiest to complete and thus provide a feeling of accomplishment. But this may not be the best use of their time. Priorities should relate to specific objectives to be accomplished over a certain time period, such as a year, a quarter, a month, a week, and even each day. Once managers have determined selling objectives, they should rank them according to their importance and assign completion dates to each one. Top-performing salespeople always set priorities in their work, based on Parkinson's Law and the concentration principle.

Parkinson's Law. **Parkinson's Law** says that work tends to expand to fill the time allotted for its completion. For instance, if salespeople have eight hours to write a sales proposal, it will probably take that much time to complete the task. But if salespeople have only four hours, they will somehow manage to complete the proposal within that time frame.

Concentration Principle. Often called the "80-20 rule," the **concentration principle** states that most of a salesperson's sales, costs, and profits come from a relatively small proportion of customers and products. Global firms like GE, Xerox, IBM, Dell, and Cisco sell their products in many countries, but a small number of countries account for a very high proportion of their sales. The same is true for smaller firms, but in their case the principle suggests a small number of companies will account for a high proportion of sales.

■ New Sales Manager Roles

Sales force automation and salesperson empowerment are dramatically changing selling. With salespeople able to access customer data 24-7, obtain training by DVD or

Web conferencing and webinars (Web seminars), and communicate with virtually anyone via e-mail, the sales manager's former roles as communications conduit, data analyst, information disseminator, and hands-on manager are also changing. Increasingly, the emphasis is moving from one-to-one coaching and motivation of field salespeople to reorganizing, training, motivating, and providing support and resources for a hybrid sales force comprised of various types of electronic contacts as well as field salespeople.[11] With increasing empowerment, salespeople are reporting to higher management levels.[12] Bristol-Myers Squibb pharmaceuticals (www.bms.com/) nearly doubled the range of control of its district sales managers and eliminated many lower-level sales managers.[13] Overall, the sales manager's job is evolving toward being channel manager—overseeing a hybrid sales force operating in diverse electronic and field channels and managing channel partner relationships.

To succeed, sales managers need to (1) build closer relationships with customers to better understand their businesses; (2) work in coordinated teams with other departments in their companies to satisfy customers; (3) treat salespeople as partners; (4) improve marketing skills, including direct marketing and e-commerce, to spot potential business opportunities; (5) develop improved motivational skills; and (6) become partners with salespeople and channel members to achieve goals. No other marketing managers will need more eclectic or adaptable skills than will sales managers.[14]

■ Customer Reviews of Performance

Many customers are conducting annual performance reviews of their suppliers and deciding which ones to keep or drop. To avoid unpleasant surprises, sales managers and salespeople should proactively ask for annual performance review meetings with customers. Obtaining regular feedback from customers is one of the most effective ways to keep from losing touch with customers. Research has shown these major reasons for customers to switch suppliers: (1) they were offered a better deal by a new supplier or (2) the sales rep failed to maintain regular contact.[15]

Time Management and Routing

After sales managers have established sales territories and assigned salespeople to them, they should turn their attention to scheduling and routing the sales force within territories. Scheduling and routing are vital to keeping productivity high and sales costs low. Unfortunately many companies ignore these tasks. Salespeople often are told either to call on as many accounts as possible or to call on only those whose potential is above a specified level.

Some companies do not take the time to route or schedule a salesperson, especially if the salesperson's sales figures are good. A good record can be misleading, however, because even if sales are high, the cost of the sales may also be high. One salesperson may be spending more time and money than necessary on overnight sales calls or wasting time on the road by taking inefficient routes. Another salesperson could be spending too much money entertaining clients or even entertaining the wrong clients. To accomplish sales objectives set for the sales force and for each territory, the sales manager must ensure proper routing and scheduling of each sales rep.

■ Managing Salesperson Time

Salespeople must be good time managers because this is one of the best ways to improve territory coverage. Think of the salesperson's use of time as a resource allocation problem, whose solution is to eliminate wasted time, increase efficiency, and maximize productivity. Some examples of time allocation problems are (1) deciding which accounts to call on; (2) dividing time between selling and paperwork; (3) allocating time between present customers, prospective customers, and service calls; and (4) allocating time to spend with demanding customers or new prospects.

Salespeople must be good time managers to control these problems and maximize time spent interacting with prospects and customers. How can salespeople maximize their productive time? An important first step is to avoid time traps.

Avoid Time Traps. Good time use requires that salespeople recognize and avoid "time traps" that can erode their effectiveness (see Table 7.4). Calling on unqualified or unprofitable prospects, failing to prioritize their work, making poor use of waiting time, and not breaking up large, long-range projects into currently manageable pieces are a few of the many time traps that sales reps can easily fall into. Reps also need a system or procedure for planning how to use their time effectively (several are described later). Different selling situations will require different approaches to time management. The sales manager must work with the salespeople to develop an effective time management procedure.

Allocate Time. In allocating time, salespeople first need to decide on the principal tasks or activities they must complete, and then determine the amount of time to allocate to each one. Although sales tasks vary widely, we can classify them into five general areas: waiting and traveling, doing face-to-face selling, making service calls, clearing administrative tasks, and prospecting. A simple way to determine how much time a salesperson is spending on each of the basic sales activities is to ask the sales-

TABLE 7.4   Common Time Traps

Calling on unqualified or unprofitable prospects	Failing to prioritize work
Insufficiently planning each day's activities	Procrastinating on major projects, resulting in redundant preparation and paperwork
Making poor territorial routing and travel plans	Inefficiently handling paperwork and keeping disorganized records
Taking long lunch hours and too many coffee breaks	Failing to break up huge, long-range projects into small, currently manageable tasks
Making poor use of waiting time between appointments	Ending workdays early, especially on Friday afternoons
Spending too much time entertaining prospects and customers	Failing to insulate oneself from interruptions or sales calls or while doing paperwork
Not using modern telecommunications equipment like a cellular phone, pager, facsimile, and laptop computer	Conducting unnecessary meetings, visits, and phone calls
Doing tasks that could be delegated to a staff person or to automated equipment	Neglecting customer service until a small problem becomes a large one that takes more time to resolve

Sales Rep: Scott Widmier **Date: May 8, 2008** **Territory: Atlanta, GA** **Day: Wednesday**	
Call 1: 9:00 a.m. Phil Piper at Centroid Wireless in Suwanee. Reorder; try to sell new products.	Travel: 20 minutes Wait: 10 min. Contact: 35 min.
Call 2: 10:00 a.m. Carolyn Crawford, BTW Co. in Lawrenceville. New prospect, just opened last month.	Travel: 20 minutes Wait: 5 min. Contact: 75 min.
Call 3: 12:00 Luncheon presentation with A&R industries in Lawrenceville. Group of 17, including VP Marketing.	Travel: 10 minutes Wait: 20 min. Contact: 60 min.
Call 4: 1:30 p.m. Bob Joyce at ACME Associates in Alpharetta. Service visit; explain new Web portal.	Travel: 30 minutes Wait: 10 min. Contact: 35 min.
Call 5: 2:30 a.m. Sid Green at Pinnacle Industries in Sandy Springs. Reorder and service visit.	Travel: 15 minutes Wait: 10 min. Contact: 30 min.
Call 6: 3:30 p.m. Laura Smith at Smith and Co. in Roswell. New prospect; found website using search engine.	Travel: 25 minutes Wait: 15 min. Contact: 40 min.
To office: 35 minutes travel **Administrative work:** 1 hr. 15 minutes	

FIGURE 7.2 Daily Activity Analysis Report

person to carry out an activity analysis for several representative days—usually five to ten. The analysis should include different days of the week as well as days in different parts of the territory. After the salesperson records time use for several days on an activity analysis sheet such as that shown in Figure 7.2, the sales manager works with the salesperson to increase the amount of time spent on productive activities.

Set Weekly and Daily Goals. The sales manager and the salesperson should work together to develop a weekly action plan. Weekly sales goals set targets for planned days, number of sales calls, number of demonstrations, and type of customer coverage. The sales call plan can set the course of action for the week as well as for each day. Figure 7.3 is a typical sales call planning sheet. Reps can prepare a custom planning format using Excel, or one of many off-the-shelf versions available with standard CRM systems.

Probably the most important aspect of sales call planning is identifying the type of customer coverage. Ranking customers by the volume of business and profit generated enables salespeople to focus on important accounts and minimize time spent with relatively unimportant ones.

In addition to sales call planning, salespeople must allocate time to selling and non-selling activities. Selling and servicing activities should be planned for the time of

Sales Rep: Mary Walfinbarger   **Week ending: September 6, 2008**
Territory: Los Angeles, CA

Planned Itinerary	**Completed Itinerary**
Number of sales calls ____	Number of sales calls ____
Number of demonstrations ____	Number of demonstrations ____
Number of A account calls ____	Number of A account calls ____
Number of B account calls ____	Number of B account calls ____
Number of C account calls ____	Number of C account calls ____

Detailed Sales Itinerary

Company	Location	Rating	Purpose
Jasmin WiFi	Bel Air	A	Reorder
Linklines Mobile	Santa Monica	B	Sell new product
GIGA News	Glendale	C	Prospect
Apple Store	Burbank	A	Reorder
AT&T Wireless	Pasadena	A	Explain new Web portal

FIGURE 7.3 Sales Call Plan

day when customers and prospects are available. To the extent possible, non-selling activities—traveling, waiting, and handling administrative work—should be done during non-prime hours, when customers are not available. Figure 7.4 illustrates this allocation.

Manage Time During Sales Calls. An often neglected aspect of time management for salespeople is how they manage their time *during* sales calls. Studies show the amount of time salespeople spend with customers does not influence performance, unless it is quality time spent with customers. Instead, sales success is related more to what takes place during the customer-salesperson interaction.[16] Therefore, just spending extra time with customers does not always lead to additional sales. Customers are more

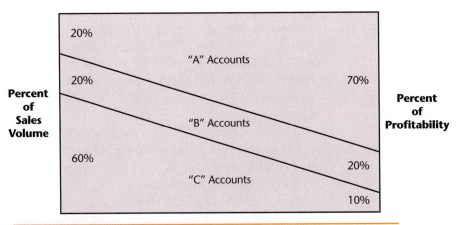

FIGURE 7.4 Customers Based on Sales Volume and Profitability

appreciative and more likely to develop partnerships with salespeople when sales calls are efficient rather than long.

Evaluate. Ideally, as the week progresses salespeople keep records on planned and actual activities, and they constantly monitor their use of time. But at the end of the week, they meet with the sales manager to review the week's activities. Together the rep and manager measure efficiency in selling activities from the sales call plan and evaluate time devoted to non-selling activities. In this manner, they can quickly detect time allocation problems and take corrective actions. Both parties should monitor time usage over time, so they can identify trends and make any needed changes to improve efficiency and productivity.

■ Routing

Territorial Routing
Devising a travel plan or pattern to use when making sales calls.

One of the most valuable tools for time management is the planning of efficient routes to cover a territory. **Territorial routing** is devising a travel plan or pattern to use when making sales calls. Routing systems may be complex, but we can develop a basic pattern by finding accounts on a map and then identifying the optimal sequence and fastest route for visiting them. Time wasted on the road is often due to simple things like having poor directions and getting lost. Salespeople who get lost run the risk of being late for an appointment, and few customers will tolerate tardiness. Indeed, some customers refuse to see latecomers. At a minimum, being late is unprofessional and makes closing the sale more difficult.

During initial training, the sales rep and sales manager usually do the routing together. After training, routing becomes the primary responsibility of the salesperson. Routing is not a difficult task for most salespeople, especially if they are familiar with the territory. But poor routing often makes the difference between closing the sale and losing it. A properly designed routing system has three primary advantages:

1. *Reduced travel time and selling costs*—Perhaps the greatest advantage of routing plans is reduced travel time and selling costs, giving salespeople more productive time to spend with customers. The main objective is to eliminate backtracking and non-selling time in completing sales calls. Studies show that as much as one-third of the field salesperson's daily working time is spent traveling. Thus, the typical sales rep spends three to four months of the year on the road. Obviously, anything that can reduce travel time and increase the salesperson's productive selling time is highly desirable.
2. *Improved territory coverage*—A routing plan also improves territory coverage. Detailed information about the number and location of customers, methods of transportation available within a territory, and call frequencies is essential in developing a routing plan that ensures orderly, thorough coverage of the market.
3. *Improved communication*—If the sales manager knows where salespeople are, it is easier to offer last-minute information or instructions. While e-mail and mobile phones generally provide instant communications, other means of contact based on a routing plan can be useful. A well-designed routing plan not only improves communication, it also helps the sales manager monitor individual salespeople.

The major disadvantage of routing is it reduces the salespersons' initiative and places him or her in a pattern that can become inflexible. Many sales executives believe the field salesperson is best able to determine the order in which to call on customers, and how long to stay. Many times a prospect can be won over with just a little more time and effort—something a formalized routing plan may not allow. Also, in changing market conditions, a strict routing plan prevents salespeople from making changes to adapt to new situations. These disadvantages are reduced by CRM systems that enable continuous updating of routing patterns. After a sale is completed, the salesperson can contact the next customer to reconfirm their appointment or adjust the routing pattern.

Routing is recommended for all companies with a field sales force, but flexibility in implementing it is important. For instance, a firm entering a new area may not know the number and location of potential customers, so a strict routing schedule is impractical. In this situation, routing plans must structure sales calls that are flexible enough to allow reps to pursue previously unknown prospects. Also, high-caliber salespeople and independent salespeople such as manufacturers' reps require a more flexible routing approach than other types of salespeople. These individuals resist a fixed routing schedule that restricts their ability to adapt to situations.

The extent to which firms use routing depends on two issues: the nature of the product and the nature of the job. If the product requires regular calls and frequent servicing, routing is definitely necessary. Driver-salespeople who sell soft drinks, tobacco, and grocery items are usually routed. In fact, routing is so important to these salespeople that an irregular call often leads to losing the account.

The nature of the job also determines whether routing is desirable. Routing is definitely needed if the job is routine. But situations that require creative selling techniques and a high-caliber sales force need a more flexible routing schedule. Finally, established companies are more likely to use a routing plan than new companies just entering a geographic area.

■ Time Management for Sales Managers

Just as salespeople need to make effective use of their time, sales managers also need to manage their time. The approach is similar for both. The sales manager identifies tasks that must be carried out and allocates time appropriately. Sales management tasks differ from company to company. Some sales managers lead a group of salespeople and personally handle a sales territory. Others may sell to a small number of major accounts while managing the sales force, and still others only manage the sales force.

Sales managers must set daily and weekly objectives. They should make an itinerary of things they need to accomplish in a particular week and rank them in order of importance. Examples might include setting up salesperson recruiting visits to two universities, working out the details for a training program for new salespeople, hiring a training consultant to present a motivational seminar to the sales force, and evaluating sales call reports for individual salespeople.

As the week progresses, sales managers, like salespeople, need to review and evaluate their performance to determine how successful they have been in accomplishing their objectives. If they haven't completed their planned tasks, then the sales managers should examine their planned time allocation and make necessary adjustments. To successfully plan and control the activities of the sales force in achieving sales goals and objectives, the sales manager first must be an effective and efficient manager of his or her own time.

CHAPTER SUMMARY

1. **Describe the basic reasons for establishing sales territories.** Escalating costs of making personal sales calls have spurred sales managers to seek more efficient and effective means of reaching customers. Sales managers are achieving these goals through time and territory management and by adopting new technology. The six basic reasons for establishing sales territories are (1) enhance market coverage, (2) keep selling costs at a minimum, (3) strengthen customer relations, (4) build a more effective sales force, (5) better evaluate the sales force, and (6) coordinate selling with other marketing functions. A CRM program may help determine the way salespeople are assigned to customers.

2. **Apply procedures for setting up sales territories.** In brief, the procedures for setting up sales territories are (1) select a geographic control unit, (2) conduct an account analysis, (3) develop a salesperson workload analysis, (4) combine geographic control units into sales territories, and (5) assign sales personnel to territories.

3. **Evaluate when and why to revise sales territories.** Sales territories are often revised when relatively new companies initially overestimate or underestimate territorial sales potential and the required salesperson workload. In other cases, the original territorial design may become outdated because of changed market conditions. Overlapping territories are still another reason for revision. Territory revision can be damaging to sales force morale unless it is carefully thought out beforehand, with input from the salespeople. When a territory is reduced, the salesperson assigned there may suffer a sharp reduction in income and the loss of key accounts developed over many years. One solution is to guarantee some portion of the salesperson's income for a year or two until the salesperson can develop his or her new, smaller territory. In any sales territory revision,

sensitive and savvy sales managers will seek out and fully consider the advice of the affected salespeople before implementing the change. Frequently, some reasonable compromise can be reached that will not adversely affect sales force morale.

4. **Apply the concept of self-management to sales and sales management.** Few jobs allow or require more self-management than personal selling does, especially now as technology enables salespeople to cover their territories from mobile virtual offices. Instead of fighting what may seem like a loss of control over the sales force, sales managers should recognize that rep self-management gives them additional time to spend on other managerial tasks. Most field salespeople set their daily agenda, sales call objectives, and even performance standards. But they also must monitor their performance and take corrective actions. Empowering salespeople enables them to serve prospects and customers faster and better.

5. **Use the techniques of scheduling and routing for sales success.** More efficient sales call planning and routing within each salesperson's territory can significantly save time, reduce costs, and improve overall profitability. Salespeople typically spend up to one-third of their time traveling to and from prospects and customers. More efficient time and territory management enables salespeople to make more frequent sales calls on current customers, call on more new prospects, and spend more time developing customer relationships through customer service—all of which should lead to more sales, greater customer loyalty, and higher profits. Numerous mathematical models have been designed to develop routing plans so salespeople maximize their selling time and minimize travel costs. Sales managers use many of these tools to design and update sales territories and routing plans.

REVIEW AND APPLICATION QUESTIONS

1. Why is it necessary to establish sales territories that are approximately equal in sales potential? [LO 1]

2. Why is it important to match the right salesperson with the right territory? [LO 1]

3. How might a company adopting a strong CRM focus assign sales reps to customers in a different way than would a company without such a focus? [LO 2]

4. What is a salesperson workload analysis report? [LO 3]

5. How should you, the sales manager, be using the latest technology? [LO 3]

6. List several factors that influence the number of sales calls a salesperson can be expected to make in a day. [LO 3]

7. What are some time traps that you personally tend to fall into? What could you do to avoid these time traps? [LO 4]

8. Is it important for a salesperson to be worried about time management during a sales call? Why or why not? [LO 5]

IT'S UP TO YOU

Internet Exercise

Think of three companies where you would like to get a sales job. Describe the business area of each firm. Use Internet resources to see what each company is doing with its time management and sales force. What type of time management system would you recommend for each company? Has each firm selected the best type of time management training approach?

Role-Playing Exercise

Datacor Software

Situation

Datacor Software, Inc. (DSI) is a small computer software company in Lexington, Massachusetts. DSI develops and markets innovative software packages. The company has several managing partners who founded the company. DSI has experienced rapid growth since its formation in 2006, but sales have not reached expectations. The main product is called HURRY-SELL. It was designed to enable sales organizations to train sales reps at their own pace and at a reasonable cost. The primary method of selling is telemarketing to end users and dealers in the United States and Canada. DSI's sales force is organized geographically, so that each of five sales reps has sole responsibility for a defined territory. Reps work from home and sell to end users almost entirely by phone but are expected to visit dealer-account purchasing executives at least twice a year. As

the sales manager says, "Dealers are in a position to move a lot of product. Therefore, I do not want reps to be strangers to these companies. There is no substitute for personal contact." Based on disappointing sales performance, the partners need to brainstorm ways to better understand why sales are not what they should be.

Role-Play Participants and Assignments

Karen Tutor, one of the founding partners, argues the entire problem is at the sales level. She says the company has set up territories, and they should be working.

Carlos Rodriguez, another partner, suggests centralizing the telemarketing activities in Lexington.

Sara Kakutani, recently hired sales manager with ten years of experience at IBM, says they need to look at how the salespeople are using their time. She also suggests trying to find out whether sales reps truly know what is expected of them.

In-Basket Exercise

You were recently promoted to sales manager of one of your company's most productive regions. After several weeks on the job you are becoming concerned about Brad, one of your veteran salespeople. Although he is quite successful as a salesperson, Brad seems to have a problem dealing with time. On several occasions you received reports from him that read "Chicago Monday, Detroit Tuesday, Chicago Wednesday." Moreover, his paperwork is late—if he turns it in at all. When you question Brad about these issues, he replies: "I just want to hit the road and sell. I don't have time for all this paperwork! Plus, I've always had the impression it's sales volume that counts with this company. In sixteen years with the company, I've always surpassed my quota!"

1. Prepare a memo explaining to Brad why his behavior is unacceptable and how it is affecting other salespeople.

2. Prepare an e-mail explaining the situation to your boss. Suggest a possible solution and ask her advice on how to deal with this situation.

 ## Ethical Dilemma

You have recently received complaints from several of your salespeople concerning one of your newer reps. Although this person is familiar with the assigned sales territories, he has gone into an adjacent sales territory several times to make a sale. He recently landed a new account you have been trying to get for years. When you question him about leaving his territory to make a sale, he claims the prospect was a "referral from a new, important client," who asked him "to call on a friend of his across town."

QUESTIONS

1. How would you handle this situation without insulting the new client or the territory-jumping salesperson?

2. What do you tell the salespeople in the territory that is being invaded by the new sales rep?

3. Are there alternatives for realigning sales territories?

 ## CASE 7.1

Manufacturers Insurance Group: Developing Territories

Ashley Roberts is a sales manager for the Manufacturers Insurance Group (MIG). MIG specializes in providing an array of policies to limit various types of manufacturer's liabilities. Essentially, MIG insures "gaps" in insurance coverage of traditional policies. Traditional policy limits are often lower for manufacturers than for other industries such as retailing due to the additional safety risks in a manufacturing environment. For example, MIG has a policy covering worker's medical costs, should they be injured on the job, above and beyond traditional policy limits. Another MIG policy provides employees with additional sick leave coverage. MIG offers over a dozen additional policies for manufacturer's employees. The additional cost of the insurance is typically split between the employer and the employee. Some manufacturers pay none of the cost, and some pay all of the cost.

Presently, MIG operates in 15 Midwestern states. In most cases salespersons' territory geographic control units are states. However, in a few instances, states are divided into two or even three territories after account analyses and workload analyses indicate a need to balance the sales potential between territories. In one case, two states were combined into one territory. MIG has decided to expand operations into five states: Alabama, Georgia, Florida, Mississippi, and Tennessee. Ashley Roberts has learned that sales potential is a function of the number of manufacturing employees. She goes to www.census.gov to find employees employed in manufacturing in each state. She finds the link to the U.S.

Statistical Abstract and finds a document under "Browse Sections," "Manufacturers," "Report 975—Manufacturers Summary by State." This document, reported in Microsoft Excel format, shows number of employees and payroll by state. Employees for each state are listed below:

- Alabama—259,100
- Georgia—419,600
- Florida—354,200
- Mississippi—169,900
- Tennessee—384,200

Although the type of manufacturing differs throughout the states, Roberts knows that sales potential depends largely on the number of employees. In the DIALOG database, she uses Dun's Market Identifiers to identify the specific manufacturers in each state. Access to this database gives her an immediate electronic file containing the names, addresses, officers, and number of employees among other data. The distribution of manufacturers by number of employees in each state identifies two patterns. First, in Atlanta, Georgia, there is a concentration of the largest manufacturers in the five-state area. The Atlanta area has a sales potential about as high as that existing in the rest of the state. Secondly, Memphis, Tennessee, also has a greater concentration of manufacturing than in other areas, except Atlanta. However, in Memphis the manufacturers are not as large as those in Atlanta, on average. Finally, potential in the remaining states is fairly evenly distributed around the states.

Regarding the workload for each account, insurance sales require a heavy time commitment with each account in the early life of the account. Thereafter, there should be steady, periodic calls on accounts to ensure proper maintenance. Regarding travel, a salesperson operating in the Atlanta area would travel much less. However, the sales potential of the very large accounts in the Atlanta area would require more time per account not only when acquiring the accounts but also while maintaining them. The larger the number of employees at an account, the more likely there would be claims, and salespersons were required to gather information and verify information related to claims from their accounts. Otherwise, the workload among the other states was pretty evenly balanced—except for Mississippi, which on average had smaller accounts. Every other state had some larger accounts in larger cities such as Miami, Birmingham, Nashville, and Memphis.

QUESTIONS

1. MIG uses states as the geographic control unit. What are the advantages of using states? Disadvantages?

2. What goal should Ashley Roberts have for determining territories in the new five-state markets?

3. How would you assign territories if you were Ashley Roberts?

4. Since the data in the Statistical Abstract are based on a report that is a few years old, what other more recent sources could Roberts use to ensure her decisions are current?

Case prepared by Ron Bush, University of West Florida.

 ## CASE 7.2

SalesTech, Inc.: Coping with Growth

SalesTech, Inc. (STI) is a sales software company located in Palo Alto, California. STI sells sales force automation software to niche markets as an add-on to larger, better-known companies selling branded CRM packages. STI's best-selling product is designed for companies selling medical devices and supplies to the health-care industry. Its major competitive advantages are the ability to recognize words and phrases associated with the medical and health-care industry in most major languages (English, French, German, Spanish, and Italian) and the user-friendly interface it has developed with companies selling contact information for prospects likely to be interested in purchasing health-care equipment and supplies. STI has several other innovative software products that appear to have significant market potential and should be ready to introduce in the next 12 to 18 months. The company's owners are Rex Sanford, a former Microsoft software engineer who has been developing the products; Hassan Raiyani, a wealthy entrepreneur who has been funding the business; and Ginny Miller, a former Cisco sales representative who has been handling most of the sales management responsibilities.

STI has experienced rapid growth since it was founded in 2004, but sales have not yet reached expectations. Average annual sales have been increasing slowly and are now about 4,250 units a year worldwide. The owners are not sure why sales have not grown as anticipated. When the company was formed, they hired a consultant from Stanford University to develop a business plan, and his projections estimated that sales would reach 11,000 units after three years (see Table 1).

STI has used three primary selling methods. One is telemarketing directly to users in economically developed countries, mostly North America, South America, European Union, and Australia. The objective of the telemarketing strategy was to maintain as much control as possible over the distribution and sales of products. The second method was to establish distributor relationships with local companies operating in the various geographic territories. A third selling method was via the company's website, which sometimes involved direct purchasing via downloads and at other times required one of the telemarketers to work with the customer.

The STI sales force was organized geographically into territories, so that each of the four sales reps has sole responsibility for a defined territory (see Figure 7.5). Except for selling to distributors and on the Internet, reps are expected to sell STI products via telephone and mail. Sales reps are generally fluent in the languages of their geographic areas, and this ability has worked well in all cases except the European Union due to the number of different languages spoken there. In addition to telemarketing activities, sales reps are expected to visit major distributors at least twice a year to build relationships and provide training on recent developments and future plans. The philosophy of senior management is that personal contact with distributors is important to ensure their full support in selling STI products.

STI's owners decided to retain the consultant who had prepared the original business plan to work with them to better understand why sales had not developed as expected. After reviewing the situation, the consultant noted the following:

- The current organizational approach is working relatively well except in the European Union. The multiple languages are creating a problem. Due to the potential of this market, it may need to be divided into several smaller markets, perhaps on a country-by-country basis.

- Telemarketing activities are both outbound and inbound. Outbound is working better than inbound, but both have problems. The inbound telemarketing calls are generated by advertisements in trade journals, booths at trade shows, and STI's website. There is a toll-free number for the sales rep in each of the four territories. The consultant suggests that perhaps inbound telemarketing activities need to be centralized and handled out of the home office in Palo Alto, or outsourced to another company that could provide 24-7 coverage. Further, because of the many languages involved, it may be necessary to have more than one company handle the telemarketing—but this could cause problems as well.

- Sales reps are expected to sell to distributors located in their geographic territory. The distributors are often small and carry a wide assortment of software packages. Sales reps have been given little support in selling to distributors. In three of the geographic territories the accounts were the result of distributors contacting STI about distribution possibilities. Channel conflicts have resulted in numerous situations where telemarketers and distributors have argued about who should get the commission on a particular sale. These conflicts are complicated because some inquiries originate from the website, and it is not clear whether the telemarketer or distributor should get the credit. The consultant recommends that the strategy in

TABLE 1 Business Plan Sales Projections in Units

PROJECTION	YEAR				
	2006	2007	2008	2009	2010
Optimistic	10,000	15,000	22,000	37,000	46,000
Likely	7,000	11,000	16,000	23,000	34,000
Pessimistic	4,000	9,000	11,000	18,000	28,000

Substantial growth was anticipated after 2007, based on market awareness and new products.

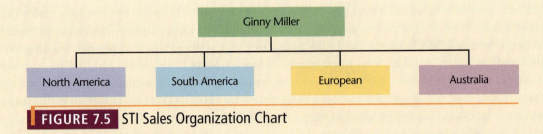

FIGURE 7.5 STI Sales Organization Chart

accepting distributors needs to be closely studied. Distributors must be highly motivated, well supported by training and technical consultation, and aggressive in contacting potential customers and providing feedback to STI management. In addition, reps need to make more frequent contact with distributors and be given more direction on how to effectively work with distributors.

■ In reviewing the four sales territories, the consultant and management conclude that the current arrangement needs reconsideration. The geographic areas are large and difficult to adequately service, and their potential differs substantially. STI attempted to become a global company too quickly and needs to consider a more focused strategy in the areas with greatest potential. This is particularly important where sales reps are expected to establish personal relationships with distributors.

■ The sales reps are typically young (ages 27 to 35), college graduates, and enthusiastic about working for the company. But a couple of problems have emerged. The two top sales reps are highly motivated by money. It appears that some of the leads generated by dealers were taken by the sales reps and classified as Internet-originated, but this has been difficult to trace. Another problem is time management. The reps have had difficulty balancing their efforts on telemarketing and distributor visits, and with the differences in time zones for the European Union and Australian reps there often is a problem in responding to inquiries in a timely manner. The consultant suggests outsourcing the telemarketing activities either to a central location in the United States that operates 24-7 or to remote locations in the appropriate time zones.

QUESTIONS

1. Which of the consultant's recommendations should be implemented, and if more than one is accepted, what is the highest priority and why?

2. Should the European Union be divided into several territories? If yes, what factors should be considered in making this decision?

3. If the sales reps' responsibilities are divided so they handle contacts only with distributors, will this help resolve the time management problems? Explain.

4. Should the two top sales reps who appear to be stealing customers from distributors be fired? If not, how should STI handle this situation?

Case prepared by Bob Erffmeyer, University of Wisconsin, Eau Claire.

Recruiting and Selecting the Sales Force

When you finish this chapter, you should be able to:

1 Follow the steps in the sales force recruitment process.

2 Identify sources of sales applicants.

3 Follow the steps in the sales force selection process.

4 Apply the criteria used to make the final selection decision.

5 Implement the sales force socialization process.

INSIDE SALES MANAGEMENT

Tere Blanca de Ulloa of Codina Realty Services

College graduates starting a career in personal sales need perseverance, discipline, and good communication skills, says Tere Blanca de Ulloa, a senior vice president at Codina Realty Services Inc., ONCOR International. As her company's most productive salesperson, de Ulloa sells and leases commercial real estate and land in Miami-Dade County, Florida. She represents owners of office buildings and land as well as tenants looking for office space. Over the years, she has found that prospective salespeople can learn effective sales techniques but often "need to polish their verbal and written communication skills," she says.

De Ulloa took a job in banking after graduating from the University of Miami with a concentration in international finance and marketing. Eighteen months later, she returned to school for a graduate degree. "The M.B.A. program gave me an overview of all the business disciplines and developed my writing and presentation skills," she says.

Then de Ulloa moved to San Diego and, at the suggestion of friends, pursued jobs in sales. Visiting the University of San Diego campus, she spotted a note on a bulletin board: "Seeking people for positions with Burroughs Corporation." De Ulloa applied, was hired, and began selling computer products to distributors after a week of sales training. Selling for Burroughs "was a terrific experience, and I developed my sales skills," she remembers. Seeking more diversity in sales contacts and wanting to apply disciplines she learned in graduate school, she looked into commercial real estate, where "each deal and client is different and finance skills are important, especially when handling investment properties."

Returning to Miami, de Ulloa was hired by Coldwell Banker Commercial Real Estate, completed its training program, and remained with the firm for about two years. The president of Codina Realty Services recruited de Ulloa when he began expanding the company fourteen years ago. Codina typically recruits through referrals, seeking candidates who have some sales experience—even in a different field. People who want to work in sales must be "absolutely hungry for the job," observes de Ulloa. "Selling is tough because you get negative reinforcement at first. When you are cold calling, the way most salespeople start, you hear 'no' from a lot of people. If you don't have discipline and perseverance, the job will not work out."

Her advice to students considering a sales career? Gain some experience in your chosen field before you graduate. "Get an internship in a company and industry that interest you," she suggests, "and try to work with the sales teams by helping with research, presentations, or marketing materials." Although an internship may not be easy to find, de Ulloa points out that successfully getting such a position demonstrates the kind of discipline and perseverance every sales professional needs.

SOURCE: Anderson, Rolph E., Alan J. Dubinsky, and Rajiv Mehta, *Personal Selling: Building Customer Relationships and Partnerships,* 2/e, p. 447. Copyright © 2007 by Houghton Mifflin Company. Reprinted with permission.

Importance of Recruiting and Selection

Sales force recruitment and selection are among the most important responsibilities of the sales manager, because to most customers and prospects the salespeople *are* the company. What salespeople say, how they handle themselves, and how they react in face-to-face interactions with customers definitely influence the firm's sales success.

Most companies recruit new people in response to business expansion or increased sales. But sales turnover also is a major catalyst to sales force recruitment. The average turnover rate for all industry groups is just under 20 percent (that is, about 20 percent of all workers leave their jobs each year), but in some industries employee turnover averages almost 100 percent. With that level of turnover, each year a company must hire a new employee for every employee currently working for the organization. High turnover rates are expensive to a company for a host of reasons. Every job takes some time to learn. During the learning period, the employee is probably unable to produce enough revenue to compensate for his or her salary. Turnover also affects customer sales and retention. Customers used to dealing with their previous sales rep may take their business elsewhere or follow an old sales rep to his or her new company. As a result, companies must incur the expense of replacing lost customers with new ones.

Due to the critical importance of recruiting and the company-wide effects of salesperson turnover, sales managers should have an effective and well-planned system for finding and selecting sales personnel. The system's value is even more obvious when we look at costs. Direct costs, such as maintaining recruiting teams and placing recruiting advertisements, as well as indirect costs, like employee time, mean businesses are spending thousands of dollars to recruit and select new people.[1]

Ineffective recruitment can force companies to hire people who don't meet their needs because not enough qualified applicants apply. Hiring the wrong person can cost a company thousands of dollars a year in training, salary, benefits, and lost productivity. But if we evaluate recruitment and selection in terms of cost versus benefits, we can greatly reduce the cost of selecting and developing new salespeople so their productivity is profitable.[2]

In this chapter we'll cover methods for sales rep recruitment and selection. Our focus is on "how to do it" from the sales manager's perspective, but the information will also help you to know what's expected when you apply for a sales position.

■ What Is Recruitment?

Recruitment is finding potential job applicants, telling them about the company, and getting them to apply. Recruitment should not simply generate applicants. It should find applicants who are *potentially good employees.* The entire sales organization ultimately depends on a successful recruiting approach.

Recruiting should be an ongoing activity at all companies. Unfortunately, many sales managers start recruiting only after someone leaves. One problem with waiting until you actually need someone is that it limits the pool of candidates you can screen and interview. Managers who constantly recruit have a useful backlog of prescreened candidates to choose from. A second problem with waiting to recruit until you have an opening is that you can fall prey to a sense of desperation and hire too quickly without proper screening. Finally, you'll lose sales opportunities to the competition during the hiring process when no one is covering the territory.

Many sales managers have little training in recruitment. As a result, they don't know the best sources to find qualified candidates, aren't properly trained in interviewing techniques or screening, and don't know how to conduct background checks on candidates.

Laws and regulations play a major role in recruitment. Sales managers must be familiar with laws that limit questions asked on applications or in interviews. For example, asking about a candidate's personal life—which may hold clues to his or her integrity, stability, or work ethic—is illegal. An HR (human resources) person often accompanies recruiters on college campus recruiting trips as one way of making sure the laws and regulations governing recruiting are followed.

Recruitment
Finding potential job applicants, telling them about the company, and getting them to apply.

The Recruitment Process

No single set of applicant characteristics or abilities can tell you as a sales manager which recruits to hire for sales positions. Different types of sales positions call for performing different activities. So you must assess each recruit's characteristics and abilities to determine whether that person is likely to do well in a particular sales position.

To ensure new recruits have the aptitude necessary to be successful in a particular type of sales job, it's best to follow systematic procedures in the **recruitment process.** The steps in this process are shown in Figure 8.1.

Newly established firms or divisions go through each step shown in Figure 8.1. Existing firms should have completed the first three steps—conduct a job analysis, prepare a job description, identify sales job qualifications—but many do not. This is one reason many firms are ineffective in recruitment and selection, and why they suf-

Recruitment Process
The step by step process through which recruitment is carried out as shown in Figure 8.2.

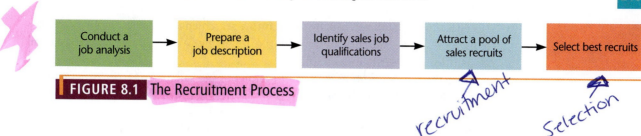

recruitment   *Selection*

FIGURE 8.1 The Recruitment Process

fer turnover problems. Firms that *have* written job descriptions and qualifications need to review them from time to time to ensure they accurately represent the current scope and activities of sales positions.

■ Job Analysis

Job Analysis
A process identifying the duties, requirements, responsibilities, and conditions of a job.

Before a company can search for a salesperson, it must know something about the sales job to be filled. To improve the process, the firm should conduct a **job analysis** to identify the duties, requirements, responsibilities, and conditions of the job. A proper job analysis has these steps:

1. Analyze the environment in which the salesperson is to work. For example:
   - What is the competition the salesperson faces?
   - What kinds of customers will be contacted, and what problems do they have?
   - What knowledge, skills, and potential are needed for this position?
2. Determine duties and responsibilities expected from the salesperson. Obtain information about these from:
   - Salespeople
   - Channel partners, if any (bus to bus)
   - Customers
   - Sales manager
   - Other marketing executives, including the advertising manager, marketing services manager, distribution manager, marketing research director, and credit manager
3. Spend time making calls with several salespeople, observing and recording the job tasks as they are actually performed. Do this for different types of customers and over a representative period of time.

■ Preparing a Job Description

Job Description
Explains to job applicants and current sales personnel what the duties and responsibilities of the sales position are.

The result of a formal job analysis is a job description, probably the single most important tool used in managing the sales force. The **job description** explains—to job applicants and current sales personnel—the duties and responsibilities of the sales position, the skills needed on the job, and on what basis the new and current employees will be evaluated. Since it will be used in recruiting, selecting, training, compensating, and evaluating the sales force, the job description should be in writing so that everyone can refer to it when needed.

Job descriptions help managers not only to supervise and motivate, but also to determine whether each salesperson has a reasonable workload.[3] Many companies provide copies of their job descriptions online. To see examples, type the keywords "job description" and a company name into a search engine. For example, Cisco Systems lists current job descriptions at the following Web address: www.cisco.com/global/EMEA/career/am/index.shtml.

Since the job description is used in evaluating the salesperson's performance, and even in terminating poorly performing employees, many of the tasks must be stated in quantitative terms. For example, the number and frequency of sales calls by type of customer, the number and types of reports to be turned in, and the number of sales promotion displays to be set up should all be included. In addition, since many tasks compete for the salesperson's time, the job description should summarize the job's priorities. Some companies give sales candidates a written job description during the initial interview. Candidates then know exactly what is expected of them before they accept the job.

Sales industry experts say many job descriptions are so brief and ambiguously written that they are of little use in the hiring process. Thus, it is important to be specific in preparing job descriptions. Table 8.1 provides a checklist for developing a job description. It is organized into six major categories: sales activities, servicing functions, account/territory management, sales promotion, executive activities, and goodwill.

■ Developing a Set of Job Qualifications

Job Qualifications
Characteristics recruits should have to perform a sales job satisfactorily.

The duties and responsibilities given in the job description should be converted into a set of **job qualifications** recruits should have to perform the sales job satisfactorily. Determining these qualifications is probably the most difficult aspect of the entire recruitment process. One reason is that the manager is dealing with people, and thus many subjective and complex characteristics come into play. Qualifications such as education and experience are included in the job description, thus making good candidates easier to identify. But most firms also try to identify personality traits that presumably make better salespersons, such as self-confidence, aggressiveness, and gregariousness. For example, a T-Mobile Wireless Sales Representative (www.themobilesolution.com) is expected to have the following qualifications: *age 18+, regular work attendance, above average interpersonal and communication skills, a desire to excel personally and financially—wireless experience a plus.*[4]

Personality Traits. Although many studies have attempted to determine which qualifications are most important for a sales position, none has developed an ideal list. Table 8.2 shows the critical characteristics sought by a *Fortune 500* company. Using a 5-point scale, the company evaluates candidates on college campuses in terms of these characteristics. Only those who score 3.5 or higher are invited to follow-up interviews at the company.

Qualifications. By knowing what the job involves, the sales manager understands the qualifications a person should have to fill the position. Overqualified people generally are not happy in a position that offers little challenge. On the other hand, people in over their head usually will not succeed. In determining the type of person best suited for a sales position, the sales manager should keep in mind certain characteristics of selling jobs:

- *Travel, sometimes overnight*—Most sales positions require some kind of travel, often overnight. People who are to be successful in sales must have no major reservations about travel or overnight trips.

TABLE 8.1 Checklist for Preparing a Sales Job Description

SALES ACTIVITIES

- Make regular calls
- Sell the product or product line
- Handle questions and objections
- Check stock; identify possible product uses
- Interpret sales points or products to customers

- Estimate customer's potential needs
- Emphasize quality
- Explain company policy on price, delivery, and credit
- Get the order

SERVICING FUNCTIONS

- Install the product or display
- Report product weaknesses and complaints
- Handle adjustments, returns, and allowances
- Handle requests for credit

- Handle special orders
- Establish priorities
- Analyze local conditions for customer

ACCOUNT/TERRITORY MANAGEMENT – done by sales manager

- Arrange route for best coverage
- Maintain sales portfolios, samples, kits, etc.

- Establish and maintain customer database
- Balance effort with customer against the potential volume

SALES PROMOTION

- Develop new prospects and accounts
- Distribute company, product, and industry information
- Make calls with customer's salespeople

- Train personnel of channel partners, etc.
- Present survey reports, layouts, and proposals

EXECUTIVE ACTIVITIES

- Develop monthly and weekly work plan
- Each night, make a daily work plan for the next day
- Organize field activity for minimum travel and maximum calls
- Prepare and submit special reports on trends and competition
- Prepare and submit statistical data requested by home office
- Investigate lost sales and reason for loss

- Prepare reports on developments, trends, new objectives, and new ways to meet objectives
- Attend sales meetings
- Build a prospect list
- Collect overdue accounts; report on faulty accounts
- Collect credit information
- Analyze work plans to determine which goals were not met and why

GOODWILL

- Counsel customers on their problems
- Build relationships with channel partners

- Maintain loyalty and respect for the company
- Attend sales meetings held by customers

- *Supervision*—Few sales jobs involve close supervision. The salesperson is in the field, traveling from one account to another, and may have contact with the home office or sales manager only every two or three days. Salespersons are in effect their own boss, determining what time to get up in the morning and start work and what time to go home. To be successful, a salesperson must be a self-starter and have a great deal of self-discipline.

- *Little work experience*—People who enter sales generally have little or no work experience. Therefore, their success on the job is hard to predict. Equally difficult is matching the job description to the individual with no track record.

TABLE 8.2	Critical Characteristics and Behaviors of Sales Recruits
Intelligence	Demonstrated in verbal expression, depth of response, analytical thought process
Decisiveness	When asked, makes definite choices, lets you know where he or she stands on issues, is not tentative
Energy and Enthusiasm	Is animated, positive, spontaneous, fast-paced
Results Orientation	Gets to the point, emphasizes achievement; responses are relevant to interview objectives
Maturity	Shows poise, self-confidence, and maturity in dress, general demeanor, and degree of relaxation
Assertiveness	Takes charge, is forceful, convincing, and persuasive
Sensitivity	Is sincere, friendly, tactful, responsive, not aloof
Openness	Responses are not canned and superficial
Tough-mindedness	Discusses persons and events critically; doesn't allow emotions to cloud perceptions

■ *High turnover*—Due to these characteristics, high employee turnover is typical in sales. Many people change from job to job, while others exit the sales profession altogether after only a short time.

Job qualifications should identify the characteristics and abilities a person must have to meet the requirements of the sales position. For example, a prospective salesperson might need any or all of the following qualifications: two years of college, at least four years of work experience, ability to make decisions under stress, specific product knowledge, technology literacy, a car, and the ability to travel.

Since recruits with *all* the most important qualifications are seldom found, managers must decide which are most important and what trade-offs they consider acceptable. For instance, can enthusiasm and high ambition substitute for relatively poor verbal skills? The answer to such questions depends on the sales job and the extent to which the recruit can be trained to overcome weaknesses.

There is no one method for every company to use in determining the qualifications of sales recruits. The logical starting point, however, is the job description. If the sales position requires technical or analytical skills, then specific educational background or work experience may be necessary. Technology companies, for example, often hire salespeople with technical backgrounds in engineering or computer science. Also, sales positions with limited supervision may necessitate hiring mature, experienced persons. For example, ADP (Automatic Data Processing—www.adp.com) hires only experienced salespeople with the skills and confidence to manage their own sales territories, exceed quota, and work hard.

Models for Success. Companies that have been in business for several years and have a large sales force usually analyze personal histories of present and past salespeople to determine job qualifications. Comparing the characteristics of good, average, and poor salespeople suggests traits that predict success in a sales career with the company. To make this analysis, firms place the information in their data warehouse and develop statistical models to differentiate high performers from low performers.

● **Technology companies, for example, often hire salespeople with technical backgrounds in engineering or computer science.**

Predictive models incorporating the unique characteristics of salespeople who failed or were fired can then enhance recruitment and selection.[5]

Sales managers rely on statistical models because they improve the manager's ability to recruit and ultimately select qualified individuals. But equally important, they help validate selection criteria, and validation is required by government regulations on equal employment opportunity in hiring. Some companies might use an outside organization such as a consulting firm specializing in personnel services, or a similar but non-competing firm, to develop job qualifications.

■ Attracting a Pool of Applicants

The next step in the recruitment and selection process is attracting a pool of applicants for the sales position. Large companies need to continuously identify, locate, and attract salespeople. Recruited candidates become the pool from which new salespeople are chosen. The quality of this pool predicts future successes or problems of the sales force.

We cannot overemphasize the importance of starting with a large pool of applicants. If there are too few applicants, the probability is high that a person with inferior selling abilities will be hired. When a firm processes large numbers of applicants, the recruiting program serves as an automatic screening system. But sales managers must be careful not to screen out good candidates. The interview process is only one screening device. Others are the recruiting sources used, such as the colleges visited or the websites and newspapers where ads are placed. An advertisement in the *Wall Street Journal,* for example, will attract a different type of recruit than an ad on Monster.com (www.monster.com).

Recruiting is not equally important in all firms. The quality of salespeople needed, the rate of turnover expected, and a firm's financial position are just a few factors that account for the difference. When higher-caliber salespeople are needed, managers must screen more applicants before finding someone who meets the hiring specifications. At firms that experience high turnover, recruiting must be continuous. Financially strong companies may have traveling recruiting teams, whereas weaker firms may rely heavily on advertisements.

Sources of Salespeople

There are many places to find recruits. Managers need to analyze potential sources to determine which produce the best recruits for the sales position to be filled. Then they should maintain a continuing relationship with these sources, even during periods when no hiring is being done. Good sources are hard to find, and goodwill must be established between the firm and the source to ensure good recruits in the future.

Some firms use only one source, while others use several. The most frequently used sources are persons within the company, competitors, non-competing companies, educational institutions, advertisements—both traditional and Internet—and employment agencies.

■ Persons within the Company

Companies often recruit salespeople from other departments, such as production or engineering, and from the non-selling section of the sales department. These people are familiar with company policies as well as the technical aspects of the product itself. The chances of finding good salespeople within the company are excellent because sales managers know the people and can assess their sales potential. In fact, many firms turn to non-sales personnel within the company as their first source of new sales recruits.

Hiring people from within the company can lift morale because a transfer to sales is often viewed as a promotion. But transferring outstanding workers from the plant or office into the sales department does not guarantee success. In some cases, hostility can arise among plant and office supervisors, who feel their personnel are being taken by the sales department. Recommendations from the present sales force and sales executives usually yield better internal prospects than those from other employees, because the people in sales understand the needed qualifications. It is better to hire candidates with selling skills instead of just shuffling employees from other departments.[6]

■ Competitors

Salespeople recruited from competitors are trained, have experience selling similar products to similar markets, and should be ready to sell almost immediately. But usually a premium must be paid to attract them from their present jobs. Some sales managers are reluctant to hire competitors' salespeople because the practice is sometimes viewed as unethical. But is trying to lure away a competitor's employees really different from attempting to take a competitor's customers or market share? No. However, recruiting a competitor's employees out of revenge is unethical. Likewise, ethical issues arise when a newly hired salesperson uses valuable proprietary information from his or her former employer to look good on the new job. Hiring a competitor's reps may also pose legal questions if they have signed a non-compete or non-solicitation agreement with their former employer. Courts today generally do not support non-compete agreements, since they can hinder someone's ability to earn a livelihood. Non-solicitation agreements, on the other hand, are more easily enforced because the salesperson has agreed not to contact customers acquired while with the former company.

Recruiting competitors' salespeople may bring other problems. Although they are highly trained and know the market and product very well, it is often hard for them to unlearn old practices. Also, they may not be compatible with the culture of the new organization and management. Finally, recruits from competitors usually are expected to switch their customers to the new business. But if they are unable to do so, their new employer may be disappointed.

We can evaluate the risk of incurring these problems by asking one question: Why is the person leaving his or her present employer? A satisfactory answer often clears up doubts and identifies a valuable employee. The difficulty arises, however, in determining the real answer. Often it's almost impossible to determine why someone is looking for another job. Good sales managers must be able to accurately evaluate the information they get.

Non-Competing Companies

Non-competing firms can provide a good source of trained and experienced salespeople, especially if they are selling similar products or selling to the same market. Even though some recruits may be unfamiliar with the recruiting firm's product line, they do have selling experience and require less training.

Companies that are either vendors or customers of the recruiting firm are also an excellent source of candidates. Recruits from these sources have some knowledge of the company from having sold to or purchased from it, and their familiarity reduces the time it takes to make them productive. Another advantage of recruits from these sources is that they are already familiar with the industry.

Educational Institutions

High schools, adult evening classes, business colleges, vocational schools, junior colleges, and universities are all sources of sales recruits. Large firms usually are successful in recruiting from universities, but small firms tend to be more successful in recruiting from smaller educational institutions or other sources.

While most college graduates lack specific sales experience, they have the education and perspective that many employers seek in potential sales representatives. College graduates tend to adapt more easily than experienced personnel and have not developed loyalties to a firm or an industry. They usually have acquired social graces, are more mature than persons of the same age without college training, and can think logically and express themselves reasonably well. Companies recruiting from campuses have found that students from universities with specialized sales programs—like Kennesaw State University (www.kennesaw.edu) in Atlanta, Georgia, and Illinois State University (www.ilstu.edu) in Normal—have a much lower turnover rate than students from other programs. Some universities even have more specific sales programs, such as the pharmaceutical sales program at the University of Southern Mississippi (www.usm.edu). Sales organizations increasingly focus their campus recruiting efforts on students who graduate from specialized sales programs.[7]

● Large fims usually are successful in recruiting from universities, but small firms tend to be more successful in recruiting from smaller educational institutions or other sources.

A problem in recruiting from college campuses is the unfavorable image some students have of sales. Recruiters report some college students accept sales positions only after they have been turned down for other jobs or rejected by law schools or medical schools. One survey asked over five hundred students to rank, in order of career preference, seven job opportunities in marketing: advertising, direct marketing, market research, product management, retailing, sales, and wholesaling. Advertising ranked first overall, and sales came in fifth—ahead of only retailing and wholesaling.[8] Despite these problems, educational institutions remain a good source of sales recruits.

■ Advertisements

Classified advertisements in newspapers, trade journals, and on the Internet are another source of recruits. The *Wall Street Journal, U.S.A. Today,* and various trade journals are used in recruiting for high-caliber sales and sales management positions. Local newspapers generally are used to recruit for lower-level sales positions.

While advertisements reach a large audience, the caliber of applicants may be second-rate. This places a burden on those doing the initial screening. Managers can also increase the quality of applicants recruited by advertisements by carefully selecting the media and describing the job qualifications specifically in the ad. To be effective, a recruiting ad must attract attention and have credibility. Include the following elements to ensure an ad's effectiveness: company name, product, territory, hiring qualifications, compensation plan, expense plan, fringe benefits, and how to contact the employer.

■ Online Recruiting

Many companies use the Internet to recruit for sales positions. One of the largest Internet recruiting sites is Monster.com (www.monster.com), a recruitment and human resources database that posts job listings from companies like Coca-Cola, Bank of America, Procter & Gamble, and General Electric. The website has thousands of resumes at any given time—about 12 percent of these postings are for sales and marketing positions. Another Internet recruitment site is JobWeb.com (www .jobweb.org), sponsored by the National Association of Colleges & Employers.

Most of the sites offer both job and resume postings as well as keyword searches and searches by state, locality, industry, company, or title. Sites like www.Careerbuilder .com, www.Monster.com, http://www.jobs4sales.com and www.Yahoo!HotJobs.com are increasingly popular, but recruiters need to go to the specific pages and departments on these sites that drill down to find applicants interested in sales. Even better is to use websites specifically tailored to the sales profession, like www .saleshead.com.[9]

An important advantage of the Internet as a recruitment source is its low cost compared to other recruitment methods. Other advantages include access to more people and a broader selection of applicants, the ability to target the type of people needed, access to people with a technical background who know computers, convenience, quicker response and turnaround, and ease of use. Recruiting online can also have its disadvantages. For example, some companies are concerned about the high volume of resumes they might receive from the Internet and their limited resources to review them.

● Many employment agencies provide a full array of services for recruiting, from searching for candidates to screening, interviewing, and recommending the best candidate.

Employment Agencies and Professional Recruiters

Third-party employment agencies and professional recruiters are among the best and the worst sources. Often the quality of results depends on the relationship between the agency or recruiter and the sales manager. So sales managers should select the agency or recruiter carefully and develop a good working relationship. The third party must clearly understand both the job description and the qualifications for the position to be filled.

In recent years, employment agencies and recruiters have steadily improved and expanded their services. They now can screen candidates so that in-house recruiters spend more time with the prospects who are most highly qualified. Many employment agencies provide a full array of services for recruiting, from searching for candidates to screening, interviewing, and recommending the best candidate.

■ Factors to Consider in Evaluating Sources

Recruiting differs substantially from company to company. Here are some factors to consider when deciding which recruiting sources to use:

- *Nature of the product*—A highly technical product requires an experienced, knowledgeable person. The firm may look at persons in its own production department, experienced persons from other companies, or candidates with specific educational backgrounds.

- *Nature of the market*—Experienced salespeople may be needed to deal with well-informed purchasing agents or with high-level executives.

- *Policy on promoting from within*—If this policy is the rule, recruiters know where to look first.

- *Sales training provided by the company*—A company that has its own sales training program can recruit inexperienced people. But if a salesperson needs to be productive quickly, it may be necessary to seek experienced recruits.

- *Personnel needs of the company*—If the company is seeking career salespeople, then MBA graduates may not be appropriate recruits, since many aspire to higher management positions.

- *Sources of successful recruits in the past*—Past sources can be used again as long as there have been no changes in the sales position.

- *Recruiting budget*—A small budget means a firm must limit its sources.

- *Legal considerations*—Civil rights laws and other regulations must be considered when a firm is deciding on sources of recruits.

Recruiters know top-rated candidates can come from any source, and they must be careful not to overlook sources because of a few poor experiences in the past. With the cost of recruiting increasing in recent years, however, it is still important to be selective. Sales managers must analyze sources and devote time to those that are most productive, while ensuring that Equal Employment Opportunity Commission (EEOC) guidelines are satisfied.

The Sales Force Selection Process

Selection Process
Activities involved in choosing candidates that best meet the qualifications and have the greatest aptitude for the job.

The recruiting process produces a pool of applicants from which to choose. The **selection process** is about choosing candidates who best meet the qualifications and have the greatest aptitude for the job. Numerous tools, techniques, and procedures can aid the selection process. For instance, applications or brief phone interviews help initially screen out candidates. In-depth interviews and tests, such as sales aptitude or psychological tests, provide further information for final candidate selection. Reference checking adds third-party comments to the selection process. None of these should be used alone. Each is designed to collect different information.

Steps in the salesperson selection process are shown in Figure 8.2. Depending on the size of the company, the number of salespeople needed, and the importance of the position to be filled, the steps will vary from company to company. For example, sales recruits for some companies may have to pass a psychological test before being invited to an in-depth interview. Other companies may not check a candidate's references until just before an offer is made, and still others may not require employment

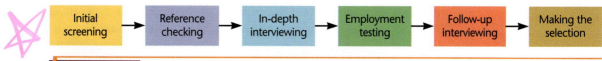

FIGURE 8.2 Steps in the Sales Force Selection Process

Note: Applicants may be rejected at any one of these steps.

tests at all. While successful selection of sales applicants does not require that all steps be completed, the more steps that are completed, the higher the probability of selecting successful salespeople.

Hiring successful candidates usually results in increased sales. But hiring the wrong person can cost a company thousands of dollars a year for training, salary and benefits, and lost sales. To avoid these losses, many companies are using technological advances such as psychological tests and statistical models in the selection process. Sales managers must remember, though, that selection tools and techniques are merely aids to sound executive judgment that can only eliminate obviously unqualified candidates and identify the more competent.[10]

■ Initial Screening

Initial Screening
Process by which undesirable job candidates are eliminated as soon as possible.

The purpose of the **initial screening** is to eliminate undesirable recruits as soon as possible. Initial screening may start with an application form or resume, a screening interview, or some type of brief test. No matter which tool is used, the shorter it is, the more it will reduce costs. But it must not be so brief that it screens out good candidates.

Application Forms. Application forms and resumes are the most widely used screening tools. An application form is an easy means of collecting the information necessary for determining an applicant's qualifications. That usually includes name, contact information, position applied for, educational background, work experience, military service, participation in social organizations, outside interests and activities, and personal references. Other important questions on an application form relate directly to the sales position for which the applicant is applying. For example:

- Why do you want this job?
- Why do you want to change jobs?
- What minimum income do you require?
- Are you willing to travel?
- Are you willing to be transferred?
- What do you want to be doing five years from now? Ten years from now?
- Are you willing to use your car for business?

Application forms differ from company to company. On all forms, however, it is illegal to include questions that are not related to the job, such as age, race, national origin, marital status, or disabilities.

An important function of application forms is to help sales managers prepare for personal interviews with sales candidates. By reviewing the application before the interview, sales managers can get an initial impression of the applicant and prepare a list of questions to ask during the interview. Specific considerations are

- Appearance of the application.
- Missing information—Are there blank spots or shortcuts that seem inconsistent with the rest of the application? Ask about these during the interview.
- Indications of instability—Does the history include more than three jobs in five years, any job held for less than one year, more than two colleges, and the like?
- Reason for job change.
- Career progression—Do the job changes represent a growth in income and responsibility?

Past behavior patterns revealed in application forms are useful predictors of future behavior, and therefore they are important for screening applicants. Table 8.3 summarizes how to use application information in selection.

Weighted Application Form
Forms that score candidates on each job attribute by assigning different values to each attribute.

Companies can use **weighted application forms** to help them distinguish between good and poor salespeople. These forms place more weight (importance) on such items as years of selling experience, employment length, career objectives, or educational level. Thus, managers can consider only applicants who rate higher than an established minimum number of points on these items, and reject those who fail to reach the cutoff point. Of course, weighted application forms must be validated for each sales position in the firm so they reflect a position's unique requirements. Also, managers should periodically reevaluate the validity of the weights, because an item's importance may change over time.

Initial Screening Interviews and Tests. Almost all companies make use of initial screening interviews or tests. Usually conducted in person or over the telephone, the interviews or tests typically last from 20 to 30 minutes and generally are given by assistant human resource managers, assistant sales managers, or sales personnel. Interviews a recruiter conducts on campus with college students, for instance, are initial screening interviews. Each recruiter talks with eight or ten students a day and selects the best ones to invite back for in-depth interviews.

TABLE 8.3   Application Items That Predict Performance and Turnover

INDICATORS OF HIGHER PERFORMANCE	INDICATORS OF LOWER TURNOVER
■ *Employment:* Currently employed at time of hiring. ■ *Prior Sales Experience:* Selling experience at most recent job ■ *Knowledge of Job Requirements:* Has an understanding of the selling position offered. ■ *Recruitment Source:* Recruited through the use of newspaper or Internet advertising rather than through unsolicited applications. ■ *Residential Moves:* Has made fewer residential moves. ■ *Education:* Has a bachelor's degree.	■ *Career Aspirations:* More interested in a career sales position than using the selling job as a steppingstone position. ■ *Employment:* Currently employed at time of hiring. ■ *Prior Sales Experience:* Selling experience at most recent job, but less overall sales experience. ■ *Employment Length:* Has spent more time at their most recent job.

Automated Screening Techniques. Both human resource officers and sales managers are increasingly using automated telephone and computer screening devices to screen job applicants. Department stores like Macy's and Neiman Marcus, for instance, require candidates to pass computer screening tests measuring honesty, personality, and other traits. Candidates answer questions at a computer, and response delays and answers that don't match up are identified. Those who pass are granted an in-person interview.[11]

Automated screening procedures speed the gathering and analysis of data from applicants. Automated devices never forget to ask a question and always ask questions the same way each time. Interestingly, people often give more truthful answers to machines than to human interviewers. Companies that use computer interviewing have found it an effective tool for streamlining the employee selection process and reducing employee turnover, while capturing data for use in future hiring or employee development.[12]

Computer screening has disadvantages. Opponents fear that electronic "profiling" will exclude those who don't fall within the desired response range, even though a person might have the skills the company really needs. Computers cannot recognize fuzzy or superficial answers or ask interviewees to elaborate, and they cannot ask follow-up questions of interviewees who drop unexpected leads. And with computer-assisted interviewing there may be an additional danger: if electronic profiling selects people who have the same personality traits, workforce diversity may decline.[13]

■ Checking References

Reference Checking
The process of following up with references provided on an application to check the credibility of a job candidate.

A company cannot be sure it has all the needed information about an applicant until it has thoroughly checked references. **Reference checking** is a screening tool that enables a company to obtain information from former and current bosses, coworkers, clients, and other professionals. One study of 150 executives of *Fortune* 1000 companies claimed that at least one-third of all resumes they received were either fraudulent or lacking in vital information.[14] Education is the area to check most closely for misrepresentation. A Notre Dame University football coach was fired because he did not have the master's degree he listed on his resume; the CEO of Lotus software company exaggerated his education and military service; and the CEO of Bausch & Lomb forfeited a bonus of more than $1 million because the MBA degree he claimed to have did not exist.[15] Sales managers will thus want to thoroughly check references and verify critical information at some point during the selection process before the final interview and selection take place.

References from teachers and former employers are generally more helpful than other types. Teachers can give an indication of intelligence, work habits, and personality traits. Former employers can be used to find out why the person left the job and how well he or she got along with others. The question "Would you rehire the applicant again if you had the chance?" tends to bring out accurate responses. Sales managers should also not overlook references from an applicant's current clients, if the candidate is an experienced salesperson. These references provide valuable clues about a candidate's selling style and whether the candidate will fit in with the company's culture.

In general, however, the quality of reference checks is questionable. Contacting the names supplied by a candidate is often a waste of time; it's unlikely serious problems will be uncovered, or the applicant wouldn't have given those names. Fearful of lawsuits, former employers are also careful not to divulge anything about an employee other than the dates the employee worked for the company. To increase the chances of getting more information, many sales managers have candidates sign a waiver releasing their former employers from liability and agreeing to let the sales manager contact additional references. If the references still won't give any information about the candidate, sales managers should ask the candidate to help. If the candidate refuses or cannot come up with other references, then the candidate probably does not have anyone that will give him or her a good recommendation.[16]

Many firms try to talk with people who know the applicant but were not listed on the application form as a reference. For reference checking to be a useful selection tool, the sales manager must be resourceful and pursue leads that are not directly given. For instance, a bit of sleuthing can find people willing to give references who may have worked with the candidate or who were his or her clients. While reference checking can be a frustrating and laborious process, many sales managers have found that even if only one significant fact is uncovered, it usually makes the effort worthwhile.

Standard Company Reviews. In addition to checking references, company policy at many firms requires standard reviews on all applicants as a condition of employment. These may include physical examinations, drug tests, and background checks—usually conducted by someone in the human resources department, rather than the sales manager. Since many of these reviews or investigations are covered in some aspect by law, they should be used with caution. Further, it may be illegal to conduct some of these investigative reviews until the company has made a job offer to the candidate in question.

- *Physical examinations*—Many sales jobs require a degree of physical activity and stamina, and therefore poor physical condition may hinder a salesperson's job performance. When sales jobs require strenuous activity, many companies insist on a thorough medical examination for all sales recruits. But physical exams or access to medical records are possible only after an offer has been made.

- *Drug tests*—Drug testing programs are used frequently in industry. Proponents of drug testing claim that it leads to a safer and more productive work environment. Critics argue that drug testing violates constitutional protection against unreasonable search and seizure and invades the individual's privacy. They also contend that screening is an attempt by employers to regulate workers' behavior off the job and that the results may be used as a tool for harassment. Opponents also raise doubts about the validity of the most widely used tests, because they are subject to high error rates. Thus, innocent persons may be falsely classified as drug abusers. As with physical exams, drug tests can be legally administered only after the company makes a job offer contingent upon a negative test result.

- *Background checks*—Many companies also conduct background checks to give them more information about a candidate. Common types include checking the applicant's workers' compensation, credit, driving, and criminal records. These checks raise legal questions, however, and may violate antidiscrimination laws such as the Americans with Disabilities Act and the Civil Rights Act of 1964. Companies that base hiring decisions on these checks must demonstrate that the information they obtain is related to the job.

■ In-Depth Interviewing

The in-depth interview is the most used and least scientific of the various tools for selecting employees. A salesperson is seldom hired without a face-to-face in-depth interview. In fact, as many as three or four interviews are usually conducted with the most desirable candidates. No other selection tool can take the place of getting to know the applicant personally. To better understand the interviewing process, go to the Cisco Systems website at www.cisco.com/global/EMEA/career/jobs/index.shtml and view the Candidate Recruitment Process Flow at the bottom of the page.

In-Depth Interview
Is the most used and least scientific of the various tools for selecting employees and is very effective for finding if an employee is right for the job through a two-way discussion involving probing questions.

In-depth interviews help the firm determine whether a person is right for the job. They bring out personal characteristics that no other selection tool can reveal. The interview also serves as a two-way channel of communication because the company as well as the applicant can ask questions and learn about each other.

Questions asked during an interview should be aimed at finding out certain things: Is the candidate qualified for the job? Does the candidate really want the job? Will this sales job help the candidate fulfill personal goals? Will the candidate find this sales position challenging enough? These questions, like those on the application form, examine the applicant's past behavior, experiences, and motivation.

When candidates have prior sales experience, use in-depth interviews to clarify their previous selling environment. This information shows whether the candidate's experience fits the job at hand. For example, an experienced candidate who was successful under a short sales cycle where sales are made daily may not be happy in an environment where the sales cycle may take years, such as with commercial airlines. Examples of information that can be obtained from an in-depth interview of experienced salespeople are shown in Table 8.4.

TABLE 8.4 Interviewing Candidates with Prior Sales Experience

- **Was the candidate a *salesperson* or an *account manager*?** Candidates responsible for obtaining new customers are different from those responsible for servicing current customers.

- **Source and quality of candidate's past sales leads?** There are substantial differences between selling to customers when qualified and highly developed leads are provided versus selling to prospects where either no or unqualified leads are furnished.

- **Length of sales cycle the candidate has been successful with?** Salespeople who thrive on long sales cycles are generally very different from those successful in short cycles.

- **Level candidate has been selling to?** Is the candidate used to dealing with channel partners or with presidents and CEOs, and how will this fit in with the sales environment of the offered job?

- **What compensation plan does the candidate succeed under?** Was the candidate successful under a salary plan in which none or very little of the compensation was at risk, or under a commission plan in which most or all of the compensation was at risk? Candidates who thrive under a commission-only plan may not feel motivated by a base salary plan. On the other hand, candidates compensated almost totally on base salary may regard the commission-only plan as too risky.

- **Has the candidate worked alone or as a team member?** Some salespeople work most effectively as members of a group, and others work best on their own. If the job requires a lot of interaction with other members of a sales team, then the candidate should be able to contribute to a team selling environment.

- **Why does the candidate want to change sales positions?** The true reason may be hard to get at, but sales managers should determine why candidates want to leave their current sales position and if the terms of the offered job will be appealing. For instance, if the salesperson wants to leave because he or she is dissatisfied with the present income, will the job offered provide the necessary increase? Likewise, if the salesperson was passed over for promotion, does the job offered provide career advancement?

> ### TABLE 8.5   Approaches Interviewers Use to Obtain Useful Information
>
> 1. Build a rapport quickly.
> 2. Structure the interview so that the interviewee clearly understands what is expected.
> 3. Elicit desired behavior by not showing disapproval or disagreement, by using humor, by showing sympathy and understanding, and by interrupting infrequently only for clarification or redirection.
> 4. Use probing, open-ended questions, and avoid yes-or-no questions.
>   Examples of typical open-ended questions:
>   - Tell me about . . .
>   - What did you like . . .
>   - How would you compare . . .
>   - Why did you decide to do that . . .
>   - Tell me about the people . . .
>   - How did you find that experience . . .
>   - How would you describe . . .
>   - How did you feel about . . .
>   - What were the differences . . .
>
>   Examples of probing techniques are reflection, paraphrasing, and phrases such as:
>   - How so . . .
>   - Because . . .
>   - In what respect . . .
> 5. Ask candidates whether they have any questions.

Sales managers use different approaches to elicit useful information, depending on their own personality, training, and work experience. Table 8.5 provides an example of an interview guide.

Types of In-depth Interviews. Interviews differ depending on the number of questions that are prepared in advance and on how much the interviewer guides the conversation. Some are highly structured interviews. Others are informal and unstructured.

In the **structured interview**, the recruiter asks each candidate the same set of standardized questions designed to determine the applicant's fitness for a sales position. Since structured interviews don't probe candidates for in-depth information, they are more often used as an initial screening tool. They're particularly useful for inexperienced interviewers because they guide the interview and ensure that all factors relevant to the candidate's qualifications are covered.

Unstructured interviews are informal and nondirected. The goal of an unstructured interview is to get the candidate to talk freely on a variety of topics. Frequently the recruiter begins the interview by saying to the candidate, "Tell me about yourself," or by asking questions such as "Why did you decide to interview with our company?" Examples of some probing questions used in unstructured interviews are presented in Table 8.6.

Several problems are associated with unstructured interviews. One is that they don't provide answers to standard questions that the interviewer can compare with other candidates' responses or with the company's experiences. Also, it's possible to spend considerable time on relatively unimportant topics. But experts say this

Structured Interview
Recruiter asks each candidate the same set of standardized questions designed to determine the applicant's fitness for a sales position.

Unstructured Interview
Informal and nondirected interview used to get a candidate to talk freely on a variety of topics.

> **TABLE 8.6   Typical Probing Questions Asked in Unstructured Interviews**
>
> *Questions that determine whether a candidate is self-motivated:*
>
> - "What is the single most important thing you want to accomplish that a sales position will enable you to accomplish?"
> - "What personal goals have you set for yourself for the next year?"
>
> *Questions that identify candidates who will work on their own to improve themselves:*
>
> - "What is one thing you really do well? How did you learn that skill?"
> - "What is the last book you read or seminar you attended? What have you done as a result?"
> - "Describe your favorite coach or instructor. What did you learn from that person?"
> - "What is the latest investment you've made in yourself?"
>
> *Questions that determine the candidate's pattern for winning or recovering from loss:*
>
> - "Describe your earliest successes."
> - "When did you first realize you were a winner?"
> - "Describe your most competitive endeavor. How did you do?"
> - "What was your last failure? How did you recover? What did you do to turn things around?"

technique is the best for probing an individual's personality and for gaining insights into the candidate's attitudes and opinions.

To administer and interpret unstructured interviews, interviewers must be well trained. Unfortunately, sales managers for many firms have had relatively little experience as interviewers, and few have ever had special training in interviewing techniques. Therefore, many firms use a combination of structured and unstructured approaches, usually referred to as a **semi-structured interview**. In semi-structured interviews the interviewer has a planned list of questions but allows time for interaction and discussion. This approach is flexible and can be tailored to meet the needs of different candidates as well as different interviewers.

Semi-Structured Interview
Combined approach in which a fixed set of questions is applied but time for discussion and interaction is left after each.

Applicants' Responsibility in an Interview. Applicants should prepare for interviews by learning about the company and trying to anticipate questions that may be asked.

 SALES MANAGEMENT IN ACTION

The Non-Interview Interview Approach

The business development manager for AT&T's wireless data division asks sales candidates just one probing question, such as: "I need to get three thousand customers on my wireless network next week. What would you do to get these customers on? You have thirty minutes to tell me." This type of unstructured, probing interview enables AT&T to observe candidates' personalities and eliminate canned responses. And because they routinely hire reps for new, unde-

fined markets, the company looks for candidates who can think quickly and offer innovative solutions.

Do you think this is an effective way to interview candidates?

SOURCES: Dave Kurlan, "Consistently Inconsistent," *Understanding the Sales Force,* May 24, 2005; http://omgevaluation.blogspot.com/2005_05_01_omgevaluation_archive.html (accessed October 2006); Michele Marchetti, "Where to Find the Next Top Performer," *Sales & Marketing Management,* December 1996, pp. 30–31.

This task is very easy today because almost all companies have websites that are easily accessed. For some sales positions it may be helpful to practice answers ahead of time. After all, applicants are "selling" themselves to the interviewer, and the objective is to make a favorable impression. A review of Tables 8.7 through 8.10 will suggest some of the questions that applicants should be prepared to answer. And just as companies make recruiting and selection a serious process, so also should candidates be shrewd job seekers. Applicants should consider whether the job is a good fit with their background, skills, and temperament; determine whether the organization's approach to getting work done matches their own; and assess whether the job and organization offer opportunities for professional growth and advancement.[17]

Applicants should ask questions during the interview to help them decide whether they want the position if it is offered to them. Table 8.7 lists questions candidates typically ask in the interview. While they're all important, some are more important than others. Sales managers need to be prepared to answer questions on these topics.

The types of questions an applicant asks also give the sales manager clues about his or her values, aspirations, and goals as well as knowledge and abilities. Candidates who ask only "what's in it for me" questions about salary, benefits, vacation policies, and promotability—or those who ask only "filler" questions, such as when the company was founded or how many employees there are—show little insight, initiative, or creativity. Applicants who ask absolutely no questions are obviously not interested at all in the job. On the other hand, top performers will ask questions that help them gain a more accurate picture of success in the job and at the company.[18]

Many sales recruits successfully pass screening interviews as well as appraisals of application forms. The in-depth personal interview is much more challenging, how-

TABLE 8.7   Questions Typically Asked by Candidates During Interviews

- Where are the entry-level positions? (Start at the division level)
- What are these positions?
- How is the training conducted? How long? Formal or informal?
- What percentage of the job will require travel?
- What is the likelihood of relocation?
- What are the starting salaries for a particular position?
- What is the typical career path of each position?
- How long will it take?
- What is the selection process like?
- What is the compensation package?
- What are the benefits?
- How am I evaluated for promotion?
- What are your selection criteria, or what do you look for most in a candidate?
- Does your company encourage furthering one's education?
- How would you describe the culture of the company?
- What criteria make someone successful in sales at your company?
- Are employees required to assume responsibilities beyond the written job description?

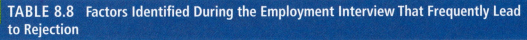

TABLE 8.8 Factors Identified During the Employment Interview That Frequently Lead to Rejection

- Poor appearance
- Overbearing, overaggressive, conceited attitude
- Inability to express self clearly; poor voice, diction, grammar
- Lack of career planning; no purpose or goals
- Lack of interest and enthusiasm; a passive, indifferent manner
- Lack of confidence and poise; nervousness
- Failure to participate in extracurricular activities
- Overemphasis on money; interest in "best dollar" offer
- Poor scholastic record
- Unwillingness to start at the bottom; the expectation of too much too soon
- Evasiveness; failure to be clear about unfavorable factors in record
- Lack of tact
- Lack of maturity
- Lack of courtesy
- Condemnation of past employers
- Lack of social understanding
- Marked dislike for hard work
- Lack of vitality
- Failure to make eye contact with interviewer
- Limp, fishy handshake
- Indecision
- Indefinite responses to questions

- Failure to ask questions about the job
- Little sense of humor
- Sloppy, poorly prepared application
- Evidence of merely shopping around for a job
- Desires job for short time only
- Lack of knowledge in field of specialization
- No interest in company or industry
- Emphasis on whom the applicant knows
- Unwillingness to relocate, if necessary
- Cynical attitude
- Low moral standards
- Laziness
- Intolerance; strong prejudice
- Narrow interests
- Evidence of wasted time
- Poor handling of personal finances
- No interest in community activities
- Inability to take criticism
- Lack of appreciation of the value of experience
- Radical ideas
- Tardiness to interview without good reason
- Failure to express appreciation for interviewer's time

ever, and many have difficulty with it. Table 8.8 lists negative factors that frequently lead to rejection of applicants during employment interviews. Sales applicants should be aware of these and avoid them whenever possible.

■ Employment Testing

Employment Test
An objective way to measure traits or characteristics of applicants for sales positions and to increase the chances of selecting good salespeople using intelligence tests or some other norming test.

Employment tests are an objective way to measure traits or characteristics of applicants for sales positions and to increase the chances of selecting good salespeople. They can identify traits and qualifications—such as intelligence, aptitude, and personality—that other selection tools cannot measure. Another reason for using tests relates to the high cost of training and hiring the sales force. A selection tool that can reduce sales force turnover and increase sales productivity is definitely desirable. Tests also provide a basis for interviewing. Questionable points noted in the test results may be probed more deeply during the interview. Six basic tests are used in selecting sales personnel:

- *Intelligence tests*—Intelligence tests measure a salesperson's general cognitive ability or intelligence as an indicator of future job performance. While not used as frequently as other tests in sales force selection, they can often be an effective tool for selecting salespeople.

- *Knowledge tests*—Knowledge tests measure what the applicant knows about a certain product, service, market, and the like.

- *Sales aptitude tests*—Sales aptitude tests measure a person's innate or acquired social skills and selling know-how as well as tact and diplomacy.

- *Vocational interest tests*—Vocational interest tests assume that a person is going to be more effective and stable if he or she has a strong interest in selling. They're more likely to be administered to high school or college students as a means of assessing career potential.

- *Attitude and lifestyle tests*—Attitude and lifestyle tests assess honesty and identify drug abusers. Typical test items include questions that ask how often the applicant drinks alcoholic beverages, whether the applicant daydreams, and how the applicant feels about drug abuse. They also include indirect questions about habits and attitudes of friends.

- *Personality tests*—Personality tests measure the behavioral traits the interviewer believes are necessary for success in selling, such as assertiveness, initiative, and extroversion. They are being used more often by sales organizations as valid forms with proven results. Personality traits measured in one popular personality test, the *Comprehensive Personality Profile,* are presented in Table 8.9.[19] Studies in the insurance and financial services industry show individuals who scored in the extremely high ranges of the emotional intensity, recognition motivation, and assertiveness scales of the *CPP* test earned 2.8 times the commission of individuals scoring in the lower ranges of these same scales.[20]

Those who are interviewing candidates should use tests designed to meet the needs of a particular job. First identify factors related to job success; then design valid and reliable tests that measure them, or purchase appropriate standardized tests. Since tests can have a cultural bias and discriminate against certain groups, their use must be continually monitored. A test may be a valid predictor for one group of recruits but not for all. Also, different scores for different groups may be equally good indicators of success in a sales job. Therefore, the company should keep records showing that the tests and questions are relevant to the job and are not screening out a large proportion of women or minorities.

Advantages and Disadvantages of Testing. Pre-employment tests are one of the most controversial tools used in the selection process. The need for application forms, reference checks, and personal interviews is seldom disputed, but there are differences of opinion about whether tests are necessary in the hiring of salespeople. Questions about the legality of testing have increased the controversy surrounding its use as a screening tool. But test data has proven useful to management in selecting sales applicants likely to be high performers. Considering the fact that a hiring mistake can cost a company as much as $100,000, any tool that helps firms make the right selection decision is welcome.

Opponents of employment tests say tests are not as objective and scientific as they are purported to be. Savvy test takers can often figure out the "right" or "wrong"

TABLE 8.9 Primary Personality Traits of the *Comprehensive Personality Profile (CPP)*

PERSONALITY TRAIT	MEASURES	HIGH-SCORING INDIVIDUALS . . .	LOW-SCORING INDIVIDUALS . . .
Emotional Intensity	Physical, mental, and social intensity levels	Are excitable, restless, and motivated toward immediate results	Are persistent, even-paced, and motivated toward security, predictability, and order
Intuition	Degree to which a person relies upon experience and feelings to make decisions or solve a problem	Dislike detailed analysis of complex subject matter and avoid situations that require deep concentration or long-term memory	Use an analytical approach to problem solving and enjoy challenges that involve deep concentration or detailed analysis
Recognition Motivation	Need for status, prestige, or acknowledgment	Are dependent upon consistent feedback from others and are motivated toward situations that provide public recognition and popularity	Seek activities that provide private recognition and self-respect
Sensitivity	Degree to which an individual expressively demonstrates warmth and caring	Are actively involved in helping and nurturing others	Are controlled and private and typically avoid open relationships
Assertiveness	Ability to influence the actions of others	Confidently assert themselves when necessary	Have difficulty saying no when confronted and are often too concerned about what others think of them
Trust	Individual's perception of the outside world	Are open, trustworthy, see others as being open and trustworthy until proven wrong, and initially give others the benefit of the doubt	Are skeptical and initially require others to "prove themselves" before trusting relationships can result
Exaggeration	Degree to which the applicant is exaggerating strengths or downplaying weaknesses in order to appear more favorable	Intentionally or unintentionally present a more favorable image regarding conformity, self-control, and moral values	Present themselves in a less favorable light and are more forthright and critical of their personal qualities

SOURCE: *User's Manual: The Comprehensive Personality Profile (CPP),* Wonderlic Personnel Test, Inc., 1998 (Bradenton, FL: CraftSystems, Inc.), http://www.craftsystems.com/ (accessed October 2006). *User's Manual: The Comprehensive Personality Profile;* Larry L. Craft, "The Career Life Insurance Agent," in *Research Brief 96-1* (Bradenton, FL: CraftSystems, Inc.), September 1996.

answers to questions. Further, critics question the methodology used to develop tests. For instance, most test consultants profile a client's top sales performers and then match test results against their personality traits. But salesperson success can be influenced by factors other than personality, such as having the best territory or the longest tenure. The result is that potentially successful salespeople may be screened out because they do not fit the stereotype.

Another problem is that many managers use tests as the sole decision factor. Recruits may look good on the basis of interviews, application forms, and reference checks. But if their test scores are low, they may not be considered further. If the score is only slightly below the acceptable level, applicants should probably be retested. Test scores should not be the sole criterion used in making hiring decisions. Rather, they should be one of several factors considered.

Tests are often misunderstood and misused, causing many sales managers to conclude they are of little value as a screening tool. For example, management sometimes believes that the highest score on the test indicates the best prospect. However, all applicants who fall within a certain range should be judged equally qualified for the job.

■ Follow-Up Interviewing

Sales managers seldom decide which candidate to hire after only one in-depth personal interview. Strong candidates often go through several interviews with more than one interviewer. Candidates who rate favorably after the in-depth interview and score in the acceptable range on employment tests are asked to come back for follow-up interviews with other members of the sales team, such as other sales managers, division managers, and sales reps. Like the in-depth interview, these follow-up interviews can be either structured or unstructured, or a combination of both, depending on the interviewer's style and the objectives of the interview.

Making the Selection

When all other steps have been completed in the selection process, the sales manager must decide whether or not to hire each applicant. The manager reviews everything known about a particular applicant from screening, reference checks, interviews, and tests. The next step is to match the applicant's goals and ambitions against present

---

SALES MANAGEMENT IN ACTION

Selecting Salespeople for Overseas Assignments

A growing concern of many U.S. corporations is selecting qualified salespeople for international markets. As U.S. companies go overseas to sell their products, they soon realize how different the selling environment and the markets are from those in the United States. Differences in ethnic compositions, religious orientations, social class, and education definitely complicate the sales force selection process for multinational corporations. Sales force recruiters at multinational companies report differences in rankings of salesperson selection criteria for overseas markets and those for U.S. markets. For example, education, cultural adaptation skills, social class, religion, and ethnicity are more important in hiring salespeople for overseas assignments.[21] Therefore, differences in the selling environments and cultures make the use of standardized selection criteria dangerous when salespeople are being selected for overseas markets.

General Electric has been a leader in global sales. A decade or so ago, GE realized that most expatriate assignments went to U.S. employees.[22] More recently, the firm has made a concerted effort to give all employees a chance for international assignments. Thus, more and more sales managers from around the world have a chance of working in foreign lands. GE has discovered that people from around the world can make good global sales managers.

SOURCE: Scott Widmier and Joe Hair, "Enhancing Global Sales Skills through Executive Education Programs," *Journal of Executive Education* 6, no. 1 (forthcoming 2007); John S. Hill and Meg Birdseye, "Salesperson Selection in Multinational Corporations: An Empirical Study," *Journal of Personal Selling & Sales Management* (summer 1989): 39–47. S. Green, F. Hassan, J. Immelt, and M. Marks et al., "In Search of Global Leaders," *Harvard Business Review,* August 2003, pp. 38–44.

and future opportunities, challenges, and other types of rewards offered by the job and the company.

Selection tools used in the sales force selection process are only aids to executive judgment. They can eliminate the obviously unqualified candidates and generally spot the more competent individuals. But since many recruits fall between these extremes, the tools can only suggest which ones will be more successful in sales. Thus, executive judgment is relied on heavily in the final selection of salespeople.

While judgment is often necessary in making a selection, sales managers should avoid letting emotion or intuition cloud the decision. Inexperienced sales managers often hire a candidate because he or she interviewed well, they "hit it off," or the manager put too much emphasis on the candidate's physical appearance. Some managers even boast of being able to decide whether to hire a sales rep after the first five minutes of the interview.

While the sales manager's intuition does matter, seasoned sales executives know that hiring completely based on intuition or emotion can prove disastrous. If the manager has any uneasy feelings about top candidates, they should be called back for another interview, and additional reference checking or testing should be done. If a company follows the logical sequence of a well-planned recruiting and selection system, the executive's intuitions will soon be transformed into objective criteria that can help compare applicants and make decisions among them.

A decision to hire is followed by a formal offer, with no unspecified details or surprises. The terms should be in writing, for the protection of both the recruit and the firm. Many companies require that all new salespeople sign contracts containing all important job-related information. Table 8.10 emphasizes some key points for sales managers to cover upon making a formal offer to a candidate.

If a chosen candidate seems to have a lot of reservations about the job, sales managers should not attempt persuasion. Such applicants are not likely to give the company their best efforts.

Sales Force Socialization

Socialization

The proper introduction of the recruit to company practices, procedures, and philosophy and the social aspects of the job through which the salesperson is integrated into the organization.

Once you've completed the process of recruiting and selecting the new salesperson, it's time to integrate that person into the organization. Sales force **socialization** is the proper introduction of the recruit to company practices, procedures, and philosophy and the social aspects of the job. The process actually begins when the potential sales candidate reads recruiting literature about the firm and attends the first interview with company representatives. Socialization is crucial in achieving a return on the sizable investment made during the recruiting and selection process. Effective development of job skills, adoption of appropriate role behaviors and organization values, and adaptation to the work group and its norms can influence a recruit's motivation, job satisfaction, and performance. With large numbers of women and minorities entering the workplace as entry-level salespersons, the socialization process takes on an increasingly critical role in a firm's future success.

Recruiting, selection, and training all play an important part in the socialization process. The most important benefits of a formal sales force socialization program include greater job satisfaction, increased employee commitment, greater job involvement, improved chance for survival of new salespeople, and the new hire's better understanding of his or her role in the company.[23]

TABLE 8.10   Key Points to Cover When Hiring a Salesperson

DUTIES OF THE SALESPERSON

- Exercise best efforts in representing the company and its products or services.
- Make no representations, warranties, or commitments binding the company without the company's prior consent. The salesperson will be personally liable and required to reimburse the company if he or she exceeds this authority.
- Forward all field inquiries or complaints in the field to the company immediately.
- Work full-time for the company without any sideline. Do not represent or form a competing business.
- Personally solicit the product, and do not hire an associate to represent the company without prior written approval.
- Maintain minimum general and automobile liability coverage.
- Attend sales meetings, both local and national.
- Call on accounts periodically, service accounts, and maintain accurate selling records and lead sheets.
- Assist in any collection efforts requested by the company.
- Promise to protect all trade secrets, customer lists, and other forms of confidential information acquired while working for the company.

COMPENSATION

1. *Salary:*
   - Specify the amount and when it is payable.

2. *Draw:*
   - Specify whether it is applied against commission.
   - Specify the amount and when it is payable.
   - Clarify that the draw can be stopped by the company at any time without prior notice when commission earnings do not exceed draw.
   - Specify that the sales rep is personally liable for repayment when draw exceeds commission earnings and the rep resigns or is fired from his or her job.
   - State that the company has the right to sell off draw and reduce the amount of commission owed on termination of the employment relationship.

3. *Bonus:*
   - Specify whether the bonus is enforceable by contract.
   - Specify the amount and when it is payable.
   - Specify that pro rata bonuses will not be given in the event the salesperson resigns or is fired prior to the date the bonus will be paid.
   - Avoid basing the bonus on a determination of profits, because this may give the salesperson the right to inspect the company's books and records.

4. *Commission:*
   - Specify the commission rate and when it is payable.
   - Avoid guaranteed shipping arrangements.
   - Specify split-commission policies if working in a team-oriented environment.
   - Specify all deductions from commissions and how and when they are computed, such as for returns, freight charges, unauthorized price concessions given by the salesperson, billing and advertising discounts, collection charges, failure of the customer to pay.
   - Specify commission for large orders, special customers, off-price goods, and reorders.

5. *Expenses:*
   - Specify the kinds and amount of expenses that are reimbursable.
   - Specify the kind of documentation the salesperson must supply in order to receive reimbursement.

TABLE 8.10 (continued)

TERRITORY

- Identify how the salesperson's territory or customers are determined (by geographic boundaries, industry or customer group, functional group, etc.).
- Clarify whether the sales rep has exclusive or non-exclusive territorial rights.
- Be sure to discuss all house accounts, and document these in writing.
- Determine how products sold in one territory and shipped in another will affect your split-commission policy.
- Clarify whether the salesperson can sell in other territories or to other groups of customers not solicited by other salespeople, such as at trade shows.
- If exclusive territorial rights are not involved, ensure that the salesperson will not receive commission for orders not actually solicited by him or her.

LENGTH OF EMPLOYMENT RELATIONSHIP

- Specify date employment is to begin.
- Specify length of employment and whether employment is at will (the salesperson can be fired any time) or for a definite term, say, two years.
- If employment is at will, specify whether notice is required. If so, say how far in advance it must be sent for the termination to be effective, and by what means (certified or regular mail).
- Never give assurances of job security if you are hiring a salesperson at will.
- If employment is for a definite term, say whether the contract is renewable under the same terms and conditions after the expiration of the original term, and whether notice must be sent to confirm this.
- Peg employment to a minimum sales quota, if applicable.

TERMINATION OF EMPLOYMENT

- Clarify when commissions stop; upon termination, upon shipment of order, upon shipment with a cutoff date to eliminate the problem of reorders.
- Avoid severance compensation arrangements.
- Specify when a final accounting will be made.
- Limit the right of the salesperson to sue for commissions within a specified period.
- Specify the prompt return of all samples, customer lists, orders, and field information, and specify a penalty for noncompliance.
- Include a restrictive covenant for additional protection in writing.

Person-Organization Fit (POF)
Describes how consistent a salesperson's beliefs and value system are with those of the organization for which he or she works.

Sales force socialization can also contribute to person-organization fit. **Person-organization fit**, or **POF**, describes how consistent a salesperson's beliefs and value system are with those of the organization for which he or she works. POF has many positive job outcomes including higher job satisfaction, lower stress, and a lower likelihood of turnover.[24]

Sales managers have a greater impact on new salespeople and improve the culture of the sales organization more successfully if they implement socialization in organized programs rather than creating a unique socialization experience for each new hire. A formal socialization program is a common learning experience all recruits go through that removes newcomers from their normal work setting and offers guidelines about the sequence and timing of progression in the organization. It offers close contact with experienced salespeople in the organization and provides social support from other members of the sales organization to reinforce the newcomer's identity.[25] Thus, socialization is a critical part of the hiring process.

There are two types of socialization. The first is **initial socialization**. This preliminary exposure to the firm begins with the recruiting and selection process and ends with the initial orientation of the salesperson to the firm's procedures and policies. The second type, **extended socialization**, makes new salespeople feel they are an integral part of the company. This is achieved by exposing new recruits to the corporate culture (values, philosophy, group norms, different work groups, corporate officers, and so on) and by helping them adapt to the new culture as quickly as possible.

■ Initial Socialization

Initial socialization occurs during recruiting, selecting, and introductory training. Let's take a closer look at each of these aspects.

Recruiting. Most firms begin the socialization process by sending the sales candidate recruiting literature that details the company's philosophy and the salesperson's role in the organization. Today, many companies post recruiting material on their Internet sites so that interested job seekers can browse through descriptions of jobs available and information about the company's culture. The IBM Internet site (www.ibm.com), for example, discusses career opportunities as well as the corporate culture at the company and explains why a recruit would want to seek a job there.

Selection. The interview process can give both the candidate and the recruiter some idea of how the new salesperson will respond to the socialization efforts of the company. For example, sales representatives may be expected to dress conservatively. By conforming to this pattern, the recruiter signals the company's expectations to the recruit. In addition, this image may yield clues about the organization's philosophy and the structure of the company.

Many firms also schedule multiple interviews at all levels of the company and in other functional departments. The purpose is not only to get multiple opinions about how well the recruit will respond to socialization efforts but also to expose candidates to the organization's culture. For example, IBM requires five or six interviews for sales recruits in an effort to find those who will be successful in the IBM culture.

Professional recruiting brochures and lengthy interview processes are typical of many large and medium-sized firms. But small firms may not be able to afford such high-quality recruiting materials. When smaller firms recruit salespeople, the firm's owner is often involved in the interviewing process. Thus, the candidate can get first-hand information about the owner's philosophy of running the business and the role of the sales force. Likewise, the owner may discern whether the candidate fits the characteristics the firm is seeking.

Introductory Training. After successfully completing the recruiting and selection process, the new recruit has some notion of the firm's corporate philosophy and the nature of the sales position. Some companies prepare detailed human resources manuals covering the company's history, product line, organization, job descriptions, and various compensation and benefit packages. By receiving such a manual before they report for work, new salespeople can quickly find answers for many of their questions concerning the company's procedures and policies.

When the salesperson reports to work for the first time, immediate placement into a field selling situation may result in improper socialization. New recruits should

Initial Socialization Begins in the recruiting process with things like brochures and is intended as a preliminary form of integrating a person into the company.

Extended Socialization Exposing new recruits to the corporate culture (values, philosophy, group norms, different work groups, corporate officers, and so on) and helping them adapt to the new culture in as short a period of time as possible.

report first to the home or regional office so they can be properly informed about the job, company procedures, policies, and so forth. Recruits should also be encouraged to ask questions about information in the human resources manual or other materials given to them prior to reporting to work.

While at the home office, sales recruits should be exposed to actual operations of the firm. Payroll procedures, expense accounts, office procedures and policies, and routine items such as parking and dining facilities should be explained by members of the human resources department or sales training staff, or by the sales manager.

■ Extended Socialization

Extended socialization programs include long-term training, job rotation, and corporate social activities. The focus of extended socialization is building esprit de corps in the sales organization.

Long-Term Training. Many large companies use long-term training programs to educate salespeople about the firm's products, customers, and competitors and to ensure that new recruits are properly socialized. For example, sales recruits for Johnson Controls, Inc. (www.johnsoncontrols.com) go through an extensive six-month training program before being assigned to their own territory. The training includes classroom lectures, independent study, and sales simulation and role-play. All these efforts are undertaken to ensure superior product knowledge and an understanding of the market and customers.

Companies that engage in extended socialization programs are seeking consistent adherence to company practices, procedures, and philosophy. In addition, they want to assist new salespeople in acquiring a high level of job skills and an understanding of appropriate role behaviors and work-group values. This standardization of values, behavior norms, and philosophy helps produce consistent sales performance results, because salespeople become highly motivated team players.

There is, however, a negative side to this type of extended socialization. Some recruits may resent being asked to "fit the mold" and may leave the firm. Through proper selection methods and accurate presentation of company expectations, managers can screen such individuals out before company resources are expended in training them.

Job Rotation. Both large and small firms use job rotation as a way to expose sales trainees to the corporate culture. Not only do the recruits learn how different departments work, but they also make social contacts and are exposed to the overall organization. This broad exposure to the firm early in their sales career helps instill a sense of belonging and camaraderie in recruits.

Corporate Social Activity. Many firms recognize the value of informal ways of socializing new employees. Company picnics, sports teams, and sales meetings all provide an opportunity for the new salesperson to interact with experienced salespersons, sales managers, and company executives in a non-threatening environment. In these types of settings, the new employee can ask questions and observe how everyone fits into the social structure of the firm. Often the recruit's spouse or significant other is included in the activity. This helps affirm the role of the new employee's partner in the successful performance of the sales job. The main problem with these kinds of activities is usually the distance between a salesperson's territory and corporate headquarters.

Corporate social activity aimed at socialization need not be elaborate or expensive. Hallway conversations and softball teams can be effective means of socializing the new salesperson. Each of these methods facilitates the major purpose—building esprit de corps within the sales organization.

CHAPTER SUMMARY

1. **Follow the steps in the sales force recruitment process.** Due to the critical importance of recruiting, sales managers should have an effective system for finding and selecting sales personnel. To ensure that new recruits have the aptitude necessary to be successful in a particular type of sales job, sales managers should follow the steps in the recruitment process: (1) conducting a job analysis, (2) preparing a job description, (3) identifying sales job qualifications, (4) attracting a pool of sales recruits, and (5) evaluating and selecting the best recruit available. Before a company can search for a particular type of salesperson, it must know something about the sales job to be filled. This is determined by conducting a job analysis and developing a job description. The job description lets prospective job applicants know exactly what the duties and responsibilities of the sales position are and on what basis employees will be evaluated. Since a job description is used in recruiting, selecting, training, compensating, and evaluating the sales force, the description should be in writing. Duties and responsibilities set forth in the job description should be converted into a set of job qualifications. Job qualifications should specifically spell out the characteristics and abilities a person must have to carry out the requirements of the sales position, such as education, previous experience, decision-making ability, product knowledge, transportation, ability to travel, and computer literacy.

2. **Identify sources of sales applicants.** Companies use several sources to find qualified applicants. The search can begin within the company by surveying the sales force for possible recruits and then seeking individuals from other departments. Some of the external sources include competitive and noncompetitive firms, educational institutions, advertisements, and employment agencies. A relatively new source of sales candidates is through online career centers. Recruiters must recognize that top-rated candidates can come from any source. However, with the increasing costs of recruiting, sales managers must be careful to devote their time to the most productive sources.

3. **Follow the steps in the sales force selection process.** Selecting good applicants is an extremely important and challenging task for the sales manager. The salesperson selection process involves choosing the candidates who best meet the qualifications and have the greatest aptitude for the job. General steps in the salesperson selection process include (1) initial screening, (2) reference checking, (3) in-depth interviewing, (4) employment testing, (5) follow-up interviewing, and (6) making the selection. In selecting salespeople, several tools are used to screen and eliminate undesirable recruits. Initial screening may start with an application form or resume, a screening interview, or some type of brief test. Application forms, as well as resumes, are the most widely used screening tools and are an easy means of collecting the information necessary to determine applicants' qualifications, such as educational background, work experience, and personal references. An important function of application forms is to help sales managers prepare for personal interviews with candidates for sales positions. Almost all companies make use of initial screening interviews or tests.

4. **Apply the criteria used to make the final selection decision.** When all other steps have been completed in the selection process, the sales manager must decide whether or not to hire each applicant. The company reviews everything known about a particular applicant, gathered from screening, reference checks, interviews, and tests. The applicant's goals and ambitions are matched against present and future opportunities, challenges, and other types of

rewards offered by the job and the company. While selection tools and techniques can eliminate the obviously unqualified candidates and generally spot the more competent individuals, some amount of judgment is typically used to make the final selection decision.

5. **Implement the sales force socialization process.** Once the process of recruiting and selection is complete, the new salesperson must be integrated into the sales force. Socialization involves the formal introduction of the recruit to company practices, procedures, and philosophy as well as the social aspects of the job. Effective development of job skills, adoption of appropriate role behaviors and organization values, and adaptation to the work group and its norms can influence a recruit's motivation, job satisfaction, and performance. There are two levels in the socialization process. Initial socialization occurs during the recruiting, selection, and introductory training processes. Extended socialization is accomplished through long-term training, job rotation, and corporate social activities.

REVIEW AND APPLICATION QUESTIONS

1. What are the steps involved in the recruiting process? [LO 1]

2. Why should sales managers conduct job analyses before recruiting salespeople? [LO 1]

3. How is the job description used in managing the sales force? [LO 1]

4. What factors should sales managers consider when deciding which recruitment source to use? Explain. [LO 2]

5. Why should sales managers develop a set of job qualifications? Is this a difficult process? Explain. [LO 3]

6. Discuss the benefits of screening tools to the selection process. How might screening tools help control the cost of salesperson selection? [LO 4]

7. What is socialization? When does it occur? Why is socialization of new salespersons important to the culture of the sales organization? [LO 5]

8. What is POF? How does socialization contribute to POF? What do you think tends to happen when an employee experiences low levels of POF? [LO 5]

IT'S UP TO YOU

Internet Exercise

In its recruiting efforts, United Parcel Service (UPS) emphasizes diversity, as described at this website: http://www.diversitycareers.com/articles/college/sumfall03/dia_ups.htm. Compare the UPS diversity efforts with those of two other companies at which you are interested in getting a sales job. Which firm has the best diversity program and why?

Role-Playing Exercise

Determing the Ethics of a Candidate

Situation

Even the sleaziest rep can look like a saint in an interview. So how can you tell if a rep is ethical before you make the job offer? There's no foolproof method, but human resources experts say sales and marketing executives need to probe candidates for important characteristics—self-discipline, honesty, openness, self-respect, levelheadedness, and a mix of aggressiveness and empathy. One way to uncover these qualities is by posing hypothetical dilemmas to potential hires. Personnel Decisions International (www.personneldecisions.com/), a global management and human resources consulting firm based in Minneapolis, uses the combined responses from the following scenarios asked during an interview to determine an overall pattern of ethics, or lack thereof, in job candidates.

- A few months after you join the company, your colleagues tell you about a diner's club card that gives 20 percent cash refunds at certain restaurants. Easy money, especially if you're just beginning to establish a territory. Since the company encourages entertaining, the salespeople reason, why not take clients to those restaurants and pocket the refunds? It won't cost the company any money. Do you join in?

- After speaking with a sales manager at a competitor's trade show booth, you spot a hard copy from the competitor's database listing 100 qualified leads from the show. You can slip it into your briefcase easily, and no one will see. What do you do?

- After meeting with a customer, you discover a competitor has low-balled your offer by 15 percent. This competitor has a reputation for offering products at the lowest possible price but failing to provide an acceptable level of service. Do you warn the customer, attempting to push him toward your offer, or walk away from the business, hoping he'll find out for himself and choose your company in the future?

- The standard rate for your product is $15,000. After negotiations with an important customer, you discover the company can realistically afford only $13,000. A few weeks later you receive the purchasing order with the original $15,000 price.

You receive a 5 percent commission on the total dollar value of the deal. Do you correct the customer's mistake, or allow the company to be billed for $15,000, hoping the error is never discovered?

- You're on a sales call, and a key customer from a *Fortune 500* company says she won't buy from you unless you match a competitor's offer. The competitor's offer includes a ten-day trip to Hawaii for the customer and her husband. What do you do?

In evaluating the responses, concern arises if the answers suggest a salesperson will do anything to make a sale—especially in ways that may jeopardize the company's reputation. For example, an unethical rep would indicate he or she would not hesitate to steal the competitor's list of qualified leads or match a potentially questionable offer by a competitor to send a client on an exotic trip. An ethical rep would warn a customer about the competitor who offers products at a low price but skimps on service. Further, ethical salespeople would raise the issue of the 20 percent diner's card with their management before proceeding. Last, in the case of the billing mistake, ethical reps will correct the error immediately to preserve the relationship of trust with the client.

Role-Play Participants and Assignments

Debbie Stuart: This sales rep argues that these practices are unacceptable.

Shane Williams: This sales rep argues that these are standard practices in the industry and should be OK.

SOURCES: http://www.personneldecisions.com/ (accessed October 2006); "Putting Reps to the Test," *Sales & Marketing Management,* December 1997, p. 38.

 ## In-Basket Exercise

You have just finished a series of interviews with a person who you feel is an excellent candidate for your firm's open sales position. She has a 3.4 grade point average and a marketing degree. The candidate has excellent communication skills, held a part-time sales job throughout college to help pay for school, and was an officer in the sales fraternity on campus. She will definitely make a great entry-level salesperson at your company. Your only concern is that another company will offer her a job before you do! Before any candidate is offered a job, your company requires that a few of the applicant's references be checked. During the process,

you discover that your ideal candidate lied on her resume and application. She was never an officer in the sales fraternity; she was only a member.

QUESTIONS

1. Given the difficulty in finding excellent candidates, what do you do with this person?

2. Would your decision change if you also find out this candidate has several speeding tickets?

3. Prepare an e-mail for the human resources department to support hiring this individual.

Ethical Dilemma

Your company uses a two-person team approach to recruit sales applicants. When visiting college campuses, two sales managers sit in on the initial employment interview and individually evaluate the applicant. You have been paired with a very successful veteran sales manager. After several interviews you notice that he always brings up sports—in particular, golfing—during the interview. At first you assumed the sports questions were a form of "ice breaker" and a good way to build rapport with the college recruits. You've come to realize, however, that your partner rates applicants poorly if they are not avid golfers and/or sports enthusiasts. This behavior is particularly upsetting to you because the veteran sales manager rejected several recruits whom you evaluated very highly. You feel that you really don't want to question his ability as a recruiter. However, you are concerned that if your evaluations of the recruits are continually different from those of the successful veteran, your own career may be jeopardized.

What do you do? If you confront the veteran sales manager, could there be any negative outcomes? Any positive ones? Are any legal ramifications possible as a result of the veteran sales manager's actions?

CASE 8.1

Vector Marketing Corporation: Recruiting and Selecting College Students

Vector Marketing Corporation, headquartered in Olean, New York, is the exclusive North American distributor of CUTCO Cutlery. Both Vector Marketing Corporation and CUTCO Cutlery Corporation are wholly owned subsidiaries of the Alcas Corporation, founded in 1949. CUTCO Cutlery is a high-quality product manufactured by CUTCO Cutlery Corporation. The product line features table knives, carving knives and forks, gourmet cookware, kitchen utensils, and selected hunting and fishing knives as well as garden tools.

Vector divides North America into seven major selling zones (six in the United States and one in Canada), with approximately 200+ year-round sales offices, called District offices, and more than 200 summer offices, called branch offices, throughout the United States and Canada. Total 2006 sales reached $177 million, which is more than double what they were just ten years ago. The growth of Vector is attributed to the outstanding quality of CUTCO as well as to managerial leadership and an outstanding sales force comprised mainly of college students who sell CUTCO full-time during the summer and part-time during the school year.

Sales representatives demonstrate CUTCO Cutlery under the direction of local office sales managers. All Vector sales representatives and office sales managers are independent sales contractors working primarily on a sales commission basis. Vector offers a base pay program for all representatives to ensure that they are paid for a sales demonstration even if the customer does not purchase any CUTCO. The representative receives whichever amount is higher at the end of each week—the base pay for appointments, or the commission. Salespeople develop sales leads almost entirely from referrals and make appointments via telephone. There is no "cold calling" or "door-to-door" solicitation.

Vector salespeople participate in a highly-recognized sales training program called Skills for Life. Basic product and sales training is conducted at the local office level, as is advanced training on selling and communication skills. Further training is offered at regional sales meetings and conferences throughout the year. Salespeople are trained to follow the Vector sales approach, which is based on "showing" rather than "selling" to alleviate the customers' pressure to buy and the representatives' pressure to sell.

Advancement within Vector is based solely on effort and performance. Sales representatives can advance to the top sales representative level of Field Sales Manager. In 2006 the average income of the top sales representatives was $10,000/year, and the very top performer earned over $100,000 (students typically work full-time during the summer and part-time during the school year). Since college students are the dominant portion of the sales force, Vector has established a scholarship program as an incentive for outstanding sales performance. Vector awards $40,000 in college scholarships annually.

An extensive customer service program is designed to support the sales force's efforts with the customer. CUTCO products are backed with a forever satisfaction guarantee. Prompt order processing and shipping enable customers to receive CUTCO within three weeks of the in-home demonstration. A toll-free number is available for customers in the event of any questions about the order. An additional benefit of the customer service program is to give the salespeople added confidence in the product they sell as well as to enhance the image of Vector as a reputable company. Vector also adheres to the Code of Ethics established by the Direct Selling Association as part of its customer service effort.

Substantial effort is focused on selecting, training, and equipping the sales force with the sales support programs needed to successfully sell CUTCO. Public relations and advertising expenses for the CUTCO product are relatively small because the product is demonstrated and sold exclusively in customer homes. Getting the word out to customers is done via the word-of-mouth referral system utilized by the sales force. Vector does, however, use newspaper classified and Web advertising plus direct mail to recruit salespeople. Additional marketing tools include a direct-mail catalog that is sent as a service to existing CUTCO owners. Sales reps who are still active in the business are eligible to receive a commission on any sales that are made through the catalog to their previous customers. Managers also receive a commission on any sales made from the catalog in the geographic area of their office. In addition, CUTCO has a website on the Internet (www.cutco.com) to provide information and communication for consumers. However, there is not an open e-commerce access because of the belief that it could significantly hinder the sales rep's efforts to generate sales.

A comprehensive sales incentive support program provides motivation for, and recognition of, sales achievements by the Vector sales representatives and field sales managers. Incentives range from cash bonuses and prizes to a recent travel incentive program for trips to locations such as Italy and Hawaii. In addition, all conferences and sales meetings include considerable emphasis on recognition and sales awards for the sales reps and managers.

Vector is part of a growing number of firms that are selling direct to consumers in their homes. The rapid success of Vector can be traced to the company's basic founding principle, which is "To be successful we must first help others to succeed." An expanding, committed sales force selling a superior product is essential to the firm's continued success.

QUESTIONS

1. What are some of the challenges in managing a sales force consisting mainly of college students?

2. Develop a profile of the ideal candidate you would select for the Vector sales position.

3. What could management do to increase the number of students applying for a sales job with Vector Marketing?

Case prepared by John Whelpley and Sarah Baker Andrus, Vector Marketing Corporation, and Mike Williams, Illinois State University.

 ## CASE 8.2

R³ Technology: Improving Recruitment and Selection

R³ Technology generates $8 million in annual revenues by providing remote recovery and repair for computer servers to companies with wholesale and retail websites. The primary competitive advantage of R³ is providing cost-effective, remote-access, 24-7 troubleshooting and repair. If the customer's website is down or is operating too slowly, the customer is effectively "out of business." Therefore, customers view this service as critical to their success.

Josh Lyons started the company while he was still in college. The technology is based on a prototype developed in his dorm to help friends with computer problems without leaving his room. In the six years since Josh graduated, sales have grown dramatically due to his unique technology. While some larger accounts are serviced with a direct sales team, most customers are served by fifteen Internet-telemarketing sales and support staff.

Until now, rapid sales growth has been the exclusive focus of the company. However, Josh is concerned because top-line growth has slowed recently, and his investors are beginning to ask questions about future growth prospects. At the suggestion of a member of the board of directors, Josh has recently started looking at customer renewal (retention) rates. He has noticed that only 65 percent of customers are renewing their contracts after one year.

Josh decides to call some of the customers who had not renewed their service contracts to explore this issue. He learns that customers "never talked to the same person twice," and they perceived "a lot of turnover" in the company. They also say that a long-term relationship with their sales support person is important to maintaining confidence in the company and its services.

This customer feedback really shocks Josh. He always thought rapid sales growth meant that customers must be satisfied. Josh begins to question if he has been too focused on technology and growth. Is the customer retention problem really related to turnover in his sales team? If so, how can he reduce turnover?

Josh has always been proud that all of his employees are either students or recent graduates of Spring College, his alma mater. He thinks it is really cool to be able to work with friends and people with the same background. The college has even recognized him as alumni of the year. Now he isn't so sure that this is a good strategy for recruiting members of the sales team. This thought is especially strong when he takes the time to calculate his employee turnover rate—72 percent! In an instant, all the parties for employees who were leaving the company for graduate school and marriage takes on a new meaning!

Recruitment and selection of salespeople at the company is informal. Usually applicants are identified by word of mouth among employees. Often because they are in a hurry to fill a position, only one applicant is brought in to be interviewed by Josh and a couple of other people who are around at the time. Since they usually know the applicant's family or friends, interviews are very personal and social. Josh always looks for people who would "fit in" with the small company culture. In fact, he doesn't think the applicant's college major and previous experience is very important, because the company provides on-the-job training.

Orientation and initial training at the company is also informal. Orientation consists of Josh talking with the new member of the sales team about how the company started and its mission, vision, and core values. Next the new employee is assigned to one of the "senior" members of the sales team for on-the-job training. Since there is no formal training system or manual, the new employee sits with the "trainer" at a workstation to learn the job. This approach seemed to work well when the company was smaller. However, Josh is beginning to wonder if the initial training process may also be contributing to the turnover problem.

Josh has promised to present a detailed plan to address customer retention at the next R^3 Technology board of directors meeting. He knows that solutions to turnover in the sales team must be addressed to improve customer retention, so he makes a list in his PDA of some key questions he must answer in preparation for the meeting.

QUESTIONS

1. What changes does R^3 Technology need to make in its recruiting process?

2. What changes does the company need to make in its selection process?

3. How can the initial orientation and training process be modified to be more efficient and effective?

Case prepared by K. Randall Russ, Belhaven College.

PART THREE

Managing and Directing Sales Force Efforts

CHAPTER **9**
Training the Sales Force

CHAPTER **10**
Sales Force Leadership

CHAPTER **11**
Sales Force Motivation

CHAPTER **12**
Sales Force Compensation

Training the Sales Force

INSIDE SALES MANAGEMENT

Robert Brodo, Executive Vice President, Advantexe Learning Solutions

How have sales management and sales training changed? That question excites Robert Brodo, executive vice president of Advantexe Learning Solutions, a national and global sales training firm based in Philadelphia.

Over the last generation, says Brodo, customers have changed, selling has changed, and sales managers' goals for sales training have evolved in turn. These influences have brought about a host of new training approaches for sales managers. Sales reps used to be trained in programs that resembled "boot camp," so they would

sell products, meet budgeted goals, and generally follow orders. Sales managers needed only to be controlling and authoritative to succeed. "Now," says Brodo, "while the old way is still effective for a few cases, most enlightened firms are looking at ways to match their sales management style to the type of business they're in. Sales managers are less like disciplinarians today, and much more like coaches."

For instance, even in a commodity business where it all comes down to price, says Brodo, sales managers can develop their reps by telling them how to make themselves unique in the customer's eyes—perhaps by being available by phone 24-7. That can help develop a great customer relationship and make the company stand out.

How do sales managers learn these coaching strategies? One way is through leadership training that teaches managers how to develop their sales reps' skills and competencies, how to give reps the right kind of feedback, how to develop reps' time-management techniques, and how to pass on their own skills, such as conflict management. Other training for sales managers sensitizes them to diversity and helps them make the most of cultural inclusion—for instance, by putting the right salespeople in the right accounts.

Computer simulations are one of the most important new sales training tools, and Brodo is a big believer in their value. These simulations work like flight simulations and give sales managers a chance to respond to realistic, customized situations with plans and objectives built around reinforcing certain sales management skills. The simulations' branched decision trees don't all end up in success. Some make it possible for the manager to make a wrong choice and "go down a very bad road," even leading to loss of one of his or her virtual reps through burnout, "checkout" (loss of motivation), or even quitting. Most such simulations take a couple of days to complete but can pack a year's worth of decisions into their scenarios.

What helps make these simulations successful, according to Brodo, is that they're preceded by careful skill assessments. "Assessments let new managers figure out for themselves what they don't know," he says, "and they're always surprised. But then they're motivated."

What's ahead? According to Brodo, simulations have a lot to offer sales managers who want to continue learning and growing. Ongoing virtual training that managers can complete at their own pace will be one of the most efficient and practical ways for making people better at what they do.

Words like *blog*, *wiki*, and *podcast* sound like a foreign language to many people. But these technologies, along with others, are quickly becoming mainstream in sales training. Dynamic databases such as external and internal wikis and blogs; podcasts via MP3 players, mobile phones, and PDAs; and online internal company help sites are just some of the access channels sales managers and their people use not just to keep in touch but also to get the most out of sales training opportunities.

With these technologies salespeople can access "take it anytime" sales instruction. Much of this "on demand" help is in the form of modules—short 5- to 10-minute videos focusing on a particular message or discussion topic. Blogs and content downloads do more than provide immediate access to needed information—they stimulate curiosity and motivate people to enroll in formal training they might not have pursued in the past.[1] These and other ways of training salespeople are the subject of this chapter.

Importance of Sales Training

Developing effective sales training programs is one of the most important parts of a sales manager's job. Information technology has made customers more knowledgeable than ever before, and they now demand more quality and service from sales interactions. In addition, more purchasing options and increased global competition have created new challenges. Sales reps must be able to call on CEOs of multibillion-dollar corporations, sell to national and global accounts, and use consultative selling approaches rather than just peddling products. An organization's sales training influences the partnerships it builds with customers and channel members. And ultimately, sales training influences the success of the organization.[2]

Sales training takes human inputs—salespeople—and develops them into successful, productive members of a marketing team. Training is a long-term, ongoing process facilitating the continual growth and productivity of salespeople. With training, salespeople continually grow in knowledge, skills, and selling techniques and develop good attitudes about their jobs, companies, and customers. Thus, sales training includes both formal and informal programs designed for sales force and channel member development to achieve the organization's overall, long-run goals.

Cisco Systems (www.cisco.com) understands the importance of training its own sales force as well as channel partners. According to Cisco's senior vice president of Worldwide Channels, in the past the company determined how to train its sales force and then adapted those methods to its channel partners. Now it looks at both its own needs and those of channel partners in developing training concepts and delivery vehicles that work for both. Cisco believes a partner-focused approach is important to future growth and is expanding its Partner E-Learning portal.[3]

Sales Training
Takes human inputs—salespeople—and develops them into successful, productive members of a marketing team.

■ Benefits of Sales Force Training

The long-term objective of sales training is increased profits. Sales training teaches effective ways to plan, sell, serve customers, and implement company procedures. Through training, management also hopes to improve customer relations, reduce sales force turnover, and achieve better sales force control. Immediate benefits of sales training include faster development of the sales force because salespeople don't have to learn as much through their own experience, greater role clarity and job satisfaction, and improved morale because training makes sales reps more successful. These benefits are summarized in Table 9.1.

■ Keys to Sales Training Success

U.S. companies spend some $100 billion annually on training, about 10 percent of which goes to sales training. The average salesperson receives about thirty-three hours of training per year. Unfortunately, some estimates indicate that only 10 to 30 percent of all training is being used on the job a month later, resulting in billions of wasted training dollars.[4] Why does so much training go to waste?

TABLE 9.1　Benefits of Training Programs

TRAINING PROGRAM INPUTS	ANTICIPATED CHANGES	LONG-RUN OUTPUTS
Initial and continuous training	Faster development	More sales force control
	Better role clarity	Better customer relations
	Improved morale	Lower turnover
	Higher job satisfaction	Increased sales
		Higher company profits

TABLE 9.2 Key Ingredients for Sales Training Success
Sales training should be . . .
1. Comprehensive
2. Customized
3. Relevant
4. Tied to measurable performance outcomes
5. Motivational
6. Reasonably paced
7. Easy to test and measure
8. Interactive
9. Cost effective
10. Embraced by top management

SOURCES: Jerry Rosen, Eileen Klockers, and Barry Aloisi, "Performance-Based Sales Training," www.tmctraining.com/read.htm (accessed October 2006); T. McCarthy, "How to Beef Up Local Sales," *Lodging Hospitality,* February 1, 2007, p. 24.

Much of the squandered training money goes to programs that aren't necessary or focuses on problems that can't be solved through training. Sales managers often request courses without assessing what their employees need. Further, managers frequently neglect to reinforce newly acquired skills. Other training programs are so poorly designed that their failure is guaranteed, and few companies evaluate their training programs or measure training's return on investment (ROI).[5]

So how can sales managers make sales training a meaningful learning experience and achieve the intended goals and objectives? In his book, *Performance-Based Sales Training,* Jerry Rosen suggests keys to sales training success for planning and implementing sales training programs (see Table 9.2). These characteristics serve as a checklist for sales training programs. When a sales manager is considering implementation of a program, he or she can use the list to evaluate the program's merit. Ideally, these attributes would describe any sales training program adopted by the company.

Developing and Implementing Sales Training

Your goal as a sales manager is to design and implement training based on the skills and experiences of your salespeople and other channel members. This means first identifying the gaps between sales force and channel member skills and the firm's objectives, and then developing programs to fill these gaps. Sales training programs often weed out individuals who slipped through the selection process but are not actually fit for the job. In this sense, sales training is an investment in a salesperson with the hope of continued productivity. Usually, however, training programs identify the skills needed and then develop those skills.

Sales training programs are a challenge to design. As the checklist in Table 9.3 shows, there are many questions to answer in the design process. By considering the questions in this table, sales managers can help make sure that the training possesses many of the attributes shown in Table 9.2. For instance, the performance needs

TABLE 9.3   Checklist for Developing Sales Training Programs

Performance Needs Analysis:

- Why do you think your sales force and/or channel partners need training?
- What is the problem?
- Why is it happening?
- What should be happening instead?
- What factors help or hinder performance?
- What improvements do you expect from the trainees?
- What improvements do you hope for in the organization?

Training Needs Analysis:

- Who will attend the training?
- What are the training objectives?
- What topics will be taught?
- How will training be presented?
- Who will present it?
- What do salespeople and channel partners already know about the topic?
- What should they be able to do afterward?
- How will success be determined and measured?

Feasibility Analysis:

- Is the training solution practical?
- Does the training have management support?
- What is the budget?
- What are the technical requirements?
- How long will the training take?
- How many people will attend?

SOURCES: Adapted from Lehman (2006); Lester (2003); Nancy Chase, "Raise Your Training ROI," *Quality,* September 1997, p. 28.

questions can help in designing a relevant program by attacking a genuine and important problem. The training needs questions address customizing the training for a specific organization. The feasibility analysis questions address cost effectiveness. Using these two checklists can help the sales manager avoid training blunders.

Sales Training Development Process
The process of designing and implementing a sales training program that begins with analyzing needs, setting objectives, developing program content, determining delivery, preparing, motivating, reinforcing, and evaluating.

■ Sales Training Development Process

Whether you are designing initial or continuing sales training programs, you need to make several planning decisions. The **sales training development process,** shown in Figure 9.1, lists the major decision areas. We examine each of these areas in the following sections.

The greatest mistake sales managers make in developing training programs is a lack of planning. Using the sales development process can help avoid this mistake. Other mistakes are giving boring content that oversimplifies the selling situation, having boring speakers, or overwhelming trainees by trying to teach too much in training sessions. Common training mistakes and their remedies are listed in Table 9.4.

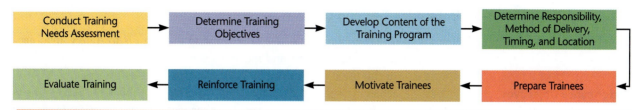

FIGURE 9.1 Sales Training Development Process

■ Conduct a Training Needs Assessment

Training Needs Assessment
The step in the sales training development process that analyzes the training needs of the sales force to determine the gaps between what they know and what they need to know.

The first step in designing an effective sales training program is to conduct a **training needs assessment**. Managers should review trainees' backgrounds and experiences to identify gaps between their qualifications and the required job activities. The pharmaceutical company Pfizer (http://pfizer.com/pfizer/main.jsp), for example, surveys salespeople and their managers to determine where salespeople need help. When the surveys are returned, salespeople meet with their managers and determine what training they should take. Managers then develop training programs with customized curricula based on the developmental needs of each salesperson.[6]

TABLE 9.4 Common Sales Training Mistakes and Avoidance Strategies

TRAINING MISTAKE	MISTAKE AVOIDANCE ACTION STRATEGY
Lack of planning	■ Use checklists in Tables 9.2 and 9.3.
No perceived reason or benefit for training in the minds of the participants	When announcing or beginning a training session, tell participants: ■ Purpose of training ■ How they will benefit ■ How they will use it
Boring content and approach	■ Make sure trainers are overprepared. ■ Customize the content to the audience. ■ Use personal illustrations to maintain interest. ■ Use appropriate technology to deliver content.
Unenthusiastic trainer	Keep a positive attitude toward the training; it will spread among the trainees.
Lack of involvement by trainees	Build involvement into the sessions by including role-plays, question-and-answer sessions, discussion and brainstorming, written activities, watching recorded sales approaches, and games.
No instruction on how to apply material learned in the field	Have trainees write a list of action steps they will practice when they leave training at the end of each session or module
No encouragement, recognition, or approval	Encourage, recognize, approve, and congratulate participation during training.
Lack of follow-up or measurement	■ Set performance objectives before training begins and determine how it will be measured. ■ Include electronic methods such as podcasts to reinforce learning. ■ Reward trainees when they apply concepts they learned in training in the field. ■ Schedule a follow-up session to discuss success stories.

SOURCE: Adapted from "Seven Fatal Sales Training Mistakes . . . And How You Can Avoid Them," *Telephone Selling Report,* www.smartbiz.com/sbs/arts/tsr26.htm (accessed October 2006).

■ Determine Training Objectives

The next step in designing an effective sales training program is to state your objectives in realistic, measurable terms and include a specific time period. Put everything in writing so you can use it later in evaluating the program's effectiveness.

The key to achieving successful results from training is to focus on **performance objectives** rather than **learning objectives**. In other words, what the sales force *does* with its newly learned skills should be more important than how much they *know*. Concentrate your objectives on changing or improving a salesperson's behavior.

You'll need specific goals and objectives. For instance, the objective of initial sales training (described later) is usually to assimilate new salespeople into the organization and develop them into top producers. A specific performance objective might be to train new salespeople to sell at least 75 percent of what experienced salespeople sell within one year after they are hired.

A primary objective of many training programs is to teach the sales force and channel members how to be more productive. Productivity usually increases with experience. But if sales training can substitute for some of the needed experience, reps can reach higher productivity levels sooner. Sales training not only helps to increase productivity faster, but higher productivity also reduces sales force turnover, which lowers hiring and training costs.

Another objective of sales training is to instill pride and demonstrate the importance of the selling function to the individual and the firm. To achieve high morale, a key to success, the sales force must realize the importance of their role in introducing innovations to markets, conveying information to customers, facilitating consumption of goods and services, serving as a channel of communication between the company and its markets, and—most important for a marketing-oriented sales organization—solving problems for customers. The overriding philosophy is that professional salespeople are advisers or consultants, not mere product pushers. Table 9.5 contrasts the two types of salespeople.

Performance Objectives
What the sales forces should be able to do after training. A specific performance objective might be to train new salespeople to sell at least 75 percent of what experienced salespeople sell within one year after they are hired.

Learning Objectives
What the sales forces should know after a managerial training session.

TABLE 9.5 New versus Old Salesperson Concepts	
SALES ADVISOR OR CONSULTANT	PRODUCT PUSHER
Develops a long-term relationship with clients	Is interested in making an immediate sale. Shows little concern for the long term
Identifies the client's problems and suggests solutions	Emphasizes a particular product's benefits regardless of a client's needs
Depends on providing helpful information and service to secure business	Uses high-pressure—sometimes unethical—tactics to close a sale
Often works as a member of a team of specialists	Works alone and has little special product knowledge
Follows through to ensure customer satisfaction	Often neglects to follow up
Works closely with headquarters marketing support staff	Ignores headquarters marketing people; thinks they are a nuisance or hindrance to field sales
Wants to participate in training to enhance selling and relationship-building skills	Does not want to participate in training; thinks he or she already knows all there is to know about selling

SALES MANAGEMENT IN ACTION

Ensuring Success for Newly Recruited University Graduates

After completing a masters program in physics at Creighton University in Omaha, Nebraska, Jeff Gross spent a year doing research and teaching undergraduates. But he felt something was missing from his professional life. He longed for more interaction with people, and he found the perfect match when he accepted a job with JCI (Johnson Controls, Inc., www.johnsoncontrols.com).

The company was looking for recent college graduates with engineering backgrounds who wanted to get into sales, but hadn't sold anything before. "It couldn't have been more perfect," says Gross. What came next was a bit of a shock. When building construction rates began making a comeback, JCI wanted more focus on sales. The company also needed consistency, and it decided to start by hiring green salespeople and molding them through an intensive sales training program. Gross, along with other rookie salespeople, first needed to spend six months learning about the marketplace, how to sell products, and how best to interact with customers.

When designing the rookie sales training program, JCI decided to take a gradual approach so trainees would have the chance to apply what they learned. The six-month program covered company orientation, product knowledge, information about the installation business and estimating skills, on-the-job training with experienced field engineers

and sales managers, sales skills development, relationship building, and a mentoring stint with an assigned sales engineer. By the end of the program, trainees had to prove they could sell on their own. To avoid sending any of the new reps out unprepared, the firm designed the last session as a sales simulation program. The new salespeople not only had to make presentations to judges and mock customers, but they had to do it in front of all their peers.

As Gross finished the training program, he felt a sense of accomplishment. Going out into the field alone, he was confident he could do the job well. "It's been a long time, and I've put all my training to use at some point during the six months," he says. "Now I just need to put it all together on my own. I think I'm ready."[7]

A lost tourist once happened upon a famous performer on the streets of New York and asked, "how do I get to Carnegie Hall?" The performer replied facetiously, "Practice, practice, practice." The same reply suggests how to develop the skills and qualities necessary to become a successful salesperson or sales manager. Sales managers must develop the proper training program to assist their people in practicing to become the best salespeople they can be.

SOURCE: http://www.johnsoncontrols.com (accessed October 2006).

Initial Sales Training Program
A type of sales training program provided to new recruits to teach them the basic selling concepts, as well as knowledge about the company and its products, competitors and the industry, and customers and the market.

Continuing Sales Training Program
A type of sales training program that seeks to improve the skills of experienced salespeople.

Training programs must also stress the idea that a professional salesperson must continually seek self-improvement. For example, you'll want to teach trainees that it pays to be up-to-date on selling techniques, new products, new uses for old products, technology to support higher productivity, and upcoming changes and emerging problems in their industry.

■ Determine Training Program Content

Sales training programs come in two types. One is an **initial sales training program**, designed for newly hired salespeople, that is comprehensive and usually lasts three to six months. A second type is a **continuing sales training program** for experienced salespeople. It's shorter and more intensive in its coverage of specialized topics.

The scope of initial sales training programs is usually broad because it must cover all aspects of the new salesperson's job. These include six basic elements: company knowledge, product knowledge, knowledge of competitors and the overall industry, customer and market knowledge, selling skills knowledge, and technology-based skills.

● **Careful planning of training content increases sales training effectiveness.**

Company Knowledge. New recruits must learn about the company's policies in general—including company benefits, office protocol, payment methods, expense accounts, and communication channels—as well as about specific selling policies. Trainees also need to know policies covering selling practices, such as how many sales calls to make per day, how to handle returns, and how to submit orders. Company knowledge is not hard to teach. Lectures are useful for explaining policies, procedures, and the rationale for them, and specific documentation for these is often accessible electronically via the company's data warehouse. After covering these issues, the training program should quickly move on to prevent boredom and loss of enthusiasm.

Product Knowledge. Trainees should not just study the company's products and how customers use them; they must also learn how to solve customers' problems. But to compete successfully, they also need to learn about and use *competitors'* products. Table 9.6 presents key topics related to the product that trainers should discuss with salespeople during product training.

Knowledge of Competitors and the Industry. Sales trainees should know about industry trends and competitive tactics—and they should know almost as much about competitors' products as they know about their own. This is the only way salespeople can compare brands, highlight advantages of their own products, and overcome customer objections.

Customer and Market Knowledge. Today's customers are more knowledgeable and have greater expectations than before. Sales channels, once a relatively simple path between manufacturer and customer with a few distributor relationships, are now a complex maze. Product cycles are shorter, and technology has modified almost every aspect of sales and supply chain management. For instance, in the software industry,

> ### TABLE 9.6 Essential Product Training Topics
>
> - What is the product?
> - Why do people buy it?
> - Who participates in the buying process?
> - How do I find and qualify buyers?
> - How do I differentiate the product (its advantages)?
> - Who are the major competitors?
> - What are strengths and weaknesses of our product and competitors' products?
> - What are the product's price and terms of sale?
> - What is the product's availability?
> - How long with the product take to arrive?

sales channels may include not only manufacturer's salespeople but also system integrators, computer resellers, and consultants that offer the product in a sale or select a competitor's product instead.

As a result, effective sales training must go beyond the basics. It no longer is enough to teach salespeople to overcome customer objections. They must be trained to create strategic relationships with customers. Table 9.7 highlights important sales training topics designed to improve partnerships with channel partners and customers.

Selling Skills Knowledge. Sales trainees must learn the selling process as well as selling techniques to apply in different situations. Basic steps of the selling process are

> ### TABLE 9.7 Training to Build Partnerships
>
> *The following skills help trainees develop customer knowledge:*
>
> - *Understand the company's products thoroughly.* Customers expect salespeople and channel partners to know how the products they sell are made, packaged, shipped, installed, operated, and so on. In short, how will the product solve their problem, and how is it different from the competitor's solution?
> - *Penetrate customers' buying organizations.* Sales reps must know how to find and communicate with decision makers in customers' organizations. They must understand and create relationships across customer functions—such as technical, operations, and finance.
> - *Know the customers' markets.* Successful partnerships are created when salespeople and channel partners understand relationships customers have with *their* customers.
> - *Relate to customers' requirements.* Sales reps must know customers' requirements, such as delivery and inventory control, and how to best meet them.
> - *Make professional sales calls.* Training programs must emphasize the importance of listening, which has overtaken presenting in importance.
> - *Become team coordinators.* Salespeople must participate in or be aware of all communication that takes place between the company and the customer.
> - *Stay in close contact with customers.* Making a sale is only the first step in a long relationship with the customer.

SOURCES: Lehman (2006); David Stamps, "Training for a New Sales Game," *Training,* July 1997, p. 46; and William Atkinson, "A New Approach to Sales Training," *Training,* March 1989, pp. 57–60.

(1) prospecting, (2) planning the call, (3) approaching the prospect, (4) making the sales presentation, (5) meeting objections, (6) closing the sale, and (7) following up.

New salespeople are often provided a list of prospects to get started. In training they learn how experienced salespeople identify and qualify their own prospects. Trainees then learn how to plan sales calls on qualified prospects, and how to gather information so they can answer the following questions: What are the objectives of the sales call? What are the customer's needs? How can my company's products satisfy these needs? How do my competitors' products satisfy the customer's needs? What objections might be raised, and how can I handle them? What kinds of presentation or support materials will I need? Answers to these questions help tailor the sales presentation to the prospect—the next step in the selling process.

Since salespeople often have only one opportunity to meet with the customer, a large part of sales training is devoted to presentation skills. Training should address skills like establishing rapport, presenting the product's benefits, identifying customer buying signals, handling customer objections, and using trial closes. Training on presentation skills also includes basics such as vocal inflection and tone of voice, eye contact, gestures, and listening. Presentation skills are often taught through role-play, which we discuss later in the chapter.

Trainees learn that the sale is not complete once they've obtained the order. A good salesperson follows up the sale to make sure he or she has answered all questions, the product arrived at the specified time and in good condition, and the customer is satisfied. Follow-up reassures the customer that he or she made a wise decision and builds customer loyalty, which can substantially increase future sales. Finally, follow-up often generates sales of complementary items or referrals of new prospects.

Technology Training. Recall from chapter 3 that sales force automation (SFA) and customer relationship management (CRM) require salespeople and sales managers to use the latest information technologies. New sales reps need to know how to use the software, what information they are required to maintain electronically about their customers and sales calls, what reports are expected, and how to use equipment and applications such as Internet portals and websites that enhance the automated sales environment. As discussed previously, sales reps who travel need to learn how to use PDAs, mobile phones, and the Internet to transmit data and communicate with individuals at other locations.

For every dollar spent on technology, sales managers should budget three dollars for training. Adoption of SFA may actually reduce salesperson effectiveness and efficiency when not supported by adequate training and support.[8] Content developed for and presented in sales training programs can improve sales force productivity and help an organization accomplish its objectives. But sales managers must be sensitive to ethical issues that can surface during training programs.

Training Delivery Decisions
Decisions made during the sales training development process that include who will train the sales force, what method will be used to transfer knowledge, where the training will take place, and when the training will occur.

Making Training Delivery Decisions

Now that you have defined the training needs of the sales force, set objectives, and determined the content of the training program, you're ready to make **training delivery decisions**. Who will conduct the training, will it be for individuals or a group, what method will you use to deliver it, and where and when will the training take place?

■ Determine Responsibility for Training

Since the trainer often both develops and delivers the training program, managers usually must select a trainer before they can design any training. Depending on the situation, responsibility for training can belong to line executives, staff trainers, or outside training specialists.

Line Sales Executives. Whether the company is large or small, line executives (sales managers, senior sales representatives, field supervisors, and division managers) often train new as well as experienced salespeople. Line sales executives are usually highly respected, and their messages tend to carry more authority than those of staff executives or outside training specialists. They are also in a better position to evaluate each trainee's ability and performance than are administrators who don't participate in training.

Even if line executives are not entirely responsible for training, they should always participate in planning and selecting training situations. Sales executives are most familiar with the needs of the entire sales force and the selling resources of the firm, and they can effectively design such programs.[9]

Staff Trainers. Staff trainers are either members of personnel, production, or office management areas, or they are company employees hired specifically to conduct sales training programs. People from elsewhere in the organization are best used in combination with other trainers, such as line sales executives or outside specialists.

If a company chooses to use staff trainers, often the best strategy is to maintain a training department. Staff trainers have the time and teaching skills necessary for sales training, and they can develop training programs for channel members to teach them how to sell the firm's products effectively.

Staff trainers hired specifically for training purposes do have disadvantages. To some extent they lack control over trainees, who often do not look up to them as they do to line sales executives. Management support of the sales trainer can help overcome this problem. Another problem is the often high cost of hiring and maintaining staff trainers. Depending on qualifications, the trainer's salary can be $100,000 or more per year.

Outside Training Specialists. Outside training specialists help many small businesses that cannot afford to have their own sales training departments. These specialists also help large companies by implementing refresher training programs and special-purpose sessions. Outside training specialists offer flexibility because they can conduct the entire training program or handle only the particular part a firm needs the most. Because their livelihood depends on their clients' satisfaction, outside trainers usually are knowledgeable, interesting, and inspiring in conducting sales training.

Before hiring outside training specialists, sales managers should make sure the specialists have not only excellent presentation and communication skills but also the sales background and practical knowledge—and therefore the credibility—that only real-world experience can provide. The trainer should also understand the company's sales problems, terminology, and sales cycle. The trainer should go on sales calls with a few reps and interview a few customers to determine what salespeople need to do to get and keep their business.

Many companies have found hiring outside training firms a useful way of consistently training sales reps. American Express (www.americanexpress.com) partnered with Forum Corporation, an international sales training company based in Boston, to create the Center for Learning Excellence, a company-wide program that trains its sales executives around the world to sell Amex's products, from credit cards to travel services to traveler's checks. Previously, Amex's 100-plus training programs were disjointed and confusing. As a result, the company's salespeople were selling differently all over the world. Now salespeople undergo competency-based assessment tests to determine what training is needed. Then they participate in one or more of the ten sales training programs developed by Forum and taught at locations around the world.[10]

■ Select Group or Individual Training

Group Training Methods
Instruction methods—such as lecture, group discussion, role-playing and conferencing—that are ideal for training groups of salespeople.

Individual Training Methods
Instruction methods—such as on-the-job training, personal conferences, and computer-based training—that are ideal when training on an individual basis.

Group training methods usually serve in formal training programs, and **individual training methods** work for informal training programs (specifically, in field training). For example, lectures and role-playing are usually effective with groups of trainees in a formal sales training program, whereas personal conferences and on-the-job training are better for individual trainees once they are in the field.

Most firms want trainees to go through formal group training before they go into the field. But some firms—for example, many insurance companies—use field training and selling first to see whether the trainee's selling ability justifies the cost of formal training.

In most situations both group and individual training methods are needed. For example, new hires may attend initial training sessions as a group and then return to their home office for on-the-job training that pairs them with more experienced salespeople. More group training follows, to teach new hires additional skills.

Instructional methods for group or individual training are presented in Table 9.8. Of course, some methods are effective for both group and individual training. For example, video presentations can show examples of sales methods during a group training session, or individual salespeople can view the videos during spare time.

Choosing Instructional Methods

There are many methods of training. Sales managers have used some of them for many years, and others have emerged more recently.

TABLE 9.8 Individual versus Group Instructional Methods

GROUP INSTRUCTIONAL METHODS	INDIVIDUAL INSTRUCTIONAL METHODS
Lectures	On-the-job training
Literature (manuals, workbooks)	Personal conference
Group discussion	Literature (manuals, workbooks, electronic
Conferencing/E-learning	message boards, etc.)
Simulation games	DVD/Video
	DVD/Video/Audio
Demonstrations	E-learning
Role-playing	Computer-based training, games
	Podcasts, wikis, etc.

■ Traditional Training Methods

Lectures. Lectures can present more information to a larger number of students in a shorter period of time than many other teaching methods can. Lectures are an efficient way to present technical data or information that requires a large amount of time to write out. Effective sales training programs use only a limited amount of lecturing, however, because lectures usually don't generate active participation. Plan lectures thoughtfully and keep sessions short, interrupting them with other activities.

Literature. Good manuals or workbooks serve as study guides and contain outlines of the presentations made throughout the training program, lists of related reading materials, learning objectives for each training session, and thought-provoking questions, cases, and problems. Other useful printed materials are company bulletins, sales and product handbooks, and technical and trade publications.

Group Discussions. In the simplest form of group discussion, the trainer leads and stimulates talk and participation by the trainees. Case studies are a good tool for stimulating group discussion. Trainees receive cases to study, and then the trainer leads a class discussion to analyze and solve the problems in the case. Group discussions also can take place via an Internet chat room, which is particularly useful when the training is being delivered to people in a wide range of geographic locations.

Role-Playing
A group method of training in which trainees play different roles in a simulated sales situation and then receive feedback on their performance.

Role-Playing. If experience is the best teacher, then a good role-playing session is the next best teacher, because role-playing is learning by doing. In **role-playing**, the trainee tries to sell a product to a hypothetical prospect (usually played by the trainer or another trainee). Role-playing can help trainees learn to handle unforeseen developments that often arise in selling situations. It also gives the trainer a chance to work with trainees on voice, poise, mannerisms, speech, and movements. All in all, role-playing impresses on trainees that knowing what to do in a selling situation is one thing, but doing it is another.

Simulation Games. Simulation games can aid in learning by allowing the trainees to assume the roles of decision makers either in their own or customers' organizations. Trainees can make decisions about the timing and size of orders, sales forecasts, advertising, pricing, and the like. Then they receive feedback on the outcomes of their decisions. Simulation games generate enthusiasm through competitive game playing, aid trainees in developing skills to correctly perceive key factors that influence customer decisions, and show the uses and value of planning techniques. They're also fun and force trainees to become actively involved in the learning process.

Simulation games have a few disadvantages. First, they're time-consuming: it usually takes three to four hours for trainees to generate decisions, and several rounds of decisions are needed for the learning process. Also, because simulation games are preprogrammed computer packages, decisions that are novel or unique seldom receive the payoff they deserve.

Demonstrations. Demonstrations can be a powerful instructional method, since learners tend to retain more information if they can actually see a product in use or a service being delivered. Even more powerful are demonstrations that allow hands-on or active participation. Trainees learning how to use SFA software, for example, can experiment with the same computer and communications accessories they'll actually use on the job. Examples in such demonstrations should reflect real-world situations the sales rep will experience.

On-the-Job Training. On-the-job training (sometimes referred to as buddy-system or suitcase training) is an individual instructional method in which an experienced salesperson is assigned to a trainee to teach him or her about the job and how to sell. Typically, experienced salespersons go on sales calls made by trainees, after which the two evaluate and analyze the call. The major advantage is that trainees can learn first-hand how actual sales calls are conducted. However, for on-the-job training to be effective, the experienced salesperson must be highly qualified to train and influence the trainee. An important disadvantage of on-the-job training is that it is very time-consuming and costly for both people.

Mentoring

A method of on-the-job training in which a sales trainee is assigned long term to an experienced sales rep or manager for the purpose of transferring knowledge and experiences.

Mentoring. **Mentoring** typically pairs a new or inexperienced sales rep with a sales manager or executive, or a more experienced senior sales rep. For example, new reps at Interpane Glass Company (www.glassonweb.com), a North Carolina maker of reflective glass used in commercial construction, learn the basics of selling by traveling with four regional sales managers, spending a week with each one. This allows reps to pick out the strengths and weaknesses of each manager and eventually develop their own style. Other mentoring programs may last for a year or more and can serve to groom high-potential candidates for managerial positions. Spending time with a sales manager gives the rep experience in thinking about executive decisions.[11]

© Jim Craigmyle / Corbis

● **On-the-job training (sometimes referred to as buddy-system or suitcase training) is an individual instructional method in which an experienced salesperson is assigned to a trainee to teach him or her about the job and how to sell.**

Personal Conferences. Managers and trainers often hesitate to use personal conferences because they assume learning cannot take place in an unstructured situation. However, experience has shown that the personal conference can be an effective learning tool, and it can establish good rapport between the trainee and the sales executive or trainer. But the trainer must be careful to avoid idle chitchat during conference time.

Audiotapes. Thousands of audiotape programs are available today that can assist salespeople in anything from selling skills to personal development. Baird Corporation, a manufacturer of analytical and optical instruments, uses low-cost audiocassette tapes to give its salespeople regular refresher courses on pre-call planning, presentations, product offerings, and various other topics. The company tries to make at least one tape per month. One recent tape included a discussion of product features for one of Baird's new products; another focused on a specific model from a competitor. Baird believes audiotapes are a worthwhile method of sales training because they use unproductive driving time for training and professional development.[12]

DVDs. In a group setting, DVDs serve a function similar to conferencing. They enable outside consultants and senior management to prerecord training messages. They also minimize travel and time-loss expenses because they can easily be mailed to remote sales offices for training seminars. Like conferencing, DVDs are impersonal; and the interaction is one-way, from presenter to trainee. Since viewers can't ask the trainer questions, a sales manager or other knowledgeable individual should be available to answer queries. One note of caution: use DVD lectures sparingly. While they are effective on a limited basis, a full day of this type of training would be boring and unlikely to meet training objectives effectively.

Computer-Based Training (CBT)

A general term used to describe any learning or training event that uses computers as the primary delivery method, such as CD-ROM, the Internet, intranet, and interactive videodisc.

Conferencing (Distance Learning)

A method of delivering training to a group of trainees located in different locations using computers, telephone lines, and satellite.

Web Conferencing

A fast growing approach where participants use a computer to communicate with several other people via the Internet

Computer-Based Training. Computer-based training (CBT) is a general term used to describe any learning or training event that uses computers as the primary delivery method.[13] Sometimes called "desktop learning," CBT-based teaching methods have the advantage of using technology to deliver on-demand, just-in-time training. Further, CBT reduces the time and cost it takes to train salespeople. CBT is also ideal when all participants need to be brought up to the same level before further group training. Organizations such as SkillSoft (www.skillsoft.com), Thomson NETg (www.netg.com), and BlueU.com (www.BlueU.com) are leading innovators in the design and development of CBT. While still an effective training approach, CBT is being replaced by Internet-based approaches.

■ Emerging Training Methods

Conferencing. Conferencing (distance learning) is any training in which participants at different locations interact electronically via telephones, satellite, or the Internet. It can take several forms, including video conferencing, audio conferencing, and conferencing on the Internet. Most forms link remote locations (sales offices) to the home office or another facility via the Internet.

In **Web conferencing**, the fastest-growing approach, participants use a computer to communicate with others via the Internet. With *screen sharing,* participants see whatever is on the presenter's screen and respond via their keyboard. Voice communication is also possible, through either a traditional telephone or Voice-over-Internet

Webinar
A variation on web conferencing, it is a seminar or web conference conducted over the Internet.

Protocol (VoIP), although sometimes text chat is used instead of voice. A **webinar**, a variation on Web conferencing, is a seminar or Web conference conducted over the Internet. In contrast to a webcast, which transmits information in one direction only, a webinar is designed to be interactive between the presenter and audience. It is live and conveys information according to an agenda, with a starting and ending time. In some cases, the presenter speaks over a telephone line, pointing out information being presented onscreen, and the audience responds over the telephone, preferably a speakerphone. But increasingly, software includes both speaking (VoIP) and visual capabilities.

Conferencing is an effective training approach. Pre-test and post-test scores of trainees show no significant difference in learning when trainees take courses via video conferencing or with an in-class instructor. Research shows the tasks that occur most frequently in educational settings—giving and receiving information, asking questions, exchanging opinions, and problem solving—are done just as effectively using telecommunications as in face-to-face meetings.

E-learning
A broad term that refers to computer-enhanced learning, although it is often extended to include the use of mobile technologies such as PDAs and MP3 players.

Internet. **E-learning** is a broad term that refers to computer-enhanced learning, although it is often extended to include the use of mobile technologies such as PDAs and MP3 players. It may include the use of Web-based teaching materials and hypermedia in general, multimedia CD-ROMs or websites, discussion boards, collaborative software, blogs, computer-aided assessment, animation, simulations, games, learning management software, electronic voting systems, and so on. Sometimes managers use a combination of more than one method.

Online Learning
A purely Web-based form of learning.

E-learning also encompasses more than **online learning**, which is purely Web-based learning. E-learning often serves for conferencing and distance learning, but it also works in conjunction with face-to-face teaching, in which case we use the term **blended learning**.[14] The term **m-learning** describes mobile technologies.

Blended Learning
A blend of E-learning used in conjunction with face-to-face teaching.

Among the e-learning methods most heavily reliant on technology are RSS feeds, blogs, podcasts, and wikis. **RSS** is a format typically associated with syndicated news and content of news-like sites, including sites like Wired.com, news-oriented community sites like Slashdot, and personal blogs. RSS feeds are not just for news. Salespeople can sign up for RSS feeds on sales training topics that are made available in discrete modules and syndicated via RSS. For example, the "recent changes" page of a sales wiki, a change log of CVS (Concurrent Versions System) check-ins, and the revision history of books and documents are available through RSS feeds. The salesperson's RSS-aware program checks the feed for changes, and when something new is posted, the program sends it out. RSS-aware programs, called news aggregators, are popular in the blogging community. Many blogs make content available in RSS format. RSS news aggregators help salespeople keep up with their favorite blogs by checking their RSS feeds and displaying new items from each of them.

M-learning
A form of learning using mobile technologies.

RSS
A format typically associated with syndicated news and content of news-like sites, including sites like Wired.com, news-oriented community sites like Slashdot, and personal blogs.

Wikis are another emerging e-learning sales training technique. A **wiki** enables contributors to create and update documents collectively, usually with no review, using a Web browser. A single page in a wiki is called a "wiki page"; the entire body of pages, which are interconnected via hyperlinks, is "the wiki." A wiki is therefore a simple, easy-to-use, user-maintained database for creating and searching information. Most general-purpose wikis are open to the public without the need to register any user account. Many edits, however, can be made in real time and appear almost instantaneously online.[15] Company-maintained wikis, such as those used for sales training, are located on private servers and require user authentication before readers can edit or sometimes even read the pages.

Wiki
A simple, easy-to-use, user-maintained database for creating and searching information.

● **Salespersons benefit from new technology.**

E-learning has been the greatest change in training to occur in the past decade. Sales forces can now train anywhere, any time. In fact, often a computer isn't even necessary. The main reasons for e-learning's popularity are that it's more convenient and cost effective than traveling around the world for a training session in a hotel conference room.[16]

Intranet. Businesses that want sales training available over the Internet can set up programs on their own internal intranets. An **intranet** uses Internet and Web technologies but is accessible only to the company's reps and others, such as supply chain members, who are given permission to access the system. Intranet-based training programs generally have more audio and video capabilities than Internet-based programs, though access can be slower and more limited based on connection speeds.

Salespeople at Sun Microsystems (www.sun.com), for example, log onto a centralized server and access a browser that steps them through intranet-delivered sales training programs. With thousands of channel members and salespeople, it would take Sun more than a year to effectively train everyone each time a new product is introduced. With its intranet-based training system, salespeople and channel members can effectively sell a new product line in three months or less.[17]

The president of The Training Clinic in Seal Beach, California (http://thetraining clinic.com), says some things still can't be taught online: "For interpersonal skills, classroom learning usually works better." The classroom offers feedback from instructors and peers—information that is crucial to the learning process. Chris von Koschembahr, a learning transformation executive with IBM, believes teaching employees first in the classroom and then incorporating e-learning is the best method. "So much of the e-learning side is more efficient and effective when you've

Intranet
Using Internet and Web technologies but those accessible only to the company's reps and others, such as supply chain members, who are given permission to access the system.

had an opportunity to meet with people you're working with," he says. "When people have had a chance to meet face-to-face, so much more can be done at a distance."[18]

■ Location of Training

Centralized Training Programs
Training programs that involve organized training schools, periodic conventions, or seminars held in a central location such as the home office.

Centralized training programs usually include organized training schools, periodic conventions, or seminars held in a central location such as the home office. In smaller firms, whose sales territories often are located near the home office, it's convenient and logical for training activities to be centralized. Organizations that hire large numbers of salespeople each year also typically use centralized training. An advantage is that trainees can quickly get acquainted with each other, top managers, and key home-office personnel. Beyond this, many experts feel that removing trainees from the distractions of their daily work and home life is conducive to learning. The major disadvantages of centralized training are the substantial expense and organizational effort required.

Decentralized Training
Training programs that use one or more different types of training, such as office instruction, use of experienced salespeople, on-the-job training, traveling sales clinics, or a type of computer-based training.

Decentralized training can include office instruction, use of experienced salespeople, on-the-job training, podcasts, blogs, webinars, and other e-learning approaches. It therefore usually takes place while trainees are actually working in the field, giving them a chance to learn and be productive at the same time and avoiding the cost of supporting nonproductive trainees while they are trained in centralized programs. Also, the branch manager or an assistant is usually responsible for decentralized training, enabling sales managers to directly evaluate the trainees.

■ Timing of Training Programs

Although training should be a continual process, management must still decide when to emphasize it. Some executives believe no one should be placed in the field before being trained to sell and given a thorough knowledge of the product, company, customers, competitors, and selling techniques. The other philosophy is to evaluate the new salesperson's desire and ability to sell before spending money and time on actual training. This philosophy places recruits in the field with minimal information about selling and evaluates them based on how well they do, considering their lack of actual training.

Insisting that salespeople be thoroughly trained before they enter the field means they should be top sales producers once they begin selling. But this can cost money and time, and it may lower the new salesperson's morale and enthusiasm because he or she may resent feeling nonproductive for the length of time it takes to become thoroughly knowledgeable. The strategy of placing new salespeople in the field first and then training them can weed out people not suited for selling, and those selected for training learn more quickly and easily because they have had previous selling experience. However, the organization can lose customers or its reputation can be seriously injured by sending untrained salespeople into the field.

Preparing, Motivating, and Coaching Trainees

In planning how, when, and where training will occur, sales managers often overlook the importance of thoroughly preparing their salespeople for training, motivating trainees to learn, and then following up with them after training. Let's look at some successful strategies for filling these needs.

■ Preparing Trainees for Training

Adults seek out learning experiences only when they see a need for them.[19] If trainees don't understand why they are being trained and what benefit they will receive from it, chances are the training will not be effective.

Pre-Training Briefing
Meeting help before training begins to let trainees know the purpose of training.

One of the most effective means of increasing the positive results of sales training is for managers to prepare their salespeople ahead of time. A **pre-training briefing** tells participants the training's purpose and objectives, why they were selected to attend, and the business need the sales manager hopes to meet. By setting goals in advance of training, the sales manager can make sure trainees are more tuned in during the training sessions and thinking about ways to apply their new skills afterward. By endorsing the training program, sales managers exert more influence on whether the training accomplishes its goals than does anything a trainer can do during the training. If it's a particularly important sales topic, a member of senior management can kick off the training to enhance its credibility and confirm corporate support. A survey before the training, as shown in Table 9.9, can help sales managers and trainers determine whether trainees are ready for the training.

So that participants arrive ready to learn, the trainer may also want to give them a *pre-test* to measure how much they know about the training topic, followed with a preview of the content. Comparing pre-test scores to *post-test* evaluations at the end of training will reveal how much trainees have absorbed.

■ Motivating Trainees During Training

If trainees aren't motivated during the training session, learning does not take place. So how do sales managers and trainers get salespeople motivated for learning? One way is by encouraging student involvement and minimizing lectures. Most sales

TABLE 9.9 Pre-Qualifying Participants for Training

A negative response to any of these statements indicates that the trainee (or the sales organization) might not be ready for the training program.

Check whether you agree or disagree with the following statements:

	AGREE	DISAGREE
I have a pretty good sense of what the class is about.		
I can see how I might use what I'll learn in the class.		
There are ways the training could help me perform my job better.		
There are ways the training could help my unit.		
What I learn in class is likely to count on my performance appraisals.		
My manager knows about the training.		
The class focuses on problems and opportunities that matter to me.		
I'm glad to have the chance to learn more about the training topic.		
My manager cares about my acquiring skills and knowledge in the area covered by the training.		
When I return to work, I'll have the tools I need to use what I learned in class.		

SOURCE: Adapted from Allison Rossett, "That Was a Great Class, But . . ." *Training & Development,* July 1997, p. 21.

training programs succeed by balancing a small amount of lecture with activities that get trainees engaged in the program, such as group discussions and role-playing. Since salespeople often thrive on being in the spotlight, have trainees present some of the material to the rest of the class. Another way is to ask questions. This approach engages trainees as well as generates feedback on learning, understanding, and misunderstanding. Involvement and interaction are necessary for in-person training as well as e-learning approaches.

Another important factor is the training environment. Sales training must feel like a safe environment, so trainees are at ease when trying different selling techniques during group activities and role-playing. Some people are hesitant to role-play in front of their peers, especially if the group is critical or if an individual feels he or she is not up to speed on certain skills. Having management present may also stifle a trainee's participation. Table 9.10 summarizes ways trainers can motivate salespeople to learn during training sessions.

■ Conducting Post-Training Reinforcement

Just as they need pre-training preparation, trainees also need follow-up on the skills and concepts they learned during training. **Coaching (developmental feedback)** is informal, give-and-take discussions between sales managers and salespeople for the

Coaching (Developmental Feedback)
Post-training reinforcement that generally involves informal, give-and-take discussions between sales managers and salespeople with the purpose of reinforcing sales training concepts, solving selling problems, and improving basic selling skills.

TABLE 9.10 Motivating Trainees During Training

- *Use positive reinforcement.* Reward trainees for learning through positive body language and words of encouragement.
- *Use active training formats and variety.* In addition to lectures, use other learning methods such as discussions, demonstrations, role-playing, visuals, games, and simulations.
- *Encourage social interaction.* Social interaction is a strong motivator. Include interaction, group discussions, and problem-solving exercises.
- *Facilitate expertise sharing.* Ask trainees to share their specialized skills, knowledge, experiences, or "secrets to success" with the rest of the class.
- *Include realistic examples and situations.* Trainees will pick up skills faster and achieve better results if they get a chance to apply ideas and techniques that mirror their real world.
- *Establish a safe environment for learning.* Eliminate fear in the training environment. Trainees might develop a list of rules to follow during the training session, such as "No criticism," "No interruptions," and "Everything said is confidential."
- *Encourage self-evaluation.* Self-evaluation is an excellent motivator. Trainees can evaluate their progress during training with self-graded quizzes or "learning scorecards."
- *Recognize early success.* Include activities trainees can learn quickly and be rewarded for before presenting the more difficult exercises.
- *Include sufficient practice.* Encourage trainees to practice their new skills on the job by scheduling follow-up evaluations.
- *Encourage goal setting.* Have trainees make a list of post-training goals or ways to use their newly acquired skills after training is completed. Schedule a follow-up meeting with trainees to measure their success.

SOURCES: Lehman (2006); David Torrence, "Motivating Trainees to Learn," *Training & Development,* March 1993, p. 55; Dean Spitzer, "20 Ways to Motivate Trainees," *Training,* December 1995, p. 52; "How to Make Your Sales Training Really Work," www.salesdoctors.com (accessed September 2006).

TABLE 9.11 Requirements for Effective Coaching	
1. Managers and salespeople must trust one another.	The sales manager's actions tell salespeople if they can be trusted. Do you expect your salespeople to do as you say or as you do? Always keep your word to your sales team, and avoid competing with them. Encourage open communication to show your salespeople they can confide in you.
2. Salespeople must respect the manager's expertise and ability.	If they are to accept instruction from managers, they must have faith in their direction. Learning is a lifelong process. Good managers stay informed, keep their skills sharp, and are never too experienced or knowledgeable to learn something new.
3. Salespeople must want to learn, grow, and change.	Positive, self-motivated salespeople are more receptive to good coaching than negative people are—and more likely to put it to good use. When you hire your next salesperson, consider attitude over experience. Experience is helpful, but teaching new skills is often easier than changing a person's thinking.
4. Coaches should have excellent teaching skills.	To teach effectively, sales managers must present material so that salespeople can absorb it easily. Provide your team with a non-threatening learning environment. Mistakes are often the best teachers—let your salespeople know that it's okay to make mistakes as long as they learn from them.
5. Coaches should be empathetic.	Coaching should never be given without remembering what it is like to be in the salesperson's shoes. Being empathetic with the salesperson is one of the best ways to ensure that the salesperson is empathetic with the customer.

SOURCES: Jim Rapp, *How to Coach Salespeople for Maximum Results,* as reported by Joseph J. Kozak in "A Coach for All Reasons," www.SellingPower.com (accessed August 2006); S. Sparrow, "Empathy, Empathy, They All Want Empathy," *Training & Coaching Today,* March 2007, pp. 16–17.

purpose of reinforcing training concepts, solving selling problems, and improving basic selling skills. Says Tony Delgado, sales and marketing education program manager for Dell Computers (www.dell.com): "Inspect what you expect. Otherwise, training will just be another exercise. Ask about training, use the tools yourself. The last thing you want is to implement a selling process and then not reinforce or use the process."[20] Requirements for effective coaching are shown in Table 9.11.

Evaluating Training Programs

Once you've carried out a sales training program, it's essential to evaluate its effectiveness and determine how well you've met your overall objectives and specific goals for the program.

Table 9.12 illustrates a four-level method to gauge effectiveness. First, the *reaction* level method measures trainees' attitudes and feelings toward the training program. Second, evaluation at the *learning* level assesses how well the trainees learned basic principles, facts, and so on during the training program. (This step requires testing trainees before and after training.) Third, *behavior*-level evaluation measures changes in behavior as a result of the training. Are trainees using their new attitudes, knowledge, and skills on the job? Questionnaires from supervisors, subordinates, and even customers can provide answers. These assessments are often subjective, however, because of personal relationships that often develop during training. Finally, at the *results* level, we measure changes in performance. Plot salespeople's performance before and after training, and compare the results against training program objectives.[21] For example, Nabisco Biscuit Company (www.nabisco.com) assessed its sales

TABLE 9.12   Training Evaluation Methods

LEVELS	MEASURES	METHODS
Reaction	Attitudes, feelings, and satisfaction with the training program	Trainees complete forms, surveys, comment sheets, and exit interviews evaluating the training experience.
Learning	Principles, facts, and techniques learned	Trainer administers tests before and after the training program.
Behavior	Changes in behavior as a result of training	Trainer observes and/or surveys trainees and managers about three months after the training program.
Results	Changes in performance, both individual and company-wide	Managers measure change in sales, profits, and costs.

SOURCES: Mendosa (1995); Honeycutt and Stevenson (1989), 217.

training return on investment using a results approach and found that for every dollar invested in sales training, there was a $122 increase in sales after the training took place.[22]

To evaluate new-hire sales trainees, Microsoft follows the four levels of evaluation model presented in Table 9.12. Its trainers measure the first two levels—reaction and learning—in the classroom. For example, in a test for product knowledge, trainees are given a time limit to create an Excel worksheet. Further evaluation of learning comes from the trainees' managers, who score reps on their presentation skills, sales skills, and product knowledge. For level three, trainers conduct follow-up interviews to measure how well reps apply their new attitudes, knowledge, and skills on the job. At the fourth level of evaluation, which measures the effect training has on the company, sales managers who have new hires working for them meet in focus groups. While the evidence is more anecdotal than scientific, past results have demonstrated the value of training.[23]

Figure 9.2 is an example of an evaluation form given to trainees to assess their reaction to the sales training program (Level 1). The trainers' sample field evaluation

	Strongly Disagree	Disagree	Neutral	Agree	Strongly Agree
The instructor was well prepared.	☐	☐	☐	☐	☐
The material was relevant to my needs.	☐	☐	☐	☐	☐
The objectives of the training program were made clear.	☐	☐	☐	☐	☐
Visual aids were effectively used.	☐	☐	☐	☐	☐

FIGURE 9.2 Training Program Evaluation Form—Evaluating Reactions

CONFIDENTIAL

Date _____

Salesperson _____   Manager _____

Date report discussed with salesperson _____

- 4 *Excellent*—skill has been effectively mastered.
- 3 *Satisfactory*—salesperson has shown improvement regarding skill.
- 2 *Unsatisfactory*—salesperson may need follow-up training for this skill.
- 1 *Poor*—Further training and follow-up are required for this skill.
- 0 *Not applicable*

Please circle the number that most closely represents your feelings.

1. *Prospecting*

New lead generation	4	3	2	1	0
Lead qualification	4	3	2	1	0
Follow-up of leads	4	3	2	1	0

2. *Call Preparation*

Determining sales call objectives	4	3	2	1	0
Prospect needs analysis	4	3	2	1	0
Competitor analysis	4	3	2	1	0
Gathering of secondary data	4	3	2	1	0

3. *Approach*

Rapport with customers	4	3	2	1	0
Use of approach methods	4	3	2	1	0

4. *Presentation Skills*

Use of sales presentation strategies	4	3	2	1	0

5. *Handling Objections*

Use of methods to deal with customer objectives	4	3	2	1	0

6. *Closing*

Use of closing techniques	4	3	2	1	0
Increase in new business	4	3	2	1	0
Increase in repeat business	4	3	2	1	0

7. *Follow-up*

Use of follow-up with customers	4	3	2	1	0
Post-sale customer satisfaction	4	3	2	1	0

FIGURE 9.3 Field Evaluation and Career Development Report—Evaluating Learning

form in Figure 9.3 assesses trainees' changes in attitudes and behaviors as a result of sales training concentrating on selling skills (Level 3).

Top-level managers are demanding concrete evidence that training is achieving its goals of changing behavior on the job (Level 3 evaluation) and contributing to the bottom line (Level 4 evaluation). Technology has also made it easier to gather data necessary to evaluate training efforts, and research has shown the effectiveness of evaluation using the four-level approach outlined here.[24]

■ Continuous Training Programs

We've focused thus far on initial sales training programs. But sales managers also must develop continuous training. Two types of continuous training—refresher training and retraining—help upgrade the present sales force. The third—managerial training—focuses on sales managers, who need to maintain and sharpen their skills so they can remain effective and efficient. Continuous training conveys information about changes in the company's policies, products, marketing strategies, and the like, helping the sales force understand and quickly adapt to changes.

■ Refresher Training

Refresher Training
A form of continuous training that seeks to upgrade the skills of the existing sales force and to maximize the value of each salesperson.

Nothing is constant except change, and nowhere is this truer than in selling. The purpose of **refresher training** is to help salespeople do their jobs better by keeping them abreast of changes in technology, products, markets, and company objectives.

Refresher training reinforces the customer-driven approach that characterizes many companies. Consider, for example, Saturn's sales philosophy (www.saturn.com). Every Saturn employee—the team in Japan, the 3,000+ sales reps in the United States, the manufacturing staff, and the corporate staff—participates in over ninety hours of training each year, the equivalent of about two-and-a-half weeks.[25]

As customers become more sophisticated in their buying strategies, salespeople need to be equally sophisticated in their selling strategies. Refresher training and education become even more vital. Some types of refresher training that can help salespeople grow and succeed at their jobs are presented in Table 9.13.

TABLE 9.13 Refresher Training Topics

TRAINING ASPECT	GOAL
Basic skills	Learn how to qualify, greet, negotiate, present, and close.
Research	Increase confidence and preparedness by learning how to use available resources and how to find necessary information about customers' and competitors' products or services.
Listening skills	Learn to ask questions and *listen* to answers.
Interpersonal skills	Learn to read others' body language and intonation, as well as how to control and adjust one's own to match that of the customer.
Team selling	Learn to think like a team player and work with other departments in the company to help meet customers' needs.
Motivation	Understand what motivates and de-motivates sales reps and how it affects their work.
Positive thinking	Learn how to take negative thoughts and turn them into positive ones—even the best reps go through slumps.
Self-esteem	Help speed recovery from rejection.
Alternate disciplines	Take training courses that employees from other departments in the company take, such as marketing and customer service, to become a better team player.
Technology	Learn how to use PDAs, mobile phones, video iPods, blogs, wikis, SFA, and other emerging technologies.

SOURCES: "Training: The New Sales Basics," *Sales & Marketing Management,* April 1995, p. 81; and Margery Weinstein, "Fill 'Er Up: How to Choose Your Learning Content," October 2006, www.trainingmag.com/msg/content_display/publications/e3i9AiDhb6qKSoQNpXSOSclqQ%3D%3D (accessed October 2006).

TABLE 9.14 Checklist for Upgrading the Sales Force

INDIVIDUAL TRAINING

- On-the-job coaching by sales supervisor
- Courses for self-instruction prepared by the training department (example: podcasts on recent developments)
- Commercial self-instruction courses (example: webinars on selling skills)
- Attendance at workshops, clinics, or seminars
- Courses at local schools for special skills (accounting, computer science, drafting, design, etc.)
- Coaching by senior salesperson (example: goes with trainee to watch sales presentation)

GROUP TRAINING

- Sales meetings
- Presentation by specialists in the firm (engineer, accountant, purchasing agent, etc.)
- Presentations by other salespeople (example: how they landed a good account)
- Workshops and seminars developed by the firm's training department
- Commercial training aids (example: podcasts or webinars on selling skills, motivation, and other topics)
- Subscriptions and RSS feeds to:
  - Journals or magazines devoted to sales, sales management, or marketing (*Sales & Marketing Management*)
  - Journals relating to the industries of key accounts
  - General business magazines (*Business Week, Dun's Review, Forbes, Nation's Business,* etc.)
  - National news magazines (*Time, U.S. News & World Report, Newsweek,* etc.)
  - Business newspapers (*Wall Street Journal, New York Times,* etc.)

Managers can plan refresher training for either individuals or groups. The nature of the salesperson's deficiencies determines which approach is most appropriate. Table 9.14 shows a checklist of ways to overcome deficiencies and upgrade the sales force.

■ Retraining

Retraining
A form of continuous training that provides instruction when a salesperson's job requirements change due to new products or new methods.

When a salesperson's job requirements change because the company has added new products or services, revised sales territories, or upgraded SFA or CRM technology, **retraining** is needed. As Eastman Kodak (www.kodak.com) prepared to launch its Advanced Photo System (APS), it realized the company's sales and marketing people would need to understand APS to promote its innovative technology and features. So, Kodak created 10 two-hour training modules based on the differences in business practices, culture, and language among the fifteen countries where the system would first be launched.[26] Designing retraining programs includes the following steps:

1. *Determine which aspects of the new job are the most important.* Cover all the bases, but know what is most essential and teach that first.
2. *Determine which aspects of the new job are the most difficult.* Some new information can be learned quickly; some takes longer. Devote more time to difficult areas of a new position or responsibility.

3. *Determine which aspects of the new job are the most prevalent.* Emphasize tasks the salesperson will do most often or spend more time on.

In designing retraining programs, sales managers should also include ways to foster positive attitudes toward the job, other salespeople, and the participants themselves. Salespeople who are satisfied with their jobs and the organization make a more loyal and productive sales force. Often sales managers face the added challenge of dissolving resistance to retraining. Established salespeople may feel that management is trying to change them, and some will resist anything that hints of change. Sales managers should support the retraining wholeheartedly once the salespeople are back on the job.

Like initial and continuous training, retraining must include topics like adaptive skills, coping skills, problem solving, and improvisation to help salespeople grow and respond to change. Topics like self-assessment, self-direction, self-monitoring, and self-reinforcement are necessary to achieve the self management required in today's selling environment. Thus, sales managers must view training from the perspective of lifelong learning and growth.[27]

■ Managerial Training

Managerial Training
Includes all training on all functions of managing salespeople, such as recruitment, planning, sales forecasting, motivation, leadership, and so forth.

Just like salespeople, sales managers must also participate in training programs to ensure that they are aware of new developments. **Managerial training** should cover all aspects of the sales manager's job, not just the training function. The purpose of the programs is to introduce new approaches to organization, planning, motivation, compensation, supervision, evaluation, and control over the areas the sales manager is responsible for. Managerial training is usually sponsored by the company itself or by professional associations, universities, training companies, or private consultants.

Managerial training should also be provided for new sales managers making the transition from personal selling or another position into management. Salespeople, in particular, often have difficulty making a successful transition into sales management, but research has shown that sales management training remains one of the most neglected areas in sales training. A recent study found that fewer than half the companies surveyed provide new sales managers with formal training. Instead, sales management training consists primarily of informal, on-the-job coaching by superiors or peers. Many of the companies that do provide formal sales management training delay it until a sales manager has been promoted to a senior-level sales management position. But a sales force will have difficulty performing at the highest levels while its sales manager is learning on the job through trial and error.[28]

Sales Training Challenges for Global Companies

Most of the sales skills taught to U.S. salespeople can be translated into other countries, but differences across cultures do need to be accounted for in training. For example, notions of time differ from country to country, and so do protocols and formalities. Even colors can convey meaning to certain cultures. Printed materials presented to Chinese trainees, for example, should be in black and white, since colors have such great significance to the Chinese. Also, the way people learn differs from culture to culture. U.S. trainees, for instance, are results oriented and tend to focus on the end result during training. The French, on the other hand, use deductive logic, emphasizing the process and how to get to the end.[29]

Cultural Similarity

	Similar	Dissimilar
Extensive	Little Training Needed	Cultural Knowledge Training
Limited	Cultural Adaptability Training	Cultural Adaptability & Cultural Knowledge Training

(left axis: Cultural Experience — Extensive / Limited)

FIGURE 9.4 Determining When Cultural Training Is Needed

Sales training programs for global companies need to be tailored to different cultures, allowing salespeople to learn in a familiar environment. Wyeth (www.wyeth.com) sells pharmaceutical products in more than a hundred countries and has tailored its sales training by designating global training managers worldwide. As a result, while sales skills taught around the globe are fairly consistent, Wyeth's training managers can adapt the program to fit the cultural differences of many countries.[30]

When designing sales training programs for global companies, sales managers must determine the type and amount of training. Figure 9.4 suggests one approach to making these decisions.[31]

The more similar the culture, the less important is training in cultural knowledge. When executives have extensive cultural experiences, they also need less training in negotiating with or managing individuals with similar language and historical backgrounds. But sales executives with limited cultural experience, particularly those confronted with very different cultures, will need extensive knowledge of differences before they begin selling to, managing, or negotiating with people from very different cultures and languages. They also will need training in adaptability skills so they can assess cultural encounters and deal with them quickly and effectively. Read about ways to ensure the success of global sales training in the *Sales Management in Action* box.

SALES MANAGEMENT IN ACTION

Making Sales Training Friendly to Other Cultures

Global competition has increased to a level never seen before, and the global marketplace is becoming increasingly crowded. Salespeople and sales managers in this environment need to know the products they are selling and how best to sell them. In a word, they need training. Here is a list of ways sales managers can better provide training to their increasingly diverse staff.

■ *Include international members on the training design team.* People already familiar with the culture of the trainees can design better training.

■ *Thoroughly research the culture of the host country.* Read about the host country's culture and politics beforehand. If possible, spend some time in the country with the salespeople to get a better idea of how culture affects the selling process.

■ *Offer English classes.* If the training class will be conducted in English, teach some English before and during training to individuals who have language difficulties. This will help these trainees deal with the vocabulary presented in class and assist in their translating information correctly and quickly enough to keep up with the instructor.

■ *Avoid idioms, jargon, slang, and humor in class.* This information often does not translate readily to other cultures.

■ *Be sensitive to nonverbal language.* Body language and facial expressions provide subtle messages regarding the level of understanding and learning that is taking place.

■ *Schedule a question-and-answer session during a class break or after class.* In some cultures it is rude to interrupt by asking questions during training. Other cultures consider volunteering a way of bragging.

■ *Include managers and others given foreign assignments in training.* All individuals sent abroad need training if the assignment is a new one, not just salespeople.[32]

CHAPTER SUMMARY

1. **Explain the importance and benefits of sales training programs.** Developing an effective sales training program is increasingly becoming a critical part of the sales manager's job. Customers are more knowledgeable than ever before, competition is stronger, and customers are demanding more quality and service from sales interactions. With the rapidly rising costs of training and the many high-technology products, sales training is gaining more respect among upper-level executives. Sales training programs should seek to continually help salespeople grow in knowledge, selling habits, and selling techniques and to develop good attitudes about themselves and their jobs, companies, and customers.

2. **Follow the steps in developing and implementing sales training programs.** Sales training design should be based on the requirements of the company and on the skills and experience of the company's salespeople. Therefore, the design process should begin with a needs assessment to determine the gap between what the sales force knows and what they should know. Once these gaps in learning are determined, then specific performance objectives can be set and the content of the training program developed. Training program delivery decisions include who will train, what method will be used to train, where training will occur, and when training will occur. Trainees should be prepared before training, motivated during training, and have new skills reinforced after training. Every well-designed training program also includes an evaluation to determine if the program's objectives have been met.

3. **Apply different instructional methods for training.** Companies must decide whether to conduct training individually or in a group setting. Usually, group training methods are used in formal training programs, and individual training methods are used in informal training programs (specifically, in field training). There are many methods of training. Lectures, group discussions, role-playing, demonstrations, simulation games, DVDs, and even computer-based training have been used for many years and are considered traditional methods. Web conferencing, Internet- and intranet-based training, and e-learning are emerging techniques.

4. **Prepare, motivate, and reinforce trainees.** If trainees don't understand why they are being trained and what benefit they will receive from it, chances are the training will not be effective. A pre-training briefing can tell participants the training's purpose and objectives, why they were selected to attend, and what business need the sales manager hopes to meet. Once training begins, student involvement should be encouraged and lecture kept to a minimum. The trainer should also ask questions to get trainees to provide feedback. Additionally, the training environment should be considered "safe" so that trainees feel at ease trying different selling techniques during group activities and role-playing. Post-training reinforcement through coaching is critical for learning to persist. Coaching generally involves informal, give-and-take discussions between sales managers and salespeople with the purpose of reinforcing sales training concepts, solving selling problems, and improving basic selling skills.

5. **Evaluate training programs.** Four levels of evaluation are used to gauge the effectiveness of a training program. First, at the *reaction* level the trainees' attitudes and feelings toward the training program are measured. Second, evaluation at the *learning* level assesses how well the trainees learned basic principles, facts, and so on during the training program. Third, *behavior*-level evaluation measures changes in behavior as a result of the training. Finally, at the *results* level changes in performance are measured by plotting salespeople's performance, before and after training, and comparing the results against training program objectives.

6. **Meet the sales training challenges of global companies.** While many of the sales skills taught to U.S. salespeople can be translated into other countries, there are differences across cultures that need to be accounted for in training. Differences include notions of time, protocols, formalities, how people learn, and even such things as color. Ways to enhance success during multicultural sales training include increased planning by the trainer, research into each

country's politics, economics, and culture, integrating local examples into the training material and discussion, including international members on the design team, avoiding unfamiliar terms and humor, paying attention to nonverbal cues, using visuals, and providing question-and-answer sessions.

REVIEW AND APPLICATION QUESTIONS

1. Why should sales training and sales force development be thought of as a long-term, ongoing process? [LO 1]

2. "Good salespeople are born, not made." Agree or disagree? [LO 1]

3. What are some of the benefits a company can expect from a well-developed sales training program? Do these benefits outweigh the costs? Why or why not? [LO 2]

4. Why is the design and implementation of sales training programs such a critical task for sales managers? Briefly discuss the planning decisions that must be made by sales managers in designing sales training programs. [LO 2]

5. Discuss the basic elements that all initial sales training programs must cover. Are these elements any different from elements of continuous training programs? [LO 3]

6. What are some of the problems that can arise when delegating the responsibility of the sales training program to line executives? To staff trainers? To outside training specialists? [LO 3]

7. How is technology affecting sales training? What benefits can sales managers realize by using e-learning methods? [LO 4]

8. Why are pre-training preparation and post-training reinforcement so critical to the success of a sales training program? What are some things a trainer could do to make the sales training class more motivational? [LO 4]

9. A pharmaceutical sales firm adopts a new SFA system that tracks customer sales calls, notes, and samples. What recommendations would you make when planning the training for this program? [LO 5]

IT'S UP TO YOU

Internet Exercise

Visit the Cisco Systems (www.cisco.com) website. Insert the keywords "sales training" in the search option, and see what you find. Prepare a brief report on the two training topics you found the most interesting.

Role-Playing Exercise

The World of Training

Situation

Sal is a sales manager for a multinational footwear company specializing in casual and athletic shoes. Traditionally, training has been limited to break-out sessions at the biannual sales conference held in Kansas City each year. But increasingly, production has moved from Korea to China and India. The company now has sales operations in twenty-five countries on four continents. Sal argues with Tom, the VP of marketing, that the traditional sales conference is inadequate given the new global focus in both production and sales. Tom says, "Training is training! It doesn't matter where the people are when they get trained, and any sales rep worth their salt doesn't need to be *retrained* more than once every two years!" Sal walks away determined to revamp the sales training program to make her division and the company more successful.

Role-Play Participants and Assignments

Sal: Take on the role of Sal, and think about what she needs to consider as she sets about addressing Tom's opinions.

Prepare a slide show, using no more than eight slides, that focuses on why the current sales approach may be inadequate.

In-Basket Exercise

You are sales manager for a large consumer goods company and have just finished your best recruiting and selection process in years. You hired six great people from college campuses around the country, and you believe a couple of them have the potential to be top salespeople.

This morning you received a surprising memo from the sales trainer. She reports that your superstar recruits are doing poorly in training. In fact, they have consistently finished last on the exams. They seem uninter- ested in the training and have indicated that since the trainer has "never been in the field, there's no point listening to her!" She has labeled your top recruits "know-it-alls" who won't respond to sales training.

1. Do you believe a problem like this is more the fault of the trainer or the recruits?

2. What concepts from this chapter may help to resolve the conflict and result in more effective training results?

Ethical Dilemma

You were recently hired as a sales representative for a large financial services organization. You will be responsible for finding individuals interested in investments and convincing them that your company is the best choice for help in managing a financial portfolio. Before going into the field, you are participating in a training program. Your sales trainer is doing a good job of teaching financial management, consumer behavior, and corporate culture. Occasionally, however, he injects personal bias into the program. For example, in an informal way he told the class that in a competitive market like financial services, "Not acknowledging the strengths of your competitors can be helpful if a client is naive." Also, several times he stated that "the best place to look for new clients is in the obituary column of a newspaper. People who have recently lost a family member are excellent prospects to call on because they usually receive large sums of money after someone dies."

QUESTIONS

1. What is your initial response to such advice? Even if such suggestions work, should they be included in a training program?

2. At the end of the training, trainees normally fill out a short questionnaire with a spot for comments. Do you think anybody would comment on these statements? Would they likely be positive or negative comments?

CASE 9.1

Hops Distributors, Inc.: Getting the Blend Right!

James Williams is the sales manager for Hops Distributors, Inc. in Kansas City, Kansas. The company is a local beer distributor, carries one of the top national brands as well as a number of imports, and currently has about 500 accounts in each of its sales territories. Hops' top management recently evaluated its accounts and decided to change from geographic-only sales territories (where reps call on all accounts in a geographic area) to a more customer-oriented strategy. The new strategy is based on segmenting customers by the number of cases of beer ordered each week. Salespeople will call on fewer accounts overall and be able to provide better service based on the number of cases each account orders. For example, a high-volume account may be called on several times a week, while an ultra-low account may be called on once a week. The four categories are (1) high-volume accounts—over 200 cases per week; (2) moderate-volume accounts—100 to 200 cases per week; (3) low-volume accounts—over 10 but under 100 cases per week; (4) ultra-low-volume accounts—10 or fewer cases per week.

In the past, salespeople were paid a base salary and received most of their compensation through commissions that gave them an incentive to grow individual accounts. James wants to make sure each salesperson has an equal chance of receiving a competitive level of compensation. He has decided to divide the first three categories of accounts evenly between four salespeople, thus giving them an equal number of accounts and approximately equal sales potential. Category 4 accounts will be covered by a single salesperson. Table 1 shows the projected case sales and commissions generated.

James has identified three major problems with this new strategy. First, Category 4 accounts make up half of all Hops accounts. The sales representative covering those accounts will have five times more accounts than the other four salespeople do. Therefore, James has decided to give the Category 4 accounts to one of his best salespeople, who can properly manage complex tasks. The second major problem is that the potential to earn commissions on Category 4 accounts is significantly lower than for any other category. That is, even though Category 4 represents half of all Hops accounts, the combined sales potential is lower than for any other category. The third issue is that most of these accounts have very little potential for growing into a Category 3 account or better. Consequently, there is little hope for the salesperson to grow commissions from these accounts.

QUESTIONS

1. Evaluate the pros and cons of the new strategy.

2. Has James properly divided the accounts? Why or why not?

3. What kind of training should Hops implement to facilitate implementation of the new territory approach?

4. What topics should be included in the training program?

Case prepared by Mike Wittmann, University of Southern Mississippi.

TABLE 1   Average Sales (Cases) and Commissions

ACCOUNT CATEGORY	NUMBER OF ACCOUNTS	AVERAGE CASES SOLD	AVERAGE TOTAL SALES (IN CASES)	AVERAGE TOTAL COMMISSIONS ($1.25 PER CASE)
1	25	350	8750	$10,937.50
2	75	180	13500	$16,875.00
3	150	60	9000	$11,250.00
4	250	8	2000	$2,500.00
Total	500	598	33250	$41,562.50

 CASE 9.2

Midwest Auto Parts, Inc.: The Value of Sales Training

The engine electrical equipment industry is almost a $4-billion-a-year industry. In recent years competition has increased from U.S. companies, but the industry clearly is facing strong competition from abroad, particularly Japan. The engine electrical equipment industry is divided into three main segments. Original equipment parts are supplied domestically to Ford, General Motors, and Chrysler. Companies supplying these parts are called original equipment manufacturers (OEMs). The second segment is called the after-market or replacement parts segment. After-market parts are supplied to wholesalers and retailers of auto parts to be sold to repair automobiles after they have left the factory. The third segment is called the non-automotive segment—it supplies parts for engines other than automobiles.

Midwest Auto Parts, Inc., sells to two of these segments—the OEM (original equipment manufacturer) parts segment and the after-market parts segment. Midwest Auto Parts has been in business for over thirty years and has manufacturing plants in the United States, Canada, and Mexico. Sales are handled by a national sales director and ten regional sales representatives. The regional sales representatives line up independent manufacturer's representatives who actually do the selling. The manufacturer's representatives are paid on a commission basis and generally carry products of several non-competing companies.

In the last couple of years the regional sales representatives have had a lot of trouble recruiting and keeping manufacturer's representatives. In the past Midwest Auto Parts simply signed the reps up, and they usually stayed with the firm. But three years ago the industry leader, Standard Motor Products, Inc., started taking away Midwest's best reps. The national sales director could not understand why the reps were going to Standard Motor Products, because she thought Midwest's commission schedule for reps was very competitive.

She knew it was important to identify why their sales reps were leaving because the cost of hiring and training new reps is time-consuming and expensive. She recently ran into one of Midwest's former reps and asked him why he quit. He replied that Standard Motor Products had offered him a sales training class and an extensive sales support package. He said the sales training class was especially helpful because it provided useful information on generating new prospects and minimizing problems with current customers through greater service.

After talking with the former rep, the sales director from Midwest began exploring some training programs. She found that workplace training has consistently been shown to affect employee retention, especially when the training identifies ways that employees can use their new knowledge to advance their careers. In addition, employee surveys have shown that opportunities to develop personal attributes and career advancement are major reasons that employees remain in their current job.

The Standard Motor Products sales support package included the following information:

■ Industry sales by region and state
■ Industry sales by customer type
■ Industry sales by product line

The package also included general information about the target market by state (Table 2). To obtain a clearer view of the market by state, company analysts began computing the payroll per employee and the percentage of large (over 100 employee) plants (Table 3).

TABLE 2 Characteristics of Four-State Market Area

AREA	EMPLOYMENT	PAYROLL	TOTAL	>100 EMPLOYEES
Georgia	1,405	$31,850,000	15	5
Virginia	451	$7,292,000	9	2
North Carolina	547	$9,379,000	9	3
South Carolina	E	D	4	2
United States	50,577	$1,082,650,000	415	83

E = 1,000–2,499   D = Figures withheld based on company request.
SOURCE: County Business Patterns, U.S. Census Bureau.

TABLE 3 Payroll and Plant Size Analysis

AREA	PAYROLL PER EMPLOYEE	PERCENTAGE OF LARGE PLANTS
Georgia	$22,669	33%
Virginia	_____	_____
North Carolina	_____	_____
South Carolina	_____	_____
United States	_____	_____

QUESTIONS

1. Analyze the payroll per employee and plant size. Which state appears to have the best-paid employees (in this industry)? Which state appears to have the greatest concentration of large plants?

2. What can Midwest Auto Parts do to keep its reps from quitting and going to work for Standard Motor Products?

3. How could the sales rep use the information provided in the sales support package?

4. What else could be helpful to include in a sales support package?

5. What kinds of topics should be emphasized in a training program for a company like Midwest Auto Parts, which employs independent manufacturers' representatives?

Case prepared by Mary Collins, Strayer University.

LEARNING OBJECTIVES

When you finish this chapter, you should be able to:

1. Understand the dynamics of leadership.
2. Contrast supervision, management, and leadership.
3. Identify the sources of power that leaders possess.
4. Apply the classic theories of leadership to sales management.
5. Apply the major contemporary theories of leadership to sales management.
6. Communicate effectively with the sales force.
7. Overcome barriers to communication with the sales force.

INSIDE SALES MANAGEMENT

Jim Travis, Vice President of Sales, Green Mountain Coffee Roasters

Leadership is a very concrete notion for Jim Travis, vice president of sales for Vermont's Green Mountain Coffee Roasters, Inc. It's all about communication.

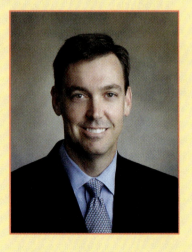

"Overcommunicate," says Travis, "and then overcommunicate again—that's my theory of leadership." Communicating is a big part of Travis's approach to leadership. In his view, if your people don't understand the top three things the organization is trying to accomplish—and if you can't convey them in about thirty seconds each—then they can't perform well, and getting your people to perform well is the goal of leading.

To improve communication with and among Green Mountain's 180 reps, Travis undertook some important changes when he arrived. First, he eliminated the weekly rep mail, a bulky FedEx or snail-mail package that had long been the company's main conduit for sales and product information. In its place he introduced a Web-based sales portal, complete with a personal dashboard for each rep that offers sales materials and real-time information about competitors as well as providing personal performance metrics. The portal also allows each rep to create a blog for sharing information across the sales team. Then Travis equipped the sales force with Blackberrys, to create accountability and ownership of sales data and to improve time management.

Next Travis brought on board a computerized system of sales cycle management training, so each rep would receive the same reinforcement of skills in prospecting, qualifying, building rapport, presenting, negotiating, and closing. Achieving consistency across the organization with the new training system helped sales managers know what to look for in their reps, and it got everyone "talking the same language, applying a common skill set," says Travis. Consistency is important to him because Green Mountain's sales force is split into two parts—one group that sells to local coffee shops, hotels, and office distributors around the country, and another that sells to big national merchandisers and grocery chains like Kroger, Publix, and Stop & Shop. Each group takes a different approach to its customers, and having common skills helps improve sales performance.

"Leadership is about increasing the reps' success," says Travis, "not mine. That's why I want everyone to be well equipped and well informed, with the tools they need to succeed. And I want them to help me challenge the system, so we can keep making sure that it's right for us."

Are leaders born or made? Travis thinks it's a little of both. "Charismatic leaders are probably born," he admits, "but a lot of management skills can be taught. How you're raised can be a big influence too," says the VP, who is also an Eagle Scout.

Travis sees three ways to achieve leadership—you can take it, you can earn it, or it can be given to you. In business, he feels, you have to earn it.

In the preceding chapters we've talked about organizing and developing the sales force. We now turn our attention to the activities that take center stage in managing and directing the sales force once we've carefully recruited, selected, and trained them. The first of these is leadership.

Some well-known researchers question whether leadership really has any observable effect on organizational effectiveness.[1] They argue that because it's so difficult to identify or even define what an effective leader is, we often work from rather romanticized ideas. Those who believe leaders do influence organizational success point to considerable evidence. For instance, behaviors central to the leadership concepts have been shown to have a big impact on organizational results.[2] The CEO of Miller Brewing Company (www.millerbrewing.com), Norman Adami, is a case in point. This charismatic and visionary leader was able to inspire a once-complacent workforce to higher performance in all functional areas of the firm, including sales. In the midst of a 15-year decline, he took over and led a dramatic turnaround of the besieged company, so that today it's nipping at the heels of Anheuser-Busch (www.anheuser-busch.com), the beverage industry leader.[3] Like other charismatic leaders—Jack Welch, former CEO of General Electric Company (www.ge.com), and Steven Jobs, CEO of Apple Computer, Inc. (www.apple.com)—Adami is an example attesting to the efficacy of leadership.

In this chapter we'll discuss relevant theories that suggest how appropriate leadership can influence the behaviors of salespeople and sales departments charged with the all-important revenue-generating task. We'll also show how the best of these theories can be applied.

Foundations of Leadership

The forces shaping business and sales management today are radically different from those of the past—they include greater diversity in the labor force, intensifying global competition, and rapid advances in technology. Globalization has brought about fiercely competitive markets in which it's increasingly difficult to remain profitable. Reengineering and downsizing have produced flatter, leaner organizations that require greater leadership at all organizational levels—not just in the executive suites.[4] Companies are placing a premium on recruiting managers with contemporary leadership potential and skills, because twenty-first century business and sales management practices are necessarily going to be significantly different from those in the past.[5]

Research on leadership theory and practice over the past three decades has been voluminous.[6] Some of the many ways to understand leadership include individual traits, behaviors, influence over people, interaction patterns, role relationships, occupation of an administrative position, and the perceptions of others regarding the legitimacy of influence.[7] Generally we can think of leadership as the process of motivating and enabling the task-related activities of team members[8] and the ability to influence them toward the achievement of goals.[9]

Leadership
The interpersonal process of communicating, inspiring, guiding, and influencing the behavior of subordinate salespeople toward attaining organizational objectives, goals, and values.

In the context of sales management, **leadership** refers to the interpersonal process of communicating, inspiring, guiding, and influencing the behavior of subordinate salespeople toward the attainment of organizational objectives, goals, and values.[10] Our definition also includes self-leadership and joint leadership by salespeople, who may influence their peers on formal and informal sales teams.[11]

There are six important elements in our formal definition of sales force leadership. First, leadership is *interpersonal* because it affects others (followers or subordinates), who should be willing to accept directions from the leader (sales manager or supervisor). Second, leadership relies on *influence*, which stems from various forms of power that we'll discuss in the chapter. This implies an unequal distribution of power in favor of the sales manager. Third, sales force leadership is the ability not only to set goals but also to guide, clarify, and chart the paths for salespeople toward goal achievement. Fourth, leaders inspire their subordinates (and sometimes their peers) to attain organizational goals. Fifth, leaders espouse ethical and moral values they expect their followers to subscribe to. Finally, as we'll discuss, leadership relies on communication to achieve goals.

Supervision, Management, and Leadership

Supervision
Tasks that deal with monitoring the daily work activities of sales subordinates.

Management
The administrative activities that include planning, organizing, staffing, directing, and controlling the operations of a firm toward attaining its goals and objectives.

Let's first distinguish between supervision, management, and leadership, which are widely considered to be overlapping functions. **Supervision is closely monitoring the daily work activities of sales subordinates.** All sales managers perform some supervisory duties, although direct supervision becomes less evident at higher levels in the sales management hierarchy. **Management**, in general, deals with administrative activities that include planning, organizing, staffing, directing, and controlling the operations of a firm toward the attainment of its goals and objectives. These efforts tend to be *primarily* focused on the non-people, policy, and decision-making functions of a firm.[12]

Although leadership and management are related, management is primarily a *learned* process of guiding subordinates in the performance of formally prescribed duties. In contrast, leadership is an *emotional* process of exercising psychological, social, and inspirational influence on the people employed by the firm. In short, it's the ability to get people to do willingly what they would not readily do on their own.[13]

Most viable organizations recognize that their people are the key to business success and that leadership and management go hand in hand. A sales manager can be an effective planner and administrator, but not possess leadership skills. Conversely, an effective leader can inspire and engender enthusiasm, but not have the requisite managerial skills. Any organization is unlikely to succeed unless it can effectively both lead *and* manage its work force.[14] It's not surprising, therefore, that today's firms are seeking sales managers who exhibit flexible leadership capabilities and skills, because the twenty-first century business and sales management environment is vastly different from the past.[15] A sales organization is a reflection of its leader. Shortcomings in sales force performance can usually be traced to inadequacy in sales management, while superior performance is generally the result of outstanding leadership by sales managers.

Leadership and Power

[handwritten: Influence inherent in the individual...]

Power

The potential capacity to influence the behavior of subordinates.

[handwritten: influence organized from his location in the org]

Central to understanding how leaders wield influence over their subordinates is the concept of power. **Power** is the potential to influence the behavior of subordinates.[16] To influence subordinates, sales managers typically can draw upon five bases or sources of power, as shown in Figure 10.1: legitimate, reward, coercive, referent, and expert.[17] The first three stem from a leader's position and are forms of position power, while the last two are forms of personal power.

[handwritten: Lee Iacocca – Chrysler dude.]

SALES MANAGER POWER

Legitimate Power	Reward Power	Coercive Power	Referent Power	Expert Power
Derived from the position occupied on the organizational structure; the sales manager has formally delegated authority to seek salesperson compliance.	The ability of the sales manager to provide subordinate salespeople with various benefits, including money, praise, or promotion and incentives such as commissions and bonuses. *[handwritten: Benefits "carrot"]*	The ability of the sales manager to obtain salesperson compliance through fear of punishment, sanctions, or by withholding rewards (includes being fired from the job). *[handwritten: Punishments "stick"]*	The ability of sales managers to influence sales force compliance based on inspiration, charisma, loyalty, and personal identification with the leader.	Subordinate compliance that is based upon the sales manager's skills, knowledge, intelligence, job-related information, and expertise.

POSITION POWER | PERSONAL POWER

FIGURE 10.1 Sources of Sales Manager Power and Influence on the Sales Force

■ Position Power Sources

Legitimate Power
Derived from the position occupied in the organizational structure, the leader has formally delegated authority to seek subordinate compliance.

Let's look at the three forms of position power available to most sales managers. **Legitimate power** is derived from the sales manager's position in the firm's hierarchical structure as well as the level of responsibility he or she is formally given. Often referred to as *authority,* legitimate power allows managers to govern sales department activities integral to achieving sales goals and objectives.

Reward Power
The leader's ability to provide subordinates with various benefits, including money, praise, or promotion.

Reward power is the ability to provide salespeople with various benefits—salary, raises, commissions, bonuses, monetary incentives, promotions, interesting job assignments, preferred work schedules, sales territories, and clients—based on performance assessment. Reward power also includes important compensation issues, which we discuss in greater detail in chapter 12.

Coercive Power
The leader's ability to obtain subordinate compliance through fear of punishment, or sanctions, or by withholding rewards including being fired from the job.

Coercive power comes from the ability to withhold rewards or punish (even up to firing) and is primarily aimed at behavior modification through fear of sanctions. Most sales managers have access to all these position power sources and can use them in appropriate situations to influence the behavior of salespeople.

■ Personal Power Sources

Referent Power
The leader's ability to influence subordinate compliance based on inspiration, charisma, loyalty, and personal identification with the leader.

Referent and expert power bases are derived from personal characteristics of the sales manager. **Referent power** actually resides with salespeople, who identify with and admire the sales manager because of his or her personal traits and charisma to such an extent that they're willing to change their behavior to resemble or be compatible with that of their leader. Superstar salespeople who perform at much higher levels than most salespeople do also have referent power. Ben Feldman, whom many call the greatest salesperson who ever lived, epitomized referent power for his New York Life Insurance (www.newyorklife.com) colleagues.[18]

Expert Power
Subordinate compliance based on the leader's skills, knowledge, intelligence, job-related information, and expertise.

Finally, **expert power** is based on the sales manager's skills, knowledge, and special abilities that enable his or her work to exhibit the highest level of expertise. For example, sales managers who are highly educated and adept at technologically complex tasks, such as using sophisticated statistical sales forecasting or territory routing software, possess expert power.

■ Sales Management Implications

The major behaviors that sales managers can influence are salesperson commitment, compliance, and resistance.[19] When salespeople make a maximum effort and enthusiastically comply with the sales manager's directions, they manifest a sense of *commitment* to accomplishing sales objectives. With *compliance,* salespersons are not as enthusiastic but still may go along. *Resistance* is the most undesirable of the three behaviors, which occurs when salespeople reject the sales manager's plans or even delay, pretend to comply with, or sabotage them. Table 10.1 presents the likelihood of eliciting each type of behavior by using the various sources of power. Sales managers who exercise expert and referent power are likely to achieve higher commitment, while those using legitimate and reward power are likely to get compliance. Sales managers displaying coercive power usually meet with resistance from salespersons, who may also experience a sense of disconnect or alienation from the job—to the detriment of their performance.

The use of expert and referent power has been associated with increased sales force performance.[20] These two types of non-coercive power tend to increase sales force

TABLE 10.1 Effects of Sales Manager Power on Salesperson Behaviors

	Power Source	Commitment	Compliance	Resistance	Motivation/ Job Effort	Job Satisfaction	Job Performance
Position Power	1. Legitimate	High	High	Medium	Medium	Medium	Medium
	2. Reward	High	High	Medium	High	High	High
	3. Coercive	Low	Medium	High	Low	Low	Low
Personal Power	4. Referent	High	Medium	Medium	High	High	High
	5. Expert	High	Medium	Medium	High	High	High

(table header spanning: LIKELIHOOD/LEVEL OF IMPACT ON:)

motivation as well. If salespeople are highly motivated by monetary rewards, a sales manager may also exercise reward power to augment performance.

Good sales managers are likely to utilize all five sources of power at one time or another. The key is to know the appropriate source of power to use for each salesperson and in each situation.

Applying Classical Leadership Theories to Twenty-First Century Sales Management

Researchers' efforts to understand how leaders influence subordinates led to the development of three broad classical schools of thought about leadership: (a) the trait approach, (b) the behavioral approach, and (c) the contingency or situational approach. We'll look at those that are germane to sales force management.

Trait Theory

The earliest leadership research—often referred to as the *Great Man* perspective—concluded that great leaders are born, not made. It focused on identifying the personal traits that characterize these people,[21] such as confidence, honesty, integrity, ambition, creativity, job-relevant knowledge, initiative, intelligence, extraversion, and drive. Later, researchers thought leadership traits were not completely inborn but could be developed through experience and learning. However, many good leaders did not possess the expected traits, and possession of the traits failed to reliably predict leadership success.

Trait theory has been widely criticized because few studies examined the same traits, and because it doesn't take into account the situational context of leadership. Stogdill completed a comprehensive review of over 100 trait theory studies, and found that only 5 percent of the traits appeared in four or more studies.[22] Moreover, there was a "chicken and egg" problem. For example, was George Washington a leader because he was self-confident, or was he self-confident because leadership responsibilities

Trait Theory
Leadership theory that focuses on identifying the qualities or personal traits of effective leaders.

were thrust upon him at a young age? Other weaknesses of trait theory were that it seldom distinguished which traits are most or least important.[23]

Sales Management Implications. Although no consistent list of sales force leader characteristics has been uncovered, many observers believe that certain qualities are needed to become an effective sales *manager*. For example, some hold that an effective sales force leader must work hard and be people oriented. Others feel he or she must have the innate ability to take risks and be a decision maker. Table 10.2 presents one perspective on the traits of a successful sales force leader.

Behavioral Styles Theory

Because of the weaknesses associated with trait theory, many leadership studies have focused on identifying patterns of **leader behavior**, or "leadership style," shifting from

Leader Behavior
The leader's manner and approach in providing direction, implementing plans, and motivating people.

TABLE 10.2   Twelve Traits of Highly Effective Sales Force Leaders
1. **Courageous.** They set courageous examples for their salespeople to follow. An example is not giving up in the face of intense competition and demanding work to win a challenging account. As General George Patton once said, "Courage is fear holding on another minute."
2. **Visionary thinkers.** They see things in a larger perspective than ordinary sales managers do. They help salespeople expand their thinking and vision to appreciate the value in developing relationships with high potential prospects that may not pay off in substantial company profits and salesperson earnings until sometime in the future.
3. **Change masters.** They can create change, motivate their salespeople to accept it, and move them in directions beneficial to all.
4. **Ethical.** They are fair and just, dedicated and conscientious in their work and relationships, and they expect the same from others.
5. **Persistent and realistic.** They set realistic goals, effectively communicate them, and maintain their commitment to them until they are accomplished.
6. **Show a sense of humor.** They exhibit a lighthearted, upbeat sense of humor that can turn difficult or routine tasks into enjoyable experiences for the sales team. They do not take themselves too seriously and tend to express their feelings in spontaneous, optimistic, and positive ways even when things are not going well.
7. **Risk takers.** They take the initiative, are independent and resourceful, and are willing to risk failure in order to succeed which, in turn, encourages their salespeople to take risks to succeed.
8. **Positive and Optimistic.** They see good even in a bad situation and have faith when others do not. They tend to be optimistic and elicit that attitude from others.
9. **Moral but not judgmental.** They value the power of truth yet are not judgmental about others in their morality.
10. **Decision oriented.** They know that not deciding is a decision, and that indecision wastes time, energy, money, and opportunity.
11. **Use power wisely.** They know that power can intimidate others, so they use it judiciously to help others achieve their full potential.
12. **Steadfast.** They continually demonstrate their commitment to their goals, their salespeople, and their company.

who the leader *is* to what the leader *does*. Some leadership behaviors were found to be more effective than others.

Consideration

Sometimes called the "human relations" approach, this dimension of behavioral styles theory seeks to engender friendship, mutual trust, respect, and support of subordinates.

Initiating Structure

Sometimes called "task orientation," this dimension of behavioral styles theory reflects the extent to which leaders organize, clearly define, and clarify the tasks subordinates need to perform in attaining firm goals.

Leadership Styles

Different patterns of leader behavior, or "styles" employed to secure subordinate compliance toward achieving organizational goals.

Ohio State University and University of Michigan Studies. Studies conducted at Ohio State University identified two composite dimensions of leader behavior: **consideration** (friendship, mutual trust, respect, support, and warmth)—sometimes called the "human relations" approach—and **initiating structure** (the extent to which leaders organize, clearly define, and clarify the tasks subordinates must perform)—sometimes called a "task orientation."[24] Although "high consideration, high initiating structure" tended to yield high employee satisfaction and performance, no single leader behavior surfaced as best for all situations. Moreover, few managers can be both task and human relations oriented.

Meanwhile, studies conducted at the University of Michigan also sought to identify those behavioral characteristics of effective leaders that were associated with building effective work teams and subordinate performance.[25] In these studies, the two dimensions of **leadership styles** identified were *employee oriented* and *production (or task) oriented*, which are very similar to leader consideration and initiating structure facets, respectively. Employee-focused leaders set high performance goals and were supportive toward subordinates. Production-centered leaders displayed less concern with people needs and were oriented toward maintaining schedules, reducing costs, making production efficient, and completing tasks; to them, people were a means to an end. The results revealed that job-centered leadership styles were associated with lower productivity and job satisfaction, while employee-oriented leadership styles led to higher work performance and job satisfaction.

Sales Management Implications. Although a review found few studies that substantiated a significant relationship between the two dimensions of leader behavior and productivity,[26] the behavioral styles approach is appealing because of the widespread belief that people can learn and apply specific leader styles. Taken together, the Ohio State and University of Michigan studies suggest four leadership styles that may be effective for sales managers in varying situations; see Table 10.3.

As shown in Quadrant 1 of the table, a *highly considerate/employee-oriented and low structured/production-oriented leadership style* is appropriate if the sales force consists of highly motivated individuals who are dedicated to the task at hand but require social support from superiors. This leadership style may be effective in influencing and managing experienced, high-performing salespeople who tend to compete with one another.

A *highly considerate/employee oriented and highly structured/production oriented leadership style* (Quadrant 2) is appropriate if the sales force requires social support from superiors, is not cohesive, and lacks a strong identity with the task at hand. This leadership is especially conducive when sales managers need to influence newly hired, inexperienced sales trainees.

When the sales force consists of highly motivated and experienced individuals who are socially mature and doing work they know and enjoy, a *low considerate/employee oriented and low structure/production oriented leadership style* (Quadrant 3) is germane.

As indicated in Quadrant 4, a *low considerate/employee oriented and high structure/production oriented leadership style* is appropriate if the sales force consists of individuals who are socially mature and highly cohesive, but who do not understand or identify with the task at hand, such as learning new technological skills that will augment their selling efforts.

TABLE 10.3 Dimensions of Behavioral Style: Directions for Leadership in Sales Management

INITIATING STRUCTURE/PRODUCTION (TASK) ORIENTATION

	Low	High
High (CONSIDERATION/EMPLOYEE ORIENTATION)	**Quadrant 1: High consideration/employee orientation and Low structure/production orientation** Leader focuses on achieving team harmony and individual need satisfaction. Less emphasis is placed on subordinate tasks. **Sales Management Implications:** Appropriate to use when experienced, high-performing salespeople tend to be too competitive with one another.	**Quadrant 2: High consideration/employee orientation and High structure/production orientation** Leadership strives to accomplish the job while maintaining a harmonious work team. Leader provides guidance on how tasks should be completed and is considerate of subordinate needs. **Sales Management Implications:** Appropriate in situations with newly hired, inexperienced sales trainees.
Low	**Quadrant 3: Low consideration/employee orientation and Low structure/production orientation** Largely passive, the leader does not provide structure and exhibits little consideration for subordinate needs allowing work and people to be self-managed. **Sales Management Implications:** Appropriate in situations with experienced, high-performing salespeople that know their tasks and enjoy work.	**Quadrant 4: Low consideration and High structure/production orientation** Leader focuses on getting the job done by structuring tasks, but exhibits little consideration for subordinate needs. **Sales Management Implications:** Appropriate in situations where experienced salespeople are required to do unpleasant, unfamiliar work.

SOURCE: Based on Ohio State Leadership Studies, "Dimensions of Leadership Style," in Edwin A. Fleishman and James G. Hunt (eds.), *Current Developments in the Study of Leadership,* Southern Illinois University Press, Carbondale, Ill., 1973. Reprinted by permission of Southern Illinois University Press; and R. Likert, "From Production-and Employee Centeredness to Systems 1-4," *Journal of Management,* 5 (1979), pp. 147–156.

Contingency Theories of Leadership

The inability to consistently explain the relationships between leadership and organizational effectiveness, and the assumption that high levels of leadership skill produce optimal results in *all* situations, are major drawbacks of the behavioral styles theory. These deficiencies gave rise to the third prominent line of thought: the contingency perspective.

Contingency theories generally suggest that an effective leadership style is largely predicated or contingent upon different situations.[27] While trait and behavioral leadership theories focus primarily on the leader, the contingency leadership approaches emphasize the interaction factors among the leader, followers, and situation-specific conditions. Interactions among the following factors have been identified as determinants of effective leadership: (1) the leader's personality and experience; (2) the expectations and behavior of superiors; (3) the characteristics, expectations, and behavior of subordinates; and (4) the behavior and expectations of peers. Implicit in this contingency perspective is the notion that leaders should be capable of adapting their leadership styles to match situational factors.

There are several contingency approaches, but we'll examine those specifically relevant to sales management: Fiedler's contingency theory of leadership, the path-goal theory of leadership, theory H, leader-member exchange model, and substitutes for leadership.

Fiedler's Contingency Theory. In developing the first comprehensive and perhaps most thoroughly researched contingency paradigm of leadership, Fred Fiedler incor-

Contingency Theory
A collection of leadership theories which suggests that an effective leadership style is largely contingent upon the interactions among the leader, followers, and situation-specific conditions.

porated leadership styles and the nature of the leadership situation.[28] Fiedler's research indicated that a leader's performance depends on two interrelated factors: (1) the degree to which the situation gives the leader control and influence and (2) the leader's basic motivation—whether toward accomplishing the task or toward having close, supportive relations with others. Leaders are motivated either by tasks or relationships, somewhat equivalent to *initiating structure* and *consideration* from the Ohio State and University of Michigan studies discussed earlier. Specifically, Fiedler tried to discover which leaders are most likely to develop high-producing teams: leaders who are very lenient or those who are highly demanding and discriminating in evaluating subordinates. His results indicate that the most effective type of leadership depends upon three situational variables:

1. *Leader-member relations*—Exerting the most important impact on the leader's power and effectiveness are his or her personal relationships with team members. Specifically, if subordinates respect, like, accept and trust the leader, leader-member relations are considered *good;* when leaders are disliked or not respected, relations are considered *poor.*

2. *Task structure*—The second most important factor in Fiedler's model is the degree to which the team's task is structured or clearly described with specific procedures to attain explicitly identifiable goals. The situation is considered *high* in structure when the task structure is well defined, *low* when tasks are ambiguous.

3. *Position power*—The third factor is the extent to which the leader can access coercive, legitimate, expert, referent, and reward power to influence subordinates. A leader with no authority to evaluate, control, and reward is considered ineffective and possesses *weak* position power. Position power is *strong* when the leader can use the power bases to effectively induce subordinates to attain desirable goals.

Situations high on all three components are considered highly favorable (see Figure 10.2) because (1) leaders can usually expect support from team members; (2) leaders can enforce their will with the legitimate power or formal authority of their positions; and (3) all members of the organization can more clearly define, delegate, control, and evaluate structured tasks.

Fiedler reported that a discriminating, task-oriented leader attitude is effective in *either* highly favorable or highly unfavorable situations. But when the situation is moderately favorable or moderately unfavorable, a more lenient and considerate leader attitude is best for higher team performance—as illustrated in the figure. When relationships with team members are moderately poor, position power is low, and a highly structured task is at hand, the leader should be permissive and accepting in behavior and attitude.

Fiedler's contingency model of leadership effectiveness suggests that we can improve team performance by modifying either the leader's style or the team's task and situation. However, he believes that most organizations cannot afford expensive selection techniques to find talented leaders who fit specific job requirements.[29] Nor does training provide adequate answers to the problems of leadership.[30] The most reasonable approach is to tailor the job to fit the leader. Since the type of leadership called for depends on the favorableness of the situation, the organization can more easily alter the job than transfer managers or train them in different styles of interaction with team members. Such factors as the power associated with the leader's

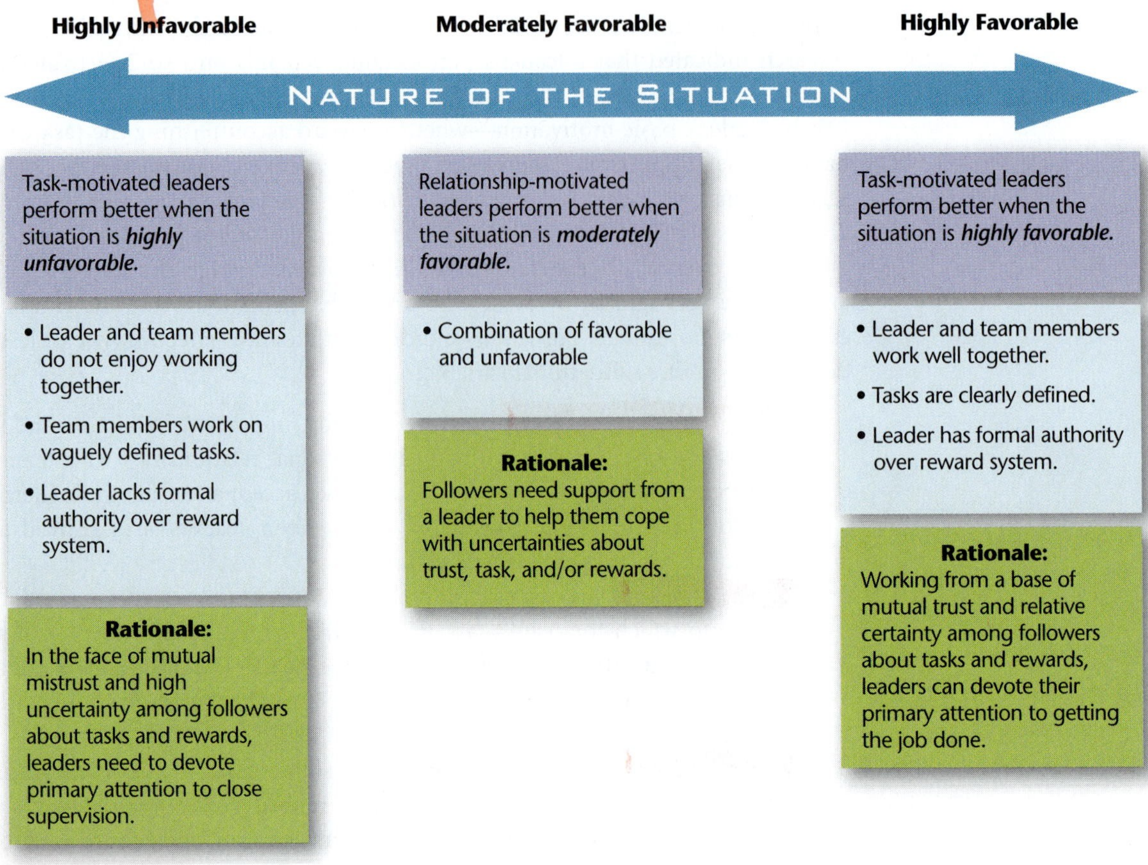

Highly Unfavorable   **Moderately Favorable**   **Highly Favorable**

NATURE OF THE SITUATION

Task-motivated leaders perform better when the situation is *highly unfavorable.*

- Leader and team members do not enjoy working together.
- Team members work on vaguely defined tasks.
- Leader lacks formal authority over reward system.

Rationale:
In the face of mutual mistrust and high uncertainty among followers about tasks and rewards, leaders need to devote primary attention to close supervision.

Relationship-motivated leaders perform better when the situation is *moderately favorable.*

- Combination of favorable and unfavorable

Rationale:
Followers need support from a leader to help them cope with uncertainties about trust, task, and/or rewards.

Task-motivated leaders perform better when the situation is *highly favorable.*

- Leader and team members work well together.
- Tasks are clearly defined.
- Leader has formal authority over reward system.

Rationale:
Working from a base of mutual trust and relative certainty among followers about tasks and rewards, leaders can devote their primary attention to getting the job done.

FIGURE 10.2 Fieldler's Contingency Theory of Leadership

SOURCE: Kreitner, Robert, *Management,* 10/e, p. 452. Copyright © 2007 by Houghton Mifflin Company. Reprinted with permission.

position, the task assigned to the team, or the composition of the team's membership can be changed.[31]

Sales Management Implications. According to Fiedler's contingency theory, both relationship-oriented and task-oriented sales managers can perform better under some situations than others. For example, a high-performing salesperson who is promoted to sales manager may fail because having a task-oriented leadership style may not match the demands of the situation. A sales manager's tasks tend to be complex and non-routine, such as motivating an older sales representative or building confidence in younger salespeople. Thus, to be an effective leader, the newly appointed sales manager will need to switch from a task-oriented to a personal, more relationship-centered style.

Path-Goal Theory
A contingency leadership theory in which the tasks (paths) to be performed and the results (goals) to be achieved by subordinates are clearly defined by the leader, who makes desirable rewards contingent upon accomplishment of organizational goals.

The Path-Goal Theory of Leadership. Path-goal theory extracts and extends the key elements of *leader consideration* and *initiating structure* around which behavioral styles theory is centered.[32] It also draws heavily on the *expectancy theory of motivation,*[33] which views motivation as a function of the degree to which increased effort will enable an individual to attain a valued outcome or reward.

The path-goal theory proposes that the leader can affect the level of satisfaction, motivation, and performance of team members by using appropriate leadership styles in several ways. The first is by making rewards contingent upon the accomplishment of organizational goals and objectives. Second, the leader can aid team members by clarifying their paths to those goals by removing obstacles to performance and by ensuring their goals are compatible with the overall objectives of the organization. And third, the leader can increase the support and rewards valued by team members by determining which rewards are important and increasing these rewards consistent with their needs and wants.[34] Therefore, a leader's behavior is effective when team members view it as an immediate or future source of satisfaction.

According to the original formulation of path-goal theory, leadership styles were codified into four dimensions (see items 1–4, below).[35] However, in a more recent reformulation of path-goal theory, four additional behavioral facets were added by House (see items 5–8).[36] These eight central behaviors, which together form the latest version of path-goal theory, include

1. *Participative leadership styles*—The leader consults with team members about work, task goals, and the paths to goals, and uses members' suggestions before making a decision. Thus, team members are able to influence decisions about their jobs.

2. *Supportive leadership styles*—The leader displays personal concern and is supportive, friendly, and sensitive to the needs of team members. This leadership style parallels *leader consideration*, the first dimension of the behavioral styles theory of leadership.

3. *Directive leadership styles*—The leader explains what the performance goal is, provides guidance and feedback, removes roadblocks, specifies rules, regulations, and procedures to be followed in accomplishing the task, schedules and coordinates work, and explains what is expected of team members. This leadership style is analogous to *initiating structure*, the second dimension of the behavioral styles theory of leadership.

4. *Achievement-oriented leadership styles*—The leader emphasizes the achievement of challenging tasks, and the importance of excellent performance, and simultaneously shows confidence that team members will perform well.

5. *Path-goal clarifying leadership styles*—The leader defines the tasks (paths), and clearly identifies the results (goals) for which subordinates are held responsible. Further, the leader clarifies that organizational goals are tied to rewards important to the needs and wants of followers.

6. *Interaction facilitation leadership styles*—The leader proactively attempts to resolve and mediate conflicts, while encouraging subordinates to coalesce, collaborate, and work as a team.

7. *Networking leadership styles*—The leader acts as a representative of the team and safeguards the team's interests when interacting with influential high-level managers.

8. *Value-based leadership styles*—The leader formulates and articulates a vision while passionately advocating support for it from followers.

While a leader can display *any or all* of these leadership styles concurrently, there are two classes of situations or contingency variables that moderate the leadership behavior-outcome relationship.[37] The first is identified as the environmental pressures and demands of the workplace, such as the task structure (the extent to which tasks are defined and have explicitly developed work procedures), the formal authority system (the amount of legitimate power employed by leaders, the extent to which policies and rules are formalized to regulate the behaviors of subordinates), and the educational level of subordinates and their relationships in the work team.[38] The second variable, subordinate contingencies, includes personal characteristics of subordinates such as experience, perceived ability, skills, and needs.

Sales Management Implications. We need to make three assumptions in order to effectively apply the path-goal theory to the sales management setting. The first is that the sales force is made up of salespeople with independent as well as collective goals. The second is that the sales manager, by virtue of seniority, has access to economic, social, and psychological bases of power. Finally, we assume that individual salespeople and sales managers interact to coordinate accomplishment of sales tasks and activities.[39] Under different conditions, sales managers should be able to use the appropriate leadership styles—shown in Figure 10.3—to motivate greater sales force effort toward achieving organizational and personal goals including sales revenues, salesperson productivity, and job satisfaction.

For example, sales managers can employ a participative leadership style by eliciting suggestions and consulting with salespersons in decision making, devising policies, and crafting sales strategies. This approach can be effective in increasing salesperson commitment, productivity, and performance. Sales managers can also employ participative leadership approaches for cultivating long-term customer relationships and even forging sales alliances with their competitors (discussed in chapter 3). Sun

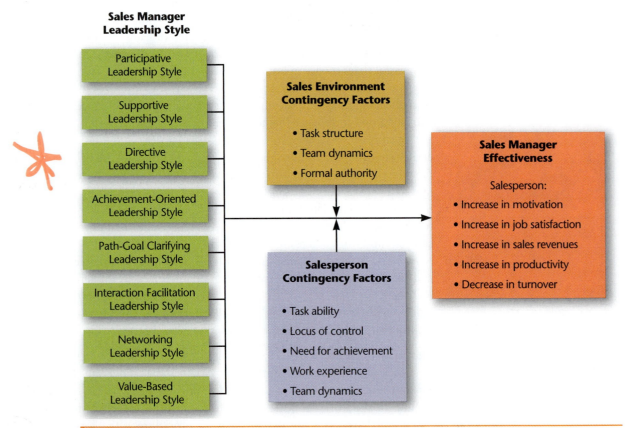

FIGURE 10.3   Extending the Path-Goal Theory of Leadership to Sales Management

● Peruse the website of 1000Ventures.com to learn cutting-edge participative management approaches for making joint decisions and to understand how participative management can help develop strategic partnerships with customers.

Microsystems (www.sun.com), a high-tech manufacturer of server hardware, workstations, and storage devices, has taken this strategy to a higher level by developing strategic partnerships with its competitors. Although the professional services division provides implementation expertise for its products, Sun does not try to develop computer solutions for customers by itself. Instead, Sun salespeople partner with software vendors and system integrators; then, as a team, they provide complete technology solutions for their customers by using participative management processes to make joint decisions. Rarely assuming the role of a "prime contractor," Sun opts to cooperate with its partners for mutual gain.[40] To augment your understanding of this cutting-edge approach, visit websites such as www.1000ventures .com/business_guide/mbs_mini_spartnerships.html, where you'll find articles, case studies, and slide shows on how participative management styles can be used for developing strategic partnerships.

Theory H. Effective leaders match their style—from task oriented to human relations oriented—to the maturity and duties of the sales force. Experienced salespeople who operate largely independently may resent a sales manager who exercises tight supervision and control over their activities. One way of visualizing possible leadership styles is to diagram them as an automobile gearshift or the capital letter *H*, as shown in Figure 10.4.[41] A sales manager may need to shift among these styles as the sales force composition and responsibilities change. Xerox's Information Systems Group (www.xerox.com), which is responsible for copier and duplicator products, became one of the first companies to teach "situational leadership" to its middle-level and new first-level managers.[42]

Continuing the analogy of the gearshift, a sales manager exercises strong pulling power in first (autocratic) and second (paternalistic) gear, with the sales force largely dependent on the sales manager for rewards and punishments. In neutral (consultative), the sales manager exerts little push or pull and allows the salespeople to

1 Autocratic		3 Democratic
	5 Consultative (neutral)	
2 Paternalistic		4 Laissez-faire

FIGURE 10.4 Leadership Styles Based on Theory H

influence management decisions. In third (democratic) and fourth (laissez faire) gear, the sales manager functions in a largely passive manner as salespeople operate quite independently. The real task of the successful sales manager is to select the style of leadership most appropriate for the individual salesperson, for the sales force as a whole, and for the particular sales situation.

No one leadership style fits all situations, and research indicates that about three-fourths of sales managers use two or more different styles to handle various members of the sales force. Effective leadership seems to call for flexibility and modification of style to match the changing sales situations. However, the sales manager must take care to be fairly consistent in handling each salesperson and team. Studies have indicated that the lowest morale usually results when a sales manager's style vacillates between an authoritarian approach at one time and a permissive approach at another. Table 10.4 presents capsule views of the five leadership styles.

Leader-Member Exchange Theory. An interesting and intuitively appealing theory, leader-member exchange was an outgrowth of the incorrect assumption that leaders

Leader-Member Exchange Theory
A contingency leadership theory in which the subordinates a leader favors are given preferential treatment and assigned to an "in-group," whereas less desirable subalterns are placed in "out-groups."

TABLE 10.4 Extending Leadership Styles Based on Theory H to Sales Management

LEADERSHIP STYLE CHARACTERISTICS

Authoritarian	Paternalistic	Consultative	Democratic	Laissez Faire
■ Tight control and rigid authority ■ Clearly defined tasks ■ Downward communication from sales manager	■ "Kindly father knows best" ■ Authority is centralized with sales manager	■ Two-way communication with sales force ■ Right to make final decision retained by sales manager	■ Much authority delegated, but sales manager retains the right to determine team consensus ■ Participatory decision making and division of work	■ Leader responsibility abdicated and authority given to sales force ■ Primarily horizontal communication between sales force peers

APPROPRIATE SITUATION FOR LEADERSHIP STYLE

Authoritarian	Paternalistic	Consultative	Democratic	Laissez Faire
■ New or inexperienced salespeople ■ Disciplinary action needed ■ Emergencies ■ Complacent sales force	■ Weak sales supervisors ■ Immature or inexperienced salespeople ■ Informal sales force leaders expressing discontent	■ Well-trained, experienced sales force ■ Sales force works well as a team	■ Small, well-informed sales force ■ Cooperative salespeople ■ Lots of time to make decisions	■ Salespeople have expert knowledge ■ Nature of work guides salespeople

INAPPROPRIATE SITUATION FOR LEADERSHIP STYLE

Authoritarian	Paternalistic	Consultative	Democratic	Laissez Faire
■ Mature, experienced salespeople ■ Teamwork and cooperation needed	■ Mature, independent salespeople ■ Strong, competent sales force	■ Inexperienced, poorly trained sales force ■ Sales force does not work well as a team	■ Larger teams of salespeople ■ Decisions must be made quickly ■ Salespeople are not sufficiently informed	■ Salespeople are reluctant to make decisions ■ Nature of work is similar

treat all their subordinates uniformly. Specifically, *not* all employees have similar relationships with their managers. Those whom a manager favors, consults, mentors, praises, trusts, and gives preferential treatment to belong to an "in-group" that researchers call "cadres." In reciprocal exchange, each in-group subordinate makes greater efforts to increase performance, and exhibits greater respect and loyalty to the manager. Those assigned to an "out-group," however, are dispensed less attention and privileges; researchers have labeled them "hired hands." Thus, the group an individual is assigned to will affect his or her short- and long-term opportunities within the firm.

Sales Management Implications. Salespersons who a sales manager regards as being very high on (a) abilities, (b) motivation to assume additional responsibility, and (c) trustworthiness are considered members of the in-group.[43] These salespersons have a high-quality relationship with their sales manager and receive considerable latitude, support, and attention. In return, they are expected to perform duties that go well beyond written job descriptions (e.g., service the sales manager's key accounts, collect overdue accounts, train inexperienced sales personnel). Salespeople whom the sales manager considers to be relatively low on the preceding three qualities belong to the out-group and thus have a formal, lower-quality, and less supporting relationship with their sales leader. The out-group salespersons—the hired hands—perform tasks defined in their job description and nothing more. Of course, sales managers do not expect nearly as much from them as they do from in-group salespersons. Further, those salespersons a sales manager considers to be desirable task members and social partners receive more favorable performance reviews and more interesting assignments than do their counterparts who are regarded as less desirable.[44] Another interesting finding is that sales managers have less favorable reactions to hired hands who perform ineffectively than to cadres who perform ineffectively.[45] While being in the in-group is desirable to most salespeople, not all have the skills to be in that sales force category. Also, a few inflexible sales managers may make early subjective assessments of their different salesperson subordinates that are difficult to overcome even if the outgroup salesperson's objective performance improves significantly.

Research has sought to determine whether certain factors differentiate cadres from hired hands. Findings to date reveal that cadres tend to have been with their managers longer and are more trusting and less suspicious of their managers than are hired hands.[46] Additionally, cadres, compared with hired hands, have been found to exhibit higher job satisfaction,[47] less role stress,[48] and higher performance.[49] Salespeople can attempt to cultivate a relationship with their sales manager that will lead to their becoming cadres.[50] Similarly, sales managers may seek to do the same with their superiors. Whether an individual has the ability or the aspiration to be a cadre, of course, is another issue. Some salespeople, as well as managers, may opt to be hired hands so as not to go beyond their "comfort zone" of industriousness. Although they may have the capacity to assume responsibilities going well beyond their job description, they may simply be satisfied with their current job situation.

The overall implications are that sales managers should focus on developing salesperson skills and enhancing salesperson motivation while displaying leadership behaviors that enable them to be perceived as trustworthy. These behaviors are instrumental in developing a close working relationship with their salespeople, who in turn will focus on performing tasks that will help them join the favorable in-group category.

Substitutes for Leadership Theory. The substitutes for leadership theory was developed because existing theories didn't account for situations in which leadership is neutralized or replaced by characteristics of the subordinates, the task, and the organization.[51] First, subordinate characteristics such as experience, need for independence, and professional orientation may serve to neutralize leadership behavior. For example, productive employees with a high level of professionalism may not need guidance on tasks. Second, challenging or intrinsically satisfying characteristics of the task itself may substitute for leadership. Finally, leadership may not be needed when company policies and practices are formal and inflexible. Preliminary research has provided support for the substitutes for leadership perspective.[52]

Sales Management Implications. The concept of substitutes for leadership is highly applicable to personal selling. In some situations, sales managers can be better leaders if they know when *not* to lead, choosing the management-by-exception approach instead. Further, the solitary nature of many sales jobs can mean that the salesperson and the sales manager will be physically separated and have little interaction. Thus sales organizations often employ their own "leadership substitutes"—mechanisms for providing salespersons with the needed guidance and support as they work alone. Here are some of the more popular substitutes:

- *Ability, experience, training, and knowledge*—Salespeople with the necessary training and preparation to perform the job in the field have less need to rely on the sales manager for job-related information or guidance.

- *Professional orientation*—Salespeople seek guidance and feedback from sales peers within the same sales team (or department) or from those outside the firm—non-competing sales representatives, or those in professional organizations like Sales and Marketing Executives International and the American Marketing Association.

- *Task-provided feedback*—The job description, goals, and other parameters can indicate to the salesperson the level of his or her job performance. For example, percent of quota achieved to date, closing of a sale, loss of a sale, and customer complaints are accurate and immediate sources of performance-related information.

- *Organizational formalization and inflexibility*—The sales organization might choose to articulate explicit plans, goals, areas of responsibility, guidelines, and ground rules and employ them in a relatively rigid way. Such structure provides impersonal, yet formalized, direction.

- *Advisory staff*—Salespeople and sales managers are supported by an array of production, advertising, marketing research, pricing, and other support staff. They thereby receive ad hoc, but ongoing, assistance as necessary.

- *Closely knit work group*—The sales organization fosters strong esprit de corps among the sales team to provide emotional support, encouragement, and friendship.

- *Compensation plans, quotas, and expense accounts*—These tools direct the salespeople toward the appropriate job behavior, providing guidance about what they should be doing on the job and how to execute their job tasks.

- *Customers and competitors*—Direct customer feedback can tell salespeople about the adequacy of their job performance, in the form of either praise or failure to make a purchase. Indirect feedback can also come in the form of complaints to the salesperson's sales manager. Competitors' actions, such as raising or lowering market prices or offering favorable terms to a particular customer, can suggest what the salesperson should do in his or her territory to be successful.

Applying Contemporary Leadership Theories to Twenty-First Century Sales Management

So, now that you're familiar with the classical theories of leadership, you're probably wondering what it will take to be a successful sales force leader in the twenty-first century? It's a fair question! The answer may well lie in the emerging schools of thought that include (a) transformational leadership, (b) Pygmalion leadership, and (c) empowerment.

■ Transformational (or Charismatic and Visionary) Leadership

Transactional Leadership
Transactional leaders identify and clarify for subordinates their job tasks and communicate to them how successfully executing those tasks will lead to job rewards.

The classic theories we've looked at so far all examine **transactional leadership** applications. In the context of sales management, transactional sales managers identify and clarify job tasks for salespeople and communicate to them how successfully executing those tasks will lead to desirable job rewards.[53] Today, however, interest is surging in *transformational* or *charismatic* leaders.[54]

Transactional leaders recognize the immediate needs of their employees and communicate to them how those needs will be met through effective performance. As transactional leaders, they determine and define the goals and work that subordinates need to achieve, suggest how to execute their tasks, and provide feedback. The goals the salesperson should achieve usually have a short-term focus, can be based on effort and/or results, may or may not be quantifiable, and will depend on the sales subordinate's position and function within the sales organization.

Goals for the salesperson often include sales volume in dollars or units, new account acquisition, customer retention rate, percent of quota achieved, willingness to assist new sales recruits, and knowledge of competition. The sales manager can reward successful performance with increased commissions, bonuses, salary increases, promotions to higher-level positions, recognition, trophies, transfers to larger territories, and praise. Conversely, the leader can react to poor performance negatively, with a wide array of contingent reinforcement methods such as reduced compensation, intensified monitoring of activities, and reassignment.

Given the nature of the selling position, most sales managers use transactional leadership and seek to stimulate and direct their sales forces with contingent reinforcement (reward or punish salespeople based on their performance). In simple terms, transactional sales leadership consists of a contract between the manager and the subordinate. An example of this relationship is typified by the sign above a sales manager's desk that reads: "No orders, No money." Research has found that this leadership approach can favorably influence salespeople's job attitudes and behavior[55] as well as sales managers' performance.[56]

Transactional leadership, which takes a short-term perspective to generate favorable results from the sales force, tends to be the most frequently used leadership approach in business today. But it has been criticized on several grounds. For example,

**Transformational
Leadership**
Transformational leaders
adopt a long-term
perspective. They gain
extraordinary commitment
from their followers
through several key
characteristics: charisma
and vision, inspiration,
intellectual stimulation, and
individual consideration.

Charisma
A mystical, inspirational
quality that few people
possess; the charismatic
leader wins the emotional
loyalty and enthusiasm of
followers.

Vision
An attractive, credible
notion of a future state that
is not readily attainable.

Visionary Leadership
The ability to create and
articulate a realistic,
credible, and attractive
vision of the future that
improves upon the present
situation.

time pressures on sales managers, poorly developed sales performance appraisal systems, unfair rewards systems for salespeople, absence of training for sales managers, and lack of control over company rewards by sales managers can all work against the effectiveness of a transactions leader.[57] Thus, another approach that has garnered the attention of sales managers is **transformational leadership**, which adopts a long-term orientation by focusing on future needs.

Transformational sales leaders activate their subordinates' higher-order needs and encourage them to substitute company needs for their own. They raise salespersons' awareness of the value of their jobs, the consequences of their actions, and their importance to the organization. The result is more committed, more satisfied employees who are encouraged to surpass their own expectations and personal objectives for the good of the sales district and the company.[58] Transformational sales managers have the ability to gain extraordinary commitment from their followers through four key characteristics: *charismatic and visionary leadership, inspiration, intellectual stimulation,* and *individualized consideration.*[59]

Charismatic and Visionary Leadership. **Charisma** has been described as a "fire that ignites followers' energy and commitment, producing results above and beyond the call of duty."[60] Charismatic leaders are known to inspire and motivate people not only to willingly do more, despite obstacles and personal sacrifice, but to transcend their own interests for the sake of the firm.[61] Charismatic sales managers have a strong emotional appeal for salespeople; it exceeds ordinary esteem, affection, admiration, and trust.[62] Such managers inspire through their confident attitudes, risk-taking tendencies, assertiveness, magnetic personalities, and often feisty approaches. Salespeople often demonstrate total and unqualified belief in and identification with the vision of charismatic sales managers.

A **vision** is an attractive, credible notion of a future state that is not readily attainable. While vision is a key ingredient of charismatic leadership, **visionary leadership** goes beyond that to include articulating a realistic, credible, and attractive future that improves upon the present.[63] Thus a visionary leader appeals to the hearts of subordinates and their desire to be part of something that has a bigger, brighter future.[64] He or she also mobilizes subordinate commitment toward the vision by communicating it and by institutionalizing change throughout the organization. Lee Iacocca, the former CEO of Chrysler (www.chrysler.com), was a quintessential transformational leader who had both charisma and vision to transform the company and its managers into agents of change. Herb Kelleher of Southwest Airlines (www.southwest.com) had the vision and foresight to know that in order to create a successful airline, he had to continuously champion his commitment to excellent customer service. Steve Jobs, CEO of Apple (www.apple.com), inspires loyalty to his vision by continually developing innovative and exciting new products. Characteristics of these charismatic leaders include (1) a vision that is clearly articulated, (2) willingness to take risks to achieve the vision, (3) sensitivity to environmental constraints, (4) sensitivity to follower needs, and (5) behaviors that are novel.[65]

Inspiration. Inspiration, another key characteristic of transformational leadership, is the ability to articulate expectations to subordinates, communicate important purposes in simple ways, and use symbols to focus their efforts. Inspirational sales managers are emotionally arousing and reassuring to their salespeople, typically because they've "been there successfully before."[66]

Intellectual Stimulation. A transformational sales leader stimulates salespeople intellectually by creating a readiness for change and by encouraging them to use ingenuity to find new approaches for solving old and continuing problems or emerging ones. These leaders are capable of devising and introducing innovative prospecting and selling strategies, controlling sales force turnover, and maintaining the organization's stability by developing imaginative ways to recruit sales personnel. Salespersons under this kind of sales manager tend to readily offer their own ideas, become inspired in their problem solving, and think more critically and creatively.

Salespeople can maintain a "learning log," which is a recording of each sales problem they confront, how they resolved it, and what they learned from it. To avoid reinventing the wheel, salespeople and their peers can review the learning log when they face similar problems in the future.[67] Sales managers at Amana Refrigeration (www .amana.com) went into the field to discover why their lead generation program did not produce a high rate of sales. They discovered that their more successful salespeople ignored most of the leads sent to them by distinguishing between customers who view the product as a commodity (and thus buy on price) and those who use it to differentiate their own products (the "real" prospects). Armed with this knowledge, Amana sales managers redirected sales force efforts toward selling to customers who were not price driven but were concerned mainly with product quality.[68]

Individualized Consideration. The fourth characteristic of transformational leadership is the manager's ability to treat each employee as an individual, supporting their career development and growth by providing mentoring, coaching, and counseling. Transformational sales managers also show genuine concern for each salesperson rather than only for tasks, policies, administrative matters, or decision making. Individualized attention paves the way for ongoing communication between the leader

© David Young-Wolff / PhotoEdit

● Sales managers can use different leadership approaches to effectively influence salespersons to go above and beyond the call of duty in helping the organization succeed.

TABLE 10.5 Extending Transactional versus Transformational Leadership to Sales Management	
TRANSACTIONAL SALES MANAGERS	**TRANSFORMATIONAL SALES MANAGERS**
■ Identify and communicate tasks to salespeople	■ *Inspiration*—effectively communicate expectations; are emotionally arousing and reassuring to salespeople
■ Recognize immediate needs of salespeople and suggest ways to meet more needs	■ *Charisma*—have a vision, a sense of mission, and a strong emotional appeal for salespeople
■ Suggest ways to execute tasks	■ *Intellectual stimulation*—help salespeople become better at identifying and solving customer problems and needs
■ Provide appropriate rewards and feedback	■ *Individual consideration*—display individual consideration to salespeople through mentoring, coaching, and counseling

and the sales subordinate; evokes personal commitment and devotion; and allays fears, anxiety, and depression. Admittedly, frequent personal contact with field salespeople is often difficult because of their physical distance from the sales manager. Nonetheless, convincing salespeople to transcend their own self-interests for the organization's benefit will be difficult without the sales leader's knowledge of, sensitivity to, and response to each salesperson's unique needs for growth and development. Bill Marriott, president of Marriott Corporation (www.marriott.com), practices individualized consideration by calling his firm's top producers every month to congratulate them. Imagine how motivating and empowering *that* phone call must be for the recipients!

Essentially, then, transformational sales leaders are not content with the status quo and tend to develop salespeople who resemble and emulate them. They seek to "transform" the salespeople's perspective from a short-run, self-oriented one to a long-run, company (or work unit) orientation.

Transformational leadership has been found to be particularly effective in non-sales work contexts. Some preliminary evidence suggests that this leadership style has a rather favorable impact on salespeople[69] and sales managers,[70] but not necessarily a greater effect than that of transactional leadership. However, the two leadership styles can be used together to provide leadership perspectives on both the company and the individual. Table 10.5 presents capsule views of transactional and transformational leadership.

■ Pygmalion Leadership

Some effective sales managers communicate high but realistic expectations to their sales subordinates, on the principle that positive thinking begets positive results. In other words, they try to shape subordinates' performance by communicating their high hopes for job success. The result is a self-fulfilling prophesy—sales managers get what they expect.

This leadership style is sometimes called the "Pygmalion" effect.[71] One reason it can work is that "when a manager communicates high expectations to a subordinate, the subordinate is likely to raise the level of his or her own performance expectations"[72] (Sales Manager: "You have outstanding selling ability, and I know you'll achieve over 125 percent of your quota for this year." Salesperson: "Gee, Boss, thanks for your support. You know what? I think that I can achieve that, too, if not more").

Salespeople can also develop high expectations for themselves without input from their managers and still perform exceedingly well (the "Galatea" effect). If, however, a sales manager articulates low expectations to a sales subordinate, low performance might well ensue (the "Golem" effect)—negative thinking leads to negative results.

To use Pygmalion leadership effectively, sales organizations should encourage their sales managers to have high performance expectations of their salespeople. At the same time, though, they should try to increase salespersons' self-confidence so that they will expect more of themselves and thus enhance their productivity. And of course, sales managers should avoid conveying low performance expectations for sales force members. Instead, they need to convince their salespeople that "they have untapped potential" and get them "to believe that they can achieve more."[73]

■ Leadership and Empowerment: Distributive Power Sharing Through Participative Management

Empowerment
The process of making partners of subordinates by giving them legitimate authority and discretion in decision making and by providing rewards tied to company performance.

In a departure from traditional leadership theories, the concept of **empowerment** focuses on distributing power to lower-level employees. Many employees experience low levels of **self-efficacy**, or feelings of powerlessness and the belief that their work does not contribute meaningfully to organizational performance. Another contributor to the spread of empowerment is the fact that organizational hierarchies are becoming flatter and require stronger leadership at lower levels.

Empowering employees means to recognize and release the potential power that people already have in their reservoir of useful knowledge, experience, and internal motivation.[74] Because it allocates decision-making authority to better resolve problems, empowerment can help alleviate employee powerlessness and improve self-efficacy.[75]

Self-Efficacy
Feelings of power and the subordinate belief in the ability to make a meaningful contribution in influencing organizational performance.

The philosophy behind empowerment is **participative management**, which gives subordinates a sense of ownership and responsibility by enabling them to play an integral role in decision making, problem solving, goal setting, and instituting organizational changes. Participative management goes above and beyond simply eliciting ideas or opinions from subordinates. To feel self-worth and self-efficacy, employees must believe their jobs have value. Having been legitimately empowered, they are more likely to contribute to the accomplishment of organization goals. Participative management is associated with other organizational effectiveness criteria such as increases in subordinate job commitment, security, challenge, and motivation.[76] Figure 10.5 applies the idea of empowerment to sales management tasks, along a continuum from high to low levels of shared power and authority.

Participative Management
The participation of employees with management in shared decision making that enables them to accomplish individual and organizational goals.

Sales managers can take several steps to ensure the success of an empowerment program. First, they should make sure that their salespeople can attain job mastery by providing any needed skills training.[77] Second, sales managers should give salespeople authority (legitimate power), responsibility, and control to make substantive decisions, including job performance procedures. In turn, salespeople should then be ready to be held accountable for results including organizational performance.[78] Third, sales managers should assign role models to mentor other salespeople in their

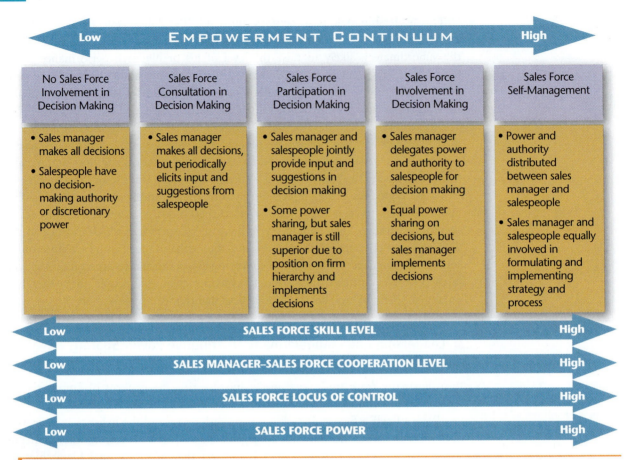

FIGURE 10.5 The Sales Manager–Salesperson Empowerment Continuum: Distributive Power Sharing Through Participative Management

work.[79] Fourth, they can use reinforcement and persuasion to raise the confidence levels of salespeople—through praise, encouragement, and feedback—and offer emotional support to relieve job stress and anxiety.[80] Fifth, they should be provided with emotional support to attenuate job stress and anxiety.[81] Sixth, to make effective decisions, sales managers should be sure their salespeople have access to financial and operational performance data.[82] Seventh, they should reward salespeople based on how much they improve the firm's bottom line. For instance, a profit-sharing program should give a share of directly attributable profits to the individual's department. Furthermore, subordinates should be fairly rewarded for work and even be allowed to choose how they get compensated.[83] Without results-based compensation and rewards, empowerment programs may not meet their intended objectives.

Sales Management Implications. Empowerment shifts decision making to lower-level employees, and this may seem counterintuitive in the context of our earlier discussion of how sales managers can judiciously use power. But recall from chapter 1 that the new definition of marketing entails "a set of processes for communicating and delivering value to customers and for managing customer relationships in ways that benefit the organization and its stakeholders."[84] Further, sales and marketing have moved from focusing on transactions to developing long-run, mutually profitable customer relationships. Acting as boundary spanners between buyers and sellers, salespeople have found that their roles have shifted significantly to include customer relationship management (CRM), "the overall process of building and maintaining profitable customer relationships by delivering superior customer value and satisfaction."[85]

So what does empowerment mean for sales management? First, because salespeople often work alone, they tend to have considerable freedom on the job. They can make decisions about whom to call (and in what order), the content of their sales presentations, the percentage of selling time versus non-selling time, and even the selling price. Given this level of job latitude, sales managers want to empower their sales staff in a way that will simultaneously control their activities and avoid inhibiting their sales productivity.[86] To bring out the creativity of their salespeople, many sales managers have empowered them by using "four levers of control":[87]

- *Diagnostic control systems*—Sales managers establish and support clear performance goals for the sales force. The system allows them to monitor and correct their sales subordinates' progress toward such goals as sales, market share, and profitability.

- *Beliefs systems*—Sales managers communicate core values and a mission to the sales force. Thus, salespersons know what is acceptable behavior as their selling situations change.

- *Boundary systems*—Sales managers specify and enforce the rules of the game. Instead of having a blank check to execute their tasks, the sales team is allowed to operate within defined limits.

- *Interactive control systems*—Sales managers encourage learning within the sales department. Rather than believing that information is power, they believe that "we all need each other's input to be successful."

These four control levers allow for empowerment without "giving away the house." Although many companies may employ some elements of each, successful sales managers make explicit use of all the levers when empowering their sales subordinates.

Second, to effectively implement an empowerment program, sales managers need to focus on (1) enhancing salesperson skills, (2) developing salesperson character, (3) creating a culture of empowerment, and (4) providing empowerment opportunities. Figure 10.6 shows ways of achieving these goals.

Third, in light of their expanding tasks in CRM that include building and maintaining long-term customer relationships, sales managers need to sufficiently empower their salespeople to effectively and efficiently perform their new roles. Empowerment may be difficult for traditional sales managers, who may perceive it as a threat to their authority, but it offers higher potential for success in today's business environment where customers expect prompt and full satisfaction of their needs. To learn more about cutting-edge leadership and empowerment issues, sales managers can enroll in leadership and empowerment training programs offered by such organizations as the Leaders Institute (www.leadersinstitute.com).

Reprinted by permission of The Leader's Institute.

● To increase their understanding of state-of-the-art leadership and empowerment processes, sales managers can enroll in training programs offered by organizations like the Leaders Institute.

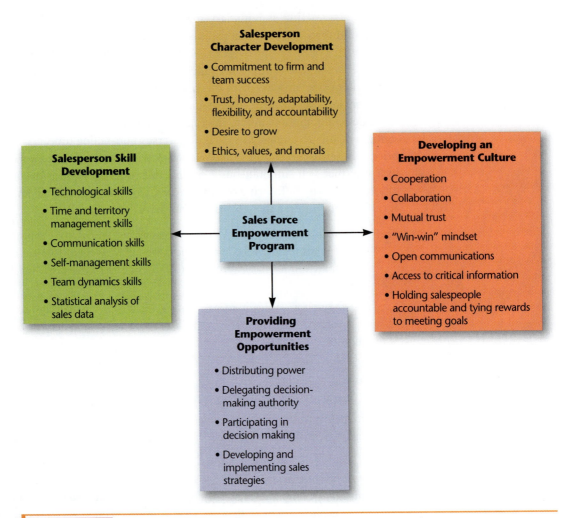

FIGURE 10.6   Implementing an Empowerment Program for the Sales Force

Other Emerging Issues in Twenty-First Century Sales Force Leadership

■ Mentoring

Mentor
Someone who systematically helps develop a subordinate's abilities through careful tutoring, personal guidance, and example.

A proven way to develop leaders is through **mentoring.** A **mentor** is someone who systematically helps develop a subordinate's abilities through careful tutoring, personal guidance, and example. Mentors are typically strong, self-confident people who do not fear an aggressive, young subordinate. They take risks in betting on perceived talent in subordinates and are an important source and stimulus for the development of leaders. Sales managers can be effective mentors by working closely with their salespeople. A form of mentoring that has recently gained popularity among sales managers is "curbstone coaching." In this practice, the sales manager remains with a salesperson during a sales call and provides a constructive critique immediately after the call. Many experts feel that tremendous improvements can be made if a sales manager can properly coach the salesperson about a sales call while the call is still fresh in his or her mind.[88] Sales managers must realize the importance of setting aside a few minutes after the sales call—either over a cup of coffee or on the way to the next appointment—to analyze what did or did not happen and what improvements can be made. If the sales manager can provide instant feedback that is truly helpful and acceptable to the salesperson, the payoff can be almost instantaneous. A few minutes of empathetic concern for the salesperson also can do a lot to boost a mentor's leadership effectiveness.

Mentoring revisits the question we asked at the beginning of the chapter: Can leaders be created? Mentors and senior sales managers can certainly create *better* leaders by helping young sales managers with various aspects of their careers.[89] For example, mentors can equip individuals with the skills, tools, and techniques to bring out their natural leadership talents. A good, solid background of information learned from mentors can also give young sales managers the confidence they need to make critical decisions. Finally, a senior member of a company can do a great deal for an entry-level employee by instilling the values of curiosity, idealism, entrepreneurism, and commitment.[90] While implementing these strategies will not necessarily guarantee a leader, they can do a great deal to bring out natural leadership talents that may be latent in an individual. For some additional insights on developing leaders for the twenty-first century, see the nearby *Sales Management in Action* box.

© Jupiter Images / Thinksotck / Alamy

● Sales managers increase salesperson productivity by mentoring and providing guidance on sales data analysis.

SALES MANAGEMENT IN ACTION

Developing Effective Sales Management Leaders in the Twenty-First Century

Intensifying global competition, multicultural customers, growing sales force diversity, and innovative sales and marketing channels have combined to make the search for effective sales management leaders increasingly urgent. These "superstar" sales managers must exhibit exceptional leadership qualities and behaviors, including the following:

- Treating salespeople more like partners or teammates than subordinates in achieving sales, profitability, and customer satisfaction goals
- Empowering salespeople by providing them with profitability information about products and services and releasing decision-making authority that enables salespeople to negotiate and satisfy customers on the spot instead of having to obtain prior approval from headquarters
- Willingness to take risks and capitalize on new opportunities for growth and improvement in all areas, instead of clinging to the status quo
- Developing closer relationships with customers and more in-depth understanding of customers' businesses
- Applying flexible motivational skills in working with a hybrid sales force across multiple sales channels, online and offline

- Communicating effectively with salespeople to inspire them to embrace and share the organizational vision
- Sharing successes with salespeople and sales support people by recognizing, rewarding, and celebrating their accomplishments, individually and collectively
- Keeping up-to-date on the latest technologies affecting buyer-seller relationships
- Learning marketing skills in order to identify potential business opportunities and recommend strategies to senior management
- Working closely with internal departments as a member of the total corporate team dedicated to satisfying customers profitably
- Continually seeking ways to exceed customer expectations and bring added value to the ongoing buyer-seller relationship
- Creating a flexible, learning and adapting environment for all members of the sales team
- Serving as a positive role model by exhibiting high standards of ethics and dedication to customer service and satisfaction

SOURCE: Updated and revised from Rolph E. Anderson, "Personal Selling and Sales Management in the New Millennium," *Journal of Personal Selling & Sales Management* 4 (fall 1996): 17–32.

■ Women as Sales Managers

All organizations need to be on guard against stereotyping. Selling and sales management traditionally have been male dominated, but in the twenty-first century, women in growing numbers are taking leadership roles in industry as well as government. A recent study indicated that salespeople of both genders responded favorably to female sales leaders. Interestingly, though, successful leadership styles of female sales managers may not be the same as those of male sales managers.[91]

Women possess many management and leadership qualities. For instance, they tend to be nurturing, interpersonally concerned, relationship oriented, socially sensitive, and expressive; to be highly involved with others; to value connection between themselves and others; and to have both a propensity for encouraging participation with subordinates and good communication skills.[92] Despite these favorable characteristics, the rise of women into sales management has not always been particularly smooth, because old stereotypes persist in some environments. For example, some men may be reluctant to work for female supervisors, whom they may see as less qualified to give them direction.

Many women sales managers therefore ask, "What leadership style should I adopt to be effective?" Some experts argue that women should use the same approaches as male sales managers. But when females use these strategies they can have different effects, sometimes leading to failure with both male and female salespeople. Some advise that women should simply do what they do best: use their own innate qualities without trying to be male "management clones." Still others argue that women sales managers should opt for an androgynous approach, using both male and female characteristics to advantage.

One recent study found that a female sales manager's contingent reward (transactional) leadership style had a far greater impact on salespeople's job performance and job commitment than did a management-by-exception or transformational leadership approach, regardless of the salesperson's gender.[93] Another investigation discovered that saleswomen were more satisfied with their female sales manager and had higher performance when led by charisma (a component of transformational leadership) and intellectual stimulation (another element of transformational leadership), respectively. Alternatively, salesmen viewed their female sales manager more favorably when she provided individualized consideration (a component of transformational leadership), and they reached higher performance levels when she used transactional and management-by-exception leadership approaches.[94]

So what does all this mean for women sales managers? The salesperson's gender may dictate which leadership style is appropriate. Women who are managing males may seriously consider emphasizing contingent reward approaches to enhance salesperson performance. This means setting objectives and establishing plans with subordinates and pointing out how goal achievement will lead to the rewards they desire. Then, managing from afar (management by exception) will allow the salesmen operational freedom in the field. When managing women, female sales managers should consider using intellectual stimulation to increase salesperson productivity. This means getting subordinates to focus on problem awareness, innovative selling techniques, adaptive selling, and reasons for good or poor performance.

Communication

At its most basic level, leadership requires communication as a way of transferring ideas, facts, thoughts, and values from one person to another. Thus, communication is an essential component of leadership.

Setting objectives and goals, organizing, staffing, forecasting, supervising, compensating, motivating, evaluating, and controlling the sales force—nearly all sales management functions—rely on communication. Open channels are especially critical when the sales organization must quickly adapt to a dynamic marketing environment. The typical manager spends more time communicating than doing anything else: 75 percent of an average day in face-to-face listening or speaking, 9 percent in writing, and 16 percent in reading.[95]

Communication
A two-way process whereby information is transferred and understood between two or more people.

Communication is a two-way process that includes listening and reading body language as well as speaking and writing. In fact, some of the best communicators follow this advice: "Always use your ears and mouth according to the number you have of each." Successful sales managers and salespeople are usually exceptionally good listeners. Many studies support the conclusion that good communication improves an organization's productivity.[96]

© 2007 Masterfile Corporation

● **Sales managers can use various techniques to communicate effectively with their salespeople.**

■ Listening

Effective Listening
Becoming familiar with the four types of listening (content listening, critical listening, empathic listening, and active listening) and knowing when to apply them.

One of the most overlooked qualities of a good communicator and thus of a good leader is *listening skill.* Listening provides managers with the bulk of the information they need to do their jobs. However, research shows that the average person is a poor listener, remembering only half of what is said during a ten-minute conversation and forgetting half of that within forty-eight hours.[97] **Effective listening** has become so necessary a component of business success that many companies now train their employees in listening.[98]

There are four basic types of listening, and they differ not only in purpose, but in the amount of feedback or interaction that occurs:

1. *Content listening*—The receiver's goal is to understand and retain information and identify key points. The receiver asks questions and takes notes as the information flows primarily in one direction—from speaker to receiver.
2. *Critical listening*—The receiver's goal is to critically evaluate the message by looking at the logic of the argument, strength of the evidence, and validity of

the conclusions. There's a great deal of interaction as the receiver tries to uncover the speaker's point of view.

3. *Empathic listening*—The receiver's goal is to understand the speaker's feelings, needs, and wants in order to solve a problem. Less interaction occurs, as the receiver is attempting to gain insights into the speaker's psyche.

4. *Active listening*—This listening technique attempts to help people resolve their differences. Before replying to the speaker's comment, the receiver must restate the ideas and feelings behind the comment to the speaker's satisfaction. The goal here is to appreciate the other person's point of view, whether or not you agree.

Sales managers as well as salespeople can use these listening modes to build better relationships with one another and with their customers. For example, sales managers can help alleviate any role ambiguities among their salespeople by honing their active listening skills. On the other hand, salespeople can learn a great deal about their customers by engaging in more empathic listening. Regardless of whether the sales management situation calls for content, critical, empathic, or active listening, sales managers can improve their listening ability by following the basic guidelines presented in Table 10.6.

TABLE 10.6   Ten Keys to Effective Listening

TO LISTEN EFFECTIVELY	THE BAD LISTENER	THE GOOD LISTENER
1. Find areas of interest.	Tunes out boring subjects.	Stays alert to opportunities. Asks, "What's in it for me?"
2. Judge content, not delivery.	Tunes out if speaker's delivery is poor.	Judges content. Doesn't focus on speaker's delivery weaknesses.
3. Hold your fire.	Tends to enter into arguments.	Doesn't judge until comprehension is complete. Interrupts only to clarify.
4. Listen for ideas.	Listens for specific facts.	Listens for central themes.
5. Be flexible.	Takes intensive notes using only one mode of listening.	Takes fewer notes. Uses four or five different listening modes depending on speaker.
6. Work at listening.	Tends to fake attention. Shows little energy output.	Strives to understand. Exhibits positive body language.
7. Resist distractions.	Is distracted easily.	Ignores distractions. Tolerates bad habits. Knows how to concentrate.
8. Exercise your mind.	Resists difficult expository material. Seeks light, recreational material.	Invites complex material as exercise for the mind.
9. Keep your mind open.	Reacts too strongly and quickly to emotional words.	Interprets emotional words. Does not overreact to them.
10. Capitalize on the fact that thought is faster than speech.	Tends to daydream when listening to slow speakers.	Challenges, anticipates, mentally summarizes, weighs the evidence. Listens between the lines to tone of voice.

SOURCE: Adapted from C. L. Bovee and J. V. Thill, *Business Communication Today,* 9/e, © 2008, p. 532. Adapted by permission of Pearson Education, Inc., Upper Saddle River, NJ.

■ Understanding Nonverbal Communication

Nonverbal Communication
Communication that takes place largely through body language, facial expressions, gestures, or body postures.

Many experts feel that nonverbal communication has more impact than verbal communication, accounting for as much as 93 percent of the emotional meaning exchanged in any interaction.[99] **Nonverbal communication** takes place largely through body language: facial expressions, gestures, and body postures. Facial expressions (such as smiles, frowns, clenched teeth, or wrinkled brows) convey messages from approval to disapproval, from understanding to confusion. Gestures (such as nodding the head or shrugging the shoulders) can signal agreement, understanding, or indifference. Body postures assumed by superiors (bowing, slouching, or standing rigidly) can significantly affect subordinates' interpretation and behavior. A timely smile, wink, or pat on the back can give salespeople positive feedback that is often more powerful than words.

Of the many forms of nonverbal communication, three of the most important to sales managers are communication via space, style of dress, and body movements. For example, some customers may feel threatened if a salesperson is too close to them, violating their personal space during the sales presentation. Dress can affect perceptions that others have not only toward an individual and his or her message but also toward the company the individual represents. To project a highly professional image, IBM (www.ibm.com) used to require its salespeople to wear conservative suits and white shirts, but such conformity was dropped when many of its business customers began allowing their employees to dress more informally. It's usually a good idea for salespeople to dress to fit the environment in which they're selling and the customers with whom they're interacting. Finally, the salesperson's ability to project confidence and professionalism by his or her posture and mannerisms and to be able to interpret the body language feedback of customers can help the communication process. Learning to skillfully read and respond to the prospect's nonverbal communication will enable salespeople to make more flexible and effective sales presentations.

Sales managers can utilize the principles of nonverbal communication in two important ways. First, they can instruct the sales force on the proper handshake, eye contact, and attire to use during visits with prospects and customers. Second, sales managers can use their own confidence and the way they dress to boost their referent power with the sales force.

To find out how effective a communicator you are and to identify areas where you might improve your skills, take the communication "test" in Figure 10.7.

■ Breaking Down Communication Barriers

Perhaps the first step in enhancing communication is to identify the barriers standing in the way. Let's look at organizational and individual barriers.

Organizational Barriers. Communication problems are likely to occur between a salesperson and a sales manager due to the structural hierarchy of most organizations. If the company objectives are not filtered down correctly to a salesperson, problems are sure to arise. A barrier to communication in this case may cause role perception problems for the salesperson and affect his or her performance.

Individual Barriers. Sales managers must be able to send clear, effective messages that the entire sales force can understand. Some individual barriers to communication

Use this scale, from 5 to 1, to respond to the following statements. (In your answers, assume you're in face-to-face interaction with another individual. Be as objective as you can!)

5-Strongly Agree; 4-Agree; 3-Neither Agree nor Disagree; 2-Disagree; 1-Strongly Disagree

When I have face-to-face communication:

___ 1. I focus only on the other person.

___ 2. I try to maintain regular eye contact when the individual is talking.

___ 3. My nonverbal gestures communicate that I am listening carefully.

___ 4. I remain genuinely interested throughout the interaction.

___ 5. I ask for more details when I do not completely understand what the individual is saying.

___ 6. I paraphrase questions to make sure I understand before answering.

___ 7. I do not interrupt another who is speaking.

___ 8. I do not change the subject frequently when communicating.

___ 9. I never try to finish another speaker's sentences.

___ 10. I try hard to understand fully what the individual is saying.

___ 11. I respond with useful statements rather than merely replying "yes" or "no."

___ 12. I offer relevant information regarding questions another asks me.

___ 13. I show eagerness and enthusiasm in my responses.

___ 14. I answer all questions at the appropriate time.

ASSESSING YOUR COMMUNICATION EFFECTIVENESS

It would be great if you scored a perfect 70, but very few people do. In fact, even if your self-rating score was 70, it might be a good idea to let a friend objectively rate you on each question. Consider how you might improve on any questions where you rated less than 5.

FIGURE 10.7 Are You An Effective Communicator?

SOURCE: Adapted from Rosemary P. Ramsey and Ravipreet S. Sohi, "Listening to Your Customers: The Impact of Perceived Salesperson Listening Behavior on Relationship Outcomes," *Journal of the Academy of Marketing Science* 25 (spring 1997): 127–37.

that sales managers should readily recognize are conflicting assumptions, semantics, emotions, and communication skills.

Two individuals can hear the same message yet have *conflicting assumptions* about its meaning. For example, a customer telephones a sales representative and asks her to ship an order "as soon as possible." The customer receives the order five days later and never orders from that salesperson again. To the customer and the salesperson, "as soon as possible" meant today. To the shipping department, it meant something totally different!

Semantics, or the meaning of words, can cause communication failure. Most words have multiple meanings; some common words can have as many as fifteen to eighteen interpretations. Communication barriers are sure to exist when two people attribute different meanings to the same words and don't know it.

All communication is influenced by *emotions*. When a person sends a message, feelings are attached to it; if the receiver of the message is unaware of or misinterprets those feelings, the intent of the message may be lost or misconstrued.

Finally, since *communication skills* vary greatly, some people are better communicators and thus better leaders than others. Some differences in communication skills are due to education and training, while others may be due to innate personality traits.

Overcoming Barriers. Sales managers can overcome the barriers to communication if they acknowledge their existence and take the time necessary to work them out. Here are some useful strategies.

- *Regulate information flow*—Too much information can cause anyone to experience information overload. Establish a system that allows priority messages to receive immediate attention, and keep messages short; in fact, many communication experts recommend limiting messages to one page.
- *Provide and elicit feedback*—We've talked about the importance of *providing* feedback. Sales managers also need to *encourage* feedback to ensure the sales force has understood the message. Respond promptly and respectfully to any non-routine communications from the sales force to show your concern for their views and to encourage their early reporting of potential territorial problems or opportunities.
- *Use simple language*—Sales managers must use words *everyone* can understand. The larger the team you are addressing, the greater the chance of miscommunication. Avoid using jargon or technical language, and be sensitive to the diversity of your audience.
- *Practice effective listening*—Become familiar with the four types of listening and know when to apply them.
- *Keep emotions in check*—Emotions are in all communications, and they sometimes can distort the message content. A highly emotional sales manager can easily convey the wrong emotional feeling in a message and create misunderstanding. Communicate when you are calm.
- *Give nonverbal cues*—Nonverbal cues help sales managers emphasize major points and express feelings. Make sure nonverbal cues reinforce your words, so you don't send mixed messages.
- *Use the grapevine*—Don't be afraid to use the grapevine. It can help you send information rapidly without having to go through formal channels, and it can be an excellent way to obtain feedback from the sales force. Make sure, however, that all information you convey is accurate and meaningful.

CHAPTER SUMMARY

1. Understand the dynamics of leadership. In the drive for competitiveness, organizations are becoming flatter and leaner. This requires greater leadership skills at all organizational levels—not just in the executive suites, because twenty-first century business and sales management practices are necessarily going to be significantly different from those in the past. Within the context of sales management, we can define *leadership* as the interpersonal process of communicating, inspiring, guiding and influencing the behavior of subordinate salespeople toward the attainment of organizational objectives, goals, and values.

2. **Contrast supervision, management, and leadership.** Supervision, management, and leadership are related, but also quite different. Supervision entails performing tasks that deal with monitoring the daily work activities of subordinates. Management is primarily a *learned* process whereby subordinates are guided by formally prescribed duties toward achieving organizational goals. In contrast, leadership is more of an *emotional* process that involves exercising psychological, social, and inspirational influence on people.

3. **Identify the sources of power that leaders possess.** Leaders may draw upon power from a variety of sources to enable them to accomplish their goals. These include *legitimate* power from formally delegated authority; *reward* power or the ability to provide subordinates with various benefits such as raises, praise, or promotion; *coercive* power, which is the ability to punish or withhold rewards; *referent* power, which is the leader's ability to inspire others; and *expert* power, based on the leader's skills, knowledge, or special abilities.

4. **Apply the classic theories of leadership to sales management.** Although there are several classical leadership theories, they can be broadly categorized into three approaches: (a) trait, (b) behavioral, and (c) contingency (situational). *Trait* theory contends that certain inherited traits such as honesty and drive determine successful leaders. *Behavioral* theory focuses on what the leader does and sees effective leadership as a result of two composite dimensions of leader behavior: consideration and initiating structure or task orientation. *Contingency* theory emphasizes the relationships among the sales manager, salespeople, and the sales situation. No one leadership style fits all situations, and sales managers often must use more than one style to handle different members of the sales force. Moreover, effective leadership usually calls for flexibility to match changing sales situations. For example, effective leaders match their style with the maturity and duties of the sales force. One way of visualizing leadership styles is to diagram them as an automobile gearshift, or the capital letter *H*. The sales manager can *shift* leadership styles from *autocratic* to *laissez*

faire as the composition and responsibilities of the sales force change.

5. **Apply the major contemporary theories of leadership to sales management.** With dynamic changes in the global business environment, three contemporary schools of leadership thought include (a) *transformational* leadership, (b) *Pygmalion* leadership, and (c) *empowerment.* Transactional or visionary leaders recognize the immediate needs of their employees and show them how their needs will be met by superior performance. Visionary or charismatic leaders inspire and motivate people to willingly do more despite obstacles and personal sacrifice. Pygmalion leaders enhance their salespeople's success by establishing high (but realistic) goals for their salespeople and communicating those aspirations to them with the expectation that sales performance will increase. That is, positive thinking begets positive results, in that sales managers get what they expect—also known as the "Pygmalion" effect.

In flatter and leaner firms, there is a need for leaders at all levels. This has given rise to a forward-thinking business philosophy known as *empowerment,* which can be defined as recognizing and releasing the potential power that people already have in their wealth of knowledge, experience, and internal motivation.

6. **Communicate effectively with the sales force.** As an essential component of leadership, sales managers must skillfully communicate with salespeople and others by setting objectives and goals, organizing, staffing, forecasting, supervising, compensating, motivating, evaluating, and controlling the sales force. *Communication* is a process whereby information is transferred and understood between two or more people; it is a two-way process involving listening as well as speaking, writing, and reading body language.

7. **Overcome barriers to communication.** Oftentimes, sales organizations have various communication barriers. Sales managers can overcome barriers to effective communication by providing feedback to subordinates, using straightforward language, understanding nonverbal language, and by staying attuned to the organizational grapevine.

REVIEW AND APPLICATION QUESTIONS

1. Is there a distinction between supervision, management, and leadership within the context of the sales department? Explain your perspective in detail. [LO 2]

2. Identify and explain the sources of power that leaders draw upon in exercising influence over their subordinates. [LO 3]

3. Define the concept of leadership. Describe what leaders do, and identify the traits of effective leaders. [LO 4]

4. Describe your understanding of the behavioral styles theory of leadership. What direction does this theory offer to sales managers? [LO 4]

5. Explain Fiedler's contingency model of leadership. What are the implications of this model for sales managers in influencing the behavior of salespeople? [LO 4]

6. Describe your understanding of the path-goal theory of leadership. What direction does it offer to sales managers for influencing the behavior of salespeople? [LO 4]

7. Describe the leader-member exchange paradigm. Discuss its implications for sales managers seeking to influence the behavior of salespeople. [LO 4]

8. Identify and discuss the reasons that empowerment has become an important progressive management concept. What are the precepts of empowerment, and what is the role of participative management? [LO 5]

9. Is the contemporary philosophy of empowerment similar to or different from the concept of power and the use of power by managers to influence subordinates? Explain your position in detail. [LO 5]

10. Identify and describe the steps that can be taken to ensure the success of an empowerment program. [LO 5]

11. Which theory of leadership do you think is most sound? Discuss which theory you might most often apply during your career in sales management. [LO 5]

12. Define communication, and suggest how sales managers can improve their own communication skills. [LO 6]

13. Think of some interactions you have had with people today. What kind of nonverbal communication took place? Were you conscious of your own nonverbal communication? [LO 7]

14. What are some common communication barriers? How can a sales manager overcome these barriers? [LO 7]

IT'S UP TO YOU

Internet Exercise

Use the Internet to find articles on contemporary leadership approaches being used by sales managers at two different organizations. How can you ascertain whether these leadership approaches are effective?

Role-Playing Exercise

Leadership Style Problems

Situation

You are the national sales manager for a large financial services firm, and one of your regional sales managers has asked you for some advice. She is anticipating problems in one of her districts, primarily due to the leadership style of one of her district sales managers. He is a highly successful sales veteran who believes in gaining compliance from his salespeople through fear and punishment. He makes it very clear to his salespeople that if they don't perform up to his standards, they *will not* receive bonuses and might even be fired. He firmly believes every salesperson can be replaced, and salesperson turnover in his district is higher than in other districts. Nevertheless, his sales district is one of the most profitable in the company. However, the sales manager says she has recently heard rumors that some of the salespeople in his district have started deliberately ignoring his communications to them, and they are making negative comments and spreading rumors about him to customers and other salespeople. None of the salespeople in his district have complained directly to her yet. But she's still worried that the salespeople in his district are becoming so turned off by his management style that some major sales force and customer problems may erupt soon and hurt the company's sales and reputation.

Role-Play Participants and Assignments

National sales manager: You must give the regional sales manager advice on how to handle the situation.

Regional sales manager: She feels the district sales manager's salespeople are nearing the point of open rebellion and that their behavior may harm the company's reputation with customers. Before discussing the situation further with the national sales manager, she needs to gather more facts and perspectives by talking first to the district sales manager and then to his salespeople.

District sales manager: He is not fully aware, and maybe not even particularly concerned, that his salespeople are becoming totally turned off by his management leadership style.

 ## In-Basket Exercise

Soon after being hired as sales manager for a large industrial products firm, you receive your first memo from the national sales manager. It addresses a serious issue that's facing not only your company, but your overall industry—it's salesperson burnout. Your company's national sales manager believes that many of the company's salespeople have plateaued and are no longer improving. He has requested your input regarding this issue at next week's regional sales meeting.

DISCUSSION QUESTIONS

1. What are you going to recommend at the upcoming meeting?
2. Is there such a thing as a "plateaued" or "burned-out" salesperson?
3. What specific things can sales managers do as leaders to revitalize their salespeople?

 ## CASE 10.1

School Suppliers, Inc.: Leading a Diverse Sales Force

School Suppliers, Inc. (SSI) is a national distributor of elementary and secondary school supplies. The company has fifty salespeople located in eight regional offices throughout the United States. The salespeople call on purchasing agents or principals at elementary and secondary schools in their assigned regions. Over the past decade, the Southeastern region has been one of the company's fastest-growing regions. Primarily because of the increasing population in Florida, SSI's Southeastern region has led the company in sales and is projected to be the strongest region for the next several years.

Howard Larsen, one of SSI's top sales reps over the past several years, was recently promoted to sales manager of the premier Southeastern region. Howard, age twenty-eight, was at first very pleased and excited to be managing one of the most promising regions within the company. After only four months as the sales manager of this region, however, he began to question his ability as a sales manager. Howard believes that he is having problems managing his salespeople.

Howard recently met with his close friend, John—who manages a large resort in the Orlando area—to discuss his problems with the sales force. He gave John a brief rundown of the situation: "Well, my problem concerns the way I'm leading my salespeople. Things seem to be going fine with five of my seven salespeople. Melissa and Jeff, who I just hired six months ago, are going great. They are both young and eager to learn. Both have been progressing well, with slight increases in sales volume over the last two months. They both have very little sales experience, so they do make a few mistakes now and then. However, both will take constructive criticism very well, as they continually want to improve their selling skills. Melissa and Jeff are both about my age. Therefore, they relate to me very well. I have no problems with my two new salespeople.

"Rhonda is perhaps one of my best salespeople. Everyone enjoys being around her. Rhonda can give the other reps a lift when they're down. Her own sales performance is exceptional. Rhonda regularly surpasses her quotas and actively seeks out new customers. Rhonda accepts my leadership as if I were the VP of marketing. I wish all my salespeople were like Rhonda.

"Robert is also a fun salesperson to manage. He's been out of college for only about two years. He's young and wants to do well in the company. Robert reminds me a lot of myself when I first started with SSI. He is very competitive and readily accepts my constructive feedback since he constantly wants to improve. I made a few sales calls with him last week, and he must have asked over twenty questions after each call about how best to handle selling activities. He sort of looks on me as a big brother, and that makes him very easy to manage. To be honest with you, Robert is good for my ego.

"George is about my age, and if he has a problem, it's that he likes to goof off too much. George is good at bringing life and laughter into the job. He is well liked by everyone. However, he spends too much time bullshooting with virtually everyone he encounters during the work day! Every so often I have to get after him to manage his time better. When I do, George picks up his pace and usually reaches his annual sales quota. George's lapses keep me on his case but I don't think he really minds being supervised. Actually, I think he realizes that a little bit of leadership now and then will help his sales performance."

"It sounds like things are going pretty well for you, Howard," John observed. "Five of your seven salespeople seem to be doing fine. Is it the other two salespeople who are causing you all that grief? I can't wait to hear about these two!"

"Well, Fred is probably my biggest problem. He's a veteran salesperson who has been with the company for over thirty years. Fred started out by selling the liberal arts textbooks. In fact, he has been the top salesperson

in the company several times in past years. However, since he's been working for me, his performance has fallen off sharply. His performance is not quite bad enough for me to recommend that he be fired. However, if it gets any worse, I'm going to have to do something.

"The biggest problem with Fred is that he doesn't listen to me. He is very hardheaded and seemingly feels insulted every time I tell him to do something. For example, the other day I told him that he wasn't spending enough time with some of his best customers. He angrily fired back that he was selling textbooks before I was born and that he has forgotten more about 'real world' selling than I've learned from textbooks.

"Recently, I've been going out of my way to work with Fred. I've asked him to go on recruiting trips with me, and I've tried to help make his job easier by offering to train him to do several sales related tasks on a laptop computer. In both instances, he rejected me by making up some feeble excuse. He refuses to listen to me, no matter how hard I try to win him over.

"Fred also shows me very little respect. He will sometimes address me as 'college boy' in sales meetings. Last week, he called me by that name in front of one of our largest accounts. I don't know how much more I can take from him.

"Warren is my other problem. Warren is about forty-eight years old and has been with the company for about ten years. He is a hard worker and normally reaches his sales quota. I thinks he resents me for having this managerial job at such a young age. It may sound paranoid, but I have the feeling that he wants my job and will do whatever he can to get it. Warren is very competitive and seems to be trying to undercut me and show people that he can do a better job managing the sales force than I can. Given his attitude, I have a difficult time being a leader to Warren because he's not a good follower.

"The way I look at it, I'm a fairly effective sales manager because five of my seven salespeople accept my leadership and are doing well. However, it really disturbs me that I can't do a better job with Fred and Warren. These two guys have the potential of being top salespeople. If they would change their attitudes and significantly improve their sales volume, I could have the best sales district in the company. I just don't know what to do to be a more effective leader to these guys!"

"I personally feel that you have nothing to worry about," said John. "You definitely have the ability to manage this sales force, or your company would never have promoted you. Howard, you need to build up your self-confidence so that these old guys don't bother you. Don't be afraid to boss them around. Remember, your company's future is with the younger and currently more successful people. I didn't become manager of a resort hotel by being afraid to boss people around."

QUESTIONS

1. Comment on Howard's leadership style. What kind of leader is he?

2. Do you agree with John's advice? Why or why not? Is John's leadership style different from Howard's? If so, how?

3. Should Howard take John's advice? Why or why not?

4. Should Howard change his leadership style in an attempt to be a more effective leader to Fred? To Warren? Why or why not?

5. Would a transactional or transformational leadership style help Howard? Please explain.

Case prepared by Scott Widmier, Kennesaw State University.

CASE 10.2

Öhlins Chemicals: Leadership and Communication Problems

Ulrik Johansson is a salesperson for Öhlins Chemicals, a Swedish-owned distributor of industrial chemicals and solvents in the European Union and the United States. Öhlins Chemicals has developed a favorable reputation in both Europe and the United States for its high-quality industrial products and excellent customer service. Early on, Ulrik realized that selling industrial products requires excellent interpersonal skills because you must deal with a small number of customers whose upper management is often involved in making the purchase decisions. Since there are relatively few customers, salespeople need to be flexible and creative in solving specific customer needs—something that Ulrik realized early would give him an advantage over some competitors' salespeople.

A few years ago, Öhlins decided to widen its product mix and enter the textile market, starting first in the United States. If Öhlins succeeded there, the plan was to introduce the textile products into European markets. To implement this basic strategy, Öhlins acquired several small independent companies in the U.S. and formed a new division—the Textile Products Division. Its group of textile products include specialty woven, knitted, and braided fabrics for aerospace, marine, industrial, recreational, and medical applications. These products have similar industrial characteristics, and the same selling approach is typically effective. Twenty-four sales territories were set up to sell the new line of textile products, and two salespeople were reassigned or hired for each sales territory. Ulrik Johansson was one of the salespeople assigned to this new division based on his excellent track record selling textile-related products for other companies before joining Öhlins.

The Öhlins textile sales force is separate from the industrial chemicals sales force. While both share the district offices, warehousing, and delivery facilities, management of the two sales forces is handled differently. Each office has a district sales manager for the industrial chemicals salespeople and another district manager in charge of the textile salespeople. In addition, Öhlins created a national sales manager position to lead the forty-eight salespeople handling the textile products line. Mike Page—a highly productive industrial chemicals salesperson who has been with Öhlins for ten years—was promoted to fill this position which reports directly to the executive vice president.

Ulrik respects and likes Mike Page, and he feels comfortable communicating directly with him even though he reports on a day-to-day basis to Joan Fleming, his district sales manager. Joan, in turn, reports directly to Mike. Ulrik's interactions with Joan are often through informal, oftentimes somewhat irreverent communications which are common in the Swedish culture. These informal communications include jokes, wisecracks, things said in jest, or sardonic comments as well as serious discussion of issues, so Joan frequently has to read between the lines to interpret the subtle real meaning of some communications from her salespeople. What's more, Joan is frustrated and irritated by some of her salespeople who seem to feel that it's acceptable to communicate directly with Mike without even talking to her first or sending her a copy of the communication. Oftentimes, in follow-ups with her about an issue raised by her salespeople, Mike has assumed that she had already seen the communication . . . and Joan sometimes is too embarrassed to tell Mike that this is the first time she's hearing about the issue.

A highly energetic and self-motivated salesperson, Ulrik has been quite successful at Öhlins. Each year he has reached or exceeded all his assigned sales volume and financial quotas. Overall, he is probably one of the top performing salespeople in the Textile Products Division. Currently, he ranks third in this year's national sales contest for Wearever, a group of new products in the textile line. Öhlin's senior management is determined to make the Wearever products successful and substantial resources have been committed to their promotion. Wearever was a departure from the usual for Öhlin because these products are purchased in bulk from suppliers, then repackaged and branded under the Öhlin's Wearever brand.

Recently, Ulrik has noticed a significant attitude change toward Öhlin products among his customers and an increasing number of complaints. In their drive to successfully sell the Wearever brand of products, Öhlins senior management seems to be ignoring or in denial about any problems. At first, the Wearever products sold well, but then distribution and warehousing problems began causing delays in shipping orders. Growing numbers of customers are not receiving their orders on time and they are becoming increasingly upset with Öhlins as a supplier. At the same time, Öhlins management insists on maintaining its profit margins on the Wearever product line and avoid hurting its quality image, so they have remained inflexible in pricing strategy for the line even while competitors are giving discounts for similar textile products. Ulrik's customers cannot understand why Öhlins refuses to offer discount terms like other suppliers and some have started buying more competitors' products. Another concern for the Öhlins sales force, in general, is the outdated customer relationship management (CRM) system being used to support sales force activities. Ulrik and other salespeople frequently have to respond to customer inquiries or plan sales calls without having important account information. As a result of these compounding problems Ulrik is losing some of his best customers.

Even beyond his declining earnings due to customer defections, Ulrik wants to be proud of his company and the products he sells, so he has contacted Öhlin's management (first Mike then Joan) to share his concerns about the growing problems. From talking to other Öhlin salespeople, Ulrik knows they are having similar frustrating experiences. It's been several months since Ulrik initially alerted Öhlin management to the Wearever product line problems, but he has heard nothing back from either Joan or Mike except perfunctory "thank you" notes from each for expressing his concerns to them. But no management action has been taken or promised to correct the continuing situation. It's almost like Öhlin management doesn't want to hear about the problems because so much is riding on the success of the Wearever product line.

Finally, Ulrik has become so exasperated with unresponsive Öhlin management that he has decided to accept a sales position with an Öhlin competitor. He is now preparing his resignation letter, which he plans to submit to Joan and Mike this coming week. As he writes, Ulrik struggles to find exactly the right words to explain his reasons for leaving.

QUESTIONS

1. How would you rate the leadership and communication skills of Öhlins management? Explain your reasoning.

2. What suggestions do you have for improving the leadership and communication skills of Öhlins sales managers?

3. What do you think Öhlins management might have done to keep Ulrik from leaving, even if all his suggestions could not readily be implemented?

4. What do you think Ulrik should say in his resignation letter to Joan and Mike? Explain your reasoning.

Case prepared by Ossi Pessama, Luleå University of Technology, Sweden.

Sales Force Motivation

LEARNING OBJECTIVES

When you finish this chapter, you should be able to:

1 Understand the nature of motivation.

2 Apply contemporary theories of motivation to sales management.

3 Design reward and incentive programs to motivate salespeople.

4 Develop sales contests and sales meetings to motivate salespeople.

5 Utilize organizational commitment, career stage, and empowerment to motivate a sales force.

INSIDE SALES MANAGEMENT

Lance Perkins of GE Medical Systems

Lance Perkins is a fair-sized company all by himself. As executive account manager for General Electric's Medical Systems unit, he helps hospitals achieve goals such as cutting costs, boosting productivity, and improving quality through annual purchases of more than $25 million worth of goods (CAT scanners, x-ray equipment, and more) and services (such as repair contracts, consulting, and financing). Perkins is the main company contact for hospitals in his territory and coordinates the sales efforts of other GE specialists. If a hospital executive mentions building plans, for instance, Perkins will suggest GE Industrial Systems, "because we sell roofing, tile, even power systems for emergency generators."

In addition to meeting monthly sales goals, Perkins must progress through a series of activity milestones leading to each sale, because nine to eighteen months may pass between an initial meeting and a signed contract. GE also evaluates the leadership skills of its sales professionals. "In this sales position, you manage a lot of other people," says Perkins. "You may have ten or twelve other salespeople who are in touch with each hospital. I establish the relationship and bring in other specialty sales reps to supplement my discussions with customers."

Working on commission, Perkins learned to identify his best sales opportunities—the 20 percent of customers who account for 80 percent of his sales volume. "Fresh in the territory, it takes at least a year before you get the pulse of the market and figure out how to work smarter instead of harder," he observes. Although he initially reacted to every lead, he gradually began focusing on larger accounts, narrowing his contact list from sixty hospitals to fewer than twelve.

Perkins spends about three days a week visiting customers. The rest of the time he sets appointments, updates customer files and sales forecasts, obtains quotes, and coordinates the work of other GE specialists through e-mail, teleconferences, and meetings. Despite his busy schedule, Perkins makes cold calls every week. "Many salespeople have call reluctance," he says. "If they don't set a time to do it, they just won't do it." Without the cold calls, the milestones, and information about past sales—such as when a service contract expires—Perkins might miss potential sales.

Instead of writing call reports about customer contacts, Perkins creates "trackers," spreadsheets listing how much money each deal will generate, what milestone each deal is at, and the probability that a deal will close—and when. He constantly reviews and revises his trackers to see which sales may close in a given month and where he needs more support from other GE personnel. Managing his time and his territory, says Perkins, "is really like running a business and trying to figure out what the cash flow will be."

SOURCE: Anderson, Rolph E., Alan J. Dubinsky, and Rajiv Mehta, *Personal Selling: Building Customer Relationships and Partnerships*, 2/e, pp. 414–415. Copyright © 2007 by Houghton Mifflin Company. Reprinted with permission.

I n an era of rapid globalization, companies from all over the world are increasingly competing for survival or vying for a bigger piece of the pie. Some business strategists observe that many firms are waging economic war against one another.[1] Others urge salespeople to use guerilla marketing tactics in the field.[2] The preceding metaphors seem appropriate because salespeople do contend at the front lines in the battlegrounds of business, and their performance will play a major role in determining whether or not their companies succeed in today's intensely competitive markets.

It's up to sales managers to make sure salespeople perform their jobs well.[3] This chapter provides a foundation for understanding sales force motivation. We'll not only review the major theories behind motivation, but we'll also show how to apply them to enhance sales force performance.

Foundations of Motivation

Motivation
The set of dynamic interpersonal processes that cause the initiation, direction, intensity, and persistence of work-related behaviors of subordinate salespeople toward attaining organizational goals and objectives.

Motivation is a multi-faceted concept that has been the subject of intensive study.[4] In general, motivation refers to the initiation, direction, intensity and persistence of behavior.[5] In the context of sales management, we can define **motivation** as the set of dynamic interpersonal processes that cause the initiation, direction, intensity, and persistence of work-related behaviors of subordinate salespeople toward the attainment of organizational goals and objectives.

There are three important elements in our definition: First, *direction* means choosing the activities toward which the individual will focus the effort (will the salesperson spend most of the time calling on prospects or on existing accounts?). Second, *intensity* refers to the amount of physical and mental effort we expend on a given activity (how many sales calls will a salesperson make per day, or how much time will he or she allocate to selling tasks?). Third, *persistence* refers to the duration of the effort an individual will exert (will the salesperson make sales calls for eight hours straight?). Salespeople with a high degree of intensity and persistence will spend time and effort on those job duties that give them the greatest chance of achieving personal and organizational goals.

Applying Contemporary Motivation Theories to Sales Management

We'll look at several theories of motivation that are specifically relevant to sales force management, each offering intuitively appealing, but slightly different, explanations for why people exert high levels of effort to reach certain goals.[6] These theories are of three types: (a) content, (b) process, and (c) reinforcement oriented. Depending on the situation and the composition of the sales force, sales managers will need to exercise their own individual judgments in deciding which motivation theory applies best.

■ Content Theories of Motivation

Content theories provide insights into employees' needs for rewards and recognition. Understanding these can help sales managers design compensation plans and rewards that motivate by meeting the needs of salespeople.

Hierarchy of Needs Theory
A need theory; based on the assumption that people are motivated by a hierarchy of psychological growth needs.

Hierarchy of Needs Theory. Maslow's well-known **hierarchy of needs theory** contends that people are motivated by a "hierarchy" of psychological growth needs.[7] In our context it implies that salespeople come to their jobs already motivated and need only the opportunity to respond to the challenges of higher-order needs. Table 11.1 presents the priority of the needs individuals seek to fulfill (beginning at the bottom) and sales managers must consider. Remember first that the higher hierarchical level of a given need, the greater its importance and strength. And second, the gratification of needs at one level in the hierarchy activates needs at the next-higher level.

Sales managers should use close personal contact to keep track of the level of needs most important to each salesperson, from the beginning trainee to the senior sales representative. To avoid becoming stagnated at one level, salespeople must be given opportunities to activate and satisfy higher-level needs which will motivate them toward superior performance.

ERG Theory
Espouses that individuals' needs can be subsumed under a three-category hierarchy of existence (physiological and safety needs), relatedness (social and esteem needs), and growth (self-actualization needs).

ERG Theory. Three need categories are posited by **ERG theory**, as follows: *existence* (Maslow's physiological and safety needs), *relatedness* (social and esteem needs), and *growth* (self-actualization needs).[8] Like the need hierarchy theory, ERG proposes that individuals will focus on higher-level needs as lower-level ones are satisfied; unlike need hierarchy theory, though, it suggests that people can move up and down the three-part hierarchy.

Sales managers can study each salesperson's location on the hierarchy and customize incentives and other ways to help each one to fulfill his or her unmet needs. This explicit positioning (preferably in writing) will tell management which people need guidance with personal problems, which could benefit from a pat on the back or a shoulder to lean on, which need retraining, which can absorb more responsibilities, and which could improve their productivity under a modified compensation plan.

TABLE 11.1 Hierarchy of Needs and Their Implications for Sales Managers

MASLOW'S HIERARCHICAL LEVELS	SALESPERSON'S NEEDS	SALES MANAGER'S TASK
Self-actualization needs	■ Self-development ■ Creativity ■ Self-fulfillment	■ Provide greater job control, freedom, self-development workshops ■ Provide greater responsibilities, promotion opportunities
Esteem needs	■ Recognition ■ Status	■ Public recognition for achievement
Social needs	■ Social interaction and friendship ■ Acceptance among peers and superiors	■ Maintain close relationships with sales force ■ Sales meetings, newsletters, e-mail, social gatherings
Safety needs	■ Freedom from worry about security of jobs, incomes, medical expenses, etc.	■ Provide a balanced package of fringe benefits
Physiological needs	■ Food, shelter, overall health, etc.	■ Be aware of general health and living conditions of individual salespeople

Needs Theory

Posits that employees develop various needs—such as for power, affiliation, and achievement—over their lifetime based on life experiences.

— based on a lifetime.

Needs Theory. Developed by David McClelland, **needs theory** says that employees develop certain needs over their lifetime based on life experiences.[9] Specifically:

1. *The need for power* reflects the drive to dominate, influence, and have authority to control others. Sales managers must recognize that many successful salespeople want greater control over their jobs and more influence on sales force decisions, so their input should be sought before important decisions are made.

2. *The need for achievement* is the strong urge to master and accomplish difficult tasks. Achievement-oriented people readily accept individual responsibility, seek challenging tasks, and are willing to take risks doing tasks that may serve as steppingstones to future rewards. These individuals receive more satisfaction from accomplishing goals and more frustration from failure or unfinished tasks than the average person does. Any achievement-related step on the "success path" may include rewards (positive incentives) or threats (negative incentives).[10]

   high locus of control →

   Sales managers should identify achievement-motivated salespeople and then give them personal responsibility for solving definable problems or achieving certain goals. Frequent, specific feedback is also essential so that these salespeople can know whether they are performing well or not. Managers may have to temper negative feedback because achievement-motivated people may resign if they feel they will be unsuccessful. Finally, competition among such salespeople can be intense and damaging to the organization unless carefully monitored and controlled.

3. *The need for affiliation* is the desire to establish friendships, to have close working relationships with peers as well as customers, and to avoid conflict. Affiliative types like to work in groups and want to be accepted by others.[11] They are less self-centered, usually help bind the group together, and are less able to tolerate traveling jobs involving long periods of solitude.

In sum, although most salespeople have general needs for achievement, affiliation, and power, sales managers should learn the dominant needs of individual salespeople in order to devise specific strategies for motivating them.

Dual Factor Theory
Based on the assumption that the job itself contains sources of satisfaction and dissatisfaction as well as motivators.

Dual Factor Theory. Also referred to as motivation-hygiene theory, the **dual factor theory** was formulated by Frederick Herzberg, who found two types of factors associated with the satisfaction or dissatisfaction of employees. Sources of satisfaction are called *motivators* because they are necessary to stimulate individuals to superior efforts. They relate to the nature or content of the job itself and include responsibility, achievement, recognition, and opportunities for growth and advancement. When present, they motivate salespeople; if absent, they demotivate them.[12]

Hygiene factors are extrinsic aspects of the job, such as company policies, pay level, fringe benefits, working conditions, and job security. They pertain to satisfying lower-level needs. When present, hygiene factors do not actually induce positive motivation in salespeople; their absence, however, leads to salesperson dissatisfaction and demotivation.[13]

According to dual factor theory, then, only motivators can motivate the sales force, while hygiene factors can be demotivating if absent or neutral at best if present. Thus, being given increased responsibility can be particularly motivating to a salesperson. Working in a lucrative territory may satisfy the salesperson, but it will probably not motivate him or her; and working in a non-lucrative territory may reduce motivation.

Notwithstanding its support in non-sales settings, the relevance of dual factor theory in the selling arena remains questionable.[14] Nonetheless, one selling authority implicitly advocates its use, stating that "Motivation is internal . . . [sales managers] can't reach inside a rep's head and flip a switch. All . . . [they] can do is create an environment in which a rep's internal motivation takes over. . . . In part that involves removing demotivators. It also involves good listening to find out what the rep's true motivators are."[15] This suggests that sales managers can improve salesperson productivity by maintaining hygiene factors (like a pleasant work environment) while providing motivators (like job enrichment) for the sales force. Some examples of job enrichment in the sales context include

- Give salespeople a *complete natural unit of work responsibility and accountability* (specific customer category assignments in a designated area).

- Grant *greater authority and job freedom* to the salespeople in accomplishing assignments (let salespeople schedule their time in their own unique way as long as organizational goals are met).

- Introduce salespeople to *new and more difficult tasks and to challenges not previously handled* (opening new accounts, selling a new product on the Internet, or being assigned a large national account).

- Assign salespeople specific or specialized *tasks enabling them to become experts* (training new salespeople on "how to close a sale").

- Send *periodic e-mails and other communications directly to the salesperson* instead of forwarding everything via the sales supervisor. (Of course, the supervisor should be kept informed about any direct communication with salespeople.)[16]

■ Process Theories of Motivation

More dynamic than content theories, process theories emphasize the kind of goals and rewards that motivate people. Specifically, they try to explain the thought process of employees and identify actions that fulfill their needs.

© Ed Bock / Corbis

● **Sales managers can improve salesperson productivity by maintaining hygiene factors (pleasant work environment) such as an on-site daycare facility for children of their salespeople.**

Equity Theory
Based on the assumption that people compare their relative work contributions and rewards with those of other individuals in similar situations.

Equity Theory. According to the **equity theory** of motivation, employees compare their relative work contributions and rewards with those of other individuals in similar situations. We experience inequity when we feel either under-rewarded or over-rewarded for our contribution relative to that of others. Although individuals may respond in unique ways to inequity, most people who feel under-rewarded decrease their work efforts; people who feel overpaid tend to increase theirs. People may also distort their perceptions of their rewards and contributions relative to those of others. Finally, individuals may leave a perceived inequitable situation by quitting the job or changing the comparison group.[17]

According to equity theory, sales managers should learn how individual sales representatives feel about how their contributions and rewards compare with those of others. If some of the salespeople perceive inequity, the sales manager needs either to alter their perceptions or, if inequity really exists, to remedy the situation.

Expectancy Theory
Based on the assumption that people are motivated to work toward a goal when they expect their efforts will pay off.

Expectancy (Effort-Performance Linkage)
The salesperson's perceived probability that exerting a given level of effort will lead to higher achievement.

Expectancy Theory. First developed by Victor Vroom[18] and modified by Campbell, Dunette, Lawler, and Weick,[19] the **expectancy theory** of motivation proposes that individuals contemplate the consequences of personal actions in choosing different alternatives to satisfy their needs. The motivation to perform is a rationally determined, carefully thought out decision process—a key feature that makes this theory appealing. This theory was first applied to marketing to explain the performance of salespeople.[20] According to expectancy theory, motivation (or effort) is a function of three elements: expectancy, instrumentality, and valence.

Expectancy is the salesperson's perception that exerting a given level of effort will lead to higher achievement. For example, the salesperson might believe that if he or she increases effort by making 10 percent more calls per day, there is a 75 percent chance of achieving quota. Salespeople will likely increase their efforts if they think doing so will improve their performance. The degree of the expectancy estimate is important, but its *accuracy* is, too. If salespeople hold inaccurate expectancy beliefs, they are likely to expend effort on the wrong job activities.

Instrumentality (Performance-Reward Linkage)
The salesperson's estimate of the probability that achieving a certain level of improved performance will lead to the attainment of designated rewards.

Instrumentality is the salesperson's estimate of the probability that achieving a certain level of improved performance will lead to the attainment of certain rewards. For instance, the salesperson might believe there is a 50 percent chance that achieving quota will lead to a salary increase. If salespeople think that performing effectively will lead to rewards, they are likely to be more motivated than otherwise. The *accuracy* of instrumentality beliefs is important. If salespeople hold inaccurate instrumentality perceptions, they're likely to focus solely on the activities for which they *think* they'll be rewarded, instead of those for which they *actually* will be.

Valence (Attractiveness of Rewards)
The desirability of a potential outcome or reward that the salesperson may receive from improved performance.

Valence is the desirability of a potential outcome or reward that the salesperson may receive from improved performance. For example, a salesperson may have a strong desire for a promotion or a pay raise. To the extent that salespeople receive highly desirable rewards, their motivation is enhanced.

Symbolically, the motivation (or effort) expended by a salesperson is a function of the probability of an expectancy estimate multiplied by the probability of the instrumentality estimate multiplied by the valence for the reward:

$$\text{Motivation} = \left[E_i \times \left(\sum_{j=1}^{n} I_j \times V_{jk} \right) \right] \tag{11.1}$$

where

E_i = probability of an expectancy (How hard will I have to work to achieve this goal?)
I_j = probability of an instrumentality (What are my chances of receiving the reward?)
V_{jk} = valence or desirability for the reward or outcome (How attractive is the reward?)

To motivate salespeople to greater efforts, then, the alert sales manager should remember that they'll ask themselves: "What's in it for me—that is, what's my payoff, what's required of me (my costs or efforts expended), and what's my probability of success?" Unless sales managers can satisfactorily anticipate and answer these questions, salespeople will not be motivated to expend greater effort.

Attribution Theory
Based on the assumption that people are motivated by their perception of why an event occurred.

Attribution Theory. Extended from psychology, **attribution theory** identifies the reasons for a given outcome.[21] It contends that people are motivated to know why an event occurred and why they succeeded or failed at a certain task. For instance, a salesperson would likely be interested in determining why he or she lost a sale and might draw up a list of attributions to explain the failure. An *internal* attribution is a reason *within* the salesperson that could affect performance (such as ability, effort, skill, and experience); an *external* attribution is an explanation that lies *beyond* the salesperson's realm of control (such as luck, territory or task difficulty, and unanticipated adverse circumstances). Whether an internal or an external rationale is given for the lost sale can influence the salesperson's subsequent behavior. A salesperson who thinks that he or she lost the sale because of poor effort or inadequate ability is likely to increase effort or seek training. However, the salesperson who perceives the sale was lost because of uncontrollable factors like bad luck or poor economic conditions will not likely change selling behavior (after all, the failure was not his or her fault, or so the salesperson feels). Management, then, must assist salespeople in making accurate attributions for success and failure; inappropriate attributions could lead them to make inappropriate responses.[22]

TABLE 11.2   Goal-Setting Procedures for Motivating Salespeople
■ Involve the salesperson actively and openly in the goal-setting process.
■ Set realistic goals.
■ Meet and reset goals when conditions beyond the control of either party change, or when they prove to be unattainable because of unrealistic assumptions.
■ Fix goals that can be measured in tangible ways, such as time or dollar volume.
■ Incorporate the development of the measurement system into the goal-setting process.
■ Consider the measurement system in terms of real-time feedback.
■ Meet promptly with sales personnel to determine the reasons for a goal shortfall.
■ Provide positive feedback on how to correct shortfalls.
■ Develop goals and a measurement system for the new corrective plan of action.
■ Provide timely public recognition for goal achievement.

The outcome of the attribution process is that salespeople can choose either to *work harder* or to *work smarter*.[23] For example, calling on more accounts or putting in more hours is working harder. Changing the type or direction of effort is working smarter. Working longer hours and contacting more clients have long been among the primary objectives of sales managers. Yet attribution theory suggests they should concentrate on motivating salespeople to make better choices about the activities they perform—in other words, to work *smarter*. Sales managers can do this by helping sales reps direct their efforts better by searching for new customers, making different presentations for different types of customers, deciding which customers to visit more often, and other strategies. By getting a better understanding of the causal attributions salespeople make, as well as the outcomes of those attributions, sales managers can add much to their understanding of sales force motivation.

Goal-Setting Theory
Attempts to increase motivation by linking rewards directly to individuals' goals.

Goal-Setting Theory. **Goal-setting theory** attempts to increase motivation by linking rewards directly to individuals' goals.[24] Sales managers should set specific goals for individual salespeople on a regular basis. These goals should be moderately difficult to achieve, but they should be the type of goals that the salesperson will want to accomplish.[25] Unlike the traditional quota system, goal-setting theory integrates other motivational theories in an attempt to develop a reward system tailored to individual needs. Several management experts predict this approach to motivation will steadily gain in popularity.[26] Procedures for helping ensure the successful implementation of goal setting are provided in Table 11.2.[27]

To learn more about cutting-edge motivation approaches, sales managers can enroll in training programs offered by specialized firms such as Sales Motivation Solutions (http://www.sales-train.com/Training-Programs.htm), shown in Figure 11.1.

Reprinted by permission of William G. Fitzpatrick, Sales Motivation Solutions, www.sales-train.com

FIGURE 11.1   Sales Motivation Training Programs

● **Visit the website of Sales Motivation Solutions to learn about contemporary sales force motivation programs and strategies sales managers can use to increase the dedicated efforts of their salespeople.**

■ Reinforcement Theory of Motivation

The reinforcement perspective focuses on a unique approach to motivating people. It deals with the consequences of behavior, which managers can modify by using rewards and penalties, since individuals tend to repeat actions that result in rewards and avoid those that lead to punishment. Also known as **organizational behavior modification (OBM)**,[28] which has been extended to the sales arena, this theory relies on the principles and techniques of learning to strengthen, maintain, or eliminate behaviors through an intentional and systematic application of rewards or punishments.[29] In essence, management engages in interventions that can influence employee behavior and thus motivation. Sales managers can take four approaches when utilizing OBM. Two increase desired behavior through positive or negative reinforcement, and two are directed at decreasing undesirable behavior through punishment or extinction (eliminating the behavior).

Positive reinforcement provides a pleasant consequence for a desired behavior, like a bonus for opening new accounts. **Negative reinforcement** allows salespeople to avoid an undesirable outcome after displaying the desired behavior—for instance, those who achieve or surpass their annual quotas keep their jobs. Both kinds of reinforcement are intended to increase the likelihood that the desired behavior (opening new accounts, meeting quotas) will be repeated in the future.[30]

Punishment provides salespeople with an undesirable outcome when they display an undesired behavior (reducing the commission because the salesperson incorrectly estimated the cost of the sale). *Extinction* provides no positive reinforcement after an undesirable behavior (the sales manager starts a sales meeting on time rather than waiting for late arrivals). Both punishment and extinction are directed at eliminating, or at least reducing the frequency of, an undesirable behavior. The ideal situation, of course, is to permanently eliminate the undesirable behavior.

Sales managers must be aware of how frequently they reinforce salesperson efforts. *Continuous reinforcement* rewards the salesperson's desired behavior *every time* it's exhibited. *Partial reinforcement* periodically boosts the desired behavior—such as by awarding a commission check only once a month rather than after every sale. Continuous reinforcement helps salespeople learn the desired behavior more quickly, but partial reinforcement often leads to more permanent learning.

For OBM to be successful, sales managers must know precisely what behaviors their salespeople should exhibit and avoid; then they should clearly articulate these behaviors and outcomes to them. Furthermore, sales managers need to determine what reinforcement schedules are necessary to bring about desired results.

Organizational Behavior Modification Theory
Involves the use of various learning techniques to strengthen, maintain, or eliminate specific behaviors by using rewards or punishments.

Positive Reinforcement
Providing salespeople with a pleasant consequence for having engaged in the desired behavior (e.g., providing a bonus for opening new accounts).

Negative Reinforcement
Avoiding an undesirable outcome after displaying the desired behavior (e.g., allowing those salespeople who achieve or surpass their annual quotas to keep their jobs).

Using Rewards and Incentive Programs for Sales Force Motivation

We now turn to one of the sales manager's most important tasks: initiating and directing salespeople's intense and persistent work-related behaviors toward attaining organizational goals and objectives. Nucor Corp. (www.nucor.com), a company that treats its workers like owners, demonstrates how a reward system can turn an underdog into an upstart nipping at the heels of giants in an industry almost decimated by intense global competition. Nucor has thrived by creating a performance culture based on a uniquely radical reward structure that motivates its work force in all functional areas—including sales.[31] Unlike many companies, Nucor managers focus their motivational skills on employees in the front line of the business by talking with them, listening to their suggestions, and accepting the occasional failure. To emphasize the importance of each person on the Nucor team, every employee's name goes on the cover of the annual report.[32] Tying employees' income to their performance,[33] Nucor exemplifies how employees will expend extraordinary effort if they are richly rewarded, treated with respect, and empowered.

So, you may now be thinking, "What administrative actions and strategies can I use to enhance sales force motivation?" Good question. The answer may well lie in the vast array of intrinsic and extrinsic rewards that can induce salespeople to exert higher levels of effort.

■ Extrinsic Rewards

Extrinsic Rewards
Those rewards controlled by managers and customers (e.g., pay, bonuses, and promotions).

Incentive Program
When salespeople achieve or surpass a specified sales quota, they are often given a monetary bonus and/or special recognition to reward them for their performance as well as to motivate them to continue this behavior.

Financial Incentives
Monetary reward for job performance; includes salary, commission, bonuses, stock options, or fringe benefits such as a company car, medical, dental and life insurance, or educational aid.

Extrinsic rewards come from the organization, usually higher management, and are mostly financial in nature. Examples include salary, commissions,[34] fringe benefits, perks, formal recognition, job promotions, employee stock ownership plans, profit sharing, gain sharing, stock options, and team-based compensation. Although they're a central part of extrinsic rewards, compensation plans and packages constitute the most important way to remunerate employees.[35] Thus, we discuss these topics separately in chapter 12. Let's look at sales incentive programs first.[36]

Sales Incentive Programs. As tools with tremendous potential motivating power, incentive spending is becoming a bigger part of many firms' budgets.[37] A recent survey indicated that more than 70 percent of the responding companies considered **incentive programs** essential to the success of their overall marketing plans.[38]

Among the more important motivators in **financial incentive** programs are cash, travel, and merchandise. When salespeople achieve or surpass a specified sales quota, they are often given a monetary bonus to reward them for their performance as well as motivate them to continue this behavior. Travel rewards are used similarly. U.S. companies now spend over $28 billion annually on incentive travel for top employees and customers.[39] Some of the more popular destinations for travel incentives are Europe and the Mediterranean, Hawaii, the Caribbean, Bermuda, Mexico, and South America. Today's salespeople want choices in travel awards tailored to their particular interests, and they often want to take their families with them. So, at a growing numbers of firms—including WebEx, a video-conferencing company—the range of travel rewards for salespeople who meet their annual sales quotas or other goals may include anything from a deep-sea fishing excursion to an African safari.[40] The most common items of merchandise used as a sales force incentive include award plaques and trophies, consumer electronics, household goods, clothing, sporting goods, and travel accessories.

An effective sales incentive program can accomplish several important goals. Perhaps the main one is to increase total sales. Sales incentive programs can also help increase the number of new accounts brought into a company. Other benefits include helping launch new products, boosting morale, and reviving old products. For help in devising creative incentives, sales managers can turn to firms, such as Incentive Logic (www.incentivelogic.com), that specialize in developing incentives to motivate the sales force (see Figure 11.2).

Reprinted by permission of Incentive Logic.

FIGURE 11.2   Sales Incentive Solutions

● **Sales managers can turn to firms such as Incentive Logic, who are specialists in implementing sales incentive solutions to increase sales force motivation.**

Sales incentive programs can be cost-effective ways to increase sales. The Incentive Marketing Association reports that the typical sales incentive program increases sales by an average of 19 percent—at a cost, as a percentage of increased sales, of only 8 percent. Over 40 percent of all participating salespeople earn awards.[41]

One study found similarities in incentive preferences among men and women in sales. For example, travel was one of the most popular awards for both men and women, and merchandise incentives valued from $100 to more than $1,000 were highly rated by both genders. The survey also showed emerging interest in less traditional incentives. Tuition assistance for themselves or their children and educational opportunities that could lead to career advancement were highly rated by both male and female salespeople.[42] The important implication for sales managers is that salespeople are willing to extend themselves if they are properly motivated.

Promotion Opportunities. An attractive career path with "promotion decision" stages at regular intervals (at least every three to five years) can keep many individuals motivated throughout most of their careers. People tend to become ego-involved with succeeding on the "fast track," and they continue to strive for the next promotion. To maximize motivational benefits from a career development plan, the sales manager must provide periodic feedback—at least yearly, but more frequently in the early stages of career development. This feedback ought to come to salespeople through a comprehensive performance evaluation. Small sales units may find informal evaluations practical; but larger sales organizations need more formalized performance evaluation systems, supported by rating forms and written narratives maintained in the employee's personnel file.

In a simplified career path, sales trainees have an introductory or trial period of up to three years. By that time, the salesperson must either be promoted to the sales development stage or be terminated. Then, no later than his or her seventh anniversary with the sales force, the individual must be either promoted to senior salesperson or let go. At this level, the individual may continue on a *career sales path* or switch to a *sales/marketing career path*. Although the decision to remain on the sales path is largely up to the individual salesperson, the opportunity to move into management depends upon performance evaluations, which we discuss in chapter 14.

■ Intrinsic Rewards

Intrinsic Rewards
Nontangible rewards that salespeople experience internally (e.g., personal growth and self esteem).

Some rewards are psychological or behavioral in nature and seek to influence and satisfy internally experienced desires. These **intrinsic rewards** come from within the salesperson and include feelings of accomplishment, personal growth and development, enhanced self-esteem, and personal worth and recognition.[43] While monetary rewards are important to individuals under thirty-five years of age, the opportunity for advancement and promotion also are strong motivators for them.[44] Table 11.3,

TABLE 11.3   What Motivates Top Sales Performers?

MOTIVATORS	DESCRIPTION
1. **Need for status**	■ Recognition is a key motivating factor for top salespeople. This group seeks power, authority, image, and reputation.
2. **Need for control**	■ While top salespeople like being with other people, they also like to be in control and enjoy influencing others.
3. **Need for respect**	■ Top sales achievers like to be seen as experts who are willing to help and advise others.
4. **Need for routine**	■ It is a misconception that successful sellers thrive on freedom. Most like to follow a routine strictly and are upset when it is interrupted.
5. **Need for accomplishment**	■ Money is only one of the many things that motivate the top sales performers. In addition to a big house, fancy cars, and nice clothes, they constantly go after new challenges in their jobs to maintain enthusiasm.
6. **Need for stimulation**	■ Most outstanding salespeople have an abundance of physical energy and thrive on challenges. Therefore, they welcome outside stimulation as a way of channeling their energy.
7. **Need for honesty**	■ Top sales achievers have a strong need to believe in the product they are selling. If they have doubts about the company or a new product line, they are apt to switch jobs.
8. **Need for commitment from upper sales management**	■ Salespeople need to be supported by their senior sales management in their quest for increasing sales. This commitment is exhibited in the form of training, mentoring, and guidance provided by sales managers.

based on several studies, shows the variety of factors that motivate top sales performers.[45] Because studies report that promotions and opportunities for growth are very attractive to salespeople in the early stages of their careers, we next discuss how sales managers can use such recognition to motivate the sales force.

Non-Financial Incentives
Psychological rewards related to the individual salesperson's intrinsic needs in that they are internally experienced payoffs (e.g., job security, relationships with superiors and coworkers, working conditions, challenging sales assignments, increasing responsibility, or rewards and recognition for special achievements).

Recognition
A non-financial reward used for motivation.

Recognition. For years, the majority of sales managers assumed that monetary rewards were most valued and therefore most motivating to salespeople. Recently, however, sales managers across all industries are beginning to realize that while monetary rewards are initially motivating, **non-financial incentives** and intrinsic rewards, such as **recognition**, are critical in drawing higher levels of performance from the sales force.[46] Vincent Alonzo, a sales consultant, says, "I'll bet you'd be hard-pressed to find anyone in sales who doesn't crave the spotlight, the excitement, the personal validation that recognition brings. If they don't crave it, they probably shouldn't be in sales."[47]

Most sales managers realize that giving salespeople symbolic motivators, such as plaques, rings, and memberships into elite sales clubs, can instill a certain pride that a paycheck or free trip cannot. Money and other incentives are soon spent or consumed, but public recognition acts as a constant reminder of a salesperson's accomplishment. Xerox Corporation (www.xerox.com) has a President's Club for its top sales achievers. As one of Xerox's top salespeople explains, "The President's Club is

TABLE 11.4   Developing a Recognition Program for Salespeople

- The program should be based on objective *performance* only. No subjective judgments should be allowed.

- Everyone must have a realistic chance to win, and there should be awards for superior performance in several categories.

- Awards should be presented in public, so that winners receive recognition in front of their peers.

- Award ceremonies must be conducted in good taste. A poorly done recognition program can leave employees uninspired to do their best.

- The awards program should be highly publicized to create awareness and involvement throughout the company.

what we all strive for because it's how our success is measured within Xerox."[48] While a free trip accompanies membership in the President's Club, the real motivator for most salespeople is being recognized as a member of that elite group. Many top-performing salespeople win company incentives year after year. What eventually becomes important is being recognized as a top salesperson. Bolstering the salesperson's ego becomes much more important than an incentive can ever be.[49] Of course, no single form of recognition works for everyone. A good recognition program begins by finding each person's "start center,"[50] which is often activated by higher-order needs, such as appreciation and admiration, that are as unique as the individual. Table 11.4 presents the factors a sales manager should consider in developing a recognition program for salespeople.

● **Public recognition and awards for achieving excellence in sales productivity can be a powerful way of motivating salespeople.**

Sales Force Motivation Strategies and Tools

Sales Motivation Strategies
Techniques used to implement motivational theories or approaches (e.g., sales contests, sales meetings, promotion opportunities, and incentive programs).

If salespeople come to take a relatively stable plan for granted, compensation systems, which are primarily designed to attain organizational goals, can become ineffective. Then the sales manager needs other **sales motivation strategies** and tools that go above and beyond rewards. For example, sales training programs can motivate salespeople by providing up-to-date knowledge about the company, customers, products, technology to employ in selling, and performance expectations that can give them more self-confidence, instill enthusiasm, and raise career aspirations.[51] But the two most popular motivational strategies are sales contests and sales meetings.

■ Sales Contests

Sales Contests
Relatively short-run competitive events designed to motivate and reward salespeople for achieving objective goals.

As a motivational device, the **sales contest** has the potential for undesirable as well as desirable results. Therefore, it is important for sales managers to understand the goals that can be accomplished through sales contests, the essential decision areas in planning contests, and the potential pitfalls associated with them. Contest themes, rules, prizes, participation, duration, promotion, and post-contest assessment are important considerations in the planning and implementation of this motivational tool. However, all planning must begin with the specific purposes, goals, and objectives of the contest.

Sales Contests: Purposes, Goals, and Objectives. Although astute sales contest planners will coordinate contests with current market conditions, contests can focus sales force attention on any particular goal area for short periods of time. The purpose of a contest may be to motivate salespeople to increase the number of new customers, develop sales of a new product, counteract sales slumps due to seasonal variations, sell a more profitable product mix, cut costs, adjust quotas, reorder salespeople's priorities, and boost morale. In addition, contests might be held to clear overstocked inventory, keep production lines running, encourage sales personnel to recruit and train newcomers, develop new prospecting methods, prepare call reports more carefully, make more sales presentations, provide greater customer service, and enhance customer satisfaction. Sometimes, contests are designed subtly to get the sales force to reinstitute good work habits while focusing on some general goal like increasing sales volume. Some contests are designed to achieve several complex goals. For example, as described in the *Sales Management in Action* box, MCI (www.mci.com) ran what may have been the first Internet-based sales contest. Several other reasons for sales contests are presented in Table 11.5.

Contests tend to produce the most effective results when only a small number of goals (one to three, ideally) are established. Goals should be consistent with the company's overall marketing strategy, understandable and achievable, and readily measurable.

Contest Themes. Sales managers should ensure that contest themes are creative, novel, timely, implementable, promotable, visibly measurable, and self-image reinforcing. Variations of sports and games in season are frequently used as a theme, as are travel routes, mock battles, races, building construction, and clothing contests (in which the salesperson can wear to meetings what he or she wins). There must be an easily understood way to measure milestones of progress. Contest themes that create

TABLE 11.5   Sales Contest Objectives and Rewards

OBJECTIVE	REWARD
Increase dollar volume	■ Prize to salespeople who increase sales (based on percentage of dollar increase over previous period). ■ Several prizes, with top producers awarded most expensive prize. Runners-up receive less expensive prizes. Points for each $1 of sales. Prizes won by fixed number who have most points.
Stimulate more orders	■ Prize for all salespeople who reach or exceed their order quota. ■ Points for each order, with fixed number of prizes to those with most points.
Increase sales orders	■ Prizes to those who make the most demonstrations and/or complete the most call reports. ■ Prizes to all who make quota of calls and demonstrations. ■ Additional prize for meeting a second quota.
Build higher unit sales	■ Points for higher dollar or unit volume (based on past averages), with prizes for those who make best showing. ■ Reach quota of new customers to earn prize. Sellers who add most customers earn prize. Several prizes, with best prizes to top producers.
Add customers	■ Points toward prize for each new customer, with bonus points for target accounts.
Secure prospects	■ Points toward prize for each new prospect, with additional points for each prospect that becomes a customer within a specified period.
Build off-season business	■ Dollar or unit-volume quota to earn prize during slow months. Two quotas: first for salesperson, second for spouse (if trip).
Push slow item	■ Points awarded for sales of slow-moving stocks, with prizes for biggest point getters.
Stimulate balanced selling	■ Prizes to those who maintain best sales record for selling entire line during specified time.
Introduce new product	■ Points toward prize for best sales record with new product. ■ Prize to salespeople who reach quota of customers who buy new product.
Increase use of displays	■ Prize to salespeople for placing quota of displays.
Stimulate dealer tie-ins	■ Prizes to salespeople who get most dealers to tie in with national advertising campaign.
Revive dead accounts	■ Prizes to salespeople who reactivate most old accounts. ■ Prizes for greatest sales volume from formerly dead accounts.
Switch users to your brand	■ Points toward prize for salespeople who switch users or owners of competitive product to yours.
Improve sales abilities	■ Prizes to salespeople who score best on examinations after training period.
Reduce costs	■ Prize to salespeople and managers who achieve best sales-to-costs ratio.
Build multiple sales	■ Prizes to salespeople with best carload or multiple-sales record.
Increase Internet usage among salespeople	■ Prizes to salespeople with most new business from web page.

great difficulties in implementation or complex measurement processes should be avoided. Above all, salespeople should be able to identify psychologically with the theme, and it must not be so juvenile or silly that mature salespeople feel childish when playing "the game." In fact many experts believe that salespeople should have input into the goals and themes of the sales contest.

The theme can be annual, such as a summer contest or a special holiday contest, both of which can be designed to persuade salespeople to put forth special efforts during vacation or holiday seasons. Novelty themes can be related to the contest objective, to current events, to seasonal sports, or to other appealing common

SALES MANAGEMENT IN ACTION

Sales Contests Go Interactive

Along with motivating its sales force, MCI (www .mci.com) wanted to give its service reps experience using the Internet. So, a sales contest called Cyber Safari was targeted to its 5000 reps who had never used the Internet before. Salespeople won points for achieving each of ten different objectives based on sales and revenues. Points could be redeemed for more than 300 prizes ranging from trips to Monte Carlo, Hawaii, and Acapulco to home fitness centers, computers, and pianos. Salespeople used their laptops to find out their current rankings in the contest and to choose from the online catalog of prizes. This interactive sales contest helped MCI achieve its highest-selling quarter in more than two years. What's more, the salespeople had competitive fun while learning new technology.

SOURCE: Andy Cohen, "Sales Contests Go Interactive," *Sales & Marketing Management,* July 1996, pp. 45–46.

denominators. Regardless of the specific contest theme adopted, it must generate enthusiasm and stimulate the salespeople to react favorably. For example, one firm held a very successful "strip the brass" contest that had the effects of fulfilling the recognition needs of salespeople. In this company, the president wore a very unusual digital watch, its marketing vice president was recognized by his elegant leather attaché case with raised edges, and the sales vice president had a wardrobe of designer shirts. During a two-week contest, replicas or reproductions of these three items were awarded to winners by the three executives (in person) based on a formula that related productivity to the value of the prizes.

Contests can be designed for the entire sales force, for those with different levels of experience (such as junior or senior salesperson), or for horizontal business segments (such as those serving different customer classes or territorial zones). Grouping salespeople for contest purposes is consistent with the hierarchical segmentation approach to motivation, and it recognizes that different levels of salespeople tend to have different needs. Contests should be customized to each separate group of participants, with appropriate goals, themes, and awards reflecting their different drive levels. For example, junior salespeople might be best motivated by the expectation of glamorous prizes, while senior salespeople might prefer a vacation trip with top officials of the company so they can share their views on company issues and later brag to their peers about their interactions with the "big bosses." In planning contests, sales managers should ensure that everyone has an equal chance to win. Otherwise, the effect will be demotivational. Suppose, for example, that banks and savings and loan institutional buyers are the best prospects for products included in the contest scope, and that some salespeople have few of these institutions in their sales territories. Clearly these employees can become cynical about the whole thing.

Contest Rules. Formulate contest rules to clarify goals and prevent abuses. Obsolete or deficient products as well as all unethical tactics must be deemed outside the ground rules of the contest. Rules should also be phrased so that they discourage salespeople from holding back orders before the contest, applying undue pressure on buyers during the contest, or suggesting that buyers can cancel their orders after the contest. However, the rules can be used to orient the contest toward specific organization goals. For instance, restricting it to accounts not reported on call sheets for two months preceding the contest period might channel contest efforts more toward selling newly developed prospects. Finally, rules must clearly define the contest time period, the action that actually constitutes a sale for contest purposes (order, delivery, payment), and the exact basis for accumulating points for prizes.

Contest Rewards and Prizes. Unless contest prizes include items that most of the participants want, the contest will not be motivating. While many salespeople will say they prefer cash, more unusual and visible awards that winners can conspicuously enjoy—such as glamorous trips, luxurious boats, cars, sporting equipment, or home entertainment systems—serve as long-lasting incentives for all participants. Consideration of the salesperson's family also is important in selecting incentives. Awards ought to be something the whole family would enjoy, ensuring their participation in cheering on their prospective winner.

Many corporations are turning to productive travel as incentives—for example, motivational sales force training in exotic settings has the advantage of being easily justified to top management, since they can combine business and pleasure, family participation, highly visible recognition, and non-taxability while giving salespeople the chance to share spirited interaction with other high producers in the company.

Salesperson Participation. Sometimes, only senior salespeople have the opportunity to compete for the chance to go to national sales conventions or to be awarded membership in an elite group such as the President's Club or the Million Dollar Sales Club. Junior salespeople are more likely to have their own contests, with awards such as a trophy and a letter of praise signed by a top company official.

© Bill Bachmann / PhotoEdit

● Using rewards like a fully paid vacation to exotic locales, sales managers can help motivate salesperson performance toward the attainment of organizational goals.

Most contests don't pit one salesperson against another, but award prizes for achieving certain individual standards of performance. Experts disagree about whether it's better to have lesser prizes that nearly everyone can win, or expensive rewards that only a few can attain. Prizes must be at least attractive enough to motivate, because token prizes with little recognition value may kill the motivational effects of the contest. On the other hand, excessively expensive prizes may overemphasize competition and hurt sales force cohesiveness.

With firms increasingly emphasizing teamwork, sales contests also have the potential to increase the motivation of an entire sales team as well as individual salespeople. The same guidelines for goals and prizes hold for team-oriented contests. The major difference is that the contest winner is a team of individuals who all receive prizes.

Contest Duration. Contests usually last between one and five months. Salespeople should have enough time to make at least one complete pass through their territories. Extra-effort pressures can be maintained for only a limited time before interest begins to lag. Contests that occur too regularly (at the same time each year) may come to seem routine and lose their incentive value. Contests that are unexpected often generate more enthusiasm.

Promoting the Contest. To build enthusiasm, the contest should be promoted with great fanfare to the sales force before it begins. Personal letters and e-mails from management can announce and reinforce the imminent contest. It's important for sales managers to announce the exact nature and rules of the contest to all salespeople simultaneously—and dramatically. Explanatory posters should be put up promptly after the contest is announced. The company's website can be used to enable salespeople, no matter where their territories are located, to follow their relative progress in the contest. Some creativity presentation of the contest progress can add to the excitement and fun of the contest. For example, model race cars might show the daily or weekly progress of each salesperson "driver" by his or her relative position on a circular race track. All participants should frequently get detailed, official feedback unless the contest is not competitive, in which case each person's progress can be conveyed confidentially.

Assessing Contest Effectiveness. A contest is like any other management tool: it requires the use of resources. Thus management will want to assess whether the resources used in the contest were wisely invested. Determine whether the results of the contest exceeded its costs, whether contest objectives were achieved, how satisfied the sales force was with the contest, and what strengths and weaknesses were inherent in the contest. Obviously, there's no point in conducting a contest if the company is not better off afterward than it was before.

Potential Pitfalls of Contests. While well-devised contests can accomplish multiple organizational and individual goals, the sales manager ought to recognize and avoid certain negative side effects. Contests can become so routine that they are expected, and sales reps consider awards as part of their yearly compensation. Another drawback is that contests can temporarily increase sales and thereby provide a means of disguising sales force shortcomings or sales management deficiencies. Like any overused incentive, the contest award eventually tends to lose its motivational effects. Professional salespeople may look on even well-designed contests as beneath their

TABLE 11.6 Why Some Sales Contest Are Losers	
Overestimating goals	Salespeople will only be frustrated by a goal they know can't be reached.
Neglecting to publicize the contest	For salespeople to be motivated and excited about the contest, they must be informed.
Rewarding only the top salespeople	If only the top twenty salespeople can win, it ultimately demotivates everyone else. Give everyone a chance to win!
Leaving spouses at home	If the prize is a trip, many salespeople don't want to go alone; thus they will not be excited about the contest.
Viewing the sales contest as a panacea	If sales and performance are drastically down, something more than a sales contest may be needed. A sales contest is not a substitute for sound marketing and sales strategies.

SOURCE: Adapted from Andy Cohen, "Why Some Contests Are Losers," *Sales & Marketing Management,* August 1996, pp. 39–40.

image, and it is always difficult to devise themes that are simultaneously fun and image enhancing. Some sales managers feel that the money put into contests would provide a more continuous incentive if it were spread among high performers as pay increases instead. This approach can increase costs, however, and there is little to substantiate the idea that it provides more benefits than contests.

While the major purpose of sales contests is to enhance motivation, many times they can end up *demotivating* the sales force. An improperly implemented sales contest can destroy morale among salespeople as well as negatively affect sales. For example, if the sales contest rewards one person each year and the same person tends to win the contest year after year, some negative side effects are bound to occur. Everyone else starts to feel like a loser. And the top performer, if it's the same person all the time, usually does not need the reward or recognition as much as some of the other salespeople do. Thus, the contest can create jealousy among the sales force as well as making the winner unpopular with his or her colleagues.

After sales contests end, some salespeople fall into a motivational valley, resulting in sales slumps. Sales managers need to provide positive encouragement to perk them up. The zeal to win contests can also lead to high-pressure selling tactics, inventory overloading, outright cheating, and neglect of other customer relationships. Some general guidelines concerning what not to do with sales contests are presented in Table 11.6. Despite shortcomings, contests can provide a flexible and valuable managerial tool if themes, rules, prizes, participation, duration, and publicity are tailored to organizational and salespeople's goals.

■ Sales Meetings

Sales Meetings
Opportunities for two-way communication and interaction among all members of the marketing team—field and headquarters.

One of the most popular means of enhancing motivation is the **sales meeting**, be it national, regional, or local. Instead of utilizing the normal one-way communication from management to salespeople, sales meetings provide opportunities for two-way communication and interaction among all members of the marketing team—field and headquarters. The company comes alive at sales meetings, and names become people as sales representatives, sales managers, marketing managers, and top company executives interact. Salespeople are able to see how their role as the field-marketing arm of the company blends with headquarters' marketing activities.

Sales meetings are strategic "halftimes" in the selling game for communicating about new-product introductions, price changes, upcoming promotional campaigns, new policies, and overall company goals. They can help motivate salespeople to greater productivity by reminding them of the rest of the company's support efforts.[52] They can even motivate by surprising, entertaining, and exciting salespeople. For example, Northwestern Mutual Life (www.nmfn.com) salespeople enjoyed one recent family-reunion-style sales meeting—which included country music star Wynona Judd—so much that each of them paid $1,000 to attend! Sun Microsystems, Inc. (www.sunw.com) held a sales meeting that included a dance party and a day of river rafting in Colorado. Straus Discount Auto (www.straussauto.com) recently staged a wrestling match as part of its sales meeting. In the tag-team match, former WWF champion Greg "The Hammer" Valentine and the company CEO took on the "Bounty Hunters." These types of creative sales meetings can boost morale and productivity for everyone involved.[53]

National, Regional, and Local Meetings. Usually held once a year, *national meetings* may include the entire sales force or only a select group of top performers. Travel and lodging expenses for national meetings are considerable, and territorial opportunities or problems must go unattended while salespeople are away. The benefits, however, may outweigh these costs. Sales representatives get the chance to exchange ideas with company management, experience a pleasant change of environment and a break in their normal routine, and even hear motivational talks by experts and/or celebrities so that they return to their territories with renewed enthusiasm. Especially when the sales force is relatively small and scattered, national conferences can be an important unifying device. *Regional conferences,* planned with a work-oriented agenda, can be less expensive for large corporations whose sales forces have more localized selling problems. *Local meetings* and seminars are the backbone of the communication system and usually give salespeople the greatest support. These regularly held meetings are important for bestowing timely recognition on salespeople, providing group interaction, and focusing sales training on solving territorial problems and creating selling opportunities.

Planning. Detailed planning is required for effective sales meetings. Regional or local meetings are generally held monthly or weekly in the regional or branch sales office, and success depends upon developing a strong agenda. Planning for national conferences, however, is much more demanding. Facilities must be reserved many months in advance, and goals, dates, programs, participants, and publicity must be arranged early on—often starting a year or more ahead of time. Usually, national sales conferences are held away from the immediate work environment, at a resort area if the purpose of the meeting is largely motivational or at a hotel close to company headquarters if work is the primary objective. Planning sales meetings involves several tasks:

■ Establish meeting goals (from both the company's and the sales representatives' perspectives).

■ Select a theme that integrates goals and communicates the overall purpose of the meeting.

■ Develop a tentative agenda or program for the meeting, and work up a preliminary budget.

■ Finalize the program and budget, and send copies of the program to all attendees.

- Coordinate closely with all participants in the program to ensure they know their roles.

- Provide handouts summarizing the main points of the meeting for salespeople to take home for further review.

- Evaluate the meeting in terms of goal achievement.

Table 11.7 presents some general guidelines for creating more memorable sales meetings.

Competitive Spirit. The sales meeting is an excellent opportunity for management to recognize sales accomplishments, to announce the names of sales leaders, and to award prizes to outstanding salespeople and sales managers. For instance, one company holds a three-day annual sales convention for district and division sales managers and their spouses. On the final evening a formal dinner is held, and manager-of-the-year trophies are given out in an "Academy Award" style that includes requests for "the envelope please." Throughout the year, the company house organ builds up to the momentous occasion when the president's spouse opens the envelope and announces the name of the manager of the year. Another firm awards stock options to sales force members and uses the weekly sales meeting to announce the paper dollar gains of salespeople who own a substantial number of company shares.

Specialized Training. Often, the national or regional sales meeting offers management an excellent opportunity to train all salespeople simultaneously (e.g., regarding how to introduce a new product or customer strategy). One manufacturer of inexpensive costume jewelry held a training session at a national sales meeting to address a delicate problem. As the firm's merchandise was being sold off its store racks, retail clerks were filling in the racks with jewelry purchased from competitors. In turn, when calling on the retail stores, company salespeople were removing competitive products from its displays. Later, store buyers instructed the clerks to put the items back on the racks. Discussions among all the salespeople at the sales meeting were fruitful in uncovering a company-wide method of dealing with this troublesome matter. Other companies hold weekly sales clinics to analyze the activity or call reports of salespeople. Unidentified copies of call reports are distributed, discussed, and criticized under the watchful eye of the sales manager.[54]

Change of Pace. The regional or national sales meeting is often a vacation with a purpose. Getting away helps salespeople unwind. Many firms hold their sales meet-

TABLE 11.7   Creating Memorable Sales Meetings
■ Before setting up and scheduling the meeting, sales managers should survey salespeople to learn what kind of information or training they would find most beneficial.
■ Choose meeting locations, entertainment, and activities that salespeople will enjoy and learn from.
■ Add a special element of surprise by not revealing ahead of time everything on the meeting's agenda—for example, a celebrity appearance or special gifts for attendees.
■ Give individual attention at the meeting by rewarding salesperson accomplishments and recognizing special contributions.

ings at resort sites, where salespeople can enjoy golf, tennis, swimming, horseback riding, winter sports, and health club facilities in between business meetings. The announcement of a resort site, accompanied by a handsome brochure, often causes prospective attendees to look forward to the meetings. Moreover, it tells them there will be more to the meeting than business.

Video Conferences. Setting up a video conference is an efficient way to link several different locations together for an interactive sales meeting. Rather than bringing the entire sales force of an organization together under one roof, video conferencing links everyone via satellite and/or interactive video. One large company celebrated its 100th anniversary by connecting over 2,000 district sales managers in five cities for a video conference. "We held a video conference for the first time because we wanted every member of the sales management family to be together simultaneously and share the excitement coming out of the celebration," reported the manager of sales meetings and conferences.[55]

A video conference is an excellent way to inform and motivate the entire sales force of a company at one time. More important, it enables top management to give everyone the same message at the same time. And a teleconference to several locations enables top management not only to speak to each location simultaneously but also to tailor the content of each of the locations' meetings without having to hold separate regional meetings. Finally, as a spokesperson for a large consumer products company put it, "We could have brought all 2,000 sales managers to a central location for one big meeting, but we wouldn't have had the same feeling that we got with only 400 people in the room."[56] Given the success many companies are experiencing with video conferences, they're likely to become a bigger part of sales meetings in the future.

Additional Perspectives in Twenty-First Century Sales Force Motivation

Let's now look at a few emerging perspectives that provide additional insights into sales force motivation.

■ Organizational and Job Commitment

Successful salespeople feel a bond between themselves and their company and work. **Organizational commitment** is identifying with and internalizing the company's values and goals and desiring to stay a viable member of the organization. **Job commitment** refers to the degree of involvement (high or low) salespeople have in their job.

When salespeople feel committed to their organization and/or job, they feel energized to be effective producers.[57] After all, their selling success will assist the firm in achieving its ends. Similarly, such success is likely to increase their positive attitudes toward—and subsequent commitment to—their job.[58] Such salespeople demonstrate strong dedication to their company and to the work itself. This sense of devotion can pack an emotional wallop. Research has found that both organizational commitment and job commitment can favorably affect salesperson motivation.[59] Furthermore, the longer salespeople stay with the firm, the more knowledgeable they become about

Organizational Commitment
When salespeople identify with and internalize the company's values and goals and desire to stay a viable member of the organization.

Job Commitment
The degree of involvement (high or low) salespeople have in their job.

their customers; consequently, they're in a position to provide improved customer service, and customer loyalty tends to rise.[60]

■ Organizational Climate

Organizational Climate
The perceptions salespeople have about their work situation and conditions.

Organizational climate consists of the perceptions salespeople have about their work situation and conditions. Whether favorable or unfavorable, the perceived climate can affect salespeople's attitudes about their job situation.

Organizational climate has four components: (1) job characteristics (role perceptions, opportunities, and problems in the job); (2) leadership characteristics (supervisory styles and salesperson/sales manager relationships); (3) organizational characteristics (company philosophy about managing salespeople); and (4) work group characteristics (formal and informal relationships among the salespeople).[61] Aspects of organizational climate that influence salesperson motivation include such factors as ethical climate, the considerateness of the sales supervisor, management's concern for sales subordinates, the level of company support and training, availability of adequate resources, the number of personal and career development opportunities, extent of trust in the sales manager, the degree of challenge in the salesperson's goals, sales manager success in obtaining upper-management support for the sales force, and the opportunity for high earnings and promotions.[62]

■ Learning Orientation versus Performance Orientation

Performance Orientation
When salespeople are especially keen on receiving favorable assessments of their skills from management and peers.

Because sales managers typically have a short-term perspective, they tend to encourage their salespeople to adopt a **performance orientation**. That is, they predispose them toward working hard and generating sales. Indeed, a performance orientation works when salespeople are especially keen on receiving favorable assessments of their skills from management and peers. But, afraid that change will lead to failure, they may doggedly continue their traditional way of doing things, even if an alternate way would be better.

Learning Orientation
When salespeople strive to discover new ways of selling effectively.

Compare this perspective to a **learning orientation**, which occurs when salespeople discover news ways of selling effectively. They're willing to take risks and try new approaches, even if doing so leads to mistakes; they value personal growth and development.[63]

More firms today are trying to enhance the learning orientation of their salespeople. Through careful and conscientious learning, salespeople *can* adopt improved methods for dealing with their customers, thus enhancing their selling skills and ultimately producing long-run gains for the firm.

Salespeople who use a learning orientation are zealous to acquire new knowledge, enhance their present skills, obtain new skills, and improve their overall performance for the firm's customers and themselves.[64] Research has found that a performance orientation affects salesperson motivation differently than a learning orientation does. Specifically, salespeople using a performance orientation have an increased propensity to "work harder" (increase their selling effort). Salespeople utilizing a learning orientation also work hard, but they are also more likely to "work smarter," gaining knowledge about various selling situations and then adapting it to the sales situation at hand.[65] Working smarter is especially effective in enhancing salesperson productivity.[66]

Some salespeople set personal goals for themselves, in addition to the organizational and individual goals that have been set for them by or in concert with their sales manager. Personal goals can give the salesperson an "extra push," particularly because they have been tailored to the individual's specific needs and the unique circumstances in their territories. In fact, salespeople who set specific goals for themselves and who believe that such goals are important to job success exert more effort than salespeople who don't take this approach.[67]

■ Salesperson's Career Cycle

Just like human lives and company products, salespeople, too, have a "life cycle" of different stages that evolve over time.[68] They pass through four distinct stages: the preparation or exploration stage, the development or establishment stage, the maturity or maintenance stage, and the decline or disengagement stage. Individuals go through these stages not only as a function of time but also because of changes in their personal and professional lives and circumstances. At each stage, salespeople have different needs, skills, requirements, goals, and performance levels. Thus motivational concerns at each career stage can vary, as shown in Table 11.8.

In the *preparation/exploration stage,* salespeople are concerned about finding an occupation in which they will succeed. They're likely to be new to the selling arena (or at least to the firm) and typically require extensive training. Their priority is to build up knowledge and skills and become conversant with the organization's procedures and policies.

When salespeople arrive at the *development/establishment stage,* they have become committed to the selling profession, seek stability in their professional and personal lives, and strongly desire professional success. This is the stage when training must be converted into productive results. The *maturity/maintenance stage* requires holding on to what has already been achieved—position, status, image, and performance level. The salesperson may reach a "rated capacity" beyond which he or she is unwilling or even unable to go. In this stage, salespeople prefer to sell smarter rather than harder and may well plateau at a desirable level.

TABLE 11.8 Motiving Salespeople Throughout Their Career

CAREER STAGE	SALESPERSON CHARACTERISTICS	SALES FORCE MOTIVATOR
Preparation/ Exploration	■ Is in early phase of career ■ Searching for comfortable position ■ Likely to change occupation	■ Use communication to build self-confidence and lower uncertainties
Development/ Establishment	■ Seeks stabilization in occupation ■ Sees career as very important ■ Strives for professional success and promotion	■ Widen criteria for success ■ Introduce rewards for meeting challenges
Maturity/ Maintenance	■ Concerned with retaining current position ■ Shows greater commitment to firm; less likely to switch jobs ■ Adapts to changes to keep performance at current level	■ Reward creativity and self-reliance ■ Emphasize techniques for working smarter
Decline/ Disengagement	■ Exhibits declining performance ■ Psychologically disengages from work ■ Preparing for retirement	■ Help reduce number of work hours ■ Assign to special sales related projects

In the *decline/disengagement stage,* salespeople may be preparing at least mentally for retirement or, if they haven't achieved much success, they may psychologically withdraw from the sales scene by making fewer calls per day or calling solely on existing accounts rather than on prospects. They may experience substantially reduced confidence in themselves and lose interest in their work.

How does motivation change from one career stage to the next? Research has found that preparation/exploration stage salespeople don't feel they're being rewarded for effective performance. In the development/establishment stage, they place heavy emphasis on receiving a promotion; in the maturity/maintenance stage, their level of motivation may be the same except for a decreased emphasis on receiving a promotion. Finally, salespeople in the decline/disengagement stage don't think they'll be rewarded for achieving their new accounts or special products quotas.[69] Another study found that salespeople in the exploration stage of their careers had greater material ambitions (desire for money and material things) than did those in subsequent stages.[70]

Career Plateauing
When a salesperson no longer grows or develops in the position, and/or the likelihood of the person receiving additional responsibility is low.

Career Plateauing. Despite the potential for substantial material and nonmaterial rewards, sales jobs are demanding, challenging, and even grueling. **Career plateauing** occurs when a salesperson no longer grows or develops in the position, or when the likelihood of the person's receiving additional responsibility is low. It occurs for three major reasons: (1) the salesperson's performance is deficient, (2) few opportunities for promotions or augmented responsibility are available in the firm, or (3) the individual has a preference or some constraint that prevents him or her from taking on added responsibility. Plateauing is a vexing motivational problem for sales managers. Although the salesperson may still be a solid performer (but not necessarily), his or her performance is likely to have decreased at least somewhat. To elevate the salesperson's desire to move ahead and to increase personal productivity becomes a daunting challenge for management.

Salespeople at a plateau can manifest a number of adverse behaviors. They may reduce the number of calls they make per day or the amount of time they spend in the field. They may feel stressed out or burned out and unable to cope with either dilemma. Performance might decline across the board, or only on selected performance criteria. The plateaued salesperson may emphasize calling on existing accounts and considerably reduce the time spent prospecting. Absenteeism or sick days could noticeably rise. Boredom, frustration, moroseness, even melancholy can envelope the individual. Unless drastic measures are taken, management may lose the services of a solid performer—and his or her behavior can even become contagious.

So what's a sales manager to do with a plateaued salesperson? Or better yet, what might be done to reduce the chances that sales force members will become plateaued? Although there are no sure-fire solutions to this problem, there are several substantive efforts sales managements can make:[71]

- Analyze and if necessary change the sales force selection process, to increase the chances of hiring salespeople with the skills or training potential necessary for increased job responsibilities.

- Review the job description of the advanced position, to determine whether the salesperson has the skills and abilities necessary to perform effectively in it.

- Provide different, more focused training for salespeople who have insufficient capacities for assuming additional responsibility but might be able to perform better in their current jobs.

- Consider changing the nature of the job—increase the number of sales activities the salespeople perform, use sales teams if feasible, and adopt relationship-selling principles to better serve customers.

- Explain to underachieving salespeople why their performance is deficient, and work out strategies for addressing the sales problems.

- Maintain competitive compensation and promotional programs for salespeople at all career stages.

- Reduce stress and burnout by changing salespeople's assignments, providing techniques for managing these "twin evils," and encourage espirit de corps within the sales organization.

- When promotional opportunities are minimal, encourage the poor performers to take early retirement or leave; provide extensive recognition in the form of titles, public praise, or pay raises to high performers who cannot yet be promoted; or coordinate personnel planning with strategic planning (match an employee's career needs with an appropriate position).

- Provide career information to salespeople—and explain the consequences of their taking on or failing to take on additional responsibility.

- Create dual career paths that can lead to improved matching of a salesperson's skills and desires with an appropriate position.

■ Empowerment and Participative Management

Empowerment
Process of making subordinates into partners by giving them legitimate authority and discretion in decision making plus rewards tied to performance.

Participative Management
The involvement of employees in shared decision making that enables them to accomplish individual and organizational goals.

In chapter 10 on sales force leadership, we talked about **empowerment** and **participative management** as ways to provide greater autonomy to employees. Now let's briefly revisit this cutting-edge business philosophy and consider its enormous potential to increase motivation.

Shifting, sharing, and delegating power to subordinates at lower organizational levels gives them the authority to make decisions about how to perform tasks and instills a sense of ownership and responsibility.[72] Empowered employees play an integral role in decision making, problem solving, goal setting, and in suggesting and instituting organizational changes. Consistent with Maslow's needs theory, empowerment and participative management can heighten subordinates' self-efficacy—the feeling that they do meaningful work and have the ability to produce valuable outcomes—thus increasing effort and motivation and leading, in turn, to higher levels of performance.[73] Note, however, that empowerment programs may not produce motivation and desirable organizational goals if subordinates are not provided with appropriate information, knowledge (through training), power, and rewards.[74]

CHAPTER SUMMARY

1. Understand the nature of motivation. In an era of rapid globalization, companies from all over the world are competing for survival, larger market share, or highest profits. Firms are quickly learning that to thrive, not merely survive, they must increasingly rely on their salespeople to "do battle" with their competitor counterparts by skillfully interacting with prospects and customers on the front lines.

Responsible for revenue-generating and customer relationship activities, salespeople can enable their firms to succeed in this intensely competitive global economy. Recognizing the crucial role salespeople play in their firm's success, sales managers must devise and employ appropriate inducement strategies to increase salesperson motivation—the set of dynamic interpersonal processes that cause the initiation, direction, intensity, and persistence of work-related behaviors—to ensure the attainment of organizational goals and objectives.

2. **Apply contemporary theories of motivation to sales management.** This chapter exposed you to the concept of motivation with an extended discussion of the relevant *contemporary* content theories of motivation (hierarchy of needs theory, ERG theory, needs theory, and dual factor theory), *process* theories of motivation (equity theory, expectancy theory, attribution theory, and goal-setting theory), and *reinforcement* theory of motivation (organizational behavior modification theory). Understanding these theories can guide sales managers in stimulating their sales forces to exert the extra efforts needed to dramatically increase sales performance.

3. **Design reward and incentive programs to motivate salespeople.** While fulfilling financial needs is important to salespeople, research indicates that today's salespeople are increasingly motivated by extrinsic (financial) rewards as well as higher-order intrinsic (non-financial) rewards—respect, accomplishment, control, status, and honesty. Giving salespeople recognition via symbolic motivators such as special vacations, gifts (plaques or jewelry), or simply verbal praise and a pat on the back can instill a certain pride that a paycheck cannot. Salespeople, in particular, can be motivated by the spotlight and personal validation that recognition brings when they succeed in their competitive work.

4. **Develop sales contests and sales meetings to motivate salespeople.** Sales managers can choose from several motivational strategies and tools to implement their general approach to inducing higher performance from the sales force. Two of the most important motivational tools are sales contests and sales meetings. These tools, if implemented correctly, can significantly enhance the performance of individual salespeople and the entire sales force.

5. **Utilize organizational commitment, career stage, and empowerment to motivate a sales force.** This chapter also discussed the emerging perspectives of organizational and job commitment, organizational climate, learning versus performance orientation, salesperson's career cycle, and empowerment of salespeople. These perspectives provide many insights for sales managers charged with motivating the diverse sales forces of the twenty-first century.

REVIEW AND APPLICATION QUESTIONS

1. Define the concept of sales force motivation. Describe the important elements in the definition of sales force motivation. [LO 1]

2. Explain the meaning of *content* theories of motivation. Identify and discuss the key features of the different content theories of motivation. [LO 2]

3. What are *process* theories of motivation? Identify and discuss the key features of the different process theories of motivation. [LO 2]

4. Outline the *reinforcement* theories of motivation. Identify and discuss the key features of the organizational behavior modification theory. [LO 2]

5. As a sales manager, which of the contemporary theories of motivation would you use to motivate your sales force? Why? [LO 2]

6. Name some extrinsic and intrinsic rewards that can be used in motivating the sales force. [LO 3]

7. Many sales managers face the problem of how to motivate top-performing salespeople who no longer respond to the incentive of more money. How would you use recognition to motivate such salespeople? What steps are involved in developing a recognition program? [LO 3]

8. Explain the major reasons for using sales contests. What makes a good sales contest? [LO 4]

9. Discuss some advantages of video conferences over the traditional sales meeting. When might a video conference be more appropriate than a sales meeting? [LO 4]

10. Distinguish between a learning versus a performance orientation. Which orientation would more likely motivate the sales force? [LO 5]

11. Identify and describe the four stages of a salesperson's career life cycle. How would you motivate salespeople in each stage? [LO 5]

IT'S UP TO YOU

Internet Exercise

Using an Internet search engine, find three firms that specialize in motivational sales training. What type of motivational approach do they seem to be advocating? Is the focus on B2B selling, B2C selling, or both? Do they imply that one motivational approach will fit the entire sales force? What are the length and cost of each program? Where is the training held? Who does the training (i.e., what are their qualifications)? What innovative topics will the sales force motivation training cover?

Role-Playing Exercise

Finding the Right Motivation Approach

Situation

Several months ago Fairlie Products, Inc. hired one of its most energetic, highly self-confident, achievement-oriented college recruits in years. Lakisha had an overall 3.5 grade point average while dual majoring in marketing and finance, was an officer in the business club, and supported herself through school with a part-time sales job—so it seemed like she couldn't miss as a new salesperson. However, Lakisha's manager, Pedro, has just finished preparing her first semi-annual performance review, and things don't look good. Not only has Lakisha fallen far behind track on her assigned sales quota for the year, but a few customers have complained about her patronizing attitude and neglect of customer service. In college, Lakisha's self-confidence and ability enabled her to succeed without needing help from anyone, so she tends to be very independent.

Role-Play Participants and Assignments

Lakisha: For the past six months, she is last in the region in sales volume and in generating new customers. But she has never failed at anything before, so she feels that she just needs more time to prove herself.

Pedro: Confident that Lakisha has the knowledge and drive to succeed, he is surprised by her poor performance. After all, she earned the highest scores in the one-month sales training class and testing that all new Fairlie salespeople must complete. Pedro knows that she can be a little brusque and impatient in dealing with people but that quality is not unusual in new salespeople who are anxious to win orders. He also feels somewhat at fault because his travel schedule for this past several months hasn't given him much time to communicate with Lakisha. At this mid-year performance evaluation meeting, Pedro first wants to find out what Lakisha thinks might be going wrong and what she plans to do to turn the situation around. Second, he wants to decide what motivational approach would be best to improve her performance because he still believes that she can be a successful salesperson for the company.

In-Basket Exercise

Today, you received your written annual evaluation from Caroline Jensen, the national sales manager for Specialty Metal Products Company. Last year, you received a large increase in salary plus a bonus because your district came in No. 1 in sales and you were named district sales manager of the year. This year, however, you're disappointed by your below-average performance evaluation, small raise, and lack of a bonus—primarily, it seems, because your district's sales performance was next to last. In reviewing your performance, Ms. Jensen noted that your district's poor performance seemed to be at least partially attributable to the sharp decline in sales by one of your senior salespeople, Roger Casey. Although her note didn't specifically say it, Ms. Jensen's comments clearly imply that she feels it's the responsibility of sales managers to keep their salespeople highly motivated so that they don't go through long sales slumps.

In a handwritten note attached to your performance evaluation, Ms. Jensen has suggested that you put Roger on notice that if his performance doesn't substantially improve in the next few months, he will be moved out of field sales and shifted to a telemarketing job contacting smaller customers. If Roger's sales don't improve and he refuses the telemarketing job, then Ms. Jensen recommends terminating him because "we can't afford to carry deadwood on the payroll."

Upon signing a copy of your performance evaluation to return to Ms. Jensen, you also attach a note explaining: "Roger and his wife went through an unpleasant divorce at the beginning of last year. After that, he seemed melancholy, distracted, and without the old fire that drove his success for many years. Based on his twenty-two years of successful sales experience prior to last year, I still think Roger has considerable potential. I knew that he was struggling last year, but I didn't want to add to his pressures at that time. Moreover, I felt that he would be able to work things out and return to his old form. Unfortunately, that didn't happen, but would you grant me six months to try to turn Roger's performance around?"

As part of your note to Ms. Jensen, provide a detailed outline of what you plan to do to motivate Roger.

Ethical Dilemma

You are the national sales manager for a large consumer goods company with a liberal travel and expense program for its salespeople. Many of your sales reps have large territories requiring a great deal of air travel. Your company always reimburses all travel expenses, but does suggest that reps "search for the best possible airfares whenever traveling." Because of rising fares, your boss has asked you to do whatever you can to hold down air travel expenses. From a preliminary investigation of your reps' travel patterns, you discovered that most reps fly with only *one* airline. When you asked individual salespeople about this, most gave the same explanation: "All airlines charge about the same fares, so I stick with the same airline so I can take advantage of the frequent-flyer programs!" Some of your reps travel so frequently that they can accumulate five to ten *free* airline tickets a year!

QUESTIONS

1. Are the reps behaving ethically by flying with only one airline? Why or why not?

2. Should any or all of the sales force's free airline tickets be given back to the company to be used for future business travel?

3. What can be done to hold down air travel costs in this situation?

CASE 11.1

Schindler Pharmaceuticals: Motivating the Sales Force

Amanda Miller, vice president of marketing at Schindler Pharmaceuticals, headquartered in Atlanta, Georgia, is beginning to question her company's various methods of motivating the sales force. Over the last year or so she has noticed a gradual decline in sales force morale. Sales among the top salespeople have been relatively flat, and from various conversations she has heard around the office, Miller believes her salespeople have become somewhat complacent and could use a good dose of motivation. Motivational techniques currently used at the company include a generous commission system, a promotion plan, sales contests, and sales meetings. In an attempt to determine whether the motivational tools at Schindler are adequate, Miller takes a close look at them.

Schindler management believes a good compensation package should include "an accelerator pedal" to jumpstart salespeople and "a steering wheel" to guide them toward achieving company goals. All Schindler salespeople are paid a regular salary between $48,000 and $75,000 a year depending on seniority plus commissions on sales volume. The commission system is set up so the higher the sales volume, the higher the commission percentage. Commissions on sales range from 6 percent to as high as 18 percent.

Miller believes this is a generous compensation plan, and the "the sky's the limit" at Schindler when it comes to salespeople's earnings as many have incomes in the low six figures. According to Miller, who believes that "salespeople are motivated by both financial and non-financial incentives," there are no apparent problems with the sales force compensation package.

Another means of motivating the salespeople is Schindler's "promotion-from-within" program. Most of its company executives started their careers in entry-level positions within the firm. All but one of the company's marketing managers started in sales. The promotion-from-within program is set up so that advancement is tied closely to performance. Salespeople who are top performers over several years are usually promoted into either sales or marketing management. Miller believes the promotion-from-within program is an excellent way to help motivate the sales force. "Each salesperson knows exactly where he or she stands and what it will take to move up the corporate ladder. If a salesperson wants to become part of the management group at Schindler, the major requirement is disciplined hard work to achieve your assigned quotas each year!" Miller, for example, began her career sixteen years ago as a sales rep for Schindler, and, thanks to her tenacious work habits, she has climbed the ladder all the way up to VP of marketing.

Schindler continually uses sales contests as a motivator for its sales force. Although the sales force is well compensated, the company conducts a special sales contest every year and is careful to make the contest a fair one. The contests are designed to reward the performances of several salespeople rather than just the top one or two performers. Contest themes highlighting corporate goals are changed yearly, as are prizes. While the prizes are usually trips to exotic vacation locations, expensive gifts such as new cars and jewelry are occasionally given, so the salespeople never know just what rewards await the winners in the sales contests. Sometimes celebrities are hired to present the awards.

Once again, Miller has a difficult time finding fault with the yearly sales contests. "We've done our homework on how to run sales contests, and I feel we're doing a first-rate job of motivating our salespeople with these contests," says Miller. "When I was a salesperson, all of us got caught up by the challenge of each year's sales contest. Not only was it great to win an expensive surprise gift, but it made us swell with pride when we heard our names announced as a winner at the annual sales meeting. I remember how the contests motivated me to sell my heart out!"

Annually, Schindler holds a national sales meeting and five regional sales meetings. The national sales meeting is held at exclusive resort areas, usually in early June. The last six years' meetings were held at Knots Berry Farm near Los Angeles, California; Colonial Manor in Williamsburg, Virginia; Kennedy Flight Center, Florida; French Quarter in New Orleans, Louisiana; Harrah's Club at Lake Tahoe, Nevada; and Disney World in Orlando, Florida. The meetings start on a Tuesday, last three days, and are considered an effective means for announcing new product lines. All of Schindler's top management and the board of directors attend, with the daytime devoted to business discussions and the evenings set aside for recreation for management, employees, and their families. The national meetings are attended by approximately 100 to 150 people. Each year, the total attendance has increased by 10 percent. The national meetings have become extremely expensive and time-consuming to prepare. On the other hand, the regional meetings have proven more productive and far less expensive, primarily because of the lower transportation and lodging costs.

The relative benefits versus costs of both the national and regional meetings are being evaluated. When the regional meetings are held, Schindler usually sends about eight top executives. The format is geared to seminars and workshops. Although the regional meetings appear to be better for technical instruction, they are not thought to be as valuable in strengthening total company morale and teamwork. While the national meetings are expensive, Miller believes they are great at building morale and improving communication between the salespeople and management. At no other time during the year do all the salespeople and key executives get to interact with each. "It is important for all employees of a company to get together once a year in order to lift spirits and increase camaraderie," says Miller. Nevertheless, Miller has reviewed the major cost factors associated with the meetings and developed the following alternatives to reduce expenditures:

- Change the format of the national meeting to include technical instruction, thus eliminating the need for the regional meetings.
- Exclude the nighttime recreational activities.
- Hold meetings at less-expensive locations.
- Send fewer top executives.
- Discourage relatives from attending the national meetings.

After evaluating the different motivational tools that Schindler employs, Miller is having difficulty finding any significant problems. However, some Schindler executives feel the outlays in time and resources on these so-called motivators are becoming excessive given the recent lackluster performance of the sales force. It is difficult for them to see how sales contests and sales meetings contribute directly to the firm's overall profitability. Some executives contend that sales contests may be counterproductive in that they cause salespeople to become too focused on sales and not customer service. And, they argue that taking the salespeople out of the field for several days to attend sales meetings doesn't make financial sense. One suggestion is to substitute video conferences for the annual national meeting and perhaps even some regional meetings. Moreover, they ask, why aren't the salespeople sufficiently motivated by salary and commissions without having to offer non-financial incentives, too?

Miller believes that to properly motivate the sales force, she needs the right balance of financial and non-financial incentives. However, she does have some concerns about non-financial incentives.

1. Do non-financial incentives help keep the salespeople happy and enthusiastic to sell? Do they reduce salesperson turnover?

2. Can a sales force accustomed to high financial and tangible incentives be further motivated with non-financial rewards? Do non-financial incentives significantly contribute to sales force productivity over the long-run?

3. How might she go about measuring the overall cost-benefit relationship for the company from non-financial rewards?

QUESTIONS

1. Critique Schlindler's current motivational tools for its sales force.

2. Would any of the theories of motivation presented in the chapter help Schindler to better motivate its salespeople? If so, which ones?

3. Do you think Miller is justified in her concerns about non-financial incentives for the Schindler sales force? Comment on each of her concerns about non-financial incentives.

4. What are the advantages and disadvantages of Schindler's promotion-from-within program? Does it help sales force productivity?

5. Do you think Miller should implement one or more of her alternatives for changing the national and regional sales meetings? Explain. What other alternatives might be considered?

6. What advice would you give Ms. Miller to help her gain Schindler executive support of non-financial incentives?

Case prepared by Mike Weber, Mercer University.

 ## CASE 11.2

Sales Actions Software, Inc.: Motivating Salespeople in Different Career Stages

Located in Wilmington, Delaware, Sales Actions Software, Inc. sells time and territory management solutions targeted at small-to-medium-size companies that cannot afford well-known brands of sales force automation or enterprise software from giant companies like SAP and Oracle. Randy Stuart, new national sales manager for the company, has been asked by its president to review and evaluate the motivational approaches currently being used with the sales force. Randy wasn't happy about this request from the president because he felt it subtly implied that he didn't know the best way to motivate his salespeople. After all Randy knew that most companies use similar motivational approaches—sales contests, sales meetings, podcasts, newsletters, individual recognition, and targeted group sales training—so, why worry about something that's working fine? The current group of motivators clearly has made Sales Actions Software a highly desirable place to work because its sales force turnover is only about 10 percent annually as compared to twice that for most competitive companies. But the president expressed concern about whether there should be different motivational approaches to match up with the different career stages of the salespeople. As he put it: "I don't see how one motivational size can fit all when our salespeople are so diverse in terms of their career stage."

After some second thoughts, Randy realized that the president probably had a good point because some of the salespeople had complained about the lack of choice in company benefits and incentives. In fact, in discussions with the head of the human resource department Randy learned that exit interviews with salespeople who had left the company in the last few years cited Sales Actions Software's incentive package as one reason for their decision to leave.

To get a better idea of the make-up of his sales force, Randy followed the advice of a sales article he had recently read dealing with career stage assessment. Using the human resource profiles for each of his salespeople, Randy assigned each salesperson to one of five career stage categories. Six of his salespeople clearly belonged in the *preparation/exploration* career stage because they were relatively new hires who were just getting into their sales careers and required considerable more sales training to be really productive. Ten salespeople seemed to be in the *development/establishment* stage as they were highly motivated to earn a good living and each was achieving his or her assigned annual sales goals. Two were still single but the other eight had children living at home. Three saleswomen with children often had a major crisis on their hands when one of their kids got sick because they had to stay home with them. The maturity/maintenance career stage best fit fourteen of the salespeople because they were established reliable performers with from ten to twenty years sales experience. Some of the younger salespeople tended to look up to these mature salespeople as role models and frequently sought their advice about sales strategies and sometimes personal matters.

Finally, Randy assigned six of the salespeople to the decline/disengagement stage because it was fairly obvious that they were mentally preparing for retirement. They tended to make fewer sales calls and called mainly on existing accounts rather than doing much prospecting. Three of these salespeople had been superstar salespeople in the past, but they were no longer performing at a superior level. They appeared to have lost some of their old confidence and desire to put up the effort to exceed their sales quotas. Nevertheless, these six salespeople had influential friends throughout the company and they knew "where all the bodies were buried." Oftentimes, they had given Randy a heads-up or advice on some upcoming issue they had heard about through their grapevine connections.

After analyzing his salespeople by career stage, Randy had an epiphany as he realized: "The president is absolutely right! No one motivational approach could possible get the maximum productivity out of such a diverse sales force. I'm going to need some combination of financial and non-financial incentives because some of my salespeople are not that motivated by high earnings any more; whereas, some others seem totally motivated by potential earnings. But what mix of motivational approaches should I use?"

To approach this problem, Randy separated the motivational approaches into financial and non-financial. He believes financial motivators are "the required cost of doing business" and need to include commissions, bonuses, and sales contests. In contrast, sales meetings, podcasts, special recognition programs, team projects, and targeted group sales training are non-financial motivators where there's more managerial flexibility.

Randy decided to review special recognition approaches first. One program, referred to as "Pacesetters," recognizes the top five salespeople in each region. These pacesetters, who are crowned the "Fabulous Five," are given recognition at monthly banquets, in the company newsletter, and on the website. At the end of the year, a national "Fabulous Five" is identified and awarded special gifts like jewelry or a luxury vacation plus a trip to company headquarters to meet with and be recognized by senior management at an elaborate banquet with a celebrity speaker. Other recognition awards, often given to salespeople at regional sales meeting, include plaques, rings, and certificates for outstanding performance in various areas like providing superior customer service, winning new customer accounts, or recommending a new cost saving or revenue generation idea.

Two types of sales force training are used—individual training via podcasts and group training at regional sales meetings. Randy was influential in adding podcasts as a training method and heavily involved in developing recent group training content and approaches. He is therefore finding it difficult to objectively evaluate these areas. The podcasts have been popular based on the number of salespeople who have downloaded them. But the production costs are relatively high, and there is no formal mechanism for evaluating their effectiveness. The group training topics typically include customer analysis, sales techniques, and developing long-run customer relationships: all of these programs are designed for junior salespeople rather than the experienced old hands. Last year, Randy sent out a lengthy questionnaire to evaluate these group training topics. Although the response rate was low, the results along with informal verbal feedback indicated the salespeople did not think the group training was very effective.

As Randy reviews the various motivational approaches, he realizes how difficult it is to measure the effectiveness of the non-financial factors for any of the career stage groups. But he believes that non-financial incentives such as public recognition can spur some salespeople to higher performance, and that they are especially important to motivate junior salespeople. He still remembers how proud he was when he received awards in front of his peers during his early selling career. In fact, Randy feels to some extent that an increase in the motivational budget might be needed instead of a reduction, and that the more important issue is how the budget is spent instead of its size. However, he will need to provide the president with well-thought-out arguments for any requested increase in his sales force motivation budget. Before requesting a budget increase, he knows that he must explain in his report to the president how he plans to motivate the salespeople in each of the four career stage groups.

QUESTIONS

1. Do you think Randy has sufficiently categorized his salespeople for motivational purposes? Why or why not? Is it practicable to provide non-financial incentives to motivate salespeople in each of the four career stage groups? Explain.

2. What role might specific non-financial factors play in motivating salespeople in different career stage categories?

3. What kind of system could be developed to evaluate the impact of intangible, non-financial motivational factors on the sales force, and how might such a system be smoothly implemented at Sales Actions Software?

4. Outline the report that Randy should send to the president of Sales Actions Software.

Case prepared by Dan Goebel, Illinois State University and Paul Christ, West Chester University.

Sales Force Compensation

LEARNING OBJECTIVES

When you finish this chapter, you should be able to:

1 Meet the challenges of developing sales force compensation plans.

2 Follow the basic steps in developing a compensation plan.

3 Compare the different methods of sales force compensation.

4 Evaluate the recent trends in sales force compensation.

5 Control the use of expense accounts and fringe benefits in compensation planning.

INSIDE SALES MANAGEMENT

J. B. Shireman, Executive Vice President of Sales and Marketing, New Belgium Brewery

New Belgium Brewery is one of many companies in the business of making and selling beer, but it's probably one of the few that doesn't pay its sales reps commissions.

"We make a couple of assumptions about our reps," says J. B. Shireman, who serves as the company's executive vice president of sales and marketing but prefers the moniker "Guru of Goodwill." "First, everyone we hire is going to be working for a pretty big part of their lives. Second, while everybody we hire needs to make money, no one is very good at what they're spending their lives doing unless they're really passionate about it. We could hire people who can do all the tasks in our selling jobs, but what we *want* are the people who have a bigger picture in mind when they come to work for us. They want more than money. They want to share in our core values and direct their passion towards our mutual achievement of those goals."

Says Shireman, "If I lose a good job candidate because that person can't see past the commission he got at his last job, then I know he wouldn't have been very successful in the long term with us anyway."

New Belgium, based in Fort Collins, Colorado, is an open-book-management company that makes its key financials available to every employee. Every department, not just sales, has in its budget a cost-per-barrel number that it has to hit. All the department budgets roll up into the company-wide profit plan, and if the company makes its numbers, then everybody benefits through profit sharing. If the company misses its numbers, no matter which department fell short, no one gets a payout. All company-wide goals are also subject to parameters for the overall health of the business as set by an internal board of directors.

"There's no way you can attract the right salespeople if you don't pay competitively," says Shireman. So New Belgium is careful to offer a highly competitive compensation package. The alcoholic beverage industry is a close-knit one, and it's relatively easy for the company to keep in touch with competitors, headhunters, and independent researchers to ensure its salary ranges and benefits are in the ballpark. About every eighteen months to two years, New Belgium also commissions a survey of compensation among its competitors to keep up to date. "We offer competitive salaries, benefits including family-friendly policies, 401k plans, expense accounts, cars, vacation and other time off, and medical and dental insurance. And we offer bonuses for meeting objectives and making efficiency gains. In our business, those are just table stakes."

So what else does the firm offer, if not commissions? New Belgium is a quirky, whimsical, offbeat, and fun place to work, says Shireman. "What do you want the brand to be?" he asks the reps. "If making and selling world-class beer is what drives you, if you want to look back on your life and say not, 'This is how much money I made,' but 'This is what I *did*,' and be proud of that, then we're a good fit for you. We want that higher level of commitment, and we can give you a sense of achievement and pride that's beyond the money."

How well does the no-commission system work? "It's a challenge every year and always will be," says Shireman. "But I believe it works better than a lot of other systems I've seen."

"**S**how me the money!" If this now famous line from the popular film *Jerry Maguire* strikes a familiar chord, you probably know that many people define success and power by the amount of money they make. If, like most people, you're not planning to become a professional athlete or entertainer, you can still have a lot of control over your income by embarking on a career in sales. Salespeople and sales managers are the direct revenue producers of their organizations, and in most organizations, those who bring in the money usually make the most. That's one reason why sales management is considered one of the fifty best jobs in America,[1] and commands six-figure compensation.[2]

Although every employee directly or indirectly affects organizational performance, the firm's revenue-generating success largely rests on the performance of individual salespeople. Thus, sales managers, who are ultimately accountable for the success of the sales organizations,[3] need to design compensations programs that clearly reward salespersons for superior performance.

How do you do this? To succinctly answer that question, let's turn to Jack Welch—the charismatic former CEO of General Electric (www.ge.com)—who states: "By rewarding stars [the top 20 percent performers] in an outsized way that is soul-satisfying and financially satisfying." Top salespeople must be openly recognized and fully compensated for excellent performance, which can also help retention.[4] While the middle 70 percent must be given more training and coaching to augment their performance, an effective reward program and compensation structure is perhaps the most powerful mechanism to motivate average performers to achieve their full potential. However, according to Welch, the bottom 10 percent who exhibit neither good results nor good behaviors should be "shown the door."[5] Welch, who regularly co-authors a column in *Business Week* magazine, believes that by moving out the bottom performers, firms can recruit new talent.[6] While his advice may sound harsh, it's hard to argue with his long-term success at General Electric.

Recall that in chapters 10 and 11, we discussed how sales managers can use leadership approaches and an array of intrinsic rewards and sales incentive strategies to motivate salespeople to higher performance levels. Many people will tell you that the compensation plan is the most direct and powerful way to motivate productive sales force behavior. So, in this chapter, we turn our attention to how sales managers can design effective compensation structures[7] and extrinsic (financial) reward programs to stimulate higher levels of effort (motivation), thus contributing to superior salesperson performance, productivity,[8] and profitability.[9]

Sales Force Compensation Plans

Compensation
All monetary payments as well as benefits used to remunerate employees for their performance.

Compensation is defined as all monetary payments as well as benefits used to remunerate employees for their performance. Constituting a central part of extrinsic rewards, compensation plans and financial packages are the most important, least ambiguous way to remunerate employees.[10] Compensation is widely recognized as the single greatest motivator of salespeople,[11] although a recent study revealed that managers frequently fail to determine what else motivates employees and to overestimate the importance of extrinsic rewards.[12] Sales compensation plans can be the "steering wheel" that enables management to directly influence salesperson performance, and should reflect a company's goals.[13]

Straight Salary
A fixed sum of money paid at regular intervals. Most appropriate for team selling, long negotiating periods, mixed promotional mixes, sales trainees, missionary selling, and in special situations such as introducing new products or developing new customer accounts.

While there are a variety of ways employees can be rewarded—as shown in Table 12.1—in general, firms use three main methods to financially compensate salespeople:

1. **Straight salary**—The salesperson receives a fixed amount of money at regular intervals, such as weekly or monthly.
2. **Straight commission**—The salesperson receives an amount that varies with results, usually sales or profits.
3. **Combination**—The salesperson receives a mix of salary and commission.

Straight Commission
Payment for a given level of sales results; based on the principle that earnings should vary with performance. Historically based on dollar or unit sales volume, but can be tied to measures of profitability.

It could very well be that salespeople respond uniquely to monetary rewards. Patrick Hughes, vice president of sales and marketing for Blue Cross Blue Shield of Massachusetts (www.bluecrossma.com), analyzed salespersons' pay plans outside his industry for assistance in revising his company's plan because as he put it, "Salespeople, despite their market specialization, have one thing in common: they want to make lots of money."[14] Nick DiBari feels that salespeople do respond uniquely to financial rewards. DiBari has achieved an impressive track record in sales; he has been the number one earner for five consecutive annual compensation surveys conducted by *Sales & Marketing Management*. (In a recent year, his annual compensation exceeded $1.5 million.) According to DiBari, most salespeople are "crusaders, builders, and competitors." They want and need to make a difference in whatever they are involved in. These people see financial compensation as a way of "keeping score" among their peers. They are, understandably, highly motivated by their "scorecard"

Combination Compensation Plan
Plan that combines two or three of the basic compensation methods (e.g., salary plus commission). This is the most widely used compensation method.

TABLE 12.1 Types of Sales Compensation Plans		
COMPENSATION PLAN	**NATURE OF REWARD**	**DESCRIPTION**
Hourly wage	Non-incentive based	Fixed pay per hour worked
Straight salary	Non-incentive based	Fixed salary paid in intervals as per contract
Straight commission	Incentive based	Pay based on sales results
Performance bonus	Incentive based	Discretionary pay based on individual or team performance
Merit Pay	Incentive based	Pay based on exemplary performance
Profit sharing	Incentive based	Pay based on profits attained
Pay-for-knowledge	Incentive based	Pay based on skill augmentation and education degree earned
Stock options	Incentive based	Financial reward of company stock either given free or purchased at a discount
Flexible pay compensation	Incentive based	Pay based on a personal choice of compensation plan and benefits selected
Combination	Incentive based	Pay that includes a fixed salary, plus variable commission based on sales levels
Health insurance	Benefits based	Non-financial benefits in compliance with employment laws
Dental insurance	Benefits based	Non-financial benefits in compliance with employment laws
Pension plans	Benefits based	Non-financial benefits in compliance with employment laws
Social security	Benefits based	Non-financial benefits in compliance with employment laws
Others (education, travel allowances, etc.)	Benefits based	Additional payments disbursed as perquisites

(paycheck).[15] To retain top performers, companies must maintain an attractive compensation package. Recruiting qualified salespeople has become so intense that some high-tech firms offer them $100,000 signing bonuses.[16]

In examining the effect of various compensations plans on company profits, a seminal study identified several types of salespeople:

- *Creatures of habit*—They try to maintain their standard of living by earning a predetermined amount of money.

- *Goal-oriented individuals*—They prefer recognition as achievers by peers and by superiors and tend to be sales-quota-oriented, with money serving mainly as a by-product of achievement.

- *Satisfiers*—They perform just well enough to keep their jobs.

- *Trade-offers*—They allocate their time according to a personally determined ratio of work and leisure that is not influenced by opportunities for increased earnings.

- *Money-oriented individuals*—They seek to maximize their earnings. These people may sacrifice family relationships, personal pleasures, and even health to increase their income.[17]

Although this classic study was conducted years ago, more recent research suggests that the classifications still hold true in today's sales environment.[18] The sales manager must identify these basic types of salespeople and design a compensation package that will maximize total sales force efforts.

Variable Pay Compensation Systems
Also known as flexible compensation systems; pay based on a personal choice of compensation plan and benefits selected.

■ Variable Pay Compensation Systems

Although the critical importance of rewards as a means of motivating employees has been well established,[19] reward preferences, reward levels, reward satisfaction, and managers', subordinates', and superiors' perceptions of the adequacy of their rewards are known to differ.[20] Moreover, compensation and perks tend to increase at the higher levels of a corporation, creating status and power differences, and reward inequality at successive hierarchical levels.[21] Studies also suggest that the importance employees assign to rewards differs according to their changing needs, career stage, and organizational level.[22] Furthermore, over the past three decades, the profile of the typical worker has changed dramatically with large numbers of minorities and women found at all organizational levels.[23] The U.S. work force now includes large numbers of dual-career households whose employers tend to provide similar, overlapping reward or benefit programs in which only one spouse can participate. And many older employees have needs for rewards and benefits that may not be consistent with their chronological age or organizational level.

Given these conditions, to be truly effective in improving productivity, management needs to design and implement reward systems, compensation structures, and benefit packages from which employees may make their own choices. Many firms have already adopted flexible, cafeteria-type compensation plans, which have become an increasingly popular alternative to standardized reward systems.[24] To learn more about designing and implementing innovative variable sales compensation plans that can be effective in augmenting sales force performance, visit websites such as www.vault.com and www.varicent.com.

Reprinted by permission of Varicent Software.

● Sales managers can employ companies like Varicent to design attractive variable compensation reward systems for their sales force.

Developing the Compensation Plan

As shown in Figure 12.1, the seven distinct stages in the process of developing a compensation plan include (1) prepare job descriptions, (2) establish specific objectives, (3) determine general levels of compensation, (4) develop the compensation mix, (5) pretest the plan, (6) administer the plan, and (7) evaluate the plan. If any of these steps are skipped or poorly executed, the compensation plan will not be as effective as it should be in motivating the sales force.

Prepare job descriptions → Establish specific objectives → Determine general levels of compensation → Develop the compensation mix → Pretest the plan → Administer the plan → Evaluate the plan

FIGURE 12.1 Stages in Developing a Compensation Plan

■ Preparing Job Descriptions

Job Description
A written description of the responsibilities and performance criteria for a particular position.

Sales managers need detailed, meaningful **job descriptions** before they can develop a compensation plan. They should systematically compare job descriptions—including responsibilities and performance criteria—to other sales positions in terms of their importance to the organization. Jobs of approximately equal value are usually assigned to the same grade level. For example, in the federal government, all jobs under civil service have been described, evaluated, and categorized vertically into grades ranging from GS-1 (the lowest) to GS-18 (the highest). On a horizontal basis, at any one civil service grade—say, GS-14—there are different jobs, such as contract administrator or accounting supervisor. The U.S. Bureau of Labor Statistics (www.bls.gov) conducts national surveys every March to adjust the GS pay levels relative to private industry. Many companies also classify their sales positions by levels of responsibility.

Sales positions typically vary on both vertical and horizontal levels. Vertical positions may be sales trainee, sales representative, and senior sales representative. Horizontal jobs may be missionary salespeople or regular salespeople. Each position, on both the vertical and horizontal scales, needs a separate job description for assignment of a minimum starting salary and a maximum salary, often determined by surveys of what other organizations are paying.

■ Establishing Specific Objectives

Compensation plans are designed to achieve certain organizational objectives, for example, larger market share, higher profit margins, introducing new products or services, winning new accounts, or reducing selling costs. Surprisingly, an "extraordinary number of American companies use sales compensation plans that are inconsistent with their marketing goals," according to research findings. About 60 percent of the companies surveyed reported that their sales managers have a difficult time trying to bring their compensation plans in line with organizational objectives.[25]

These findings are both dramatic and rather puzzling, since it appears that the procedure for establishing compensation goals that are consistent with organizational goals is relatively straightforward. Ready availability of sales data means that it is easier to measure the productivity of salespeople than that of most other types of employees. Moreover, firms can measure achievement of other organizational objectives, even when few sales are being made. For example, the number of sales presentations made to customers may be an important objective for making potential buyers aware of company offerings. Another objective might be to increase the conversion ratio (orders as a percentage of sales presentations).

Any compensation plan may have several objectives, depending upon the needs of the specific company, sales manager, or salesperson. From the company's vantage point, the plan should stress:

- *Control*—Sales managers prefer a plan that allows maximum control over how salespeople allocate their time.
- *Economy*—Sales managers want a plan that offers a desirable balance between sales costs and sales results.
- *Motivation*—Sales managers want a plan that can motivate their salespeople to optimal performance.

● **Sales managers can increase overall sales force productivity by designing compensation systems that recognize exemplary performance and reward salespeople accordingly.**

© John Coletti / Indexstock.com

■ *Simplicity*—Sales managers like a plan that is simple to administer, easily explainable to salespeople, and sufficiently flexible to ensure timely adjustments to changing market conditions and organizational goals.

From the standpoint of sales representatives, the compensation plan should offer:

■ *Income regularity*—Salespeople want to be protected from drastic fluctuations in income so that regular monthly expenses for home mortgage, food, and utilities can be paid without hardship.

■ *Reward for superior performance*—Salespeople like compensation in direct relationship to the amount of effort they expend and the results they obtain. Superior performance should reap superior rewards.

■ *Fairness*—Salespeople want their earnings to be equitable in terms of their experience and ability, the pay of coworkers, competitor's sales reps, and the cost of living.[26]

It's not easy for a single compensation plan to achieve all these objectives, especially since some objectives, such as economy and income regularity, tend to conflict.

Because their marketing situations and objectives are so diverse, organizations use a wide variety of compensation plans, from simple to complex, across industries. Regardless of the sophistication of the plan, it is important for sales force morale that sales reps be able to calculate their own expected earnings over a given pay period to facilitate their personal financial planning.

■ Determining General Levels of Compensation

Companies and industries with low average levels of compensation tend to suffer high turnover rates. Therefore, the level of compensation should be sufficiently competitive to attract and retain competent salespeople.

Several factors determine the basic level of pay for a sales force. The most significant ones are (1) the skills, experience, and education required to do the work successfully; (2) the level of income for comparable jobs in the company; and (3) the level of income for comparable jobs in the industry (that is, the competitive environment). The relative importance of each of these factors will vary from one situation to another.

One approach to establishing general pay levels for sales positions is to assign numerical values to each job requirement. For instance, previous experience in sales might be rated high for a particular sales job (say, 8 on a scale of 1 to 10), and a college major in marketing may receive a value of 6. For another selling job, sales experience may be worth only 4. Sum the point values for all requirements to compare the importance of different sales jobs within and outside the organization. From this analysis, managers can obtain a rank order of jobs and assign a range of basic income to each level, as shown in the simple example in Table 12.2.

Usually, there is some overlap in salaries among the different job rankings, to allow for growth within each position based on the individual's experience, skills, and performance. For example, in civil service positions there is a range of salaries depending upon the individual's position in that grade level. Similarly, in the corporate world, a recent compensation survey found that top-performing salespeople earned higher compensation than some senior executives and more than 2.5 times the staff average.[27]

Living Costs. Beyond the general level of compensation, any plan should be sufficiently flexible to adjust to area living costs. *Sales & Marketing Management* publishes an annual "Survey of Selling Costs," which identifies living costs by selected metropolitan area. Sales managers can use this information to help establish the level of compensation for particular areas.

Earnings Ceilings. Should there be a ceiling on what an outstanding sales representative can earn? More specifically, should salespeople be able to earn more than their bosses? Although there are arguments on both sides of the issue, the answer depends on circumstances and management philosophies. Where ceilings are placed on earnings,

TABLE 12.2 Sales Position Analysis

Job Requirements	Experience	Education	Test Scores	Total Possible Score
Total numerical values	**10**	**6**	**10**	**26**

		MINIMUM SCORES REQUIRED			

Sales Position	Experience	Education	Position Scores	Totals	Pay Level
Sales trainee	4	3	3	10	High
Sales representative	6	4	6	16	Higher than salary for sales trainee
Senior sales representative	8	4	8	20	Higher than salary for sales representative

management must set reasonable sales quotas to avoid discouraging the sales force. In many progressive companies, no limits are placed on a salesperson's earnings as long as selling costs are kept within acceptable limits. For example, James B. Horton, president and chief executive officer of Hall Publications, Inc. (www.hallpublications.com), is a strong advocate of no ceilings on the salaries of sales representatives. When Horton was publisher of *Psychology Today,* an ad salesman made the most money in the company, the sales manager made the second most, and Horton made the third most. Horton thought this was excellent. "All I wished was that I had five more salesmen like that. . . . As the guy sells more, he gets more commission. Because of the salary component of the structure, my sales cost per page came down."[28]

■ Developing the Compensation Mix

Compensation Mix
The relationship between salary, commission, and other incentives.

Most contemporary sales organizations have found that a **compensation mix** of salary, commission, and/or bonus is more effective in achieving objectives and goals than salary or commission alone. Essential in this mix is the relationship between the regular salary and incentive pay.

Costs for Alternative Compensation Mixes. Sales managers need to consider the costs of alternative compensation mixes before drawing up a compensation plan. Generally, straight-commission plans are most efficient at lower levels. Recognizing this, companies often shift from commissioned sales agents to salaried salespeople once sales volume has reached the critical level.

Table 12.3 illustrates, by means of a hypothetical example, the impact on costs of alternative compensation mixes for three salespeople. At the lower sales volumes, the

TABLE 12.3 Comparison of Costs for Alternative Compensation Mixes

SALESPEOPLE	COMPENSATION METHOD		
Antonelli	Straight commission (10%) of $ sales		
Bartholomew	Straight salary ($2,500/month)		
Cumar	Salary ($1,200/month) plus commission (5% of $ sales)		

Sales Volumes	Name	Compensation Costs	Cost-to-Sales Ratio (%)
$10,000	Antonelli	$1,000	10.0
	Bartholomew	2,500	25.0
	Cumar	1,700	17.0
15,000	Antonelli	$1,500	10.0
	Bartholomew	2,500	16.7
	Cumar	1,950	13.0
20,000	Antonelli	$2,000	10.0
	Bartholomew	2,500	12.5
	Cumar	2,200	11.0
25,000	Antonelli	$2,500	10.0
	Bartholomew	2,500	10.0
	Cumar	2,450	9.8
30,000	Antonelli	$3,000	10.0
	Bartholomew	2,500	8.3
	Cumar	2,700	9.0

straight-commission plan is the most cost efficient. At the highest sales volume, however, straight salary is preferable. Salary plus commission is most efficient at a slightly lower sales volume. Each compensation plan ought to be evaluated in view of the alternatives at different sales levels.

In considering the breakdown of salary and incentives, sales managers must decide what degree of control is needed over the sales force activities, what amount of incentive is required to reach objectives and goals, and what the total costs are for the different compensation mixes. After answering these questions, sales managers must decide what proportion of each salesperson's total income should be earned through incentives and whether the incentive pay schedule should be fixed, regressive, or progressive.

Proportion for Salary. Salaries should enable salespeople to meet everyday living expenses while encouraging them to perform tasks that are not directly measurable by sales, such as servicing customer accounts. But they should not be so high as to make the salesperson complacent or content with salary alone. In most plans, about 70 to 80 percent of the salesperson's total income is fixed salary. However, there is definitely a trend to increase incentives to salespeople in all industries.

Bonus
Payments made at the discretion of management for specific achievements.

Proportion for Incentives. Commission and **bonus** are the incentive parts of the compensation plan, and they typically require the salesperson to achieve some predetermined sales quota. Incentives are about 20 percent of base salary for salespeople at consumer products companies, and about 25 percent of base for reps at industrial products companies. However, for salespeople in business services, incentive pay may be as high as 50 to 70 percent over their base salary.[29]

Progressive Incentives
Increase the percentage of commission or bonus awarded as sales volume rises. Best when profit margins climb significantly after the break-even point is reached.

Fixed, Progressive, or Regressive Incentives. Fixed commission or bonus rates are the easiest to compute, but they do not offer salespeople much incentive for seeking higher, increasingly difficult levels of sales. **Progressive incentive** rates, which steps up the percentage of commission or bonus awarded as sales volume grows past designated levels, are best when profit margins climb significantly after the break-even point is reached. Conversely, **regressive incentives** decline as sales increase: for example, 6 percent for all sales less than 1,000 units, 4 percent for all sales from 1,000 to 1,500 units, and 2 percent for all sales over 1,500 units. Firms use regressive commission rates if there is a high probability of windfall sales and a propensity to overload customer inventories. In choosing among fixed, progressive, or regressive commission plans, sales managers need to estimate the potential effects of each plan on overall profits.

Regressive Incentives
Decrease the percentage of commission or bonus awarded as sales volume increases. Usually used where there is a high probability of "windfall" sales and a propensity to overload customer inventories.

Splitting Commissions. A special administrative problem for sales managers is how to split commissions when two or more people worked on closing a sale. For example, a key account sales rep may call on the customer's headquarters, while other salespeople call on the customer's branch offices. Because disagreements may develop afterward as to who is most responsible for the sale, management should decide in advance how to divide commissions.

Fringe Benefits
Indirect financial awards that help to provide salespeople with personal security and job satisfaction.

Types of Incentives. Companies may consider a host of **fringe benefits** to reward high-performing executives (see Table 12.4). Although many are reserved for top-level management, fringes such as a company car and stock options are frequently made

TABLE 12.4 Types of Fringe Benefits	
Company car	Low- or no-interest loans
Supplemental life insurance	Deferred compensation
Tax return preparation	Supplemental retirement benefits
Supplemental medical insurance	First-class air travel
Personal tax and financial planning	Relocation allowance
Country club membership	Stock options

available to the sales force. Others, such as club memberships, are often given to salespeople to entertain customers. While Congress has limited some tax deductions that companies can claim for "entertainment facilities"—such as yachts, resorts, and hunting lodges—business-related entertainment expenses are still legitimate tax deductions.

Stock Options. To retain top-quality people, sales organizations may offer stock options in proportion to the salesperson's productivity. A *stock option* is simply an awarded opportunity (an option) to purchase stock in the company at some future date at a preset price—usually lower than the prevailing market value. If the shares rise in price, the individual may buy them at the lower, preset price, sell them at a profit, and pay tax on the profit. When the price of the firm's stock is climbing, salespeople and managers may be reluctant to leave without exercising the options available at some future date. If stock options are awarded according to productivity, the company's hold on top performers increases. Some companies allow salespeople to

© JupiterImages / Comstock Images / Alamy

● Sales managers can offer fringe benefits such as membership at a country club, which top salespersons can use for entertaining their clients during sales negotiations.

SALES MANAGEMENT IN ACTION

Stock Option Inducements in Compensation Packages

Ruth Bronsen, a sales manager for an office equipment manufacturer, earns approximately $165,000 annually in salary and bonus. In an effort to secure her services, a competitor offers the same salary plus stock options. If Bronsen accepts the competitor's offer, she will receive an official statement granting her the right to buy 5,000 shares of the company's stock for $10 per share at some future date (when the market price is expected to be higher), usually two or three years hence so that management can evaluate her performance before she obtains windfall profits on the stock option. Some companies have terminated underperforming managers prior to the required waiting time for exercising the stock option, so many managers now insist upon an employment contract that extends beyond the exercise date of the stock option.

make contributions for each sales order, which the companies match, to a special equity fund. When salespeople leave early, their own contributions are returned to them but they forfeit the company's contributions. These types of incentives are called "golden handcuffs," since they tend to hold people to a company. The nearby *Sales Management in Action* box explains how stock options work.

■ Pretesting the Plan

Managers must pretest and evaluate any compensation plan before adopting it. To identify its probable impact on profits, they need to compute the sales and potential earnings the new plan would have offered each salesperson over the past several years. The firm can then pretest the proposed plan in one or more sales divisions. This pretest should run long enough to evaluate its effect on achievement of organizational objectives. If the limited trial is successful, then the plan can be implemented throughout the sales force. Finally, because people often resist change, it is critical that committees of key affected employees help develop, approve, and implement any proposed new plan.

■ Administering the Plan

A compensation plan should be fair, easy to understand, simple to calculate, and flexible. As market conditions and organizational objectives change, the plan may need to be altered.

Sales are not always a fair or adequate measure of a salesperson's contribution. In times of product and service shortages, for example, getting supplies to customers may become the company's major short-run objective. In general, the increasing demands on salespeople to perform such non-selling activities have led management to reevaluate basic compensation plans. Since only about a third of a salesperson's workday is typically spent in face-to-face selling, it is important to have a compensation plan that reinforces effective and efficient planning and time management by salespeople.

Most sales managers feel they should not disclose peer pay to the sales force. Pay experts generally fear that salary disclosure can lead salespeople to demand justification for pay differentials and increase friction and jealousy among employees. Therefore, most firms limit information to expected scheduling of raises and, perhaps, the prescribed range of salaries within different job categories.

But it's also possible that *lack* of pay information may negatively affect employee performance and satisfaction. Pay secrecy prevents people from judging their progress in relative terms. Some research has supported the position that greater disclosure can positively influence performance, satisfaction with pay, and acceptance of company promotional policies. One warning, though: Salespeople seem to become less satisfied with their superiors (at least initially) after implementation of open-pay policies. Also, organizations not capable of objectively measuring performance are likely to have difficulty with an open-pay system.

■ Evaluating the Plan

Before a compensation plan is set in concrete, even for a relatively short period, the firm should thoroughly evaluate it for consistency with the sales managers' goals of attracting desirable people, keeping them, and motivating them to achieve organizational goals. Once it's established, management must then continually review and evaluate the compensation plan to determine its ongoing effectiveness. This review can be done on a quarterly, semiannual, or annual basis.

Advantages and Disadvantages of Different Compensation Methods

In the next several pages, we review the advantages and disadvantages of various compensation methods under changing market conditions and different sales objectives.

■ Straight Salary

Even though sales recruits will often claim that compensation *level* is far more important to them than compensation *method,* many will reject any plan that creates wide variability in their income. These security-oriented people prefer a base salary or drawing account so that they can depend on some regular income to meet basic living expenses. This becomes even more important when sales are infrequent and seasonal.

Straight salary is most appropriate in the following situations:

- *Team selling situations*—Several people—for example, a coordinating salesperson, a technical engineer, a marketing service representative, and a member of marketing management—cooperate as a team in making a sale. IBM incorporates this approach in selling computer systems.

- *Long negotiating periods*—A year or more may be needed to make a complex sale of a system of products and services or big-ticket items, such as private jets.

- *Mixed promotional situations*—Advertising sometimes plays a vital role in selling, and the relationship between a salesperson's efforts and advertising may be difficult to evaluate. This is also true of "inside-outside" sales forces.

- *Learning periods*—During the first year, a salary is usually required to attract new recruits into selling and to compensate the trainee, at least until commissions are large enough to provide an adequate living standard.

- *Missionary selling*—Missionary selling jobs are non-selling jobs aimed at developing goodwill among customers (such as physicians, pharmacies, hospitals, museums, or government agencies that serve as product deciders or recommenders for their own patients, clients, or customers) by providing them with information, advice, service, and assistance in prescribing, recommending, or merchandising (setting up educational displays or products).

- *Special conditions*—Introducing a new line of products, opening up new territories, calling on new customer accounts, or selling in unusual market conditions (e.g., rising gas prices) are all special situations that may create salespeople anxiety about their earnings unless they have the security of a guaranteed salary.

At Xerox Corporation (www.xerox.com), district managers are expected to be in tune with any unusual conditions in the marketplace so they can make adjustments in the compensation plan for their sales force. For instance, salespeople (who are directly affected by an unusual market condition) have the option of switching from a combination compensation plan to a 100 percent straight-salary plan. This plan flexibility avoids instability of income and promotes satisfaction with the compensation plan in general. To ensure timely responses to the needs of the sales force and to monitor any changes in the environment, Xerox Corporation (www.xerox.com) also evaluates its compensation plans each quarter.

Since earnings under a straight-salary method are independent of any productivity measures such as sales, profits, sales calls, or presentations, this method gives salespeople the security of a precise income. From the managerial perspective, the chief advantage of the straight-salary plan is that salespeople can direct their activities toward company objectives. Many successful companies pay their salespeople on a straight-salary basis. Straight-salary plans are widespread in the aerospace, petroleum, and chemical industries, where service and engineering skills are particularly important to customers. In these industries, salespeople are more likely to think of themselves as customer consultants or sales engineers and often do not even carry the title "sales representative." Under a straight-salary plan, high productivity can be rewarded by annual salary increases. Overall, the straight-salary method of compensation has these advantages and disadvantages:

Advantages

- Provides security to salespeople, since they know their basic living expenses will be covered
- Helps develop a sense of loyalty to the company
- Increases flexibility in territorial assignments because salespeople are less likely to become attached to certain sales territories and customers
- Gives a higher degree of company control over salespeople's activities
- Permits rapid adaptation of sales force efforts to changing market demands and company objectives
- Is simple to administer

Disadvantages

- Provides no financial incentive to put forth extra effort
- May increase selling costs because salaries continue even when sales are not being made

- Often leads to income inequities, since the least productive salespeople tend to be overpaid, and the most productive underpaid
- Leads to adequate, but not superior, performance

■ Straight Commission

Straight-commission plans provide strong incentives rather than security, and they tend to result in higher productivity and earning levels for salespeople than do salary-based compensation plans in similar organizations. Straight-commission plans are common in industries such as real estate, insurance, door-to-door sales, and party-based sales—such as Mary Kay Cosmetics (www.marykay.com) or Tupperware (www .tupperware.com).

Commissions are paid only for measurable achievements (usually sales volume), so straight-commission plans offer rewards and risks much like those assumed by entrepreneurs. To increase sales productivity, the CBS Station Group (www.cbs.com) eliminated its salary structure for salespeople and adopted an all-commission plan.[30]

When compensated by straight commissions, less productive salespeople eventually resign, whereas under a guaranteed salary system, the sales manager would usually have to fire them.

Application of commission plans requires the sales manager to decide:

1. The base, or unit, upon which the commissions will be paid (dollar sales, units sold, or gross profits)
2. The rate to be paid per unit (usually expressed as a percentage of sales or gross profit)
3. The point at which commissions start (after selling the first unit or after reaching a sales quota)
4. The time when the commissions are paid (when the order is obtained, shipped, or paid for)

If salespeople are not paid their commission until the order is shipped, they will likely pressure plant managers to ship promptly. This means customer service is being improved at the same time that salespeople are looking out for themselves.

Companies without large working capital often use commissions as a method of keeping selling costs directly related to sales. Some companies prefer to use part-time salespeople or independent manufacturers' agents on straight commission, to avoid the administrative costs associated with collecting federal social security taxes, unemployment taxes, and income taxes. Whenever the company is not very concerned about service or developing long-term customer relationships, commissions are an effective way to obtain high sales.

Profitability. Though commissions ought to be related to profits, management is often reluctant to reveal profit margins to salespeople for fear that they may quit and take the information to competitors. Yet salespeople should be able to compute their expected income. One solution to this dilemma is to divide products into profit groups and assign a different commission rate to each group.

Draw
A sum of money paid against future commissions. A "guaranteed draw" is one that does not have to be repaid in the event of insufficient commissions.

Drawing Accounts. Commission plans may include a **draw**, which is a sum of money paid against future commissions. A *guaranteed draw* is one that does not have to be repaid by the salesperson if he or she earns insufficient commissions. Thus, it acts like a salary but is lower than a straight salary would be. Commissions may be paid under varying conditions and times. Salespeople may receive commissions on all orders written, accepted, shipped, or paid for during a given period.

A draw, or advance, against future commissions is one way of giving salespeople the security of a fixed income while providing an incentive for greater productivity. As indicated in Table 12.5, a salesperson may receive a weekly draw of $2,500, with 10 percent commission on all sales. Note that this sales rep's balance was negative until week 8, when sales volume reached a high enough level for total commissions earned to exceed the total draw against commissions. Throughout these weeks, however, the sales rep had some income security due to the fixed $2,500 draw. With a high positive balance, the salesperson might reasonably request an increase in the draw. Generally, management's objective is to set the draw high enough to offer the needed security but low enough to prevent salespeople from falling too far behind their offsetting commission earnings. Some sales managers put upper limits on permissible negative draw balances.

If a salesperson's balance is negative at the end of the quarter, it is usually carried over to the next quarter. If this situation continues, however, the company should consider reducing the draw amount or switching the sales rep to straight commission. In cases where a salesperson leaves with a negative balance on the statement, legal precedent does not call for the terminated employee to repay the draw. Some companies use a negative commission system to control a sales rep's efforts. For example, if a customer terminates a machine lease, the salesperson assigned to that particular account would lose the original commission paid when the machine was placed. This type of policy helps ensure that salespeople do not neglect present or long-term customers. Many experts believe that whenever a sales force has a large amount of pay at

TABLE 12.5 Salesperson's Earnings Statement with a Weekly Draw and 10 Percent Commision

WEEK	SALES VOLUME	EARNED COMMISSIONS	WEEKLY DRAW	BALANCE
1	0	0	$2,500	−$2,500
2	$10,000	$1,000	2,500	−4,000
3	15,000	1,500	2,500	−5,000
4	25,000	2,500	2,500	−5,000
5	30,000	3,000	2,500	−4,500
6	40,000	4,000	2,500	−3,000
7	45,000	4,500	2,500	−1,000
8	50,000	5,000	2,500	+1,500
9	45,000	4,500	2,500	+3,500
10	55,000	5,500	2,500	+6,500
11	60,000	6,000	2,500	+10,000
12	63,000	6,300	2,500	+13,800
13	75,000	7,500	2,500	+18,800
Totals	$453,000	$51,300	$32,500	+$18,800

risk and more than 20 percent variation in earnings from month to month, the sales manager should consider whether the benefits of the draw program outweigh its negative points.[31]

The following are some advantages and disadvantages of straight-commission plans.

Advantages

- Income is directly related to productivity.
- Commission is easy to calculate, so salespeople may keep track of their earnings.
- There is no ceiling on potential earnings.
- Money is not tied up in salaries, because commissions are paid only when revenues are generated.
- Costs are proportional to sales.
- Salespeople have maximum work freedom.
- Poorly performing salespeople eliminate themselves by quitting.
- Income is based strictly on accomplishments, not on subjective evaluations by sales managers.

Disadvantages

- Excessive emphasis may be placed on sales volume rather than profitable sales.
- Salespeople have little loyalty to the company.
- Because of extreme fluctuations in earnings, many salespeople may face uncertainty about meeting daily living expenses for their families.
- There may be high sales force turnover rates when business conditions are slow.
- Non-selling activities like service, missionary sales, and displays are often neglected.
- Salespeople may overload customers with inventory, thereby straining long-term customer relationships.
- Windfall earnings may come about under good business conditions, which may be disturbing to sales management.
- Flexibility to split territories or transfer salespeople is diminished because of limited means of control over the sales force.
- Sales managers may become lax about recruiting, selecting, and supervising, since they may consider marginal salespeople acceptable under this compensation plan.

Bonus Compensation Plans. Bonus plans provide a lump sum of money or stock for some exceptional performance, such as making quota, obtaining a new customer account, or selling a desired product mix. Firms may pay bonuses for individual performances or group achievements and give them in the current period, distribute them over several time periods, or defer them until after retirement, when the salesperson is earning less money and will pay less tax. Most companies pay salespeople their incentive earnings annually. It is usually best for bonuses to be paid as soon as possible so they positively reinforce the desired salesperson behavior. If paid annually or semiannually, a bonus tends to lose its effectiveness in stimulating superior performance. Finally, sales managers should not routinely allocate equal bonuses to all members of a team who achieve a certain goal. Instead, recognize individual contributions to the goal achievement so that marginal contributors are not rewarded equally with high producers. Probably the major advantage of bonus plans is their flexibility, allowing managers to quickly adapt individual and group efforts toward changing organizational objectives.

■ Combination Compensation Plans

Combination compensation plans combine two or three of the basic compensation methods. They usually include commissions and bonuses to motivate reps to achieve volume or profit goals, and salary to help attain less quantifiable goals, such as customer service, expense control, and long-run sales development. Combination plans are the most widely used of all compensation methods and more than 70 percent of companies favor them.[32]

The critical factor in a combination compensation plan is the selection of a target salary-and-incentive mix. The decision is not an arbitrary one. The sales manager needs to offer a salary high enough to attract talent, and an incentive sufficient to motivate. That means being familiar with the competitive compensation environment and the amount of incentive that will motivate the sales force, given the nature of the sales job. The compensation leverage ratio varies among companies, but it is generally 70 to 80 percent salary and 20 to 30 percent incentive.

No compensation plan will fit all situations. Combination compensation plans, however, are the most flexible of all approaches. These are some combination compensation plans that fit a variety of conditions:

- *Salary plus commissions*—This combination is best when management wants to get high sales without sacrificing customer service. It is good for new salespeople, since it provides more security than straight commission.
- *Salary plus bonus*—This combination is preferred for achieving long-run objectives, such as selling large installations or product systems or achieving a desired customer mix.
- *Salary plus commission plus bonus*—This plan is appropriate for seasonal sales, when there are frequent inventory imbalances and when management wants to focus on certain products or customers.
- *Commission plus bonus*—This plan is usually applied to group efforts, in which some salespeople call on central buyers or buying committees while others call on store managers.

Here are the main advantages and disadvantages of a combination compensation plan.

Advantages

- Provides the greatest flexibility and control over salespeople, in that all desirable activities can be rewarded
- Provides security plus incentive
- Allows frequent, immediate reinforcement of desired sales behavior

Reprinted by permission of Centive.

● **Sales managers can turn to specialist firms such as Centive to design combination compensation plans that can be effective in increasing sales force performance.**

Disadvantages

■ Can be complex and easily misunderstood

■ Can be expensive to administer, particularly if not computerized

■ May fail to achieve management objectives if not carefully conceived

Which compensation method pays salespeople the most money? A recent survey revealed that a salary and incentive combination yielded the highest total pay to top salespeople.[33]

Visit various websites, such as www.centive.com, to learn more about sales force compensation programs and to review case studies, white papers, industry research, and available webinars that can augment your understanding of sales force reward systems and compensation plans.

Trends in Sales Compensation

Many recent changes in salesperson compensation are expected to continue during the years ahead. These trends include

■ Tying the sales compensation plan to productivity as well as retention

■ Inclusion of customer satisfaction in the sales compensation plan

■ More emphasis on international sales compensation

■ Compensation for Productivity and Retention

Companies are beginning to view sales compensation plans more broadly—as an investment in future sales productivity and retention of desired salespeople and sales managers. Thus they are becoming more generous in compensating sales managers as well as salespeople.[34]

Due to years of cost cutting and downsizing, companies' sales forces have become rather lean. This puts added pressure on sales managers to retain good salespeople. So sales compensation plans must now not only attract new recruits, but retain the current salespeople as well. Increasingly, sales managers are offering high starting salaries and signing bonuses to attract new salespeople. At the same time, adjustments are being made to improve existing salespeople's compensation plans to keep morale high.[35]

■ Inclusion of Customer Satisfaction in the Compensation Plan

Another important trend in the business environment is the growing emphasis on customer satisfaction and relationship building. Managers are recognizing that high levels of customer satisfaction and retention are critical to profitability. Firms such as IBM (www.ibm.com), Xerox (www.xerox.com), Saturn (www.saturn.com), Infiniti (www.infiniti.com), and DaimlerChrysler (www.daimlerchrysler.com) have incorporated customer satisfaction-based incentives (CSBI) into their sales compensation plans.[36] For example, salespeople at IBM have a significant amount of their incentives determined by customer satisfaction ratings. Other companies use customer satisfaction ratings to determine year-end bonuses for salespeople. One survey found that 26 percent of companies measure customer satisfaction as part of a sales compensation plan, and these firms reported they are likely to continue CSBI systems in the future.[37]

Another related trend in sales compensation is customer sales teams and key account programs. Many *Fortune 500* companies are moving their salespeople into account-based teams. These companies believe they can better serve their customers by adopting a more customer-focused structure for their salespeople and compensation plan.[38] Key account salespeople or customer sales teams who call on the largest and most profitable customers are often the highest-paid salespeople in their companies. Their compensation plans are also tied to customer satisfaction. A national account manager for Monsanto (www.monsanto.com), with 15 percent of his compensation based on customer surveys, says, "You have to get your compensation tied to the relationships you have with your customers or upper management won't understand [how much you're worth]."[39]

■ International Sales Compensation

As U.S. firms continue to expand into international markets, they are being confronted with a range of circumstances that require them to adjust their sales compensation plans for indigenous salespeople.[40] For example, in the Far East, sales volume is the primary indicator of success, compensation is tied almost exclusively to this factor, and less weight should be placed on non-selling activities when developing a compensation plan. With wide cultural differences throughout the world, U.S. companies must carefully assess each country's culture before tailoring a sales compensation plan for that market.[41]

■ Commission for Sales Managers

While we've focused on methods of compensating salespeople, we should not overlook the obvious fact that sales managers are concerned about their own compensation, too. Logically, sales managers' compensation ought to be closely tied to the performance of the sales force.

Developing a sales manager's compensation plan can be challenging. First, the responsibilities of a sales manager are neither purely sales nor purely management. Good sales managers strike a balance between these two distinct goals: they continually strive for short-term sales, yet must also meet long-term corporate goals. Therefore, developing a sales manager's compensation plan solely on the basis of yearly sales performance may not be appropriate. Second, designing a sales manager's compensation plan is further complicated by the expectations of other functional areas of the organization. For example, financial executives may expect sales managers to control selling costs and be compensated accordingly, while marketing executives may want to reward a sales manager for emphasizing new products, market share growth, and the long-term image of the company. So companies should consider a blend of sales-oriented goals as well as organizational goals when developing a compensation plan for sales managers.[42]

Expense Accounts and Fringe Benefits

Expense Account
Financial accounts that enable sales representatives to carry out necessary selling activities.

Expense accounts enable sales representatives to carry out necessary selling activities, while fringe benefits help provide them with personal security and job satisfaction. Although neither should be a means of augmenting income, salespeople often see them as important parts of the total compensation package, so we discuss them in this chapter. (We dealt with sales contests and other indirect monetary incentives used as motivational devices in chapter 10.)

■ Acknowledging the Importance of Selling Expenses

The costs associated with supporting salespeople in the field have been rapidly increasing and are expected to continue rising for the foreseeable future. The major sales expense categories—other than salary, commissions, and bonuses—are meals and entertainment, air travel, automobile rentals, and lodging. The increasing cost of lodging during the late 1980s single-handedly pushed the selling cost index to an all-time high. More recently, sales managers are beginning to voice concern over automobile expenses, because the costs of new cars and ongoing maintenance have also driven up the price of putting salespeople on the road.[43] To make matters even worse, skyrocketing gasoline prices in recent years have increased the costs associated not only with automobiles but also with air travel.

While selling costs have increased, they do represent expenses that are necessary and important for salespeople to carry out their jobs. In fact, sales managers have been known to consider travel and entertainment expenses as both "a tool and a curse." Firms must continue budgeting for these expenses, which are often critical to the company's sales growth and overall image. Many U.S. companies seem to have found that "Entertainment is to the businessman what fertilizer is to the farmer . . . it increases the yield." Some firms take business expenditures one step further, as the nearby *Sales Management in Action* box demonstrates.

To accomplish sales objectives, every effective sales force must incur expenses. However, it is probably more realistic to see these not as expenses, but as investments that will yield future dividends (as in the *Sales Management in Action* box). Because salespeople usually spend their own money for daily expenses, it is especially important to their morale that these outlays be quickly reimbursed. Most firms reimburse salespeople for items such as meals, lodging, auto expenses, business and personal phone calls home, drinks, and laundry costs while on the road.

■ Designing the Expense Plan

Any well-designed expense plan requires several building blocks. These are flexibility, equitability, legitimacy, simplicity, and affordability of administration.

Flexibility. A plan that tries to relate selling expenses only to sales may discourage longer-run profitable sales activities, such as prospecting for new customers or providing special services. Thus, expense plans need to accommodate these other objectives.

Equitability. An expense plan should be sufficiently flexible to ensure equal treatment of all salespeople regardless of their territory or sales assignment. Thus, the plan

SALES MANAGEMENT IN ACTION

Corporations Toe the Party Line

The Tax Reform Act of 1986 reduced the amount of entertainment expenses that can be written off from 100 percent to 80 percent, and the days of "scandalous" entertaining appeared to be over. Nonetheless, many multinational firms continue to lavishly entertain their best customers and probably will continue to do so, even if the expenditure is not deductible at all. In fact, entertainment was "business as usual" at a recent Super Bowl, where 50-yard-line tickets were sold out at $2,500 or more each.

One of the most sought-after events on the corporate calendar is the Lawn Tennis Championships at the All England Lawn Tennis and Croquet Club—better known as Wimbledon. Seagram's is among the

hundreds of multinational corporations that entertain guests at Wimbledon each year. Competition for space is tremendous, but Merrill Lynch, IBM, British Petroleum, and Avis were among the fortunate few to fete prized clients with traditional tournament fare of champagne, cold salmon, and strawberries with cream. To help build company-customer relationships, Wexford International invited 60 of its customers and suppliers to a two-day golf tournament at a New Jersey country club. All this entertaining seems to be based on a business belief that companies and customers who play together, tend to stay together.

should take into account regional cost differences for food, lodging, and travel as well as expense variations for handling different types of customers or for doing different sales tasks. Each year *Sales & Marketing Management* calculates a selling cost index (SCI) for a typical five-day week for a salesperson working in each of eighty metropolitan markets. This index is used by many firms to determine appropriate reimbursement levels.

Legitimacy. The plan should simply reimburse legitimate expenses, with neither profits nor losses for salespeople whether on the road or at the home office. Expense allowances should never be used in lieu of compensation. This would weaken the sales manager's control over the basic compensation plan, encourage expense padding, and violate federal income tax laws. Only expense accounts that reimburse salespeople for legitimate business expenses are non-taxable.

Simplicity. Expense-account reimbursement policies must avoid legalistic language. Salespeople should easily understand which expenses are reimbursable so they have clear guidelines for making expenditures.

Affordability. Too many organizations require excessive and redundant paperwork for reimbursement of expenses. An efficient expense control plan should minimize the clerical burdens for the reps and the sales office staff.

■ Controlling Expenses through Reimbursement

Although salespeople on straight commission often pay their own expenses out of commissions, most companies reimburse their salespeople for legitimate selling expenses. Three basic reimbursement plans are widely used: unlimited, limited, and combination.

Unlimited Reimbursement Plans. By far the most popular method of expense control, unlimited reimbursement allows salespeople to be reimbursed for all their necessary selling and travel expenses. No limit is put on total expenses, but sales reps must regularly submit itemized records of their expenditures. With the flexibility provided by unlimited payment plans, the expense variations in serving different customer types and territories or in performing diverse selling tasks are easily handled. This unlimited aspect may tempt some salespeople to be extravagant or to pad their expense accounts. While its flexibility allows sales managers some control in directing sales force activities, an unlimited payment plan tends to make forecasts of selling costs more difficult.

Limited Reimbursement Plans. Under limited payment plans, expense reimbursement is restricted either to a flat dollar amount for a given time period (usually a day or week) or to an allowable cost per item (such as for a motel room, daily meals, or each mile of travel). To develop a limited payment plan, managers must study past company records to learn what the costs of meals, lodging, and travel have been over the years (using dollars adjusted for inflation). With this plan, sales managers can predict and budget expenses more accurately, reduce expense account padding, and establish unequivocal guidelines for spending by salespeople.

There are disadvantages, however. Salespeople may feel a limited plan indicates management's lack of trust. Such plans restrict those unusual (perhaps unallowable) expenses that might win or save a customer. And they make salespeople too expense conscious, to the possible detriment of sales and profits. They also tempt salespeople to switch reporting of expenditures from one time period to another, to avoid going over expense ceilings. Finally, they require frequent revision of expense ceilings during inflationary periods; this may lead to confusion among salespeople about the current ceiling level.

Combination Reimbursement Plans. Sales managers may consider a combination of the unlimited and limited expense reimbursement programs, in order to secure the advantages of both. One approach sets limits on certain items such as food and lodging but not on transportation. Another variation of the combination plan relates expenses to sales. For example, the salesperson may be reimbursed for expenses up to 5 percent of net sales or be awarded a bonus for keeping expenses below 5 percent of net sales. Probably the greatest advantage of this approach is that it ensures

● **Although firms readily cover traveling expenses, sales managers should remember that keeping a close watch on expenses is an effective way of increasing profitability.**

that expenses do not get out of line in relation to sales. The major disadvantage is that it diverts some of the sales rep's attention from obtaining profitable sales to worrying about expense ratios.

■ Curbing Abuses of Expense Reimbursement Plans

Since few salespeople can afford frequent company travel on their personal funds, some means of immediate funding must be available to them. Unfortunately, travel advances have been a source of much waste and abuse. It is a temptation for salespeople to draw a larger advance than needed for a trip and to spend the full amount. Some companies have resorted to credit cards for salespeople, but these have proved so painless to use that travel expenses have been known to jump as much as 25 percent as the salespeople upgrade their out-of-town lifestyle.

■ Adjusting to Rising Selling Costs

As the costs of sales calls climb, many companies are being forced to rethink their selling strategies and tactics. One survey indicated that approximately 60 percent of companies take steps to make sure they're getting the best deals on all their travel arrangements.[44] More companies today are planning well in advance to get better airfares and shopping airlines, hotels, car rental agencies and websites to ensure they are getting the lowest possible prices. One of the most interesting responses to rising travel and entertainment expenses comes from a manufacturing company that recently developed a video to use in place of face-to-face sales calls. Its sales force now does about two-thirds less traveling. According to the marketing manager of the firm, the use of the video saves the company about $30,000 to $40,000 per year in travel and lodging costs alone. The increasing use of the Internet is also helping to lower travel expenses for many companies. One of the key jobs of today's sales managers is to find creative ways to control rising personal selling costs.

CHAPTER SUMMARY

1. **Meet the challenges of developing sales force compensation plans.** Developing a sales compensation plan is one of the most difficult tasks facing sales managers. In general, most salespeople are motivated by money, and for many salespeople the amount of money they make represents their "scorecard" of how well they are performing. The difficulty lies in developing a sales compensation plan that isn't too comfortable in that it fosters complacency, or one that is so aggressive in its goals that it actually demotivates the sales force. All salespeople are somewhat different, and to develop a plan to satisfy everyone is extremely challenging but a goal worth striving for.

2. **Follow the basic steps in developing a compensation plan.** When new compensation plans are developed or existing ones are revised, a systematic process should be followed. The seven distinct steps in the process of developing a compensation plan are to prepare job descriptions, establish specific objectives, determine general levels of compensation, develop the compensation mix, pretest the plan, administer the plan, and evaluate the plan.

3. **Compare the different methods of sales force compensation.** The three basic methods of sales compensation are straight salary, straight commission, and combination plans. Straight salary has the advantages of providing security, developing a sense

of loyalty, providing more control over salespeople, and being simple to administer. Its disadvantages are that it may cause a lack of incentive, increase selling costs, and lead to adequate but not superior performance. Straight commission has the advantages of relating income directly to sales, basing income strictly on accomplishments with no ceiling, and ensuring that costs are proportional to sales. The disadvantages of straight commission include an overemphasis on sales, neglect of non-selling activities, erratic earnings, and a loss of control by sales managers. Combination plans often provide the greatest flexibility and control while also providing security plus incentive. The disadvantages of a combination plan include the difficulty and expense in administering the plan.

4. Evaluate the recent trends in sales force compensation. The changing business environment has affected sales compensation planning for sales managers. Recent trends in sales compensation include tying sales compensation to retention as well as productivity, including customer satisfaction measures in the compensation plan, and growing emphasis on compensation for international salespeople.

5. Control the use of expense accounts and fringe benefits in compensation planning. Expense accounts enable salespeople to carry out necessary selling activities, while fringe benefits help provide them with personal security and job satisfaction. Although expense allowances and fringe benefits should not be used as a means of supplementing salespeople's income, they are often perceived by salespeople as important parts of their total compensation package. Any well-designed expense plan requires several building blocks. These basic criteria are flexibility, equitability, legitimacy, simplicity, and affordability of administration.

REVIEW AND APPLICATION QUESTIONS

1. Do you believe that most salespeople can be effectively "steered" by financial compensation? Explain. [LO 1]

2. What compensation mix do you think is best for creative selling of intangible goods, like estate planning advice? What mix would be best for a missionary salesperson (drug detail person) calling on physicians? A salesperson for large factory machines? A rep for office equipment? [LO 1]

3. What would be the ideal compensation package for the type of sales career you would consider? Would this "ideal" package change over the course of your career? [LO 1]

4. Identify and describe the various steps involved in devising a compensation plan. [LO 2]

5. What would you suggest to reduce selling costs? Do you think selling costs are like profitable investments and thus should not necessarily be reduced? Explain your answer. [LO 2]

6. Describe the advantages and disadvantages of different compensation methods. [LO 3]

7. What are the essential criteria for designing and implementing a sound bonus incentive program? [LO 3]

8. Discuss some of the recent trends in developing sales force compensation programs. [LO 4]

9. What method of reimbursing sales expenses would be best for a life insurance salesperson, a computer hardware sales rep, or an account executive who sells commercial time for a television station? [LO 5]

IT'S UP TO YOU

Internet Exercise

Use the Internet to access MyWorkTools (www.myworktools.com) and other similar knowledge exchange websites. Based on your research, develop a comprehensive sales force compensation checklist identifying financial rewards for remunerating the sales force.

Role-Playing Exercise

Justifying the New Compensation Plan

Situation

You are the national sales manager for a large medical products company that sells a broad line of products to hospitals and pharmacies. After several years of fine-tuning your sales force compensation plan, you feel you've finally got it right to achieve corporate goals while maximizing sales force productivity. In brief, this plan, which was implemented six months ago, gives salespeople a weekly draw of $3,000 plus 5 percent commission on sales, a 20 percent bonus for making quota, a 3 percent bonus for signing up each new account, and a special 5 percent commission on designated medical equipment that the company's product managers want emphasized. Your salespeople seem to like the new plan, and sales are steadily growing since its implementation. In fact, it looks as if each sales force region is going to reach its sales volume goals for the first time in years. The company doesn't provide executives below vice president with detailed profitability data so you are not able to calculate profits for different market factors (customer, product, territory, or salesperson), so your focus is on achieving the company's sales goals.

Today, you received a confidential memo from the vice president of finance for your company. In it, she informed you that a detailed financial analysis of revenues and expenses has revealed that the company is *losing* money in several areas and that cost reductions must be made throughout the company. An executive meeting has been scheduled for next week, and she has requested that you come prepared to discuss in depth the new sales force compensation plan.

Role-Play Participants and Assignments

National sales manager: You feel that you will be on the defensive at this meeting and will have to justify the sales force compensation plan to the senior executives.

Vice president of finance: She will come prepared with profitability data about sales territories, products, and customers. And, she will be asking tough, detailed questions about the new sales force compensation plan.

Other senior executives: They will probably ask many wide-ranging questions about sales force compensation, revenues, sales expenses, and profits.

 In-Basket Exercise

After getting your first cup of coffee at work this morning before reading your e-mails, you notice a red envelope in your in-basket mail. You immediately recognize that distinctive red color as urgent correspondence from your company's national sales manager. Quickly opening the envelope and reading the letter inside, you're surprised to read that the company is getting a "rising tide of customer complaints" about poor customer service by your company's salespeople . . . and customer retention levels have "declined in each of the past three years." From the blunt wording of his letter, it's obvious that the national sales manager is under pressure to do something quickly to satisfy senior management. The last sentence of his letter puts it directly:

"I want 'well-thought-out ideas with supporting pro and con arguments' for changes in our sales force compensation plan by the end of the week from each sales manager." The company's current sales force compensation plan provides a relatively low salary and no team bonus but generous individual sales commissions. Since becoming a district sales manager, you have felt that some of the highest-earning salespeople might be neglecting customer service to maximum their commissions. "Wow," you think to yourself, "this is going to be a six-cups-of-coffee day."

Outline a new sales force compensation plan to improve customer service and retention without hurting sales force motivation.

Ethical Dilemma

You were recently hired as a sales manager for a successful financial services firm, and you're beginning to question the company's compensation plan. Salespeople are compensated on a salary-plus-commission basis. However, after a salesperson reaches a certain level of sales, commissions can run as high as 20 percent. This high commission rate, which can apply to over 100 different services, may be creating a situation that's not serving your customers well. After only a month on the job, you've received several calls from irate customers complaining that your company salespeople are too aggressive and have confused them into buying more financial service products than they need. You discuss this with one of your top salespeople, and he downplays the issue, stating: "With our compensation system, selling only a few extra service products to each customer can mean the difference between earning $75,000 and $125,000 a year. And selling customers some extra financial services isn't really hurting them at all. In fact, everyone benefits!"

DISCUSSION QUESTIONS

1. Is this salesperson acting unethically? Why or why not?

2. Should your company's compensation plan be changed? Why or why not?

3. How would you revise the compensation plan?

CASE 12.1

Syntel, Inc.: The Role of Compensation in Salesperson Turnover

Syntel, Inc. is an established domestic manufacturer of industrial air compressors and other related products. Over the years, the company has worked with major retail chains such as Home Depot, Lowes, and Wal-Mart to develop efficient air compressors for the industrial and commercial markets. In turn, the large retailers sold the compressors under their own brand names to painters, carpenters, bricklayers, and other people in small businesses. Syntel's own brand of smaller compressors is sold to small retail chains. Syntel's image as experts in air compressor manufacturing continues to be highly positive among both the companies and the customers it serves.

During the 1990s, Syntel and many of the companies purchasing its small air compressors recognized the growing trend in the do-it-yourself market. More consumers were taking an active interest in home-improvement projects and automotive repairs. This led to a growing market for do-it-yourself products. During this time, the marketing vice president and sales manager of Syntel took an especially active interest in the demand for the company's smaller commercial line of air compressors. Close monitoring of the sales of small air compressors revealed that as consumers became more involved in do-it-yourself projects, many discovered the benefits of using small air compressors for their home and automotive projects.

As a result of the rapid growth of this market during the 1990s, Syntel considered manufacturing a small, lightweight air compressor. After conducting several marketing research studies, Syntel developed a prototype of the product for further consumer testing and possible commercialization. The prototype had the following characteristics: a 0.5-horsepower motor and easy portability since it weighed only 18 pounds; it did not require lubricating and was virtually maintenance-free; it could do more than fifty tasks around the house; and it came with a 12-foot cord plus a kit of accessories. Syntel conducted additional research in the consumer market and found that consumers especially liked its portability, its regulator dial, its ability to be attached to a wall in the garage or workshop, and its attractive design. Syntel then decided to enter the in-home consumer market with its new lightweight air compressor.

In developing the in-home air compressor market, Syntel faced the traditional problems of bringing a new product to market, but it also needed to expand its sales force. Historically, the firm produced private-label air compressors for mass merchandisers. But it also sold to major accounts such as Tru-Value Hardware, Ace Hardware, and large independent distributors. Unit sales were large, but there were a limited number of customers. The company had six full-time salespeople and a sales manager. To gain national distribution as quickly as possible, the firm contracted with a large number of manufacturers' agents (oftentimes called manufacturers' reps) who collectively covered the United States. They called on smaller accounts and/or accounts that Syntel could not cover with its own small sales force. The manufacturers' reps were compensated through commissions which were computed on either a per-unit basis or a sliding-scale percentage of their invoice totals. Initially, both Syntel and the manufacturers' reps benefited. As the product became more accepted in distribution channels, the manufacturers' reps began to "cherry-pick" their larger accounts and ignored the smaller accounts in their territories. Recognizing this, Syntel decided to enlarge the size of its own internal sales force and hired sixteen new salespeople. Compensation was salary plus benefits, and the new salespeople's role was to call on accounts the manufacturers' reps were bypassing. At the time of the decision to hire the "junior salespeople," the original six internal salespeople were promoted to national account managers, handling only the largest customers like Lowes, Home Depot, Wal-Mart, and Target. Their compensation would be salary and benefits in addition to a year-end bonus based on volume and profitability.

After a few years of having three different groups of salespeople (junior, national account, and manufacturers' reps), Syntel faced a serious problem with its junior salespeople. The junior salespeople complained that the manufacturers' reps continued to cherry pick the large accounts in their territories, thus earning large commissions, while they had to make three times the sales calls for a lower salary. In addition, junior salespeople felt

the old guard had an unfair advantage with their national accounts. Not only were they making considerably more with a salary plus bonus opportunity, but they had fewer sales duties. A summary of the annual compensation for each category of salesperson is shown in Table 1.

Despite the unusual makeup of Syntel's sales force, sales increased rapidly. The do-it-yourself market grew faster than Syntel management had anticipated. With the growth, however, came a great deal of competition. Although Syntel's sales force strategy had weaknesses, management felt they were doing an adequate job in the in-home consumer market. Turnover remained high (50 percent or more in some years) among the new salespeople, but there was never any problem hiring additional salespeople. By 2008, Syntel's internal sales force had grown to thirty-two salespeople (six senior national accounts reps and twenty-six new junior salespeople).

As competition in the in-home market slowed the sales growth rate, Syntel management began thinking about separately targeting the small contractor segment of the market. As the consumer market expanded, the small contractor segment was being virtually forgotten or was assumed to be part of the consumer market segment. Some experts were projecting the home-improvement market would surpass $175 billion by the year 2010. Many of the products aimed at the home-improvement market were actually purchased by the thousands of small contractors throughout the United States.

While the tremendous growth during the past decade left many unsolved problems within Syntel's sales force, management wants to get a jump on the competition in the relatively neglected small contractor market.

TABLE 1 Compensation and Turnover for Syntel's Sales Force

| Type of Salesperson | COMPENSATION | | | | Turnover (%) |
	Commission	Average Yearly Salary	Year-End Bonus	Benefits	
National account managers (6)	None	$90,000–$110,000	$15,000–$20,000	$10,000–$12,000	0
Manufacturers' reps	$50,000–$75,000	None	None	None	0
Junior salespeople (26)	None	$45,000–$60,000	None	$10,000–$12,000	50+

QUESTIONS

1. Should Syntel enter the small contractor segment with its product? Why or why not?

2. Give some suggestions on how the high turnover problem among Syntel's junior salespeople might be solved.

3. What major questions must be answered before Syntel makes the decision to enter the small contractor market? Should its sales force structure and three compensation plans remain the same? Why or why not?

4. Assuming Syntel enters the small contractor market and remains in the in-home consumer market, recommend a compensation program for the entire sales force. Be specific in your recommendations by considering each of the seven steps in developing a compensation plan.

5. Would any of the recent compensation trends help Syntel? Why or why not?

Case prepared by Jim Boles, Georgia State University.

CASE 12.2

Sun-Sweet Citrus Supply, Inc.: Compensation and Sales Expenses

Sun-Sweet Citrus Supply (SCS), located in Orlando, Florida, is a wholesaler of citrus farming supplies and equipment, particularly heavy-duty equipment such as pickers, forklifts, fruit washers, driers, and crating machines. Since being established thirty years ago, SCS has become a well-known industry name, earning a reputation as one of the best in the industry.

David Collins assumed the position of sales manager for SCS less than two weeks ago. He was recruited from a large wholesaler of mining supplies in Louisville, Kentucky. When David's secretary presented him with the sales expense accounts for the past week, he almost fainted. He quickly asked her to double-check the figures, but she assured him they were correct. David had been in sales too long not to recognize padded expense accounts.

After checking the expense account records of the ten SCS salespeople for the past six months, David realized that last week's expenses were not unusual for the salespeople. But, they were way out of line compared to industry norms. He quickly picked up the phone and summoned to his office any salesperson that happened to be in the office on that particular day. Kimberly Rolwood happened to be that most unlucky person.

When initially questioned about her expense account, Kimberly was a bit uncomfortable. After a few minutes, she suggested to David that he check with the CEO on this matter, stating that he must have forgotten to mention how the expense accounts were handled. After David insisted, Kimberly finally remarked that this was the way the salespeople got part of their pay each month thereby making up for the low salaries at SCS. David thanked Kimberly for telling him this, but he was still upset about the practice.

The next morning David immediately took up the matter with the CEO and found that Kimberly had indeed told the truth about the way padding expense accounts was viewed at SCS. David was very distressed, since he strongly objected to the practice. Not only was it illegal, but he thought it reflected poor judgment by management because compensation and rewards should be tied to employee performance. After reflecting on it for several days, David met with the CEO again. He told him he very much disapproved of the way the expense accounts were being handled and requested permission to change the reimbursement procedures so they would be more in line with industry norms. David got the go-ahead from the CEO to take whatever measures he believed were best for the company.

That afternoon David sat in his office pondering the situation and how best to resolve it. He wanted honest expense reporting, but wondered if it should be an open expense system or one with limits on the various types of expenditures salespeople were allowed to make. He also wondered how he would adjust the sales force's salaries to compensate for the tighter restrictions on expense accounts. David knew that to attract and retain qualified employees, their pay should be linked to competitive market rates for that industry. He also knew that employees increase their performance when an organization implements a pay-for-performance method of pay.

TABLE 1 Sales Force Compensation and Selling Expenses

	SCS	INDUSTRY AVERAGE
Compensation		
Salary	$50,000–$65,000	$70,000–$85,000
Commission	$10,000–$15,000	$15,000–$20,000
Year End Bonus	None	$8,000–$12,000
Selling Expenses as a Percentage of Sales		
Meals & Entertainment	8–12%	2–4%
Air Travel	5–8%	4–5%
Lodging	7–10%	5–6%
Miscellaneous	4–6%	1–3%
Total Expenses as a Percentage of Sales	24–36%	12–18%

In researching the farm equipment industry for background on resolving the CSC sales compensation and expenses problem, David found the information presented in Table 1. The information revealed exactly what Kimberly admitted, David suspected, and the CEO knew all along—the SCS sales force was taking advantage of the tradition of padding the expense account. Instead of paying a competitive market rate of compensation, SCS paid much less than the industry average and expected its salespeople to make up the difference by padding their expense accounts. David understood that the way a company compensates employees sends a clear message about what management believes is important, and that its approach to sales force compensation could cause SCS employees to believe the company is unfair and unethical in other business practices.

QUESTIONS

1. Should any changes be made in the sales force compensation and expense reimbursement plans at SCS? Why or why not?

2. Given the long tradition of using sales expense reimbursement to supplement salaries, how should David explain the need for changes and go about implementing them to (a) ensure senior SCS management does not feel embarrassed, and (b) to avoid creating a morale problem among the sales force? What might David do to increase involvement and support for changing the current compensation and expense reimbursement plans?

3. What basic type of compensation and expense reimbursement plans should David propose for the SCS sales force? Why?

4. Design precise compensation and expense reimbursement plans for SCS. Fully justify your recommendations.

Case prepared by Mary Collins, Strayer University.

Controlling and Evaluating Sales Force Performance

CHAPTER **13**
Sales Volume, Costs, and Profitability Analysis

CHAPTER **14**
Sales Force Performance Evaluation

CHAPTER 13

Sales Volume, Costs, and Profitability Analysis

LEARNING OBJECTIVES

When you finish this chapter, you should be able to:

1. Understand the framework for a sales force organization audit.

2. Discuss the sources of information and need for sales volume, costs, and profitability analyses.

3. Outline the procedures for conducting sales analyses by territory, sales representative, product line, and customer.

4. Describe the procedure for marketing costs and profitability analyses.

5. Articulate the arguments for using contribution costs versus full costs.

6. Illustrate the concept of and ways to improve return on assets managed (ROAM).

INSIDE SALES MANAGEMENT

Mike Andrews, Vice President of Sales and Marketing, J. A. Riggs

How do you manage profitability when your inventory costs are largely out of your control?

That's the challenge Mike Andrews faces every day. Andrews is the vice president of sales and marketing for J. A. Riggs, the sole Caterpillar Inc. dealership for the state of Arkansas. It's a $250 million business in which the cheapest equipment products, such as Skid Steer loaders, sell for upwards of $25,000—and the largest tractors can sell for $1.5 million.

Caterpillar Inc. publishes the list prices of its product line, with Riggs setting the customer sale prices. Competition in the marketplace leaves little wiggle room to price excessively. Margins are relatively small—the dealer might pay $90,000 for a vehicle or equipment it hopes to sell for $100,000. But Andrews relies on several different opportunities for profitability. The selling price, which the sales manager and rep arrive at together for each customer, is only one of them.

"All machinery breaks down eventually," says Andrews, and although Caterpillar Inc. can be depended on to produce a high-quality and saleable product, one of Riggs' most profitable lines is parts and service after the sale. Most Riggs customers plan on keeping their purchases for many years, and it's critical to keep them in safe and efficient working condition. Dealer after-sale support adds value to each transaction and is required to maintain profit margins. Another profit center for Riggs is the rental equipment it offers customers—some customers prefer to rent rather than own the equipment.

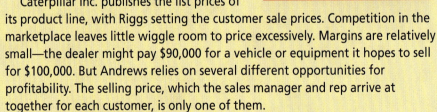

"Offering customers cost-effective solutions to their business problems keeps them coming to you rather than competition," says Andrews.

Still another big part of managing profitability is managing controllable costs. Each of Riggs' twenty-seven sales reps is a profit center, with an expected profitability rate and a sales plan. Each rep costs the company about $75,000 a year in salary, commission, travel costs, and expense accounts. "They're fairly expensive employees," says Andrews, "and if they don't produce the revenues, profitability, and market share required, it shows up very quickly. Every sales manager's dream is to hire the right people for the job." Managing sales reps to get the best performance is a real balancing act between training and motivation. Reps who don't bring in the expected revenue don't stay on the payroll for long.

But profitability doesn't end there. While the dealership can't control what it pays for its inventory, it can manage that inventory to keep its profitability high. So Andrews keeps an eye on customer trends to refine his forecast of their equipment needs and project exactly what he'll need to have on hand as far as two years ahead of time. It can take up to a year and a half to get some larger vehicles from Caterpillar Inc., and Andrews can't use up resources keeping such big-ticket items sitting on the lot. In fact, the larger the equipment, usually the farther in advance he needs to plan for it. "Our inventory plan has to match our sales forecast," says Andrews. "All the pieces of our business plan have to work together to keep us profitable."

W e've covered organizing and developing the sales force in *Part Two*, then managing and directing in *Part Three*. Now, in *Part Four*, we'll examine two critical areas that fall within the realm of controlling and evaluating sales force performance. First, in this chapter, we'll concentrate on sales volume, costs, and profitability analyses as key determinants of overall sales force effectiveness and efficiency. Our second topic—evaluating salesperson performance—focuses on the individual salesperson level and will be discussed in chapter 14.

Some sales managers stress selling activities and sales volume while neglecting cost controls and profitability analysis. Although analyzing sales volume metrics is helpful in evaluating and controlling sales effectiveness, it neglects the profitability of sales efforts—and high volume does not ensure high profits.[1] With the ever-increasing costs of selling, it's important that sales managers emphasize the profitability of sales efforts.[2] This requires analyzing costs and profitability by important market segments (customers, product lines, and territories) and organizational units.[3] From such analyses, sales managers can redirect resources and expenditures to those areas where the return per dollar spent is highest. In this process, they should be able to assess the impact of formal and informal control mechanisms on the sales organization and salespersons, as well as on customers.[4] Thus, in this chapter we will show you how to analyze sales volume, costs, and profitability in order to assess overall sales force productivity.[5]

Framework for Sales Force Organization Audit

Sales Force Audit
A comprehensive, systematic, diagnostic, and prescriptive tool designed to assess the adequacy of a firm's sales management process and to provide direction for improved performance and prescription for needed changes.

Analysis of overall sales organization performance can be best approached through a **sales force audit**—a comprehensive, systematic, diagnostic, and prescriptive tool designed to assess the adequacy of a firm's sales management process and to provide direction for improved performance and the prescription for needed changes.[6] The approach sales managers use in conducting an audit depends on the purpose and perceived importance of the evaluation, the availability of evaluation information, management philosophy toward performance appraisals, evaluation skills of the raters, and the way the firm uses the planning process. As shown in Figure 13.1, a sales force organization audit includes an evaluation of four areas:

- *Sales force organization environment*—Evaluates the external environmental factors (economic, sociocultural, competitive, technological, and political-legal) and the intra-organizational factors (company structure, sales-marketing department linkages, marketing mix).

Sales Management Functions

Evaluation of:

- Sales Force Organization
- Sales Force Recruitment
- Sales Force Selection
- Sales Force Training
- Sales Forecasting
- Sales Budgeting
- Territory Coverage and Routing Management
- Ethical Standards and Behavior
- Setting of Sales Force and Individual Salesperson Quotas
- Sales Volume
- Selling Costs
- Profitability by Market and Organizational Segments
- Overall Sales Force Performance

Sales Force Organization Planning System

Evaluation of:

- Sales Force Goals and Objectives
- Development of the Sales Management Program
- Deployment of the Sales Management Program

Program for Auditing the Sales Force Organization

Sales Manager Evaluation

Evaluation of Sales Manager's:

- Leadership Skills
- Motivation Skills
- Salesperson Empowerment Skills
- Participatory Decision-Making Skills
- Communication Skills

Environment of the Sales Force Organization

Evaluation of External Environmental Factors:

- Competitive Environment
- Political-Legal Environment
- Technological Environment
- Economic Environment
- Sociocultural Environment
- Target Market (Consumers and Organizational Buyers)

Evaluation of Intraorganizational Environmental Factors:

- Organizational Hierarchy
- Sales and Functional Departmental Linkages
- Sales and Marketing Departmental Linkages
- Development of the Strategic Marketing Program
- Development of the Marketing Process

FIGURE 13.1 Conceptual Model for a Sales Force Organization Audit

SOURCE: Dubinksy, Alan J., and Richard W. Hansen, "Improving Marketing Productivity: The 80/20 Principle Revisited." *California Management Review* 25/1 (Fall 1982): 96–105.

■ *Sales force organization planning system*—Evaluates the sales department's goals and objectives, its overall sales management program, and the program's deployment.

■ *Sales manager*—Assesses the adequacy of sales management at all levels in terms of leadership, motivation, and communication skills as well as in empowering salespeople and seeking their participation in decision making.

■ *Sales management functions*—Assesses the major sales management functions of recruitment, training, compensation, supervision, forecasting, evaluation, quotas, sales, costs, and profitability analyses.

When investigating each of these areas, the sales management auditor will first acquire a wealth of information for identifying the sales organization's weaknesses and strengths and then offer advice about what the firm should do to address any deficiencies. Sales personnel, customers, the sales and marketing support teams, other company personnel, internal company documents (marketing plan, sales plan, policy manuals, and surveys), industry publications, trade association information, and readily available published reports, newspapers, books, and periodicals can all provide information. Auditors must be objective and unbiased, so oftentimes they will come from outside the sales organization or even outside the company.

Some managers suggest that a detailed audit is an extravagance or questionable luxury, given the cost and time required. They prefer conducting audits only after some major problem has emerged. Waiting, however, until competition has become fierce, market share has eroded, key salespeople are leaving in droves, or profitability has headed south may make it too late to take corrective action that works. Therefore, it's advisable for sales managers to conduct a sales force audit regularly, at least once a year. The cost of an audit is often easily offset by the potentially substantial returns from taking timely corrective action to solve sales force problems early before they become large.

To learn more about conducting effective sales force organization audits, sales managers can enroll in comprehensive training programs offered by firms such as ES Research Group (www.esresearch .com).

● **Sales managers can employ the services of firms such as the ES Research Group that specialize in conducting an unbiased, comprehensive, systematic, diagnostic, and prescriptive sales audit to assess the sales management organization.**

Sales Volume, Costs, and Profitability Analysis

It usually takes a long time to complete a comprehensive assessment of the sales department's effectiveness and efficiency. However, let's now turn our discussion to conducting an analysis of sales volume, costs, and profitability because these are the key factors by which we can quickly gauge the performance of the sales department. Because total sales (or even profits, for that matter) provide an incomplete picture of a firm's sales patterns, sales managers also should evaluate costs and profitability at the same time to reveal strengths and weaknesses of the company's different marketing units.

In analyzing the productivity of sales force efforts, sales managers should note the linkages among sales volume, selling costs, and profits by market segments.[7] To determine the profitability of different market segments, it's necessary first to analyze the sources of sales volume and then to subtract the costs for producing those sales. Although the analytical task seems straightforward, it does present challenges, especially in assigning marketing costs (such as advertising, administration, or warehouse and office rent) that are indirect or common to more than one market segment.

Since selling costs are really a subcategory of marketing costs, and because a combination of selling and marketing costs are required to produce sales, we'll use the more general term *marketing costs analysis*. And, because sales managers are more interested in profitability than in costs, we'll use *marketing profitability analysis* to describe the overall process of sales volume, costs, and profitability analysis.

Marketing profitability analysis requires an in-depth analysis of the elements making up an organization's profit-and-loss or income statements. It reclassifies the traditional accounting statement expenses into cost centers according to the purposes or functions for which the expenses (costs) were incurred. For example, a sales organization may pay employees for performing such functions as direct selling, order processing, or sales administration. These salaries can be further allocated to territories, products, customers, or salespeople. This type of analysis can be invaluable to sales managers for eliminating or adding new selling activities or for changing the allocation of current efforts.[8] Let's discuss sales volume analysis first.

■ Sales Volume Analysis

Collecting, classifying, comparing, and evaluating an organization's sales figures is a process referred to as sales volume analysis. All organizations collect and classify sales data as the framework upon which to construct their accounting records and statements. To sales managers, sales figures are the most immediately visible and readily available means to judge how well the organization is performing. They regularly use sales analyses to compare current performance to past sales, competitors' sales, or forecasted sales. From these evaluations, management decides the direction and scale of future sales efforts. In some companies, sales figures are not always readily available due to a long sales cycle, as described in the *Sales Management in Action* box.

Sales Volume Analysis
The collection, classification, comparison, and evaluation of an organization's sales figures.

Key Considerations in Sales Volume Analysis. Because a **sales volume analysis** will try to identify deviations between actual and expected sales performance of some marketing unit, and then recommend action based on that identification, sales managers first need answers to the following questions:[9]

- *How will we define a sale?* We can think of a sale in three ways: it can occur (a) when an order is taken, (b) when it is shipped, or (c) when the customer pays. Most companies consider a sale to take place at the time of shipment, but some keep records for all three definitions to analyze what volume and type of orders make it through each of the stages. Whatever the definition, the firm must apply it consistently if sales comparisons across time periods are to be meaningful.

- *How will we measure sales?* Will we measure sales in dollars, physical units, and/or as a percentage of total sales (product A sales as a percentage of total sales)?

- *At what organizational level will we conduct the sales analysis?* Will we analyze the overall sales organization, or will we analyze it by region, district, or territory?

SALES MANAGEMENT IN ACTION

Sales Timing Can Be Everything

Sales at Sire Technologies (www.siretechnologies .com), a Salt Lake City software company selling to state and local governments, were unpredictable—up dramatically one quarter and sharply down the next. Sire didn't know how much money was coming in and when, so planning became virtually impossible. Sales negotiations with government agencies are known for bureaucratic delays, and Sire sales reps must persuade large committees made up of employees across several departments before closing its typical software sale of $20,000 to $80,000.

To bring some predictability to sales, Sires hired a new sales manager with analytical skills in sales costs. He identified six distinct steps in the Sire selling process, ranging from identifying prospects to signing a contract. Utilizing Salesforce.com, an off-the-shelf CRM product, he began collecting and tracking key data at each stage. In this analytical process, the sales manager learned that his salespeople needed at least thirty-two leads in the pipeline at any one time to generate a single sale. Each salesperson's process was monitored daily for potential problems such as too few leads or infrequent contact with specific prospects. The salespeople were then counseled about how to get things back on track. By analyzing daily progress in each sales stage, this resourceful sales manager was able to reduce Sire's quarterly revenue variations to less than 20 percent, and planning for Sire Technologies became a new reality.

SOURCE: http://www.siretechnologies.com/dotnetnuke/Default.aspx; http://www.businessweek.com/magazine/content/07_09/b4023444.htm ?chan=search (accessed September 13, 2007).

- *How will we break down the sales analysis?* Common categories include sales by territory, product (or product line), customer group (or individual customer), customer size, customer type (consumer, industrial, government, institutional) method of sale (phone, catalog, in-person, e-commerce), order size, distribution method, and salesperson.

- *What will we use as our basis (or bases) of comparison?* Popular bases include sales in prior periods, the fiscal period's sales forecast or sales quota, competitors' sales (or market share), and average sales for the period.

- *What information sources will we use?* Customer invoices, cash register receipts, salesperson call reports, salesperson expense reports, individual customer or prospect records, financial records, credit memos, and warranty cards can all provide information for conducting the sales analysis.

The most illuminating kind of sales analysis disaggregates the sales information into multiple marketing units or cross classifications. A territory-by-customer sales analysis will be more revealing than merely a territory or customer sales analysis alone. Similarly, a three-way sales analysis (territory-by-customer-by-product) will uncover more information than a two-way (territory-by-customer) sales analysis. Additional gradations of sales information can be especially valuable in identifying weaknesses and strengths in the marketing units. Too much disaggregation of the data, though, may result in information overload—management is simply inundated with sales information with which to make decisions. Thus, sales managers need to make a trade-off between the specificity of the sales information they desire and the time and resources they have to expend on the sales analysis.

Sources of Sales Information. Depending upon the depth of sales analyses and the breakdown desired, the sources of sales information will vary widely. In a simple sales

● A sales manager can ascertain how effective and efficient the sales force has been by examining sales, costs, and profitability data by different market segments or organization units which can be used to design and implement more suitable sales strategies for accomplishing organizational objectives.

analysis, only aggregate sales figures are needed for the desired market segment. But for comparisons with quotas, market potential, historical sales, or industrial averages, the sales manager will want much more information collected and classified. A sales invoice is the most important single source of sales information, but most companies utilize other sources as well, depending on the types of analysis desired. Major sources of sales information are shown in Table 13.1.

Collecting Sales Data. Firms usually report their sales figures in both dollars and units because inflation can distort dollar comparisons across different time periods. Sales data are frequently subcategorized by territories, product types, customer classes, order sizes, method of sales, time period, organizational unit, or salespersons to provide more meaningful information to management. Each subcategory can be further broken out for more in-depth analysis. For example, sales by territory breaks down into product types, customer classes, and so on, as shown in Figure 13.2.

Total Sales Volume. In any sales analysis, total sales volume figures are usually the first ones studied. Sales managers want to know the trend of sales over the past several years in terms of units and constant (un-inflated) dollars. Comparing relative changes in total industry sales with company sales gives the sales manager a benchmark for performance against competitors. Trends in company market share (company sales/industry sales) are excellent indicators of relative competitive performance. In Table 13.2, CENTREX Company's sales volume has risen faster than industry sales from 2002 through 2008, and sales (in constant dollars) have continued to increase. Even though these aggregate sales figures indicate that all is going well, an aggressive

TABLE 13.1 Sources and Types of Sales Information	
SOURCES AND TYPES	**DESCRIPTION OF DATA**
Sales invoice	Customer name and address; products or services bought, sales in units and dollars; name of salesperson; customer's industry and/or trade channel; terms of sales, including discounts and allowances; method of payment; mode of shipment and freight costs
Salesperson's call reports	Prospects and customers called upon; names of persons contacted; products presented or discussed; prospect's or customer's product needs and usage; orders obtained
Salesperson's expense accounts	Itemized daily expenses for travel, lodging, food, and entertainment of prospects and customers
Individual prospect/ Customer records	Prospect or customer name and address; customer's industry or trade channel; number of calls by company salesperson; sales in dollars and units; estimated annual usage of each product type sold by the company; annual purchases from the company
Internal financial records	Sales by major market segments (territories, customers, products, or salespersons); direct selling expenses; administrative costs; costs and profits by market segments
Warranty cards	Basic demographic data on customers; where purchased; price paid; reasons for purchase; service expected
Store audits	Dollar or unit sales volume; market share in product category
Consumer diaries	Dollar or unit purchases by package size, brands, prices, special deals, and type of outlets where purchased
Test markets	Dollar or unit purchases; market share; repeat purchases; impact of different marketing expenses on sales

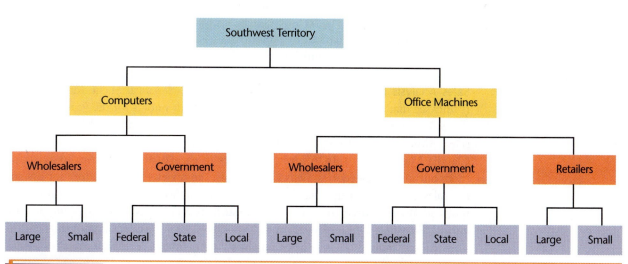

FIGURE 13.2 Subcategories of a Sales Territory

TABLE 13.2 CENTREX Company Sales versus Industry Sales (in thousands of dollars)*

YEAR	INDUSTRY SALES	COMPANY SALES	COMPANY MARKET SHARE
2002	$15,689	$2,359	15.04%
2003	16,912	2,782	16.45
2004	17,776	3,373	18.98
2005	18,234	3,519	19.30
2006	18,982	3,712	19.56
2007	19,871	3,916	19.71
2008	20,466	4,231	20.67

*Inflation-adjusted dollars

sales manager would resist the temptation to be complacent and go ahead with a more in-depth sales analysis to see how sales force productivity might be improved.[10]

With the press of other duties, sales managers are often lulled into inattention to sales analyses when total sales figures appear favorable, because they forget the *iceberg principle.* Only about 10 percent of a floating iceberg is visible above the surface of the water. Yet it is the underlying 90 percent that can sink a mighty ship, when the captain superficially evaluates the iceberg based on its visible part. Favorable total figures can easily hide unprofitable market segments and unproductive sales activities. To uncover more of the iceberg, it is necessary to divide total sales figures into their successively smaller components. For example, we might start with an analysis of sales volume by territory, and then subdivide territorial sales to the individual salespeople who generated those sales. Next, we might assign each salesperson's sales to product lines. Finally, we can subdivide product-line sales into customer classes. Each sales manager will need to decide what type and how many breakdowns are needed to get at the desired underlying explanations for sales volume figures. Through this sequential process, sales managers can unravel the outer covering at each top-to-bottom hierarchical level to see exactly where sales revenue originates, as illustrated in Figure 13.3. Working with our data from Table 13.2, we can break out 2008 sales data by geographical territory, as shown in Table 13.3.

Sales Analysis by Territory. Scanning the territorial classification in Table 13.3, we readily see that all the territories met or exceeded their quotas for the year, except for the Midwest region, which achieved 98 percent of quota and had the highest total sales. Although everything looks good, CENTREX Company's new sales manager, Claudia Middleton, wants to investigate sales in each of the territories by breaking them out into subcategories. Before doing this, she reviews the procedure for assigning sales quotas to ensure that each quota was assigned fairly and based on one or more sound measurements of potential, such as *Sales & Marketing Management's* annual "Survey of Buying Power Index." Middleton also considers any unusual conditions in the individual territories (such as more intense competition or a union strike) that might have adversely affected sales; or conversely, an anticipated shortage of the company's product that may have created windfall sales to customers stocking up in order to guide further sales analysis. If quota was barely achieved in a territory

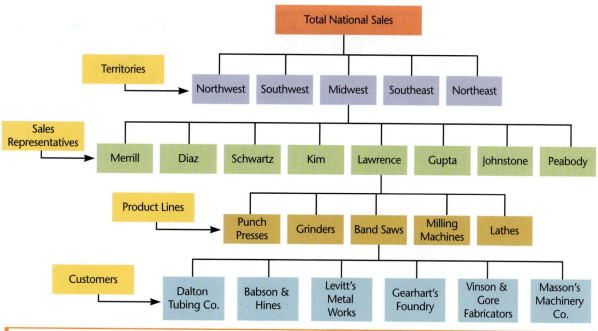

FIGURE 13.3 CENTREX Company: Hierarchical Analysis of Sales Volumes by Market Segments

where industry demand was sharply up during the year, further investigation is called for. After considering each territorial circumstance for the period, the sales manager can start with the territory that suggests the most promise for productivity improvement. Since the Midwest territory was the only one to fall short of quota (.98), Middleton begins with that region's sales, broken out by sales representative, as shown in Table 13.4. Upon finding that the lowest-performing sales rep was Jared Lawrence, who reached only 82 percent of his quota, she decides to dig deeper into Lawrence's sales for the year.

Sales Analysis by Product Line. Table 13.5 shows that Lawrence did a good job of reaching product quotas—except for band saws, for which he achieved only 20 percent of quota. In checking with the company's production manager, the sales manager learns there were no unusual quality control problems, shortages, or delivery

TABLE 13.3   CENTREX Company 2008 Sales Analysis by Territory (in thousands of dollars)

TERRITORY	QUOTA	ACTUAL	INDEX PERFORMANCE (ACTUAL SALES/QUOTA)
Northeast	845	848	1.00
Southeast	820	840	1.02
Midwest	890	870	.98
Northwest	815	843	1.03
Southwest	830	830	1.00
Totals	4,200	4,231	1.01

TABLE 13.4 CENTREX Company, 2008, Midwest Territory: Sales by Sales Representative

SALES REPRESENTATIVE	QUOTA	ACTUAL	INDEX PERFORMANCE (ACTUAL SALES/QUOTA)
Kim	106	110	1.04
Johnstone	95	93	.98
Merrill	110	112	1.02
Schwartz	115	117	1.02
Peabody	110	109	1.02
Lawrence	130	106	.82
Diaz	116	116	1.00
Gupta	108	107	.99
Totals	890	870	.98

problems on band saws. Furthermore, the marketing vice president said that there had been no recent change in the marketing mix for band saws in any territory and that total sales for band saws were running slightly ahead of last year. To probe a little deeper, Middleton decides to ask her sales administration assistant for a breakout of Lawrence's sales of band saws by customer.

Analysis of band saw sales by customer, shown in Table 13.6, reveals that one customer, Babson & Hines, accounted for Lawrence's poor performance on that product line. Babson & Hines was Lawrence's biggest customer and had been targeted for 80 percent of his entire sales quota for band saws. With a change of purchasing agent at Babson & Hines, the customer had switched to another supplier, leaving Lawrence out in the cold. Embarrassed about losing such a large account, which he had begun taking for granted, Lawrence said nothing to the new sales manager, hoping that he might regain some of the business later in the year or make it up by increasing sales on other product lines. Lawrence did not expect his deception to be picked up, because the previous sales manager seldom analyzed sales by market segments as long as overall sales were favorable. Claudia Middleton has a private conference with

TABLE 13.5 CENTREX Company Sales Representative Lawrence's 2008 Sales by Product Line ($10,000's)

PRODUCT LINE	QUOTA	ACTUAL	INDEX PERFORMANCE (ACTUAL SALES/QUOTA)
Lathes	53	52	.98
Milling machines	44	49	1.11
Band saws	60	12	.20
Grinders	37	44	1.19
Punch presses	46	47	1.02
Totals	240	192	.82

TABLE 13.6 CENTREX Company Sales Representative Lawrence's 2008 Sales by Customer

PRODUCT LINE	QUOTA	ACTUAL	INDEX PERFORMANCE (ACTUAL SALES/QUOTA)
Masson's Machinery Co.	1	1	1.00
Vinson & Gore Fabricators	2	2	1.00
Gearhart's Foundry	1	1	1.00
Levitt's Metal Works	1	1	1.00
Babson & Hines	24	0	0.00
Dalton Tubing Co.	1	1	1.00
Totals	30	6	.20

Lawrence following the next monthly sales meeting. She explains to him that in the future, she expects to be alerted immediately about sales problems so that she might provide assistance. Lawrence, relieved that he was not reprimanded for his mistake in judgment, leaves Middleton's office feeling respect for his manager's thorough analysis of sales force operations.

Concentration Principle
Assertion that a relatively small percentage (20 percent) of products, customers, orders, sales territories, and salespeople account for a large percentage (80 percent) of profits.

Lawrence's sales by customer illustrate the validity of the **concentration principle** (sometimes called the 80-20 rule), which asserts that the major portion (80 percent) of any organization's sales, costs, or profits often come from a small proportion (20 percent) of customers or products. If Lawrence had allocated his selling time with customers in proportion to sales, he might have retained the Babson & Hines account. Many progressive companies today use telesalespeople to make telephone and e-mail calls on small customer accounts, so that field salespeople can spend more time with large accounts. Beyond revealing all kinds of valuable information about "who, what, where, when, and how" sales revenue is generated, sales volume analysis lays the foundation for the next stage in profitability analysis—the in-depth study of the costs of achieving sales.

■ Profitability Analysis

Although a sales analysis is a useful control tool, it does not give the complete picture of the sales organization's effectiveness. Recall that the sales analysis focuses on the results generated by the sales force. It says nothing, however, about the attendant costs, profitability, and return on investment that the results produced. Thus, cost and profitability analysis complements a sales analysis.

Historically, sales managers have not been very cost or profit oriented. This is not to say that they don't recognize the need for profitable sales volume. They often make the mistake, though, of treating volume and cost control as two separate entities. Some sales leaders are so motivated to generate sales that they give little consideration to the costs of obtaining those sales. Others are shortsighted about cost-volume relationships. Furthermore, some sales managers incorrectly assume that the more their salespeople sell, the more money their firm is making. Sales managers, in pursuit of sales, are often reluctant to delete unprofitable products, drop unprofitable customers, or eliminate unprofitable territories. An ever-growing number of sales organizations are emphasizing a profit perspective in their evaluation process.[11]

Marketing costs analysis goes beyond sales volume analysis to investigate the costs incurred and the profits generated from sales volume. By subtracting the costs identified with the sales revenue from various market segments or organizational units, we can determine the profit contributions of the segments and units.[12]

Sales managers should utilize all their resources to achieve that balance between sales volume and costs that will result in the highest long-run organizational profits. But it is often difficult to decide how to allocate these resources, because the precise impact of expenditures on different elements of the marketing mix—like advertising, sales promotion materials, sales calls, and post-purchase service—isn't readily measurable. Any effective marketing costs analysis requires cooperation among the sales manager, the headquarters marketing team, and the accounting department. One way to understand this need for integrated efforts is to consider input-output efficiency.

Input-Output Efficiency. We need different mixes and levels of selling and supporting marketing efforts to achieve different sales objectives. The relationship between these inputs (marketing efforts) and the outputs (sales goals) is known as **input-output efficiency**.[13] To illustrate, suppose a regional sales division of MicroComputer Solutions Corporation has the objective of selling 2,000 new office computers during the year. The input is the mix and level of direct selling and supporting marketing efforts required to achieve the output, the sales objective. It is projected that to help introduce the new product to prospective customers, the sales force will have to make 3,000 additional sales calls during the year, and twenty advertisements will be needed in selected trade magazines. In addition, the sales manager estimates that the inside office sales force will accept about 600 collect telephone calls inquiring about the new machines. A summary of these activities is presented in Table 13.7.

By dividing the dollar outputs by the dollar inputs ($1,000,000/$320,900), we derive an efficiency ratio of 3.116.

Minimum Average Costs. Many organizations fail to function most efficiently because they don't operate near the optimal point on their average cost curves, representing selling and supporting marketing costs. Instead of making 3,000 sales calls, it may be more efficient, based on a $10,000 market survey, to mail out 6,000 sales promotion brochures about the new product and make only 1,500 sales calls on the best prospects identified by marketing research. By reallocating the mixture of direct selling and marketing support activities, the firm might achieve the same sales goal with greater efficiency ($1,000,000/$186,900 = 5.35), as shown in Table 13.8.

Input-Output Efficiency
The relationship between marketing efforts (inputs) and sales (output) is a measure of a sales organization's efficiency.

TABLE 13.7 MicroComputer Solutions Corporation: An Illustration of Input-Output Efficiency

SALES EFFORTS (INPUTS)	$	SALES GOALS (OUTPUTS)	$
3,000 sales calls @ $100	$300,000	Sell 2,000 new computers ($1,000 each) @ $500 gross margin	$1,000,000
600 telephone calls @ $1.50	900		
20 trade magazine ads @ $1,000	20,000		
Totals	$320,900		$1,000,000

TABLE 13.8 MicroComputer Solutions Corporation: An Illustration of Minimum Average Costs			
SALES EFFORTS (INPUTS)	$	SALES GOALS (OUTPUTS)	$
1500 sales calls @ $100	$150,000	Sell 2,000 new computers ($1,000 each) @ $500 gross margin	$1,000,000
600 telephone calls @ $1.50	900		
1 market survey @ $10,000	10,000		
6,000 sales promotion brochures @ $1.00	6,000		
20 trade magazine ads @ $1,000	20,000		
Totals	$186,900		$1,000,000

Cooperation Between Marketing and Accounting Departments. Sales organizations often incur high average costs for selling tasks because they over-utilize direct selling activities and under-utilize their marketing support team. By cooperating with the marketing specialists in advertising, marketing research, or sales promotion, the sales force can often function much more efficiently. It behooves sales managers to attempt to operate at the optimal point on their average selling cost curve. As you can see in Figure 13.4, typically an optimal number of sales calls are required to operate at the lowest average selling cost per unit. At S1, reps are making an insufficient number of sales calls to produce desired sales, so per unit costs are high at C1. At S3 the sales manager is relying too heavily on costly sales calls, so per unit costs remain too high at C3. Only at S2 is the optimal number of sales calls being made to achieve the lowest per unit costs at C2. Beyond this optimal point, the sales manager ought to shift from sales calls to other marketing and promotional activities.

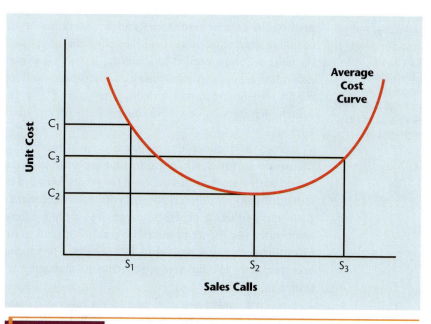

FIGURE 13.4 Average Per Unit Sales Cost Curve for Direct Selling

Historically, accounting systems have been concerned mainly with reporting aggregate financial data to stockholders and creditors in order to raise outside funds. Gradually, accounting statements were redesigned to provide analysis of production costs for internal management use. But only in recent years, with the widespread use of computers, have accountants seriously turned their attention to marketing costs analysis.

Due to their critical function as the revenue-producing arm of the company, marketing activities often constitute a company's largest total expenditures. To progressive accounting and marketing departments, marketing costs analysis offers rewarding opportunities to cooperate in improving overall productivity. Three continuing problems account for the long neglect of marketing costs analyses by accounting systems: (1) inadequate communication, (2) lack of marketing costs standards, and (3) inability to collect and analyze the huge volume of marketing data.

Inadequate communication between marketing and accounting managers arises partially from their different perspectives on the use of cost data. Accountants tend to see costs as an end, something to be reduced. Marketers, however, see costs largely as a means to an end or benefit—usually sales. Sales managers are particularly sensitive to potentially adverse effects on sales if marketing expenditures are curtailed too much.

Accounting cost analysis is primarily designed to provide a historical financial record of overall company operations and to ensure that production costs stay within established standards. By contrast, marketing cost analysis is more concerned with future decisions; it seeks to learn the specific cost and profit contributions of different marketing efforts. While recognizing their different perspectives on cost analysis, marketing and accounting managers should try to cooperate with one another for the overall benefit of company productivity.

Lack of marketing costs standards has slowed the development of marketing costs analysis. However, based on experience and research, **standard costs** that include labor, material, and machinery resources needed to produce a certain output can be predicted and standardized as norms in conducting production costs analyses. Unfortunately, the marketing outlays needed to produce a given level of sales are much less predictable, because results vary widely depending on the marketing mix selected for changing marketing scenarios. Marketing managers seldom can precisely determine the costs of inputs needed to achieve a desired sales level. Moreover, many marketing expenditures, such as advertising and customer service, don't have an immediate, readily measurable impact on sales. They work over a period of time, making it difficult to identify sales results in one period with the marketing costs to achieve those sales.

Standard Costs
Predetermined costs, based on experience and research studies, for achieving certain levels of volume. In production there are usually standard costs for direct labor, materials, and factory overhead. Marketing costs are much more difficult to standardize since they tend to be generated from non-repetitive activities.

In conventional accounting practice, most marketing expenses are charged off in the period incurred, while production costs are identified with per unit output that is held in inventory until sold. Even the terms *costs* and *expenses* highlight the accountant's difficulties with marketing operations. Accountants tend to speak of production costs and marketing expenses, suggestive of their different levels of specificity. Marketers often use the terms interchangeably but tend to think of marketing expenses as investments that will pay off in future sales. The challenge remains for accountants and marketers to find new approaches to managing marketing costs for improved profitability.

Inability to collect and analyze the huge volume of marketing data has long hindered the progress of marketing costs analysis. But with more sophisticated collection and

● **Managers from the sales, marketing, finance, and accounting departments can work together to correctly calculate profitability by territory, market segments, product lines, and salesperson.**

© Tom Carter / PhotoEdit

analysis software, the mass of marketing data has become increasingly manageable. Today, even small firms often have access to the latest computer software, which can handle the countless calculations necessary to compile and analyze marketing information in a timely fashion for decisions on sales force efforts and other marketing activities. Today's sales managers can also receive full-color managerial charts and graphs, directly from computers, summarizing the mountains of marketing sales volume, costs, and profit data in almost any form desired. Computer graphics enable sales managers to identify and respond more quickly to opportunities and challenges in the marketplace.

Costs versus Expenses
Two terms that are often used interchangeably in describing marketing costs analysis. But costs tend to be specific and directly related to volume output, while expenses are more general or indirect expenditures (e.g., we tend to say production costs and marketing expenses).

Benefits of Marketing Costs and Profitability Analysis. Two terms—**costs** and **expenses**—have often been used interchangeably in describing marketing costs analysis. But costs tend to be specific and directly related to volume output, while expenses are more general or indirect expenditures; therefore, we tend to say *production costs* and *marketing expenses*. Marketing costs analysis recognizes that sales are achieved through marketing expenditures that contribute uniquely to profits. By identifying the productivity of different marketing expenditures, sales managers are able to improve the precision and productivity of their decisions in (1) allocating sales force efforts and sales department resources, (2) preparing sales department budgets, and (3) obtaining support for the sales force from other elements of the company's marketing mix.[14]

Several sales volume, marketing costs, and profitability analysis management software programs are available from vendors such as Salesforce.com (www.salesforce .com), CB Software Systems (www. cbsoftware.com), Program URL (www.programurl

.com), and SYSPRO (www.syspro.com). You can compare the top six sales analysis computer software programs at www.2020software.com. Some sales managers employ the services of specialized companies like Hyperion Solutions Corporation (www.hyperion.com) to collect, organize, and analyze data to improve the performance of the overall sales organization.

In addition to diligently analyzing costs and profits by market segments using the latest software programs, resourceful and insightful sales managers often can spot inefficiencies needing correction by applying their common sense—with sometimes surprising benefits, as explained in the *Sales Management in Action* box.

Profitability Analysis Procedure. In conducting a marketing costs (or profitability) analysis for a sales organization, sales managers can approach the analysis systematically by following these steps: (1) Specify the purpose of the analysis, (2) identify functional cost centers, (3) convert natural expenses into functional costs, (4) allocate functional costs to segments, and (5) determine profit contribution of segments (Figure 13.5). Let's discuss each of these steps.

Reprinted by permission of Oracle.

● Sales managers can use sales revenue, marketing costs, and profitability analysis management software programs available from vendors like Hyperion Solutions Corporation to systematically collect, organize, and analyze data to improve sales force performance.

SALES MANAGEMENT IN ACTION

Using Common Sense in Sales Analysis: Three Examples

A sales manager for a medical device company observed that the commissions earned by salespeople varied dramatically with the "best" salespeople receiving up to ten times the dollar commissions of the apparently "worst" salespeople. Checking further, he found that the sales potential for the company's territories had not been updated in years. After updating the relative potential for the sales territories assigned different salespeople, he found that the salespeople with the highest commissions typically were assigned the highest potential sales territories. In essence, the company was rewarding the sales territory, not the salesperson's successful efforts.

An alert industrial products sales manager noticed that a territory that ranked fourth highest out of 250 territories in sales for the company had been vacant (no assigned salesperson) for many months. Further analysis revealed that the territory had huge potential, so company sales could be significantly increased by assigning salespeople to work this territory.

After reviewing rising sales force travel expenses, a consumer products sales manager decided that it didn't make economic sense for the field salespeople to be calling on low-potential, remotely located customers. So, in the future, these accounts were to be covered by teleselling, direct mail, e-mail, and the company's Internet and extranet websites. By saving the travel time and costs expended in covering small accounts, salespeople were able to spend more face-to-face selling time with their larger accounts, and profits increased. What's more, the direct sales force retained over 80 percent of their total sales volume. Two additional benefits of reduced travel included more nights at home for their salespeople and higher sales force morale.

SOURCE: Andris A. Zoltners and Sally E. Lorimer, "Sales Territory Alignment: An Overlooked Productivity Tool," *Journal of Personal Selling & Sales Management,* vol. 20, no. 3 (summer 2000): 139–50. Copyright © 2000 by PSE National Educational Foundation.

FIGURE 13.5 Marketing Profitability Analysis Procedure

Fixed Costs
Those costs that do not change with sales volume (e.g., salaries of the sales administration staff, office rent, and fire insurance).

Variable Costs
Those costs that vary with sales volume, for example, travel outlays for salespeople calling on customers or commissions based on sales volume.

Direct Costs
Those costs that can be entirely identified with or traced to a particular function or market segment such as a territory, customer, or product. In a territorial analysis, for example, each territory would be assigned the cost of salaries for those salespeople working exclusively in that territory.

Indirect Costs
Sometimes called common costs, which are incurred for more than one function or segment and thus must be allocated on some reasonable basis. For example, the sales manager's salary or office utilities would have to be spread among sales functions, sales territories, and other segments.

Functional Costs
Reclassified natural expenses into the activities or functions for which they were incurred (e.g., "salary expense" reclassified into direct selling, transportation, or advertising function salaries).

Specify the Purpose. Sales managers must first decide the precise purpose of the analysis. That is, what do they want to determine the profitability of—sales territories, sales representatives, customers, product lines, or organizational units such as district or branch offices? Depending upon the answer to this question, the treatment of marketing costs will vary. Some costs may be direct for one segment but indirect for another. For instance, a salesperson's salary is a direct cost to an assigned territory but indirect with regard to the different product lines or customer classes that he or she sells in that territory. Even compensation usually breaks down into **fixed costs** (salary) and **variable costs** (commission based on sales). By specifying the precise purpose of the analysis, sales managers are able to classify expenses as **direct** or **indirect costs** and as fixed or variable costs.[15]

Identify Functional Cost Centers. **Functional costs** refer to reclassified natural expenses into the activities or functions for which they were incurred (e.g., "salary expense" reclassified into direct selling, transportation, or advertising function salaries).

As shown in Table 13.9, we can broadly categorize functional cost centers for sales organizations into (1) order-getting costs and (2) order-filling costs. Order-getting costs pertain to those activities that obtain sales orders, such as direct selling and advertising expenditures. Order-filling costs relate to those activities that follow the sale (such as order processing, packing, shipping, and delivery) and are necessary to fill a customer's purchase order. Each functional cost center should contain a homogeneous group of directly related expenses instead of arbitrarily allocated ones.

Convert Natural Expenses into Functional Accounts. In marketing costs analysis, **natural accounting expenses** (the traditional expense categories like salaries, rent, depreciation, etc.) used in accounting statements must be reassigned to categories based on the purpose of each expense. Because nearly all expense data are collected by the organization's accounting system, analysis ought to start with the traditional

TABLE 13.9 Functional Accounts for Marketing Profitability Analysis	
ORDER-GETTING COSTS	**ORDER-FILLING COSTS**
Sales promotion and publicity	Product packing and shipping
Product and package design	Transportation and delivery
Advertising	Customer service
Sales discounts and allowances	Warehousing
Sales administration	Inventory control
Credit	Accounts receivable collection

Natural Expenses
The traditional expense categories, such as salaries, rent, depreciation, and so on, used in accounting statements.

accounting statements. The most important of these is the profit-and-loss (or income) statement, which takes this basic form:

Sales − Cost of goods sold = Gross margin − Expenses = Net Profit

Traditional income statements are of limited value to sales managers because they fail to reveal the costs of performing different marketing activities. Working with the simplified income statement for the CENTREX Company Sales Department in Table 13.10, we have assigned the natural expense accounts to functional accounts in Table 13.11.

Salaries were spread to the functional areas where the recipients work. As Table 13.11 indicates, about $590,190 went to salespeople and the sales manager, $21,400 to a sales promotion specialist employed part-time in the sales office, $25,650 to an advertising specialist, $64,250 to two people in sales administration, $31,000 to a billing clerk, $27,340 to a marketing research staff specialist, and $71,280 to two people in the shipping department. Besides their regular salaries, all salespeople received a commission of 2 percent on sales. Since these commissions were directly related to sales, the entire $169,334 was charged off to the direct selling function. Travel expenses included $151,491 for food, lodging, and entertainment expenses incurred in direct selling efforts, and $1,003 spent by the marketing research specialist while coordinating a market study. As both natural and functional accounts, advertising in selected trade magazines required $45,000, and sales promotion materials cost $20,115. Postage expenses were incurred to some degree for every functional cost center but largely for the packing and shipping area. Expenditures for supplies, which were also spread over all the functional accounts, amounted to $160,623—again mainly for packing and shipping. Finally, the sales department had to pay $188,606 in rent, and these costs are allocated to the functional areas in proportion to the floor space used by each activity.

TABLE 13.10   CENTREX Company Sales Department Income Statement

ACCOUNTS	$ EXPENSES	$ INCOME/PROFIT
Sales		11,466,683
Cost of goods sold		6,923,491
Gross margin		4,543,192
Sales Expenses Salaries	831,110	
Commissions	169,334	
Travel	151,491	
Sales promotion	20,115	
Advertising	45,000	
Postage	62,078	
Supplies	160,623	
Rent	188,606	1,628,357
Net Profit		$2,914,835

TABLE 13.11 CENTREX Company: Natural Expenses Assigned to Functional Areas

				FUNCTIONAL ACCOUNTS				
Natural Expenses		Direct Selling	Sales Promotion	Adver-tising	Sales Adminis-tration	Order Processing and Billing	Marketing Research	Packing and Shipping
Salaries	$831,110	$590,190	$21,400	$25,650	$64,250	$31,000	$27,340	$71,280
Commissions	169,334	169,334						
Travel	151,491	150,488					1,003	
Sales promotion	20,115		20,115					
Advertising	45,000			45,000				
Postage	62,078	3,000	9,671	212	689	794	493	47,219
Supplies	160,623	7,716	21,247	2,023	183	928	2,101	126,425
Rent	188,606	79,186	8,200	5,300	15,100	23,400	12,150	45,270
	$1,628,357	$999,914	$80,633	$78,185	$80,222	$56,122	$43,087	$290,194

Allocate Functional Costs to Segments. To discover the profitability of separate organizational units or particular market segments, the sales manager must allocate the functional costs incurred by the unit or in serving the segment. He or she needs to examine each marketing function or activity to find the factor that most affects the volume of work. In making the cost allocations, the sales manager can consider several bases, including selling time, number of sales calls, and actual space occupied.

Another frequently used but improper basis is to allocate functional costs according to sales volume. This approach tends to penalize sales productivity and efficiency. For example, if one sales territory accounted for 20 percent of total regional sales, it would be charged with 20 percent of the sales administration function costs of $80,222 in Table 13.10, regardless of the actual expenses and proportion of time spent by the sales manager and his or her staff in working with that territory. In contrast, a particularly worrisome territory may have taken up 40 percent of total sales administration expenses and personnel time but be allocated only 5 percent of those functional costs to match its low sales volume. Using sales volume to allocate functional costs contravenes the very purpose of marketing costs analysis, since it ignores the actual costs incurred in different business segments while relying on a simple but irrelevant basis. Therefore, sales managers should allocate functional costs according to measurable variables that have a cause-and-effect relationship with the functional cost category. That is, the costs should change in proportion to the performance of the activity; so direct selling costs, for instance, should increase directly with the number of sales calls. Several bases for allocating functional costs to different identifiable segments are provided in Table 13.12.

Full Costs or Contribution Margin? Since marketing costs contain direct, indirect, fixed, and variable amounts, another major decision is whether to allocate full costs or only marginal costs (direct and variable) to the segments. Costs that are fixed and indirect are usually impossible to assign to segments except arbitrarily. Advocates of

TABLE 13.12 Functional Cost Centers and Bases of Allocation

Functional Costs	BASES OF ALLOCATION		
	To Sales Territories	To Products	To Customers
Direct selling costs			
Salaries, incentive pay, travel, and other expenses of salespeople	Direct	Selling time devoted to each product	Number of sales calls multiplied by average time per call
Indirect selling costs			
Sales administration, sales training, marketing, research, field supervision	Equal charge to each salesperson	Selling time devoted to each product	Selling time devoted to each customer
Sales promotion costs			
Consumer or trade Promotions, e.g., trade discounts, coupons, contests, and point-of-purchase displays	Direct	Direct	Direct
Advertising expenditures			
Advertising department salaries and expenses, media costs	Direct or by circulation of media	Direct or by media space given each product	Charged equally to each account
Marketing research			
Cost of gathering information	Time spent researching each territory	Time spent researching each product	Time spent researching each customer
Transportation			
Cost of delivering goods to customers	Classification rate × weights of products	Classification rate × weights of products	Bills of lading
Order processing and billing	Number of customer orders	Number of customer orders	Number of customer orders
Packing and shipping	Number of shipping units, weights, or size of units	Number of shipping units, weights, or size of units	Number of shipping units, weights, or size of units

the full-cost (or net profit) approach argue that all costs can be allocated on some reasonable basis. Using the full-cost approach, we allocate total costs (whether variable, fixed, direct, or indirect), and determine the profitability of each segment by deducting cost of goods sold from net sales to arrive at gross margin. Then we deduct all other costs or operating expenses to derive net income for the segment.

Contribution Margin
The sales price less direct costs and variable costs equals the amount the sale contributes to profits (contribution margin).

On the other side of the controversy, proponents of the **contribution margin** (the sales price less direct costs and variable costs equals the amount the sale contributes to profits) approach claim that it's misleading to allocate costs that are not controllable and, therefore, not considered in marketing decisions. They believe only costs that are controllable (direct and variable) and traceable to a particular segment should be subtracted from the revenue produced by that segment. The reasoning is that these variable and direct costs would disappear if the segment were eliminated, while all other costs (fixed and indirect) would continue and have to be absorbed by other segments. Moreover, any segment that produces revenues in excess of its direct and variable costs is making a contribution to profits by helping cover the organization's fixed expenses or common costs. In Table 13.13, we can see the essential differ-

© Johnny Come Lately / Alamy

● **A better understanding of sale force organization effectiveness and efficiency can be attained by critically examining sales, costs and profitability data across product lines, customer types, geographic territories, and other market segments.**

ences between the full-cost and the contribution margin approaches to marketing costs analysis. Under the contribution margin concept, costs are categorized as either variable or fixed without regard to whether they pertain to manufacturing, marketing, or administrative activities. Then all the variable costs are deducted from dollar sales to determine the segment's contribution margin.

TABLE 13.13 Marketing Profitability Analysis: Full-Cost Approach versus the Contribution Margin Approach	
FULL-COST APPROACH	**CONTRIBUTION MARGIN APPROACH**
Sales	**Sales**
Less: Cost of goods sold	**Less:** Variable manufacturing costs
Equal: Gross margin	**Less:** Other variable costs directly traceable to the market segment
Less: Operating expenses (including the segment's allocated share of company administrative and general expenses)	**Equal:** Contribution margin
Equal: Segment net income	**Less:** Fixed costs directly traceable to products; Fixed costs directly traceable to the market segment
	Equal: Segment net income

Advantages of Contribution Margin. The trend in marketing profitability analysis favors the contribution margin approach, for two primary reasons. First, arbitrarily allocating fixed and indirect costs to segments merely confuses profitability analysis, since these costs continue even if the apparently unprofitable segments are eliminated. Second, the contribution margin approach considers the interrelationships among marketing activities and the synergism of their efforts. One marketing activity, such as advertising, both benefits from and supports other activities such as personal selling or sales promotion. Similarly, one product in a multi-product line helps promote the image and sell the entire line.

We'll use the income statement for the CENTREX Company, depicted in Table 13.10, to compare the two approaches to allocating functional costs. As you can see in Table 13.14, the full-cost method shows product A suffering a net loss of $1,488 and product B earning a net profit of $682,154. From this analysis, management might decide to de-emphasize or even drop product A. However, the full-cost approach allocated $1,027,718 of administrative expenses on the basis of product A's percentage of total sales ($5,287,141 product A sales ÷ $11,466,683 total sales = .46 × $2,234,169 total administrative expenses = $1,027,718 product A administrative expenses). Thus, the arbitrary allocation of fixed costs was responsible for product A's net loss. Switching to the contribution margin approach (see Table 13.15) reveals that product A contributes $1,026,230 to covering total fixed administrative expenses of $2,234,169. If product A were eliminated, current total net profit of $680,666 would turn into a net loss of $345,564 because product B's contribution margin would be insufficient to absorb the additional burden of administrative costs. Progressive companies keep track of the profit contribution of sales regions and products on a monthly basis so timely marketing mix adjustments can be made.

Determine Profit Contribution of Segments. Although some sales managers still avoid cutting costs because they fear sales will simultaneously decline, more astute sales managers want to identify unprofitable customer accounts, products, or territories that can be served less frequently or dropped. Unprofitable segments are endemic problems in virtually all sales organizations. In some companies, up to 50 percent of business elements lose money. Illustrating the concentration principle, studies have found that often one-third of products, customers, orders, sales territories, and salespeople account for two-thirds of profits. Studying profit contributions by segments invariably rewards the sales manager far beyond the time spent in the analyses.

TABLE 13.14   CENTREX Company Income Statement by Product Lines: The Full-Cost Approach

	TOTALS	PRODUCT A	PRODUCT B
Sales	$11,466,683	$5,287,141	$6,179,542
Cost of goods sold	6,923,491	3,562,734	3,360,757
Gross margin	$4,543,192	$1,724,407	$2,818,785
Expenses:			
Sales expenses	$1,628,357	698,177	$930,180
Administrative	2,234,169	1,027,718	1,206,451
Total expenses	$3,862,526	$1,725,895	$2,136,631
Net Profit (loss)	$680,666	$(1,488)	$682,154

TABLE 13.15 CENTREX Company Income Statement by Product Lines: The Contribution Margin Approach

	TOTALS	PRODUCT A	PRODUCT B
Sales	$11,466,683	$5,287,141	$6,179,542
Variable costs:			
Cost of goods sold	6,923,491	3,562,734	3,360,757
Sales expenses	1,628,357	698,177	930,180
Total variable costs	$8,551,848	$4,260,911	$4,290,937
Contribution margin	$2,914,835	$1,026,230	$1,888,605
Fixed costs:			
Administrative expense	$2,234,169		
Net Profit	$680,666		

We can examine profit contributions by segments in two basic ways: (1) by individual segments or (2) by cross-classification of segments. When we study them individually, we examine segment categories sequentially; thus, the analysis may proceed from determining the profitability by one segment category, such as product class, and then move to territory or customer type, and so on until we have investigated all segments. In a cross-classification analysis, we relate one segment to or define it more specifically by other segments. For instance, the sales manager may want to know the profitability of product X, sold to customer B, in territory 2.

In Table 13.16, we analyze the profitability of segments separately. All segments (products, territories, and customers) appear profitable when examined one at a time. But when we conduct cross-classification analysis of the three segments in Table 13.17, we learn that product Y is losing money with customer A in territory 1, and product Y is yielding only a low-profit contribution with customer D in territory 2. An alert sales manager would probably want to probe further by requesting a cross-classification that includes a breakdown by salesperson as well. Without seeing the interrelationships of segment profitability as provided in a cross-classification analysis, a sales manager might erroneously assume that all the individual segments are profitable.

TABLE 13.16 Marketing Profitability of Individual Market Segments

MARKET SEGMENTS	PRODUCT X	PRODUCT Y	TERRITORY 1	TERRITORY 2	CUSTOMER A	CUSTOMER B	CUSTOMER C	CUSTOMER D
Sales	$805	$2,995	$1,610	$2,150	$710	$900	$800	$1,350
Variable costs	−520	−2,340	−1,210	−1,650	−540	−670	−550	−1,100
Direct fixed costs	−198	−460	−308	−350	−138	−170	−145	−205
Market segment profit contribution	$87	$155	$92	$150	$32	$60	$105	$45

TABLE 13.17   Marketing Profitability of Segments Analyzed via Cross-Classification

	TERRITORY 1		TERRITORY 2	
Product X	Customer A	Customer B	Customer C	Customer D
Sales	$190	$120	$185	$310
Variable costs	−115	−73	−128	−204
Direct fixed costs	−41	−32	−39	−86
Market segment profit contribution	$34	$15	$18	$20

	TERRITORY 1		TERRITORY 2	
Product Y	Customer A	Customer B	Customer C	Customer D
Sales	$520	$780	$615	$1,040
Variable costs	−425	−597	−422	−896
Direct fixed costs	−97	−138	−106	−119
Market segment profit contribution	−$2	$45	$87	$25

■ Underlying Problems

Merely determining that certain cross-classified segments are unprofitable is not sufficient. The sales manager must next discover *why*. Have the salespeople been adequately motivated? Are they making efficient and effective use of their time? Is the competitive situation in these segments unique? Are product quality, customer service, and warranties satisfactory? Are prices competitive? How compatible and effective is the marketing mix supporting the field sales representatives? These plus many other questions should be asked and answered.

As important as marketing profitability analysis is, it merely uncovers symptoms. It's up to the sales manager to discover the specific underlying problems before attempting to improve profitability by making various decisions, such as dropping segments, changing incentive plans, retraining or firing salespeople, or altering the marketing mix. Sales managers should not hesitate to obtain the help of marketing research specialists to identify problems and recommend solutions for improved segment profitability.

■ Return on Assets Managed (ROAM)

Profitability analysis is invaluable for comparing sales productivity by segment with the cost of activities performed to achieve those sales. Yet a critical financial management tool missing from profitability calculations is the total value of company assets (working capital in the form of accounts receivable and inventory) required to support the sales force functions. The return on assets managed (ROAM) by each segment of the business measures how productively the assets have been employed. We avoid using the term return on investment (ROI) here, since it usually refers more narrowly to capital investment (non-current assets) and owner's investment (net worth or equity capital). As shown in Table 13.18, ROAM is the product of the profit margin on sales (net profit/sales) and inventory turnover (sales/total assets).

TABLE 13.18 Calculating Return on Assets Managed

$$\text{ROAM} = \frac{\text{net profit}}{\text{sales}} \times \frac{\text{sales}}{\text{total assets used}}$$

When applied to segment analysis on the basis of the contribution margin, the formula becomes:

$$\text{ROAM} = \frac{\text{segment contribution margin}}{\text{segment sales}} \times \frac{\text{segment sales}}{\text{additional assets used by the segment}}$$

$$\text{ROAM} = \frac{\$1,026,230}{\$5,287,141} \times \frac{\$5,287,141}{\$11,257,387} = 0.09116$$

Using the data in Table 13.15, we can compute ROAM for product A (see Table 13.18). Assume product A required an investment in accounts receivable of $2,493,889 plus an inventory of $8,763,498 (for total current assets of $11,257,387) in order to achieve its sales of $5,287,141 and its contribution margin of $1,026,230. By substituting these figures in the formula (see Table 13.18), we derive a ROAM of 9.12 percent.

Despite the obvious usefulness of ROAM calculations, one study found that only about 1 of 10 industrial firms regularly use the tool, although nearly one-third analyzed profitability by customer, salesperson, and territory.[16] One criticism aimed at the ROAM approach is that it tends to neglect the opportunity costs for capital invested in the assets.[17] Nevertheless, the most successful sales managers of today and tomorrow may gain a winning edge on other sales managers (in the eyes of superiors) by conducting marketing profitability analyses by market segments and making full use of ROAM.

Improving Return on Assets Managed. To increase the return on assets managed for specific segments, the sales manager has three options: (1) to raise the profit margin on sales, (2) to increase total sales while maintaining profit margins, and (3) to decrease the relative dollar value of assets necessary to achieve sales. Raising the profit margins on sales requires the sales manager to conduct profitability analyses by segments to identify those that are yielding inadequate contribution margins. Then, he or she must decide to de-emphasize or eliminate efforts in these segments.

Increasing total sales while maintaining profit margins on sales requires the sales manager to seek more effective and efficient marketing mixes, so that the sales organization operates near its minimal average costs per unit of sales (as discussed earlier in this chapter). Market testing, under reasonably controlled conditions, may be necessary to find this optimal mix of headquarters and field marketing efforts. Therefore, it is vital for sales managers to include on their sales department staff a marketing research specialist who works closely with the headquarters marketing research department as well as with the field marketing representatives.

Decreasing the assets needed to obtain sales requires sales managers to cooperate with inventory managers to find that optimal trade-off between inventory levels and out-of-stocks. Both sales managers and accounting managers need to monitor the level of accounts receivable to ensure they remain within predetermined standards.

Increasing Sales Force Productivity and Profits

Revolutionary and evolutionary changes in analytical software and telecommunications technologies are helping sales managers in their unrelenting efforts to lower selling costs and increase sales force productivity,[18] and the possibilities for the future seem virtually unlimited.[19] With increasingly sophisticated software tools, the sales department and other functional areas (marketing, accounting, finance, operations) throughout a company can work synergistically to identify unprofitable market segments and take timely corrective actions that will significantly increase profits.[20] To motivate him to regularly conduct in-depth sales volume, marketing costs, and profitability analyses, one sales manager keeps a plaque on his wall with Benjamin Franklin's famous quote: "A penny saved is a penny earned."

CHAPTER SUMMARY

1. **Understand the framework for a sales force organization audit.** This chapter discussed the importance of conducting a sales volume, costs, and profitability analysis to assess the effectiveness of the sales force organization. Examining the performance of the overall sales organization can be accomplished through an in-depth sales force audit—a comprehensive, systematic, diagnostic, and prescriptive tool designed to assess the adequacy of a firm's sales management process and to provide direction for improved performance and the prescription for needed changes.[21] A sales force organization audit constitutes an assessment of four key issues: (1) sales force organization environment, (2) sales management functions, (3) sales force organization planning system, and (4) sales manager qualities.

2. **Discuss the sources of information and need for sales volume, costs, and profitability analyses.** Although the *sales invoice* is the most important source of sales information, there are many other sources, too. Among the most important sources of sales information are salesperson call reports, expense accounts, prospect and customer records, internal financial records, warranty cards, cash register receipts, store audits, consumer diaries, and test markets results.

3. **Outline the procedures for conducting sales analyses by territory, sales representative, product line, and customer.** Sales volume, costs,

and profitability analyses involve the collection, classification, comparison, and evaluation of sales, costs, and profit figures by such subcategories as product types, customer classes, territories, and salespeople. Marketing costs analysis goes beyond sales volume analysis to determine the costs involved in generating sales. To determine the profit contributions of various market segments, marketing costs involved in generating the sales revenue must be subtracted. Using the concept of input-output efficiency, sales managers should consider several mixes and levels of selling and supporting marketing efforts to achieve different sales objectives. Especially important to improving overall company productivity is increased cooperation and understanding between the marketing and the accounting departments. Indeed, one of the sales manager's most important jobs is to use profitability analyses to increase the productivity and efficiency of sales force efforts by allocating resources to market segments providing the highest return per dollar spent.[22]

4. **Describe the procedure for marketing costs and profitability analyses.** Sales analysis, whether by territory, sales rep, product line, or customer, involves five major steps: (1) specify the purpose of the analysis, (2) identify functional cost centers, (3) convert natural expenses into functional costs, (4) allocate functional costs to segments, and (5) determine the profit contribution of segments.

5. Articulate the arguments for using contribution costs versus full costs. Since marketing costs contain direct, indirect, fixed, and variable amounts, a critical decision is whether to allocate full costs or only marginal costs (direct and variable) to the market segments being analyzed. Advocates of the full-cost approach argue that all costs should be and can be allocated on some reasonable basis. Proponents of the contribution margin approach claim that it is misleading to allocate costs that are not controllable—and thus not appropriately considered in marketing decisions. They believe that only costs that are controllable (direct and variable) and traceable to a particular market segment should be subtracted from the revenue produced by that segment.

The trend in marketing profitability analysis favors the contribution margin approach.

6. Illustrate the concept of and ways to improve return on assets managed (ROAM). The return on assets managed (ROAM) by each market segment of the business measures how productively the assets, such as accounts receivable and inventory, have been employed. ROAM is the product of the profit margin on sales (net profit/sales) and inventory turnover (sales/total assets). Sales managers have three basic ways to increase ROAM: (1) raise the profit margin on sales, (2) increase total sales while maintaining profit margins, or (3) decrease the relative dollar value of assets necessary to achieve sales.

REVIEW AND APPLICATION QUESTIONS

1. Define a sales audit, and explain the four areas that constitute a sales force organization audit. [LO 1]

2. Identify and describe some sources and types of sales information that can be used for conducting a sales volume, marketing costs, and profitability analysis. What is the need to conduct these analyses? [LO 2]

3. How might the sales manager obtain greater cooperation with the accounting manager or marketing controller? Do you think sales managers have a communication problem in dealing with accounting managers? Explain. [LO 4]

4. Why has accounting generally focused on production costs instead of marketing costs analysis? [LO 4]

5. Do you think that we will ever develop standardized costs for marketing activities? Why or why not? [LO 4]

6. Discuss the benefits of conducting a sales volume, marketing costs, and profitability analysis. [LO 4]

7. Which side of the controversy between full-cost and contribution margin approaches to allocating marketing costs do you support? Why? [LO 5]

8. Why aren't more sales managers concerned about their return on assets managed (ROAM)? What would you suggest to increase their use of ROAM? [LO 6]

IT'S UP TO YOU

Internet Excercise

Use the Internet to access MyWorkTools (www.myworktools.com), and other similar knowledge exchange websites. Based on your research, develop a comprehensive sales analysis checklist.

Role-Playing Exercise

Preparing for the Seminar

Situation

Your national sales manager thinks that you, a district sales manager with a recent MBA and a dual major in marketing and finance, would be the best of his sales managers to help lead a seminar on sales volume, marketing costs, and profitability analysis. Staff people have been doing these analyses in the past, but the CEO has decided that he wants all sales managers to become familiar with the process and procedures and eventually take over from the staff people. Your national sales manager left a voice mail message on your cell phone this Tuesday afternoon asking you to prepare an opening seminar presentation for this coming Monday on (1) the overall purpose of sales volume, marketing costs, and profitability analyses, and (2) the sources of sales information.

Role-Play Participants and Assignments

District sales manager: Although you did earn a dual major in marketing and finance for your MBA, you're not very comfortable with accounting concepts and procedures. So, you're apprehensive about not being able to answer all the questions the other sales managers might come up with at the seminar. Some of them, in fact, might enjoy seeing you look foolish. To help prepare, you've asked two sales manager friends of yours from other companies to come over to your house Saturday afternoon to hear your presentation and ask challenging questions.

Two sales manager friends: Although they have been sales managers for several years, they have done only basic sales volume analyses—not marketing costs or profitability analyses. Nevertheless, they agree to come over to listen and to ask questions.

In-Basket Exercise

You are the national sales manager for a large and successful consumer products company. Today, your in-basket contains a memo from the company's chief operating officer. In the memo she indicates that, although sales have been increasing steadily, she would like you to cut your selling costs by approximately 15 percent to prepare for a projected sharp downturn in the economy. In addition, she feels that it would be beneficial to the organization if you could be "precise" in identifying those particular costs you plan to cut back to achieve the 15 percent reduction. She also states that the sales quotas for your sales force are not being lowered. In her words: "We must learn to achieve our annual goals by more creative and efficient use of our limited resources." She would like to meet with you on Friday to discuss these issues.

QUESTIONS

1. How are you going to respond to this memo?
2. Can you successfully argue against the COO's demands? If so, how?

Ethical Dilemma

You are the sales manager of the Northwest region for a medium-sized software manufacturer, and you're knee-deep in the process of analyzing quarterly sales volume, marketing costs, and profitability by different market segments. One thing surprises you: personal selling expenses seem about 10 percent higher this quarter than for the same quarter last year, even though inflation is up only about 2 percent. These increased selling costs are hurting profits compared to last year. Your company has a policy of reimbursing salespeople for all their legitimate selling costs—hotel, meals, travel, and customer entertainment expenses—although salespeople were expected not to spend extravagantly. Last year's sales were off company-wide because of a downturn in demand for your software products, which are a bit dated in comparison to those offered by competitors. You've heard that some salespeople are angry that their earnings are down, and it's rumored they feel the company is letting them down by not developing new software products for them to sell. To make up for their lower earnings, some salespeople are taking their families and friends out to dinner and entertainment and claiming on their expense accounts that they entertained customers. Although you consider such behavior unethical and unprofessional, you understand the frustration of the salespeople and their anger toward the company. You've decided this behavior needs to be dealt with forthrightly, but you don't want to make the salespeople even angrier. You've called a general meeting for all your salespeople this Friday morning, and you're now trying to work out exactly what you're going to say and anticipate their reaction.

DISCUSSION QUESTIONS

1. How will you start off your comments to the salespeople who may be quite defensive about their behavior with regard to selling costs?

2. Since the salespeople seem to resent the company's failure to develop new software products for them to sell and apparently have made this an excuse for inflating their sales expenses, how will you handle this sensitive area?

3. What will you tell the salespeople about your future policy on reimbursing sales expenses?

4. In closing this meeting, will you promise or offer the salespeople anything to make them feel better?

 ## CASE 13.1

Fabrizia Pasta Company: The Value of Financial Reports

The Fabrizia Pasta Company was started in 1999 by Anthony (Little Tony) Columbo in Hackensack, New Jersey. Little Tony had previously worked for Mama Corlini's restaurant for six years as an assistant to the chef and was promoted to head chef after three years. As head chef for Mama, Little Tony received many awards for his pasta and sauces and had several newspaper articles written about him. In fact, he became a local celebrity in the restaurant business in the Hackensack area, and many of his friends and family members believed he should start a business to market his pasta and sauces. After considering it for a couple of years, Little Tony quit his job and put all his savings into the Fabrizia Pasta Company.

At first Little Tony concentrated his efforts on establishing his business on a regional basis. He made all the pasta and sauces himself, while his brothers Vinnie and Franco called on grocery stores and supermarkets in the New Jersey and surrounding East Coast area. Sales of Little Tony's pasta and sauces were better than anyone expected. Many of the grocery store managers who purchased the pasta were quite taken by his products and suggested that Little Tony sell them to national supermarket chains. Within two years after Little Tony started the company, his pasta and sauces were being sold in all of the forty-eight contiguous states.

Over the years Little Tony added several new sauces and related product lines to his menu of products. A line of pizzas, olive oil, spumoni, and spices soon carried the "Little Tony's" trade name. By 2007 Little Tony had sixty-two employees, including twenty-eight salespeople and three regional sales managers. Gino Biagio had been one of the three regional sales managers for the past five years, and when Little Tony decided he needed a national sales manager he picked Gino. The first month on the new job went smoothly as Gino traveled through the other two regions to introduce himself. But after returning to the home office, Gino began to realize being national sales manager involved a lot of paperwork and required him to spend much more time in the office as well as in scheduled and unscheduled meetings. He did not like the paperwork or the time in the office, but he knew being national sales manager required him to grasp the "big picture" and to prepare and understand numerous reports.

At the end of the first three months, Gino received several reports from Fabrizia's financial department summarizing quarterly sales and profits (see Table 1). In reviewing these reports, Gino saw that two of the company's regions have earned healthy net profits for the quarter, but the Midwestern region has a net loss of $40,269. Sales in the Midwestern region were

TABLE 1   Income Statement by Sales Regions

	EASTERN REGION	MIDWESTERN REGION	WESTERN REGION
Sales	$8,697,328	$6,543,121	$9,214,864
Variable costs:			
Cost of goods sold	5,128,540	5,210,533	6,420,432
Selling expenses	1,233,457	1,025,732	1,072,117
Fixed costs:			
Administrative expenses	433,163	347,125	416,274
Total costs	$6,795,160	$6,583,390	$7,908,823
Net Profit	$1,902,168	$(40,269)	$1,306,041

$2.1 million less than those in the Eastern region and nearly $2.7 million less than those in the Western region. Yet selling expenses clearly were too high in the Midwestern region. Ninety percent of sales force compensation was straight salary, and Gino remembered that the Midwestern region had a lot of senior salespeople who were highly paid. Unless the compensation system changed, there wasn't much Gino could do about selling expenses in the region. One way to solve the problem might be simply to close the Midwestern sales region. It certainly did not make sense to keep losing money there. Gino wondered what the impact on the company would be if the Midwestern region were shut down.

Another financial report dealt with sales and profits by product in each region (see Table 2). The company grouped its products into two basic categories: pasta and other products. This report showed that the only unprofitable product was pasta sold in the Midwestern region. Again, Gino wondered what would happen to overall company profits if pasta were dropped in the Midwestern region.

While looking at several other reports provided by Fabrizia's financial department, Gino was drawn to one that showed each region's investment in inventory and accounts receivable (see Table 3). He was not sure what to do with this report, but he was extremely surprised to see how high accounts receivable and inventory were. Overall, Gino recognized there were problems; but being new in this job, he was not sure how to analyze the data or what to do.

TABLE 2   Income Statement by Product

EASTERN REGION

	Pasta	Other Products
Sales	$5,362,192	$3,335,136
Variable costs:		
Cost of goods sold	3,347,134	1,781,406
Selling expenses	703,118	530,339
Fixed costs:		
Administrative expenses	245,791	187,372
Total Costs	$4,296,043	$2,499,117
Net Profit	$1,066,149	$836,019

MIDWESTERN REGION

	Pasta	Other Products
Sales	$3,612,446	$2,930,675
Variable costs:		
Cost of goods sold	3,060,050	2,150,483
Selling expenses	678,694	347,038
Fixed costs:		
Administrative expenses	189,987	157,138
Total Costs	$3,928,731	$2,654,659
Net Profit	($316,285)	$276,016

WESTERN REGION

	Pasta	Other Products
Sales	$5,423,517	$3,791,347
Variable costs:		
Cost of goods sold	4,003,862	2,416,570
Selling expenses	621,664	450,453
Fixed costs:		
Administrative expenses	250,123	166,151
Total Costs	$4,875,652	$3,033,174
Net Profit	$547,865	$758,173

TABLE 3 Accounts Receivable and Inventory by Product and Region		
EASTERN REGION		
	Pasta	Other Products
Accounts Receivable	$3,120,449	$1,872,312
Inventory	8,881,479	5,122,376
MIDWESTERN REGION		
Accounts Receivable	$2,120,287	$1,540,601
Inventory	7,297,128	6,482,120
WESTERN REGION		
Accounts Receivable	$2,311,483	$2,481,040
Inventory	8,421,677	7,120,432

QUESTIONS

1. What else besides high selling expenses might be contributing to the Midwestern region's problems?

2. What corrective action might Gino take, given the information provided in the reports?

3. Should Gino drop the Midwestern region? Or stop selling pasta in this region? Justify your recommendation.

4. What other financial reports should Gino request from the financial department to better understand the situation? Explain.

Case prepared by Mark Leach, Loyola Marymount University.

CASE 13.2

J.B.'s Restaurant Supply: How CRM Data Is Used to Justify Change

J.B.'s Restaurant Supply is located in Ocala, Florida, and serves full-service restaurants throughout central and northern Florida as well as much of southern Georgia. The company was originally built around a base of customers operating independent restaurants in the I-75 corridor in central Florida. J.B.'s provides all types of restaurant supplies, from small items such as napkins to large items such as industrial equipment. J.B.'s has recently implemented a customer relationship management (CRM) system that includes a number of sales force automation processes. It's hoped that unnecessary sales calls will be eliminated with the new system.

The new CRM system provides a wealth of data, such as the ROI for each customer. After analyzing the report, the firm's sales managers arrive at several conclusions:

■ Customers in larger metropolitan areas like Orlando are more profitable than customers in rural areas such as Lake City.

■ Customers operating Italian- and Mexican-style restaurants are less profitable than those operating other types of restaurants.

■ National chains like Olive Garden and Flemings are among the most profitable customers.

■ Independents are less profitable than chain customers.

■ Salespeople with less than two years of experience or more than twenty years of experience generate less profit than do other salespeople.

Sales managers at J.B.'s are considering making some changes in an effort to improve the company's performance. Although you would expect everybody to be interested in higher profits, many of the changes have proved to be controversial. The following changes have been announced based on an increased emphasis on profitability:

■ The sales force will be reassigned so the more experienced salespeople are assigned only to chain accounts.

■ J.B.'s will expand service into the areas of Mobile, Alabama, and Atlanta, Georgia.

■ J.B.'s will no longer make face-to-face sales calls to independent restaurant owners. In the future, communications with less-profitable customers will be handled via the Internet and an occasional telephone call.

QUESTIONS

1. Will these changes help make J.B.'s more profitable? Explain.

2. Do you agree that all of the changes are in J.B.'s long-term best interests?

3. What potential problems could result from making these changes just as proposed?

4. Are there additional changes you would suggest?

Case prepared by Kathrynn Pounders, Louisiana State University.

Sales Force Performance Evaluation

LEARNING OBJECTIVES

When you finish this chapter, you should be able to:

1 Carry out the sales force performance evaluation process using the outcome-based, behavior-based, and professional development measures.

2 Establish different types of sales goals and objectives, and develop the sales plan.

3 Set sales force performance standards.

4 Allocate resources and efforts through sales quotas.

5 List the major steps in the sales force performance evaluation monitoring system (PEMS).

6 Provide feedback and evaluation, and improve sales force performance.

7 Apply twenty-first century sales force performance appraisal methods.

INSIDE SALES MANAGEMENT

Tom Cunningham, Senior Sales Manager, Boeing Rotorcraft Systems

Boeing Rotorcraft Systems, a division of the Boeing Company, is a world leader in the design, development, and manufacture of transport and combat helicopters—the Apache, Chinook, and Osprey craft—for customers all over the world. Because it makes such a complex product, the company measures its sales cycle not in months, but in years. So, for senior sales manager Tom Cunningham, interim benchmarks are critical for measuring and evaluating the performance and personal development of his business development staff.

"When we start a campaign," says Cunningham, "we set an objective, identify issues that must be solved, build strategies to overcome them, and implement action plans to accomplish those strategies. I measure my team against the successful implementation of the action plans, using interim milestones several times a year. This means we can have frequent course checks and corrections on the way to the objective."

Performance evaluation at Boeing Rotorcraft also includes some qualitative measures. "There are behaviors that are expected," says Cunningham, "in the areas of honesty, integrity, integration with other Boeing and stakeholder interests, as well as skill development. We assign relevant tasks in these areas at the beginning of the year and measure them throughout the year. This year Boeing also began measuring all leaders against a new set of leadership attributes."

There are three mandatory measurements every year—when the business development staff sets its sales objectives, during an interim evaluation, and finally at the year-end review. The outcome of the year-end review influences the staff's compensation for the coming year. Good reviews, demonstrating the employee's ability to perform required marketing tasks and to master leadership skills, can lead to more important assignments and recognition, and eventually to broader responsibilities within the company.

Evaluating performance can be a bit uncomfortable for both the manager and the employee. "Everyone has characteristics that are positive, and some that are negative," says Cunningham. "But each person working for me has a personal development plan. I focus on eliminating the negative traits and rewarding the positive."

That makes the annual review a profitable learning experience. As Cunningham sees it, the learning works both ways. "Our performance evaluation process isn't new," he says. "I refine it every year based on lessons learned during the year and changing expectations of the company."

N ow that you know how to assess the effectiveness of the overall sales force organization, this final chapter will introduce you to the process and methods used in evaluating the performance of individual salespeople—an equally important component of controlling and monitoring the sales program. The success of the sales organization and the company depends largely on the performance of individual salespeople, who are responsible for the all-important revenue-generating and customer relationship activities.[1] Appraising the performance of individual salespeople often results in sales managers taking appropriate measures to improve the productivity and performance of each salesperson.[2]

Sales Force Performance Appraisal

Salesperson Performance Appraisal
A systematic process for (1) establishing whether the salesperson's job behavior contributes to the fulfillment of a firm's sales objectives and for (2) providing feedback to the individual.

Performance is perhaps the single most important factor of concern to sales managers because the central purpose of the sales organization is to increase sales, market share, and profits.[3] **Salesperson performance appraisal** can be defined as a systematic process for (1) establishing whether the salesperson's job behavior contributes to the fulfillment of a firm's sales objectives and (2) providing specific feedback to the individual. Before we start our analysis of sales performance appraisal procedures and methods, we need to discuss the purpose, challenges, and methods of conducting salesperson evaluations.

■ Purpose of Salesperson Performance Appraisals

The central reason to evaluate salespeople is to determine their performance and compare it with the established goals. Evaluation implies a process of systematically uncovering deviations between goals and accomplishments. When weaknesses are identified, the sales managers can devise and implement corrective methods. When strengths are identified, management can use this information as a valuable aid in anticipating and dealing with problems in future periods.[4]

Performance appraisals help ensure that managers (1) recognize high-performing salespeople with increased compensation, awards, and promotion—or deny these benefits to poor performers and, when necessary, dismiss them; (2) identify training needs of salespeople; (3) anticipate sales force personnel requirements; (4) devise criteria for recruiting and selecting new salespeople; (5) mentor salespeople about their careers; (6) motivate and influence salespeople through leadership; (7) revise sales performance standards, policies, and evaluation procedures as appropriate; and (8) most importantly, augment salespeople's future performance.

One sales expert stresses the importance of a sound performance evaluation as follows:

> a sound appraisal system . . . not only helps sales managers improve communications with their salespeople and other employees, it also increases personal motivation and provides a sound basis for achieving organizational goals. . . . [it can] improve a sales team's ability to focus energy on establishing meaningful targets and developing collective "ownership" for achieving tactical and strategic objectives.[5]

■ Challenges in Salesperson Performance Appraisals

Evaluating salespeople is a challenging task, complicated by the nature of the selling job. First, salespeople typically work alone in the field and may have little direct contact with their sales managers. Second, salespeople have more information about their sales territories than do their managers. They may use this information to their advantage, and to the possible disadvantage of their sales managers. In fact, research has found that information asymmetry between salespeople and their sales managers often leads to dysfunctional job behaviors.[6]

Third, salespeople engage in a multitude of activities. Determining which tasks to evaluate—and their relative significance—is not straightforward. Fourth, sales managers often do a poor job of evaluating salespeople simply because they dislike the task. They tend to feel uncomfortable having to assess the performance of their subordinates, and salespeople dislike being evaluated (particularly if the evaluation is negative). Yet, interestingly, one study reveals that positive performance feedback can enhance role clarity, satisfaction with the sales manager, and salesperson performance; moreover, even negative feedback can increase role clarity.[7]

And fifth, several factors that are truly beyond the salesperson's control contribute to the individual's performance.[8] These include differences in territory potentials, physical disparities in territories, competitive intensity, variations in company support, time allocation between account development and account maintenance, and salesperson tenure in and acclimation to the territory. Sales managers often overlook these uncontrollable factors during evaluations either because they forget, there's no system for including them or they don't know how to do so ("This is the way we've always done it!"), or the needed information to evaluate them is unavailable.

■ Timing of Salesperson Performance Appraisals

Several studies indicate that performance appraisals are usually conducted by the salesperson's immediate supervisor and occasionally by a higher-level sales manager.

Appraisals normally occur once a year, but sometimes semiannually and even quarterly. Evaluations include both objective (quantitative) and subjective (qualitative) measures. These are assigned different weights, usually with greater emphasis on objective measures. Sales managers generally provide feedback in both written and oral form.[9]

A Contemporary Approach to Sales Force Performance Evaluation

Using a systematic process for sales force performance evaluation—as shown in Figure 14.1—the sales management team's first step is to determine objectives and goals

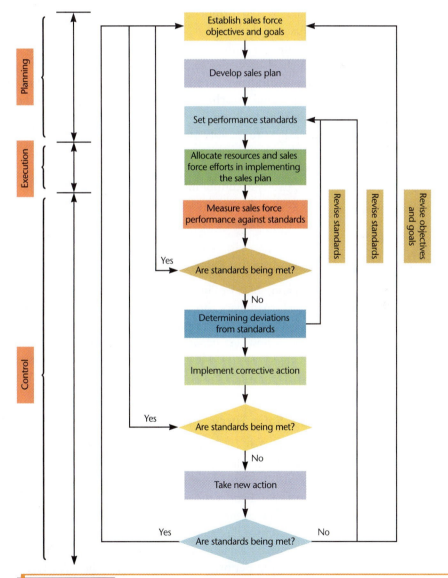

FIGURE 14.1 Sales Force Performance Evaluation Process

SOURCE: Adapted from D. J. Dalrymple and L. J. Parsons, *Marketing Management,* 2nd ed. (New York: Wiley, 1980): 622. Reprinted with permission of John Wiley & Sons, Inc.

for the sales organization. Next, they develop the sales plan with specific strategies and tactics for achieving the objectives and goals. They set performance standards for all sales activities and decide how best to allocate resources and sales force efforts. Then it's time to put the plan into action. Finally, the team will monitor performance continuously, compare it to preset standards, and—if needed—make corrective decisions to bring any deviations back into line.

In the following subsections, we describe each step of the sales force evaluation process in greater detail.

■ Establish Sales Goals and Objectives

After top management establishes the company's goals and objectives, the performance measurement and evaluation process for the sales organization can begin. The initial step is to formulate sales goals, the long-run aspirations that usually aren't easy to quantify. For instance, the sales organization may have a goal of being recognized by customers as the most service-oriented sales force in the industry. When long-run sales goals have been determined, the sales manager can focus on the shorter-run, more quantifiable targets, called sales objectives. For example, annual objectives might include reaching 100 percent of sales quota, keeping sales expenses within assigned budgets, improving the ratio of selling to non-selling time by 20 percent, or increasing profitability on sales by 10 percent.

After sales management has set sales goals and objectives, the next step is to ensure that salespeople understand, approve, and enthusiastically support them. Without open, two-way communication connecting these to the salespeople's personal goals, sales goals and objectives may become little more than "wish lists" without the organizational commitment needed for achievement.

■ Develop the Sales Plan

Goals and objectives indicate the "destination," but it takes a sales plan to provide the detailed "road map" showing how to get there. As outlined in Table 14.1, the sales plan includes four major parts: (1) *situation analysis,* which identifies where the sales organization is now; (2) *opportunities and problems,* which indicate where it wants to go; (3) *action programs,* which outline how best to get there; and (4) *performance evaluation systems,* which measure how much progress is being made toward the destination.

■ Set Sales Force Performance Standards

Performance Standards
Planned achievement levels that the sales organization expects to reach at progressive intervals throughout the year; an agreement between subordinate and superior as to what level of performance is acceptable in some future period.

The next step is to set performance standards for the sales force. **Performance standards** are planned achievement levels that the sales organization expects to reach at progressive intervals throughout the year. They represent agreements between subordinates and superiors as to what level of performance is expected in some future period. One of the best ways to formalize this general agreement is in a detailed job description for the sales subordinate. An example of a job description for a sales representative for a major oil corporation is provided in Table 14.2.

In setting performance standards for the sales force, managers need to consider *efforts expended* as well as *results obtained.* Some variables bearing on performance are outside the sales representative's control, so results alone may not be objective measures. For instance, in many types of selling, there's a time lapse between efforts and

> ## TABLE 14.1 The Sales Plan
>
> **I. Situation Analysis: "Where are we now?"**
> - **A.** *Market situation and competitive environment*
>   1. Size of the market (by major segments)
>   2. Dynamics in the marketplace (e.g., shifts in customer purchasing behavior and competitive strategy changes)
>   3. Market shares (by competitors, products, and customer classes)
>   4. Strengths and weaknesses (of each competitor's sales organization and products relative to ours)
> - **B.** *Product sales situation*
>   1. Product types (by line items, sizes, models, etc.)
>   2. Sales and distribution data (by geographic regions, territories, customer categories, or sales representatives)
>   3. Markets served (by types of customer segments or end users)
>   4. Customer profiles (by purchasing patterns and servicing needs)
>
> **II. Opportunities and Problems: "Where do we want to go?"**
> - **A.** *Internal* (Marketing and sales, R&D and technical, manufacturing/operations, financial, organization, personnel, etc.)
> - **B.** *External* (market segments, competition, economic, political, legal, social, or international)
> - **C.** *Planning assumptions and constraints*
>   1. Internal company environment (estimate stability of objectives, goals, resources, management)
>   2. External market environment (estimate short-run and long-run marketing environment conditions)
> - **D.** *Sales forecasts*
> - **E.** *Contingency planning* (based on different sets of assumptions from those in C, above)
>
> **III. Action programs: "What's the best way to get there?"**
> - **A.** *Strategies and tactics* (convert sales forecasts into resource, production, service, quotas, and budget needs)
>
> **IV. Performance evaluation systems: "How much progress are we making toward our destination?"**
> - **A.** *Set standards* of performance
> - **B.** *Evaluate actual performance* versus planned standards
> - **C.** *Take necessary corrective action* on variances from plan

results. This is especially true in business-to-business (B2B) sales, where tangible results may require several months of intense sales efforts before the prospective buyer makes a final decision. That's why sales managers must use qualitative as well as quantitative measures.

Key Sales Force Performance Factors. Although sales managers are becoming more profit oriented in their focus,[10] the percentage of sales quota achieved has long been the ultimate performance criterion for salespeople. But because sales figures don't provide a complete assessment of a salesperson's job, most sales managers employ several variables to evaluate salesperson performance.

All such standards should be (1) relevant to job performance, (2) stable and consistent irrespective of the evaluator, and (3) capable of discriminating between outstanding, average, and poor performance. Variables in the larger marketing system

---

TABLE 14.2 Job Description for a Sales Representative

Position: **Sales Representative**
Immediate Supervisor: District Sales Manager

Purpose of Job: To manage a designated territory so that assigned objectives are achieved in the following categories: sales/profit, accounts receivable, rent income, and retail efficiency. These objectives can be largely accomplished by developing a strong network of dealers, salaried service station managers, consignees, agents, and distributors.

Regular Assigned Duties:

1. Plan and organize work in accordance with the TEAM system to achieve sales/profit plan in all categories.
   a. Analyze the accounts in the territory, using the *Quarterly Review and Replanning Guide,* to determine the opportunities and problems that can affect sales/profits, accounts receivable, rent income, and retail efficiency; determine what action plans would realize the opportunities and solve the problems.
   b. Prioritize opportunities and problems, determine which should be accomplished each quarter, and set objectives accordingly.
   c. Schedule and plan sales calls and set target dates to accomplish objectives.
2. Call on accounts on a planned basis.
   a. Solicit orders.
   b. Counsel dealers/managers and wholesalers on money management, hours, planned merchandising, appearance, and driveway service; implement plans, programs, and methods that will contribute to the territory's objectives.
   c. Keep accounts receivable within established credit limits and collect all monies as required.
   d. Maintain dealer business in line with company objectives. Renew existing dealers' leases with consideration given to the interests of dealers and/or wholesalers as well as the firm.
   e. Conduct dealer meetings on subjects that can best be handled by group counseling and selling.
3. Recruit and interview lessee dealer/manager prospects following selection procedures; recommend acceptable candidates for management approval; arrange for training; negotiate and propose loans where applicable; install new dealers/managers under installation guide. As required, recruit consignees.
4. Investigate customer complaints, resolve or, where necessary, refer to others for their handling.
5. Recommend appropriate maintenance of corporation-owned buildings and equipment.
6. Keep abreast of competitive activity in the territory and, as required, advise dealers and the district sales manager.
7. Handle correspondence and reports pertinent to the territory and maintain adequate records.

---

such as product quality, price differences, and the level of promotional support should not distort the performance standards selected for measurement of sales force achievement.

Figure 14.2 shows three kinds of evaluation criteria for assessing salesperson effectiveness: (1) outcome-based measures, (2) behavior-based measures, and (3) professional development measures. Let's look at each criterion.

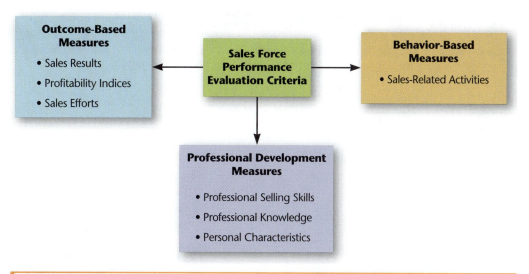

FIGURE 14.2 Sales Force Performance Evaluation: Outcome-Based, Behavior-Based, and Professional Development Measures

Outcome-Based Performance Standards
Performance criteria that can be objectively measured (number of sales calls made each month).

Outcome-Based Measures. Results generated by the salesperson fall into three categories: (1) sales results, (2) profitability indices, and (3) sales efforts (see Table 14.3, part 1). Specific **outcome-based performance measures** include sales volume, percent of quota, market share, gross margin, contribution margin, number of orders, average order size, number of new accounts, and number of lost accounts. Outcome-based performance criteria generally require relatively little monitoring of salespeople and minimal managerial direction or effort because they rely on straightforward, objective measures of results.[11] In sales organizations that emphasize use of outcome-based criteria, salespeople tend to be especially focused on the bottom-line, extrinsically motivated, and self-oriented; but they also tend to be less accepting of supervisory direction.[12] The essence of outcome-based criteria is that they are quantitative and, therefore, objective. They afford easy comparison with a salesperson's prior performance as well as with the performance of peers. However, performance measures, like the number of sales calls made, tend to affect sales or expenses directly and can be evaluated objectively.

Behavior-Based Performance Standards
Performance criteria that can be subjectively measured (e.g., product knowledge).

Behavior-Based Measures. Each sales organization has to develop its own subjective **behavior-based performance measures** for evaluating the less-quantifiable sales-related activities. Examples of these qualitative criteria appear in Table 14.3, part 2. Sales managers tend to avoid using subjective criteria to evaluate salespeople because they reflect observations and opinions instead of objective measurements. Nevertheless, it's still important to consider subjective or qualitative measures in any evaluation because they can significantly affect a salesperson's performance and the company's reputation. It's vital for sales managers to develop an evaluation system that clearly identifies sales force goals and standards and encourages salespeople to perform in the desired manner.

Professional Development Measures. Professional development criteria have a more indirect and longer-run impact on sales, so sales managers must evaluate them largely

TABLE 14.3   Sales Force Performance Evaluation: Outcome-Based, Behavior-Based, and Professional Development Measures

1. OUTCOME-BASED MEASURES

(a) Sales Results

Sales Orders:
- Number of orders obtained
- Average order size (units or dollars)
- Batting average (orders/sales calls)
- Number of orders canceled by customers

Sales Volume:
- Dollar sales volume
- Unit sales volume
- By customer type
- By product category
- Translated into market share
- Percentage of sales quota achieved

Customer Accounts:
- Number of new accounts
- Number of lost accounts
- Percentage of accounts sold
- Number of overdue accounts
- Dollar amount of accounts receivables
- Collections made of accounts receivable

(b) Profitability Indices

Profitability Indicators:
- Gross profit margin
- Net profit contribution
- Net profit margin by customer type
- Net profit margin by product category
- Return on investment
- Return on sales
- Return on sales costs
- Return on assets
- Return on assets managed

(c) Sales Efforts

Sales Calls:
- Number made on current customers
- Number made on potential new accounts
- Average time spent per call
- Number of sales presentations
- Selling time versus non-selling time
- Call frequency ratio per customer type

Selling Expenses:
- Average per sales call
- As percentage of sales volume
- As percentage of sales quota
- By customer type
- By product category
- Direct selling expense ratios
- Indirect selling expense ratios

Customer Service:
- Number of service calls
- Displays set up
- Delivery cost per unit sold
- Months of inventory held by customer type
- Number of customer complaints
- Percentage of goods returned

2. BEHAVIOR-BASED MEASURES

Sales-Related Activities:
- Territory management: sales call preparation, scheduling, routing, and time utilization
- Marketing intelligence: new product ideas, competitive activities, new customer preferences
- Follow-up with customers
- Using promotional brochures and correspondence with current and potential accounts
- Customer relations
- Report preparation and timely submission

3. PROFESSIONAL DEVELOPMENT MEASURES

Professional Selling Skills:
- Product knowledge
- Customer knowledge
- Understanding of selling techniques
- Execution of selling techniques
- Quality of sales presentations
- Communication skills
- Cooperation with sales team
- Punctuality
- Patience
- Initiative
- Resourcefulness
- Customer feedback (positive and negative)
- Dependability
- Empathy
- Enthusiasm
- Judgment

TABLE 14.3   (continued)

3. PROFESSIONAL DEVELOPMENT MEASURES

Professional Knowledge:

- Willingness and ability to acquire new capacities
- Sales management potential
- Knowledge of the company and its policies
- Knowledge of competitors' products and marketing and sales strategies
- Use of marketing and technical backup teams

Personal Characteristics:

- Enthusiasm
- Motivation
- Judgment
- Good citizenship
- Ethical code of conduct
- Physical appearance
- Ambition
- Stability

on a subjective basis. These criteria, identified in part 3 of Table 14.3, fall into three areas: (1) professional selling skills, such as the salesperson's product and customer knowledge; (2) professional knowledge of company and competitors, such as awareness of organizational policies and marketing and sales strategies; and (3) personal characteristics, such as enthusiasm, judgment, an ethical code of conduct, and personal appearance. Not all successful salespeople possess all or even most of these qualities. Research indicates that in many selling situations, some qualities are more important than others for success.[13] Sales managers place considerable emphasis on personal characteristics, and they are the most frequently used category of the three foregoing evaluation criteria.[14]

Combining Sales Performance Evaluation Criteria. Although some firms may opt for outcome-based criteria and others for behavior-based criteria, sales managers tend to

© Michael Newmann / PhotoEdit

● **The number of sales calls made is one among many measures of sales performance.**

adopt a hybrid approach that maximizes the strengths and reduces the limitations of each.[15] But what specific criteria should sales management actually use to assess its salespeople's performance?

The appropriate combination of appraisal criteria depends on the specific selling framework and on the broad corporate, marketing, and selling objectives of the firm. In establishing goals for individual salespeople, sales managers should choose criteria that focus on the most important features of the sales job, provide a complete picture of the salesperson's performance, and are generally controllable by the salesperson. Obviously, these concerns need to be weighed against the availability of the information and the time and cost of using it.

Sources of Information for Sales Performance Evaluations.
Supervision and evaluation are interdependent and continuous processes. Field sales managers cannot work closely with subordinates without becoming aware of their strengths and weaknesses. Moreover, salespeople often discuss each other with members of management. Customers and prospects frequently praise or complain about different salespeople. A certain amount of informal, subjective appraisal of salespeople and their selling activities is both inevitable and desirable.

A major step toward improving the evaluation method occurs when the procedures become systematic, which may be very rare.[16] To assist in providing a systematic appraisal system, sales managers should collect evaluative information from a variety of sources.[17] The final rating of a salesperson's performance should be a composite of information received from many sources, with each source appropriately weighted. Company records, customers, sales management, and the salesperson's own input can provide valuable evaluative information that is both outcome and behavior-based.

For example, the obvious source of quantitative information is the record kept by the company. For example, how did the salesperson do based on number of orders, sales volume, gross margin, and selling costs? Such information about "how much" (available from company records) can be supplemented by information from other sources. Field sales managers are in a position to discuss the quality of the salesperson's sales presentations, his or her work habits, rapport with customers and prospects, devotion to work, mental attitude, and integrity. Through regular interaction and/or joint sales calls, the sales manager can glean a wealth of information about the salesperson's performance. Also, time and activity studies of salesperson activities can indicate how much time is spent in various selling and non-selling activities and whether those time expenditures are worthwhile.

Activity reports turned in by salespeople provide valuable information about efforts such as prospecting methods, number and frequency of calls, number of presentations, time spent in entertaining clients, and the like. These reports are especially useful when combined with informal comments and solicited remarks from prospects or customers. Given the customer orientation pervasive in selling, input from buyers is easy for the sales manager to obtain during order-verification phone calls or through questionnaires that seek information for improving the seller's offerings and services to customers.

■ Allocate Resources and Sales Force Efforts

In the next step of the performance appraisal process (Figure 14.1), sales managers should allocate resources (human, financial, and material) and sales force efforts for implementing the sales plan. Sales managers control sales force efforts and activities by using quotas as well as standards for appraising the performance of individual salespeople (i.e., outcome-based, behavioral-based, and professional development criteria). Hence, to achieve desired sales goals and productivity objectives,[18] sales managers set sales quotas for their salespeople and for different sales units.

Sales Quota
A specific, quantitative goal, usually established in terms of sales volume; important in planning, control, and evaluation of sales activities.

Sales Unit
An individual salesperson, sales territory, branch office, district, region, dealer or distributor.

Types of Sales Quotas. A **sales quota** is a goal with a given time period assigned to a particular **sales unit** (such as a sales region, district, branch, territory, or individual salesperson).[19] It is a numerical target representing a standard of performance that is expected from the sales unit or salesperson. Quotas are a supplement to direct supervision, like goal setting[20] (see Chapter 11). Thus, they free up some of the sales manager's time for non-supervisory duties.[21]

Sales quotas have several purposes, including the following:

- To help motivate salespeople by providing a goal as an incentive
- To provide quantitative performance standards
- To control and direct salespeople's activities and efforts[22]
- To evaluate the performance of salespeople[23]
- To aid in controlling use of selling expenses

Not all sales organizations use quotas for all these reasons. In fact, the purpose for a quota dictates the kind of quota a firm utilizes. For example, if management wants to increase profitability, it will most likely adopt a cost-reduction or profit-oriented quota. If it wishes to enhance market share, it will use a sales-volume-oriented quota. Results of a study of 3,000 salespeople indicate how the intent of a quota may be blunted through salespeople's efforts (or lack thereof); specifically, up to 85 percent of salespeople have no documented plan for reaching their sales goals, thus suggesting they think their quotas can be achieved with minimal planning and by relying on ad hoc sales tactics.[24]

Regardless of the kind of sales quota and its purpose, a quota plan (consisting of all quotas used in the sales department) ideally should possess the following features:[25]

- Realistically attainable
- Clear and precise in its definition
- Based on objective accuracy instead of subjectivity
- Easy to administer
- Allow for flexibility
- Seen as equitable by all the salespeople
- Include only quotas that represent critical salesperson tasks or responsibilities
- Enable regular feedback to salespeople about quota achievement progress

One sales management expert offers additional requirements by suggesting that (1) quotas should be attainable, but only with effort; (2) unreachable quotas are not motivating, but frustrating; (3) "creampuff" quotas do not induce extra effort; and (4) quotas should pertain to a salesperson's activities, not personality.[26]

What sales managers hope to accomplish will be a critical factor in determining the kind of quotas they use. The rationale to use a specific type of sales quota is largely predicated by the quantitative and qualitative sales goals a salesperson is expected to achieve in a given time frame. Figure 14.3 shows four types of sales quotas: (1) sales

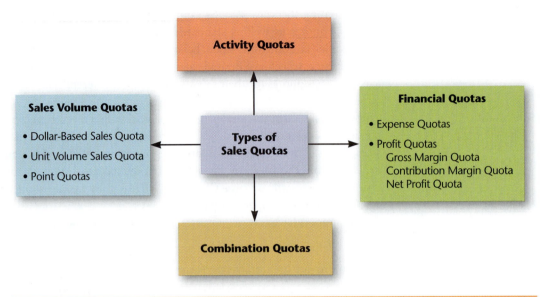

FIGURE 14.3 Types of Sales Quotas

volume, (2) financial, (3) activity, and (4) combination. Let's look at them more closely.

Sales Volume Quotas. A sales volume quota represents a sales goal (usually expressed in dollars or units). It is the most frequently used kind of quota because it is easy to understand and relates to a major sales department objective—generating sales. Sales volume quotas allow sales managers to aggregate different types of products, customers, or other market segments into a summary figure for comparison over time. Here are the three variants of sales volume quotas:

1. *Dollar-based sales quota*—A dollar-based sales quota is typically used when a firm sells a large number of different products, prices are relatively stable, and prices reflect management's selling priorities (e.g., salespeople should emphasize one product line over another). Dollar-based quotas allow managers to compare sales to other dollar figures such as selling expenses or commissions.

2. *Unit volume quota*—A unit volume quota expresses the quantity of a product to be sold. A unit quota is especially advisable when sales reps are selling big-ticket items. Stating the quota in units can reduce the adverse impact that a dollar-based quota could have on salesperson morale and motivation. For instance, a quota of $1 million may look daunting to a salesperson even though each unit is $50,000. But, if the quota is set on a per unit basis, twenty units seems much more reasonable. Companies selling a relatively small number of products with prices that are unstable also use unit-volume quotas.

3. *Point quotas*—To avoid having salespeople concentrate their selling efforts on a few easy-to-sell products or customers, sales managers often employ point quotas in lieu of or in addition to sales volume and unit volume quotas. Point quotas assign points that typically vary across products; this helps management encourage its salespeople to stress certain products over others. Some companies require salespeople to reach all point quotas before earning bonuses, thus ensuring a desired mix of product sales.

In setting sales volume quotas, the sales manager should start by comparing territorial potential with the salesperson's history of sales there. The salesperson and sales manager should always work together in developing a territory sales quota.

Sales volume quotas are generally established for a certain time period—and the shorter the time period, the more effective the quota. For this reason, many companies establish monthly or quarterly quotas unless sales are seasonal. For example, an annual quota guides college textbook sales reps because even though they work when school is in session (September to June), most of their orders do not come in until July and August, when many schools are closed for summer vacation.

Financial Quotas. Rather than focusing on sales volume, financial quotas are established to control gross margin and net profit or expenses. Like sales volume quotas, these quotas can be applied to salespeople, regions, and product lines. Without **financial quotas**, many salespeople will gravitate toward easier sales whether they are the most profitable or not. Financial quotas help make salespeople aware of the cost and profit implications of their sales. By manipulating financial quotas, the sales manager can shift salespeople's efforts toward achieving specific company goals such as introducing new products, increasing market share in a given territory, developing new accounts, changing the customer mix, or attaining higher profit margins.

Financial quotas have taken on increased importance as sales managers have begun to assume greater profit responsibility. Most successful companies realize that not all sales are profitable, so sales managers must be held accountable for the profit generated within their respective territories. There are two kinds of financial quotas:

1. *Expense quotas.* Stated either as a percentage of sales or as a dollar amount, an **expense quota** is designed to make salespeople aware of the costs involved in their selling efforts. The idea behind its use is to force salespeople to be accountable for the expenses they incur. Only those expenses they can control (travel, entertainment, and lodging) belong in an expense quota. If salespeople start to pay too much heed to selling costs, however, they may overlook important selling activities like customer service.

2. *Profit quotas.* Profit quotas focus on the profit generated through the sales department's selling efforts. A *gross margin quota* (sales − cost of goods sold = gross margin) makes sense when products have distinctly different production costs (and thus different gross margins). Management tends to set a higher quota for products having a larger gross margin than for those with lower margins. Some firms use a *contribution margin quota* (gross margin − direct selling expenses = contribution margin) when management wants salespeople to stress certain products and take responsibility for the expenses they can control (direct selling expenses). Other companies opt for a *net profit quota* (sales − cost of goods sold − direct selling expenses − indirect selling expenses = net profit). Managers selecting this kind of quota argue that ultimately the firm has to cover all expenses; therefore, they feel that sales personnel should be responsible for their role in reaching that level of profitability.

Sales departments tend to prefer gross margin or contribution margin quotas over net profit quotas. Net profit quotas, after all, include expenses that salespeople have little or no control over (like the sales manager's salary); thus the value of holding them responsible for such costs is questionable. Profit quotas are especially appropriate when salespeople engage in activities that can dramatically influence company

Financial Quotas
Those established to control expenses, gross margin, or net profit for the various sales units.

Expense Quotas
Those designed to make the salespeople aware of the costs involved in their selling efforts.

profit (like emphasizing one product line over another, or lavishly entertaining customers). Sales managers can use these quotas to emphasize to high-volume salespeople that the company would rather have large profits than large sales volume. For example, Sam Barone sells the highest volume for Oracle Fasteners Company; however, he stresses the easy-to-sell, low-margin products. Kaye Garcia, on the other hand, sells at somewhat lower volume, but she sells more expensive items carrying a greater profit margin. As shown in Table 14.4, although Barone sold $15,000 more than Garcia did, his profit margin was almost $8,000 less than hers due to the type of product each of them emphasized.

This illustration is important to management because it points out the need to control the salesperson's selling emphasis. Salespeople receive an emotional boost every time they make a sale, so naturally they are going to try to make as many sales as possible. To do this, they may emphasize the easy-to-sell items. By spending too much time on less-profitable products, the reps limit the company's opportunity to earn higher profits from its high-margin products. Granted, it may take a salesperson longer to sell higher-priced products, but the higher profits usually are well worth it to the company.

Salespeople also tend to spend more time calling on customers they feel more comfortable with. These customers, however, may not purchase in large quantities or may require many services. Thus, they can be far less profitable than other customers. Setting a quota on net profits encourages the sale of high-margin products over low-margin products.

While profit quotas are very desirable to some companies, they have some disadvantages. First, gross-margin or net-profit quotas are the hardest for salespeople to understand. Much of the cost information (particularly production costs) needed may not be readily available to them. Moreover, salespeople may not know they have achieved their quotas without frequent updates. Thus, because it is more difficult for them to know how well they're doing at any given time, they can get frustrated and lose motivation. Second, external factors such as competition, economic conditions, or internal restrictions (i.e., the inability to negotiate on price) affect the salesperson's net profit. Thus, profit quotas may be unfair because of the many uncontrollable factors.

Visit the website of a firm like ConvertMoreSales .com (www.convertmoresales.com/roi_survey.php) to learn more about sales quotas, financial performance calculators, sales performance indicators, and sales skills assessments. At the website, you can also review free resources such as sales articles, company testimonials, and case studies to augment your understanding of sales force performance appraisals.

● To increase your knowledge of how sales quotas, financial performance calculators, and sales performance indicators are used in sales force performance appraisals, visit the website of firms like ConvertMoreSales.com.

Activity Quotas
Those designed to control the many activities the salesperson is responsible for.

Activity Quotas. To ensure that salespeople are conducting their tasks conscientiously, many companies require them to meet **activity quotas**, which are designed to control the many activities for which the salesperson is responsible. These quotas serve as

TABLE 14.4 Ratio of Sales Volume to Net Profit					
			$ VOLUME PER MONTH		$ PROFIT MARGIN PER MONTH
	$ Sales Price Per Unit	$ Profit Margin Per Unit (%)	Sam Barone	Kaye Garcia	Sam Barone	Kaye Garcia
Product A	20	15.00 (75%)	5,000	30,000	3,750	22,500
Product B	5	3.00 (66%)	5,000	2,500	3,000	1,500
Product C	2	.50 (25%)	40,000	2,500	10,000	625
Totals			$50,000	$35,000	$16,750	$24,625

guidelines for younger, inexperienced sales reps who may tend to overemphasize the wrong activities.

The first step in setting an activity quota is to determine the salesperson's most important activities over a designated time period. These activities might include making sales calls on new prospects, setting up dealer displays, or providing special customer service. Before setting activity quotas, management should do research on how long it takes to perform these duties, how long it takes to travel throughout each territory, which activities should be given priority, and how much priority to give each activity. Finally, management must set a target level of performance, usually expressed as a frequency (see Table 14.5).

Activity quotas can be advantageous to both the salesperson and sales manager. If they plan their work carefully, salespeople should have no trouble meeting their daily activity obligations. Activity quotas also allow management to control the salesperson's selling efforts. Thus, they allow management to recognize sales reps for performing important non-selling activities and maintaining contact with infrequent customers who buy in large quantities. Finally, they quickly identify unmotivated, underperforming salespeople so that the manager can take corrective action.

One problem with activity quotas is that salespeople may not be motivated to perform their activities effectively; they may just go through the motions. So it's wise to use activity quotas in conjunction with sales volume quotas. Any slouching by the salesperson that is not revealed by the activity quota is sure to be indicated later by the sales volume quota. However, salespeople may become so preoccupied with the sales volume quota that they acquire bad habits—pressing for a quick sale, covering only large or existing accounts, and trying to bypass necessary stages in the selling process. For example, the salesperson may make the presentation before qualifying the prospect and waste time trying to sell to a person who lacks the ability to buy. Certain products may require several sales calls, yet because the salesperson is anxious to

TABLE 14.5 Common Types of Activity Quotas
■ Number of current customers or new prospects called on
■ Number of product demonstrations made
■ Number of displays set up
■ Number of new accounts established
■ Number of service calls made
■ Number of dealer training sessions given

● In evaluating the overall performance of salespeople, sales managers should consider the accomplishment of various tasks assigned in activity quotas.

reach his or her sales volume quota, the buyer feels uncomfortably pushed and the negotiations are cut off early. For these reasons, activity quotas are generally best for salespeople who perform numerous non-selling functions.

Combination Quotas
Those used when management wants to control the performance of both the selling and non-selling activities of the sales force.

Combination Quotas. To control salesperson performance of both selling and non-selling activities, sales managers make use of **combination quotas**. They generally use points as a common measuring tool to overcome the difficulty of evaluating the different units used by the other quotas. For example, dollars are used to measure sales volume, and the number of prospects called on is used to measure activities; by converting each unit to points, the sales manager can readily measure the salesperson's overall performance. Sales managers do this by computing the percentage attained for a specific quota and then multiplying this by a point weight designed to show the relative importance of achieving that quota. This calculation is done for each individual quota and then all points are added together to provide a total score for the salesperson.

This method is shown in Table 14.6. Here, three sales reps are being evaluated on their attainment of three separate quotas: net profit, sales volume, and the number of

TABLE 14.6 Combination Quotas

Salesperson: Lanesha Freedman	Quota	Actual	% of Quota	Weight	Quota × Weight
Net Profit	$50,000	$48,000	96	4	384
Sales volume	$100,000	$75,000	75	3	225
Number of New Accounts	25	22	88	1	88
Total Score = 697/8 = 87.125				8	697
Salesperson: Julie Cangelosi	Quota	Actual	% of Quota	Weight	Quota × Weight
Net Profit	$80,000	$52,000	65	4	260
Sales volume	$125,000	$105,000	84	3	252
Number of New Accounts	25	25	100	1	100
Total Score = 612/8 = 76.5				8	612
Salesperson: Chris Kwan	Quota	Actual	% of Quota	Weight	Quota × Weight
Net Profit	$50,000	$38,000	76	4	304
Sales volume	$75,000	$73,000	97	3	291
Number of New Accounts	15	9	60	1	60
Total Score = 655/8 = 81.875				8	655

new accounts established. Lanesha Freedman has the highest point total even though she had the lowest sales volume percentage of the three reps; she attained an extremely high percentage of her net-profit quota. Obviously, Freedman stressed the company's high-margin products. Julie Cangelosi did an excellent job establishing new accounts; however, the company did not assign as much importance to this quota as it did to the others. Chris Kwan came very close to attaining his full quota, but he did not do well in setting up new accounts.

This illustration points out some of the problems of combination quotas. First, they're difficult for salespeople to understand. Sales reps may get confused and put more emphasis on the less important activities. Second, salespeople have a hard time assessing their own performance and thus do not know what needs to be improved. Therefore, it's important for the three salespeople evaluated in our Table 14.6 example to have computer access for up-to-the-minute feedback on their ongoing relative performances in obtaining new accounts, net profits, and sales volume versus assigned quotas. There is always room for managerial creativity in setting sales goals and working with customers, as explained in the *Sales Management in Action* box.

Administration of Sales Quotas. For the quota system to effectively plan, control, and evaluate the sales effort, salespeople must be willing to cooperate with their sales managers. Some welcome the challenge of having their performance strictly monitored and measured, although many other salespeople dislike quotas. They become anxious and nervous when they are being evaluated so closely. Thus, management must "sell" the salespeople on the fairness and accuracy of assigned quotas and assure them that the quotas are a way for them to measure their own progress and reasonably attainable if the salespeople willingly accept them and expend an honest effort.

SALES MANAGEMENT IN ACTION

Merging Seller and Buyer Sales Goals

A few years ago, Procter & Gamble (www.pg.com) dropped some of its traditional sales quotas to form business development teams with its largest customers, such as Wal-Mart. Instead of focusing largely on P&G needs by trying to sell as many boxes of its products as possible into distribution channels, the business development team goal is to ensure optimal success for the entire collaborative supply chain by considering seller and buyer goals together. As business development partners with its major channel member customers, P&G has found a way to work synergistically to achieve win-win goal outcomes. Approximately 45 percent of P&G's U.S. sales and over a third of its international sales are now using this business development team approach for mutual goal setting and achieving.

SOURCES: Clinton Wilder and John Soat, "The Trust Imperative: Collaborative Business Means a Broader Set of Ethics That Places a Premium on True Partnership," *Information Week,* July 30, 2001, p. 6; Ronald Alsop, "Sales Know-How Is Only a Footnote for Most MBA Programs," *Wall Street Journal,* April 11, 2006, p. C1; http://www.ugs.com/CaseStudyWeb/dispatch/viewCaseStudy.html?id=235.

Set Realistic Quotas. Salespeople must be motivated to sell effectively. If they feel their assigned quota is unrealistic, they will not be motivated to attain it. And if recognition, compensation, or job security is not dependent on quotas, then many salespeople may be less concerned about attaining any of them.

In setting quotas, different companies have different theories of attainability and motivation in mind. For example, some sales managers believe in setting an average quota and then rewarding salespeople according to the percentage of quota achieved. This approach rewards salespeople for average work, but it also motivates many to continue working hard to achieve greater rewards for significantly exceeding quota. Xerox Corporation (www.xerox.com), on the other hand, sets quotas very high and rewards salespeople only for performance above and beyond their quotas. Xerox believes that rewards are for those who put forth an excellent performance, and that higher goals motivate most salespeople more. Easily achieved goals may cause some salespeople to slow down once they reach that lower bar.

To set accurate quotas, sales managers must closely relate them to territorial potentials while using sound, objective executive judgment. They must analyze the different markets and territories and make adjustments to ensure that quotas are fairly assigned based on market facts, so that salespeople willingly accept them.

Create Understandable Quotas. Make the quota plan understandable, and carefully explain it to salespeople; otherwise, they may feel that management is trying to coerce them into giving more effort without comparable rewards. If salespeople fully understand their assigned quotas, they're more likely to view them as fair, accurate, and attainable.

Include the Salesperson in Quota Setting. Management can ease the sales reps' understanding of quotas by allowing them to participate in the quota-setting procedure. This not only enhances understanding, but significantly reduces questions of inaccuracy, unfairness, and unattainability. The amount of input the salespeople should have depends on their experience, the amount of market information available, and the company's management philosophy.

TABLE 14.7 Performance Evaluation Sheet

Salesperson: Delroy Hawkins Territory: Florida	Actual	Quota	% of Quota
October 2008	$22,765	$25,000	91.1
October 2007	$21,050	$19,500	107.9
Year to Date: 2008	$267,567	$300,000	89.2
Projection: 2008	$321,081	$300,000	107.0

Keep the Sales Force Updated. Keeping salespeople updated on their performance relative to their assigned quotas reinforces the importance of the quotas, allows them to see their progress, and enables them to take timely corrective action to improve their performance. Sales managers should try to keep in close personal contact with their salespeople to encourage them and offer advice toward attaining quotas.

Maintain Control. Continuously monitor and analyze individual salesperson performance, and then regularly provide up-to-the-minute information to each salesperson about progress toward his or her quota. Via e-mail or an intranet website, you can provide weekly or monthly charts, or a ranking of the entire sales force based on actual performance compared with quota. Some managers feel this disclosed ranking creates a competitive atmosphere that encourages poorly ranked salespeople to try harder so as not to be embarrassed. Others feel it can produce more harm than good, and they prefer to provide each sales rep with a chart monitoring just his or her progress toward the quota. One of these charts is shown in Table 14.7.

■ Measure Sales Force Performance Against Standards

Performance Evaluation Monitoring System (PEMS)
System designed to provide feedback to salespeople on performance, to help salespeople modify or change their behavior, and to provide information to sales managers on which to make decisions on promotion, transfer, and compensation of salespeople.

In smaller companies, the **performance evaluation monitoring system (PEMS)** may be largely informal, relying on the firsthand observations of supervisors. As an organization grows, managers are less able to closely monitor each employee's daily activities. So they turn to a more formalized PEMS.

Companies differ greatly in their approach to PEMS. Lockheed-Martin (www.lockheedmartin.com) requires managers in its Aerospace Division to write broad essays describing an individual's strengths and weaknesses. Most companies, however, try to quantify managerial observations and judgments by means of performance results, behavior, or personal characteristics. In their rush to develop quantifiable scores, organizations can lose sight of what they want the PEMS to do. Performance appraisal systems should help do three essential things for the sales manager and salespeople: (1) provide feedback to each salesperson on individual job performance, (2) help salespeople modify or change their behavior to include more effective work habits, and (3) provide information to sales managers to help in making decisions about promotion, transfer, and compensation of salespeople.

There are three successive stages in the effective implementation of a PEMS.

1. *Performance planning*—probably the most important phase of the PEMS; it allows the salesperson to ask the sales manager three key questions: "Where am I going?" "How will I get there?" "How will I be measured?"

2. *Performance appraisal*—a continuous interpersonal process whereby sales managers give individual salespeople immediate feedback—recognition, praise, correction, or comment—on each specific task, project, or goal accomplished.

3. *Performance review*—a periodic review of past performance appraisals summarizes where the salesperson is in his or her personal development. It should answer the question "How am I doing?" and lead into the next performance planning stage.

Even though the three PEMS stages lead into one another, sales managers should not assume they can deal with all three simultaneously in once-a-year, overall performance evaluations. *Performance planning* lays out goals and plans for achieving them, and explains how the individual will be evaluated. A well-constructed MBO program (discussed later) can be invaluable in this stage. *Performance appraisals* are day-by-day mini-evaluations on specific performances, while the *performance review* is a periodic summing up of these daily appraisals so that the salesperson can see where he or she stands.

Types of Performance Appraisal Techniques. Sales managers have a variety of evaluation techniques at their disposal. Each one, however, has limitations as well as strengths. When selecting evaluation approaches, consider the degree to which a particular method possesses the following characteristics:[27]

- *Job relatedness*—The evaluation method should accurately reflect the job behavior that leads to performance.
- *Reliability*—The method's measurement should be stable over time and consistent across raters.
- *Validity*—The method should accurately reflect what it is intended to measure.
- *Standardization*—The evaluation instrument and the way it is administered should be consistent throughout the sales organization.
- *Practicality*—The method should be easy to understand and use for both sales managers and salespeople, and neither too costly nor time consuming.
- *Comparability*—The method should allow for easy comparison across sales force members (those in the same and different jobs and in the same and different geographical areas).
- *Discriminability*—The method must be able to determine performance differences across salespeople.
- *Usefulness*—The method should be helpful for making decisions about promotion, compensation, and termination.

Sales managers should be required to periodically summarize each salesperson's performance in a permanent record, for the benefit of the salesperson in tracking his or her progress and for the review of other sales and marketing managers. Ultimately, the nature of the sales job and the purpose of the evaluation process should determine which evaluation techniques sales managers use. Sales managers may use multiple evaluation methods simply because the sales job is complex (selling enterprise software, for instance), or they may opt for one approach if the job is relatively straight-forward (detail salesperson, for example).[28] The evaluation method they use should be related to the decision that will flow from the evaluation (promotion, compensation, termination, and so on).[29] Four widely used evaluation techniques are

(1) descriptive statements, (2) graphic rating scales, (3) behaviorally anchored rating scales, and (4) management by objectives. Let's look at each one.

Descriptive Statements. Usually used in conjunction with some form of graphic rating scale, descriptive statements about a salesperson may be short responses to a series of specific criteria such as job knowledge, territorial management, customer relations, personal qualities, or sales results. Another approach, which various organizations including the military use, calls for an overall portrait of the individual's abilities, potential, and specific performance during this evaluation period. This essay-type appraisal backs up and should be consistent with quantitative ratings on different performance criteria. One overriding problem with descriptive statements is their subjectivity, both in the writing and the interpretation. Many sales managers fall into some predictable pattern of being too harsh, too lenient, or too neutral in their comments, so the appraisal is not well balanced. Moreover, many evaluators are simply not very capable writers, so their use of words may fail to accurately portray the salesperson. All sales managers need specific training in performance evaluation, particularly with making descriptive statements.

Graphic Rating Scales. There are several formats for the graphic rating scale, a kind of report-card-type rating. But in all cases, the sales manager must assign an individual a scale value for various traits, skills, or sales-related results. Two ways of doing this are the "semantic differential" and Likert-type scales. The semantic differential uses polar extremes to anchor several scale segments, usually five or seven, as shown in Figure 14.4. The manager rates the salesperson on some quality, such as product knowledge, from a numerical low of 1 (poor) to a high of 7 (excellent).[30]

Likert-type scales provide descriptive anchors under each segment of the scale, as shown in Figure 14.5, so the sales manager can select which overall term best applies.

Sales managers should try to avoid these report-card graphic ratings of generalized abilities, traits, or performances of individual sales reps. The word anchors are not very meaningful because of their subjective interpretation by the rater, the wide variation among salespeople, and their vague connection with actual performance.

Behaviorally Anchored Rating Scales. Many rating systems attempt to overcome their inherent limitations by asking the sales manager to justify extremely high or low ratings. But this requirement tends to cause managers to avoid using scale extremes, resulting in a clustering of ratings. Another approach is to use a **behaviorally anchored rating scale (BARS)**, shown in Figure 14.6. The BARS concentrates on measuring behaviors key to performance that individual salespersons can control.

Behaviorally Anchored Rating Scales (BARS)
Concentrates on measuring behaviors key to performance that the individual salesperson can control.

Product Knowledge

Poor ___ ___ ___ ___ ___ ✕ ___ Excellent
     1   2   3   4   5   6   7

FIGURE 14.4 Semantic Differential Graphic Rating Scale

Product Knowledge

Unsatisfactory	Below average	Average	Above average	Outstanding

×

FIGURE 14.5 Likert-Type Graphic Rating Scale

Consideration of specific behaviors also allows different sales managers to arrive at more consistent and objective evaluations, since the rating factors have similar interpretations.[31]

There are four basic steps to constructing a sales-oriented BARS:

1. *Identify critical incidents.* Sales managers, salespeople, and customers describe specific critical incidents of effective and ineffective sales performance behavior and provide an actual example. These critical incidents are then condensed by the sales manager into a smaller number of performance categories. Some studies have obtained over a hundred critical incidents for a sales job before reducing them to about ten sales performance dimensions.

2. *Refine critical incidents into performance dimensions.* The sales managers and salespeople who are developing the performance appraisal analyze the reduced set of critical incidents and then refine them into a still smaller set of performance dimensions—usually 5 to 12—defined in general terms. The critical

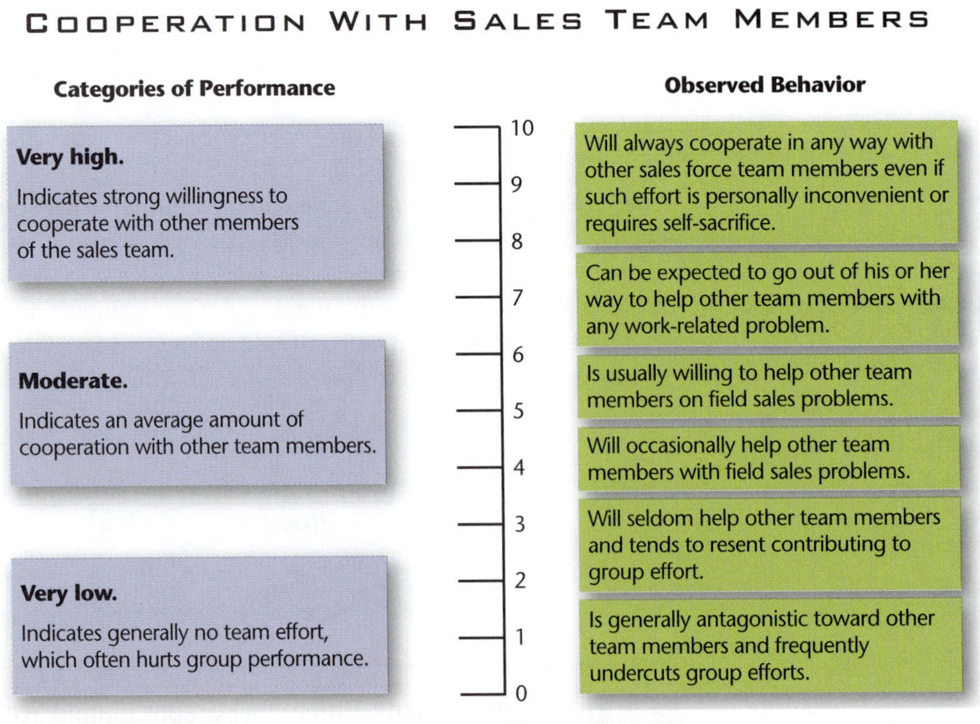

COOPERATION WITH SALES TEAM MEMBERS

Categories of Performance

Very high.
Indicates strong willingness to cooperate with other members of the sales team.

Moderate.
Indicates an average amount of cooperation with other team members.

Very low.
Indicates generally no team effort, which often hurts group performance.

Scale: 10, 9, 8, 7, 6, 5, 4, 3, 2, 1, 0

Observed Behavior

Will always cooperate in any way with other sales force team members even if such effort is personally inconvenient or requires self-sacrifice.

Can be expected to go out of his or her way to help other team members with any work-related problem.

Is usually willing to help other team members on field sales problems.

Will occasionally help other team members with field sales problems.

Will seldom help other team members and tends to resent contributing to group effort.

Is generally antagonistic toward other team members and frequently undercuts group efforts.

FIGURE 14.6 Behaviorally Anchored Rating Scale

incidents are then provided to another knowledgeable group of salespeople, who assign the incidents to appropriate performance dimensions. An incident is usually retained for the final BARS if 60 percent or more of the second sales group assign it to the same dimension as the first group.

3. *Rate the effectiveness of the described behaviors.* The second sales group rates the behavior described in the critical incidents as to how accurately it represents performance on the dimension, usually on a scale of 0 to 10. Incidents that have the lowest standard deviations (indicating greater agreement among raters) are kept for the final BARS.

4. *Select a set of incidents as behavioral anchors for the performance dimension.* The final BARS consists of vertical scales, one for each dimension to be evaluated, anchored by the six or eight retained incidents.

Although a true behavioral anchored rating scale takes time to develop, it is usually worth the extra effort because it allows for more precise, objective, and consistent ratings of salesperson by different sales managers.

Management by Objectives. Sales managers are responsible for setting many sales performance standards for salespeople, but the salespeople must understand and accept these standards before developing their own plans for achievement. In **management by objectives (MBO)**, the sales manager and the sales representative jointly agree on the salesperson's specific goals or performance targets for the coming period. If they help set their own performance targets, salespeople are more likely to be committed to them and to devise realistic plans for their accomplishment.

In some companies, salespeople must prepare an annual "territorial marketing plan" outlining their strategy for obtaining new customers and increasing sales to current customers. This ensures that salespeople and sales managers agree on how goals are to be achieved—particularly when they participate in setting objectives and have give-and-take discussions about how to improve performances. Information derived from these territorial plans helps sales managers to more objectively evaluate the individual performances of salespeople. This process also encourages salespeople to do a better job of planning their work and reporting their activities.

At many companies, each salesperson has a written plan, reviewed quarterly with the sales manager. Periodic performance monitoring ensures sales reps are making acceptable progress toward goals and provides guidance for altering the planned strategies and tactics to get back on target. The final step is an annual performance evaluation, which leads to the setting of new objectives for the coming year. The MBO cycle is illustrated in Figure 14.7. The process is essentially the same whether applied to the entire sales force or to an individual salesperson. With each successive MBO cycle, sales managers and salespeople should find the process works more efficiently.

Sales managers should stress four principles in using MBO:

1. *Open communication*—Only a free exchange of views between sales manager and salesperson will result in realistic future commitments and agreement on specific actions needed to achieve goals and objectives.

2. *Mutual participation and agreement*—The salesperson must be an uninhibited, full participant in the MBO process with the sales manager, so that there is mutual understanding and agreement on objectives, plans, and performance evaluation.

Management by Objectives (MBO) Involves mutual goal setting devised by the sales manager and the salesperson, who jointly agree on the salesperson's specific goals or performance targets for the coming period.

FIGURE 14.7 The MBO Cycle for the Sales Force

3. *Coinciding goals*—Personal goals of the individual salesperson must be integrated with the overall goals of the organization so they are mutually reinforcing.
4. *Rewards for performance*—High-performing salespeople ought to be rewarded through public recognition as well as increased financial compensation. Public recognition enhances the value of the reward for high-achieving individuals and generally helps inspire other salespeople to do better.

Comparisons Between Salespeople. Many rating systems force sales managers to assign an overall score to each salesperson for comparison with other salespeople. Various formats have been used for such comparisons for salespeople, for example:

Compared to other salespeople I know doing the same job, this salesperson's performance is:

__ Not quite as strong as most others
__ About equal to most others
__ Stronger than most others
__ Far superior to most others

Comparison rating enables the sales manager to call all his or her salespeople "outstanding," even though some are more outstanding than others. A more direct comparison is rank ordering of all salespeople. Large sales organizations often gather several evaluations from different sales supervisors and managers for each salesperson. However, because each evaluator has his or her own tendency to be tougher or easier than other sales supervisors in rating salespeople, it is difficult to compare salespeople doing essentially the same job across sales districts. One way to minimize rater bias is to consider prior evaluations of each rater. In Table 14.8(a), first-year salesperson Ruth Saworski has been evaluated by five different sales superiors and has an overall average rating of 80. As a matter of policy, the company has set 80 as the standard or average rating for salespeople. In Table 14.8(b), Ruth has been compared with four

TABLE 14.8 Evaluation of Salesperson Ruth Saworski

(A) RATINGS OF RUTH SAWORSKI BY DIFFERENT SALES SUPERVISORS AND MANAGERS

Rating	Rated By
80	John Becker, Assistant Sales Supervisor
85	Melinda Rao, Sales Supervisor
75	Kathy O'Shannon, Assistant Sales Manager
80	Andrew Rumanski, Sales Manager
80	Donovan James, Regional Sales Manager

80 = Composite rating

(B) COMPARISON OF FIRST-YEAR SALESPEOPLE

Composite Ratings	Ranking	Salesperson
88	1	Kathy Donnelly
82	2	Richard Staubach
80	3	Ruth Saworski
78	4	Charles Bruno
72	5	Janelle DePass

(C) RELATIVE EVALUATION FOR SALESPERSON RUTH SAWORSKI

Rating	Rated by	Number of Prior Ratings	Weight Assigned Rating	Rater's Average Rating	Simple Normalized Rating
80	Becker	4	1	80	80
85	Rao	8	1	85	80
75	O'Shannon	7	1	80	75
80	Rumanski	18	2	90	70
80	James	15	2	87	73

Simple Normalized Rating: = Rating + (Company Standard Rating − Rater's Average Rating). To illustrate for Rumanski, $80 + (80 − 90) = 70$.

Weighting Factor = Weight assigned rater × Number of prior ratings. For example, for James $2 × 15 = 30$. Total weighting factors = 85 or $(4 + 8 + 7 + 36 + 30)$.

Weighted Normalized Rating = (Weighting Factor × Simple Normalized Rating) − (Weighting Factors). Thus, Ruth Saworski's weighted normalized rating would be figured as follows:

Becker	(4 × 80)	320/85 = 3.76
Rao	(8 × 80)	640/85 = 7.53
O'Shannon	(7 × 75)	525/85 = 6.18
Rumanski	(36 × 70)	2,520/85 = 29.65
James	(30 × 73)	2,190/85 = 25.76

6,195/85 = **72.88** Weighted normalized rating for Ruth Saworski

other first-year salespeople who are doing essentially the same work but have been rated by different sales supervisors. This comparison indicates that Ruth is about average in performance. But when we look at all others rated by the same sales supervisors and normalized to the company standard score in Table 14.8(c), Ruth is really a *below-average* performer. Her weighted normalized rating (which gives higher weight to raters who have considerably more prior ratings) is only 72.88, compared to the company's standard average rating of 80.

Comparisons like this provide for more overall objectivity of ratings by comparing performances based on normalized or standardized assessments. They prevent raters from unfairly inflating their own people's ratings because the individual ratings establish a pattern to be used in normalization. In other words, each rating assigned by a sales manager is compared to his or her average rating.

Sales Force Evaluation Bias. Regardless of the evaluation criteria or methods, sales manager bias inevitably creeps into the evaluation process. To err is indeed human. But besides generating ill will and low morale, bias can lead to litigation against the firm (and the manager) if it strays to illegal personnel practices. Numerous studies have uncovered various management biases or errors that occur during salesperson performance appraisals.[32] Sales managers' social perceptions and judgments are likely to produce the different kinds of biases or limitations that are identified in Table 14.9.[33]

Providing Feedback and Improving Sales Force Performance

Sales managers must provide prompt, explicit, and meaningful feedback to their salespeople if they are to improve performance; otherwise the performance evaluation process is short-circuited and provides limited value for the salesperson or the company. Most sales managers readily give positive feedback to salespeople who are performing well, but many are reluctant to provide candid feedback to those who are performing poorly. Yet, the poor performing salespeople are most in need of feedback about how to improve performance.

■ Providing Feedback on Salesperson Performance

Earning praise from the boss can pack a real emotional wallop for successful salespeople. Such formal recognition enhances self-esteem, self-confidence, and motivation, and can spur many salespeople to even higher accomplishments. It also can provide direction and guidelines for future behavior because it indicates to the effective performers what they are doing well.

Even the poor and marginal salesperson should be promptly informed of his or her progress, standing, and need for improvement. Sales managers frequently hesitate to dismiss an ineffective producer. They hope (usually in error) that the poor performer will leave voluntarily, or they are reluctant to throw away the investment they made in recruiting and training the salesperson, or they fear legal reprisal if they dismiss the individual. Caution is commendable, but once it's clear that a salesperson is unlikely to improve, termination should be prompt so the manager's efforts can be redirected toward developing higher achieving salespeople. Jack Welch, former CEO of General Electric (www.ge.com), did not tolerate poor performance; annual evaluations at GE weeded out the bottom 10 percent of managers, as explained in the *Sales Management in Action* box.

TABLE 14.9 Limitations of Sales Force Evaluation Systems

Stereotyping—A sales manager develops a belief about some group as a whole (such as women) and then applies that belief to a salesperson in that group without considering the salesperson as an individual.

Contrast error—A sales manager allows the impression he has formed of one salesperson to affect the evaluation of another.

Similar-to-me error—The sales manager more favorably evaluates salespeople who are more similar to her on certain characteristics (attitudes, beliefs, interests, race, gender, and other demographic characteristics).

First-impression error—The sales manager permits his first judgment about a salesperson to strongly affect subsequent evaluations, regardless of change that has occurred within the salesperson.

Leniency or harshness error—The sales manager rates the salesperson at the extremes of the rating continuum (poor to outstanding) on all job criteria.

Escalation of commitment error—The sales manager evaluates salespeople she has hired (or recommended hiring) more highly than she evaluates others.

Fundamental attribution error—The sales manager attributes salesperson performance to certain factors within that individual (like ability, effort, and skill) rather than to situational factors (such as environment, competition, luck).

Self-serving bias—The sales manager attributes his salespeople's successes to his own efforts while attributing his salespeople's failures to their efforts.

Central tendency—Some sales managers may be reluctant to take a stand, so they rate salespeople near the middle of the scale on all rating factors. Thus, little distinction is made among salespeople, providing minimal information for compensation or promotion decisions.

Psychological resistance to negative evaluations—A few sales managers suffer emotional distress when providing negative evaluations to salespeople, so they tend to avoid making negative evaluations.

Political concerns—To look good themselves and avoid creating problems on their watch, some sales managers will avoid giving any rating that is not acceptable to the individual salesperson.

Fear of reprisal—Due to fear of reprisal for discriminating among employees, some sales managers are especially careful to avoid giving negative ratings to anyone who might take legal action.

Varying evaluation standards—Some sales managers have very high standards and rate harshly; others may be relatively lenient.

Interpersonal bias—The sales manager's personal likes and dislikes may influence his or her evaluations of salespeople. The chemistry between two people may be poor, and resultant friction can lead to evaluation bias. Conversely, salespeople may use personal influence techniques with the sales manager to bias their evaluations upward.

Questionable personality traits—Although many rating forms include personality traits (such as enthusiasm, resourcefulness, or intelligence) as indicators of selling performance, there is little research evidence to support this approach.

Organization use—Sales managers often give higher ratings to salespeople when the evaluation is for compensation or promotion purposes because they want to keep their people happy and see them do well in comparison to other organizational units. When appraisals are mainly for personal development of subordinates, however, sales managers tend to be more objective and willing to point out areas needing improvement.

Recency bias—Some sales managers are influenced too much by recent performance when evaluating individual performance, so behavior earlier in the rating period is neglected.

No outcome focus—Too many rating systems seem to have questionable validity and limited value for directing the growth and development of salespeople. They tend to rely on rating factors believed to be related to performance, but fail to indicate how the salesperson might improve performance.[34]

Inadequate sampling of job activities—Some sales managers may not know about or adequately observe behavior of all the activities in a given salesperson's assignment. Thus, the evaluation fails to include all important aspects of the job, or job tasks may be included that are not part of the current job.

SALES MANAGEMENT IN ACTION

Grading Managerial Performance

Jack Welch, former CEO of General Electric, insisted that his managers grade their subordinate managers as A, B, or C performers. Moreover, he demanded that the bottom 10 percent of all managers each year be fired, so any manager graded "C" was at risk of losing his or her job. In this GE evaluation system, A-rated managers were those who demonstrated the critical four E's: *energy, energize, edge* (toughness), *execute*. The C-rated managers were considered a drain on the organization, sapping the strength of others. In Welch's view, it was demotivating for other managers to see poorly performing managers kept on the payroll.

Although these tough evaluations appeared to work well for GE, other CEOs found them difficult to copy in their own companies. For example, when Jacques Nasser, former CEO of Ford Motor Company, adopted Welch's practice of rating managers A, B, and C, then firing the lowest-rated 10 percent, he triggered a Ford management rebellion that was a factor in his termination as CEO.

SOURCES: Jack Welch and John A. Byrne, *Jack: Straight from the Guts* (Clayton, VIC: Warner Business Books, 2003); http://news.com/The+folly+of+forced+rankings/2009-1069_3-950200.html; Robert Slater, *Jack Welch on Leadership* (New York: McGraw-Hill, 2004); Jack Welch and Suzy Welch, *Winning* (New York: HarperCollins, 2005).

Sales managers generally use one of the following approaches to provide feedback:[35]

- *Tell and sell*—The sales manager discusses both the positive and negative aspects of the salesperson's performance, makes a case for the validity of the evaluation, and seeks to get the salesperson to commit to performance improvement.

- *Tell and listen*—The sales manager describes the strengths and weaknesses in the salesperson's performance, listens to the salesperson's reaction to the results, and counsels in a nondirective way.

- *Problem solving*—The salesperson evaluates his or her own performance and reviews it with the sales manager in relation to previously agreed-upon goals. This approach seeks solutions to performance difficulties rather than simply focusing on them.

All three approaches have merit, depending on the situation. But the problem-solving alternative is preferable in most selling situations, for several reasons. First, it takes a proactive stance. Rather than waiting for problems to arise and react accordingly, salespeople (in concert with their manager) can try to identify situations that may need special attention in the future and then draw up a plan of action to prepare for them. Second, given the dynamism of the selling environment, being future oriented and seeking to uncover potential problems and opportunities before they develop will provide salespeople with enhanced ability to adapt. And third, given that field sales personnel often work alone, they must be able to diagnose a situation and take appropriate action in the absence of a sales manager. The problem-solving approach provides salespeople with this experience.

■ Improving Sales Force Performance

After making a detailed evaluation, management must take action based on that performance appraisal. In this context, as Wotruba and Simpson suggest:

An evaluation program is of little benefit unless management carries through to the final stage: action. Isolating weakness and strengths is not an end in itself,

● **Sales managers should provide prompt appraisal feedback so that salespeople can take timely measures to correct and augment their performance.**

because problems are not self-correcting and benefits are not self-generating. Yet, no action following diagnosis is an action—one that implies that the situation cannot be improved. Such situations rarely occur.[36]

At times management may feel uncomfortable admitting that the company, rather than the sales force member, is at fault. For example, the selling goals may have been set arbitrarily. When the salesperson's performance is below expectations through no fault of his or her own, then the company clearly is the culprit. In such instances, sales managers might revise the policies and/or plans or the various strategies used in their implementation, or they might adjust the objectives or standards to make them more realistic. When the salesperson is the ultimate reason for the lack of success, then taking corrective action requires reallocating the salesperson's effort, enhancing the individual's personal development, or modifying the organizational procedures or methods of operation.[37]

Before the sales manager presents an appraisal, the sales subordinate should be making a self-evaluation based on the same performance criteria, including suggesting ways to improve.[38] When the sales manager and the salesperson meet, they compare evaluations, discuss and reconcile discrepancies in evaluation perceptions, identify strengths and weaknesses in sales performance, uncover reasons for the performance-standard variances, and take corrective action (exploit the salesperson's strengths and reduce or seek to eliminate any weaknesses). The appraisal interview should be an informal, two-way exchange that focuses on the causes rather than the results of the performance. The salesperson should be permitted to react to each segment of the appraisal, to suggest modifications of ratings, to explain any unique circumstances, and to recommend methods for the salesperson and management together to improve the individual's performance. In many ways, the appraisal interview is the beginning of an MBO plan; the salesperson and management work together in developing a set of goals, including standards of performance for the next selling period. A final step is establishing the means for reaching these goals through self-development activities, formal retraining, or field-related actions by the salesperson's immediate supervisor.

A truly constructive performance evaluation can go a long way toward overcoming the angst associated with the process. Rather than viewing the evaluation as a report card, the sales manager and salesperson should consider it a progress report that provides feedback on how the salesperson is doing and outlines the path forward to attaining desired goals.

Emerging Perspectives in Twenty-First Century Sales Force Performance Appraisals

We now focus on three emerging perspectives on sales force performance evaluation. Each perspective offers important insights for the person being evaluated as well as the evaluator.

■ 360-Degree Performance Appraisals

360-Degree Performance Appraisal
A performance evaluation system that provides a salesperson with comparative pooled and anonymous feedback from the sales manager, peers on the sales team, subordinates, and clients; often includes a self-assessment.

Traditional sales force performance evaluation has been a top-down process, with sales managers evaluating salesperson performance. But salespeople interact with various constituents, not just their managers. So an innovative method called **360-degree performance appraisal**—shown in Figure 14.8—systematically elicits information on a salesperson's skills, abilities, and behaviors from all internal and external constituents with whom the salesperson has ongoing contact—the sales manager, sales team peers, subordinates, other departmental coworkers, purchasing managers, and accounts payable managers. It also includes a salesperson self-assessment,[39] thus providing performance feedback from many different perspectives.[40]

Salespeople can select their appraisers, but to gather data honestly, all ratings are confidential. The data gathering is both multidirectional and multidimensional, though this means it can also be expensive and time consuming. Generally, 360-degree performance appraisals are able to capture information that other evaluation methods can't.[41] For example, because this method elicits input from customers, sales managers can understand their needs and in the process make adjustments to better serve them. Input from a salesperson's peers can help the manager reassign team members as needed to resolve conflict and improve cooperation and harmony. The statistically pooled results of this appraisal system are a rich source of information. Salespeople can use the feedback to make improvements in areas where they are deficient with the aim of augmenting performance and thus facilitating their growth and career development.[42] To facilitate 360-degree performance appraisals, sales managers can turn to companies such as SuccessFactors, Inc. (www.successfactors.com), Alinea Group (www.alineagroup.com), and Perseus Development Corporation (www.perseus

FIGURE 14.8 360-Degree Performance Appraisals

.com) that specialize in conducting these types of assessments. Alternatively, they can enroll in training seminars offered by companies like Sales Training America (www.salestrainingamerica.com) to learn how this innovative performance appraisal technique can boost company performance.

● To learn more about how the innovative 360-degree performance appraisal technique can be used to augment company performance, sales managers can enroll in training seminars offered by firms such as Sales Training America.

Although 360-degree performance evaluations have not supplanted traditional top-down assessments, they're gaining popularity. They fit well with flattening organizational structures, greater empowerment of employees, and working in teams, which we discuss next.

■ Performance Appraisals of Team Selling

Appraising an individual salesperson's performance is a challenge; trying to evaluate members of a sales team, as a team and as individuals, can be even more complex. Problems include the use of systems that were established for individual evaluations, the difficulty of distinguishing between individual salesperson and group output, the need to customize performance measures to the type of team, and the problems of measuring inputs from cross-functional team members.[43]

Just like individual appraisal, team performance evaluation starts with selecting the relevant performance criteria and assessment methods. Both sales managers and team members should be part of the process. Some firms use a matrix that requires sales managers to identify the critical tasks of each team member, the relative importance of individual and group performance on each task, and the actual performance level on each task. Other companies ask each team member to rate all the other members on several critical performance dimensions like teamwork, leadership, productivity, and team relations. The sales manager then merges the ratings from all team members and arrives at a composite picture of team performance.

■ Performance Review Ranking System

Another recent trend is performance review ranking,[44] used by several firms that include Cisco Systems (www.cisco.com), Intel (www.intel.com), Hewlett-Packard (www.hp.com), and Microsoft (www.microsoft.com).[45] Sales managers evaluate each of their salespeople by ranking them on multiple performance dimensions using a scale, such as A = excellent, B = above average, C = average, and so on. Another approach is to place salespeople in performance categories of the top 20 percent, the middle 70 percent, and the bottom 10 percent. In so doing, firms such as General Electric (www.ge.com) have created meritocracies. How? By rewarding stars (top performers) in an "outsized way that is soul-satisfying and financially satisfying; by developing the middle 70% with training and coaching; and the bottom 10% that have neither good results nor good behaviors are 'shown the door.'"[46] Proponents of this system say that by moving out the bottom performers, managers can make room for new talent.[47] Although this method imposes a high degree of standardization, comparability, and discriminability, it has a poor standing on the remaining five features of performance appraisal techniques we discussed earlier. It is based on subjective evaluations and can produce skewed results.[48]

In this chapter, we have discussed different concepts, approaches, and procedures for conducting sales force performance evaluations. Given the wide variety of market situations, company goals, and sales force compositions, there is no one best way to always perform this essential sales management function. Therefore, it is up to the sales manager to assess the overall sales environment and determine the approach that seems to work best for evaluating and improving the performance of his or her particular sales force.

CHAPTER SUMMARY

1. **Carry out the sales force performance evaluation process using the outcome-based, behavior-based, and professional development measures.** Stages in the sales force performance appraisal process include (1) establish sales goals and objectives; (2) develop the sales plan; (3) set sales force performance standards; (4) allocate resources and sales force efforts; (5) devise a plan for sales force performance improvement; (6) conduct the sales force performance evaluation process; and (7) provide feedback on sales force performance appraisals. Outcome-based measures can be separated into sales

efforts, sales results, and profitability indices. Sales efforts include such measures as number of sales calls made, selling expenses as a percentage of sales volume, and number of service calls. Sales results include measures such as number of orders obtained, dollar sales volume, number of new accounts, and collections of accounts receivable. Profitability indices include net profit contribution, and performance as measured by financial/economic indicators, such as return on investment, return on sales, return on assets, and return on assets managed. Behavior-based outcomes include sales-related activities such as customer relations, territory management, report preparation and timely submission, product knowledge, and personal characteristics. Successful sales organizations usually employ a mixture of quantitative and qualitative performance standards. Competence assessment, which tries to determine the characteristics needed to do a job rather than the specific tasks of the job, has been successfully used to select high-achieving salespeople. Professional development measures for assessing sales force performance include professional selling skills, professional knowledge, and personal characteristics.

2. **Establish different types of sales goals and objectives, and develop the sales plan.** After establishing long-run sales goals, the sales manager can focus on the shorter-run, more quantifiable targets, called sales objectives, that should be aligned to the company's goals and objectives. For example, these goals may be to become the most service-oriented sales force in the industry or to increase profitability on sales by 10 percent. If these sales goals and objectives are not communicated to salespeople, they can become little more than "wish lists" without the organizational commitment needed for achievement. In essence, the sales plan provides the detailed "road map" showing how to achieve sales goals and objectives. It includes four major parts: (1) situation analysis, (2) opportunities and problems, (3) action programs, and (4) performance evaluation systems.

3. **Set sales force performance standards.** Performance standards are planned achievement levels the sales organization expects to reach at progressive intervals throughout the year. Ideally, they should be agreements between subordinates and superiors as to what level of performance is to be acceptable in some future period, and they should be formalized based on the detailed job description for the sales subordinate. In setting performance standards for the sales force, managers need to consider *efforts expended* as well as *results obtained*. Business-to-business sales may require several months of intense sales efforts before the prospective buyer makes a final decision. Thus, where there's a time lag between effort and tangible results, sales managers must use qualitative, as well as quantitative, measures in setting sales performance standards.

4. **Allocate resources and efforts through sales quotas.** There are four types of sales quotas: sales volume, financial, activity, and combination. The

rationale to use a specific type of sales quota is largely based on the quantitative and qualitative sales goals a salesperson is expected to achieve in a given time frame. Three variants of volumes quotas are dollar-based sales quotas, unit volume quotas, and point quotas. Two categories of financial quotas are expense quotas and profit quotas. Activity quotas are measured by factors such as the number of prospects called on, number of demonstrations made, number of displays set up, and number of new accounts established. Combination quotas are used when management wants to control the performance of both the selling and non-selling activities of the sales force. These quotas generally use points as a common measuring tool to overcome the difficulty of evaluating the different units used across quotas.

5. **List the major steps in the sales force performance evaluation monitoring system (PEMS).** An effective performance evaluation monitoring system (PEMS) has three stages: performance planning, performance appraisal, and performance review. Specific steps in the performance measurement and evaluation process include (a) establish sales goals and objectives, (b) develop the sales plan, (c) set performance standards, (d) allocate resources and sales force efforts in implementing the sales plan, and (e) evaluate sales force performance and implement corrective actions, if needed.

6. **Provide feedback and evaluation, and improve sales force performance.** Four widely used evaluation techniques are descriptive statements, graphic rating scales, behaviorally anchored rating scales (BARS), and management by objectives (MBO). Descriptive statements about a salesperson may be short responses to a series of specific criteria such as job knowledge, territorial management, customer relations, personal qualities, or sales results. Two commonly employed devices in graphic rating scales are "semantic differential" and Likert-type scales. The semantic differential uses bipolar adjective extremes to anchor several scale segments. Likert-type scales provide descriptive anchors under each segment of the scale. BARS, which concentrates on measuring behaviors key to performance that the individual salesperson can control, includes four basic steps: (a) identify critical incidents, (b) refine critical incidents into performance dimensions, (c) rate the effectiveness of the described behaviors, and (d) select a set of incidents as behavioral

anchors for the performance dimension. MBO involves mutual goal setting by the sales manager and the sales representative, who jointly agree on the salesperson's specific goals or performance targets for the coming period. Traditional performance evaluation systems have limitations including central tendency, varying evaluation standards, psychological resistance to negative evaluations, recent performance bias, no outcome focus, inadequate sampling of job activities, political concerns, fear of reprisal, interpersonal bias, questionable personality traits, and the influence of special organizational use. Prompt evaluation feedback should be provided to salespeople, so they can take measures to enhance their performance by improving selling skills and ultimately their sales performance through sales training programs.

7. **Apply twenty-first century sales force performance appraisal methods.** Current developments in the area of sales force performance appraisals include 360-degree performance perspectives, performance appraisals of team selling, and perfor-

mance review ranking systems. Just as in evaluating individual sales force members, team performance evaluation involves selecting the relevant performance criteria and employing appropriate appraisal methods. The 360-degree performance appraisal process systematically elicits information on a salesperson's skills, abilities, and behaviors from various individuals with whom the salesperson is in ongoing contact—all internal and external constituents, including the sales manager, sales team peers, sales subordinates, other departmental coworkers, purchasing managers, and accounts payable managers. Also included is a self-assessment, thus providing appraisal from many different perspectives. Performance review ranking entails sales managers evaluating each of their salespeople by ranking them using multiple performance dimensions and then placing them in different performance categories using a scale (e.g., A = excellent performance, B = above-average performance, C = average performance, D = satisfactory performance, and E = subpar performance).

REVIEW AND APPLICATION QUESTIONS

1. Identify outcome-based, behavior-based, and professional development measures that could be used for sales force performance evaluations. In your opinion, which of these three categories of measures are most important for evaluating salespeople? Explain. [LO 1]

2. Explain the multiple purposes for employing sales quotas. [LO 4]

3. What are the features of an effective quota plan? [LO 4]

4. Identify and describe the four major types of sales quotas. Be sure to describe the different kinds of sales volume quotas and financial quotas. In your opinion, which of these types of quotas can be most effective for evaluating salespeople? Explain. [LO 4]

5. Name the three stages in a performance evaluation monitoring systems (PEMS), and describe the sales manager's role in each stage. In your work experience, what procedure or process has your superior used to evaluate you? [LO 5]

6. Identify and explain the characteristics different types of performance appraisal techniques should possess. [LO 5]

7. Explain the key features for each of these widely used evaluation techniques: descriptive statements, graphic rating scales, behaviorally anchored rating scales, and management by objectives. [LO 5]

8. Identify and describe the various limitations of sales force evaluation systems. Do you have any personal experience with these limitations as either a rater or a ratee? Describe your experience. [LO 6]

9. Explain the necessity of providing feedback on sales force performance appraisals. [LO 6]

10. Describe the key features and advantages and disadvantages of 360-degree performance appraisals. Can a 360-degree performance appraisal help reduce appraisal bias? Why do you think this form of performance evaluation is being increasingly used? Explain. [LO 7]

11. Describe how a performance review ranking system can be used in evaluating sales force performance. [LO 7]

IT'S UP TO YOU

Internet Exercise

Use the Internet to access MyWorkTools (www .myworktools.com), and other similar knowledge exchange websites. Based on your research, develop a comprehensive sales force performance evaluation checklist.

Role-Playing Exercise

Appraising Salesperson Performance

Situation

As a district sales manager, you conduct semiannual performance evaluations with each of your salespeople. You have been using the MBO approach to setting various annual quotas with each salesperson. Last year, all the salespeople agreed readily on the quotas that you jointly set. One of your salespeople, Raj Srinivasan, is not on track to reach several of his assigned quotas this year. Normally, in the semiannual performance of a salesperson, you jointly explore ways to take corrective action to get back on track toward achieving the assigned yearly quotas. After only a few minutes into his evaluation, Raj interrupts to complain that his sales quotas were set too high this year and that it is not possible for him to achieve them.

Role-Play Participants and Assignments

District sales manager: You are somewhat irritated by Raj's complaint about his quotas being set too high because he agreed to them and signed the letter establishing them for the year. Nevertheless, Raj has been an above-average salesperson for nearly five years at your company, so you're willing to patiently listen to his reasoning.

Raj: You are upset because you're fearful that you won't reach some of your assigned quotas for the year. At this six-month evaluation point, you're lagging significantly behind on some of the quotas. One of your complaints is that your territory was reduced at the beginning of the year when a new salesperson was hired. Several salespeople besides you were asked to give up a small part of their territories to create a new territory for the incoming salesperson. You feel that this reduction in territory has hurt your achievement of some quotas.

In-Basket Exercise

You were just hired as the national sales manager for a large retail organization, and your first task is to assess the company's salesperson evaluation system. You've asked several of the sales managers how they currently evaluate their salespeople. They all have indicated that their sales reps are ranked according to quarterly sales volume and that raises are based on these rankings. All the sales managers seem to believe this system provides a fair and objective annual appraisal of salespeople, even though you know it has many limitations. However, you suspect their apparent satisfaction with the current system may really reflect their desire to avoid the extra work required to revise it.

Write a diplomatic but firm memorandum to all your subordinate sales managers expressing why you think the current sales force evaluation system needs to be revised and updated. In a concluding paragraph, ask them to provide feedback on how to improve the salesperson evaluation system within three weeks. Perhaps you can offer an award for the best proposal.

Ethical Dilemma

One of your subordinate sales managers has just turned in a highly negative performance evaluation for the only female member of her sales force by assigning her to the *unsatisfactory* performance category. Her evaluation of the twenty-four-year-old saleswoman, who was hired out of college two years ago, seems to be largely subjective and provides very little quantitative or objective written narrative support. The evaluation does not mention any failure to reach an assigned quota, complaints from customers, lack of product knowledge, or any other performance negative. Instead, the evaluation describes the saleswoman as self-centered, flippant with office staff, and detrimental to employee morale. In reviewing this saleswoman's quantitative and qualitative performance for the year, you note that she has met all her quotas and received several letters from customers praising her for outstanding service. You suspect that the sales manager may resent this young woman for some reason and want her removed from her sales force. You realize you're facing a dilemma that needs to be resolved promptly. On one side, the young saleswoman may leave if she receives this highly negative evaluation. On the other side, your subordinate sales manager may take a job with a competitor if she thinks you're not supportive of her evaluation of the saleswoman. You don't want to lose either person, because both are performing well. How will you handle this delicate situation?

CASE 14.1

FUTSUCO Electronics: Rewarding Performance

FUTSUCO Electronics manufactures and distributes a wide range of consumer and industrial electronics products. The company has been very successful, becoming a leader in a highly competitive industry. Top management attributes much of this success to the drive for continuous improvement existing within the company.

Senior executives encourage an aggressive, results-oriented environment in an effort to keep the company among the industry leaders globally. As part of this philosophy, the human resources department recently introduced 360-degree feedback as a component of the performance evaluation system. A 360-degree feedback approach involves assessing employees based on information provided by their supervisor, by the people they work with, and by customers. In addition, employees are asked to evaluate their own performance.

Input for the 360-degree feedback process is obtained using questionnaires tailored to the position of the person being evaluated. One example is the 360-Degree Feedback Questionnaire for sales representatives as shown in Figure 1. It asks about specific factors such as assessing territory market potential, influencing and selling, and managing the territory, as well as about more generally applicable topics such as communicating and managing self-development. Once completed, questionnaires are returned to the human resources department where individual factors are scored and totaled.

Questionnaire results are then provided to the ratee's supervisor or manager, who shares them with the individual in an appraisal interview during which objective performance measures (e.g., meeting sales targets) are also discussed. In the interview, the salesperson presents an appraisal of his or her own performance (see Figure 2) for the previous year. This system is used to evaluate performance and set targets or quotas, and it is a significant factor in determining bonuses at the end of the year.

Supria Menon was hired by FUTSUCO three years ago, right after she graduated from college. In her initial sales training, Supria was one of the top performers and was identified as a future outstanding salesperson at FUTSUCO. During her first two years at FUTSUCO the bonuses were marginal, but she accepted the situation because she viewed this period as one for learning and self-improvement. Supria has just finished her third year with FUTSUCO, and this time she is upset with her year-end bonus. She believes the past year was her best year yet and that she deserves a much larger bonus. Supria's 360-Degree Feedback Questionnaire from her sales manager was outstanding. She received a rating

Please complete this questionnaire about the person named below. The questionnaire results will be combined with others into a confidential report to him or her. Only ratings by the supervisor/manager will be identified. All other ratings are anonymous. After completing this questionnaire, please return it to the Human Relations Department in the envelope provided.

Name of person being assessed

Name of person giving feedback

Your relationship to person being assessed ___ Self ___ Manager/Supervisor ___ Peer ___ Client

Directions	Rating Scale			
Please **circle** the number that reflects your view.	**1** = Exceeds expectations **2** = Meets expectations **3** = Below expectations **NA** = Not applicable or don't know			
1. Assessing territory market potential, setting objectives, and developing territory marketing plans				
a. Analyzing sales and market data	1	2	3	NA
b. Setting sales and product support objectives	1	2	3	NA
c. Developing territory marketing plans	1	2	3	NA
2. Managing the territory				
a. Maintaining customer records	1	2	3	NA
b. Preparing call plans	1	2	3	NA
c. Developing work plans	1	2	3	NA
d. Budgeting and controlling expenses	1	2	3	NA
e. Handling administrative work	1	2	3	NA
3. Influencing and selling				
a. Maintaining relationships with key influential contacts	1	2	3	NA
b. Establishing productive relationships with customers and their staff	1	2	3	NA
c. Identifying and confirming customer needs	1	2	3	NA
d. Making effective sales presentations	1	2	3	NA
e. Handling objections and closing	1	2	3	NA
f. Implementing corporate policies	1	2	3	NA
g. Developing new business opportunities	1	2	3	NA
4. Communicating and maintaining effective working relationships				
a. Maintaining productive relationships with sales manager	1	2	3	NA
b. Developing productive relationships with appropriate corporate staff	1	2	3	NA
c. Contributing to the development of a strong team effort in the organization	1	2	3	NA
5. Managing self-development/acquiring product knowledge				
a. Gaining and maintaining product knowledge	1	2	3	NA
b. Participating in development programs	1	2	3	NA
c. Evaluating and improving job skills	1	2	3	NA
d. Managing his/her own career development	1	2	3	NA
e. Keeping up with the latest technology	1	2	3	NA

FIGURE 1 360-Degree Feedback Questionnaire

FUTSUCO Electronics
Your Self-Appraisal Form
Directions

As part of a review of performance being conducted in your division, you are asked to complete a self-appraisal of your performance. The subject matter should include an opinion of what you feel are your major strengths and weaknesses and your accomplishments in reaching your goals for the past year. If you have not met your goals, then provide explanations for not meeting goals. You should also define areas concerning your job on which you and your sales manager agree as well as areas where you feel you do not quite see eye to eye. Also, comment on what you think can be done to help you do a better job at FUTSUCO.

It is important to understand that the performance review session is a method that enables you and your manager not only to discuss your performance but also to agree on mutually acceptable goals and seek ways to meet your needs as well as those of the company. The session should not be considered an inquisition or fault-finding process. When you meet with your sales manager, be sure to freely discuss all matters pertaining to your performance and your job.

After your performance review session, your sales manager will submit your self-appraisal form and 360-Degree Performance Appraisal plus a summary of your discussion to the Human Relations Department, which maintains a confidential file on your job performance at FUTSUCO. Remember that this session is designed to help you progress in this company. Its success depends on cooperation between you and your sales manager.

Strengths

1. _____
2. _____
3. _____
4. _____
5. _____

Weaknesses

1. _____
2. _____
3. _____
4. _____
5. _____

Objectives
(Met and not met. If not met, please explain.)

_____
_____
_____
_____
_____
_____
_____

FIGURE 2 Salesperson Self-Appraisal Form

---

of 1 (Exceeds Expectations) on all items except 3f, 4a, and 4b. For these items, she received a rating of 2 (Meets Expectations). Her total score for the 360-Degree Feedback Questionnaire was 66. Supria also feels she did exceptionally well on her Self-Appraisal Form. All the goals she set for the year were met, and any weaknesses that were listed have been overcome. Everything seemed to go well during Supria's management appraisal interview, and her sales manager said he was impressed with Supria's progress and performance. After talking with several of her close friends on FUTSUCO's sales force, however, Supria found that some of her peers with scores of 55 to 60 on the 360-Degree Feedback Questionnaire received similar or even higher yearly bonuses.

QUESTIONS

1. What are the reasons for Supria's unsatisfactory year-end bonus?

2. Do you see any weaknesses with FUTSUCO's sales force evaluation system? What are they? Comment on both the 360-Degree Appraisal Form and the Self-Appraisal Form.

3. Are there areas that need to be evaluated that are not included in FUTSUCO's 360-Degree Appraisal Form? If so, what are they? Should weights be assigned to any of the factors listed in the 360-Degree Appraisal Form? Explain.

4. What should Supria do?

5. Develop an alternative evaluation system for FUTSUCO. Support your recommended system.

Case prepared by Jose Casal, New Jersey Institute of Technology, Newark, NJ.

CASE 14.2

Midwest Risk Management: Performance Evaluation Systems

Douglas Powell, the southern district sales manager for Midwest Risk Management, has just returned from his company's annual sales and marketing meeting. At the meeting the vice president of marketing announced the company's intentions to expand into the professional liability insurance market. Doug was instructed to take five salespeople from his sales staff of twenty-five and have them start developing the professional liability markets in his area, concentrating on lawyers and CPAs. In addition, he was given a first-year operating objective of obtaining a 10 percent penetration for the professional liability market in the southern district.

The selling tasks required in developing the market for professional liability insurance products are quite different from those needed to sell the personal lines of insurance and risk management products. Doug was confident his district salespeople could do the job, but he was unsure about how to effectively assess their performance.

Background

The Midwest Risk Management Insurance Agency was started in 1987 by Rick Henderson and Shane Williams, each with experience working as insurance agents for national companies. The firm began as an independent agency selling personal lines of insurance, such as life, accident, and health coverage. After five years, the agency had almost $80 million of life, accident, and health coverage in force and employed ten agents who worked on commission and covered three states in the Midwest.

In 1998, the name of the company was changed to Midwest Risk Management to reflect its geographic growth and plans for product diversification. By this time, the company had approximately seventy agents working in four regional offices, with customers in five Midwestern states. The agency began to offer basic employee benefit plans, consisting of life, accident, and health insurance programs to small businesses with less than fifty employees. By 1998, Midwest had over $950 million of life, accident, and health insurance coverage in effect, with a sales force of 105 agents in five states.

Doug Powell has been the sales manager for the southern district since 1995. Under his supervision, the district has been either first or second in premium income generated. In addition, the level of turnover among the southern district's sales force was traditionally the lowest of the four regional offices in the company.

Midwest Risk agents sold life, accident, and health insurance policies underwritten by various national insurance carriers. Midwest Risk collected the premiums from the individual customers and kept an agreed-upon percentage of each premium payment to cover its sales expenses, administrative overhead, and profits. Part of that premium percentage went to pay the commissions of the agent who sold the policy. Agents were paid commissions based on a percentage of the premiums they generated. In addition, they received a base salary and quarterly bonuses for attainment of quotas. Quotas were developed by evaluating the market potential for writing new policies or adding to existing coverage. This potential was compared with the current estimated level of market penetration. Then, quotas were derived by mutual agreement between the sales agent and sales manager to increase market penetration.

Doug attributed the productivity of the southern district to the talent of the sales force personnel and his ability to identify and reward the most effective salespeople. The current appraisal system consisted of Doug's comparison of each agent's premium income produced for the current year compared with the income generated from the previous year. Exceptions were noted and discussed with the individual agent. Doug then prepared an evaluation of each individual on the district sales force along with recommendations for increases in commission rates or salary bases. This report was forwarded to the vice president of marketing and was approved or revisions were suggested. This system had been developed by Doug when he became district manager and he felt confident about it. The people on his sales force had told him they felt the process adequately rewarded the best performers.

Lawyers, CPA's, engineers, or any individual who provides advice or services based on acquired expertise needs protection from lawsuits by clients. Professional liability insurance is designed for such needs. Frequently, one of the benefits provided by professional organizations is the endorsement of various insurance products for organization members at group rates. The individual members are typically contacted by the endorsed company through direct mail, followed by a sales call from the representative.

Doug knows that the company's decision to enter the professional liability insurance market will require that his salespeople perform a set of sales tasks quite different from those they are accustomed to performing. If Midwest Risk could become the endorsed supplier of professional liability coverage for bar associations or CPA organizations in each market of the southern district, the sales force would have access to a customer group of high potential. Gaining the endorsement of local professional organizations would do much to ensure the successful market penetration for professional liability insurance.

The salespeople involved in the professional liability market will spend a large portion of *their time* contacting officers of the target professional organizations, making presentations, and performing various missionary selling tasks in an attempt to win the organizations' endorsements. Consequently, any evaluation of the performance of the professional liability salespeople should take into account the amount of effort devoted to "non-selling" tasks.

In an attempt to handle this challenge, Doug wrote down the selling tasks required to sell life, accident, and health insurance (see Table 1). Beside the list of activities, he noted the percent of total effort his district salespeople typically devoted to each job. Doug listed the selling tasks he envisioned as necessary in developing and servicing a market for professional liability insurance. In the last column of the table he placed question marks alongside the entries, since he was uncertain about the percent of effort needed for each task.

Looking at the two lists of activities, Doug began to realize that the selling tasks themselves were not so different but that the amount of time devoted to each task by the two types of salespeople was what would change. Keeping that fact in mind, Doug began to try to think of ways in which he could develop an evaluation system that was flexible enough to encompass the activities of both types of sales jobs.

QUESTIONS

1. Could the vice president of marketing be premature in expanding into the professional liability market? Develop a sales plan for Doug to follow as he enters this new market.

2. Evaluate Doug's current appraisal system for his agents. What are the current strengths and weaknesses of this system?

3. Given the operating objectives for the professional liability market, which selling activities should be emphasized for the professional liability sales force? How much effort should be devoted to each sales task?

4. How would you develop standards of performance or quotas for the professional liability sales force?

5. How would you compare the productivity of the professional liability sales force with the performance of the life, accident, and health insurance sales force?

6. Will any changes be necessary in the compensation package? If so, what?

Case prepared by Jim Strong, California State University, Dominguez Hills and Paul Christ, West Chester University.

TABLE 1   Descriptions of Required Selling Tasks

Life, Accident, and Health Insurance	Percent of Effort	Professional Liability Insurance	Percent of Effort
1. Prospecting for new accounts	0.20	1. Prospecting for new accounts (identifying new professional groups)	?
2. Contacting prospects	0.10	2. Obtaining endorsements for client-affiliated professional groups	?
3. Qualifying prospects	0.05	3. Contacting prospects (group contacts through mass mailings)	?
4. Presenting the sales message	0.20	4. Qualifying prospects	?
5. Meeting customer objections	0.10	5. Presenting the sales message	?
6. Closing the sale	0.05	6. Meeting customer objections	?
7. Servicing the account	0.30	7. Closing the sale	?
		8. Servicing the account	?
		9. Maintaining client and professional group relationships	?

Notes

Chapter 1

[1] M. R. Czinkota, M. Kotabe, and D. Mercer, *Marketing Management: Text and Cases* (Maiden, MA: Blackwell Publishing, 1997), 494; Charles W. Lamb Jr., Joseph F. Hair Jr., and Carl McDaniel, *Marketing*, 8th ed. (Mason, OH: Thompson/Southwestern, 2006), 554; Rolph Anderson, Alan Dubinsky, and Rajiv Mehta, *Personal Selling: Building Customer Relationships and Partnerships* (Boston: Houghton Mifflin, 2007), 4–5.

[2] William C. Moncrief and Greg W. Marshall, "The Evolution of the Seven Steps of Selling," *Industrial Marketing Management* 34 (2005): 13–22; Rolph Anderson, "Personal Selling and Sales Management in the New Millennium," *Journal of Personal Selling & Sales Management* XVI (Fall 1996): 17–32.

[3] Bert Rosenbloom and Rolph Anderson, "The Sales Manager: Tomorrow's Super Marketer," *Business Horizons,* March–April 1984, pp. 50–56.

[4] William Keenan Jr. "The Death of the Sales Manager," *Sales and Marketing Management* 150 (April 1998).

[5] William A. Stimpson, "A Deming-Inspired Management Code of Ethics," *Quality Progress,* February 2005, pp. 67–68; "Firms Making Ethics a Part of Corporate Life," *Mobile Register,* April 16, 1995, p. 6F.

[6] "Marketing Redefined," *Marketing News,* September 14, 2004, p. 16.

[7] Ibid.

[8] John F. Tanner Jr., Michael Ahearne, Thomas W. Leigh, Charlotte H. Mason, and William C. Moncrief, "CRM in Sales-Intensive Organizations: A Review and Future Directions," *Journal of Personal Selling & Sales Management* 25 (spring 2005): 169–80; Alex R. Zablah, Danny N. Bellenger, and Wesley J. Johnston, "An Evaluation of Divergent Perspectives on Customer Relationship Management: Towards a Common Understanding of an Emerging Phenomenon," *Industrial Marketing Management* 33 (2004): 475–89; Srini Srinivasan, Rolph Anderson, and Kishore Ponnavolu, "Customer Loyalty in E-Commerce: An Exploration of Its Antecedents and Consequences," *Journal of Retailing* 78 (January 2002): 41–50; Grahame Dowling, "Customer Relationship Management: In B2C Markets, Often Less Is More," *California Management Review* 44, no. 3 (spring 2002): 87–104; Sudhi Seshadri and Randhir Mishra, "Relationship Marketing and Contract Theory," *Industrial Marketing Management* 33 (2004): 513–26.

[9] George Day, "Capabilities for Forging Customer Relationships," *Marketing Science Institute Report 00–118* (2001), Cambridge, MA.

[10] Frederick Hong-kit Yim, Rolph E. Anderson, and Srinivasan Swaminathan, "Customer Relationship Management: Its Dimensions and Effect on Customer Outcomes," *Journal of Personal Selling & Sales Management* 24 (Fall 2004): 263–78; James Boles, Thomas Brashear, Danny Bellenger, and Hiram Barksdale Jr., "Relationship Selling Behaviors: Antecedents and Relationship with Performance," *Journal of Business & Industrial Marketing* 18, no. 2/3 (2003): 141–62; Sally Rao and Chad Perry, "Thinking About Relationship Marketing: Where Are We Now? *Journal of Business & Industrial Marketing* 17, no. 7 (2002): 598–614; Christian Gronroos, "The Relationship Marketing Process: Communication, Interaction, Dialogue, Value," *Journal of Business & Industrial Marketing* 19, no. 2 (2004): 99–113.

[11] Fernando Jaramillo, Jay Prakash Mulki, and Greg W. Marshall, "A Meta-Analysis of the Relationship Between Organizational Commitment and Salesperson Job Performance: 25 Years of Research," *Journal of Business Research* 58 (2005): 705–14.

[12] Andy Cohen, "Who Needs A Sales Force, Anyway?" *Marketing & Sales Management,* February 1999, p. 13.

[13] Dominique Rouzies, Erin Anderson, Ajay K. Kohli, and Ronald E. Michaels et al., "Sales and Marketing Integration: A Proposed Framework," *Journal of Personal Selling & Sales Management* 25, no. 2 (spring 2005): 113–24.

[14] Rouzies et al., "Sales and Marketing Integration"; Troy G. Miller and Eric P. Gist, *Selling in Turbulent Times* (New York: Accenture-Economist Intelligence Unit Survey, 2003).

[15] Czinkota et al., *Marketing Management.*

[16] Phil Kitchen and Don Schultz, "A Multi-Country Comparison of the Drive for IMC," *Journal of Advertising Research* 39 (1999): 21; Bill Cook, "Integrated Marketing Communications: Performing Together," *Journal of Advertising Research* 37, no. 5 (1997): 5.

[17] Eli Jones, Steven P. Brown, Andris A. Zoltners, and Barton A. Weitz, "The Changing Environment of Selling and Sales Management," *Journal of Personal Selling & Sales Management* 25, no. 2 (spring 2005): 105–12.

[18] Adapted and updated from Rolph E. Anderson, "Personal Selling and Sales Management in the New Millennium," *Journal of Personal Selling & Sales Management* 16 (fall 1996): 17–32.

[19] Julie Bennett, "Selling Technology Can Be a Taxing Task and Top Salespeople Are Tough to Find," *Wall Street Journal,* April 5, 2005, p. B7. For other insights on sales force automation, see Michael Fielding, "Four Technologies That B-to-B Marketers Can Leverage Now," *Marketing News,* May 1, 2005, pp. 13–14; Stephen Baker and Heather Green, "Blogs Will Change Your Business," *Business Week,* May 2, 2005, pp. 56–67; Cheri Speier and Viswanath Venkatesh, "The Hidden Minefields in the Adoption of Sales Force Automation Technologies," *Journal of Marketing* 66 (July 2002): 98–111; Devon S. Johnson and

Sundar Bharadwaj, "Digitization of Selling Activity and Sales Force Performance: An Empirical Investigation," *Academy of Marketing Science Journal* 33 (Winter 2005): 3–18.

20. Leroy Robinson Jr., Greg W. Marshall, and Miriam B. Stamps, "Sales Force Use of Technology: Antecedents to Technology Acceptance," *Journal of Business Research* 20 (2004): 1–9.

21. Melanie Berger, "It's Your Move," *Sales & Marketing Management,* March 1998, pp. 46–53.

22. Rolph Anderson, Alan Dubinsky, and Rajiv Mehta, "Sales Managers: Marketing's Best Example of the Peter Principle?" *Business Horizons,* January–February 1999, pp. 19–26; Jack Carew, "When Salespeople Evaluate Their Managers . . . ," *Sales & Marketing Management,* March 1989, pp. 24–27.

23. Anderson et al., "Marketing's Best Example of the Peter Principle?"

24. Ibid.

25. Rajiv Mehta, Rolph Anderson, and James Strong, "An Empirical Investigation of Sales Management Training for Sales Managers," *Journal of Personal Selling & Sales Management* 27 (summer 1997): 53–66.

26. "Industrial Newsletter," *Sales & Marketing Management,* June 4, 1984, p. 29.

27. Adapted and updated from Anderson, "Personal Selling."

Chapter 2

1. Adapted from M. Goulston, "Tiger Woods Doesn't Cheat: How to Be Ethical and Profitable," *Sales and Service Excellence,* July 2005, p. 10; J. G., "Shades of Gray," *Sales & Marketing Management* 156 (November 2004): 26.

2. Ronald F. Duska, "Ethical Issues with Annuities: Some Situations for Reflection," *Journal of Financial Service Professionals* 58 (September 2004): 38–42.

3. http://www.ti.com/corp/docs/company/citizen/ethics/index.shtml (accessed February 20, 2007; K. Larick, "The New Crisis in Business Management," *Fortune,* April 20, 1992, p. 176.

4. http://multimedia.verizon.com/responsibility/ethics/index.aspx (accessed February 20, 2007); Sue Gaines, "Handling Out Halos," *Business Ethics,* March–April 1994, p. 21.

5. James B. Deconinck, "The Influence of Ethical Control Systems and Moral Intensity on Sales Managers' Ethical Perceptions and Behavioral Intentions," *Marketing Management Journal* 15 (fall 2005): 123–31.

6. E. F. Schultz and J. D. Opdyke, "At Annuity University Agents Learn How to Pitch to Seniors," *Wall Street Journal,* July 2, 2002, p. B1.

7. Patricia Knowles and Anusorn Singhapakdi, "Distinguishing Sales Professionals from their Marketing Counterparts: An Empirical Inquiry," *Marketing Management Journal* 10, no. 2 (2000): 41–53.

8. S. J. Vitell, K. Rallapalli, and A. Singhapakdi, "Marketing Norms: The Influence of Personal Moral Philosophies and Organizational Ethical Culture," *Journal of the Academy of Marketing Science* 21 (fall 1993): 331–37.

9. Eugene Sivadas, Susan Kleiser, James Kellaris, and Robert Dahlstrom, "Moral Philosophy, Ethical Evaluations, and Sales Manager Hiring Practices," *Journal of Personal Selling & Sales Management* 23 (winter 2002–2003): 7–21.

10. Bulent Menguc, "Organizational Consequences, Marketing Ethics and Salesperson Supervision: Further Empirical Evidence," *Journal of Business Ethics* 17 (March 1998): 333–52.

11. Donald Robin, Eric Reidenbach, and Barry J. Babin, "The Nature, Measurement and Stability of Ethical Judgments in the Workplace," *Psychological Reports* 80 (1997): 563–80.

12. Ibid.

13. Ken Bass, Time Barnett, and Gene Brown, "The Moral Philosophy of Sales Managers and Its Influence on Ethical Decision Making," *Journal of Personal Selling & Sales Management* 18 (spring 1998): 1–17; Alan J. Dubinsky, Rajan Nataraajan, and Wen-Yeh Huang, "The Influence of Moral Philosophy on Retail Salespeople's Ethical Perceptions," *Journal of Consumer Affairs* 38, no. 2 (2004): 297.

14. Bass et al., "Moral Philosophy of Sales Managers"; Sergio Román and Jose L. Munuera, "Determinants and Consequences of Ethical Behaviour: An Empirical Study of Salespeople," *European Journal of Marketing* 39, no. 5/6 (2005): 473–95.

15. Sivadas et al., "Moral Philosophy, Ethical Evaluations."

16. Ibid.

17. Joseph A. Bellizzi, "Disciplining Top-Performing Unethical Salespeople: Examining the Moderating Effects of Ethical Seriousness and Consequences," *Psychology & Marketing* 23 (February 2006): 181–201.

18. Joseph A. Bellizi and R. D. Hasty, "Supervising Unethical Sales Force Behavior: Do Men and Women Managers Discipline Men and Women Subordinates Uniformly?" *Journal of Business Ethics* 40 (October 2002): 155–66.

19. Barry J. Babin, James S. Boles, and Donald P. Robin, "Representing the Perceived Ethical Work Climate Among Marketing Employees," *Journal of the Academy of Marketing Science* 28 (summer 2000): 345–59.

20. Charles H. Schwepker Jr. and Michael D. Hartline, "Managing the Ethical Climate of Customer-Contact Service Employees," *Journal of Service Research* 7 (May 2005): 377–97.

21. Charles H. Schwepker and David J. Good, "The Impact of Sales Quotas on Moral Judgment in the Financial Services Industry," *Journal of Services Marketing* 13, no. 1 (2005): 35–58.

22. Román and Munuera, "Determinants and Consequences."

23. Babin et al., "Perceived Ethical Work Climate"; Schwepker and Hartline, "Managing the Ethical Climate."

24 Jay Prakash Mulki, Fernando Jaramillo, and William B. Locander, "Effects of Ethical Climate and Supervisory Trust on Salesperson's Job Attitudes and Intentions to Quit," *Journal of Personal Selling & Sales Management* 26 (winter 2006): 19–26.

25 William A. Weeks, Terry W. Loe, Lawrence R. Chonko, and Carlos Ruy Martinez et al., "Cognitive Moral Development and the Impact of Perceived Organizational Ethical Climate on the Search for Sales Force Excellence: A Cross-Cultural Study," *Journal of Personal Selling & Sales Management* 26 (spring 2006): 205–17.

26 Marc Gunther, "Money and Morals at GE," *Fortune*, November 15, 2004, pp. 176–82.

27 "Clinton Lifts Ban on Trade with Vietnam," *Wall Street Journal*, February 4, 1994, p. A12.

28 "Singapore Remains a Graft-Free Haven," *Straits Times*, April 9, 1996, p. 3.96.

29 Weeks et al., "Cognitive Moral Development."

30 Román and Munuera, "Determinants and Consequences."

Chapter 3

1 *Marketing Research* (2006), "Is CRM c-r-u-m-m-y?"

2 Elizabeth Bennet, "CRM Before There was CRM," *Baseline*, July 2006, p. 49.

3 Adrian Payne and Frow Pennie, "A Strategic Framework for Customer Relationship Management," *Journal of Marketing* 69 (October 2005): 167–76.

4 Werner Reinartz, Manfred Kraft, and Wayne D. Hoyer, "The Customer Relationship Management Process: Its Measurement and Impact on Performance," *Journal of Marketing Research* 41 (August 2004): 293–305.

5 Don Peppers and Martha Rogers, *The One-to-One Fieldbook: The Complete Toolkit for Implementing a 1 to 1 Marketing Program* (London: Piakus, 1999).

6 Taken from the following sources: Kelly Shermach, "Growing Acceptance of Cookies," *Sales and Marketing Management*, September 2006, p. 20; Bill Britt, "Customized Publishing on the Rise," *Marketing*, October 18, 2006, p. 15.

7 Roy Church, "New Perspectives on the History of Products, Firms, Marketing and Consumers in Britain and the United States in the Nineteenth Century," *Economic History Review* 52, no. 3 (1999): 405–35.

8 Ibid.

9 Eli Jones, Paul Busch, and Peter Dacin, "Firm Market Orientation and Salesperson Customer Orientation: Interpersonal and Intrapersonal Influences on Customer Service and Retention in Business-to-Business Buyer-Seller Relationships," *Journal of Business Research* 56 (2003): 323–40.

10 Roland T. Rust, Katherine Lemon, and Das Narayandas, *Customer Equity Management* (Upper Saddle River, NJ: Prentice Hall, 2005).

11 David T. Wilson, "Deep Relationships: The Case of the Vanishing Salesperson," *Journal of Personal Selling & Sales Management* 20 (winter 2000): 53–61.

12 M. Viswanathan and E. Olson, "Organizational Purchasing Analysis for Sales Management," *Journal of Personal Selling & Sales Management* 12 (winter 1992): 45–57.

13 Christian Gronroos, "The Relationship Marketing Process: Communication, Interaction, Dialogue, Value," *Journal of Business & Industrial Marketing* 19, no. 2 (2004): 99–113; James Boles, Thomas Brashear, Danny Bellenger, and Hiram Barksdale Jr., "Relationship Selling Behaviors: Antecedents and Relationship with Performance," *Journal of Business & Industrial Marketing* 18, no. 2/3 (2003): 141–62.

14 Rolph Anderson and Srini Srinivasan, "E-Satisfaction and E-Loyalty: A Contingency Framework," *Psychology and Marketing* 20 (February 2003): 123–38.

15 Eli Jones, Lawrence B. Chonko, and James A. Roberts, "Creating a Partnership-Oriented, Knowledge Creation Culture in Strategic Sales Alliances: A Conceptual Framework," *Journal of Business & Industrial Marketing* 18, no. 4/5 (2003): 336–52; Michael K Rich, "Requirements for Successful Marketing Alliances," *Journal of Business & Industrial Marketing* 18, no. 4/5 (2003): 447–56.

16 Atilla Yaprak, S. Tamer Cavusgil, and Destin Kandemir, "Alliance Orientation: Conceptualization, Measurement and Impact on Market Performance," *Journal of the Academy of Marketing Science* 34 (summer 2006): 324–40.

17 Fred Selnes and James Sallis, "Promoting Relationship Learning," *Journal of Marketing* 59 (July 2003): 80–107.

18 "Strategic Partnerships," http://www.giantstepsmts.com/strategicpartnerships.htm (accessed February 25, 2007).

19 Wilson, "Deep Relationships."

20 Lee Yikuan and S. T. Cavusgil, "Enhancing Alliance Performance: The Effects of Contractual-Based Versus Relational-Based Governance," *Journal of Business Research* 59 (August 2006): 896–905.

21 S. J. Carson, A. Madhok, and T. Wu, "Uncertainty, Opportunism, and Governance: The Effects of Volatility and Ambiguity on Formal and Relational Contracting," *Academy of Management Journal* 49 (May 2006): 1058–77.

22 T. Cavusgil, S. Deligonul, and C. Zhang, "Curbing Foreign Distributor Opportunism: An Examination of Trust, Contracts, and the Legal Environment in International Channel Relationships," *Journal of International Marketing* 12, no. 2 (2004): 7–27.

23 Babin, B. J. and J. S. Attaway (2000), "Atmospheric Affect as a Tool for Creating Value and Gaining Share of Customer," *Journal of Business Research*, 49 (2), 91–99.

24 Peppers, Don and Martha Rogers (2005), "Hail to the Customer," *Sales & Marketing Management*, 157 (October), 1.

25 Peppers and Rogers, *One-to-One Fieldbook*.

26 Lewis, M. (2005), "Price Reality Check," *Cabinet Maker*, 5428 (3/4), 19–21.

27 See William Boulding, Richard Staelin, Michael Ehret, and Wesley J. Johnston, "Customer Relationship Management: What Is Known, Potential Pitfalls, and Where to Go," *Journal of Marketing* 69 (October 2005): 155–66.

28 *CRM Magazine,* "Customer Service on Demand: Avoiding the Pitfalls," June 2006, pp. 6–9.

29 *Precision Marketing,* "Nintendo Tours Universities to Push Pet Game," December 9, 2005, p. 2.

30 Timothy D. Landry, Todd J. Arnold, and Aaron Arndt, "A Compendium of Sales-Related Literature in Customer Relationship Management Processes and Technologies with Managerial Implications," *Journal of Personal Selling & Sales Management* 25 (summer 2005): 231–51.

31 Patricia Van Arnum, Erik Greb, and Douglas McCormick, "Pharmaceutical Technology's 2005 Manufacturing Rating," *Pharmaceutical Technology* 30 (July 2006): 36–50.

32 Martin LaMonica, "IBM to Beef Up Sales Staff," News.com (March 24, 2005), http://news.com/IBM%20to%20beef%20up%20software%20sales%20staff/2100-1012_3-5634664.html (accessed November 19, 2006).

33 Bennet, "CRM Before There was CRM."

34 Raman Pushkala, C. Michael Wittmann, and Nancy A. Rausen, "Leveraging CRM for Sales: The Role of Organizational Capabilities in Successful CRM Implementation," *Journal of Personal Selling & Sales Management* 26 (winter 2006): 39–53.

35 Matthias Meyer and Lutz M. Kolbe, "Integration of Customer Relationship Management: Status Quo and Implications for Research and Practice," *Journal of Strategic Marketing* 13 (September 2005): 175–98.

36 Mary E. Morrison, "WebEx Clears Up Cloud of Poor Delivery with a Clean Database," *B to B,* September 12, 2006, p. 23.

37 Jaymeen R. Shah and Mirza B. Murtaza, "Effective Customer Relationship Management through Web Services," *Journal of Computer Information Systems* 46 (fall 2005): 98, 109.

38 Ronald Jelinick, Michael Ahearne, John Mathieu, and Miles Schillewaert, "A Longitudinal Examination of Individual, Organizational and Contextual Factors on Sales Technology Adoption and Job Performance," *Journal of Marketing, Theory and Practice* 14 (winter 2006): 7–23.

39 Deva Rangarajan, Eli Jones, and Wynne Chin, "Impact of Sales Force Automation on Technology-Related Stress, Effort, and Technology Usage among Salespeople," *Industrial Marketing Management* 34 (May 2005): 345–54. Jelinick et al., "Longitudinal Examination."

40 Melanie Berger, "It's Your Move," *Sales & Marketing Management* (March 1998): 46–53.

41 Colin Beasty, "How Sales Teams Should Use CRM," *CRM,* February 2006, pp. 30–34.

42 Sometimes referred to as CHAID.

43 Stephen Baker, "Math Will Rock Your World," *Business Week,* January 23, 2006, pp. 54–62.

44 *CRM,* "The 2006 Market Leaders," October 2006, pp. 30–39.

45 *CRM,* "Replicate Sales Success: Clone Your Salespeople," September 2006, p. 4.

46 Thomas Daniel, "Firms Are Unhappy with CRM," *Computer Weekly,* January 23, 2003, p. 4.

47 Barry Trailer and Jim Dickie, "Understanding What Your Sales Manager Is Up Against," *Harvard Business Review,* July/August 2006, pp. 48–55.

48 See for example S. Jayachandran, S. Sharma, P. Kaufman, and R. Pushkala, "The Role of Relational Information Processes and Technology Use in Customer Relationship Management," *Journal of Marketing* 69 (October 2005): 177–92; *Institute of Management & Administration,* "A Look at Why CRM Fails and How You Can Prevent It," *Institute of Management & Administration,* 2 (February 2002): 1–14; Trailor and Dickie, "What Your Sales Manager Is Up Against."

49 Betsy Cummings, "Proving the Sales Process," *Sales and Marketing Management* 158 (June 2006): 15.

Chapter 4

1 Many of the tables in this chapter have been adapted from Rolph Anderson, Alan Dubinsky, and Rajiv Mehta, *Personal Selling: Building Customer Relationships and Partnerships,* 2nd ed. (Boston: Houghton Mifflin, 2007)

2 Julie T. Johnson, Hiram C. Barksdale, and James S. Boles, "The Strategic Role of the Salesperson in Reducing Customer Defection in Business Relationships," *Journal of Personal Selling & Sales Management* 21 (Spring 2001): 123–24.

3 Frederick Hong-kit Yim, Rolph E. Anderson, and Srinivasan Swaminathan, "Customer Relationship Management: Its Dimensions and Effect on Customer Outcomes," *Journal of Personal Selling and Sales Management* 24 (Fall 2004): 263–78.

4 *Occupational Outlook Handbook, 2004–05* (Washington, D.C.: Bureau of Labor Statistics, U.S. Department of Labor, 2004); and "Occupational Employment Projections to 2012," *Monthly Labor Review* (Washington, D.C.: Bureau of Labor Statistics, U.S. Department of Labor, February 2004).

5 "The 2004 Compensation Survey," *Sales and Marketing Management* 156 (May 2004): 28–35.

6 Julie Bennett, "Selling Technology Can Be a Taxing Task and Top Salespeople Are Tough to Find," *Wall Street Journal,* April 5, 2005, p. B7.

7 Rolph Anderson, Alan Dubinsky, and Rajiv Mehta, *Personal Selling: Building Customer Relationships and Partnerships* (Boston: Houghton Mifflin, 2007), 22.

8 F. B. Evans, "Selling as a Dyadic Relationship—A New Approach," *American Behavioral Scientist* 6 (May 1963): 76–79. Other studies supporting Evan's results include M. S. Gadel, "Concentration by Salesmen on Congenial Prospects," *Journal of Marketing* 28 (April 1964): 64–66; Arch G. Woodside and J. W. Davenport Jr., "The Effect of Salesman Similarity and Expertise on Consumer Purchasing Behavior,"

Journal of Marketing Research 11 (May 1974): 198–202; Edward A. Riordan et al., "The Unsold Prospect: Dyadic and Attitudinal Determinants," *Journal of Marketing Research* 14 (November 1977): 530–537; Lawrence A. Crosby, Kenneth R. Evans, and Deborah Cowles, "Relationship Quality in Services Selling: An Interpersonal Influence Perspective," *Journal of Marketing* 54 (July 1990): 68–81.

9 J. David Lichtenthal and Thomas Tellefsen, "Toward a Theory of Business Buyer-Seller Similarity," *Journal of Personal Selling & Sales Management* 21 (Winter 2001): 1–14.

10 Lichtenthal and Tellefsen, "Theory of Business Buyer-Seller Similarity"; Herbert M. Greenberg and Jeanne Greenberg, "Job Matching for Better Sales Performance," *Harvard Business Review* (September–October 1980), pp. 128–33; Robert J. Zimmer and Paul S. Hugstad, "A Contingency Approach to Specializing Industrial Sales Force," *Journal of Personal Selling & Sales Management* 1 (Spring/Summer 1981): 27–35.

11 http://www.sellingpower.com/magazine/abstract/ v25n3_abstract.asp (accessed April 20, 2005).

12 "Thriving on Order," *INC.,* December 1989, p. 49.

13 For an alternative view of the seven-stage selling process, see William C. Moncrief and Greg W. Marshall, "The Evolution of the Seven Steps of Selling," *Industrial Marketing Management* 34 (2005): 13–22.

14 Rolph Anderson and Srini Srinivasan, "Make Profits Soar with the 8Cs of Customer Loyalty," *LeBow Business Knowledge,* June 2003, p. 2.

15 Adapted in part from Charles Futrell, *Fundamentals of Selling: Customers for Life Through Service,* 9th ed. (New York: McGraw-Hill/Irwin, 2006).

16 Susan Del Vecchio, James Zemanek, Roger McIntyre, and Reid Claxton, "Updating the Adaptive Selling Behaviors: Tactics to Keep and Tactics to Discard," *Journal of Marketing Management* 20 (2004): 859–76; Barton Weitz, Harish Sujan, and Mita Sujan, "Knowledge, Motivation, and Adaptive Behavior: A Framework for Improving Selling Effectiveness," *Journal of Marketing* (October 1986): 174–91.

17 Jerry R. Goolsby, Rosemary L. Lagace, and Michael L. Boorom, "Psychological Adaptiveness and Sales Performance," *Journal of Personal Selling & Sales Management* 12 (Spring 1992): 51–66.

18 Stephen S. Porter and Lawrence W. Inks, "Cognitive Complexity and Salesperson Adaptability: An Exploratory Investigation," *Journal of Personal Selling & Sales Management* 20 (Winter 2000): 15–21.

19 Marvin A. Jolson, "Canned Adaptiveness: A New Direction for Modern Salesmanship," *Business Horizons* 32 (January–February 1989): 7–12.

20 Frederick Reichheld and Earl Sasser Jr., "Why Satisfied Customers Defect," *Harvard Business Review,* November–December 1995, p. 88; Frederick F. Reichheld, Robert G. Markey Jr., and Christopher Hopton, "The Loyalty Effect—The Relationship Between Loyalty and Profits," *European Business Journal* (2000): 134–39.

21 Anderson et al., *Personal Selling,* 19.

22 James L. Heskett, Thomas O. Jones, Gary W. Loveman, W. Early Sasser Jr., and Leonard A. Schlesinger, "Putting the Service-Profit Chain to Work," *Harvard Business Review,* March–April 1994, pp. 165–66; Rebecca Piirto Healt, "Loyalty for Sale: Everybody's Doing Frequency Marketing—But Only a Few Companies Are Doing It Well," *Marketing Tools,* July 1997, p. 65; Kenneth Carlton Cooper, "The Relational Enterprise," *Customer Relationship Management,* July 2002, pp. 42–45.

23 Philip Kotler and Gary Armstrong, *Principles of Marketing,* 10th ed. (Upper Saddle River, NJ: Prentice-Hall, 2004): 16.

24 Don Peppers and Martha Rogers, *Managing Customer Relationships: A Strategic Framework.* (Hoboken, NJ: Wiley, 2004): 6.

25 Don Peppers, "Banking on Strong Customer Relationships," *Inside 1to1* (March 16, 2000), www.1to1.com/publications.

26 Rolph E. Anderson and Wen-yeh (Rene) Huang, "Empowering Salespeople: Personal, Managerial, and Organizational Perspectives," *Psychology and Marketing,* February 2006, pp. 139–59.

27 William G. Zikmund, Raymond McLeod Jr., and Faye W. Gilbert, *Customer Relationship Management: Integrating Marketing Strategy and Information Technology* (New York: Wiley, 2003).

28 Rolph Anderson, "Personal Selling and Sales Management in the New Millennium," *Journal of Personal Selling & Sales Management* 16 (Fall 1996): 17–32.

Chapter 5

1 http://press.weather.com/index.php/press_releases/96.html (accessed October 19, 2006).

2 Chris Whisenant, "The Politics of Forecasting in Sales and Operations Planning," *Journal of Business Forecasting* 25 (summer 2006): 17–19. Exhibit adapted from material on page 18.

3 M. Muzumdar and J. Fontanella, "The Secrets to S&OP Success," *Supply Chain Management Review,* April 2006, pp. 34–41.

4 Ibid.

5 S. Tillet and J. Shwartz, "Delta Syncs Data, Ops," *Internet Week,* June 25, 2001, pp. 1–2.

6 Gail S. Mock and Dwight E. Thomas, "The Volume Forecasting Process: Linking Customers with Factories," *Journal of Business Forecasting* (spring 1992): 3–4.

7 www.census.gov/epcd/www/naics.html (accessed October 20, 2006).

8 Ibid.

9 "Nokia and Coca-Cola Put Nokia's Local Marketing Solution to the Test at 3GSM," www.10meters.com/Nokia_coke.html (accessed November 2006).

10. "Q3 DSP Shipments Healthy, Q4 Slowing, Firm Says," *Electronic News,* November 7, 2005, p. N.

11. Charles C. Holt, "Forecasting Seasonals and Trends by Exponentially Weighted Moving Averages," *Journal of Economic and Social Measurement* 29 (2001): 123–25.

12. N. Kulendran and J. Shan, "Forecasting China's Monthly Inbound Travel Demand," *Journal of Travel & Tourism Marketing* 13 (2002): 5–29.

15. Muzumdar and Fontanella, "Secrets to S&OP Success."

16. www.ibm.com (accessed November 2006).

15. Mike Thacker, "Why They Are Wrong, Why Does That Matter?" *Logistics and Transportation Focus,* November 2001, pp. 24–29.

Chapter 6

1. Jeff Thull, "Selling in Era 3: How to Leverage Value to Win—and Keep—Profitable Customers," *American Salesman,* January 2004, pp. 12–14.

2. http://www.ibm.com (accessed March 2007).

3. Gary Anthes, "Portal Powers GE Sales," *Computerworld,* June 2, 2003, and http://www.computerworld.com/developmenttopics/development/webdev/story/0,10801,81624,00.html (accessed March 2007).

4. Dennis Callahan, "Acumen Debuts Sales Planning Tool," July 12, 2002, *E-Week.com,* http://www.eweek.com/article2/0,4149,374081,00.asp?kc&EWTOV10311KTX1K2200440, and http://www.acumen-software.com/ (accessed March 2007).

5. http://www.ibm.com and http://www-304.ibm.com/jct09002c/isv/marketing/industrynetworks/benefits/rtm_workshop.html (accessed November 2006).

6. http://www.matrixmanager.com (accessed March 2007).

7. Thomas Sy and Laura D'Annunzio, "Challenges and Strategies of Matrix Organizations: Top-Level and Mid-Level Managers' Perspectives," *Human Resource Planning,* January 2005, pp. 39–48.

8. Thomas Sy and Stephane Cote, "Emotional Intelligence: A Key Ability to Succeed in the Matrix Organization," *Journal of Management Development* 23, no. 5 (2004): 437–55.

9. David Andelman, "Betting on the 'Net,'" *Sales & Marketing Management,* June 1995, pp. 47–59.

10. Christian Homburg, John Workman, and Ove Jensen, "Fundamental Changes in Marketing Organization: The Movement Toward a Customer-Focused Organizational Structure," *Journal of the Academy of Marketing Science* (Fall 2000): 459–78.

11. Dennis B. Arnett, Barry Macy, and James B. Wilcox, "The Role of Core Selling Teams in Supplier-Buyer Relationships," Journal of Personal Selling & Sales Management (winter 2005): 27–42.

12. Eli Jones, Andrea L. Dixon, Larry Chonko, and Joseph Cannon, "Key Accounts and Team Selling: A Review, Framework, and Research Agenda," *Journal of Personal Selling & Sales Management* 25 (spring 2005): 181–98.

13. Bulent Menguc and Tansu Barker, "Re-Examining Field Sales Unit Performance: Insights from the Resource-Based View and Dynamic Capabilities Perspective," *European Journal of Marketing* 39 (2005): 885–909.

14. Jones et al., "Key Accounts and Team Selling."

15. http://www.walmartstores.com (accessed March 2007).

16. Scott Hensley, "As Drug-Sales Teams Multiple, Doctors Start to Tune Them Out," *Wall Street Journal Online,* June 12, 2003, pp. 1–4.

17. Charles Shaw, "The Rep and the Future—Which Is Now," *Agency Sales Magazine,* January 2001, pp. 28–30.

18. Michele Marchetti, "Can You Build a Salesforce?" *Sales & Marketing Management,* January 2000, pp. 56–61.

Chapter 7

1. Lehman, Jeff, *The Sales Manager's Mentor* (Seattle, WA: Mentor Press LLC, 2006); and Rolph Anderson, "Personal Selling and Sales Management in the New Millennium," *Journal of Personal Selling & Sales Management* 4 (fall 1996): 17–32.

2. Sara Calabro, "Measuring Up," *Sales & Marketing Management,* March 2005, pp. 22–28.

3. Mathew Arnold, Mathew, "Flexible Forces," *Medical Marketing and Media,* November 2005, pp. 36–41.

4. Alan Dubinsky and Thomas Ingram, "A Portfolio Approach to Account Profitability," *Industrial Marketing Management* 13 (February 1984): 33–41; Raymond W. Laforge, Clifford E. Young, and B. Curtis Hamm, "Increasing Sales Call Productivity through Improved Sales Call Allocation Strategies," *Journal of Personal Selling & Sales Management* 3 (November 1983): 54.

5. Rolph Anderson, "Personal Selling and Sales Management in the New Millennium," *Journal of Personal Selling & Sales Management* 4 (fall 1996): 17–32.

6. http://www.crmondemand.com (accessed November 2006).

7. Greg Marshall, William Moncrief, and Felicia Lassk, "The Current State of Sales Force Activities," *Industrial Marketing Management* 28 (January 1999): 87–98.

8. *Sales & Marketing Management,* March 1998, p. 96.

9. Dave Kahle, "Strategic Planning for Salespeople," http://www.davekahle.com/article/strategic.htm (accessed October 2006); William A. Weeks and Lynn R. Kahle, "Salespeople's Time Use and Performance," *Journal of Personal Selling & Sales Management* 10 (winter 1990): 29–37.

10. Rolph Anderson, *Professional Personal Selling* (Englewood Cliffs, NJ: Prentice Hall, 1991), 514.

11. Lehman, *Sales Manager's Mentor;* Anderson, "Personal Selling and Sales Management."

12 Tony Seideman, "Who Needs Managers," *Sales & Marketing Management,* June 1994, p. 15.

13 http://www.bms.com/ (accessed October 2006); Wally Wood, "Reinventing the Sales Force," *Across the Board,* April 1994, p. 24.

14 Lehman, *Sales Manager's Mentor;* Anderson, "Personal Selling and Sales Management."

15 D. Kahle, "Strategic Planning for Salespeople."

16 D. Kahle, "Strategic Planning for Salespeople"; Weeks and L. Kahle, "Salespeople's Time Use and Performance."

Chapter 8

1 Jeff Lehman, *The Sales Manager's Mentor* (Seattle, WA: Mentor Press LLC, 2006).

2 Betsy Cummings, "Star Search," *Sales & Marketing Management,* July 2005, pp. 23–27.

3 Michele Marchetti, "Warp Speed," *Sales & Marketing Management,* January 2005, p. 16.

4 http://www.jobs4sales.com/seekers/search/ details.cfm?jn=231304 (accessed October 2006).

5 Lehman, *Sales Manager's Mentor;* Michele Marchetti, "Letting Go of Low Performers," *Sales & Marketing Management,* July 2005, p. 16.

6 Chris Taylor, "The Pioneers," *Sales & Marketing Management,* February 2005, pp. 32–37.

7 Cummings, "Star Search."

8 Andy Cohen, "Sales Strikes Out on Campuses," *Sales & Marketing Management,* November 1997, p. 13.

9 Cummings, "Star Search."

10 Lehman, *Sales Manager's Mentor.*

11 "Hiring Top Sales Performers," *Workforce Management,* May 2006; http://www.swlearning.com/management/hrm_news/ selection_0706_001.html (accessed October 2006); Stephanie Armour, "Firms Key Up PCs for Job Screening," *USA Today,* October 20, 1997, p. 6B.

12 "SalesMax for Selecting Salespeople," http://www .selectassesstrain.com/ssa-smintro.asp (accessed October 2006).

13 Profiles International, "Improve Sales," http://www .profilesinternational.com/SOL_SalesHiring.aspx (accessed October 2006); Linda Thornburg, "Computer-Assisted Interviewing Shortens Hiring Cycle," *HRMagazine,* February 1998, http://www.shrm.org.

14 Christopher J. Bachler, "Resume Fraud: Lies, Omissions and Exaggerations," *Personnel Journal* 74 (June 1995): 50–60.

15 Dana Telford and Adrian Gostick, "Hiring Character," *Sales & Marketing Management,* June 2005, pp. 39–42.

16 AAIM Management Association, "Talent Acquisition Solutions," http://www.aaimstl.org/tas.asp (accessed October 2006); Anne Field, "Would You Hire This Person Again?" *Business Week,* June 9, 1997.

17 Lehman, *Sales Manager's Mentor;* Richard Koonce, "Spotting Red Flags in a Job Interview," *Training & Development,* February 1997, p. 15.

18 Paul Green, "More Than a Gut Feeling," http://www.rctm.com/ Products/recruitretention/6512.htm?pcategory=17017 (accessed October 2006); Paul Falcone, "Questions Make the Candidate," *HR Focus,* December 1996, p. 15.

19 *User's Manual: The Comprehensive Personality Profile (CPP),* Wonderlic Personnel Test, Inc., 1998 (Bradenton, FL: CraftSystems, Inc.); http://www.craftsystems.com/ (accessed October 2006).

20 *User's Manual: The Comprehensive Personality Profile;* Larry L. Craft, "The Career Life Insurance Agent," in *Research Brief 96-1* (Bradenton, FL: CraftSystems, Inc.), September 1996.

21 Scott Widmier and Joe Hair, "Enhancing Global Sales Skills through Executive Education Programs," *Journal of Executive Education* 6, no. 1 (forthcoming 2007); John S. Hill and Meg Birdseye, "Salesperson Selection in Multinational Corporations: An Empirical Study," *Journal of Personal Selling & Sales Management* (summer 1989): 39–47.

22 S. Green, F. Hassan, J. Immelt, and M. Marks et al., "In Search of Global Leaders," *Harvard Business Review,* August 2003, pp. 38–44.

23 Alan J. Dubinsky, Roy D. Howell, Thomas N. Ingram, and Danny N. Bellenger, "Salesforce Socialization," *Journal of Marketing* 50 (October 1986): 201–03.

24 S. Foley, D. L. Kidder, and G. N. Powell, "The Perceived Glass Ceiling and Justice Perceptions: An Investigation of Hispanic Law Associates," *Journal of Management* 28, no. 4 (August 1, 2002): 471–96.

25 Tara Lopez and Amy McMillan-Capehart, "How Outgroup Salespeople Fit In or Fail to Fit In: A Proposed Acculturation Effects Framework," *Journal of Personal Selling & Sales Management* 22, no. 4 (fall 2002): 297–309; E. Stephen Grant and Alan J. Bush, "Salesforce Socialization Tactics: Building Organizational Value Congruence," *Journal of Personal Selling & Sales Management* 16 (summer 1996): 17–32.

Chapter 9

1 Margery Weinstein, "On Demand Is in Demand: Using Technology to Train," http://www.trainingmag.com/msg/ content_display/publications/e3iQAg%2FoQ3k4zuIR0PtOV9 psQ%3D%3D (accessed October 2006); Rebecca Aronauer, "Sales Training: The Classroom vs. E-Learning," http://www.trainingmag.com/msg/content_display/sales/ e3ilMzAQHc3EHJ6eS1OZWTAvw%3D%3D (accessed October 2006).

2 William Cron, Greg Marshall, Jagdip Singh, and Rosanne Spiro et al., "Salesperson Selection, Training, and Development," *Journal of Personal Selling & Sales Management* 25, no. 2 (spring 2005): 123–36.

3 Jennifer Follett, "Cisco Channel Chief Vows Partner Training Push," October 2006, http://www.crn.com/sections/breakingnews/breakingnews.jhtml;jsessionid=XED3QVFCAPELYQSNDLPSKHSCJUNN2JVN?articleId=193302511 (accessed October 2006).

4 Margot Lester, "The ROI of Training," September 8, 2003, http://www.larta.org/lavox/articlelinks/2003/030908_roi.asp (accessed July 2006); Nancy Chase, "Raise Your Training ROI," *Quality,* September 1, 1997, p. 28; and Sarah Lorge, "Getting into Their Heads," *Sales & Marketing Management,* February 1998, pp. 58–67.

5 Lehman, Jeff, *The Sales Manager's Mentor* (Seattle, WA: Mentor Press LLC, 2006); Margot Lester, "ROI of Training."

6 *Medical Marketing & Media,* November 2003, www.imshealth.com/vgn/images/portal/cit_40000873/4463832111953_eprint.pdf (accessed October 2006).

7 http://www.johnsoncontrols.com (accessed October 2006).

8 M. Ahearne, R. Jelinek, and A. Rapp, "Moving Beyond the Direct Effect of SFA Adoption on Salesperson Performance: Training and Support as Key Moderating Factors," *Industrial Marketing Management* 34 (2005): 379–88.

9 William F. Kenner, "Sales Managers as Trainers," *Selling Power,* September 2006, pp. 24–26.

10 http://www.sellingpower.com and http://www.americanexpress.com (accessed September 2006).

11 Lehman, *Sales Manager's Mentor.*

12 "Training: An Ear for Learning," *Sales & Marketing Management,* August 1995, pp. 30–31.

13 "Distinctions and Definitions of Learning Technologies," *Training & Development,* November 1997, p. 48.

14 http://www.wikipedia.com (accessed October 2006).

15 Ibid.

16 Rebecca Aronauer, "Sales Training: The Classroom vs. E-Learning," October 2006, http://www.trainingmag.com/msg/content_display/sales/e3ilMzAQHc3EHJ6eS1OZWTAvw%3D%3D (accessed October 2006).

17 http://www.sun.com (accessed September 2006); Robert M. Kahn, "21st Century Training," *Sales & Marketing Management,* June 1997, pp. 81–88.

18 Aronauer, "Sales Training: The Classroom vs. E-Learning."

19 Stephen Brookfield, "Adult Learning: An Overview," http://www.nl.edu/academics/cas/ace/facultypapers/StephenBrookfield_AdultLearning.cfm (accessed October 2006); Lorge, "Getting into Their Heads."

20 "The Experts Talk About Training," *Sales & Marketing Management,* February 1998, p. 62.

21 Rick Mendosa, "Is There a Payoff?" *Sales & Marketing Management,* June 1995, pp. 64–71; Beverly Geber, "Does Your Training Make a Difference? Prove It!" *Training,* March 1995, p. 27; and Earl D. Honeycutt and Thomas H. Stevenson, "Evaluating Sales Training Programs," *Industrial Marketing Management* 18 (1989): 215–22.

22 Robert Klein, "Nabisco Sales Soar After Sales Training," *Marketing News,* 6 January 1997, p. 23.

23 http://www.microsoft.com (accessed August 2006).

24 Mark P. Leach and Annie H. Liu, "Investigating Interrelationships Among Sales Training Evaluation Methods," *Journal of Personal Selling & Sales Management* 23, no. 4 (fall 2003): 327–40.

25 http://www.saturn.com, "America's Best Sales Forces: Saturn," *Sales & Marketing Management* (accessed August 2006).

26 http://www.kodak.com (accessed September 2006).

27 Cron et al., "Salesperson Selection, Training, and Development."

28 Rolph Anderson, Rajiv Mehta, and James Strong, "An Empirical Investigation of Sales Management Training Programs for Sales Managers," *Journal of Personal Selling & Sales Management* 17 (July 1997): 53.

29 Cynthia L. Kemper, "Global Training's Critical Success Factors," *Training & Development,* February 1998, pp. 35–37; Andy Cohen, "Small World, Big Challenge," *Sales & Marketing Management,* June 1996, pp. 69–73.

30 http://www.wyeth.com (accessed October 2006).

31 Scott Widmier and Joe Hair, "Enhancing Global Sales Skills through Executive Education Programs," *Journal of Executive Education* 6, no. 1 (forthcoming 2007).

32 Zhuoran Huang, "Making Training Friendly to Other Cultures," *Training & Development,* September 1996, pp. 13–14; Cynthia L. Kemper, "Global Training's Critical Success Factors," *Training & Development,* February 1998, pp. 35–37; Cohen, "Small World, Big Challenge."

Chapter 10

1 J. R. Meindl, S. B. Ehrlich, J. M. Dukerich, "The Romance of Leadership," *Administrative Science Quarterly* 30 (March 1985): 78–102; J. Pfeffer, "The Ambiguity of Leadership," *Academy of Management Review* 2 (January 1977): 104–112.

2 C. A. Martin and A. J. Bush, "Psychological Climate, Empowerment, Leadership Style, and Customer-Oriented Selling: An Analysis of the Sales Manager-Salesperson Dyad," *Journal of the Academy of Marketing Science* 34 (summer 2006): 419–38; A. J. Dubinsky, F. J. Yammarino, M. A. Jolson, and W. D. Spangler, "Transformational Leadership: An Initial Investigation in Sales Management," *Journal of Personal Selling & Sales Management* 15 (spring 1995): 17–31; B. M. Bass and B. J. Avolio, *Improving Organizational Effectiveness Through Transformational Leadership* (Thousands Oaks, CA: Sage, 1994); B. M. Bass and B. J. Avolio, "From Transactional to Transformational Leadership: Learning to Share the Vision," *Organizational Dynamics* 18 (winter 1990): 19–31; B. M. Bass, "Leadership: Good, Better, Best," *Organizational Dynamics* 13 (winter 1985): 26–40; D. A. Waldman, B. M. Bass, and Walter O Einstein, "Leadership and Outcomes of Performance Appraisal Processes," *Journal of Occupational Psychology* 60 (September 1987): 177–86.

3 A. Carter, "It's Norman Time," *Business Week,* May 29, 2006, pp. 64–68.

4 J. M. Kouzes and B. Z. Posner, *The Leadership Challenge,* 3rd ed. (San Francisco: Jossey-Bass Pfeiffer, 2003).

5 W. Bennis and R. Townsend, *Reinventing Leadership* (New York: William Morrow, 1995).

6 G. Yukl, *Leadership in Organizations,* 6th ed. (Upper Saddle River, NJ: Pearson Prentice Hall, 2006); B. M. Bass, *Bass & Stogdill's Handbook of Leadership: Theory, Research, and Managerial Applications,* 3rd ed. (New York: Free Press, 1990); R. J. House and M. L. Baetz, "Leadership: Some Empirical Generalizations and New Research Generalizations," in *Research in Organizational Behavior,* L. L. Cummings and B. M. Staw, eds. (Greenwich, CT: JAI Press, 1979).

7 Yukl, *Leadership in Organizations;* Bass, *Bass & Stogdill's Handbook of Leadership.*

8 J. A. F. Stoner, R. E. Freeman, and D. R. Gilbert Jr., *Management,* 6th ed. (Englewood Cliffs, NJ: Prentice Hall, 1995).

9 S. P. Robbins and M. Coulter, *Management,* 6th ed. (Upper Saddle River, NJ: Pearson Prentice Hall, 2006); Jerome A. Colletti and Mary S. Fiss, "The Ultimately Accountable Job Leading Today's Sales Organization," *Harvard Business Review,* July–August 2006, pp. 125–31.

10 This definition is drawn from various sources: A. J. Dubrin, *Leadership: Research Findings, Practice and Skills,* 2nd ed. (Boston: Houghton Mifflin, 1998); F. J. Yammarino, F. Dansereau, and C. J. Kennedy, "A Multiple-Level Multidimensional Approach to Leadership: Viewing Leadership through an Elephant's Eye," *Organizational Dynamics* (winter 2001): 149–63.

11 T. N. Ingram, R. W. LaForge, R. A. Avila, and C. H. Schwepker et al., *Sales Management: Analysis and Decision Making,* 4th ed. (Mason, OH: Thomson South-Western, 2006); T. N. Ingram, R. W. LaForge, and T. W. Leigh, "Selling in the New Millennium: A Joint Agenda," *Industrial Marketing Management* 31, no. 6, (2002): 559–67; Thomas N. Ingram, Raymond W. LaForge, William B. Locander, and Scott B. MacKenzie et al., "New Directions in Sales Leadership Research," *Journal of Personal Selling & Sales Management* (spring 2005): 137–54.

12 Colletti and Fiss, "Ultimately Accountable Job"; William B. Locander and David L. Luechauer, "Are We There Yet?" *Marketing Management,* November–December 2005, pp. 50–52; Dianne Ledingham, Mark Kovac, and Heidi Locke Simon, "The New Science of Sales Force Productivity," *Harvard Business Review,* September 2006, pp. 124–33; Edward C. Bursk "Low-Pressure Selling," *Harvard Business Review,* July–August 2006, pp. 150–62; Barry Trailer and Jim Dickie, "Understanding What Your Sales Manager Is Up Against," *Harvard Business Review,* July–August 2006, pp. 48–55.

13 Ingram et al., "New Directions in Sales Leadership Research."

14 Erin Anderson and Vincent Onyemah, "How Right Should the Customer Be?" *Harvard Business Review,* July–August 2006, pp. 59–67; J. Whitfield, "Leadership, Power, Productivity and You!" *Marketing Times,* September–October 1985, pp. 7–8.

15 Bennis and Townsend, *Reinventing Leadership.*

16 Bass, *Bass & Stogdill's Handbook of Leadership;* Yukl, *Leadership in Organizations.*

17 T. R. Hinkin and C. A. Scrieshiem, "Development and Application of New Scales to Measure the French and Raven (1959) Bases of Social Power," *Journal of Applied Psychology* (August 1989): 561–67; P. Busch, "The Sales Manager's Bases of Social Power and Influence upon the Sales Force," *Journal of Marketing* (summer 1980): 91–101; P. Busch and D. Wilson, "An Experimental Analysis of a Salesman's Expert and Referent Bases of Social Power in the Buyer-Seller Dyad," *Journal of Marketing Research* (February 1976): 3–11. For other perspectives on sources of power, see: B. Rosenbloom, *Marketing Channels: A Management View* (Mason, OH: Thomson South-Western, 2004); A. T. Coughlan, E. Anderson, L. W. Stern, and A. I. Ansary, *Marketing Channels,* 7th ed. (Upper Saddle River, NJ: Pearson Prentice Hall, 2006).

18 A. H. Thomson, *The Feldman Method: The Words and Working Philosophy of the World's Greatest Insurance Salesman* (Lynbrook, NY: Farnsworth, 1980); "The Selling Legacy of Ben Feldman," prospectingprofessor.blogs.com/ prospecting_professor/success_stories/index.html (accessed September 4, 2006).

19 G. Yukl and T. Tabor, "The Effective Use of Managerial Power," *Personnel Journal* (March–April 1983): 37–44.

20 Michael Ahearne, John Mathieu, and Adam Rapp, "To Empower or Not to Empower Your Sales Force? An Empirical Examination of the Influence of Leadership and Empowerment Behavior on Customer Satisfaction and Performance," *Journal of Applied Psychology* 90, no. 5, (2005): 945–55; D. Helbriegel and J. W. Slocum Jr., *Management* (Reading, MA: Addison-Wesley, 1986): 447.

21 For example, see: S. C. Koch and K. W. Irle, "Prophesysing Army Promotion," *Journal of Applied Psychology* 4 (1920): 73–87; Ralph M. Stogdill, "Personal Factors Associated with Leadership: A Survey of the Literature," *Journal of Psychology* 25 (1948): 35–71; R. M. Stogdill and A. E. Cooms (eds.), *Leader Behavior: Its Description and Measurement, Research Monograph No. 88* (Columbus, OH: Ohio State University, Bureau of Business Research, 1957).

22 Bass, *Bass & Stogdill's Handbook of Leadership.*

23 A. W. Gouldner (ed.), *Studies in Leadership* (New York: Harper 1950): 23–24, 31–35.

24 Stogdill and Cooms, *Leader Behavior.*

25 R. Likert, "From Production- and Employee-Centeredness to Systems 1–4," *Journal of Management* 5 (1979): 147–56.

26 A. K. Korman, "Consideration, Initiating Structure, and Organizational Criteria—A Review," *Personnel Psychology* 19 (1966): 349–62.

27 S. Kerr et al. "Towards a Contingency Theory of Leadership Based upon the Consideration and Initiating Structure

Literature," *Organizational Behavior & Human Performance* 12 (1974): 62–82.

[28] F. E. Fiedler, *A Theory of Leadership Effectiveness* (New York: McGraw-Hill, 1967.

[29] F. E. Fiedler, "The Leadership Game: Matching the Man to the Situation," *Organizational Dynamics* 4 (Winter 1976): 6–16.

[30] F. E. Fiedler, "The Trouble with Leadership Is that It Doesn't Train Leaders," *Psychology Today,* February 1973, pp. 23–30.

[31] O. Behling and C. Schriesheim, *Organizational Behavior: Theory, Research and Application* (Boston: Allyn and Bacon, 1976).

[32] M. G. Evans, "The Effects of Supervisory Behavior on the Path-Goal Relationship," *Organizational Behavior and Human Performance* 51 (May 1970): 277–98.

[33] R. J. House, "A Path-Goal Theory of Leader Effectiveness," *Administrative Science Quarterly* 16 (September 1971): 321–38; R. J. House and T. R. Mitchell, "A Path-Goal Theory of Leadership," *Journal of Contemporary Business* 3 (autumn 1974): 81–97; M. G. Evans, "Extensions of a Path-Goal Theory of Motivation," *Journal of Applied Psychology* 59 (April 1974): 172–78; M. G. Evans, "Path-Goal Theory of Leadership," in *Leadership,* L. L. Neider and C. A. Scriesheim, eds. (Greenwich, CT: Information Age Publishing, 2002): 115–38.

[34] House, "Path-Goal Theory of Leader Effectiveness"; House and Mitchell, "Path-Goal Theory of Leadership."

[35] House, "Path-Goal Theory of Leader Effectiveness"; House and Mitchell, "Path-Goal Theory of Leadership"; R. J. House and G. Dessler, "The Path-Goal Theory of Leadership: Some Post Hoc and A Priori Tests," in *Contingency Approaches to Leadership,* James Hunt and Lars Larson, eds. (Carbondale, IL: Southern Illinois University Press, 1974).

[36] R. J. House, "Path-Goal Theory of Leadership: Lessons, Legacy, and a Reformulated Theory," *Leadership Quarterly* 7 (autumn 1996): 323–52.

[37] Frank V. Cespedes, Alston Gardner, Steve Kerr, and Randall D. Kelley et al., "Old Hand or New Blood?" *Harvard Business Review,* July–August 2006, pp. 28–40; Ingram et al., "New Directions in Sales Leadership Research."

[38] House and Mitchell, "Path-Goal Theory of Leadership."

[39] Martin and Bush, "Psychological Climate, Empowerment, Leadership Style, and Customer-Oriented Selling."

[40] "Strategic Partnerships," www.giantstepsmts.com/partnerships.htm.

[41] Discussion of "Theory H" is largely based on T. F. Stroh, *Effective Psychology for Sales Managers* (West Nyack, NY: Parker Publishing, 1974): 59–70.

[42] R. A. Gumpert and R. K. Hambleton, "Situational Leadership: How Xerox Managers Fine-Tune Managerial Styles to Employee Maturity and Task Needs," *Management Review,* December 1979, pp. 8–12.

[43] S. B. Castleberry and J. F. Tanner, "The Manager-Salesperson Relationship: An Exploratory Examination of the Vertical-Dyad Linkage Model," *Journal of Personal Selling & Sales Management* 6 (November 1986): 29–37.

[44] T. E. DeCarlo and T. W. Leigh, "Impact of Salesperson Attraction on Sales Managers' Attributions and Feedback," *Journal of Marketing,* 60 (April 1996): 47–66.

[45] C. O. Swift and C. Campbell, "The Effect of Vertical Exchange Relationships on the Performance Attributions and Subsequent Actions of Sales Managers," *Journal of Personal Selling & Sales Management* 15 (fall 1995): 45–56.

[46] Lagace, "Leader-Member Exchange."

[47] Lagace, "Leader-Member Exchange"; Tanner and Castleberry, "Vertical Exchange Quality and Performance."

[48] Tanner and Castleberry, "Vertical Exchange Quality and Performance"; Tanner, Dunn, and Chonko, "Vertical Exchange and Salesperson Stress."

[49] Tanner and Castleberry, "Vertical Exchange Quality and Performance."

[50] Tara Lopez and Amy McMillan-Capehart, "How Outgroup Salespeople Fit in or Fail to Fit in: A Proposed Acculturation Effects Framework," *Journal of Personal Selling & Sales Management* (fall 2002): 297–309.

[51] S. Kerr and J. M. Jermier, "Substitutes for Leadership: Their Meaning and Measurement," *Organizational Behavior & Human Performance* (December 1978): 375–403.

[52] C. C. Mang and H. P. Sims Jr., "Leading Workers to Lead Themselves: The External Leadership of Self-Managing Work Teams," *Administrative Science Quarterly* 32 (March 1987): 106–29.

[53] Bass, *Bass & Stogdill's Handbook of Leadership.*

[54] Steven J. Skinner and Scott W. Kelley, "Transforming Sales Organizations Through Appreciative Inquiry," *Psychology & Marketing* 23, no. 2 (2006): 77–93.

[55] Dubinsky et al., "Transformational Leadership."

[56] F. A. Russ, K. M. McNeilly, and J. Comer, "Leadership, Decision Making and Performance of Sales Managers," *Journal of Personal Selling & Sales Management* (summer 1996): 1–5.

[57] B. J. Avolio and B. M. Bass, "Transformational Leadership, Charisma and Beyond," in *Emerging Leadership Vistas,* J. G. Hunt et al., eds. (Lexington, MA: Lexington Books, 1988), 29–49.

[58] Russ et al., "Leadership, Decision Making and Performance of Sales Managers."

[59] B. M. Bass, *Leadership and Performance Beyond Expectations* (New York: Free Press, 1985).

[60] K. J. Klein and R. J. House, "On Fire: Charismatic Leadership and Levels of Analysis," *Leadership Quarterly* 6, no. 2 (1995): 183–98.

[61] Walter A. Friedman, "Give Me That Old-Time Motivation," *Harvard Business Review,* July–August 2006, p. 24.

[62] Dubinsky et al., "Transformational Leadership."

[63] Robbins and Coulter, *Management*; N. H. Snyder and M. Graves, "Leadership and Vision," *Business Horizons* (January–February 1994): 1.

[64] Clayton M. Christensen, Matt Marx, and Howard H. Stevenson, "The Tools of Cooperation and Change," *Harvard Business Review*, October 2006, pp. 73–80.

[65] J. A. Conger and R. N. Kanungo, *Charismatic Leadership in Organizations* (Thousand Oaks, CA: Sage, 1998).

[66] Dubinsky et al., "Transformational Leadership."

[67] D. Stavros, "We Kept Reinventing the Wheel," *What's Working in Sales Management*, September 10, 1997, p. 5.

[68] B. Marcil, "We Knocked on Too Many Doors That Would Never Open," *What's Working in Sales Management*, July 23, 1997, p. 5.

[69] A. J. Dubinsky, F. J. Yammarino, and M. A. Jolson, "Closeness of Supervision and Salesperson Work Outcomes: An Alternative Perspective," *Journal of Business Research* 29 (March 1994): 225–37; F. J. Yammarino, A. J. Dubinsky, L. B. Comer, and M. A. Jolson, "Women and Transformational and Contingent Reward Leadership: A Multiple-Levels-of-Analysis Perspective," *Academy of Management Journal* 40, no. 1 (1997): 205–22.

[70] Russ et al., "Leadership, Decision Making and Performance of Sales Managers."

[71] R. J. Markin and C. M. Lillis, "Sales Managers Get What They Expect," *Business Horizons* 18 (June 1975): 51–58.

[72] D. Eden, "Leadership and Expectations: Pygmalion Effects and Other Self-Fulfilling Prophecies in Organizations," *Leadership Quarterly* 3 (winter 1992): 271–305.

[73] Ibid.

[74] W. A. Randolph and M. Sashkin, "Can Organizational Empowerment Work in Multinational Settings?" *Academy of Management Executive* 16 (February 2002): 104; S. E. Seibert, S. R. Silver, and W. A. Randolph, "Taking Empowerment to the Next Level: A Multiple-Level Model of Empowerment," *Academy of Management Journal* 47 (June 2004): 332–49; H. Mintzberg, "Enough Leadership," *Harvard Business Review*, November 2004, p. 22.

[75] R. C. Ford and M. D. Fottler, "Empowerment: A Matter of Degree," *Academy of Management Executive* 9, no. 3 (1995): 21–31.

[76] M. Sashkin, "Participative Management Is an Ethical Imperative," *Organizational Dynamics* 12 (spring 1984): 4–22.

[77] Clayton M. Christensen, Matt Marx, and Howard H. Stevenson, "The Tools of Cooperation and Change," *Harvard Business Review*, October 2006, pp. 73–80; Ashraf M. Attia, Earl D. Honeycutt Jr., and Mark P. Leach, "A Three-Stage Model for Assessing and Improving Sales Force Training and Development," *Journal of Personal Selling & Sales Management* 25 (Summer 2005): 253–68; Mark P. Leach, Annie H. Liu, and Wesley J. Johnston, "The Role of Self-Regulation Training in Developing the Motivation Management Capabilities of

Salespeople," *Journal of Personal Selling & Sales Management* 25 (summer 2005): 269–81. R. Forrester, "Empowerment: Rejuvenating a Potent Idea," *Academy of Management Executive*, 14 (3) 2000): 67–80.

[78] R. Semler, "How We Went Digital Without a Strategy," *Harvard Business Review*, September–October 2000, pp. 51–58.

[79] Thomas G. Brashear, Danny N. Bellenger, James S. Boles, and Hiram C. Barksdale Jr., "An Exploratory Study of the Relative Effectiveness of Different Types of Sales Force Mentors," *Journal of Personal Selling & Sales Management* 26 (winter 2006): 7–18.

[80] Ford and Fottler, "Empowerment: A Matter of Degree."

[81] R.C. Ford and M.D. Fottler, "Empowerment: A Matter of Degree," *Academy of Management Executive*, 9 (3) 1995, pp: 21–31.

[82] D. E. Bowen and E. E. Lawler III, "The Empowerment of Service Workers: What, Why, How, and When," *Sloan Management Review* 33 (spring 1992): 31–39; R. W. Coy and J. A. Belohav, "An Exploratory Analysis of Employee Participation," *Group & Organization Management* 20 (March 1995): 4–17.

[83] Seibert et al., "Taking Empowerment to the Next Level"; A. Podolske, "Giving Employees a Voice in Pay Structures," *Business Ethics*, March–April 1998, p. 12.

[84] Dictionary of Marketing Terms: www.marketingpower.com.

[85] R. E. Anderson and R. Huang, "Empowering Salespeople: Personal Managerial and Organizational Perspectives," *Psychology & Marketing* 23 (February 2006): 139–59; P. Kotler and G. Armstrong, *Principles of Marketing*, 10th ed. (Upper Saddle River, NJ: Pearson Education International, 2004), 16.

[86] Michael Ahearne, John Mathieu, and Adam Rapp, "To Empower or Not to Empower Your Sales Force? An Empirical Examination of the Influence of Leadership and Empowerment Behavior on Customer Satisfaction and Performance," *Journal of Applied Psychology* 90, no. 5 (2005): 945–955.

[87] R. Simons, "Control in an Age of Empowerment," *Harvard Business Review*, March–April 1995, pp. 80–88.

[88] T. L. Quick, "Curbstone Coaching," *Sales & Marketing Management*, July 1990, pp. 100–101.

[89] Thomas G. Brashear, Danny N. Bellenger, James S. Boles, and Hiram C. Barksdale Jr., "An Exploratory Study of the Relative Effectiveness of Different Types of Sales Force Mentors," *Journal of Personal Selling & Sales Management* 26 (Winter 2006): 7–18

[90] C. O. Longenecker and M. J. Neubert, "The Practices of Effective Managerial Coaches," *Business Horizons* 48 (2005): 493–500; Erin Anderson and Vincent Onyemah, "How Right Should the Customer Be?" *Harvard Business Review*, July–August 2006, pp. 59–67.

[91] L. B. Comer, M. A. Jolson, A. J. Dubinsky, and F. J. Yammarino, "When the Sales Manager Is a Woman: An Exploration in

the Relationship between Salespeople's Gender and Their Responses to Leadership Styles," *Journal of Personal Selling & Sales Management* (fall 1995): 17–32.

92 A. J. Dubinsky, L. B. Comer, M. A. Jolson, and F. J. Yammarino, "How Should Women Sales Managers Lead Their Sales Personnel?" *Journal of Business & Industrial Marketing* 11, no. 2 (1996): 47–59.

93 Ibid.

94 Comer et al., "When the Sales Manager Is a Woman."

95 C. L. Bovee and J. V. Thill, *Business Communication Today,* 9th ed. (Upper Saddle River, NJ: Pearson Prentice Hall, 2008).

96 E. Rogers and R. Rogers, *Communications in Organizations* (New York: Free Press, 1976).

97 P. Morgan and H. K. Baker, "Building a Professional Image: Improving Listening Behavior," *Supervisory Management,* November 1985, pp. 35–36.

98 Bovee and Thill, *Business Communication Today.*

99 M. L. Hickson III and D. W. Stacks, *Nonverbal Communications: Studies and Applications* (Dubuque, IA: Wm. C. Brown, 1985.

Chapter 11

1 Al Ries and Jack Trout, *Marketing Warfare* (New York: McGraw-Hill, 1997).

2 Jay Conrad Levinson, *Guerrilla Marketing: Secrets for Making Big Profits from Your Small Business,* 3rd ed. (Boston: Houghton Mifflin, 1998); Jay Conrad Levinson and Seth Godin, *The Guerrilla Marketing Handbook* (Boston: Houghton Mifflin, 1994).

3 Jerome A. Colletti and Mary S. Fiss, "The Ultimately Accountable Job: Leading Today's Sales Organization," *Harvard Business Review,* July–August 2006, pp. 125–31.

4 Walter A. Friedman "Give Me That Old-Time Motivation," *Harvard Business Review,* July–August 2006, pp. 24; David Mayer and Herbert M. Greenberg, "What Makes a Good Salesman," Harvard Business Review, July–August 2006, pp. 164–71; Diane Coutu, "Leveraging the Psychology of the Salesperson: A Conversation with Psychologist and Anthropologist G. Clotaire Rapaille," *Harvard Business Review,* July–August 2006, pp. 42–47; Mrugank V. Thakor and Ashwin W. Joshi, "Motivating Salesperson Customer Orientation: Insights from the Job Characteristics Model," *Journal of Business Research* 58, no. 5 (2005): 584–92; Thomas N. Ingram, Raymond W. LaForge, William B. Locander, and Scott B. MacKenzie et al., "New Directions in Sales Leadership Research," *Journal of Personal Selling & Sales Management* 25 (spring 2005): 137–54.

5 C. Pinder, *Work Motivation* (Glenview, IL: Scott, Foresman, 1984).

6 *Harvard Business Review on Motivating People* (Cambridge, MA: Harvard Business School Press Books, 2003).

7 Abraham H. Maslow, *Motivation and Personality* (New York: Harper & Row, 1954).

8 Clayton P. Alderfer, *Existence, Relatedness, and Growth* (New York: Free Press, 1972).

9 David C. McClelland, *Human Motivation* (Glenview, IL: Scott, Foresman, 1985).

10 Douglas Amyx and Bruce L. Alford, "The Effects of Salesperson Need for Achievement and Sales Manager Leader Reward Behavior," *Journal of Personal Selling & Sales Management* 25 (fall 2005): 345–59.

11 Saul W. Gellerman, *Motivation and Productivity* (Stanford, CA: American Management Association, 1978): 115–41, reviewing Stanley Schacter, *The Psychology of Affiliation* (Stanford, CA: Stanford University Press, 1959).

12 Dianne Ledingham, Mark Kovac, and Heidi Locke Simon, "The New Science of Sales Force Productivity," *Harvard Business Review,* September 2006, pp. 124–33; Frederick Herzberg, "One More Time: How Do You Motivate Employees?" *Harvard Business Review,* January 2003, pp. 4–11; Frederick B. Herzberg, Bernard Mausner, and Barbara Snyderman, *The Motivation to Work* (New York: Wiley, 1959).

13 Ibid.

14 Robert L. Berl, Nicholas C. Williamson, and Terry Powell, "Industrial Salesforce Motivation: A Critique and Test of Maslow's Hierarchy of Need," *Journal of Personal Selling & Sales Management* 4 (May 1984): 33–39; David D. Shipley and Julia A. Kiely, "Industrial Salesforce Motivation and Herzberg's Dual Factor Theory: A UK Perspective," *Journal of Personal Selling & Sales Management* 6 (May 1986): 9–16.

15 Tom Reilly, "Motivation Isn't External," *What's Working in Sales Management,* September 10, 1997, pp. 3.

16 Herzberg, "One More Time."

17 P. S. Goodman and A. Friedman, "An Examination of Adams' Theory of Inequity," *Administrative Science Quarterly* 16 (1971): 271–88.

18 Victor Vroom, *Work and Motivation* (New York: Wiley, 1964).

19 John P. Campbell, Marvin D. Dunnette, Edward E. Lawler III, and Karl E. Weick Jr., *Managerial Behavior, Performance, and Effectiveness* (New York: McGraw-Hill, 1970).

20 R. P. Bagozzi, "Salesforce Performance and Satisfaction as a Function of Individual Difference, Interpersonal and Situational Factors," *Journal of Marketing Research* 15 (November 1978): 517–31; Ajay Kohli, "Some Unexplored Supervisory Behaviors and Their Influence on Salespeople's Role Clarity, Specific Self-Esteem, Job Satisfaction, and Motivation," *Journal of Marketing Research* 22 (November 1985): 424–33; R. Kenneth Teas, "Performance-Reward Instrumentalities and the Motivation of Salespeople," *Journal of Retailing* 58 (fall 1982): 4–26; R. Kenneth Teas and James C. McElroy, "Causal Attributions and Expectancy Estimates: A Framework for Understanding the Dynamics of Salesforce Motivation," *Journal of Marketing* 50 (January 1986): 75–86;

P. Tyagi, "Relative Importance of Key Job Dimensions and Leadership Behaviors in Motivating Salesperson Work Performance," *Journal of Marketing* 49 (summer 1985): 76–86; Neil M. Ford, G. A. Churchill, and O. C. Walker Jr., *Sales Force Performance* (Lexington, MA: D. C. Heath, 1985).

21 Mark S. Johnson, "A Bibliometric Review of the Contribution of Attribution Theory to Sales Management," *Journal of Personal Selling & Sales Management* 26 (spring 2006): 181–95; Andrea L. Dixon, Lukas P. Forbes, and Susan M. B. Schertzer, "Early Success: How Attributions for Sales Success Shape Inexperienced Salespersons' Behavioral Intentions," *Journal of Personal Selling & Sales Management* (winter 2005): 67–77; Harish Sujan, "Smarter versus Harder: An Exploratory Attributional Analysis of Salespeople's Motivations," *Journal of Marketing Research* (February 1986): 41–49; Teas and McElroy, "Causal Attributions."

22 Michael L. Mallin and Michael Mayo, "Why Did I Lose? A Conservation of Resources View of Salesperson Failure Attributions," *Journal of Personal Selling & Sales Management* (fall 2006): 345–57; Eric Fang, Kenneth R. Evans, and Timothy D. Landry, "Control Systems' Effect on Attributional Processes and Sales Outcomes: A Cybernetic Information-Processing Perspective," *Journal of the Academy of Marketing Science* 33, no. 4 (2005): 553–74; Andrea L. Dixon and Susan M. B. Schertzer, "Bouncing Back: How Salesperson Optimism and Self-Efficacy Influence Attributions and Behaviors Following Failure," *Journal of Personal Selling & Sales Management* (fall 2005): 361–69.

23 Harish Sujan and Barton A. Weitz, "The Psychology of Motivation," *Marketing Communications,* January 1986, pp. 24–28.

24 Eric Fang, Kenneth R. Evans, and Shaoming Zou, "The Moderating Effect of Goal-Setting Characteristics on the Sales Control Systems–Job Performance Relationship," *Journal of Business Research* 58, no. 9 (2005): 1214–22; Eric G. Harris, John C. Mowen, and Tom J. Brown, "Re-Examining Salesperson Goal Orientations: Personality Influencers, Customer Orientation, and Work Satisfaction," *Journal of the Academy of Marketing Science* 33, no. 1 (2005): 19–35; Mark Cotteleer, Edward Inderrieden, and Felissa Lee, "Selling the Sales Force on Automation," *Harvard Business Review,* July–August 2006, pp. 18–22.

25 Cotteleer et al., "Selling the Sales Force on Automation"; Ledingham et al., "New Science of Sales Force Productivity."

26 J. Sterling Livingston, "Pygmalion in Management," *Harvard Business Review,* January 2003, pp. 4–12; Dov Eden, "Pygmalion, Goal Setting and Expectancy: Compatible Ways to Boost Productivity," *Academy of Management Review* 13 (October 1988): 639–52; Gary P. Yatham, Miriam Erez, and Edwin A. Locke, "Resolving Scientific Disputes by the Joint Design of Crucial Experiments by the Erez-Yatham Dispute Regarding Participation in Goal-Setting," *Journal of Applied Psychology* 73 (November 1988): 753–72.

27 Robert A. Weaver, "Set Goals to Tap Self-Motivation," *Business Marketing,* December 1985, pp. 55.

28 B. F. Skinner, *Science and Human Behavior* (New York: Macmillan, 1953); A. D. Stajkovic and F. Luthans, "A Meta Analysis of the Effects of Organizational Behavior Modification on Task Performance, 1975–1995," *Academy of Management Journal* 40 (October 1997): 1122–49.

29 Robert A. Scott, John E. Swan, M. Elizabeth Wilson, and Jenny J. Roberts, "Organizational Behavior Modification: A General Motivational Tool for Sales Management," *Journal of Personal Selling & Sales Management* 6 (August 1986): 61–70.

30 Ronald Jelinek and Michael Ahearne, "The Enemy Within: Examining Salesperson Deviance and its Determinants," *Journal of Personal Selling & Sales Management* 26 (fall 2006): 327–44; Charles H. Schwepker Jr. and David J. Good, "Understanding Sales Quotas: An Exploratory Investigation of Consequences of Failure," *Journal of Business & Industrial Marketing* 19 (1, 2004): 39–48. See also Ledingham et al., "New Science of Sales Force Productivity."

31 N. Byrnes, "The Art of Motivation," *Business Week,* May 1, 2006, pp. 56–62.

32 Ibid., pp. 57.

33 Philip Kotler, Neil Rackham, and Suj Krishnaswamy, "Ending the War Between Sales & Marketing," *Harvard Business Review,* July–August 2006, pp. 68–78; Andris A. Zoltners, Prabhakant Sinha, and Sally E. Lorimer, "Match Your Sales Force Structure to Your Business Life Cycle," *Harvard Business Review,* July–August 2006, pp. 81–89.

34 Tará Burnthorne Lopez, Christopher D. Hopkins, and Mary Anne Raymond, "Reward Preferences of Salespeople: How Do Commissions Rate?" *Journal of Personal Selling & Sales Management* 26 (fall 2006): 381–90.

35 Barry Trailer and Jim Dickie, "Understanding What Your Sales Manager Is Up Against," *Harvard Business Review,* July–August 2006, pp. 48–55; Steven P. Brown, Kenneth R. Evans, Murali K. Mantrala, and Goutam Challagalla, "Adapting Motivation, Control, and Compensation Research to A New Environment," *Journal of Personal Selling & Sales Management* 25 (spring 2005): 156–67; Edward C. Bursk, "Low-Pressure Selling," *Harvard Business Review,* July–August 2006, pp. 150–62; Frank V. Cespedes, Alston Gardner, Steve Kerr, and Randall D. Kelley et al., "Old Hand or New Blood?" *Harvard Business Review,* July–August 2006, 28–40; Chester A. Schriesheim, Stephanie L. Castro, Xiaohua (Tracy) Zhou, and Leslie A. DeChurch, "An investigation of path-goal and transformational leadership theory predictions at the individual level of analysis," *Leadership Quarterly,* 17, February 2006: 21–38

36 Clayton M. Christensen, Matt Marx, and Howard H. Stevenson, "The Tools of Cooperation and Change," *Harvard Business Review,* October 2006: 73–80.

37 William H. Murphy, "In Pursuit of Short-Term Goals: Anticipating the Unintended Consequences of Using Special Incentives to Motivate the Sales Force," *Journal of Business Research* 57 (2004): 1265–75.

38 "All Levels of Sales Reps Post Impressive Earnings Gains," *American Salesman,* March 1997, pp. 18–20.

39 Martha C. White, "Bon Voyage as a Bonus," *New York Times,* March 13, 2007, pp. C9; http://www.nytimes.com/2007/03/13/business/13incentive.html?_r=1&oref=slogin (accessed April 2007).

40 Ibid.

41 "Survey Facts 1989," *Incentive,* December 1989, pp. 21–37.

42 "Business and Incentive Strategies," *American Salesman,* January 1994, pp. 22–24.

43 Colletti and Fiss, "Ultimately Accountable Job"; Erin Anderson and Vincent Onyemah, "How Right Should the Customer Be?" *Harvard Business Review,* July–August 2006, pp. 59–67; Ledingham et al., "New Science of Sales Force Productivity."

44 See R. C. Smyth and M. J. Murphy, *Compensating and Motivating Salesmen* (New York: American Management Association, 1969); A. Haring and M. L. Morris, *Contests, Prizes, Awards for Sales Motivation* (New York: Sales and Marketing Executives International, 1968; D. A. Welks, *Incentive Plans for Salesmen* (New York: The National Industrial Conference Board, 1970).

45 See C. P. Alderfer, "An Empirical Test of a New Theory of Human Needs," *Organizational Behavior and Human Performance* 4 (1969): 142–75; Herzberg et al., *Motivation to Work;* Edward E. Lawler III, *Pay and Organizational Effectiveness: A Psychological View* (New York: McGraw-Hill, 1971); R. L. Opsahl and M. D. Dunnette, "The Role of Financial Compensation in Industrial Motivation," *Psychological Bulletin* 66 (1966): 94–118; Vincent Alonzo, "Selling Changes," *Incentive,* September 1996, pp. 45–46.

46 Philip Evans and Bob Wolf, "Collaboration Rules," *Harvard Business Review,* July–August 2006, pp. 96–104.

47 Vincent Alonzo, "Recognition? Who Needs It?" *Sales & Marketing Management,* July 1996, pp. 45–46.

48 Leslie Brennan, "Sales Secrets of the Incentive Starts," *Sales & Marketing Management,* April 1990, pp. 92–100.

49 Ibid.

50 Herzberg, "One More Time."

51 Mark P. Leach, Annie H. Liu, and Wesley J. Johnston, "The Role of Self-Regulation Training in Developing the Motivation Management Capabilities of Salespeople," *Journal of Personal Selling & Sales Management* 25 (summer 2005): 269–81; Deva Rangarajan, Eli Jones, and Wynne Chin, "Impact of Sales Force Automation on Technology-Related Stress, Effort, and Technology Usage Among Salespeople," *Industrial Marketing Management* 34, no. 4 (2005): 345–54.

52 For a detailed discussion of sales meetings, see Rolph Anderson and Bert Rosenbloom, "Conducting Successful Sales Meetings," in John L. DiGaetani (ed.), *The Handbook of Executive Communication* (Homewood, IL: Dow Jones-Irwin, 1986): 611–32.

53 Chad Kaydo, "Unforgettable Meetings," *Sales & Marketing Management,* February 1998, pp. 71–76.

54 Karen Hitchcock, "Should Work Be Fun?" *Sales Manager's Bulletin: Special Report,* 1407, Section II (August 30, 1997): 3.

55 "How Avon Rings Their Chimes," Sales & Marketing Management, November 1986, pp. 117–18.

56 Ibid., pp. 118.

57 George J. Avlonitis and Nikolaos G. Panagopoulos, "Role Stress, Attitudes, and Job Outcomes in Business-To-Business Selling: Does the Type of Selling Situation Matter?" *Journal of Personal Selling & Sales Management* 26 (winter 2006): 67–77.

58 Fernando Jaramillo, Jay Prakash Mulki, and Greg W. Marshall, "A Meta-Analysis of the Relationship Between Organizational Commitment and Salesperson Job Performance: 25 Years of Research," *Journal of Business Research* 58 (June 2005): 705–14; Jay Prakash Mulki, Fernando Jaramillo, and William B. Locander, "Effects of Ethical Climate and Supervisory Trust on Salesperson's Job Attitudes and Intentions to Quit," *Journal of Personal Selling & Sales Management* 26 (winter 2006): 19–26; Elizabeth J. Rozell, Charles E. Pettijohn, and R. Stephen Parker, "Customer-Oriented Selling: Exploring the Roles of Emotional Intelligence and Organizational Commitment," *Psychology and Marketing* 21, no. 6 (2004): 405–24.

59 Alan J. Dubinsky and Steven J. Skinner, "Impact of Job Characteristics on Retail Salespeople's Reactions to Their Jobs," *Journal of Retailing* 60 (summer 1984): 35–63; Thomas N. Ingram, Keun S. Lee, and Steven J. Skinner, "An Empirical Assessment of Salesperson Motivation, Commitment, and Job Outcomes," *Journal of Personal Selling & Sales Management* 9 (fall 1989): 25–33; Thomas N. Ingram, Keun S. Lee, and George H. Lucas, "Commitment and Involvement: Assessing a Sales Force Typology," *Journal of the Academy of Marketing Science* 19 (summer 1991): 187–97; Jeffrey K. Sager and Mark W. Johnston, "Antecedents and Outcomes of Organizational Commitment: A Study of Salespeople," *Journal of Personal Selling & Sales Management* 9 (spring 1989): 30–41.

60 Frederick F. Reichheld, "Loyalty-Based Management," *Harvard Business Review,* March–April 1993, pp. 64–73.

61 Ingram et al., "New Directions in Sales Leadership Research"; William A. Weeks, Terry W. Loe, Lawrence B. Chonko, and Kirk Wakefield, "The Effect of Perceived Ethical Climate on the Search for Sales Force Excellence," *Journal of Personal Selling & Sales Management* 24 (summer 2004): 199–214; Mulki et al., "Effects of Ethical Climate and Supervisory Trust."

62 Sergio Román and Salvador Ruiz, "Relationship Outcomes of Perceived Ethical Sales Behavior: The Customer's Perspective," *Journal of Business Research* 58, no. 4 (2005): 439–45; Emin Babakus, David W. Cravens, Mark Johnston, and William C. Moncrief, "Examining the Role of Organizational Variables in the Salesperson Job Satisfaction Model," *Journal of Personal Selling & Sales Management* 16 (Summer 1996): 33–46; Pradeep K. Tyagi, "Perceived Organizational Climate and the Process of Salesperson Motivation," *Journal of Marketing Research* 19 (May 1982): 240–54; Thomas N. Ingram and Danny N. Bellenger, "Personal and Organizational Variables:

Their Relative Effect on Reward Valences of Industrial Salespeople," *Journal of Marketing Research* 20 (May 1983): 198–205; Pradeep K. Tyagi, "Relative Importance of Key Job Dimensions and Leadership Behaviors in Motivating Salesperson Work Performance," *Journal of Marketing* 49 (summer 1985): 76–86; Schwepker and Good, "Understanding Sales Quotas."

63 Lawrence S. Silver, Sean Dwyer, and Bruce Alford, "Learning and Performance Goal Orientation of Salespeople Revisited: The Role of Performance-Approach and Performance-Avoidance Orientations," *Journal of Personal Selling & Sales Management* 26 (winter 2006): 27–38; Harris et al., "Re-Examining Salesperson Goal Orientations."

64 Lawrence B. Chonko, Alan J. Dubinsky, Eli Jones, and James A. Roberts, "Organizational and Individual Learning in the Sales Force: An Agenda for Sales Research," *Journal of Business Research* 56 (2003): 935–46; Sanjog Misra, Edieal J. Pinker, and Robert A. Shumsky, "Sales Force Design with Experience-Based Learning," *IIE Transactions* 36, no. 10 (2004), 941–52.

65 Harish Sujan, Barton A. Weitz, and Nirmalya Kumar, "Learning Orientation, Working Smart, and Effective Selling," *Journal of Marketing* 58 (January 1994): 39–52.

66 Harish Sujan, Barton A. Weitz, and Mita Sujan, "Increasing Sales Productivity by Getting Salespeople to Work Smarter," *Journal of Personal Selling & Sales Management* 8 (August 1988): 9–19.

67 Thomas R. Wotruba and Edwin K. Simpson, *Sales Management: Text and Cases* (Boston: PWS-Kent Publishing, 1992).

68 Bulent Menguc and Shahid N. Bhuian, "Career Stage Effects on Job Characteristic—Job Satisfaction Relationships Among Guest Worker Salespersons," *Journal of Personal Selling & Sales Management* 24 (summer 2004): 215–27; William L. Cron, "Industrial Salesperson Development: A Career Stages Perspective," *Journal of Marketing* 48 (fall 1984): 41–52; Marvin A. Jolson, "The Salesman's Career Cycle," *Journal of Marketing* 38 (July 1974): 39–46.

69 William L. Cron, Alan J. Dubinsky, and Ronald E. Michaels, "The Influence of Career Stages on Components of Salesperson Motivation," *Journal of Marketing* 52 (January 1988): 78–92.

70 John C. Hafer, "An Empirical Investigation of the Salesperson's Career Stage Perspective," *Journal of Personal Selling & Sales Management* 6 (November 1986): 1–7.

71 Daniel C. Feldman and Barton A. Weitz, "Career Plateaus in the Salesforce: Understanding and Removing Blockages to Employee Growth," *Journal of Personal Selling & Sales Management* 8 (November 1988): 23–32.

72 R. E. Anderson and R. Huang, "Empowering Salespeople: Personal Managerial and Organizational Perspectives," *Psychology & Marketing* 23 (February 2006): 139–59; J. A. Conger and R. N. Kanungo, "The Empowerment Process: Integrating Theory and Practice," *Academy of Management Review* 13 (1988): 471–82.

73 Michael Ahearne, John Mathieu, and Adam Rapp, "To Empower or Not to Empower Your Sales Force? An Empirical Examination of the Influence of Leadership and Empowerment Behavior on Customer Satisfaction and Performance," *Journal of Applied Psychology* 90, no. 5 (2005): 945–55; R. C. Ford and M. D. Fottler, "Empowerment: A Matter of Degree," *Academy of Management Executive* 3 (1995): 21–31; M. Sashkin, "Participative Management Is an Ethical Imperative," *Organizational Dynamics* 12 (spring 1984): 4–22; J. A. Wagner III, "Participation's Effect on Performance and Satisfaction: A Reconsideration of Research Evidence," *Academy of Management Review* 19, no. 2 (1994): 312–30.

74 Ahearne et al., "To Empower or Not to Empower Your Sales Force?"; Anderson and Huang, "Empowering Salespeople"; Steven J. Skinner and Scott W. Kelley, "Transforming Sales Organizations Through Appreciative Inquiry," *Psychology & Marketing* 23, no. 2 (2006): 77–93; D. E. Bowen and E. E. Lawler III, "The Empowerment of Service Workers: What, Why, How, and When," *Sloan Management Review* 33 (spring 1992): 31–39.

Chapter 12

1 http://money.cnn.com/magazines/moneymag/bestjobs/top50/index.html (accessed January 2007).

2 http://money.cnn.com/magazines/moneymag/bestjobs/snapshots/21.html (accessed January 2007).

3 Jerome A. Colletti and Mary S. Fiss, "The Ultimately Accountable Job: Leading Today's Sales Organization," *Harvard Business Review,* July–August 2006, pp. 125–31.

4 Thomas G. Brashear, Chris Manolis, and Charles M. Brooks, "The Effects of Control, Trust, and Justice on Salesperson Turnover," *Journal of Business Research* 58 (March 2005): 241–49; Praveen Aggarwal, John Tanner Jr., and Stephen Castleberry, "Factors Affecting Propensity to Leave: A Study of Salespeople," *Journal of Marketing Management* 14 (1, 2004): 90–102.

5 Jack Welch and Suzy Welch, "The Case for 20-70-10," *Business Week,* October 2, 2006, p. 108; Jack Welch and Suzy Welch, "Send the Jerks Packing," *Business Week,* November 13, 2006, p. 136.

6 J. Welch and S. Welch, "The Case for 20-70-10."

7 "Now Is the Time to Redesign Your Sales Comp Plan," *Report on Salary Surveys,* April 2005, pp. 1–13.

8 Dianne Ledingham, Mark Kovac, and Heidi Locke Simon, "The New Science of Sales Force Productivity," *Harvard Business Review,* September 2006, pp. 124–33; Steven P. Brown, Kenneth R. Evans, Murali K. Mantrala, and Goutam Challagalla, "Adapting Motivation, Control, and Compensation Research to A New Environment," *Journal of Personal Selling & Sales Management* 25 (spring 2005): 156–67.

9 Colin Beasty, "Dangling the Carrot: Drive Your Sales Force to Profitability," *CRM Magazine,* January 2006, pp. 22–26.

10 Barry Trailer and Jim Dickie, "Understanding What Your Sales Manager Is Up Against," *Harvard Business Review,* July–August 2006, pp. 48–55; Brown et al., "Adapting Motivation, Control, and Compensation Research"; Edward C. Bursk, "Low-Pressure Selling," *Harvard Business Review,* July–August 2006, pp. 150–62; Frank V. Cespedes, Alston Gardner, Steve Kerr, and Randall D. Kelley et al., "Old Hand or New Blood?" *Harvard Business Review,* July–August 2006, pp. 28–40.

11 Michelle Bangert, "Performance Pays," *Security Distributing & Marketing,* March 2006, pp. 84–88.

12 "What Motivates People? You Might Be Surprised," *Corporate Meetings & Incentives,* March 2003, pp. 31–32; See also Michael L. Mallin and Michael Mayo, "Why Did I Lose? A Conservation of Resources View of Salesperson Failure Attributions," *Journal of Personal Selling & Sales Management* 26 (fall 2006): 345–57; Andrea L. Dixon and Susan M. B. Schertzer, "Bouncing Back: How Salesperson Optimism and Self-Efficacy Influence Attributions and Behaviors Following Failure," *Journal of Personal Selling & Sales Management* 25 (fall 2005): 361–69.

13 Bangert, "Performance Pays."

14 Michele Mavchetti, "Developing a Competitive Pay Plan," Sales & Marketing Management, (April 1997): 69.

15 Nick DiBari, "Straight Talk," *Sales & Marketing Management,* (October 1984): 48.

16 Michele Mavchetti, "Master Motivators," *Sales & Marketing Management,* 4 (April 1998): 39–44.

17 Rene Y. Darmon, "Salesmen's Response to Financial Incentives: An Empirical Study," *Journal of Marketing Research,* (November 1974): 418–26.

18 Bangert, "Performance Pays"; Beasty, "Dangling the Carrot"; Tará Burnthorne Lopez, Christopher D. Hopkins, and Mary Anne Raymond, "Reward Preferences of Salespeople: How Do Commissions Rate?" *Journal of Personal Selling & Sales Management* 26 (fall 2006): 381–90; "Motivation/Incentives," Sales & Marketing Management, April 2006, p. 18; Julia Chang, Christine Galea, and Julie Barker, "Happy Sales Force, Happy Returns," *Sales & Marketing Management,* March 2006, pp. 32–34; "Rewards to Keep 'Em Empowered Motivated," *Sales & Marketing Management,* March 2006, pp. 35–37; Masha Zager, "Firing Up the Sales Force," *Rural Telecommunications,* May–June 2005, pp. 28–35; "Motivation/Incentives," *Sales & Marketing Management,* November 2005, p. 22; Brown et al., "Adapting Motivation, Control, and Compensation Research"; "What Motivates People? You Might Be Surprised," *Corporate Meetings & Incentives,* March 2003, pp. 31–32; Patricia K. Zingheim and Jay R. Schuster, "Sales Reward Solutions," *Compensation & Benefits Review,* September–October 2004, pp. 21–26.

19 E. E. Lawler, "The Design of Effective Reward Systems," in *Handbook of Organizational Behavior,* ed. J. W. Lorsch (Englewood Cliffs, NJ: Prentice Hall, 1987), 255–71; J. Hale, "Strategic Rewards: Keeping Your Best Talent from Walking Out the Door," *Compensation Benefits Management* 14 (summer 1998): 39–50.

20 Alan Dubinsky, Rolph E. Anderson, and Rajiv Mehta, "Importance of Alternative Rewards: Impact of Managerial Level," *Industrial Marketing Management* 29 (2000): 427–40; E. E. Lawler, "Managers' Perceptions of Their Subordinates' Pay and of Their Superiors' Pay," *Personnel Psychology* 18 (winter 1965): 413–22.

21 E. E. Lawler, "The Strategic Design of Reward Systems," in *Readings in Personnel and Human Resource Management,* ed. R. S. Schuler and S. A. Youngblood (St. Paul, MN: West Publishing, 1984): 253–69; T. Mahoney, "Multiple Pay Contingencies: Strategic Design of Compensation," *Human Resource Management* 28 (1990): 337–47; J. Pfeffer and A. Davis-Blake, "Understanding Organizational Wage Structures: A Resource Dependence Approach," *Academy of Management Journal* 30 (1987): 437–55.

22 Dubinsky et al., "Importance of Alternative Rewards"; S. A. Lynn, L. T. Cao, and B. C. Horn, "The Influence of Career Stage on the Work Attitudes of Male and Female Accounting Professionals," *Journal of Organizational Behavior* 17 (1996): 135–50.

23 B. Beck, "Women and Work: A Survey," *The Economist,* July 18, 1998, pp. 1–16.

24 Lynette J. Ryals and Beth Rogers, "Sales Compensation Plans—One Size Does Not Fit All," *Journal of Targeting, Measurement & Analysis for Marketing* 13 (June 2005): 354–62; R. Broderick, "Innovative Reward Systems for the Changing Workplace," *Compensation & Benefits Management* 4 (autumn 1995): 70–73; B. Leonard, "Perks Give Way to Life-Cycle Benefit Plans," *HRMagazine,* March 1995, pp. 45–47.

25 *Marketing News,* November 7, 1986, p. 1.

26 Philip Kotler and Kevin Lane Keller, *Marketing Management,* 12th ed. (Upper Saddle River, NJ: Pearson Prentice Hall, 2006). Additional perspectives on compensation plans can be found in Mike Emerson and Mike Marks, "Rethinking Sales Compensation," *Industrial Distribution,* August 2006, pp. 45–46; Chang et al., "Happy Sales Force, Happy Returns"; Ryals and Rogers, "Sales Compensation Plans"; Tará Burnthorne Lopez, Christopher D. Hopkins, and Mary Anne Raymond, "Reward Preferences of Salespeople: How Do Commissions Rate?" *Journal of Personal Selling & Sales Management* 26 (fall 2006): 381–90; Brown et al., "Adapting Motivation, Control, and Compensation Research"; Bangert, "Performance Pays"; Christine Galea, "Compensation Plan Redux," *Sales & Marketing Management,* October 2005, p. 1; Sunil Erevelles, Indranil Dutta, and Carolyn Galantine, "Sales Force Compensation Plans Incorporating Multidimensional Sales Effort and Salesperson Efficiency," *Journal of Personal Selling & Sales Management* 24 (spring 2004): 101–12.

27 "Sales Compensation," *Controller's Report,* July 2006, p. 4; Christine Galea, "The 2005 Compensation Survey," *Sales & Marketing Management,* May 2005, pp. 24–29.

28 Barbara Love (ed.), "Does Your Compensation Plan Inspire Sales?" *Folio,* March 1985, pp. 74–85.

29 *Dartnell's 30th Sales Force Compensation Survey* (Chicago: Dartnell Corporation, 1999).

30 Richard Katz and Claude Brodeaser, "All Commission, All the Time," *Mediaweek,* June 30, 1997, p. 5.

31 Rick Dogen, "Don't Be Too Quick on the Draw," *Sales & Marketing Management,* September 1988, pp. 58–65.

32 "All Levels of Sales Reps Post Impressive Earnings Gains," *American Salesman,* March 1997, pp. 18–20.

33 Galea, "2005 Compensation Survey"; "3 Surveys Find Sales Professionals' Compensation is Beginning to Soar," *Report on Salary Surveys,* July 2005, pp. 1–11; *Dartnell's 30th Sales Force Compensation Survey.*

34 Andy Cohen, "They're In the Money," *Leading Edge,* December 1996, p. 15.

35 Michele Mavchetti, "Master Motivators," *Sales & Marketing Management,* April 1998, p. 39.

36 Ira Sager, Gary McWilliam and Robert Hof, "IBM Leans on Its Sales Force," *Business Week,* February 7, 1994, p. 110.

37 "Managers Handbook: What Salespeople Are Paid," *Sales & Marketing Management,* February 1995, pp. 30–32.

38 Vincent Alonzo, "Selling Changes," *Incentive,* September 1996, pp. 45–46.

39 Michele Mavchetti, "Itching Prime Pay Plans," *Sales & Marketing Management,* August 1997, p. 104.

40 Frank Zaret, "Adapting Distribution and Compensation to Cultural Needs," *Market Facts,* September–October 1989, pp. 26–27.

41 Michael Segalla, Dominique Rouziès, Madeleine Besson, and Barton A. Weitz, "A Cross-National Investigation of Incentive Sales Compensation," *International Journal of Research in Marketing* 23 (December 2006): 419–33.

42 Thomas Mott, "Hot Ticket: Incentive Pay for Field Sales Managers," *Sales & Marketing Management,* March 1989, pp. 21–22.

43 William Keenan Jr., "Are You Getting Your Money's Worth?" *Sales & Marketing Management,* May 1989, pp. 46–52.

44 Ibid.

Chapter 13

1 Gary S. Tubridy, "Stay on Top of the Bottom Line!" *Sales & Marketing Management,* May 1990, pp. 56–60.

2 Jerome A. Colletti and Mary S. Fiss, "The Ultimately Accountable Job: Leading Today's Sales Organization," *Harvard Business Review,* July–August 2006, pp. 125–31.

3 Artur Baldauf, David W. Cravens, and Nigel F. Piercy, "Sales Management Control Research—Synthesis and an Agenda for Future Research," *Journal of Personal Selling & Sales Management* 25 (winter 2005): 7–26.

4 Erin Anderson and Vincent Onyemah, "How Right Should the Customer Be?" *Harvard Business Review,* July–August 2006, pp. 59–67; Eric Fang, Kenneth R. Evans, and Timothy D. Landry, "Control Systems' Effect on Attributional Processes and Sales Outcomes: A Cybernetic Information-Processing Perspective," *Journal of the Academy of Marketing Science* 33, no. 4 (2005): 553–74; David W. Cravens, Felicia G. Lassk, George S. Low, and Greg W. Marshall et al., "Formal and Informal Management Control Combinations in Sales Organizations: The Impact on Salesperson Consequences," *Journal of Business Research* 57, no. 3 (2004): 241–48; Charles H. Schwepker Jr. and David J. Good, "Marketing Control and Sales Force Customer Orientation," *Journal of Personal Selling & Sales Management* 24 (summer 2004): 167–79.

5 Dianne Ledingham, Mark Kovac, and Heidi Locke Simon, "The New Science of Sales Force Productivity," *Harvard Business Review,* September 2006, pp. 124–33.

6 Alan J. Dubinsky and Richard W. Hansen, "The Sales Force Management Audit," *California Management Review* 24 (winter 1981): 86–95.

7 Ledingham et al., "New Science of Sales Force Productivity."

8 See, for example, Bulent Menguc and Tansu Barker, "Re-Examining Field Sales Unit Performance: Insights from the Resource-Based View and Dynamic Capabilities Perspective," *European Journal of Marketing* 39, no. 7–8 (2005): 885–909; Robert A. Howell and Stephen R. Soucy, "Customer Profitability—As Critical as Product Profitability," *Management Accounting,* October 1990, pp. 43–47; Fred Selnes, "Analyzing Marketing Profitability: Sales Are a Dangerous Cost Driver," *European Journal of Marketing* 216, no. 2 (1992): 15–26.

9 Mark W. Johnston and Greg W. Marshall, *Churchill, Ford, and Walker's Sales Force Management* (New York: McGraw-Hill/Irwin, 2006); T. N. Ingram, R. W. LaForge, R. A. Avila, and C. H. Schwepker et al., *Sales Management: Analysis and Decision Making* (Mason, OH: Thomson South-Western, 2006); T. N. Ingram, R. W. LaForge, W. B. Locander, and S. B. MacKenzie et al., "New Directions in Sales Leadership Research," *Journal of Personal Selling & Sales Management,* (Spring 2005): 137–54.

10 Ledingham et al., "New Science of Sales Force Productivity."

11 Artur Baldauf, David W. Cravens, and Nigel F. Piercy, "Sales Management Control Research—Synthesis and an Agenda for Future Research," *Journal of Personal Selling & Sales Management* 25 (winter 2005): 7–26; Donald W. Jackson, John L. Schlachter, and William G. Wolfe, "Examining the Bases Utilized for Evaluating Salespeople's Performance," *Journal of Personal Selling & Sales Management* 15 (fall 1995): 57–66.

12 For more insights on marketing costs analysis, see Lisa M. Ellram, "Activity-Based Costing and Total Cost of Ownership: A Critical Linkage," *Journal of Cost Management* (winter 1995): 22–30.

13 See B. Rosenbloom, *Marketing Channels: A Management View* (Mason, OH: Thomson South-Western, 2004).

14 Ledingham et al., "New Science of Sales Force Productivity."

15 For further insights, see Robin Cooper and Robert S. Kaplan, "Profit Priorities from Activity-Based Costing," *Harvard Business Review,* May–June 1993, p. 130; Raghu

Tadepalli, "Marketing Control: Reconceptualization and Implementation Using the Feedforward Method," *European Journal of Marketing* 26, no. 1 (1992): 24–40.

16 Donald W. Jackson, Jr., Lonnie L. Ostrom, and Kenneth R. Evans, "Measures Used to Evaluate Industrial Marketing Activities," *Industrial Marketing Management* 11 (October 1982): 269–74.

17 William L. Cron and Michael Levy, "Sales Management Performance Evaluation: A Residual Income Perspective," *Journal of Personal Selling & Sales Management* 7 (August 1987): 57–66.

18 Ledingham et al., "New Science of Sales Force Productivity"; Earl D. Honeycutt, "Technology Improves Sales Performance— Doesn't It? An Introduction to the Special Issue on Selling and Sales Technology," *Industrial Marketing Management* 34, no. 4 (2005): 301–4. This section also draws heavily from Rolph Anderson, "Personal Selling and Sales Management in the New Millennium," *Journal of Personal Selling & Sales Management* 16 (summer 1996): 17–32.

19 Gary K. Hunter and William D. Perreault Jr., "Sales Technology Orientation, Information Effectiveness, and Sales Performance," *Journal of Personal Selling & Sales Management* 26 (spring 2006): 95–113; Devon S. Johnson and Sundar Bharadwaj, "Digitization of Selling Activity and Sales Force Performance: An Empirical Investigation," *Journal of the Academy of Marketing Research* 33, no. 1 (2005): 3–18; Ko Dong-Gil and Alan R. Dennis, "Sales Force Automation and Sales Performance: Do Experience and Expertise Matter?" *Journal of Personal Selling & Sales Management* 24 (fall 2004): 311–22.

20 Michael Ahearne, Ronald Jelinek, and Adam Rapp, "Moving Beyond the Direct Effect of SFA Adoption on Salesperson Performance: Training and Support as Key Moderating Factors," *Industrial Marketing Management* 34, no. 4 (2005): 379–88; Michael Ahearne, Narasimhan Srinivasan, and Luke Weinstein, "Effect of Technology on Sales Performance: Progressing from Technology Acceptance to Technology Usage and Consequence," *Journal of Personal Selling & Sales Management* 24 (fall 2004): 297–310.

21 Dubinsky and Hansen, "Sales Force Management Audit."

22 Colletti and Fiss, "Ultimately Accountable Job."

Chapter 14

1 Charles H. Schwepker Jr. and David J. Good, "Marketing Control and Sales Force Customer Orientation," *Journal of Personal Selling & Sales Management* 24 (summer 2004): 167–79.

2 Dianne Ledingham, Mark Kovac, and Heidi Locke Simon, "The New Science of Sales Force Productivity," *Harvard Business Review,* September 2006, pp. 124–33.

3 Jerome A. Colletti and Mary S. Fiss, "The Ultimately Accountable Job: Leading Today's Sales Organization," *Harvard Business Review,* July–August 2006, pp. 125–31;

Barry Trailer and Jim Dickie, "Understanding What Your Sales Manager Is Up Against," *Harvard Business Review,* July–August 2006, pp. 48–55.

4 Gary L. Hunter, "Information Overload: Guidance for Identifying When Information Becomes Detrimental to Sales Force Performance," *Journal of Personal Selling & Sales Management* 24 (spring 2004): 91–100.

5 G. A. Bricker, "Performance Agreements: The Key to Increasing Motivation," *Sales & Marketing Management* 144 (February 1992): 69–70.

6 Sridhar N. Ramaswami, Srini S. Srinivasan, and Stephen A. Gorton, "Information Asymmetry Between Salesperson and Supervisor: Postulates from Agency and Social Exchange Theories," *Journal of Personal Selling & Sales Management* 17 (summer 1997): 29–50.

7 Bernard J. Jaworski and Ajay K. Kohli, "Supervisory Feedback: Alternative Types and Their Impact on Salespeople's Performance and Satisfaction," *Journal of Marketing Research* 28 (May 1991): 190–201.

8 Artur Baldauf, David W. Cravens, and Nigel F. Piercy, "Sales Management Control Research: Synthesis and an Agenda for Future Research," *Journal of Personal Selling & Sales Management* 25 (winter 2005): 7–26.

9 Donald W. Jackson, John L. Schlachter, and William G. Wolfe, "Examining the Bases Utilized for Evaluating Salespeople's Performance," *Journal of Personal Selling & Sales Management* 15 (fall 1995): 57–66; Michael H. Morris, Duane L. Davis, Jeffrey W. Allen, and Ramon A. Avila et al., "Assessing the Relationships Among Performance Measures, Managerial Practices, and Satisfaction When Evaluating the Salesforce: A Replication and Extension," *Journal of Personal Selling & Sales Management* 11 (summer 1991): 25–36.

10 Donald W. Jackson, John L. Schlachter, and William G. Wolfe, "Examining the Bases Utilized for Evaluating Salespeople's Performance," *Journal of Personal Selling & Sales Management* 15 (fall 1995): 57–66.

11 Erin Anderson and Richard L. Oliver, "Perspectives on Behavior-Based versus Outcome-Based Salesforce Control Systems," *Journal of Marketing* 51 (October 1987): 76–88.

12 Richard L. Oliver and Erin Anderson, "Behavior- and Outcome-Based Sales Control Systems: Evidence and Consequences of Pure-Form and Hybrid Governance," *Journal of Personal Selling & Sales Management* 15 (fall 1995): 1–16.

13 Gilbert A Churchill, Neil M. Ford, Steven W. Hartley, and O. C. Walker, "The Determinants of Salesperson Performance," *Journal of Marketing Research* 22 (May 1985): 103–18; James M. Comer and Alan J. Dubinsky, *Managing the Successful Sales Force* (Lexington, MA: Lexington Books, 1985).

14 Donald W. Jackson, John L. Schlachter, and William G. Wolfe, "Examining the Bases Utilized for Evaluating Salespeople's Performance," *Journal of Personal Selling & Sales Management* 15 (fall 1995): 57–66.

15 Oliver and Anderson, "Behavior- and Outcome-Based Sales Control Systems."

16 Morris et al., "Assessing the Relationships Among Performance Measures."

17 Hunter, "Information Overload."

18 Ledingham et al., "New Science of Sales Force Productivity."

19 Bulent Menguc and Tansu Barker, "Re-Examining Field Sales Unit Performance: Insights from the Resource-Based View and Dynamic Capabilities Perspective," *European Journal of Marketing* 39, no. 7–8 (2005): 885–909.

20 Eric G. Harris, John C. Mowen, and Tom J. Brown, "Re-Examining Salesperson Goal Orientations: Personality Influencers, Customer Orientation, and Work Satisfaction," *Journal of the Academy of Marketing Science* 33, no. 1 (2005): 19–35; Lawrence S. Silver, Sean Dwyer, and Bruce Alford, "Learning and Performance Goal Orientation of Salespeople Revisited: The Role of Performance-Approach and Performance-Avoidance Orientations," *Journal of Personal Selling & Sales Management* 26 (winter 2006): 27–38; Eric Fang, Kenneth R. Evans, and Shaoming Zou, "The Moderating Effect of Goal-Setting Characteristics on the Sales Control Systems–Job Performance Relationship," *Journal of Business Research* 58, no. 9 (2005): 1214–22.

21 Terry L. Childers, Alan J. Dubinsky, and Steven J. Skinner, "Leadership Substitutes as Moderators of Sales Supervisory Behavior," *Journal of Business Research* 21 (December 1990): 368–82.

22 Eric Fang, Kenneth R. Evans, and Timothy D. Landry, "Control Systems' Effect on Attributional Processes and Sales Outcomes: A Cybernetic Information-Processing Perspective," *Journal of the Academy of Marketing Science* 33 (4, 2005): 553–74; David W. Cravens, Felicia G. Lassk, George S. Low, and Greg W. Marshall et al., "Formal and Informal Management Control Combinations in Sales Organizations: The Impact on Salesperson Consequences," *Journal of Business Research* 57, no. 3 (2004): 241–48.

23 Schwepker and Good, "Understanding Sales Quotas."

24 Performax Sales & Marketing Group, "Most Reps Don't Think They Need a Sales Strategy," *What's Working in Sales Management,* July 9, 1997, p. 4.

25 Gilbert A. Churchill, Neil M. Ford, and Orville C. Walker, *Sales Force Management* (Chicago: Irwin, 1997).

26 Tom Reilly, "Key Points about Goals," *What's Working in Sales Management,* July 9, 1997, p. 3.

27 Mark R. Edwards, W. Theodore Cummings, and John L. Schlachter, "The Paris–Peoria Solution: Innovations in Appraising Regional and International Sales Personnel," *Journal of Personal Selling & Sales Management* 4 (November 1984): 26–39.

28 Jan P. Muczyk and Myron Gable, "Managing Sales Performance Through a Comprehensive Performance Appraisal System," *Journal of Personal Selling & Sales Management* 7 (May 1987): 41–52.

29 W. E. Patton and Ronald H. King, "The Use of Human Judgment Models in Evaluating Sales Force Performance," *Journal of Personal Selling & Sales Management* 5 (May 1985): 1–14.

30 Tom Atkinson and Ron Koprowski, "Finding the Weak Links," *Harvard Business Review,* July–August 2006, pp. 22–23.

31 Benton Canougher and John M. Ivancevich, "BARS Performance Rating for Sales Force Personnel," *Journal of Marketing Research* 42 (July 1978): 87–95.

32 Alan J. Dubinsky, Steven J. Skinner, and Tommy Whittler, "Evaluating Sales Personnel: An Attribution Theory Perspective," *Journal of Personal Selling & Sales Management* 9 (spring 1989): 9–21; Marshall and Mowen, "An Experimental Investigation of the Outcome Bias"; Greg W. Marshall, John C. Mowen, and Keith J. Fabes, "The Impact of Territory Difficulty and Self versus Other Ratings on Managerial Evaluations of Sales Personnel," *Journal of Personal Selling & Sales Management* 12 (fall 1992): 35–48; John C. Mowen, Stephen W. Brown, and Donald W. Jackson, "Cognitive Biases in Sales Management Evaluations," *Journal of Personal Selling and Sales Management,* 1 (fall–winter 1981): 83–88; John C. Mowen, Janet E. Keith, Stephen W. Brown, and Donald W. Jackson, "Utilizing Effort and Task Difficulty Information in Evaluating Salespeople," *Journal of Marketing Research* 22 (May 1985): 185–91; John C. Mowen, Keith J. Fabes, and Raymond W. LaForge, "Effects of Territory, Situation, and Rater on Salesperson Evaluation," *Journal of Personal Selling & Sales Management* 6 (May 1986): 1–8.

33 Robert A. Baron and Jerald Greenberg, *Behavior in Organizations* (Boston: Allyn and Bacon, 1990); Gentry et al., "Salesperson Evaluation"; Andrew D. Szilagyi and Marc J. Wallace, *Organizational Behavior and Performance* (Glenview, IL: Scott, Foresman, 1990); For other insights see Morris et al., "Assessing the Relationships Among Performance Measures"; James W. Gentry, John C. Mowen, and Lori Tasaki, "Salesperson Evaluation: A Systematic Structure for Reducing Judgmental Biases," *Journal of Personal Selling & Sales Management* 11 (spring 1991): 27–38.

34 See Greg W. Marshall and John C. Mowen, "An Experimental Investigation of the Outcome Bias in Salesperson Performance Evaluations," *Journal of Personal Selling & Sales Management* 13 (summer 1993): 31–47.

35 Szilagyi and Wallace, *Organizational Behavior and Performance.*

36 Thomas R. Wotruba and Edwin K. Simpson, *Sales Management: Text and Cases* (Boston: PWS-Kent Publishing Company, 1992).

37 Ibid.

38 Mark P. Leach, Annie H. Liu, and Wesley J. Johnston, "The Role of Self-Regulation Training in Developing the Motivation Management Capabilities of Salespeople," *Journal of Personal Selling & Sales Management* 25 (summer 2005): 269–81.

39 Fernando Jaramillo, François A. Carrillat, and William B. Locander, "A Meta-Analytic Comparison of Managerial Ratings and Self-Evaluations," *Journal of Personal Selling & Sales Management* 25 (fall 2005): 315–28.

40 Mary N. Vinson, "The Pros and Cons of 360-Degree Feedback: Making It Work," *Training and Development,* April 1996, pp. 11–12; Walter N. Tornow, "Editor's Note: Introduction to Special Issue on 360-Degree Feedback," *Human Resource Management* 32 (summer–fall 1993): 211–19; Brian Riley, "360-Degree Feedback Can Change Your Life," *Fortune,* October 17, 1994, pp. 93–100.

41 Ginka Toegel and Jay Conger, "360-Degree Assessment: Time for Reinvention," *Academy of Management Learning & Education* 2 (September 2003): 297; Lauren Keller Johnson, "Retooling 360s for Better Performance," *Harvard Business School Working Knowledge* (February 2004): http://hbswk.hbs .edu/archive/3935.html (accessed January 2007).

42 Leach et al., "Role of Self-Regulation Training"; Robert Hoffman, "Ten Reasons You Should Be Using 360-Degree Feedback," *HRMagazine,* April 1995, p. 82.

43 William C. Moncrief and Shannon H. Shipp, *Sales Management: Strategy, Technology, Skills* (Reading, MA: Addison-Wesley, 1997).

44 Matthew Boyle, "Perilous Roads Ahead," *Fortune,* May 28, 2001, pp. 187–88; Carol Hymowitz, "Ranking Systems Gain Popularity But Have Many Staffers Riled," *Wall Street Journal,* May 15, 2001, p. B1.

45 Boyle, "Perilous Roads Ahead."

46 Jack Welch and Suzy Welch, "The Case for 20-70-10," *Business Week,* October 2, 2006, p. 108; Jack Welch and Suzy Welch, "Send the Jerks Packing," *Business Week,* November 13, 2006, p. 136.

47 J. Welch and S. Welch, "Case for 20-70-10."

48 Hymowitz, "Ranking Systems."

Glossary

360-Degree Performance Appraisal A performance evaluation system that provides a salesperson with comparative pooled and anonymous feedback from the sales manager, peers on the sales team, subordinates, and clients; often includes a self-assessment. (14)

Acceptability How culturally or socially acceptable we perceive an action to be. (2)

Activity Quotas Those quotas designed to control the many activities the salesperson is responsible for. (14)

Adaptive Selling Modifying each sales presentation and demonstration to accommodate each individual prospect. (4)

Analytical CRM Focuses on aggregating customer information electronically, allowing for better identification of target markets and opportunities for cross-selling. (3)

Approach The first face-to-face contact with the prospect. (4)

ARIMA (Autoregressive Integrated Moving Average) A sophisticated forecasting approach based on the moving average concept. (5)

Attribution Theory Theory based on the assumption that people are motivated by their perception of why an event occurred. (11)

Behaviorally Anchored Rating Scales (BARS) Concentrates on measuring behaviors key to performance that the individual salesperson can control. (14)

Behavior-Based Performance Standards Performance criteria that can be subjectively measured (e.g., product knowledge). (14)

Blended Learning A blend of E-learning used in conjunction with face-to face teaching. (9)

Bonus Payments made at the discretion of management for specific achievements. (12)

Boundary Spanner Someone who performs his or her job in the "boundary" between a company and a customer. (2)

Breakdown Approach A way of developing forecasts based on general economic conditions, typically projected gross national product (GNP) in constant dollars along with projections of consumer and wholesale price indexes, interest rates, unemployment levels, and federal government expenditures. (5)

Budget Variances Differences between actual results and sales budget expectations. (5)

Budgeting An operational planning process expressed in financial terms. (5)

Build-Up Approach A way of developing forecasts based on *primary research,* new data collected for the specific purpose at hand. (5)

Business Ethics The study of how businesspeople behave when facing a situation with moral consequences. (2)

Business Portfolio Matrix A method of segmenting the company's activities into groups of well-defined businesses for which distinct strategies are developed. (6)

Buying Power Index (BPI) A weighted combination of population, income, and retail sales, expressed as a percentage of the national potential, to identify a given market's ability to buy. (5)

Canned (or Programmed) Selling Any highly structured or patterned selling approach. (4)

Career Plateauing When a salesperson no longer grows or develops in the position, and/or the likelihood of the person receiving additional responsibility is low. (11)

Causal/Association Methods Methods that attempt to identify the factors affecting sales and determine the nature of the relationship between them. (5)

Centralized Training Programs Training programs that involve organized training schools, periodic conventions, or seminars held in a central location such as the home office. (9)

Charisma A mystical, inspirational quality that few people possess; the charismatic leader wins the emotional loyalty and enthusiasm of followers. (10)

Click-Stream Analysis Involves drawing conclusions based on the path a customer takes while navigating information on the company website. (3)

Close The stage in the PSP where the salesperson tries to obtain the prospect's agreement to purchase the product. (4)

Coaching (Developmental Feedback) Post-training reinforcement that generally involves informal, give-and-take discussions between sales managers and salespeople with the purpose of reinforcing sales training concepts, solving selling problems, and improving basic selling skills. (9)

Codes of Ethics Written expression of a firm's values, listing specific behaviors that are consistent or inconsistent with those values. (2)

Coercive Power The leader's ability to obtain subordinate compliance through fear of punishment, or sanctions, or by withholding rewards including being fired from the job. (10)

Combination Compensation Plan Plan that combines two or three of the basic compensation methods (e.g., salary plus commission). This is the most widely used compensation method. (12)

Combination Quotas Those quotas used when management wants to control the performance of both the selling and non-selling activities of the sales force. (14)

Communication A two-way process whereby information is transferred and understood between two or more people. (10)

Compensation All monetary payments as well as benefits used to remunerate employees for their performance. (12)

Compensation Mix The relationship between salary, commission, and other incentives. (12)

Computer-Based Training (CBT) A general term used to describe any learning or training event that uses computers as the primary delivery method, such as CD-ROM, the Internet, intranet, and interactive videodisc. (9)

Concentration Principle Assertion that a relatively small percentage (20 percent) of products, customers, orders, sales territories, and salespeople account for a large percentage (80 percent) of profits. (7, 13)

Conferencing (Distance Learning) A method of delivering training to a group of trainees located in different locations using computers, telephone lines, and satellite. (9)

Consideration Sometimes called the "human relations" approach, this dimension of behavioral styles theory seeks to engender friendship, mutual trust, respect, and support of subordinates. (10)

Consolidated Metropolitan Statistical Area (CMSA) An MSA that has a population of 1 million or more. (7)

Contingency Events that are conceivable, but less likely than those based directly on the forecast. (5)

Contingency Planning A backup plan to the one adopted; a contingency plan is executed only if events occur beyond the control of the major plan. (6)

Contingency Theory A collection of leadership theories which suggests that an effective leadership style is largely contingent upon the interactions among the leader, followers, and situation-specific conditions. (10)

Continuing Sales Training Program A type of sales training program that seeks to improve the skills of experienced salespeople. (9)

Contractualism The extent to which an act is consistent with stated or implied contracts and/or laws. (2)

Contribution Margin The sales price less direct costs and variable costs equals the amount the sale contributes to profits (contribution margin). (13)

Cooling-Off Rules FTC regulation requiring door-to-door salespeople to give written notice to customers placing orders of $25 or more that they can cancel their purchase within three days. (2)

Correlation Analysis A statistical approach analyzing the way variables are related to one another or *move together* in some way. (5)

Correlation Coefficient A measure of how much two variables are related to one another. (5)

Costs versus Expenses Two terms that are often used interchangeably in describing marketing costs analysis. But costs tend to be specific and directly related to volume output, while expenses are more general or indirect expenditures (e.g., we tend to say production costs and marketing expenses). (13)

Counting Methods Forecasting approaches that tabulate responses to questions on surveys or count the numbers of buyers or purchases. (5)

Critical Path The sequence of tasks to be completed, the time to complete each activity, and the responsible individuals. (6)

CRM A systematic integration of information, technology, and human resources, all oriented toward (1) providing maximum value to customers and (2) maximizing the value obtained from customers. (3)

CRM Intelligence Results when CRM software converts information into data that can be used in solving a sales manager's problem. (3)

Customer Commitment Represents the bonding, or affective attachment, between a customer and a sales firm. (3)

Customer Lifetime Value The monetary amount representing the worth of a customer to a firm over the foreseeable life of a relationship. (3)

Customer Portfolios Sets of customers who have something in common. (3)

Customer Relationship Management (CRM) A company-wide effort to satisfy customers across all "touch" points and provide personalized treatment of the most valued customers in order to increase customer retention and profitability. (1)

Customer Retention Refers to the percentage of customers who will repeatedly purchase products from the selling firm. (3)

Customer Share Represents the proportion of resources a customer spends with one among a set of competing suppliers. (3)

Customer Value The net positive worth resulting from participation in exchange. (3)

Customer Vulnerability State in which customers are at a disadvantage relative to the company. (2)

Customer-Centric The customer becomes the heart of the business process. (2)

Customer-Oriented Salesperson Motivated primarily by matching up customers with products that best address their needs. (3)

D&B—Dun's Market Identifiers (DMI) A directory file produced by D&B, Inc. that contains basic company data, executive names and titles, corporate linkages, DUNS Numbers, organization status, and other marketing information on over 17 million U.S. business establishment locations, including public, private, and government organizations. (7)

Data Mining Exploratory statistical analysis of the data in the data warehouse; aimed at revealing relationships that allow customers to be targeted more accurately. (3)

Data Warehouse An electronic storage center containing data records from diverse information systems that are shared across all functional departments. (3)

Database Marketing A computerized process for analyzing customer databases in a way that allows more effective selling by tailoring product and promotional offerings to a specific customer's sales patterns. (3)

Decentralized Training Training programs that use one or more different types of training, such as office instruction, use of experienced salespeople, on-the-job training, traveling sales clinics, or a type of computer-based training. (3)

Deliverability Refers to the proportion of e-mail sent that is successfully delivered to the intended recipient. (3)

Deontological A term used to represent decision processes that are rule based or idealistic. (2)

Dialectic Planning An approach to planning that calls for making a new set of assumptions—sometimes directly opposite—and reevaluating all previous planning decisions. (6)

Differentiated Marketing Dealing with different groups of customers by offering a unique product for each group. (3)

Direct Costs Those costs that can be entirely identified with or traced to a particular function or market segment such as a territory, customer, or product. In a territorial analysis, for example, each territory would be assigned the cost of salaries for those salespeople working exclusively in that territory. (13)

Draw A sum of money paid against future commissions. A "guaranteed draw" is one that does not have to be repaid in the event of insufficient commissions. (12)

Dual Factor Theory Based on the assumption that the job itself contains sources of satisfaction and dissatisfaction as well as motivators. (11)

Econometric Models Models developed to trace economic conditions in the United States by industry, with the objective of capturing, in the form of equations, complex interrelationships among the factors affecting either the total economy or the industry's or company's sales. (5)

Effective Listening Becoming familiar with the four types of listening (content listening, critical listening, empathic listening, and active listening) and knowing when to apply them. (10)

Effectiveness Describes results-oriented behavior that focuses on achieving sales goals. (7)

Efficiency Describes cost-oriented behavior that focuses on making the best possible use of the salesperson's time and efforts. (7)

E-learning A broad term that refers to computer-enhanced learning, although it is often extended to include the use of mobile technologies such as PDAs and MP3 players. (9)

Employment Test An objective way to measure traits or characteristics of applicants for sales positions and to increase the chances of selecting good salespeople using intelligence tests, or some other norming test. (8)

Empowerment Process of making subordinates into partners by giving them legitimate authority and discretion in decision making plus rewards tied to performance. (10, 11)

Equity Theory Based on the assumption that people compare their relative work contributions and rewards with those of other individuals in similar situations. (11)

ERG Theory Espouses that individuals' needs can be subsumed under a three-category hierarchy of existence (physiological and safety needs), relatedness (social and esteem needs), and growth (self-actualization needs). (11)

Ethical Dilemma A situation with alternate courses of action, each having different moral implications. (2)

Ethical Maturity State achieved when individuals place the moral treatment of others ahead of short-term personal gain. (2)

Ethical Stress Ambiguity about not knowing what to do in a given situation; conflict between multiple courses of action, each with different moral implications for the people involved. (2)

Ethical Work Climate The way employees view their work environment on moral dimensions. (2)

Expectancy (Effort-Performance Linkage) The salesperson's perceived probability that exerting a given level of effort will lead to higher achievement. (11)

Expectancy Theory Based on the assumption that people are motivated to work toward a goal when they expect their efforts will pay off. (11)

Expense Account Financial accounts that enable sales representatives to carry out necessary selling activities. (12)

Expense Quotas Those designed to make the salespeople aware of the costs involved in their selling efforts. (14)

Expert Power Subordinate compliance based on the leader's skills, knowledge, intelligence, job-related information, and expertise. (10)

Exponential Smoothing A type of moving average that represents the weighted sum of all past numbers in a time series, placing the heaviest weight on the most recent data. (5)

Extended Socialization Exposing new recruits to the corporate culture (values, philosophy, group norms, different work groups, corporate officers, and so on) and

helping them adapt to the new culture in as short a period of time as possible. (8)

Extrinsic Rewards Those rewards controlled by managers and customers (e.g., pay, bonuses, and promotions). (11)

Financial Incentives Monetary reward for job performance; includes salary, commission, bonuses, stock options, or fringe benefits such as a company car, medical, dental and life insurance, or educational aid. (11)

Financial Quotas Those quotas established to control expenses, gross margin, or net profit for the various sales units. (14)

Fixed Costs Those costs that do not change with sales volume (e.g., salaries of the sales administration staff, office rent, and fire insurance). (13)

Follow-Up Customer service provided not just after the sale is closed, but throughout the PSP. (4)

Fringe Benefits Indirect financial awards that help to provide salespeople with personal security and job satisfaction. (12)

Functional Costs Reclassified natural expenses into the activities or functions for which they were incurred (e.g., "salary expense" reclassified into direct selling, transportation, or advertising function salaries). (13)

Goals General, long-range destinations. (6)

Goal-Setting Theory Attempts to increase motivation by linking rewards directly to individuals' goals. (11)

Governance The mechanism that helps ensure the exchange is fair to all parties involved. (3)

Green River Ordinances Local ordinances requiring nonresidents to obtain a license from city authorities to sell goods or services direct to consumers in that vicinity. (2)

Group Training Methods Instruction methods—such as lecture, group discussion, role-playing, and conferencing—that are ideal for training groups of salespeople. (9)

Hierarchy of Needs Theory A need theory; based on the assumption that people are motivated by a hierarchy of psychological growth needs. (11)

Ideals A set of principles by which individuals decide morality. (2)

Incentive Program When salespeople achieve or surpass a specified sales quota, they are often given a monetary bonus and/or special recognition to reward them for their performance as well as to motivate them to continue this behavior. (11)

In-Depth Interview The most used and least scientific of the various tools for selecting employees; is very effective for finding if an employee is right for the job through a two-way discussion involving probing questions. (8)

Indirect Costs Sometimes called common costs; are incurred for more than one function or segment and thus must be allocated on some reasonable basis. For example, the sales manager's salary or office utilities would have to be spread among sales functions, sales territories, and other segments. (13)

Individual Training Methods Instruction methods—such as on-the-job training, personal conferences, and computer-based training—that are ideal when training on an individual basis. (9)

Initial Sales Training Program A type of sales training program provided to new recruits to teach them the basic selling concepts, as well as knowledge about the company and its products, competitors and the industry, and customers and the market. (9)

Initial Screening Process by which undesirable job candidates are eliminated as soon as possible. (8)

Initial Socialization Begins in the recruiting process with things like brochures and is intended as a preliminary form of integrating a person into the company. (8)

Initiating Structure Sometimes called "task orientation," this dimension of behavioral styles theory reflects the extent to which leaders organize, clearly define, and clarify the tasks subordinates need to perform in attaining firm goals. (10)

Input-Output Efficiency The relationship between marketing efforts (inputs) and sales (output) is a measure of a sales organization's efficiency. (13)

Input-Output Models Complex systems showing the amount of input required from each industry for a specified output of another industry. (5)

Instrumentality (Performance-Reward Linkage) The salesperson's estimate of the probability that achieving a certain level of improved performance will lead to the attainment of designated rewards. (11)

Integrated Marketing Communication (IMC) The coordination of promotional elements (advertising, personal selling, sales promotion, public relations, direct marketing, and publicity) with other marketing mix elements (product, pricing, and distribution). (1)

Intranet Using Internet and Web technologies but those accessible only to the company's reps and others, such as supply chain members, who are given permission to access the system. (9)

Intrinsic Rewards Nontangible rewards that salespeople experience internally (e.g., personal growth and self esteem). (11)

Invalid Objections Irrelevant, untruthful delaying actions or hidden reasons for not buying. (4)

Job Analysis A process identifying the duties, requirements, responsibilities, and conditions of a job. (8)

Job Commitment The degree of involvement (high or low) salespeople have in their job. (11)

Job Description A written description of the responsibilities and performance criteria for a particular position. (8, 12)

Job Qualifications Characteristics recruits should have to perform a sales job satisfactorily. (8)

Jury of Executive Opinion Sales forecast method based on key managers' best estimates of sales in a given planning horizon. (5)

Key Accounts High-volume, important customers that require added attention from the sales organization. (6)

Lead The name and address or telephone number of a person or organization potentially needing the company's products or services. (4)

Leader Behavior The leader's manner and approach in providing direction, implementing plans, and motivating people. (10)

Leader-Member Exchange Theory A contingency leadership theory in which the subordinates a leader favors are given preferential treatment and assigned to an "in-group," whereas less desirable subalterns are placed in "out-groups." (10)

Leadership The interpersonal process of communicating, inspiring, guiding, and influencing the behavior of subordinate salespeople toward attaining organizational objectives, goals, and values. (10)

Leadership Styles Different patterns of leader behavior, or "styles" employed to secure subordinate compliance toward achieving organizational goals. (10)

Learning Objectives What the sales forces should know after a managerial training session. (9)

Learning Orientation When salespeople strive to discover new ways of selling effectively. (11)

Legitimate Power Power derived from the position occupied in the organizational structure where the leader has formally delegated authority to seek subordinate compliance. (10)

Macroenvironment Largely uncontrollable factors—such as technology, competition, economy, laws, culture, and ethics—that are continuously changing and to which sales managers must adapt in overseeing the sales force. (10)

Management The administrative activities that include planning, organizing, staffing, directing, and controlling the operations of a firm toward attaining its goals and objectives. (10)

Management by Objectives (MBO) Involves mutual goal setting devised by the sales manager and the salesperson, who jointly agree on the salesperson's specific goals or performance targets for the coming period. (10)

Managerial Training Includes all training functions of managing salespeople, such as recruitment, planning, sales forecasting, motivation, leadership, and so forth. (9)

Market Capacity Refers to the units the market will absorb if the product or service is free. (6)

Market Development A strategy for opening up new markets for current products. (6)

Market Orientation Companies focus on making what could be sold, not selling what is made. A market-oriented firm focuses all activities on providing value for customers. (3)

Market Penetration A strategy focusing on increasing sales of current products in current markets by more intensive marketing efforts. (6)

Market Potential The maximum possible sales for an entire industry; a quantitative estimate, in either physical or monetary units, of the total sales for a product within a market. (5, 6)

Market Share/Market Growth Matrix A matrix displaying alternative methods for growing sales. (6)

Marketing An organizational function and a set of processes for creating, communicating, and delivering value to customers and for managing customer relationships in ways that benefit the organization and its stakeholders. (1)

Marketing Automation System Taking SFA even further, this system monitors and integrates all aspects of a firm's marketing program. (3)

Mass Marketing A way of dealing with customers by offering the same product to the entire market. (3)

Mentor Someone who systematically helps develop a subordinate's abilities through careful tutoring, personal guidance, and example. (10)

Mentoring A method of on-the-job training in which a sales trainee is assigned long term to an experienced sales rep or manager for the purpose of transferring knowledge and experiences. (9)

Metropolitan Statistical Areas (MSAs) Areas that serve as territories; they can include a major city as well as the surrounding suburban and satellite cities. (7)

M-learning A form of learning using mobile technologies. (9)

Moral Equity The inherent fairness or justice in a situation. (2)

Moral Judgment A person's evaluation of the situation from an ethical perspective. (2)

Moral Philosophy A systematic tool for recognizing and resolving decisions about what is right and wrong. (2)

Motivation The set of dynamic interpersonal processes that cause the initiation, direction, intensity, and persistence of work-related behaviors of subordinate salespeople toward attaining organizational goals and objectives. (11)

Moving Average Forecasts developed mathematically based on sales in recent time periods. (5)

Multiple Regression A tool for forecasting a dependent variable like sales using several independent variables simultaneously. (5)

Mutual Loyalty Occurs when both buyer and seller are committed to each other and avoid behaviors that may damage the relationship. (3)

NAICS (North American Industrial Classification System) A system for categorizing firms, formally adopted beginning with the 2002 Economic Census and the publication of the *2002 U.S. NAICS Manual.* (5)

Naïve Forecast The simplest judgment method, which assumes, naively, that the next period's sales will be the same as they were in the previous period. (5)

Natural Expenses The traditional expense categories, such as salaries, rent, depreciation, and so on, used in accounting statements. (13)

Needs Theory Posits that employees develop various needs—such as for power, affiliation, and achievement—over their lifetime based on life experiences. (11)

Negative Reinforcement Avoiding an undesirable outcome after displaying the desired behavior (e.g., allowing those salespeople who achieve or surpass their annual quotas to keep their jobs). (11)

Niche Marketing Offering a specialized product to an individual customer segment with specialized needs. (3)

Non-Financial Incentives Psychological rewards related to the individual salesperson's intrinsic needs in that they are internally experienced payoffs (e.g., job security, relationships with superiors and coworkers, working conditions, challenging sales assignments, increasing responsibility, or rewards and recognition for special achievements). (11)

Nonquantitative Forecasting Techniques Subjective forecasts based on knowledgeable people's opinions instead of being analytically derived. (5)

Nonverbal Communication Communication that takes place largely through body language, facial expressions, gestures, or body postures. (10)

North American Product Classification System (NAPCS) A system for categorizing consumer products and service industries. (5)

Objection Anything that the prospect or customer says or does that impedes the sales negotiations. (4)

Objectives Specific results desired within a designated time frame—usually the period covered by the annual sales plan. (6)

One-to-One Marketing Involves matching individual products with individual customers. (3)

Online Learning A purely Web-based form of learning. (9)

Operational CRM Focused on using information to improve internal efficiencies. (3)

Opportunistic Behavior One fact of all relationships is that sometimes, one firm may take advantage of another firm. (3)

Organizational Behavior Modification Theory Involves the use of various learning techniques to strengthen, maintain, or eliminate specific behaviors by using rewards or punishments. (11)

Organizational Climate Employees' perceptions of and attitudes about the organizational culture; the perceptions salespeople have about their work situations and conditions. (1, 2)

Organizational Commitment When salespeople identify with and internalize the company's values and goals and desire to stay a viable member of the organization. (11)

Outcome-Based Performance Standards Performance criteria that can be objectively measured (e.g., number of sales calls made each month). (14)

Parkinson's Law A theory that work tends to expand to fill the time allotted for its completion. (7)

Participative Management The involvement of employees in shared decision making that enables them to accomplish individual and organization goals. (10, 11)

Path-Goal Theory A contingency leadership theory in which the tasks (paths) to be performed and the results (goals) to be achieved by subordinates are clearly defined by the leader, who makes desirable rewards contingent upon accomplishment of organizational goals. (10)

Peer Behavior A dimension of ethical climate that is the extent to which employees view coworkers as having high moral standards. (2)

Performance Evaluation Monitoring System (PEMS) System designed to provide feedback to salespeople on performance, to help salespeople modify or change their behavior, and to provide information to sales managers on which to make decisions on promotion, transfer, and compensation of salespeople. (14)

Performance Objectives What the sales forces should be able to do after training. A specific performance objective might be to train new salespeople to sell at least 75 percent of what experienced salespeople sell within one year after they are hired. (9)

Performance Orientation When salespeople are especially keen on receiving favorable assessments of their skills from management and peers. (11)

Performance Standards Planned achievement levels that the sales organization expects to reach at progressive intervals throughout the year; an agreement between subordinate and superior as to what level of performance is acceptable in some future period. (14)

Person-Organization Fit (POF) Describes how consistent a salesperson's beliefs and value system are with those of the organization for which he or she works. (8)

Policies Predetermined approaches for handling routine matters or reoccurring situations. (6)

Policies and Rules Principles that govern selling and marketing conduct within the firm, sometimes summarized in a code of ethics. (2)

Positive Reinforcement Providing salespeople with a pleasant consequence for having engaged in the desired behavior (e.g., providing a bonus for opening new accounts). (11)

Power The potential capacity to influence the behavior of subordinates. (10)

Preapproach The approach-planning stage of the PSP. (4)

Pre-Training Briefing Meeting help before training begins to let trainees know the purpose of training. (9)

Price Discrimination Discriminating among different customers on price or terms of sale when the discrimination has a harmful effect on competition. (2)

Procedures Detailed descriptions of specific steps for carrying out actions. (6)

Product Development The creation of new or improved products for current markets by adding new sizes, models with new features, alternative quality versions, or creative new alternatives to satisfy the same basic needs. (6)

Product Portfolio The set of products that a customer is responsible for selling. (3)

Production Orientation Companies focus on processes allowing large-scale, efficient, and economic production. (3)

Progressive Incentives Increase the percentage of commission or bonus awarded as sales volume rises. Best when profit margins climb significantly after the break-even point is reached. (12)

Prospecting First step in the PSP, wherein salespeople find leads and qualify them on four criteria: need, authority, money, and eligibility to buy. (4)

Purchase Intentions The likelihood customers will actually purchase a given product. (5)

Push Technology Involves using data stored about a particular customer or customer group; helps send the particular customer information and promotional material when the data suggests the customer will be interested in a purchase. (3)

Quotas Sales goals for different sales territories and individual salespeople. (5)

Rational-Based Governance Involves arrangements for sharing information and tasks between the buying and selling firms, but falls short of spelling out specific obligations for each party. (3)

Recognition A non-financial reward used for motivation. (11)

Recruitment Finding potential job applicants, telling them about the company, and getting them to apply. (8)

Recruitment Process The step-by-step process through which recruitment is carried out. (8)

Reference Checking The process of following up with references provided on an application to check the credibility of a job candidate. (8)

Referent Power The leader's ability to influence subordinate compliance based on inspiration, charisma, loyalty, and personal identification with the leader. (10)

Refresher Training A form of continuous training that seeks to upgrade the skills of the existing sales force and to maximize the value of each salesperson. (9)

Regression Analysis A statistical approach to predicting a dependent variable such as sales, using one or more independent variables such as advertising expenditures. (5)

Regressive Incentives Decrease the percentage of commission or bonus awarded as sales volume increases. Usually used where there is a high probability of "windfall" sales and a propensity to overload customer inventories. (12)

Relational Exchange Recognition, by both buyer and seller, that each transaction is merely one in a series of purchase agreements between a buyer and a seller. (3)

Relativism A moral philosophy by which individuals reach moral decisions based more on the actions they perceive to be acceptable *given a particular situation.* (2)

Retraining A form of continuous training that provides instruction when a salesperson's job requirements change due to new products or new methods. (9)

Reward Power The leader's ability to provide subordinates with various benefits, including money, praise, or promotion. (10)

Role-Playing A group method of training in which trainees play different roles in a simulated sales situation and then receive feedback on their performance. (9)

ROTI, or Return on Time Invested A financial concept that helps salespeople spend their time more profitably with prospects and customers. (7)

RSS A format typically associated with syndicated news and content of news-like sites, including sites like Wired.com, news-oriented community sites like Slashdot, and personal blogs. (9)

Sales and Operational Planning Process (S&OP) An organized process that uses sales inputs to forecast business for upcoming periods of varying length. (5)

Sales Budget A financial sales plan outlining how to allocate resources and selling efforts to achieve the sales forecast. (5)

Sales Contests Relatively short-run competitive events designed to motivate and reward salespeople for achieving objective goals. (11)

Sales Emphasis A dimension of ethical climate that is the extent to which employees feel pressured to prioritize increased sales, profits, margins, or other financial returns over all other concerns. (2)

Sales Exchange The act of trading economic resources (usually money) for a specific set of benefits offered by a company. (3)

Sales Force Audit A comprehensive, systematic, diagnostic, and prescriptive tool designed to assess the adequacy of a firm's sales management process and to provide direction for improved performance and prescription for needed changes. (13)

Sales Force Automation (SFA) An integrated system of computer software and hardware used to perform certain routine sales functions that formerly were performed with independent and often manual systems. (1, 3)

Sales Force Composite Sales forecast method based on sales force estimates of sales in the planning horizon. (5)

Sales Forecast A prediction of the future market potential for a specific product. (5)

Sales Management The function of planning, directing, and controlling the personal selling activities of a business unit, including recruiting, selecting, training, equipping, assigning, routing, supervising, paying, and motivating as these tasks apply to the sales force. (1)

Sales Management Ethics The specific component of business ethics that deals with ethically managing the sales function. (2)

Sales Meetings Opportunities for two-way communication and interaction among all members of the marketing team—field and headquarters. (11)

Sales Motivation Strategies Techniques used to implement motivational theories or approaches (e.g., sales contests, sales meetings, promotion opportunities, and incentive programs). (11)

Sales-Oriented Salesperson Motivated to maximize sales from each contact even if a product does not best match customer needs and desires. (3)

Sales Potential The maximum possible sales for a company; the portion of market potential that one among a set of competing firms can reasonably expect to obtain. (5, 6)

Sales Quota A specific, quantitative goal, usually established in terms of sales volume; important in planning, control, and evaluation of sales activities. (14)

Sales Territory A specific geographic area that contains present and potential customers and is assigned to a particular salesperson. (7)

Sales Training Takes human inputs—salespeople—and develops them into successful, productive members of a marketing team. (9)

Sales Training Development Process The process of designing and implementing a sales training program that begins with analyzing needs, setting objectives, developing program content, determining delivery, preparing, motivating, reinforcing, and evaluating. (9)

Sales Unit An individual salesperson, sales territory, branch office, district, region, dealer, or distributor. (14)

Sales Volume Analysis The collection, classification, comparison, and evaluation of an organization's sales figures. (13)

Salesperson Performance Appraisal A systematic process of (1) establishing whether the salesperson's job behavior contributes to the fulfillment of a firm's sales objectives and (2) providing feedback to the individual. (14)

Salesperson Workload Analysis An estimate of the time and effort required to cover each geographic control unit. (7)

Scatter Diagram Graph that plots one variable against another to see whether there is a relationship. (5)

Selection Process Activities involved in choosing candidates that best meet the qualifications and have the greatest aptitude for the job. (8)

Self-Efficacy Feelings of power and the subordinate belief in the ability to make a meaningful contribution in influencing organizational performance. (10)

Semi-Structured Interview Combined approach in which a fixed set of questions is applied but time for discussion and interaction is left after each. (8)

Situational Ethics A behavior acceptable in one situation can be unacceptable in another. (2)

SMART Objectives A method of setting sales call objectives that are **s**pecific, **m**easurable, **a**chievable, **r**elational, and **t**emporal. (4)

Socialization The proper introduction of the recruit to company practices, procedures, and philosophy and the social aspects of the job through which the salesperson is integrated into the organization. (8)

Stakeholders Company employees, suppliers, financial community, media, stockholders, special interest groups, governments, and the general public—all of whom have a stake, interest, and frequently an opinion about sales force activities. (1)

Standard Costs Predetermined costs, based on experience and research studies, for achieving certain levels of volume. In production there are usually standard costs for direct labor, materials, and factory overhead. Marketing costs are much more difficult to standardize since they tend to be generated from non-repetitive activities. (13)

Standard Industrial Classification (SIC) A uniform numbering system for categorizing nearly all industries according to their particular product or operation. (5)

Straight Commission Payment for a given level of sales results; based on the principle that earnings should vary with performance. Historically based on dollar or unit sales volume, but can be tied to measures of profitability. (12)

Straight Salary A fixed sum of money paid at regular intervals. Most appropriate for team selling, long negotiating periods, mixed promotional mixes, sales trainees, missionary selling, and in special situations such as introducing new products or developing new customer accounts. (12)

Strategic Business Units (SBUs) Logical divisions of major businesses within multiple product companies. (6)

Strategic Partnerships Occur when the goals, strategies, and resources of buyers and sellers become so interconnected and intertwined that they develop an integrated, symbiotic relationship although still retaining their independent identities. (3)

Strategy An overall program of action for using resources to achieve a goal or objective. (6)

Strategy Planning The process of setting overall objectives, allocating resources, and developing broad courses of action. (6)

Structured Interview Recruiter asks each candidate the same set of standardized questions designed to determine the applicant's fitness for a sales position. (8)

Supervision Tasks that deal with monitoring the daily work activities of sales subordinates. (10)

Surveys of Buying Intentions Surveys that ask customers about their intentions to buy various products over a specified period. (5)

Tactics Day-to-day actions that make up the strategic plan. (6)

Team Selling The grouping of several individuals in an organization to sell products and services to all relevant decision makers. (6)

Teleology A philosophy that defines morality based on the *consequences* of the behavior. (2)

Territorial Routing Devising a travel plan or pattern to use when making sales calls. (7)

Test Marketing A popular counting forecasting method for consumer packaged goods products. (5)

Time-Series Technique Use of historical data to predict future sales. (5)

Touchpoint Refers to points in time when the customer and the company come together, either personally or virtually. (3)

Trading Area A geographic region consisting of a city and the surrounding areas that serve as the dominant retail or wholesale center for the region. (7)

Training Delivery Decisions Decisions made during the sales training development process that include who will train the sales force, what method will be used to transfer knowledge, where the training will take place, and when the training will occur. (9)

Training Needs Assessment The step in the sales training development process that analyzes the training needs of the sales force to determine the gaps between what they know and what they need to know. (9)

Trait Theory Leadership theory that focuses on identifying the qualities or personal traits of effective leaders. (10)

Transactional Leadership Transactional leaders identify and clarify for subordinates their job tasks and communicate to them how successfully executing those tasks will lead to job rewards. (10)

Transactional Selling Exists when a sales firm acts consistently with the view that each and every interaction with a customer is a unique and independent event. (3)

Transformational Leadership Transformational leaders adopt a long-term perspective. They gain extraordinary commitment from their followers through several key characteristics: charisma and vision, inspiration, intellectual stimulation, and individual consideration. (10)

Trend Analysis A quantitative forecast whereby the dependent variable is sales, and the independent variable is time. (5)

Trial Close Any well-placed attempt to close the sale; can be used early and often throughout the PSP. (4)

Trust and Responsibility Dimension that defines how far people are trusted to behave in a responsible way and are held personally responsible for their actions. (2)

Uniform Commercial Code A basic set of guidelines adopted by most states that set forth the rules of contracts and the law pertaining to sales. (2)

Unstructured Interview Informal and nondirected interview used to get a candidate to talk freely on a variety of topics. (8)

Valence (Attractiveness of Rewards) The desirability of a potential outcome or reward that the salesperson may receive from improved performance. (11)

Valid Objections Sincere concerns that the prospect needs to have addressed before he or she will be willing to buy. (4)

Value An individual's selective perception of the worth of some activity, object, or idea. (3)

Variable Costs Those costs that vary with sales volume, for example, travel outlays for salespeople calling on customers or commissions based on sales volume. (13)

Variable Pay Compensation Systems Also known as flexible compensation systems; pay based on a personal choice of compensation plan and benefits selected. (12)

Vertical Integration A pattern of controlling and perhaps acquiring assets and resources at different levels of the marketing channel. (3)

Vision An attractive, credible notion of a future state that is not readily attainable. (10)

Visionary Leadership The ability to create and articulate a realistic, credible, and attractive vision of the future that improves upon the present situation. (10)

Web Conferencing A fast growing approach where participants use a computer to communicate with several other people via the Internet. (9)

Webinar A variation on web conferencing, is a seminar or web conference conducted over the Internet. (9)

Weighted Application Form forms that score candidates on each job attribute by assigning different values to each attribute. (8)

Wheel of Personal Selling Depiction of the seven stages of the personal selling process (PSP) as a continuous cycle of stages carried out by professionals in the field of sales. (4)

Wiki A simple, easy-to-use, user-maintained database for creating and searching information. (9)

Subject Index

NOTE: Page references followed by *f* refer to figures; page references followed by *t* refer to tables.

A

ABCs ("always be closing"), 105–106
acceptability, 36
account analysis, 188, 189*f*
accounting departments, marketing and, 401–403
account managers, 5
accuracy, 136
active listening, 311
activity quotas, 436–438, 437*t*
adaptive selling, 98–100
advertising, 12, 220–222
after-market segment, 280
analytical CRM, 72–73
annual sales budgets, 138–141, 141*t*
application forms, for jobs, 223–224
approach stage of selling process, 92, 96–97, 97*t*, 98*f*, 99*t*, 100*t*
ARIMA (autoregressive integrated moving average) model, 131
ask-for-help close, 105*t*, 106
ask-for-the-order close, 105*t*
assistant sales managers, 5
assumptive close, 104*t*
attitude and lifestyle tests, 232
attribution theory, 328
automated screening techniques, 225
average cost curve, 401*f*

B

background checks, of job candidates, 226
behavior, ethics and, 33
behavioral forces, 16, 16*t*
behaviorally anchored rating scale (BARS), 444–445, 444*f*
behavioral styles theory of leadership, 288–290, 290*t*
behavior-based performance measures, 429, 429*f*, 430–431*t*
blended learning, 264
body language, 312
bonuses, 365, 372–373

boomerang technique, 103, 103*t*, 104*t*
boundary spanners, 30–32, 31*t*
branch sales managers, 5
breakdown approach, 124–125
budgeting. *See also* forecasting and budgeting
    annual sales budget preparation, 138–141, 141*t*
        budget variances, 138, 138*t*
        planning, 137–138, 138*t*
build-up approach, 125–126, 125*f*
business deceptions, 45
business defamation, 45–46
business ethics, 30. *See also* ethics
business portfolio matrix, 156–157, 156*f*
business-to-business (B2B) sales. *See also* selling process
    CRM and, 79
    megatrends in, 18
Buying Power Index (BPI) (*S&MM*), 123

C

"cadres," 297
canned selling, 98–100
career cycle, motivation and, 342, 345–347, 345*t*
career plateauing, 346–347
"cash cows," 156, 156*f*
causal/association methods, 131
centralized training programs, 266
"certified" used cars, 38
charismatic leadership, 299–302
civil service grades, 361
classical leadership theories, 287
    behavioral styles theory, 288–290, 288*t*, 290*t*
    contingency theories, 290–299, 292*f*, 294*f*, 295*f*, 296*t*
    trait theory, 287–288
Clayton Act, 41–46
click-stream analysis, 78
closing stage of selling process, 92, 103–106, 104–105*t*
coaching (developmental feedback), 266–269, 269*t*
codes of ethics, 32–34
coercive power, 285*f*, 286, 287*t*
collusion, 44
combination compensation plans, 358–360, 359*t*, 373–374

combination quotas, 438–439, 439t
combination reimbursement plans, 378–379
combination salary and commission, 9
combination sales organizations, 166, 166f
communication, leadership and, 309–314, 311t, 313f
comparison rating, 446–448, 447t
compensation, 9, 356–358, 379–382
  case examples, 382–385, 383t, 385t
  defined, 358
  developing plans, 360–368, 360f, 363t, 364t, 366t
  expense accounts and fringe benefits, 376–379
  territory revision and, 192–193
  trends in, 374–375
  types of plans, 358–360, 359t
  types of plans, advantages and disadvantages, 368–374, 371t
compensation mix, 364–367, 364t, 366t
competition
  among salespeople, 338–339
  globalization and training, 274–275, 275f
  recruiting and, 218–219
  training and, 256
comprehensibility, 136
Comprehensive Personality Profile (CPP), 232, 233t
COMPUSTAT (Standard & Poor's), 96t
computer-based training (CBT), 263
computer screening tests, 225
concentration principle, 196, 399
conferencing (distance learning), 263
conflicting assumptions, 313
consolidated metropolitan statistical areas (CMSAs), 187
consultative problem solving strategy, 99t
contemporary leadership theories, 299
  empowerment and, 303–306, 304f, 306f
  Pygmalion leadership, 302–303
  transformational leadership, 299–302, 302t
content listening, 310–311
content theories of motivation
  dual factor theory, 326
  ERG theory, 324
  hierarchy of needs theory, 324, 325t
  needs theory, 325
contests, as incentives, 335–340, 336t, 340t
contingencies, 121
contingency planning, 161
contingency theories of leadership, 290–299, 292f, 294f, 295f, 296t
continuing sales training programs, 255–258
contractualism, 36
contribution margin, 407–411, 409t, 411t
contribution margin quotas, 435

ConvertMoreSales.com, 436
Cooling-Off Rules, 47
coordinating, budgeting and, 137–138
corporate social activities, 239–240
correlation analysis, 131
cost/benefit analysis, 137
costs *vs.* expenses, 403–404
counties, as geographic control units, 186
counting methods, 127–129
creativity, 168
"creatures of habit," 359
critical listening, 310–311
critical path, 157–159
CRM—On Demand (Siebel), 193
cross-functional teams (CFTs), 158
culture, training and, 274–275, 275f
"curbstone coaching," 306–307
customer-centric firms, 62
customer coercion, 45. *See also* ethics
customer commitment, 68
customer complaints, 100–103, 100t, 101–102t, 103t, 108t
customer lifetime value (CLV), 67–70
customer loyalty, 67–70
customer/market-oriented sales organizations, 165–166, 165f
customer needs, 60–61
customer-oriented salespeople, 62
customer portfolios, 72
customer relationship management (CRM), 10–11, 15, 56–57, 80–83. *See also* time and territory management
  case examples of, 83–86
  CRM Intelligence, 77
  customer loyalty, lifetime value and, 67–70
  defined, 57–58
  implementation, 79t
  need for, 20
  relationship orientations and, 58–62, 58f, 61t
  repeat business and, 62–67
  sales territories and, 184
  selling process and, 70–74, 90, 90t, 108–110, 109t
  software application vendors, 78t, 80
  successes/failures of, 78–80
  technology and, 74–78, 75f
customer retention, 63–64
customers, based on sales volume and profitability, 200f, 399t
customer satisfaction, 160, 374–375
customer share, 68
customer value, 62
customer vulnerability, 31–32

D

database marketing, 77
data mining, 77
data warehouse, 77
D&B—Dun's Market Identifiers (DMI), 186
decentralized training programs, 266
defamation, 45–46
deliverability, 74
Delphi method, 136
deontological process, 35
depth selling strategy, 99t
descriptive performance appraisal statements, 443
dialectic planning, 160
DIALOG Database Catalogue (D&B, Inc.), 186
Dictionary of Marketing Terms (AMA), 3
differentiated marketing, 58, 59
direct costs, 405
direct marketing, 90
direct store-door (DSD) delivery, 177
distance learning (conferencing), 263
district sales managers, 5
division sales managers, 5
"dogs," 156f, 157
dollar-based sales quotas, 434
dollar cost of selling time, 195t
"door-to-door" sales, 90
draw, 370–372, 371t
drug tests, of job candidates, 226
dual factor theory, 326
Dun's Market Identifiers (DMI) (D&B, Inc.), 186

E

econometric models, 135
effective listening, 310–311, 311t
efficiency, 196
E-learning, 264–265
e-mail, 73–74
emotions, communication and, 313
empathic listening, 311
employment agencies, 221
employment testing, 231–234, 233t
empowerment, 303–306, 304f, 306f, 347
Equal Employment Opportunity Commission
    (EEOC), 222
equalized workload method, 168–169
equity theory, 327
ERG (existence, relatedness, growth) theory, 324
erroneous sales forecasts, impact of, 121t
ethics, 28–29, 50–53
    case examples, 53–55

checklist for sales managers, 49, 50t
codes of ethics, 32–34
defined, 29–30
ethical dilemma, 36
ethical maturity, 48
ethical philosophies and moral judgments, 34–38
ethical stress, 48
ethical work climate, 38–41, 49f
key legislation and, 42–43t
legal considerations and, 41–47, 47–48
practice of, among sales force, 47–50
recruiting and, 218–219
salespeople as boundary spanners and, 30–32, 31t
unethical selling-related behaviors, 37t
unfair advantages/disadvantages in sales, 31t
Excel (Microsoft), 133
expectancy (effort-performance linkage), 327–328
expectancy theory, 327–328
expense accounts, 376–379
expense quotas, 435
expenses, costs *vs.*, 403–404
expert power, 285f, 286, 287t
exponential smoothing, 130–131
extended socialization, 239–240
extrinsic rewards, 331–332

F

federal regulation, 41–47
Federal Trade Commission Improvement Act, 42, 45
feedback, 448–452
Feel, Felt, Found technique, 102, 103t
Fiedler's Contingency Theory, 290–292, 292f
field sales forces, marketing support teams and,
    12–13
field sales managers, 5
financial compensation, 9
financial incentive programs, 331
financial knowledge, 20
financial quotas, 435–436
fixed costs, 405
flexibility, 136–137
follow-up interviews, 234–235
follow-up stage of selling process, 92, 106–108,
    107t, 108t
forecasting and budgeting, 6, 13, 118–119, 141–144
    case examples, 144–147, 145t, 146t
    erroneous sales forecasts, 121t
    evaluating forecasting approaches, 136–137
    forecasting, defined, 119
    forecasting approaches and techniques, 124–135,
        125f, 126f, 130t, 132f, 133f

forecasting and budgeting (*cont.*)
  forecasts, defined, 119, 120
  industry-wide predictions, 139
  NAICS Codes, 123–124, 124*t*
  new product development and, 135
  operational planning and, 119–124, 122*f*
  sales budget planning, 137–138, 138*t*
  sales budget preparation, 138–141, 141*t*
formula strategy, 99*t*
fringe benefits, 365–366, 366*t*, 376–379
full-cost approach, 407–410, 410*t*
functional costs, 405, 405*t*, 407, 408*t*
functional organizations, 162, 162*f*
function-oriented sales organizations, 164–165, 164*f*
f-values, 134

"Galatea" effect, 303
geographic control units, 185–188, 190
geographic sales organizations, 164, 164*f*. *See also* time and territory management
globalization
  leadership and, 284, 308
  training and, 274–275, 275*f*
"goal-oriented individuals," 359
goals. *See also* performance evaluation
  planning and, 150–151, 150*t*, 153–154, 154*t*
  time management and, 199–200
goal-setting theory, 329, 329*t*
"Golem" effect, 303
governance, 66–67
graphic rating performance appraisal scales, 443, 443*f*
Green River Ordinances, 47
gross national product (GNP), 125
group training methods, 260*t*, 260
guaranteed draw, 370–371

hierarchy of needs theory, 324, 325*t*
hiring, 234–235. *See also* recruitment and selection
hybrid sales forces, 22

ideals, 35
incentive programs, 364–367, 364*t*, 366*t*. *See also* compensation
  defined, 331
  for motivation, 330–334, 333*t*, 334*t*

income. *See* compensation
incremental productivity method, 169–170
in-depth interviews, 227
indirect costs, 405
individualized consideration, 301–302
individual training methods, 260*t*, 260
industry averages, 159–160, 159*t*
informal organizational structure, 163
information management tools, 18
initial sales training programs, 255–258
initial screening, 223–225, 224*t*
initial socialization, 238–239
initiating structure, 289
innovation, 168
input-output models, 135, 400
inspiration, 300
Instant Yellow Pages Service, 188
instructional methods, 260, 261–262
instrumentality (performance-reward linkage), 328
integrated marketing communication (IMC), 14
intellectual stimulation, 301
intelligence tests, 232
international regulation, 46
international sales compensation, 375
Internet communications, 13
interviews, for selection process, 227–231, 227*t*, 228*t*, 229*t*, 230*t*, 231*t*
intranets, 265–266
intrinsic rewards, 332–334
invalid objections, 100–103, 101–102*t*

job analysis, 213
job commitment, 343–344
job descriptions, 213–214, 215*t*
  compensation and, 361
  performance standards and, 428*t*
job qualifications, 214–217
jury of executive opinion, 126–127

K

key account managers (KAM), 5
key accounts, 165
knowledge tests, 232

L

leader-member exchange theory, 296–297

leadership, 8, 282–283, 314–317. *See also* motivation
  behavioral styles theory of, 288–290, 290*t*
  case examples, 317–320
  communication and, 309–314, 311*t*, 313*f*
  contingency theories of, 290–299, 292*f*, 294*f*,
    295*f*, 296*t*
  defined, 284
  empowerment and, 303–306, 304*f*, 306*f*
  ethics and, 49
  globalization and, 284, 308
  mentoring and, 306–309
  power and, 285–287, 285*f*, 287*t*
  Pygmalion, 302–303
  styles, 288, 289
  supervision, management, and, 284–285
  trait theory of, 287–288, 288*t*
  transactional, 299, 302*t*
  transformational, 299–302, 302*t*
  women in, 308–309
leads, 93, 94*t*, 180–181. *See also* time and territory
  management
"learning logs," 301
learning objectives, 254–255
learning orientation, 344–345
legal issues
  ethics and, 41–47
  key legislation, 42–43*t*
  recruiting and, 212
legitimate power, 285*f*, 286, 287*t*
lifetime value, 108
Likert-type graphic rating scale, 443–444, 443*f*
limited reimbursement plans, 378
line-and-staff organizations, 162, 162*f*
line organizations, 161–162, 161*f*
line sales executives, 259
listening, 310–311, 311*t*

M

management, defined, 284–285. *See also* compensation;
  leadership; motivation; sales managers; training
management by objectives (MBO), 157, 445–446, 446*f*
managerial expectations, 159–160, 159*t*
managerial forces, 16t, 18
managerial training, 274
manufacturer representatives, 7, 171
market capacity, 154–155
market development, 13, 155
marketing, 20. *See also* profitability analysis; sales force
  organization
  defined, 10
  establishing sales territories and, 183–184

  management, 11–13
  mass marketing, 58, 59
  one-to-one marketing, 58, 60
marketing automation systems, 76
marketing costs analysis, 401–403
marketing representatives, 5
marketing research, 13
marketing support teams, 12–13
market orientation, production orientation and,
    61–62, 61*t*
market-oriented sales organizations, 165–166, 165*f*
market penetration, 155
market potential, 6, 120, 154–155
market share/market growth matrix, 156–157, 156*f*
mass marketing, 58, 59
megatrends, in sales management, 16–18, 16*t*
mentoring, 262, 306–309
mentors, 306
metropolitan statistical areas (MSAs), 187
minimum average costs, 400, 401*t*
m-learning, 264
"money-oriented individuals," 359
moral equity, 36
moral judgment, 36
moral philosophy, 34–38
motivation, 8–9, 322–323, 347–350. *See also* leadership
  career cycle and, 345–347, 345*t*
  case examples, 350–354
  content theories of, 324–326, 325*t*
  defined, 323–324
  empowerment and participative management, 347
  learning orientation *vs.* performance orientation,
    344–345
  organizational and job commitment, 343–344
  organizational climate, 344
  process theories of, 326–329, 329*t*
  reinforcement theory of, 330
  rewards and incentive programs for, 330–334,
    333*t*, 334*t*
  sales motivation strategies, defined, 335
  sales motivation training programs, 329*f*
  strategies and tools, 335–343, 336*t*, 340*t*, 342*t*
  of trainees, 266–269, 268*t*
moving averages, 129–130, 131
multiple regression, 132–135, 133*f*
mutual loyalty, 65–66

N

naïve forecasts, 126
national account managers (NAM), 5
national sales managers, 5

natural accounting expenses, 405–406
need satisfaction strategy, 99*t*
needs theory, 325
negative commission system, 371–372
negative reinforcement, 330
negotiating sales resistance stage of selling process, 92, 100–103, 100*t*, 101–102*t*
net profit quotas, 435, 437*t*
new product development, 135
niche marketing, 58, 59
non-compete agreements, 218–219
non-financial compensation, 9
non-financial incentives, 333
nonquantitative forecasting techniques, 126–129, 126*f*, 136–137
nonverbal communication, 312
North American Industrial Classification System (NAICS), 123–124, 124*t*
North American Product Classification System (NAPCS), 124

O

objections, overcoming, 100–103, 100*t*, 101–102*t*, 103*t*, 108*t*
objectives, 150–151, 150*t*, 153–154, 154*t*. *See also* performance evaluation
  compensation and, 361–362
  for sales contests, 336*t*
  for training, 254–255
one-to-one marketing, 58, 60
online learning, 264
on-the-job training, 262
operational CRM, 72–73
operational planning, 119–124
opportunistic manner of behavior, 66–67
orders, ethics and, 45
organizational behavior modification (OBM), 330
organizational climate, 39, 344
organizational commitment, 343–344
organizational structure, 161
  functional, 162, 162*f*
  informal, 163
  line, 161–162, 161*f*
  line-and-staff, 162, 162*f*
  matrix, 162–163, 163*f*
organizing. *See* sales force organization
original equipment manufacturers (OEMs), 280
outcome-based performance measures, 429, 429*f*, 430–431*t*
outside training specialists, 259–260
overseas assignments, 234

P

Parkinson's Law, 196
participative management, 303, 347
past performance standard, 159–160, 159*t*
path-goal theory of leadership, 292–295, 294*f*
peer behavior, 39
performance. *See also* motivation; performance evaluation
  expert and referent power and, 286–287
  improving, 450–452
  motivation and, 334*t*
  predictors of, 224*t*
Performance-Based Sales Training (Rosen), 251
performance evaluation, 9, 18, 422–423, 454–458. *See also* sales volume, costs, and profitability analysis
  allocating resources for, 432–441, 434*f*, 437*t*, 439*t*, 441*t*
  case examples, 458–462, 459*f*, 460*f*, 462*t*
  customer reviews and, 197
  developing sales plan for, 426, 427*t*
  establishing goals and objectives for, 426
  limitations of, 449*t*
  measuring performance against standards, 441–448, 443*f*, 444*f*, 446*f*, 447*t*
  merging seller and buyer sales goals, 440
  performance evaluation monitoring system (PEMS), 441–442
  performance measures, 159–160, 159*t*
  performance objectives, 254–255
  performance orientation, 344–345
  performance review ranking, 454
  performance standards, 426–432, 427*t*, 428*t*, 429*f*
  providing feedback and, 448–452
  salesperson performance appraisal, 423–425
  selection of sales managers, 18–19
  setting performance standards for, 426–432, 428*t*, 429*f*, 430–431*t*
  systematic process for, 425–426, 425*f*
  of team selling, 453–454
  360-degree performance appraisal, 452–453, 453*f*
  training and, 19
personality tests, 232
personality traits, 214, 216*t*
personal selling careers, 89, 91. *See also individual names of job titles*
personnel. *See* performance evaluation; recruitment and selection
person-organization fit (POF), 237
persuasive communication, 98

PERT (program evaluation and review technique)
  diagrams, 157–159
"Peter Principle," 18–19
physical examinations, of job candidates, 226
planning. *See* sales force organization
planning and organizing, 6–7, 148–149, 172–174
  budgeting and, 137
  case examples, 174–178
  process of, 151–160, 152*f*
  purpose and levels of, 149–151, 150*t*
  sales force size and, 167–171
  team selling, 166–167
  unsuccessful planning and, 160–161
point quotas, 434
policies and rules, 39, 151
positive reinforcement, 330
power, leadership and, 285–287, 285*f*, 287*t*
preapproach stage of selling process, 92, 93–95,
  94*t*, 96*t*, 97*f*
prenotification, 93–94
pre-training briefing, 267
price discrimination, 41–46
price fixing, 44
primary research, 125
"prime contractor" roles, 65, 295
"problem children," 156, 156*f*
procedures, 151
process theories of motivation, 326
  attribution theory, 328
  equity theory, 327
  expectancy theory, 327–328
  goal-setting theory, 329, 329*t*
product description, 45
product development, 13, 155–156
production
  CRM and, 72–73
  market orientation and, 61–62, 61*t*
productivity, 181–182
product-oriented sales organizations, 164, 164*f*
product portfolios, 72
product publicity, 12
professional development performance measures,
  429–431, 429*f*, 430–431*t*
profitability analysis, 9, 392, 399–411. *See also* sales
  volume, costs, and profitability analysis
  average cost curve, 401*f*
  cooperation between marketing and accounting
    departments, 401–403
  costs *vs.* expenses, 403–404
  cross-classification, 412*t*
  full-cost *vs.* contribution margin, 408–410, 409*t*
  functional costs, 405, 405*t*, 408*t*

input-output efficiency, 400
  marketing profitability analysis procedure,
    404–405, 405*f*
  minimum average costs, 400, 401*t*
  natural accounting expenses, 405–406, 406*t*, 407*t*
  problems of, 412
  profitable segments, 410–411, 410*t*, 411*t*
profit quotas, 435
programmed selling, 98–100
progressive incentives, 365
promotion opportunities, 332
prospecting and qualifying stage of selling process,
  92, 93
public relations, 13
puppy dog close, 104*t*, 106
push technology, 73–74
Pygmalion leadership, 302–303

Q

quantitative forecasting techniques, 126*f*, 129–135,
  130*t*, 132*f*, 133*f*, 136–137

R

reciprocity, 44
recognition, 334, 334*t*
recruitment and selection, 8, 210–211, 240–243
  case examples, 243–244
  hiring, 234–235
  importance of, 211–212
  recruiters, 221
  recruitment, defined, 212
  recruitment process, 212–222, 213*f*, 215*t*, 216*t*
  sales force socialization, 235–240, 236–237*t*
  selection process, 222–234, 223*f*, 224*t*, 227*t*, 228*t*,
    229*t*, 230*t*, 231*t*, 233–234*t*
  training and, 255
reference checking, 225–226
referent power, 285*f*, 286, 287*t*
refresher training, 272, 272*t*
regional sales managers, 5
regression analysis, 131
  econometric models, 135
  multiple regression, 132–135, 133*f*
  simple, 132
regressive incentives, 365
reimbursement, for expenses, 377–379
reinforcement theory of motivation, 330
relational-based governance, 66–67

relational exchange, 63–64, 63t. *See also* customer relationship management (CRM)
  measuring opportunism in, 67f
  risks of, 69–70
relationship orientations, CRM and, 58–62, 58f, 61t
relativism, 35
replacement parts segment, 280
resource allocation, performance appraisal and, 432–441, 434f, 437t, 439t, 441t
responsibility, 39
restraint of trade, 44
resumes, 223–224
retraining, 273–274
return on assets managed (ROAM), 412–413
reward power, 285f, 286, 287t
rewards
  extrinsic rewards, 331–332
  intrinsic rewards, 332–334
  for sales contests, 336t
  selling process and CRM training, 110
Robinson-Patman Act, 41–46
role-playing, 261
ROTI (return on time invested), 196
routing patterns, 7, 197–202. *See also* time and territory management
RSS, 264
rules. *See* policies and rules
R^2 values, 134–135. *See also* multiple regression

S

salary. *See* compensation
sales aids, 12
sales analysis, defined, 392–393. *See also* sales volume, costs, and profitability analysis
sales analysts, 5
sales and operational planning process (S&OP), 121–123, 122f
sales aptitude tests, 232
sales budgets, 6, 137–138. *See also* forecasting and budgeting
sales budget software, 140
sales calls, time management during, 200–201
sales contests, 335–340, 336t
sales department organization, 163. *See also* sales force organization
  combination, 166, 166f
  customer/market-oriented, 165–166, 165f
  functional, 164–165, 164f
  geographic, 164, 164f
  product, 164, 164f

sales emphasis, 39–40
sales engineers, 5
sales exchange, 62
sales force automation (SFA), 17, 74–76, 153
sales force composite, 127
sales force development
  guidelines for, 167
  quality of, 171–172
sales force organization
  developing sales organizations and, 167
  high-quality sales organizations and, 171–172
  organization types, 161–163, 161f, 162f, 163f
  sales department organization types, 163–166, 164f, 165f
sales force organization audits, 390–391, 390f
sales forecasts, defined, 120. *See also* forecasting and budgeting
sales management ethics, 30. *See also* ethics
sales management performance evaluation, 18–20
sales management roles, 2–3, 22–24. *See also* customer relationship management (CRM); ethics; selling process
  case examples, 25–27
  defined, 3, 4
  development of, 20–21
  expanding roles of sales managers, 10–11
  macroenvironment of, 15–18
  marketing management and, 11–14
  performance evaluation, 18–20
  qualities of sales managers, 11, 12
  responsibilities of sales managers, 4–9
  time and territory management and, 196–197
  time management and, 202
  types, titles, hierarchy of, 4, 5t, 6f, 19f
  yesterday's *vs.* today's, 21t, 90t
sales managers. *See also* performance evaluation
  commission for, 375
  ethics checklist for, 49, 50t
  managerial training, 274
sales meetings, 340–343, 342t
sales motivation strategies, 335. *See also* motivation
sales-oriented salespeople, 62
salespeople, 5. *See also* compensation; motivation; performance evaluation; time and territory management
  assigning, to territories, 190–191
  as boundary spanners, 30–32, 31t
  competition among, 338–339
  ethical behavior of, 36
  salesperson performance appraisal, 423–425
  salesperson workload analysis, 188–189
  self-management by, 193–197, 194t, 195t

styles of, 62
territory revision and, 192–193
time allocation of, 195t, 198t, 199f, 200f
sales position analysis, 363t
sales potential, 6, 120, 154–155, 170–171
sales presentation training programs, 98f
sales promotion, 12
sales quotas, 7, 120, 433–434, 434f
administration of, 439–441
combination quotas, 438–439, 439t
sales volume quotas, 434–438, 434f, 437t
selling process and CRM training, 110
sales representatives, 5
sales supervisors, 5
sales territories, 182. See also time and territory
management
alignment and optimization, 190
combining geographic control units into, 190
establishing, 182–184
revising, 191–193
setting up, 184–191
sales training, 248–249, 276–278
case examples, 278–281, 279t, 280t, 281t
challenges for global companies, 274–275
delivery decisions for, 258–260, 260t
developing and implementing, 251–258, 252t, 253f,
253t, 254t, 257t
development process, 252, 253t
evaluating, 269–274, 270f, 270t, 271f, 272t, 273t
importance of, 249–251, 250t, 251t
instructional methods for, 260–266
preparing, motivating, coaching trainees, 266–269,
267t, 268t, 269t
recruiting and, 255
sales training, defined, 250
technology and, 249, 263–266
sales training managers, 5
sales units, 443–444
sales volume, costs, and profitability analysis, 391–392,
414–417. See also performance evaluation
budgeting and, 138
case examples, 417–420, 418t, 419t
increasing productivity and profits, 414
managing profitability and, 388–389
profitability analysis, 399–412, 400t, 401f, 401t, 405f,
405t, 406t, 409t, 410t, 411t, 412t
return on assets managed (ROAM), 412–413
sales force audits and, 390–391, 390f
sales volume analysis, 97, 200f, 392–399, 395t, 396t,
397f, 397t, 398t, 399t, 404
sales volume quotas, 434–438, 434f, 437t
"satisfiers," 359

scatter diagrams, 131, 132f-1p
seeding, 93
selection process, 222–223. See also recruitment and
selection
employment testing, 231–234, 233t
hiring and, 234–235
initial screening, 223–225, 224t
interviews, 227–231, 227t, 228t, 229t, 230t, 231t
for overseas assignments, 234
reference checking, 225–226
socialization and, 236–237t, 238–240
standard company reviews, 226
steps in, 223f
self-efficacy, 303
self-management, 193–197, 215. See also time and
territory management
selling costs, 9, 183, 392. See also profitability analysis
compensation and, 376
costs vs. expenses, 403–404
dollar cost of, 195t
selling process, 88–89, 111–113
case examples, 114–115
CRM and, 70–74, 90, 108–110, 109t
personal selling career opportunities, 89, 91
roles of salespeople, 89–92, 90t
stages of, 92
approach stage, 96–97, 97t, 98f, 99t, 100t
closing stage, 103–106, 104–105t
follow up stage, 106–108, 107t, 108t
negotiating sales resistance, 100–103, 100t,
101–102t
preapproach stage, 93–95, 94t, 96t, 97f
prospecting and qualifying stage, 93
wheel of personal selling, 92–93, 93f
semantic differential graphic rating scale,
443–444, 443f
semantics, 313
semi-structured interviews, 229
senior account executives, 5
Sherman Antitrust Act, 41–46
situational ethics, 35
size of sales force, 167–171
SMART objectives, 96–97
socialization, 235–238, 236–237t
extended, 239–240
initial socialization, 238–239
societal satisfaction, 160
staff trainers, 259
stakeholders, 4, 157
standard company reviews, 226
standard costs, 402
standard error of the estimate, 134

Standard Industrial Classification Manual (U.S. OMB), 123–124
"stars," 156, 156*f*
"start center," 334
states
    as geographic control units, 186
    regulations of, 47
stimulus-response strategy, 99*t*
stock options, 366–367
straight commission, 9, 358–360, 359*t*, 370–373, 371*t*
straight salary, 9, 358–360, 359*t*, 368–370, 371*t*
strategic business units (SBUs), 156
strategic partnerships, 64–66
strategy, defined, 151
strategy planning, defined, 155
structured interviews, 228
substitutes for leadership theory, 298–299
supervision, 284–285. *See also* leadership; sales
    managers
surveys of buying intentions, 127–128

T

tactics, 151, 158*f*
Tax Reform Act of 1986, 377
team selling
    performance appraisals and, 453–454
    strategy, 99*t*, 166–167
technology
    CRM and, 73–74, 73–78, 75*f*
    megatrends in, 16–17, 16*t*
    motivation and, 343
    in time and territory management, 196–197
    training and, 249, 258, 263–266
telemarketing, 207–208
teleology, 35
territorial routing, 201–202
test marketing, 128–129
Theory H, 295–296, 295*f*
Thomas Register of American Manufacturers (Thomas Publishing Company), 95, 96*t*, 97*f*
360-degree performance appraisal, 452–453, 453*f*
tie-in sales, 45
time allocation, of salespeople, 195*t*
    common time traps, 198*t*
    daily activity analysis report, 199*f*
    sales call plan, 200*f*
time and territory management, 180–181
    case examples, 205–208, 207*t*, 208*f*
    establishing territories, 182–184
    productivity and, 181–182
    revising territories, 191–193

sales territories, defined, 182
    self-management and, 193–197, 194*t*, 195*t*
    setting up territories, 184–191
    time management and routing, 197–202, 198*t*, 199*f*, 200*f*
timeliness, 136
time-series techniques, 129, 130*t*
timing, of training programs, 266
touchpoints, 62
"trade-offers," 359
trade shows, 12
trading areas, 187–188
training, 8
    CRM and, 80, 110
    evaluation of, 269–274, 270*f*, 270*t*, 271*f*
    inadequate, 19
    sales meetings, 342
    sales motivation programs, 329*f*
    sales presentation training programs, 98*f*
    socialization and, 238–239
training delivery decisions, 258–260
training needs assessment, 253
trait theory of leadership, 287–288, 288*t*
transactional leadership, 299, 302*t*
transactional selling, 62–63
transformational leadership, 299–302, 302*t*
travel time. *See* time and territory management
trend analyses, 132
trial closes, 106, 107*t*
trust, 39
turnover rate, 211, 216, 224*t*

U

Uniform Commercial Code, 47
unit volume sales quotas, 434
unlimited reimbursement plans, 378
unordered goods, 45
unstructured interviews, 228–229, 229*t*
U.S. Bureau of Labor Statistics, 361

V

valence (attractiveness of rewards), 328
valid objections, 100–103, 101–102*t*
value, 70–71
variable compensation systems, 360
variable costs, 405
vertical integration, 66
vice presidents of sales, 5
video conferences, 343

vision, 300
visionary leadership, 299–302
vocational interest tests, 232
vulnerability, 31–32

Web technology, 73–74. *See also* technology
   conferencing, 263–264
    customer data integration and dissemination, 75
    webinars, 264

weighted application forms, 224
wheel of personal selling, 92–93, 93*f*
wikis, 264
women, as sales managers, 308–309

zip codes, as geographic control units, 186
zone sales managers, 5

Name Index

NOTE: Page references followed by *f* refer to figures; page references followed by *t* refer to tables.

A

Abbott Laboratories, 34
ABI/Inform, 96*t*
Accenture, 64
Acumen Software Services Inc., 153
Adami, Norman, 283
ADP (Automatic Data Processing), 216
Advantexe Learning Solutions, 248–249
AFLAC, 155
Alcas Corporation, 243–244
Alcoa Aluminum, 163
Alinea Group, 452–453
Alonzo, Vincent, 333
Amana Refrigeration, 301
American Airlines, 77
American Association of Advertising Agencies, 33
American Express, 259–260
American Marketing Association (AMA), 3
American Standard Company, 44
Andrews, Mike, 388–389
Anheuser-Busch, 283
Apple Computer, 136, 283, 300
AT&T, 160, 229
Avis, 377

B

Baird Corporation, 263
Bausch & Lomb, 225
Beiersdorf, 148–149
Blanca de Ulloa, Tere, 210–211
Blue Cross Blue Shield, 358
Bluetooth, 129
BlueU.com, 263
Boeing, 165
Boeing Company, 422–423
Boston Consulting Group (BCG), 156
"Bounty Hunters," 341
Bridgestone Tire Company, 66, 73, 155–156
Bristol-Myers Squibb, 197
British Petroleum, 377

Brodo, Robert, 248–249
Burdis, Jean, 180–181

C

Cadillac, 108
Campbell Soup Co., 156
Caterpillar, 66–67, 388–389
CB Software Systems, 403
CBS Station Group, 370
Centive, 374
Chrysler, 300
Cigna, 32
Cisco Systems, 15
    E-sales Web portal initiative, 185
    interviewing process by, 227
    job descriptions of, 214
    performance review ranking of, 454
    training by, 250
Citicorp, 77
Coca-Cola, 128–129
Codina Realty Services, 210–211
Consumer Federation of America, 48
Cunningham, Tom, 422–423
CUTCO Cutlery, 243–244
Cypress Pharmaceuticals, 68

D

DaimlerChrysler, 38, 374–375
Delgado, Tony, 269
Dell, 269
Dendrite, 17
DHL, 180–181
DiBari, Nick, 358
Direct Selling Association of America, 33, 244
Dow Jones Sustainability Index, 41
Dun & Bradstreet, 96*t*, 186
DuPont, 89, 95

E

Eastman Kodak, 273
Economic Information Systems, 96*t*

eFunds, 56–57
Eli Lilly, 135
EMCO, 133
Empower Geographics, 190
Empowerment Group, 98, 98*f*
ES Research Group, 391

F

Federal Trade Commission, 42, 45, 47
Feldman, Ben, 286
Firestone, 155–156
Forbes, 96*t*
Ford Motor Company, 38, 69, 77, 450
Fortune, 96*t*
Forum Corporation, 260

F

General Dynamics, 32
General Electric, 41, 357
   leadership of, 283
   Medical Systems, 322–323
   performance evaluation by, 448, 450
   sales force selection by, 234
   sales planning by, 152–153
General Motors, 77, 99, 107–108
Gillette, 165
Green Mountain Coffee Roasters, 282–283
Gross, Jeff, 255

H

Hallmark Insights, 331
Hall Publications, Inc., 364
Harrah's Entertainment, Inc., 77
Harris Interactive, 76
Heidrick and Struggles, 19
Hertz, 99
Herzberg, Frederick, 326
Hewlett-Packard, 20, 71, 91, 454
High Probability Selling, 103, 103*f*
Hitachi, 80
Holiday Inns, 156
Hollenbeck, Joel, 2–3
Home Depot, 107–108
Honeywell, 151
Hoover's Online, 96*t*
Hopkins, Ewell, 118–119
Horton, James B., 364

Houghton Mifflin Company, 2–3
Hubbell, Anne, 88–89
Hughes, Patrick, 358
Hurd, Mark, 71, 91
Hyperion Solutions Corporation, 404

I

Iacocca, Lee, 300
IBM
   compensation, 374–375, 377
   nonverbal communication by, 312
   organizational planning by, 150–151
   sales budget planning by, 140
   sales force management by, 72
   sales force organization by, 163, 165
   training, 265–266
Illinois State University, 219
Inc., 96*t*
Industry Data Sources, 96*t*
Infiniti, 374–375
Intel, 454
Interactive Sales Manager (ISM), 153
InterContinental Hotels Group, 156

J

J. A. Riggs, 388–389
JCI (Johnson Controls, Inc.), 255
Jobs, Steven, 283, 300
JobWeb.com, 221
John Deere, 66–67

K

Kelleher, Herb, 300
Kennesaw State University, 219
KeyCorp, 110
Kimberly Clark, 77
Kodak, 88–89
Kraft General Foods, 20, 77, 163

L

Lawn Tennis Championships (Wimbledon), 377
Leaders Institute, 305–306
Leno, Jay, 92
Lexus, 108
Lockheed-Martin, 165, 441

Lotus, 225
Lyons, Josh, 244–245

M

Marriott, Bill, 302
Marriott Corporation, 302
Mary Kay Cosmetics, 370
Maslow, Abraham, 324, 325t
Matrix Manager, 162
McClelland, David, 325
MCI, 337
Merck, 64
Merrill Lynch, 377
Microsoft, 64, 133, 270, 454
Midwest Auto Parts, Inc., 279–280
Miller Brewing Company, 283
Monsanto, 375
Monster.com, 220–221
Moody's Industrial Manuals, 96t
Morgan Holland & Company, 118–119
Mulcahy, Anne, 91

N

Nabisco Biscuit Company, 269–270
Nasser, Jacques, 450
National Association of Colleges & Employers, 221
New Belgium Brewery, 356–357
New York Life Insurance, 286
Nintendo, 70
Nokia, 128–129
Northwestern Mutual Life, 341
Notre Dame University, 225
Novartis, 71
Nucor Corp., 330–331

O

Ohio State University, 289
1000ventures.com, 295

P

PepsiCo, Inc., 171
Perkins, Lance, 322–323
Perry, Robert, 28–29
Perseus Development Corporation, 452–453
Pfizer, 253

Pizza Hut, 107–108
PokerTek Inc., 28–29
Procter & Gamble, 89, 164, 167, 440
Program URL, 403–404
Psychology Today, 364

Q

Quaker Oats, 171

R

Rand-McNally, 188
Reader's Digest, 57
realtor.org, 40
Red Star Yeast Co., 14
Rosen, Jerry, 251
R^3 Technology, 244–245

S

Sainsbury's, 60
Salesforce.com, 10, 77, 403
Sales & Marketing Management (S&MM), 124
    Buying Power Index (BPI), 123
    industry predictions by, 139
    selling cost index (SCI), 377
    "Survey of Selling Costs," 358–359, 363
    on trading areas, 188
Sales Training America, 453
SAP, 77, 140
Saturn, 272, 374–375
Seagram's, 377
Shell Oil, 163
Shireman, J. B., 356–357
Siebel Systems, 77, 193
Sire Technologies, 393
SkillSoft, 263
Sky Network, 60
Slashdot, 264
Smart, Jane, 64
Southwest Airlines, 300
SPSS, 133
SPX Cooling Technologies, 11
Standard & Poor's, 96t
Straus Discount Auto, 341
SuccessFactors, Inc., 452–453
Sun Microsystems, 65, 294–295, 341
SYSPRO, 404

T

Tesco, 60
Texaco, 160
Texas Instruments, 32, 160
Thomas Publishing Company, 95, 96*t*, 97*f*
Thomson NETg, 263
Training Clinic, 265
Travis, Jim, 282–283
Tupperware, 370

U

Unica, 60–61
University of Michigan, 289
University of Southern Mississippi, 219
U.S. Census Bureau, 96*t*
U.S. NAICS Manual (2002), 123–124. 124*t*
U.S. Office of Management and Budget
     (OMB), 123

V

Valentine, Greg "The Hammer," 341
Varicent, 360
Vault, 360
Vector Marketing Corporation, 243–244
Verizon Corporation, 32
Verna, Nikki, 148–149
von Koschembahr, Chris, 265–266
Vroom, Victor, 327

W

Walgreens, 68
Wal-Mart, 167
Weather Channel, 119–120
WebEx, Inc., 74
Welch, Jack, 283, 357–358, 448, 450
Westinghouse, 163
Wexford International, 377
Wimbledon, 377
Wired.com, 264
Woods, Tiger, 29
Wroblewski, Julie, 56–57
Wyeth, 184, 275

X

Xerox Corporation, 91
     compensation, 369, 374–375
     leadership of, 295
     quotas, 440
     sales force motivation by, 333–334

Y

Yellow Pages, 96*t*, 188